WITHOUT CONSENT OR CONTRACT

ROBERT WILLIAM FOGEL

WITHOUT CONSENT OR CONTRACT
The Rise and Fall of American Slavery

W. W. NORTON & COMPANY · NEW YORK · LONDON

The text of this book is composed in Bodoni with display type set in Beton Medium
Agency and Bold Condensed. Composition and manufacturing by The Haddon
Craftsmen, Inc.
Book design by Charlotte Staub.

Library of Congress Cataloging-in-Publication Data

Fogel, Robert William.
    Without consent or contract / Robert W. Fogel.
      p. cm.
    Bibliography: p.
    Includes index.
    1. Slavery—United States—History. 2. Slavery—United States—
Anti-slavery movements. I. Title.
E441.F63 1989
306'.362'0973—dc19   88-23839

                    ISBN 0-393-01887-3

W.W. Norton & Company, Inc., 500 Fifth Avenue, New York, N.Y. 10110
W.W. Norton & Company Ltd., 37 Great Russell Street, London WC1B 3NU
                    2 3 4 5 6 7 8 9 0

To Stanley L. Engerman,
who shares responsibility for most of the ideas
in this book
and
To Marilyn Coopersmith,
for all that she has done as an administrator
of research, as a collaborator,
and as a critic

PUBLISHER'S NOTE

This is the primary volume of *Without Consent or Contract*. It is a nontechnical summary and interpretation of findings by the director of a research group that has spent the past twenty-four years studying various aspects of the slave system. Subtitled *The Rise and Fall of American Slavery*, this volume includes a full set of relevant charts, maps, tables, notes, references, an index, and acknowledgments.

Three companion volumes to *Without Consent or Contract* are available for those who are concerned with its technical foundations. The first, subtitled *Evidence and Methods*, contains an array of research reports on the evidence and procedures that underlie the primary volume. The other two are subtitled *Technical Papers: Markets and Production* and *Technical Papers: Conditions of Slave Life and the Transition to Freedom*. They contain a selection of the principal papers produced by collaborators in this research project since its inception in 1965. Papers that were previously published have been revised to take account of new research, but many of the papers are published here for the first time. The full canon of research on slavery and related topics by the contributors is listed at the end of the last volume.

CONTENTS

DISCOVERIES AND DILEMMAS

The controversies of historians of slavery have been so intense and protracted during the past three decades that they have caught the attention of the entire history profession and periodically broken into the news. Such controversies may signal important intellectual progress or they may merely be the fuss produced by trendy misadventures. As scholarly passions abated, it became clear that a genuine revolution in knowledge was taking place. The intellectual turmoil was precipitated partly by the relatively sudden, vast expansion of information on the operation of slave systems and partly by the new techniques of analysis that were employed to assess this information. The result has been a transformation in perceptions of the nature of American slavery, of the black experience under it, of the ideological and political struggles against the system, and of the nature of the moral problem of slavery.[1]

It was the moral implications of some of the recent research rather than mere professional rivalries that accounted for the crackling atmosphere of these debates. The discovery that slaves were effective workers who had developed a much stronger family life, a more varied set of occupational skills, and a richer, more distinct culture than previously recognized created an agonizing dilemma. Did these findings enhance black history by revealing a hitherto undisclosed record of achievement under adversity? Or did they diminish the moral horror of slavery and constitute (no matter how innocent the intention) an apologia for centuries of exploitation? Did the findings rob blacks of a history of resistance to slavery and cast them instead in the role of collaborators in their own oppression?

These questions represent only one level of the debates over the findings. Some scholars insisted that the findings must have been in error, that they were the product either of unrepresentative samples of evidence or of outrageous errors in the technical analysis of the evidence. Others contended that the moral implications were so pernicious that the findings should have been suppressed, even if factually correct. But a more common concern was that the findings could serve to misdirect the discussion of the slavery into unproductive and potentially harmful channels.

The ultimate issues of this book are moral issues. They are not nearly as simple as many of us were taught to believe, nor is their relevance limited to the bygone era of slavery. Quite the contrary, many of the moral issues of Lincoln's time have reappeared and are involved in divisive debates of our own time that go well beyond ethnic or class relationships. To confront the moral problem of slavery, then, is not only to gain a deeper perspective on our past but also to understand the issues of our own time in a new way.

Since the moral problem of slavery must be viewed in historical context, it is necessary to review all the major results of the new slavery research.[2] The discussion focuses initially on the economic findings because the production of the great agricultural staples of the Western Hemisphere, and their sale on the world market, were the roots and trunk of modern slavery. It was virtually uninterrupted economic success for more than 200 years that made this tree thrive and grow to monstrous proportions. To understand the significance of the struggle against slavery one must, therefore, come to grips with what many scholars see as the unwelcome and ominous paradox that emerged from the new findings on the economics of slavery: Although the slave system was horribly retrogressive in its social, political, and ideological aspects, it was quite advanced by the standards of the time in its technology and economic organization. The paradox is only apparent. It collapses under scrutiny, not because the new economic findings are false, but because the paradox rests on the widely held assumption that technological efficiency is inherently good. It is this beguiling assumption that is false and, when applied to slavery, insidious.[3]

One must also come to grips with the moral dilemma that impaled leaders of the American Revolution and confounded other enlightened men of goodwill throughout the Western world for the better part of a century. The root of the dilemma was the rationalistic doctrine of natural rights which linked freedom and justice with the inviolability of property and which was the philosophical platform of the Revolution. Men who rebelled because the confiscatory taxes of Parliament and the arbitrary regulations of the Crown had diminished their wealth were bound to be confounded by the demand for the compulsory abolition of slavery. Despite anguish and desire, most of the founding fathers and their intellectual heirs were unable to find an apt solution to the conflict between the natural right of the enslaved to their freedom and the natural right of the masters to the security of their property.

It was mystics who led the escape from the dilemma. Rejecting the rationalism of the Revolutionary generation, they denounced slavery as an unmitigated evil, incapable of being justified by material gain or any other worldly consideration. Certain that they were divinely inspired, they declared that slavery was not just *a* sin, but an extraordinary sin, a sin so corrupting that persistence in it, or complicity with it, infected every aspect of life and created an insurmountable barrier to both personal and national salvation. Although the abolitionists were initially condemned as an isolated and fanatical sect even within the churches from which they sprung, their creed gradually gained numerous adherents. However, in the course of the struggle to transform a religious movement into a political one, the mystical content of the abolitionist creed became secularized and the original appeal to disinterested benevolence became overlaid with expedient political and economic arguments.

Even if this book were concerned with the purely economic aspects of slavery, it would have to take account of the many new points brought to light by historians of the ideological and political struggle to end slavery. The slave economy did not operate in a vacuum. Both its original economic successes and its ultimate collapse were heavily influenced by the legal and political conditions that affected its cost of production and its access to markets. Nor can one assess adequately the moral implications of the slave economy and the struggle to end it without an appreciation of those aspects of slave life and culture that have been developed recently by the "new" social historians.

However large the role of economic considerations in the origins and spread of American slavery, once established, the slave system of production had powerful ramifications in other spheres. As it evolved, slavery became the principal factor controlling relations between whites and blacks in the United States, with consequences that still shape the course of American life. Moreover, the struggle over slavery affected all aspects of politics, not only in America but around the world, producing slogans, ideologies, policies, and alignments that are still active and that deeply influence the politics of our own age. Political forces, not economic ones, were the overriding factors in the destruction of slavery. If the foes of slavery had waited for economic forces to do their work for them, America might still be a slave society, and democracy, as we know it, might have been a subject only for history books.

The point is not merely that the economic, cultural, ideological, and political aspects of slavery have to be viewed in an integrated way. It is that the various trains of slavery research are converging and that a new synthesis on the nature of the slave system and the struggle to end it is beginning to emerge. This emerging synthesis is the cumulative result of an avalanche of new evidence and of penetrating insights by numerous scholars. Although the research process has been halting, uneven, begrudging, often tenuous, sometimes breaking down altogether, the direction of movement has not reversed itself, and the momentum, if anything, appears to be increasing.

The pages that follow provide one picture of the emerging synthesis. It is not a final picture because research on American slavery is far from complete. Nor is it a totally different picture from the one that emerged during the first surge of slavery research after World War II. Perhaps it is not surprising that an additional decade of investigation and reflection would show that some findings that seemed so novel in the mid-1970s were prefigured in earlier work, and that some of the novelty arose from exaggeration and misconception rather than from new evidence and deeper insights. Yet even when the exaggerated claims are discounted and the misconceptions are corrected, there remains a marked leap in knowledge. The emerging synthesis of slavery research is not only a fusion of various new analytical techniques, and various new bodies of evidence, and various new perspectives; it is also a fusion of past work and new work, of old perspectives and recent ones.

This book combines analytical and narrative history. I have endeavored to make it a good story, one that will be edifying and intriguing to a wide range of readers. The book contains three subplots. One is the story of American slavery as an economic and social system (Chapters 1–6); the second is the story of the ideological and political struggle to abolish the system (Chapters 7–10). These two subplots, woven together, constitute "The Rise and Fall of American Slavery." The third subplot is the story of scholarly efforts (especially during the last three decades) to ferret out the "true" story of American slavery (to tell it "wie es eigentlich gewesen"). If instead of the current subtitle I had sought one that announced all three subplots, I might have used the following: "The Story of the Rise and Fall of American Slavery, as Filtered Through the Minds and Experiences of Historians Who Came of Age Shortly Before, During, or After World War II."

The third subplot is more implicit than explicit. It is developed mainly through comments on the central issues covered by each of the chapters and by contrasting points on which a wide consensus appears to have been reached with those that remain contentious. In order not to impede the flow of the story, most references to particular scholars have been eliminated from the text,* with the exception of Chapter 6 and the Afterword. Because differences of opinion among the experts on slave culture are still quite wide, Chapter 6 is more a survey of recent attempts

---

*These scholars are identified in the endnotes, and the companion volumes contain extensive discussions of the historiography of the slave system and of the antislavery struggle.

to uncover aspects of that culture than a synthesis, with some comments on what has been achieved so far.

The Afterword differs from all the other chapters. By design, it has a highly personal voice. It focuses on the way that I have struggled to make moral sense of my own findings as well as those of various colleagues. I think of it as the answer I would give to my sons if they asked why slavery was terrible. It should be understood that the answer given in the Afterword is not "the truth." It is the response of a person, perhaps more knowledgeable on the subject than his questioners but nevertheless the product of his age, trying to define what he believes is of lasting value in the story, as he understands it.

With this book I close an intellectual journey that has lasted more than two decades. I began it, like many other cliometricians, not because I was especially interested in the history of American slavery, but because an accident of scholarship made the economics of slavery a major testing ground for the application of cliometric methods.[4] Once drawn into the subject, however, it was the substance of the issues that maintained my interest. Although my principal professional expertise was, and is, in the areas of economics and demography, I found myself led down a road that forced me to grapple with the work of colleagues in cultural, political, and religious history. It has been a thrilling journey filled with unexpected discoveries that have transformed my views about slavery more than I dreamed they could be.

Research on American slavery continues to advance rapidly. The best work, whether its methodology is traditional or cliometric, whether its subject matter is economic, political, cultural, or religious history, is "scientific" in the Continental sense of the word (which I increasingly have come to believe is the most relevant sense). Such work is based on a thorough and often ingenious analysis of important bodies of evidence (some quantitative, some qualitative), conducted by open-minded scholars striving to be as unbiased as possible, who are impelled by an insatiable curiosity about facts and circumstances, and who long to know what actually happened. My current research is far from the subject of this book, so I can no longer contribute to the literature on slavery, but I will remain an avid consumer of it. There are still many mysteries to be solved and I am eager to know how they will turn out.

PART ONE

SLAVERY AS AN ECONOMIC AND SOCIAL SYSTEM

CHAPTER ONE

SLAVERY IN THE NEW WORLD

Slavery is not only one of the most ancient but also one of the most long-lived forms of economic and social organization. It came into being at the dawn of civilization, when mankind passed from hunting and nomadic pastoral life into primitive agriculture. And although legally sanctioned slavery was outlawed in its last bastion—the Arabian peninsula—in 1970, slavery is still practiced covertly in parts of Asia, Africa, and South America.

THE ORIGINS OF THE ATLANTIC SLAVE TRADE

Over the ages the incidence of slavery has waxed and waned. One high-water mark was reached during the first two centuries of the Roman Empire when, according to some estimates, three out of every four residents of the Italian peninsula—21 million people—lived in bondage.[1] Eventually, Roman slavery was transformed into serfdom, a form of servitude that mitigated some of the harsher features of the older system.

While serfdom was the most characteristic condition of labor in Europe during the Middle Ages, slavery was never fully eradicated. The Italians imported slaves from the area of the Black Sea during the thirteenth century. And the Moors captured during the interminable religious wars were enslaved on the Iberian peninsula along with Slavs and captives from the Levant.

Black slaves were imported into Europe during the Middle Ages through the Moslem countries of North Africa. Until the Portuguese exploration of the west coast of Africa, however, such imports were quite small. About the middle of the fifteenth century, the Portuguese established trading posts along the west coast of Africa below the Sahara and shortly thereafter began to make relatively large purchases of black slaves. Soon the average imports of slaves into the Iberian peninsula and the Iberian-controlled islands off the coast of Africa (the Canaries, the Madeiras, and São Thomé) rose to about 1,000 per year. By the time Columbus set sail on his first expedition across the Atlantic, accumulated imports of black slaves into the Old World were probably in excess of 25,000. Although blacks continued to be imported into the Old World until the beginning of the eighteenth century, it was the New World that became the great market for slaves.

It is customary to date the beginning of the New World traffic in Africans to the year 1502, when the first references to blacks appear in the documents of Spanish colonial administrators. The end of this trade did not come until the 1860s. Over the three and a half centuries between these dates about 9,900,000 Africans were forcibly transported across the Atlantic. Brazil was by far the largest single participant in the traffic, accounting for 41 percent of the total. British- and French-owned colonies in the Caribbean and the far-flung Spanish-American empire were the destination of 47 percent. Dutch, Danish, and Swedish colonies took another 5 percent. The remaining 7 percent represent the share of the United States (or the colonies that eventually became the United States) in the Atlantic slave trade.[2]

To those who identify slavery with cotton and tobacco, the small size of the U.S. share in the slave trade may seem surprising. The temporal pattern of slave imports, however, clearly reveals that the course of the Atlantic slave trade cannot be explained by the demand for these crops. Over 75 percent of all slaves were imported between 1451 and 1810. This fact clearly rules out cotton as a dominant factor in the traffic since the production of cotton was still in its infancy in 1810. There was also an enormous increase in the extent of the Atlantic slave trade during the eighteenth century. This fact rules out the possibility of a major role for tobacco: During the eighteenth century, tobacco imports into Europe increased at an average annual rate of about 350 tons per annum. Since an average slave hand could produce about a ton of tobacco yearly, the total increase in the tobacco trade over the century required an increase of about 70,000 hands, a minuscule fraction of the 5.7 million slaves imported during the same period.[3]

It was Europe's sweet tooth, rather than its addiction to tobacco or its infatuation with cotton cloth, that determined the extent of the Atlantic slave trade (Figure 1). Sugar was the greatest of the slave crops. Between 60 and 70 percent of all the Africans who survived the Atlantic voyages ended up in one or another of Europe's sugar colonies.

The first of these colonies was in the Mediterranean. Sugar was introduced into the Levant in the seventh century by the Arabs. Europeans became familiar with it during the Crusades. Prior to that time honey was the only sweetening agent available to them. After taking over the Arab sugar industry in Palestine, the Normans and Venetians promoted the production of sugar in the Mediterranean islands of Cyprus, Crete, and Sicily. From the twelfth to the fifteenth centuries these colo-

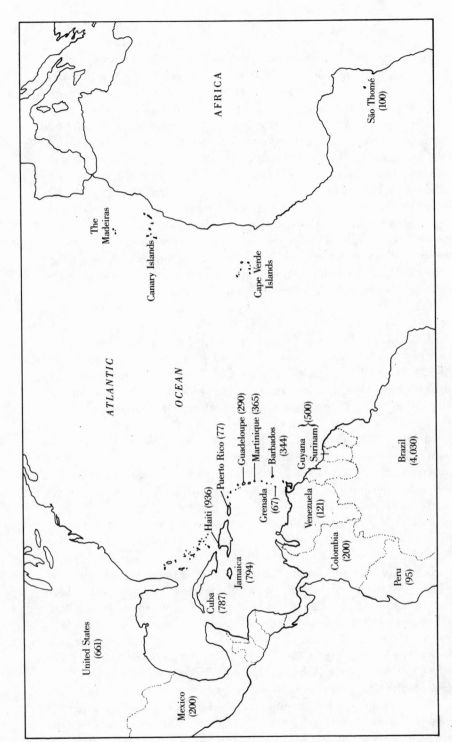

Figure 1. The principal importers of black slaves, 1451–1870 (imports in thousands).

nies shipped sugar to all parts of Europe. Moreover, the sugar produced there was grown on plantations that utilized slave labor. While the slaves were primarily white, in these islands Europeans developed the institutional apparatus that was eventually applied to blacks.

The rapid growth of European demand for sugar led the Spanish and Portuguese to extend sugar cultivation to the Iberian peninsula and to the Iberian-owned Atlantic islands off the coast of Africa. Here, as in the Mediterranean, slaves on plantations provided the labor for the new industry. While some of these bondsmen were natives of the newly conquered islands, as in the Cape Verde archipelago, most were blacks imported from Africa. For the first century of the Atlantic slave trade, the scope of imports was determined almost exclusively by the needs of the sugar planters in the Canaries, the Madeiras, and São Thomé. Of the 130,000 blacks imported between 1451 and 1559, 90 percent were sent to these islands and only 10 percent to the New World.

During the last half of the sixteenth century, the center of sugar production and of black slavery shifted across the Atlantic to the Western Hemisphere. By 1600 Brazil had emerged as Europe's leading supplier of sugar. Cane was also grown in substantial quantities in Mexico, Peru, Cuba, and Haiti. Although the Old World colonies continued to plant the crop, their absolute and relative shares of the European market declined rapidly. By the close of the seventeenth century sugar production all but disappeared from the Madeiras, the Cape Verde Islands, the Canaries, and São Thomé. The end of sugar production also marked the end of slaves imported into these territories.

The sugar monopoly of the Spanish and Portuguese was broken during the seventeenth century when the British, French, and Dutch became major powers in the Caribbean. The British venture into sugar production began in Barbados during the second quarter of the seventeenth century. In 1655 the British seized Jamaica from the Spanish and shortly thereafter began developing sugar plantations on that island. During the eighteenth century the output of sugar grew rapidly, not only in these colonies but throughout the British West Indies. It has been estimated that the annual export of the sugar crop in the British West Indies in 1787 stood at 106,000 tons, more than five times as much as the exports of Brazil in the same year. The British continued to expand their grip on sugar production, partly by acquiring additional territory during the Napoleonic Wars, so that by 1806 its West Indian colonies accounted for 55 percent of the sugar trade.

The development of the sugar culture in French Caribbean possessions was also spectacular. Haiti (then called Saint Domingue) was the principal sugar colony of the French. The French promoted plantations in that territory from the early seventeenth century until the Haitians revolted against their rule in 1794. By 1787 Haiti was shipping about 86,000 tons and production elsewhere brought the sugar trade of French Caribbean possessions to 125,000 tons. In contrast to Britain and France, Spain had been largely squeezed out of the international sugar trade, ranking a poor fourth in 1787 with slightly over 6 percent of exports. However, its colonies reemerged as a major sugar supplier in the nineteenth century, after the development of extensive plantations in Cuba and Puerto Rico. Sugar was also an important crop in Dutch Guiana (located on the northcentral coast of South America, in terrain that embraces the modern nations of Guyana and Surinam), and in the Danish island of St. Croix. Together they contributed slightly more to the sugar trade in 1787 than the Spanish colonies.[4]

The great majority of the slaves brought into the British, French, and Dutch Caribbean colonies were engaged in sugar production and its ancillary industries. In the 1820s in the British West Indies between two-thirds and three-quarters of the slaves were directly or indirectly engaged in sugar production.[5] In Brazil, perhaps 40 percent of the slaves imported were involved in sugar culture, and in Spanish America the share was probably between 30 and 50 percent. Mining, which probably stood second to sugar in the demand for labor, claimed about 20 percent of the slaves in Brazil. The balance of the blacks brought to the New World were utilized in the production of such diverse crops as coffee, cocoa, tobacco, indigo, hemp, cotton, and rice. Of the relatively small percentage of Africans engaged in urban pursuits, most were usually servants or manual laborers, although some became artisans. However, it is probable that by the mid-eighteenth century most of the urban occupations were held by creoles, slaves born in the New World, rather than by recent arrivals.[6]

SOME GENERAL CHARACTERISTICS OF NEW WORLD SLAVERY

Between 1600 and 1800, New World slaves represented less than a fifth of the population of the Western Hemisphere and less than 1 percent of the world's population.[7] Yet, during this long period and extending into the nineteenth century as well, slave-produced commodities dominated the channels of world trade. Sugar was the single most important of the internationally traded commodities, dwarfing in value the trade in grain, meat, fish, tobacco, cattle, spices, cloth, or metals. Shortly before the American Revolution sugar by itself accounted for about a fifth of all English imports and with the addition of tobacco, coffee, cotton, and rum, the share of slave-produced commodities in England's imports was about 30 percent.[8] The impact of slavery on world trade did not end there.

Much of England's shipping was engaged in transporting either sugar to Europe, slaves from Africa to the New World, or manufactured goods from England to the slave colonies. Toward the end of the eighteenth century more than half of Britain's exports were bound for one or another of the slave colonies. It was not just Britain but also France, Spain, Portugal, Holland, and Denmark that thrived on buying from or selling to slave colonies. "The whole of western France—the great ports of Bordeaux and Nantes, the cordage and sail-making industries of Brittany, the textile manufacture of Cholet, the seaport and inland refineries—all developed in great part on sugar and its derived demand."9

This intimate connection with trade, especially long-distance trade, differentiates New World slavery from the general form of slavery of the ancient world, or that in Africa and the Middle East in more recent times. Slaves in these societies were usually part of household economies, producing goods or services that would be consumed mainly by themselves and their families, by their masters, or by other members of their masters' households. The same was true of the European serfs. The fruits of their labor were usually consumed on the manors to which they were tied. Indeed, whether bound or free, less than 20 percent of the output of most European agriculturalists during the seventeenth or eighteenth centuries was destined to be exchanged on the market. But about 80 percent of the output of sugar plantations was sold on the world markets. Some New World slave societies grew so little besides sugar that they had to depend on imports, often produced by free farmers or fishermen, to feed their slaves. And so on the eve of the American Revolution most of the corn exports of the thirteen colonies and over 90 percent of livestock, dairy, and vegetable exports were sold to the West Indies.10

Another feature of New World slavery was the large scale of the enterprises on which slaves labored. In the beginning—before 1650 in the British West Indies or before 1725 in the Chesapeake Bay reigon—most slaves lived and worked on fairly small farms. In Barbados prior to 1650, for example, more than three-quarters of the island's population was white. These early colonists were usually Englishmen of modest means. Most were indentured servants but some were landowners whose farms were fairly small, generally under 50 acres. Most of the landowners employed only a few laborers each—at first English indentured servants and later on, also African slaves. But whether farmers, indentured servants, or slaves, those who labored in the fields generally did so in traditional ways, each working on a multitude of tasks, with little supervision, and at a traditional pace. The early pattern in the Chesapeake region was similar. As late as 1725 the *median* slave plantation in the Chesapeake had about 10 slaves.11

The advent of the sugar culture, beginning in Barbados about 1640, transformed the British West Indies. The replacement of tobacco by sugar not only changed the main market crop but also the lives of the agriculturalists. Small farms were rapidly consolidated into plantations. White and black hands who had farmed in traditional ways were replaced by large gangs of slaves, working in lock step, and moving methodically across vast fields. As early as 1680, the median size of a plantation in Barbados had increased to about 60 slaves. Over the decades the typical plantation in the West Indies became larger and larger. In Jamaica in 1832, on the eve of the abolition of British slavery, the median plantation contained about 150 slaves, and nearly one out of every four bondsmen lived on units containing at least 250 slaves.[12]

Whether sugar came early (as in the British West Indies) or late (as in Cuba), it always transformed the society, greatly increasing the ratio of slaves to free men, as well as the average size of the slave plantation. Cuba did not begin to specialize in sugar until late in the eighteenth century. At the beginning of the 1760s, when Massachusetts merchants and Virginia planters were starting to grumble about English policies, Cuba was still a relatively lightly settled island of small farms specializing in cattle and tobacco, with some coffee plantations. In 1774, about a decade after the beginning of the Cuban shift to sugar, 57 percent of the population was still white and another 20 percent was free black. Most of the slaves, who made up less than a quarter of the population, had probably arrived during the preceding decade. In the pre-sugar era a significant fraction of slaves were engaged in domestic service and those who worked in the fields usually did so on relatively small farms, often alongside their masters. Between 1774 and the census of 1841 the slave population increased by more than tenfold, due mainly to imports of Africans. And so the Barbados syndrome of the seventeenth century was reproduced in Cuba a century and a half later: Sugar pushed out tobacco; slaves pushed out free laborers; large slave plantations pushed out small ones; gang labor pushed out traditional methods of farming. By the middle of the nineteenth century slaves constituted nearly half of the Cuban population and, as in other sugar economies, the majority lived and worked on large plantations.[13]

The large slave plantations of the Western Hemisphere required huge capital investments, not only to cover the purchase price of the slaves but also to cover the cost of the land, buildings, work animals and other livestock, irrigation works, implements, and, in the case of sugar, machinery. Toward the end of the eighteenth century, the typical Jamaican sugar plantation operated with about 200 hands and had a capital value of about £26,400 (about $154,000 in 1860 dollars or about $21 million in 1986 dollars) of which land and buildings, including the sugar-refining machinery, represented half.[14] There were no U.S. factories of this size until the second decade of the nineteenth century.[15] As late as 1860 the average value of the capital invested in an American cotton textile factory was just $109,000 and the average number of employees was just 130. Throughout the eighteenth century, the great slave plantations of the sugar colonies, with profits averaging about 10 percent on invested capital, were the largest privately owned enterprises of the age and their owners were among the richest of all men. The same can be said of the great cotton plantations in the United States on the eve of the Civil War.[16]

The sugar plantations were not only large but also used some of the most advanced technology of their age. Every sugar plantation of any size had a sugar factory upon it that employed about 20 percent of its labor force. The factory operations included grinding the cane between huge rollers in order to extract the juice, filtering the juice to remove impurities, boiling the juice to clarify and crystallize it, curing sugar in vessels that allowed the molasses to drip out, and distilling molasses into rum. On the medium and large plantations these factories housed some of the most expensive and elaborate industrial equipment of the day. In Louisiana, on Thomas Pugh's Madewood Plantation for example, the sugar factory was a brick building 40 feet wide and 340 feet long (longer than a Manhattan block) and laid with iron rails so that cars could bring the cane right into the factory.[17]

In Cuba, planters enthusiastically promoted railroad construction. "The railroads were created to serve the sugar industry." Plans for rail connections between the sugar-growing regions and the ports began in 1830, just five years after the first successful steam railroad opened in England, and "within a short time . . . were in service in all the major sugar producing areas of the island." Planters also covered their plantations with narrow-gauged railroads to facilitate the delivery of sugar cane, as well as fuel, from the fields and forest portions of their plantations to the factory. Even planters who did not lay track on their fields did so within their factories to facilitate the movement of cane juice and sugar from operation to operation. The railroads within factories not only freed labor for other tasks but reduced the hazard to the slaves by mechanizing the transportation of hot cylinders.[18]

Sugar planters were also quick to use steam engines in their grinding operations. The first experiment with the use of steam to power sugar-rolling mills in the United States took place in 1822. That it was an economical technique was not at all obvious at first. While steam increased the crushing capacity of the mills and raised the yield of juice extracted from the stalks, the early steam-powered mills were very expensive and they required large quantities of costly fuel. Subsequent improvements cut the cost of such mills in half and raised their efficiency.

Within a decade after they were introduced, one-fourth of U.S. sugar estates had converted to steam mills and by 1860 the figure had climbed to 75 percent. It is interesting to note that as late as 1869 less than 63 percent of cotton textile mills had converted to steam. While sugar planters embraced this technology more rapidly and completely than did the textile manufacturers, its consequences were quite different in the two sectors. Steam power appears to have increased the scale of sugar factories, especially in Cuba, but it did not lead to the far-reaching transformation of economic activity that it stimulated in manufacturing.[19]

Sugar planters led the way in still another major technological innovation—the development of a new industrial labor discipline. This was at once their greatest technological achievement, the foundation of their economic success, and the ugliest aspect of their system. In considering this feature of New World slavery, it must be remembered that throughout the medieval era, custom controlled the pattern of European labor and the distribution of the product between serfs and lords. The lords did not set the exact hours of labor, strictly supervise the quality of field work, limit the number of holidays, or penalize inadequate yields, although there were bailiffs who supervised labor services on the lords' lands. The rhythm of work, which developed gradually over centuries, was generally slow and variable and the mode of labor was highly individualistic.

Every nation that has gone down the road of industrialization has had to come to grips with the difficult problem of converting peasants into industrial laborers. As recently as the 1920s and 1930s Stalin complained about the dogged resistance of Russian *muzhiks* to the demands of modern assembly lines; a century earlier British manufacturers had complained about the bad industrial habits of their rural recruits, finding them to be entirely lacking in discipline while on the job and constantly indulging in illicit holidays that came to be called "Saints Mondays" and "Saints Tuesdays."[20] Operatives fiercely resisted the regimentation required by the new mode of labor. According to Andrew Ure, an apostle of the factory system, it was "nearly impossible to convert persons past the age of puberty, whether drawn from rural or from handicraft occupations, into useful factory hands. After struggling for a while to conquer their listless or restive habits, they either renounce the employment spontaneously or are dismissed by overlookers on account of inattention."[21] This resistance reflected not the laziness or innate incompetence of the workers but their unwillingness to be dehumanized, to be reduced to cogs in a labor process "that seemed as inhuman as the machines that thundered in the factory and shed."[22]

The industrial discipline, so difficult to bring about in the factories

of free England and free New England, was achieved on sugar plantations more than a century earlier—partly because sugar production lent
itself to a minute division of labor, partly because of the invention of the
gang system, which provided a powerful instrument for the supervision
and control of labor, and partly because of the extraordinary degree of
force that planters were allowed to bring to bear on enslaved black
labor.[23] The gang system did not come into being everywhere at the same
moment of time. It developed gradually, over many decades, and the
process of development began in different places at different times. The
rate of growth in the size of plantations was certainly a factor affecting
its development, as was the nature of the crop. The gang system developed first on large sugar plantations and later spread to rice, coffee,
cotton, and, to a lesser extent, tobacco.[24]

There were, of course, significant differences in the operation of the
gang system from sugar plantation to sugar plantation and even greater
differences between sugar and cotton plantations. But certain features
were common to gang-system plantations regardless of location or crop.
The most basic of these was the division of the complex activities during
each phase of production—planting, cultivating, and harvesting—into a
series of relatively simple tasks that could be closely monitored. The
gang system thus gave rise to an elaborate division of labor that rested,
in the first instance, on a division between those slaves who worked in
gangs and those who did not. During the late eighteenth century about
half of the adult male slaves (age 16 or over) and five-sixths of the adult
female slaves on West Indian sugar plantations labored in gangs. Of the
males exempt from field work, about 20 percent held managerial jobs
(supervised other slaves) or were craftsmen and the balance worked in
semi-skilled jobs or in jobs reserved for the aged and the lame. The
division of labor on U.S. cotton plantations was similar, although the
proportion of adult males exempt from gang labor was smaller—closer
to 25 percent than to 50 percent. On both sugar and cotton plantations
field slaves usually worked in gangs of 10 to 20 hands, each of which
was headed by a "driver"—a slave who, with whip in hand, pushed his
gang to achieve the assigned task.[25]

Contemporary accounts underscore the importance that U.S. cotton
planters attached to the organization of their slaves into highly coordinated and precisely functioning gangs. "A plantation might be considered as a piece of machinery," said Bennet H. Barrow in his Highland
plantation rules. "To operate successfully, all its parts should be uniform
and exact, and its impelling force regular and steady."[26] "Driving," the
establishment of a rigid gang discipline, was considered the crux of a
successful operation. Observers, such as Robert Russell, said that the
discipline of plantation life was "almost as strict as that of our military

system."[27] Frederick Law Olmsted described one instance in which he observed two very large hoe gangs "moving across the field in parallel lines, with a considerable degree of precision." He reported that he "repeatedly rode through the lines at a canter, with other horsemen, often coming upon them suddenly, without producing the smallest change or interruption in the dogged action of the labourers."[28]

Each work gang was based on an internal division of labor that not only assigned every member of the gang to a precise task but simultaneously made his or her performance dependent on the actions of the others. On the McDuffie plantation the planting gang was divided into three classes:

> 1st, the best hands, embracing those of good judgment and quick motion. 2nd, those of the weakest and most inefficient class. 3rd, the second class of hoe hands. Thus classified, the first class will run ahead and open a small hole about seven to ten inches apart, into which the second class drop from four to five cotton seed, and the third class follow and cover with a rake.[29]

Interdependence and tension were also promoted between gangs, especially during the period of cultivation when the field labor force was divided into plow gangs and hoe gangs. The hoe hands chopped out the weeds that surrounded the cotton plants as well as excessive sprouts. The plow gangs followed behind, stirring the soil near the rows of cotton plants and tossing it back around the plants. Thus, the hoe and plow gangs each put the other under an assembly line type of pressure. The hoeing had to be completed in time to permit the plow hands to carry out their tasks. At the same time the progress of the hoeing, which entailed lighter labor than plowing, set a pace for the plow gang. The drivers or overseers moved back and forth between the two gangs, exhorting and prodding each to keep up with the pace of the other, as well as inspecting the quality of the work. In cotton picking, which did not lend itself as naturally to interdependence as did planting and cultivating, planters sought to promote intensity of effort by dividing hands into competing gangs and offering bonuses on a daily and weekly basis to the gang that picked the most. They also made extensive use of the so-called task methods. These were, literally, time-motion studies on the basis of which a daily quota for each hand was established.[30]

In addition to assembly line methods and time-motion studies to ensure maximum intensity of effort in a particular operation, planters sought to allocate their slaves among jobs in such a manner as to achieve "full-capacity" utilization of each person. In this connection slaves were given "hand" ratings—generally ranging from one-eighth to a full hand—according to their age, sex, and physical ability. The strongest hands were put into field work, with the ablest of these given tasks that would set the pace for the others. Plow gangs were composed primarily of men in their twenties or early thirties. Less sturdy men and boys, as well as prime-aged women, were in the hoe gangs. Older women were occupied in such domestic jobs as house servants and nurses; older men worked as gardeners, servants, and stock minders. Analysis of the records of the Kollock plantation in Georgia in 1860 indicates that the "hand"-to-slave ratio was 0.9 in field work but only 0.6 in non-field work.[31]

Data on the cotton-picking rates of pregnant women and nursing mothers provide still another illustration of the degree to which planters succeeded in utilizing all those in the labor force. Down to the last week before birth, pregnant women picked three-quarters or more of the amount that was normal for women of corresponding ages who were neither pregnant nor nursing. Only during the month following childbirth was there a sharp reduction in the amount of cotton picked. Some mothers started to return to field work during the second or third week after birth. By the second month after birth, picking rates reached two-thirds of the level for non-nursing mothers. By the third month, the level rose to over 90 percent.[32]

It is sometimes said that the principal function of the gang system was to increase the average number of hours that a slave worked beyond that which was typical of free labor. There is evidence suggesting that the hours of work on slave plantations exceeded those of subsistence farmers in Europe and America before the Industrial Revolution and also of subsistence farmers in the underdeveloped nations of the world today. Nevertheless, it was product per worker and not the number of hours that planters sought to maximize. Many discovered that the way to achieve this objective was not by pushing the number of working hours to the outer limit but by coupling increases in the intensity of labor per hour with a reduction in the total number of hours worked. One planter, for example, experimented with the number and frequency of the rest breaks he should provide during the day, and reached the conclusion that, in addition to the breakfast and lunch breaks, a five-minute rest every half hour increased the productivity of the slaves by 15 percent. Such rest breaks, it was noted, also increased the pace and productivity of the mules.[33] Recent studies of the labor routine on U.S. cotton plantations have revealed that the average workweek during the spring, summer, and fall was about 58 hours, well below the 72 hours thought to have prevailed in English textile mills during the first quarter of the nineteenth century and also below the 60-hour week of northern commercial farmers in the United States during the first quarter of the twentieth century.[34]

SOME SPECIAL ASPECTS OF THE EVOLUTION OF SLAVERY IN THE UNITED STATES

The United States stood apart from the other slave-importing territories, not only because of its comparatively small share in the Atlantic slave trade, but also because of the minor role played by its sugar industry in the growth of U.S. slavery. The commercial production of sugar in Louisiana did not begin until 1795, barely a decade before the United States withdrew from the international slave trade. At the time of the U.S. annexation of Louisiana, annual sugar production was a mere 5,000 tons. Even at its antebellum peak, sugar was never more than a minor southern crop that utilized less than 10 percent of the slave labor force.[35]

The absence of the sugar culture had a profound effect on the development of slavery in the U.S. colonies. For one thing, it affected the rate at which the slave labor force grew, both in absolute numbers and in relative importance. While African labor was introduced into Virginia earlier than in Barbados, there were six times as many blacks in the British Caribbean in 1700 as there were in all of the North American colonies. Some 80 years after the first group of slaves landed in Virginia, the black population of that colony was just 16,000, while all the other North American colonies contained a mere 11,000 blacks. In the British Caribbean the slave population climbed to 60,000 within 30 years after the beginning of the British presence. It took her North American colonies 110 years to reach the same absolute level, despite the higher rate of natural increase of slaves in North America and the high mortality rate in the Caribbean.[36]

As late as 1680 the relatively few slaves in Britain's North American colonies (under 7,000) were widely distributed in general farming and domestic occupations, but a concentration of slave labor in tobacco had already begun to develop in the Chesapeake. By the middle of the 1730s, the slave population had risen to about 120,000 with tobacco production requiring the concentrated effort of perhaps a third of the hands and rice another tenth. Thus, the majority of slaves were still employed mainly in general farming, in domestic service, in crafts, or in other non-farm occupations. This basic pattern continued for the next three decades, although by the mid-1760s the share of the labor of slave hands claimed by the three principal plantation crops—tobacco, rice, and indigo—had risen to a bit over 50 percent and there were rapidly growing slave populations in the Carolinas and Georgia. Allowing for the slaves en-

gaged in crafts, domestic service, and secondary-market products, plantations specializing in these three crops may have accounted for two-thirds
of the slave labor.[37]

Cotton did not emerge as a major southern crop until the beginning
of the nineteenth century, after the cotton gin lowered the cost of fiber
(see Figure 2). At the beginning of the nineteenth century about 11
percent of all slaves lived on cotton plantations. With the swelling
demand, production rose so rapidly that by 1850 the proportion engaged
on cotton plantations had risen to about 64 percent. The tobacco share
had dwindled to 12 percent; sugar was next with 5 percent; rice had
about 4 percent; and indigo was no longer commercially produced in the
South.[38]

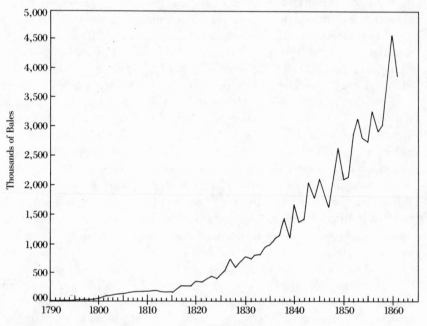

Figure 2. The course of U.S. cotton production, 1791–1861.

The differences in the U.S. and West Indian patterns of crop specialization led to striking differences in the ratios of blacks to total population.[39] As early as 1650, blacks formed 25 percent of the population in
the British Caribbean. In 1770 the ratio stood at 91 percent. The experience in the French Caribbean was similar. By contrast, blacks formed
only 4 percent of the population of the North American colonies in 1650
and rose to a pre-Revolutionary peak of 22 percent in 1770. In the
southern U.S. colonies the percentages for 1650 and 1770 were 3 and

40, respectively. Thus, while blacks were the overwhelming majority of the population and labor force of the Caribbean during most of the colonial era, they were generally a minority of the population of the U.S. colonies and for most of the colonial period a relatively small minority, even in the South. It was only toward the middle of the eighteenth century, after slaves became geographically concentrated, that they emerged as the majority of the population in certain counties.[40]

The U.S. pattern of crop specialization also affected the size of the units on which slaves lived and had far-reaching effects on the development of slave culture. During the colonial era, the median size of tobacco plantations remained below 20 slaves, and it increased only slightly thereafter. Slaves who labored in tobacco typically worked on plantations consisting of a white family and a few slave families; even large tobacco plantations were usually organized as a series of small units.[41] Cotton plantations were not much larger; the median in 1860 was 35 slaves. The biggest plantations in the United States were in rice and sugar. There were about 100 slaves on the typical Louisiana sugar plantation in 1860. Although this figure exceeds the averages for tobacco, cotton, and even rice, it falls below the averages of sugar estates in the Caribbean or Brazil.[42] And so, U.S. slave plantations were dwarfed by those of the West Indies. Blacks in these islands, particularly in Jamaica, had relatively little contact with the European culture of the white slave owner both because of the small percentage of whites who lived there and because of the enormous size of the typical plantation. But blacks in the U.S. colonies were usually a minority of the population and, even toward the end of the antebellum era, lived on relatively small units (generally fewer than seven or eight families), which brought them into continuous contact with their white masters.

U.S. slaves were not only in closer contact with European culture, they were also more removed from their African origins than were slaves in the Caribbean. Down through the end of the eighteenth century and into the nineteenth century, the majority of the slave populations of the British and French Caribbean islands and of Brazil were born in Africa because Africans were continually imported to offset the high death rates there. Indeed, as late as 1800, one-quarter of the population of Jamaica consisted of Africans who had arrived in the New World within the previous decade. On the other hand, creoles (slaves born in the New World) made up the majority of the slave population in the U.S. colonies as early as 1740 (Figure 3). By the time of Washington's presidency, the African-born component of the black population had shrunk to a bit over 20 percent. It hovered close to this share from 1780 to 1810 and then rapidly headed toward zero. By 1850 all but a minute fraction of U.S.

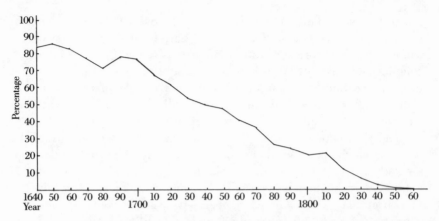

Figure 3. Foreign-born blacks as a percentage of all U.S. blacks, 1640–1860.

slaves were native born, and most of them were third-, fourth-, or fifth-generation Americans. This finding does not contradict the view that African heritage played a large role in shaping the culture of blacks, but it does serve to emphasize the extent to which black culture had, by 1860, been exposed to indigenous American influences.[43]

The rapid decline in the relative share of Africans in the U.S. black population during the last half of the eighteenth century was not due to a decline in imports (Figure 4). With the exception of the decade of the American Revolution, which brought with it a sharp decline in all international commerce, the trend in imports of slaves into the United States was strongly upward from 1620 until the end of legal U.S. involvement in the international slave trade in 1808. It has been frequently asserted that slavery was dying in the United States from the end of the Revolution until 1810 and that if it had not been for the rise of the cotton culture, slavery would have passed from existence long before the Civil War. This proposition rests partly on erroneous but widely cited estimates of slave imports for the period from 1790 to 1810 put forward by Henry Carey. Revised estimates show that far from declining, slave imports were higher in this period than in any previous 20-year period of U.S. history. There were, in fact, almost as many Africans brought into the United States during the 30 years from 1780 to 1810 as during the previous 160 years.[44]

While the imports of Africans certainly contributed to the growth in the slave population of the U.S. colonies, they were of secondary importance in explaining that growth after 1720. Natural increase was by far the more significant factor during the eighteenth and nineteenth centuries—another respect in which the U.S. experience differed from that of Latin America. In the British and French West Indies, in Dutch Guiana, and in Brazil, the death rate of slaves was so high and the birth rate so

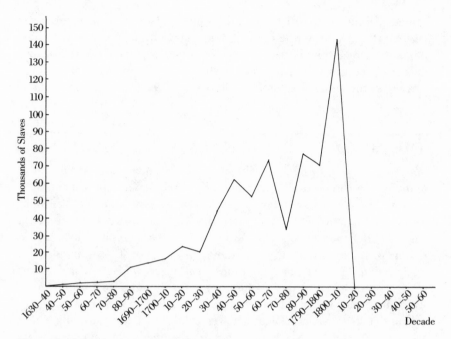

Figure 4. U.S. imports of slaves per decade, 1630–1860.

low that these territories could not sustain their population levels without large and continuous importations of Africans.

Whatever the factors responsible for the high rate of natural increase experienced by U.S. slaves, its consequences were clear. Despite their low rates of importations, which initially caused the growth of the U.S. slave population to lag behind that of the Caribbean, the U.S. colonies not only overtook but far exceeded the rate of growth of the slave populations elsewhere in the hemisphere. By 1720, the annual rate of natural increase in the United States was greater than the annual increase due to importations. And although the absolute level of importations was high after the Revolution, importations contributed only half as much to the growth of the black population as did natural increase. Even these statements underestimate the impact of the favorable demographic experience for they fail to take into account the unfavorable demographic experience elsewhere. In 1800 there were 1,002,000 blacks in the United States. But if the United States had duplicated the demographic experience of the West Indies, its black population in 1800 would have been only 186,000.[45]

Thus, the United States became the leading user of slave labor in the New World, not because it participated heavily in the slave trade but because of the unusually high rate of natural increase. By 1825 there were about 1,750,000 slaves in the southern United States. This represented 36 percent of all of the slaves in the New World in that year. Despite its peripheral role in the Atlantic slave trade, the size of its slave population and the success of its plantation system during the three decades preceding the Civil War made the South the greatest center of slavery in the New World and the bulwark of resistance to the abolition of slavery.[46]

THE CONTEST BETWEEN SLAVE AND FREE LABOR

Why did slavery become dominant in the economy and society of so many of the New World settlements?[47] Three factors are usually cited. Alternative sources of labor were scarce; European labor was more expensive than African labor; Africans could endure the rigors of the tropics better than Europeans. While each of these factors played a role, no one of them individually, or their joint sum, constitutes an adequate explanation. Traditional explanations treat the rise of New World slavery as if it occurred by default—merely because a superior form of labor, free labor, was not available, was too expensive, or somehow could not operate in the tropics. These answers slide past the most distinctive feature of New World slavery, the feature that made planters prefer slave to free labor even when free labor was relatively abundant, and even in climates, such as those of Maryland and Virginia, that were as congenial to Europeans as to Africans.

This feature is the enormous, almost unconstrained degree of force available to masters who wanted and needed to transform ancient modes of labor into a new industrial discipline. Centuries of tradition made it difficult to achieve that desired conversion without force; and the more rapid the rate of conversion the greater the amount of force that was necessary. Centuries of tradition also shielded European laborers from the degree of force that was permitted against African or Afro-American slaves. It is true that a certain amount of force was involved in the system of indentured servitude under which most Europeans reached the New World before 1800. But the degree of force involved in that case was not much greater than had been traditional in European society, it was closely monitored by the courts, and it was constrained by the character of the contract covering such servitude.[48]

It should be kept in mind that African labor and slave labor were not necessarily synonymous. In Cuba there were nearly as many free African or Afro-American laborers prior to the sugar revolution as there were slaves. In Puerto Rico, free blacks outnumbered slaves by 3 to 1 throughout the first third of the nineteenth century. In Mexico, slavery gradually dissolved itself during the seventeenth and eighteenth centuries as more and more slaves were voluntarily manumitted. But in the sugar colonies, and in economies based on the other crops that lent themselves to the gang system, slavery surged forward, manumissions were sharply curtailed, and free labor was not only unsought but was often, quite literally, pushed out. Barbados and Jamaica are cases in point. Not only did large plantations replace small freeholds there, but the white indentured servants originally called upon to work as artisans and tradesmen on the sugar estates were gradually replaced by slaves.[49]

Colonies and occupations in which slavery existed as a marginal institution should be distinguished from those in which slavery was indispensable to the economy on which it was based. Slavery was marginal in the northern U.S. colonies because no major crops lent themselves to the gang system.[50] It was marginal in Mexico and Peru because sugar remained a secondary crop until late in the nineteenth century. It was marginal in most urban occupations because slavery was not needed to alter the rhythm of work. In the case of the artisan crafts, the gang system could not be applied effectively. After the Industrial Revolution the factories provided a number of devices for transforming the rhythm of labor that were excellent alternatives to the gang system—although some southern manufacturers found that slaves could be used to undermine the resistance of free workers. A student of urban slavery has shown that the cities of the South provided a convenient reservoir for slave labor. During periods when the rural demand for slaves rose more rapidly than the supply, slaves were pulled from the cities. When the rural demand lagged behind supply, slaves were sent from the plantations to the cities. But urban enterprises did not require slavery to become competitive in the marketplace.[51]

In sugar production, on the other hand, free labor was vanquished almost everywhere by the gang system. Where small-scale production persisted, it was largely for local markets protected by tariffs and the like or aided by some special local advantage. When the gang system was extended to rice, coffee, and cotton, it also conquered these crops and left small-scale farmers with minor fractions of these markets.

Not all the victories of the gang system were so decisive. The penetration of tobacco farming by slave labor proceeded more slowly and was never as complete as it became in sugar, rice, coffee, or cotton. Recent analyses of the initial surge (1680 to 1710) in the importation of slaves into the tobacco region of the Chesapeake do not suggest that the switch to slave labor stemmed from a desire to change the mode of labor. It appears to have been induced by a rise in the price of servants (indentured English laborers) abetted by a more limited decline in slave prices, which made slaves relatively inexpensive for about three decades. The slaves imported during this period were not hustled into gangs but labored much in the manner of the servants they were replacing. Analysis of probate records in two Chesapeake counties shows that at the turn of the eighteenth century the average number of slaves plus servants per estate was about the same as it had been 30 years earlier—two or three bound persons per estate. The slave share of the bound labor, however, had risen from one-third to two-thirds of the total.[52]

Although gang-system plantations became more important as time wore on, they never became dominant in tobacco. An analysis of the farms in the tobacco region of Kentucky and Tennessee revealed that 65 percent of the tobacco crop in 1860 was produced on free or small slave farms. Large-scale plantations, those with 51 or more slaves, accounted for less than 10 percent of the region's tobacco output. The failure of gang-system plantations to sweep aside traditional farming was due not to entrepreneurial failure or moral reservations, but to biological characteristics of the tobacco plant which limited opportunities for the division of labor and for the organization of production on an assembly line basis.[53]

Political and cultural factors also affected the outcome of the contest between slave and free labor. The growth of capitalism in England during the seventeenth and eighteenth centuries led the Crown and Parliament to encourage the formation of large-scale slave plantations. Since these "capitalist plantations" were producing commodities eagerly demanded at home, English governing authorities were prepared to stimulate them with subsidies, where necessary, and to remove legal impediments. Ironically, the English tradition of representative government meant that the formulation of the laws that gave legal definition to the institution of slavery was left to colonial legislatures dominated by slaveholders. These legislatures passed a series of statutes during the seventeenth century that quite literally deprived Africans of their humanity in a legal sense, reducing them to the status of mere property—deprived not only of economic and political freedom but also of the right to marry or to be set free, even if it was the master's wish, except by an act of the legislature.[54]

Among the British colonies it was Barbados that led the way in the establishment of slave codes. Its enactments were closely followed in Jamaica, Virginia, and elsewhere. The Barbados codes did not emerge in full bloom but gradually developed as planters gained experience with the new mode of labor and from time to time petitioned the legislature for a variety of prerogatives in the management of their slaves, petitions to which the legislature dutifully responded. Within a few decades planters were granted the right to apply unlimited force to compel labor. At the mere behest of a planter, courts would order the dismemberment or death of a slave. Planters were also shielded from prosecution if, in the attempt to compel the labor of a slave, the slave should be killed. In all this, sharp distinctions were drawn between the status of a white servant and a black slave, and a racist ideology was steadily evolved to justify the distinction. Before the end of the seventeenth century, the planters of the British colonies were granted that which some British manufacturers 100 years later might have desired, but never dared to request: a labor force stripped of every right that could have impeded their industrial designs. As nearly as the law could bring it about, slaves were to be as compliant a factor of production as the mills that ground the cane or the mules that pulled the carts. Planters had the license to establish whatever institutions and to use whatever force they deemed necessary to achieve that goal.

Political policies and cultural factors in the Spanish colonies, on the other hand, tended to inhibit the development of gang-system plantations. As a consequence, Mexico, Peru, Cuba, and Puerto Rico, which all had climates and soils eminently suited for the large-scale production of sugar, did not become significant producers of this crop for the international market until three centuries after they were conquered by Spain. Cuba and Puerto Rico turned to large-scale sugar production late in the eighteenth century; Mexico and Peru did so at the end of the nineteenth century, after the abolition of slavery. For most of the colonial era the majority of the slaves in the Spanish colonies were generally employed in small-scale enterprises. In Peru and Mexico slaves were heavily concentrated in producing a wide array of agricultural commodities intended for the domestic market rather than for export, with considerable numbers employed as domestics or craftsmen in the cities. Some slaves were employed in mines, but they were generally a minority of the miners.[55]

Part of the explanation for this pattern may be related to the fact that slavery in the Spanish colonies started early in the sixteenth century, when capitalist classes were weaker in Spain than they were in Britain a century later. The major factors, however, seem to have been the autocracy of the Spanish Crown and the heavy interference of the Spanish Church in commercial affairs. Ironically, the Crown's resistance to democracy meant that the laws governing the use of slaves were made in Spain rather than by the slaveholders in the colonies. While the Crown's decisions regarding slavery and the slave trade were influenced by the needs and petitions of the colonial slaveholders, they were also influenced by pressures from the Church and by considerations related to its rivalries and wars with other imperial powers.

Several scholars have placed special emphasis on the role of the Spanish Church, identifying it as "the prime arbiter" of the social and intellectual life in Spain's New World colonies. "Not only did it define the moral basis of society and determine the limits of its intellectual world view, but," according to this interpretation, "it also sanctified and legalized the most basic human relationships." The principal objective of the Spanish Church in the colonies was to bring all the "primitive" heathens—Indians as well as Africans—into its fold. Conceding the right of the colonists to the labor of the Indians and Africans, the Spanish Church nevertheless insisted on its right to determine the "moral, religious, and even social" conditions under which this labor was conducted. It was the aim of the Spanish Church to preserve as much of the legal personality of the slave as possible, including "the right to full Christian communion, and through the sanctity of the Spanish Church, the right to marriage and parenthood." These principles, it is argued, led the Spanish Church to defend the right of slaves to personal security, to private property, and to the purchase of their own freedom. Voluntary manumission was promoted through a system called *coartación* under which a slave could petition a court to set the price at which he could purchase his freedom. "Once a slave became *coartado* he had a whole range of rights, including the right to change masters if he could find a purchaser for his remaining price and to buy his freedom as soon as he was able."[56] Other scholars contest this view on the ground that it exaggerates the extent of the influence of the Spanish Church and minimizes the extent of the cruelty and brutality of Spanish slavery, which sanctioned whipping, "mutilation of body members," including castration, and "slow death" as forms of punishment.[57]

Whatever the forces influencing the Spanish Crown, and leaving the debate over the relative mildness or harshness of the day-to-day treatment of slaves for later consideration, the weight of evidence indicates that decrees of the Crown severely restricted the rise of large-scale, gang-system plantations—of capitalist plantations that produced primarily for a world market. To begin with, the Spanish Crown limited the importation of slaves below the level desired by the planters. Although smuggling reduced their effectiveness, these restrictions nevertheless raised the cost of obtaining slaves and so reduced the supply. Moreover, the fact that slaves could marry, even against the wishes of the master, and that married families could not be separated, certainly restricted the economic latitude of masters, especially when the spouse was a free person. Although these provisions were often evaded, as in Brazil, evasion was less than universal. In Mexico, for example, the government sent inspectors to make unannounced visits to plantations, mines, and mills. Moreover, masters were tried for excessive brutality and other violations of the slave codes before both secular and religious courts in response to petitions by slaves or by sympathetic free persons. Similarly, while masters might have had ways of getting around the slave's right to self-purchase, the number of free blacks increased much more rapidly in the Spanish than in the British or French colonies. It is probable that as early as 1592 a fourth of Mexico's blacks were freedmen.[58]

Further evidence of the critical role of the political factor is to be found in Cuba's dramatic turn to sugar and the gang system, which coincided with a shift of political power from metropolitan Spain to Cuban planters. This political shift was initially reflected in the removal of restrictions on the importation of slaves, which began on a temporary basis in the 1760s and was finally made permanent in 1789. The growing power of the planters also served to undermine the new code governing the treatment of slaves that was issued by the Crown in the same year. So fierce and effective was planter opposition that the code was not even published by the authorities in Havana. And so restrictions on planter behavior disintegrated. Planters in Cuba, as in Barbados during the seventeenth century, gained a virtually free hand—free at least from the interference of the state—for about a half century. It was during this period that the gang system flourished.[59]

The outcome of the contest between slave and free labor thus turned on a combination of technological, economic, political, and cultural factors. Technological and economic conditions were necessary but, by themselves, were not sufficient to tip the scales in favor of slave labor. For the gang system to succeed there had to be a set of crops that allowed the division of the production process into a series of simple and easily monitored tasks. There also had to be a rapidly growing demand for such crops. Even so, the gang system flourished only where political and legal conditions kept the cost of operating gang-system plantations low. To operate effectively the system required an adequate supply of slaves, wide latitude in the use of the force needed to achieve an industrial discipline, and freedom to reallocate its labor force as economic conditions might dictate. Just how much interference with optimum conditions a slave economy could tolerate varied from time to time and place to place, depending on such factors as the relative supply of free labor, the levels of demand for those commodities in which the gang system had an advantage, the relative advantage of an unfettered gang system in the production of specific crops, and the skill of particular planters in the management of their enterprises. From the early sixteenth century until the end of the eighteenth century or beyond, the relevant factors conspired in the southern United States and in the British Caribbean to promote the victory of slave over free labor. When the scales began to tip in the other direction, it was due mainly to adverse developments in the ideological and political arenas. These ideological and political reversals, as we shall see, had far-reaching economic consequences.

CHAPTER TWO

OCCUPATIONAL PATTERNS

By examining the structures of slave occupations and their variations, one can identify some of the underlying forces that shaped the
social order of slave societies. Economists usually define the structure of
an economy by the distribution of output, or of the labor force, among
economic activities. The distribution of labor is the measure of choice
in this chapter because the wider availability of data on labor skills
increases the range of comparisons. Censuses taken in Trinidad, the
former British slave colony off the coast of Venezuela, contain unusually
good data for a comparison with the structure of slave occupations in the
U.S. South. Because the South and Trinidad were so different in size,
crop mix, ethnic composition, demographic conditions, history, and legal
regulations, this comparison provides an excellent starting point for
identifying both the variable and the stable features of occupational
structures across gang-system economies. Where data permit, the comparison is extended to other slave economies.[1]

SOME OCCUPATIONAL PATTERNS

The most striking variation in occupational patterns is that between
gang-system economies and economies in which slavery was economically marginal. In the gang-system economies of the nineteenth century
the great majority of slaves labored in agriculture, the urban proportion
of the population was generally under 10 percent, and the proportion of
slaves engaged in domestic services ranged between 10 and 20 percent,
depending on the size of the urban sector. In societies where slavery was
economically marginal, such as in Peru during the late sixteenth and
early seventeenth centuries, in Mexico about the same period, or in Cuba
before 1760, the share of slaves in the total population was smaller, and
a large proportion, perhaps a majority, of the slaves worked in cities.
Even the rural slaves tended to work on small produce farms close to
the cities.[2]

Within these cities most of the females and a fair proportion of the
males were domestics. However, the urban males were found mainly in

the handicrafts, transportation, construction, church, or government institutions, including military service. The hiring of slaves was common
in urban areas, sometimes predominant. Artisans and other skilled
slaves were often allowed to hire themselves out. They sought their own
jobs and bargained over wages with their employers as free artisans did,
but had to pay their masters either a fixed periodic sum or a fixed
percentage of their income. Such relative freedom affected the quality of
life and also gave slave artisans a strong position in the labor markets.[3]

Slavery was also marginal in the cities of such gang-system societies
as the cotton South and nineteenth-century Cuba. In cities where the
proportions of slave and white artisans were fairly even, sharp conflicts
often arose. A recent study described the pressure periodically put on
the legislatures of Charleston, Norfolk, Richmond, and Savannah by
white artisans who appealed for ordinances that would restrict the activities of slaves. In cities where slave artisans and freedmen predominated,
blacks sometimes became a powerful force in the labor market, so much
so that in Cuba "when massive white peasant immigration got under way
in the nineteenth century, the unskilled European peasants found the
labor market already heavily controlled by Negroes, and this control was
never broken."[4]

In gang-system economies the crafts and other non-gang occupations
were more heavily concentrated on the great plantations than in the
cities. For example, about 90 percent of slave managers and craftsmen
in Jamaica in 1834 worked on plantations. The urban/rural distribution
of craftsmen and managers in the United States during the late antebellum era was quite similar. Craftsmen on large plantations were not as
regimented as gang laborers but generally lacked the freedoms of their
urban counterparts. Many labored exclusively on the plantations to
which they were attached. Only a minority appear to have been hired out
to neighboring plantations or free farms. Some plantation-based artisans,
like their urban counterparts, sought their own employment. But in the
rural sector this appears to have been uncommon.[5]

Slaves were not always so prominent in the crafts and in the management of gang-system plantations. The timing of their entry into higher
occupations is another way in which gang-system and marginal slave
economies differed. In Mexico, Colombia, Bolivia, Peru, and Chile slaves
were found in the higher occupations from the very beginning of Spanish
colonization. An uncertain number, perhaps a few hundred, were even
assistants to the conquistadors in expeditions into new territories and
enjoyed the spoils of conquest. Some slave soldiers became free, some
rose to be conquistadors, and some became slaveholders themselves. By
the 1570s it was no longer possible to gain entry into the ruling elites
by accomplishing great military feats. But slaves continued to serve in

the military or police organizations, as personal servants to the ruling elite, and as artisans.[6]

The entry of slaves into higher occupations was more protracted and hesitant in gang-system economies. The fragmentary data suggest that during the third quarter of the seventeenth century most of the craft and managerial posts on sugar plantations in Barbados were held by whites. In 1676 the island's legislature prohibited slaves from entering skilled crafts "so as to reserve these occupations for Christian artisans." The process by which such restrictions were overcome is obscure and the point at which slaves became predominant in the crafts cannot as yet be established with precision, although it probably occurred sometime between the 1720s and 1770s.[7]

The circumstances of the shift to slave managers are even more obscure, but debates about their role in the development of slave culture have focused new attention on them. In the Chesapeake region at the beginning of the eighteenth century it was common for small groups of slaves to live and work by themselves on properties that were remote from the masters' homes—which suggests that slaves were probably in charge of these groups. But such arrangements appear to pre-date a gang-system organization. Little is known about the origins of the use of drivers—individuals who headed relatively small (usually 10 to 30 hands), task-oriented gangs—but that post probably became necessary as soon as plantations grew beyond the size of a single task-oriented gang. Sketchy evidence suggests that in the British West Indies during the seventeenth century some of those who performed the function of drivers were white indentured servants, but from the second or third quarter of the eighteenth century on, it appears that they were, as a rule, slaves. The West Indian shift toward slave managers continued through the eighteenth century and into the nineteenth century. By the 1780s and 1790s the Jamaican headmen in most crafts were slaves, although the head boiler was usually still white. Thomas Roughley's guide to planters suggests a change by the mid-1820s: The head boiler in Jamaica was often a slave.[8]

In the British colonies of North America there are references to slave drivers in the mid-eighteenth century, but it is not known how many were responsible directly to masters rather than to hired white overseers. The growth of slave participation in the management of large U.S. plantations appears to have been checked by 1850, if not sooner. As fears of abolitionist attempts to foment slave revolts intensified, new laws were passed, and old laws were more vigorously enforced, in order to limit the off-plantation movements of slaves, to limit unsupervised meetings of slaves, to prohibit schools that taught slaves to read and write, and to require the presence of white overseers on intermediate and large slave plantations. According to Carter Woodson, the tendency toward the amelioration of slavery in the United States was reversed after 1825. This reversal does not appear to have led to a sizable replacement of slave craftsmen by whites, at least not on large plantations. But after 1840 the proportion of large plantations on which slaves were the chief non-ownership managers probably began to decline. The rate of decline appears to have increased during the decade of the 1850s, although even in 1860 slaves were probably still the chief non-ownership managers on about half of all large plantations.[9]

The shift from white to slave managers and artisans was more or less completed by the beginning of the nineteenth century and the slave occupational structures remained fairly stable thereafter in most gang-system economies. Analysis of the division between field and non-field hands in the agricultural sectors of three gang-system economies (Jamaica, Trinidad, and Surinam) for which censuses are available shows that those who labored in the field varied from 72 to 80 percent. But not all field laborers worked in gangs. From 10 to 30 percent labored on plantations that were too small for the gang system to be effective. Including the urban slaves, it appears that between 44 and 57 percent of the adult slaves in Surinam, Jamaica, and Trinidad were gang labor-ers. The United States in 1850 fell near the low end of this range, despite its relatively small urban sector, because about one-quarter of the adult U.S. slaves on farms were attached to units with 15 or fewer slaves and these small units did not generally rely on the gang system.[10]

So even in societies appropriately characterized as gang-system economies, 35 to 65 percent of adult slaves were not in gangs. Large fractions of the labor force escaped gang regimentation for three reasons: slavery remained viable in tobacco and in other crops where small units accounted for substantial shares of total production; the intermediate and large slave plantations required up to a third of their slaves in manage-rial, craft, and other support occupations; and from 5 to 20 percent of the slaves labored in transportation and urban industries that served the agricultural sector or processed its products. The notion that gang-system economies were monoculture economies risks misunderstanding. They were economies in which one staple crop was usually more important than the other staple crops, but the principal crop in each case was far from being an exclusive one. In Trinidad in 1813 sugar plantations accounted for a bit less than 50 percent of the labor force; in Jamaica in 1832 about 50 percent of the labor force was directly engaged in sugar production, with perhaps another 20 percent engaged in cattle pens and other enterprises connected to sugar estates; in the United States in 1850 cotton plantations absorbed about 64 percent of the labor force.[11]

It does not follow that because U.S. cotton plantations absorbed 64 percent of the slave labor force (about 1,400,000 slaves aged 10 and over) all of these workers were engaged in cotton production. Some 250,000 were managers, artisans, semi-skilled workers, or domestics who were not engaged in field tasks. Moreover, not all of the labor time of the remaining 1,150,000 field hands was spent in producing cotton. Even on farms where cotton was the primary market crop, most of the labor time of slaves was devoted to activities other than the growing of cotton. This paradox is easily resolved. Nearly 100 percent of all cotton was shipped off the farm, but most of the output of grains, vegetables, and meat was consumed on the farm. Cotton was, of course, the single most important crop on the intermediate and large cotton plantations, requiring about 38 percent of the labor time of slaves. However, the growing of corn and the care of livestock together took nearly as much of the labor time of slaves—about 31 percent. The remaining 31 percent of the working time of slave hands was divided among land improvements, the construction of fences and buildings, the raising of other crops (potatoes, peas, etc.), domestic duties, and home manufacturing (especially the production of clothes).[12]

THE EFFECT OF GENDER, STATURE, AND COLOR ON THE ALLOCATION OF ELITE OCCUPATIONS

For the United States and Jamaica information on the sexual division of labor thus far has been derived from samples. But as can be seen from Figure 5, these samples show sexual patterns of employment similar to those revealed by the censuses for Surinam and Trinidad. Perhaps the most surprising discovery is that a larger proportion of the females than the males were engaged as field hands. The proportion of adult women who were field hands ranged from a low of 66 percent on one Jamaican sugar plantation to a high of 84 percent in Trinidad. The corresponding range for adult males was 42 to 71 percent. There was also a marked sexual division of labor among the field hands. Two cliometricians have pointed out that the plow gangs on the large cotton plantations were not only exclusively male, but were composed largely of males in their twenties or early thirties. The hoe gangs were composed mainly of women and boys or older men. Women also predominated in cotton picking, outnumbering adult men in a ratio of about 5 to 4. It appears that the sexual division of field work tended to be somewhat less rigid on plantations of intermediate size (16 to 50 slaves). Women were occasionally found in the plow gangs on such farms, apparently because of a shortage of males who could be so employed.[13]

The distribution of non-field occupations also displayed a distinct sexual division of labor. Females were rarely craftsmen and were only

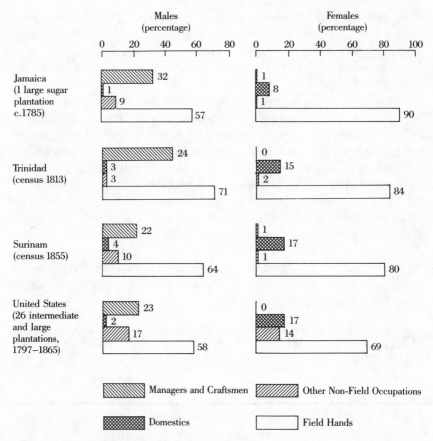

Figure 5. The occupational distribution of adult slaves on plantations, by gender, in four gang-system economies. For Jamaica, Trinidad, and the United States, adults are defined as persons aged 17 or older. Totals may not add to 100 due to rounding.

occasionally managers, and then, more often than not, managed units in which females or children predominated. They sometimes headed the domestic staff of a planter's household or functioned as the drivers of the weeding or trash gangs, which were composed mainly of children, the aged, or the physically impaired. The most common non-field occupation for women was as domestics, except in the sample of Jamaican sugar plantations where the owners were usually absentees. When owners were away, the domestic staffs were limited to the minimum needed to take care of their idle mansions. But when the owners were in residence, the domestic staffs were increased severalfold—to approximately the levels prevailing in the other economies. In the United States, especially on the intermediate and large cotton plantations, women were also employed in cloth houses where they spun and wove cloth. About 10 percent of all women over age 40 who were fit enough to be in the labor force were employed in cloth production. They were joined by some girls and some men who were lame or otherwise too enfeebled to engage in the field work.[14]

Figure 5 not only shows that the elite occupations[15] of managers and artisans were almost exclusively male in all four economies, but that managers and craftsmen represented about 20 percent of the adult male labor force in each of these cases. We do not yet know the relative importance of all the factors that contributed to this overwhelming male dominance, but stature and physical strength were surely important. Blacksmiths, coopers, carpenters, boilers, and other artisans are referred to as elites because they had occupations that brought them higher incomes, better living conditions, greater security, and more freedom than was allowed to field hands. But one should not assume that these occupations brought shorter hours or released artisans from heavy manual labor. Blacksmiths spent long days wielding heavy hammers and pumping bellows. Coopers built and moved heavy tierces and hogsheads. Strength and stature were clearly desirable qualities for such tasks.

Strength and stature also entered into the selection of drivers, partly because drivers, who rose before the field hands and went to bed after them, had to be vigorous enough to sustain the pace of the gangs and partly for psychological reasons. Drivers were usually

> of an imposing physical presence capable of commanding respect from the other slaves. Ex-slaves described the drivers as, for example, "a great, big cullud man," "a large tall, black man," "a burly fellow . . . severe in the extreme." Armed with a whip and outfitted in high leather boots and greatcoat, all emblematic of plantation authority, the driver exuded an aura of power.[16]

Drivers were generally chosen in their late thirties or early forties and usually had long tenure. They were tall, hard workers, good farmers, and articulate, and they usually had the respect of their fellow slaves.

Some aspects of this characterization are supported by quantitative evidence derived from the Trinidad census.[17] These data indicate that the proportion of slaves who were drivers reached a peak at age 60, that creoles were three times as likely to be drivers as Africans, but that light-skinned creoles were no more likely to be drivers than dark-skinned creoles. As for height, other things being equal, a male who was three inches taller than the typical adult male was 62 percent more likely to be a driver than one who was three inches shorter than the typical male. On average, drivers were an inch and a half taller than the men (and five inches taller than the women) who labored in the gangs.

Advantage in height also increased the likelihood that men would be

selected as craftsmen and that women would be chosen as domestics. In
the case of male domestics the effect was reversed. African-born men who
held domestic jobs between ages 25 and 45 were nearly two inches
shorter than their counterparts who labored in the fields. Apparently, if
prime-aged African men were chosen to be domestics it was usually
because their weakness diminished their usefulness as manual laborers,
but taller women were preferred for the household staff even though their
stature would generally have added to their productivity as field hands.[18]

In Trinidad color and ethnicity had even more powerful effects than
stature on who was selected for which occupation. Light-skinned males
were more than twice as likely to be artisans or hold another non-field
job as dark-skinned males. But it was in the selection of female domestics
that color counted most. A light woman was over six times as likely to
be chosen for a domestic as a dark woman. Among dark-skinned persons,
creoles were about twice as likely as Africans to be artisans or to hold
other non-field jobs.[19]

It has been suggested that planters exploited the skills that African-
born slaves brought with them.[20] The evidence in the Trinidad census
suggests that if there was a policy of exploiting African ethnic specialties,
its effects were quite weak. Slaves of the Mandingo ethnicity were more
likely to be boilers and slaves of Congo ethnicity were more likely to be
carpenters or coopers than other African-born slaves. While these tendencies may have reflected ethnic specialties, as some have argued, the
differences were slight. On the other hand, planters were relying heavily
on the importation of slaves born in the other West Indian colonies to
fill their craft slots because of the shortage of Trinidadians with such
skills. Creoles born outside of Trinidad were four times as likely as
Africans to be carpenters, two times as likely to be coopers, and four
times as likely to be masons.

The preceding discussion of the effect of color and ethnic origin on
the selection of slaves for various occupations should not be misunderstood. Although light-skinned creoles were more likely to be selected as
artisans and domestics than either dark creoles or Africans, the fact
remains that 86 percent of the elite occupations in Trinidad were held
by dark-skinned slaves, and two-thirds of these were Africans because
there were not enough light-skinned creoles to fill all these posts. Thus,
while planters had a strong bias in favor of assigning the children of
mixed unions to elite jobs, black slaves were not prevented from acquiring managerial and craft skills. Despite the bias, blacks outnumbered
slaves descended from mixed unions by 10 to 1 in all the artisan crafts
and managerial occupations. Light-skinned slaves were such a small
percentage of the total population of all Trinidad slaves that even when
they were heavily favored in the assignment of elite jobs, planters still

had to look to dark-skinned slaves to fill most of the posts.

Studies of the New Orleans slave records also point to the effect of color on selection for elite jobs, although the effect was much weaker in the United States than in Trinidad. The difference between the United States and Trinidad is most strikingly revealed by the distribution of light-skinned slaves between field and non-field occupations. In Trinidad only one out of every eight light-skinned slaves was employed as a field hand. But in the New Orleans records of slave sales the great majority of light-skinned slaves were field hands.[21]

THE AVAILABILITY OF ELITE OCCUPATIONS

So far we have considered which slaves were chosen to become managers, craftsmen, and domestics. It is also important to consider the factors that determined how large a proportion of slave occupations would be non-field occupations as well as the composition of such occupations. Technology was obviously a factor since each crop required a particular set of skills. Boilers and potters were needed in sugar production but not in rice, cotton, or tobacco. Although coopers made the tierces and hogsheads in which sugar, rice, and tobacco were shipped, cotton was not shipped in tierces or any other type of barrel. Economics was a factor since more than one technology could be employed to produce each crop. Such considerations as the relative prices of skilled and unskilled slaves, or the level of interest rates, for example, led some sugar planters to substitute high-yield steam mills for low-yield horse- or water-powered mills. The switch to steam raised the ratio of boilers and engineers relative to field hands. Politics and culture were factors since they could lead planters to substitute whites for slaves in various occupations, or vice versa.

It is easier to list the factors that influenced the availability of elite occupations than to know how much significance to attach to each of them. The difficulty stems from the absence of sufficiently detailed information on slave occupations, especially information that makes it possible to relate the distribution of occupations to principal crop and plantation size and to study these relationships over time. The Trinidad census of slave occupations of 1813 is a rarity, and it was not examined in detail until quite recently because it was never published. The problem is more difficult for the United States. Since no southwide census of occupations was ever conducted for slaves, scholars have been scouring archives for alternative sources of information. Some occupational information has been found in the probate records of those southern courts that required the executors of estates to list the occupation and price of each slave; some in surviving plantation business records that are deposited in

archives across the South; some in Civil War muster rolls that contain
information on the civilian occupations of all enlistees in the Union
Army, including ex-slaves; and some in the biographical narratives of
ex-slaves. The search has yielded a rich harvest of information on the
factors that determined the proportion of elite occupations—not all of
which was anticipated.[22]

Size of the plantation was by far the most important factor affecting
the proportion of elite occupations, but the influence of plantation size
on the proportion of elite occupations was not the same over all size
classes. It is useful to divide slave farms and plantations into three
classes: small slave plantations with between 1 and 15 slaves; intermediate plantations with between 16 and 50 slaves; and large plantations with
51 or more slaves. Farms with 15 or fewer slaves were generally too
small to employ the gang system but those with 16 or more were almost
always based on the gang system in the economies considered in this
section. As is shown by Figure 6, the proportion of elite slots in the class
of small plantations in Trinidad was only about half of the corresponding
proportions for the intermediate and large plantations. Less reliable data
indicate that the pattern was similar in the South.[23]

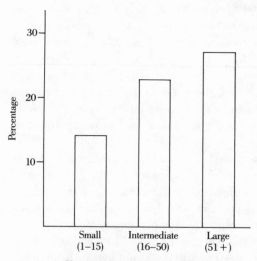

Figure 6. Elite occupations as a percentage of all adult slave occupations, by plantation size (Trinidad, c.1813). Small plantations in Trinidad accounted for
just 12 percent of adult slaves in agriculture and the intermediate-sized
plantations for another 31 percent. The large plantations thus employed
57 percent of the slaves in the agricultural sector of Trinidad. The
corresponding figure for large plantations in the United States in 1860
was about 30 percent.

More detailed analyses of the data for Trinidad revealed that virtually all intermediate and large plantations had elite slots; but on small
plantations 4 out of every 10 slaves lived on units that had none. Thus,
variation in the proportion of plantations without elite slots was the
principal factor influencing availability. That so many small plantations
failed to provide opportunities for entry into elite occupations supports
the proposition, considered more fully in Chapter 6, that the culture of
slaves on large plantations differed significantly from that which prevailed on small ones.

Plantation size not only controlled the proportion of elite slots available to slaves, but also affected the composition of these slots. Domestics
dominated elite occupations on small plantations in both the United
States and Trinidad, but were a minority on very large plantations. It
appears that one of the first acts of self-indulgence among these petty
(small) slaveholders was the purchase of a servant.[24] In Trinidad the
proportion of domestics on very large plantations was low because so
many of their owners were absentees, but the large U.S. slaveowners
were generally in residence and maintained substantial household staffs.
Even so, the ratio of domestics to field hands was lower on the large U.S.
plantations than on the small ones. The very large plantations of Trinidad were almost all sugar plantations. The factory aspects of production
on these plantations resulted in a much higher ratio of craftsmen to field
hands than on the smaller plantations. On plantations with 100 or more
slaves there were 4.5 field hands per craftsman, while on smaller plantations there were 28 field hands per craftsman.

Variations in the occupational mix had a substantial impact on the
sexual composition of the elite labor force. Both in the United States and
in Trinidad the female proportion of the elite labor force declined with
plantation size. In Trinidad females accounted for nearly 60 percent of
elite occupations on small plantations but for just 21 percent on large
plantations. In the United States the variation in the sex ratio was not
quite as extreme, but the general pattern was similar.

On the intermediate and large plantations of both economies the
upper echelon of the occupational hierarchy was heavily dominated by
males. Here men had nearly a complete monopoly of the most prestigious
jobs. All but two of over 1,300 craftsmen on intermediate and large
Trinidad plantations were men. The male to female ratio among craftsmen on the corresponding U.S. plantations was 74 to 1. The situation
with respect to drivers and other slave managers was quite similar. Male
domination of the occupational elite was mitigated on the intermediate
plantations but, in general, it was reversed only on the small plantations.
The reversal took place not because women gained access to male occupations, although there was some tendency in this direction, but because

slaves in domestic occupations, which were heavily female, outnumbered those in all the other elite occupations.[25]

Crop specialization also affected the mix of elite occupations, and had some influence on the overall share of the slave population in these occupations. But the effect on slave occupations is not consistent in all of the available data sets. This ambiguous result with respect to overall shares does not contradict the proposition that different crops required different skills. Sugar plantations had a higher ratio of craftsmen to field hands than did coffee, cotton, or cocoa plantations, but they also had fewer domestics and other non-field occupations.[26]

One significant difference in the composition of elite occupations between the United States and Trinidad was in the ratio of drivers to field hands. Slaves were much more tightly managed in the South than in Trinidad. On the plantations in the Olson sample the ratio of adult field hands to all drivers was about 15 to 1; the corresponding ratio for Trinidad was 30 to 1.[27] The data in the gang-system sample also indicate that the U.S. ratio of drivers to slaves changed over time. On plantations of moderately large size (about 50 slaves), the ratio of drivers per adult hand rose quite rapidly between 1800 and 1830, the years during which the gang system was spreading rapidly. It reached a plateau about 1830 and stayed there for the remainder of the decade. Then the number of drivers per hand began to fall slowly during the 1840s and more rapidly during the 1850s. This finding suggests that the political factors that led some planters to substitute whites for blacks in the management of their slaves began to have an effect a full two decades before the beginning of the Civil War and that this effect accelerated rapidly as the political struggle over slavery intensified.[28]

THE LIFE CYCLE IN OCCUPATIONS

Slaves began to enter the labor force at a very early age and those who survived usually remained productive until quite advanced ages. It is true that some slaves became too sick to be productive, but down to their 60th birthday those so incapacitated were generally less than 10 percent of their cohort.[29] Indeed, it was not until age 75 that the annual net earnings, or profit, from a cohort became negative (Figure 7). Thus, one characteristic of gang-system plantations was their effectiveness in extracting labor from a slave at practically every age from early childhood until each one stepped into his or her grave. In the free economy of the North and South approximately one-third of the population was in the labor force, but among slaves the labor force participation rate was two-thirds.[30] Masters achieved this high rate of labor utilization by rating the labor requirements of the various jobs as well as the slaves, and then attempting to match slaves and jobs as closely as possible. Sometimes political and ideological considerations, or just plain whim, were allowed to override the purely economic considerations (the reluctance of West Indian planters to assign light-skinned slaves to gang labor is a case in point), but as a rule the assignments were strongly related to the "hand" ratings described in Chapter 1.[31]

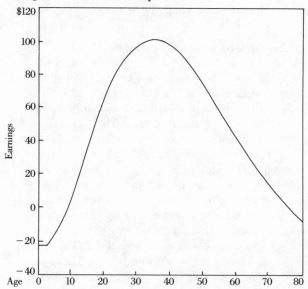

Figure 7. Annual net earnings from male slaves by age, about 1850, Old South. Shown are the average annual earnings at different ages that U.S. slave-holders derived from each male slave in the states or the Old South: Maryland, Virginia, North Carolina, South Carolina, and Georgia. Net earnings are the difference between the income earned by a slave and the cost to the planter of maintaining him. Net earnings were negative until age 9. Then they became positive and rose to a peak at age 35. It is interesting to note that earnings of 65-year-olds were still positive and, on average, brought an owner as much net income as a slave in the mid-teens. This does not mean that every slave aged 65 produced a positive net income for his owner. Some of the elderly were a net loss. However, the income earned by the able-bodied among the elderly was more than enough to compensate for the burden imposed by the in-capacitated. The average net income from slaves remained positive until they reached their late 70s. Even after that age the average burden was quite low, since a fair share of the slaves who survived into their 80s still produced positive net incomes.

Because of this policy, the typical slave did not hold the same occupation throughout his or her life but generally held different jobs at different stages of life. Children began to enter the labor force as early as age 3 or 4.[32] Some were taken into the master's house to be servants (child servants were very fashionable among southern planters), while others were assigned to field work in special children's gangs called "trash gangs" in the United States and "weeding gangs" in Jamaica. Planters attached great importance to the early and, from their viewpoint, proper introduction of children into the labor force. Much was revealed about the mind of the planter on this point by Thomas Roughley, a Jamaican planter. The weeding gang, he wrote,

> forming the rising generation, from which, in progress of time, all the vacancies occuring in the different branches of slave population are filled up, comes next to be considered. Their merits are great in their sphere. The expectations formed of them are still greater, when contemplated in a future point of view. They are drivers, cattlemen, mulemen, carpenters, coopers, and masons, as it were in embryo. Their genius and strength rises and ripens with their years, as they are made emulous by proper treatment. . . . How pleasing, how gratifying, how replete with humanity it is to see a swarm of healthy, active, cheerful, pliant, straight, handsome creole negro boys and girls going to, and returning from the puerile field work allotted to them, clean and free from disease or blemish. . . . Negro children, after they pass five or six years of age, if free from the yaws, or other scrophula, and are healthy, should be taken from the nurse in the negro houses, and put under the tuition of the driveress, who has the conducting of the weeding gang. It is . . . best to send them with those of their own age, to associate together in industrious habits; not to overact any part with them, but by degrees to conform them to the minor field work. . . .
>
> . . . They should be encouraged when they do their work well, and when the sun is unusually powerful, with a drink made of water, sugar, and lime juice, such being cooling and wholesome for them. They should be minutely examined and cleaned from chegoes; their heads and bodies from itch or scrophula; which last, when discovered, they should immediately be put under the care of the hothouse doctor, physicked and rubbed with proper ointment, and not sent to work till they are cured. Their cleanliness should be exemplary, their meals always strengthened with a small quantity of salt pork or fish, and some kind of garden stuff, such as peas or beans. . . .
>
> When any of these children becomes 12 years old, and are healthy, they are fit subjects to be drafted into the second gang, going on thus progressively from one gang to the other, till they are incorporated with the great gang, or most effective veteran corps of the estate. . . .[33]

By subjecting the information contained in 2,200 narratives of southern ex-slaves to quantitative analysis, it has been possible to reconstruct the ages of entry into the labor force during the late antebellum era. By age 7, over 40 percent of the boys and half of the girls had entered the labor force, and the process was virtually completed by age 12. Children began to be shifted from childhood to adult jobs as they matured. At about age 11, the more rapidly maturing boys in housework began the transfer to adult field jobs, and that process was generally completed by age 15 or 16. The data in Olson's sample generally confirm the pattern found in the ex-slave narratives. They reveal that among slaves aged 16–20, about 83 percent of the males and 89 percent of the females were field hands. The movement into adult jobs appears to have lagged somewhat in Trinidad and might also have been delayed a bit in Jamaica and Surinam.[34]

There were important differences in the work patterns of boys and girls. One of these was first suggested by a comparison of age profiles of earnings from male and female slaves. Figure 8 shows that for most of the ages during the life cycle, female earnings were below those of males by 20 to 40 percent, but that between ages 5 and 17 female earnings exceeded those of males. The hypothesis that the early advantage in female earnings was probably due to a more rapid rate of maturing among women than men has been supported by data which reveal that prior to age 16 women had higher cotton-picking rates than men, and that girls entered the labor force at a more rapid rate than boys. On this last point, interestingly enough, the Trinidad pattern differs from the U.S. pattern. Males entered the labor force a bit earlier than females in Trinidad.[35]

The third phase of the occupational cycle generally began in the mid-twenties in Trinidad and from 5 to 10 years later in the United States, when robust males began to be transferred from field work into the craft or managerial slots, and robust females became house servants. Later on, as increasing age reduced vigor, men were shifted into such occupations as gardeners and watchmen, and women became nurses for infants and young children as well as for the sick. On the larger U.S. plantations many of the older and infirm slaves, particularly females, were set to work in the cloth houses where they spun cotton, wove cloth, and then cut and sewed the cloth into garments.

This life cycle in slave occupations has now been found in all the available samples that give occupation by age, not only in the United States and Trinidad, but also in Brazil and Jamaica. It may well have been a universal feature of mature gang-system plantations throughout the New World, although the pattern varied from place to place. Available evidence rules out the possibility that this life cycle was a consequence of the closing of the international slave trade. A quite similar cycle has been found for Maryland during the period 1730–1779.[36]

The pattern of entry into the elite occupations, particularly into the crafts, is quite different from that normally found in free societies during

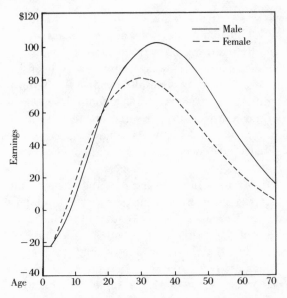

Figure 8. Annual net earnings from slaves by age and gender, c.1850, Old South.
Annual maintenance costs averaged about $25 per child. Beginning at
about age 4, when children began to enter the labor force, their earnings
partially offset their maintenance costs. By age 8 the net earnings of a
cohort of girls was zero. This means that girls of this age who had already
entered the labor force were earning enough not only to offset their own
maintenance costs, but also the maintenance costs of those 8-year-old
girls who had not yet entered the labor force. Boys did not reach the
"break-even" age until they were 9. From ages 5 through 17, the annual
net earnings from females exceeded that from males, probably because
girls matured more rapidly than boys.

the eighteenth and nineteenth centuries. In the free North or in England
during this period a boy was typically apprenticed to a carpenter, blacksmith, or other craftsmen in his early teens and remained in that occupation for the balance of his life. In the absence of a marked differential
in mortality rates between craftsmen and other occupations, the proportion of craftsmen in the labor force would remain constant over all
subsequent ages. As we have seen, the slave pattern was much different.
Slaves were underrepresented in the crafts in their late teens and twenties and overrepresented at later ages. The age pattern suggests that the
selection of slaves for training in the crafts was delayed by 5 to 10 years
as compared with free persons. Normally such a delay would be uneconomical, since the earlier the investment is made in occupational
training, the more years there are to reap the return on that investment.[37] Why was the slave pattern so different?

It has been suggested that the difference was due to the unwillingness
of masters to let their slaves compete for craft jobs off their plantations.

According to this hypothesis many slaves were trained for the crafts at young ages but could not practice them until the older craftsmen on their plantations died.[38] But even if slaves were not free to move, their masters were free to sell them. At age 35 the price of a blacksmith exceeded that of an ordinary hand by 53 percent (a differential of about $450 in the Old South in 1850). Consequently, if a blacksmith had been in excess supply on a given plantation, his master would have had a strong incentive to sell him rather than to retain him for the replacement of an older man a decade later, a replacement that could have been obtained through the market when needed. The hypothesis thus implies that craftsmen, particularly young craftsmen, should have been overrepresented in slave markets. The data on slave sales in the New Orleans market, however, indicate that they were substantially underrepresented. Only 3.3 percent of the sales of males age 16 and over were of craftsmen. The comparable figures for craftsmen belonging to ongoing plantations was 11.0 percent in the probate sample and 15.9 percent in the Olson sample of business records.[39]

Another possibility is that the life cycle might be a statistical artifact, that all persons bound for elite occupations were actually appointed at an early age and that they became an increasing proportion of their cohort as they aged because their mortality rates were much more favorable than those in non-elite jobs. Such differential mortality rates may have contributed something to the life-cycle pattern of occupations for the various slave societies, but they are hardly likely to explain more than a small fraction of the doubling of the craft share of occupations between the late teens and the late thirties.[40] For mortality rates to explain this leap, the death rate among prime-aged field hands would have had to have been more than five times as high as most estimates indicate. Moreover, the share of slaves in crafts reached a peak at about age 33 in Trinidad and then declined while the share of other non-field occupations increased through the entire range of ages.[41] The share of domestics in the labor force declined until about the late twenties and then started to rise. Those varied patterns cannot be explained by differential mortality rates.

An alternative explanation is suggested by antebellum documents that instruct plantation managers to select craftsmen from among the ablest of the field hands. Such instructions indicate that elite jobs later in life were held out to field hands as a reward for high levels of productivity. If such an incentive scheme were successful, the increased output of field hands competing for the limited number of opportunities could have more than offset the reduced period over which masters had to amortize their investment in the training of an artisan. Still another factor appears to be related to the efforts of masters to exploit the principle of comparative advantage. Although some elite jobs required considerable strength, such others as stock and storehouse minders, gardeners, coachmen, weavers, nurses, and seamstresses did not. As slaves aged and their productivity in field work declined, masters were able to increase their profits by shifting slaves into those occupations in which their experience and reliability gave them a comparative advantage over stronger slaves at younger ages.[42]

THE CULTURAL SIGNIFICANCE OF THE OCCUPATIONAL HIERARCHY

However primitive the gang-system plantations of early Brazil and Barbados may have been, however undifferentiated and brutal the toil of their black captives, however exclusive their reliance on force, the later gang-system plantations throughout the New World gave rise to complex slave societies marked by a significant degree of social differentiation and an elaborate occupational hierarchy. These hierarchies were, after some hesitation, quite intentionally promoted by planters who saw them as a means of stabilizing slave society and making it tractable. The critical decision made by the planters, the decision that allowed the eventual emergence of a many-sided and often quasi-autonomous slave society, was the switch from whites to slaves as the source of personnel for their various managerial and craft slots. While hired whites were never totally eliminated from the top of the management, especially on the great estates, the number of whites per plantation was greatly diminished during the eighteenth century and well into the nineteenth century. In the case of Jamaica, it has been estimated that in 1832, even on estates with over 100 slaves, there were an average of just two whites per plantation, counting women and children. A similar pattern is revealed by data from the U.S. census of 1860. Whether on plantations with just one slave or with over 100, there were an average of about six whites per plantation—a fraction more than the average size of a southern rural white family in 1860. The majority of the large plantations, those with more than 50 slaves, averaged only about 1.5 adult white males per plantation.[43] The policy of relying on slaves to staff most of the key craft and managerial posts was not without its risks. However, the opportunities for reducing outlays and for creating a more stable slave community appear to have outweighed whatever fears planters might have had that their policies would encourage slaves to become too independent.

Planters not only promoted the slave occupational hierarchy but quite systematically sought to influence its character. It was not by default or merely the subconscious operation of prejudice that color, ethnicity, physique, gender, and family connections became instruments of preferential entry into the occupational hierarchy. That these avenues were the consequence of deliberate policy is plainly revealed by Roughley in such documents as his guide to Jamaican planters. Yet despite all that planters did to create and shape the slave occupational hierarchies, once created, these hierarchies assumed certain independent aspects. The tendency was especially marked on great plantations with occupational elites that were not only large but multilayered. There the whites were quite remote from the mass of the slaves, and quasi-autonomous black societies emerged. Scholars have made substantial progress in attempting to reconstruct the cultures of such societies. The most progress has been made in the United States where large collections of autobiographies and biographical narratives by ex-slaves have survived.[44] These have provided rich insights into the minds and aspirations of slaves and the array of personalities on both large and small plantations. Before delving more deeply into the sources and varieties of slave culture, we need to consider the economic and demographic forces that governed the operation of slave systems in the New World.

CHAPTER THREE

UNRAVELING SOME ECONOMIC RIDDLES

Down through the end of the eighteenth century and well into the nineteenth century, it was widely assumed that slavery was a vigorous and highly profitable economic system. That proposition was not seriously challenged by British leaders of the antislavery movement during their 50-year campaign to outlaw the trade in slaves and slavery as a labor system in all parts of the British empire. They conducted the campaign primarily on moral and humanitarian grounds. It was the West Indian plantation owners rather than the abolitionists who continually interjected economic issues, claiming that the attacks of the abolitionists were harmful to the economic welfare of Great Britain, ruinous to the economic interests of the planter class, and a serious threat to property rights in general. British abolitionists were generally defensive on these issues, insisting that the reforms they sought could be accomplished without harming the economic interests of either the planter class or the nation.[1]

In the United States the antislavery struggle was also conducted primarily on moral and humanitarian grounds from pre-Revolutionary times until the mid-1850s. Indeed, such abolitionist leaders as William Lloyd Garrison adamantly resisted all proposals to shift the basis of their assault from religious to economic grounds, proposals that emanated from the more worldly leaders of the movement. To turn their appeal from the conscience "to the pocketbook," from "the duty of Christian reformation" to "the love of political preferment,"[2] he warned, would inevitably corrupt and subvert the moral principles on which their movement was based. Nevertheless, the principal basis of the antislavery appeal did suddenly shift from "Christian duty" to "the pocketbook." The shift took place between 1854 and 1856 and the political success was immediate and spectacular.[3] The new approach transformed the antislavery movement from a minor political factor into a powerful political force that could control the national agenda. This relatively brief and successful struggle for power tossed up a complicated set of economic issues that since the 1850s have been at or near the center of debate on the nature of the slave system and the cause of its downfall.[4]

PROFITS AND PROSPECTS IN THE BRITISH WEST INDIES AND THE UNITED STATES

For the British West Indies, as for the United States, the question of profitability has become intertwined with interpretations of the politics of antislavery. Some scholars have argued that Parliament first voted for the abolition of the slave trade and then voted for the emancipation of slaves because the sugar colonies fell on hard times that greatly diminished their value to the mother country. The decline in West Indian profits has been dated from the 1770s and has been attributed to both a flagging demand for West Indian sugar and a decay in the quality of West Indian entrepreneurship.

It has been possible to reconstruct the course of profits in the West Indies from the records of plantations on several of the islands. These records show that from the early days of slavery in Barbados down to the eve of emancipation in 1834, West Indian slaveholders generally reaped a high rate of return on their investment. There were times and places, such as Barbados during the 1650s, in which rates of return averaged as high as 40 to 50 percent per annum. But that was due to the sharp rise in the price of sugar that occurred when the war between the Dutch and the Portuguese disrupted the shipment of Brazilian sugar to Europe. There were also times when the average rate of return in the West Indies fell below 4 percent per annum, as during the American Revolution, which not only cut off the cheap supply of foodstuffs from the mainland but also interfered with the shipment of sugar to England. Barring such exceptional circumstances, the profit rate averaged about 10 percent per annum. Even during the 14 years immediately preceding emancipation, when the British government reduced the tariffs protecting West Indian sugar and increased the restriction on the rights of owners to manage and to sell their slaves, the average rate of return to slaveowners was still about 7 percent.[5]

Although it has been argued that the British demand for sugar was stagnating because of increasing competition from Cuba and Puerto Rico, the high tariff effectively excluded foreign sugar from the British markets. During the decade before the British abolition of slavery, 1825–1834, foreign sugar accounted for a minor share (just 6 percent) of Britain's imports. Far from declining, the British demand for sugar increased substantially between the early 1790s and the early 1830s. The rate of increase was both rapid and steady during the last 20 years of the period, when Cuban competition was supposed to have become especially troublesome.[6]

Although obscured by short-term cycles, the downward trend in sugar prices after 1790 was quite gradual (see Figure 9).[7] This decline was not brought about by Spanish competition, but by the rising productivity of West Indian plantations that were shifting to more fertile soils in colonies that Britain acquired from the French, Dutch, and Spanish as booty of war.[8] The available evidence indicates that the average productivity of Jamaican sugar plantations was also increasing, but British restrictions on the internal slave trade prevented Jamaica from catching up with the newer colonies.

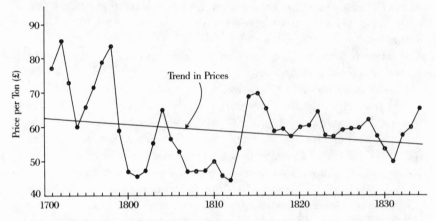

Figure 9. Real London price of West Indian sugar, including duty (£ of 1821–1825). Although the price of sugar fluctuated wildly in the short run, from 1790 to the end of the Napoleonic Wars the trend was downward at a rate of 0.31 percent per year. This moderate secular trend imposed no real hardship on producers in the newly developed slave colonies, who were increasing production sharply to meet rising demand; it may have been something of a burden to planters on older, depleted soils in Jamaica.

Beginning in 1806, Great Britain severely limited the trade in slaves between her West Indian colonies and after 1825 it precluded virtually all inter-island movements. Nevertheless, by utilizing slaves imported before the ban, planters on the lush lands of Trinidad and British Guiana gradually increased sugar production, and so the trend in British sugar prices gradually moved downward. Such large differentials appeared in the productivity of labor and in the rate of profit between the newer colonies and Jamaica that during the 1820s slaves sold in Trinidad and British Guiana brought twice the price of those sold in Jamaica. Because plantations on worn-out land could not match the productivity of the newer colonies, the average rate of profit in Jamaica during 1820–1834 declined to 5.3 percent, but the profit rate in Trinidad and Guiana was 13.3 percent. Planters in the older colonies clamored for the right to redeploy their slaves on the new lands, but their petitions were denied

by a Parliament and government that were inching toward the decision
to abolish slavery in all of their colonies.[9]

In the American case the basic profitability of slavery was obscured
by the disruptive effects of the Revolution on the southern economy and
by cyclical misfortunes in rice and tobacco. Of the South's three principal
export staples before the Revolution, indigo suffered the most. Cut out
of the British system of imperial tariff preferences and bereft of her
bounties, U.S. producers could not withstand the competition of the West
Indies and other British colonies. By 1800 indigo had dwindled from a
major export crop, which had occupied about 10 percent of the slave
labor force before the Revolution, to one of no commercial consequence,
sometimes grown by farmers in small quantities mainly for home consumption or local markets. Rice producers, who accounted for a fifth of
the slave labor force before the Revolution, fared only slightly better.
Although exports regained the pre-Revolutionary level by 1790, the rice
industry stagnated for most of the next 60 years, relieved only by a
moderate expansion between the 1820s and the 1840s.[10]

Tobacco planters, who absorbed about 40 percent of slave labor just
before the Revolution, made the best recovery. By 1786 exports were up
to pre-Revolutionary levels and favorable prices caused the industry to
spread to new regions in South Carolina, Georgia, Kentucky, and Tennessee. The subsequent history of tobacco was marked by periods of
booming demand that lasted for about a decade or more sandwiched
between periods of depression that were nearly as protracted. The misfortunes of tobacco markets created difficulties for slaveowners that were
reflected in the prices of slaves in the eastern tobacco region. But one
should not confuse the sagging of prices with a declining demand for
slaves. The demand for slaves in the eastern tobacco region showed a
strong, but moderate, upward trend throughout the half century preceding the Civil War, although the rate of growth fluctuated from decade
to decade. Despite the difficulties they encountered in world markets for
tobacco, eastern planters continued to find that slaves were effective
workers who, at the prevailing prices for slave labor, provided a generally profitable means of raising their crops. Even during the depths of
the tobacco depressions of 1826–1832 and 1840–1848, which were
caused by the rise of tobacco fields and increased duties in Europe, the
upward course of their demand for slaves hesitated only briefly. There
was never a time between the American Revolution and the Civil War
that slaveholders in the Old South became so pessimistic about the
economic future of the peculiar institution that their demand for slaves
went into a period of sustained decline.[11]

In the western cotton states, the demand for slaves did not turn
downward or falter, even during the two depression decades. The sharp,

sustained declines in the price of cotton during these years did no more than slow the pace at which western planters increased their demand for slaves. And so over the half century from 1810 to 1860, the region's demand for slaves increased twentyfold. Although the rate of growth in demand moderated as the years wore on, it remained well in excess of the natural rate of increase of the slave population. A continuation of rising demand for slaves in the West, a new surge of demand in the eastern tobacco region, and a slowdown in the rate of natural increase of the slave population all combined to double slave prices between the mid 1840s and the Civil War, which reflected both the high level of immediate profits and the bounding optimism of slaveowners regarding future prospects.[12]

A FLEXIBLE, HIGHLY DEVELOPED FORM OF CAPITALISM

Evidence of the responsiveness of slaveowners to prices and other economic signals is quite evident throughout the period from the Revolution to the Civil War. Production in all of the major southern staples waxed and waned in response to prices. Indigo disappeared as a commercial product in less than a decade (between 1792 and 1800), once the price turned against it. Planters in upper Georgia and South Carolina who moved into tobacco during the post-Revolutionary boom in demand moved out of it after the War of 1812, shifting from tobacco to cotton as the demand for cotton surged upward and the price of tobacco declined toward depression levels. Planters in Maryland, Virginia, and North Carolina shifted between tobacco and grains in response to changes in their relative prices. Tobacco production in these states languished from the early 1790s to the mid-1840s, when tobacco prices leaped sharply upward and remained above the long-term trend until the outbreak of the Civil War. Eastern planters, responding rapidly to each new surge in demand, more than doubled tobacco output between 1849 and 1859, pushing its price back toward a normal level.[13]

By far the most dramatic evidence of the responsiveness of slaveholders to market signals was the way in which they adjusted to the booming demand for cotton. As late as 1809 cotton was a secondary crop for southern agriculture, with production concentrated mainly in South Carolina and eastern Georgia. Just 7 percent of the crop was raised to the west of this area and probably just 10 percent of the slave labor force across the entire South was engaged in its production. During the next three decades the cotton crop increased nearly tenfold and the share of the western states leaped from 7 to 64 percent.

The depression decade of the 1840s interrupted this dual process of

mammoth increases in the size of the cotton crop and a westward shift
in the locus of its production. But the process resumed during the next
decade when booming world markets led to a doubling of the crop. By
the eve of the Civil War the westward shift was completed, with three-
quarters of the richest crop in southern history coming from states which,
at the start of Washington's administration, had been virtually uninhab-
ited.[14]

The correlation in the geographic movements of cotton and slaves
(see Figure 10) was dictated by biology and economics.[15] Cotton could
be grown successfully in a long belt stretching mainly from South Carolina through Texas. The bounds of this belt were determined largely, but
not exclusively, by climatic conditions since the cotton culture requires
a minimum of two hundred frostless days and ample rainfall. Tempera-
ture set the northern boundary, and rainfall the western one.

Not all land within these boundaries was equally suitable for cotton.
The black-belt lands of Alabama and Texas were more congenial to it
than the sandy soils of the Carolina Piedmont or the marshes of the
coastal plains, except for long-staple cotton. The best cotton lands of all
were the alluvial soils of the Mississippi flood plain. As long as tobacco
and grains were the principal market crops of the South, as they were
down to the end of the eighteenth century, it was efficient to concentrate
labor and other resources in regions that bordered on the Chesapeake
Bay. But as the demand for cotton grew relative to other southern
commodities, efficiency dictated a reallocation of labor and other resources to the best western lands.

Between 1790 and 1860 some 835,000 slaves were moved into the
western cotton states. The tempo of interregional slave movements accelerated with time. The traffic during the last half of the 70-year period
was three times as large as during the first half. The main exporting
states were Maryland, Virginia, and the Carolinas. Together they supplied over 85 percent of the migrants. The four largest importers were
Alabama, Mississippi, Louisiana, and Texas, which together received
about 75 percent of the displaced blacks. The impact of the movement
of slaves on the rates of growth of the slave populations of the exporting
and importing states was quite substantial. By 1860 the exporting states
had just 60 percent of the slave population they would have had if they
had grown at the national average. On the other hand, the slave population of the importing states swelled to several times the level that would
have been obtained if these states had grown at the national average.[16]

The westward shift of cotton and slaves was also stimulated by
breakthroughs in transportation. The response of slaveowners to steamboats and railroads reveals the eagerness with which they sought to bend
the industrial technology of the nineteenth century to their advantage.

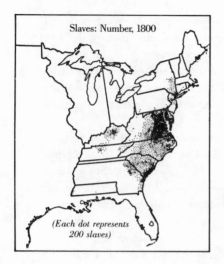

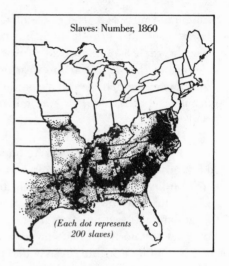

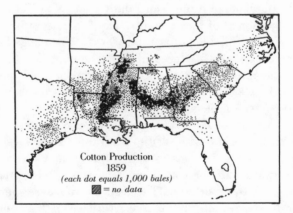

Figure 10. The westward movement of cotton and slaves, 1800–1860.

Although the steamboat was originally developed on the Hudson River, it was on the Mississippi that this innovation achieved its swiftest and most impressive successes. Steamboat traffic grew at phenomenal rates after 1811 and there were such major improvements in boat design and in engines that efficiency rose fourfold in a quarter of a century, which sent the cost of river transportation plummeting downward.[17]

It is sometimes argued that the preference of slaveowners for steamboats over railroads revealed their antipathy toward new technology. But the first U.S. railroad, the Baltimore and Ohio, was constructed in Maryland beginning in 1828. Other southern cities including "Norfolk, Charleston, and Savannah each feverishly projected lines westward to gain control of such commerce as might be developed in the interior." It was not lack of enthusiasm for the railroad but practical economics that made steamboats the preferred means of transporting the region's freight. Down to the end of the antebellum era, the steamboat was not only cheaper but more reliable than the railroad and often speedier in the delivery of cotton and other bulky commodities. Even so, southern enthusiasm for railroads led to the construction of more than 9,500 miles of railroad track by 1860, about one-third of the nation's total, and more than the mileage of France, Germany, or Great Britain, the European leaders.[18]

The South was also in the forefront of the effort to gather and disseminate economic intelligence. Southern planters had at their fingertips reports on the transactions in cotton, tobacco, rice, sugar, and other commodities, not only for all of the leading southern markets but also for the leading cities of the North and of Europe. Produce exchanges, cotton exchanges, brokerage houses, and financial institutions published (first weekly, then daily) listings of commodity prices and other economic indicators in bulletins and newspapers commonly called "Prices Current." It was determination to exploit every avenue for gathering economic information that caused the South to string telegraph lines across the entire region as soon as that means of communication was developed. The first two cities to be connected were Baltimore and Washington in 1844. By 1852 every major southern city was linked to the new network. It was a point of pride that New Orleans had telegraphic communication with New York sooner than Chicago did.[19]

Cliometricians have not as yet been able to resolve the debate over the form of the interregional slave movement. Were most slaves sold by owners in the East to traders who transported them to western markets where they were resold, or did the majority go west with owners who relocated plantations? Estimates of the proportion shipped to the West by traders range between 16 and 60 percent.[20]

Cliometric analyses of the slave trade have, however, demonstrated the business acumen with which masters valued their chattel and the limited role of sentimentality in effecting their economic decisions. How many masters were constrained by emotional attachments to individual slaves, by antipathy to the business of slave trading, or by a loathing to tear husbands from wives is still a matter of conjecture. Such sentiments were, however, balanced against the interests and conveniences of the masters. There were planters who, like George Washington, said that they were determined to resist all but the most urgent pressures to enter the market for slaves, although in Washington's case the flight of his cook led him to consider the purchase of a replacement. Others were more like Jefferson, who made no apologies for selling recalcitrant slaves and purchased new ones when he was shorthanded.[21]

When they did enter the slave market, masters assessed each purchase with as much shrewdness and concern for value as any western horse trader or northern manufacturer. Probate records and invoices of slave sales reveal that the prices were systematically affected by such characteristics of slaves as their age, gender, health, skills, and reliability. There were also distinct seasonal patterns in slave sales. As one might expect in an agricultural economy, the largest proportion were sold during the first quarter of the year, the quarter between the end of the harvest and the beginning of planting. Moreover, the prices that slaves brought were 10 percent higher during this slack season than during September, which was close to the peak of the harvest.[22]

Age had by far the greatest influence on prices, as shown by Figure 11.[23] Although prices varied at each age, as one would expect of slaves who differed in health, attitudes, and capabilities, the distribution displays a quite definite pattern. On average, prices rose until the late twenties and then declined. The decline was slow at first but then became more rapid, until advanced ages were reached. Masters put a price on each skill and defect of a slave (see Figure 12). As compared with a male field hand of the same age, blacksmiths brought a premium of about 55 percent and carpenters about 45 percent.[24] Slaves who were in poor health or who were crippled sold at substantial discounts. Masters even put a price on "virtues" and "vices." Slaves labeled as runaways, lazy, thieves, drunks, suicidals, or having "heredity vices" sold for average discounts of up to 65 percent as compared with slaves of the same age who were "fully guaranteed."[25]

The slave trade was one of the ugliest aspects of American slavery and probably was one of the most effective issues in rallying support for the antislavery cause. Foes of slavery condemned the practice on moral and political grounds, arguing that the interstate traffic in people provided the planters of the older states with the bulk of their profit and was indispensable for maintaining the profits of slaveholders as a class.

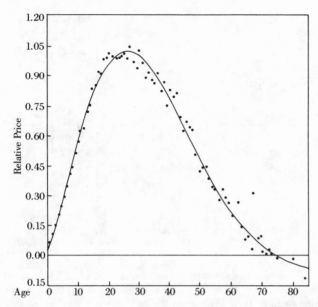

Figure 11. Averages of prices relative to age for male slaves in the Old South. Each point represents the average price of slaves at a given age. The curve fitted to these points is called an age-price profile. Notice that the average price of slaves remained positive until the mid-70s. This means that although some slaves in their early 70s were too sick to earn their upkeep, other slaves at that age earned enough to support themselves as well as the disabled members of their cohort and still leave a profit for their masters.

Yet, interstate slave trading could not have accounted for a significant fraction of the profits of the slaveowning class and may actually have reduced their collective profit.[26] Professional traders, those who purchased slaves in one state and resold them in another, did earn a regular profit for that "service," and may even have reaped some windfall gains. Since such windfalls came at the expense of other slaveholders, they were merely transfers within the slaveholding class and so did not add to its total profit.

Whether or not the masters as a class actually profited from the westward movement turns on a complicated set of trade-offs.[27] Slaveowners understood that from the purely economic standpoint, the westward march of slavery was not an unmixed blending. Virginia planters complained loudly and frequently about the depressing effect of western tobacco on the world price of that commodity. Recent cliometric work has confirmed the suspicions of Virginians that the competition from western tobacco did more to depress the prices of their slaves than the interstate slave trade did to raise it. The doubling of slave prices in

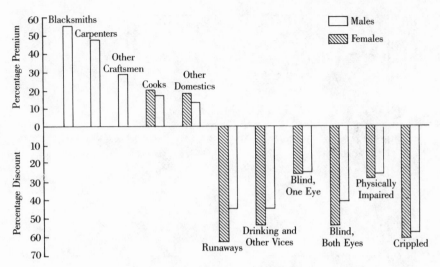

Figure 12. Premiums and discounts in slave prices for various skills and "defects."
This diagram shows that there was little difference between the way in
which planters priced their slaves and the way they priced their other
capital assets. They were as precise in valuing human attributes as those
of their livestock or equipment. The premiums and discounts are measured relative to the price of a healthy field hand of the same age and
gender (the zero premium).

Virginia during the late 1840s and the 1850s owed relatively little to the
western demand for slaves and much to the resurgence in the European
demand for tobacco during those years.[28]

While the tobacco interests (eastern and western combined) may have
suffered from the westward movement, the cotton interests probably did
not. Some eastern cotton planters were made worse off, but the gain to
planters in the West more than offset these losses. Cotton planters as a
class gained for two reasons. One is that the world demand for cotton
increased so rapidly that bringing the highly fertile western lands into
production did not reduce the total revenues of cotton planters. The other
is that by responding so quickly to the burgeoning world demand for
cotton, on lands far more suited for cotton than existed anywhere else
in the world, U.S. planters slowed the expansion of cotton production in
the West Indies, Brazil, India, and elsewhere. As a consequence, the U.S.
share of the world's market for cotton rose quite dramatically as the
westward march progressed. Cotton growers in the West Indies and India
could compete quite well with cotton grown in Virginia and the Carolinas, but not with cotton coming from the Alabama black belt or the
Mississippi alluvium.[29]

The congressional battles of the 1840s and 1850s over the extension
of slavery into the territories were not due to the degradation of eastern

soils, or any sort of land shortage whatsoever. Analysis of census data reveals no evidence of the decline in labor productivity on the farms of the Old South that would have been caused by a decline in the quantity or quality of land per worker. In fact, the cotton boom put very little pressure on southern supplies of land because cotton was not a land-intensive crop.[30] The 1850 crop was grown on just 6 percent of the improved land in the farms of the cotton states. If slaveowners had been confined to the counties that they already occupied in 1850, and if they had been barred from adding to the total acreage already improved in 1850, they could still have doubled cotton production over the next decade merely by shifting about one-fifteenth of the land normally planted in other crops into cotton.[31] This is quite close to what actually happened. Much of the increase in cotton production during the decade of the 1850s, especially the leap in production after 1856, came not from the spread of the culture to new counties or new farms, but from the expansion of output in counties that were already major producers at the beginning of the decade.

The surging demand for cotton during the 1850s put far more pressure on the South's labor supply than on its supply of land. Between 1850 and 1860 southern farmers shifted about 3 million acres of land from corn to cotton, but this shift did not release enough labor because cotton required about 70 percent more labor per acre than did corn. To meet this extra labor requirement planters drew slaves out of the cities and from the small slave farms by bidding up the price of slave labor. And so the decade of the 1850s witnessed both a decline in the urban share of the slave population and a rise in the share of the slave population working on gang-system farms that specialized in cotton. The surging demand for slave labor by cotton planters after 1846 pushed the real price of slaves to higher levels than they had ever previously achieved, not because the demand for cotton increased more rapidly during the 1850s than during all previous decades, but because the share of the slave labor force demanded by cotton planters at these prices was larger than ever before.[32]

The struggle over the expansion of slavery into the territories, despite the rhetorical references to economics, was almost a purely political issue. Radical abolitionists denounced the "political" antislavery leaders for paying too much attention to the territorial issue. As the radicals saw it, this issue only served to divert the abolitionist movement into harmless channels, and so they called on antislavery leaders to fight slavery where it was, rather than where it was not. On strictly economic grounds, the radical position was sound. Slavery could not have been damaged economically by denying it access to lands in Kansas, or anywhere else outside of the states in which it was already well established by the

1840s. Yet, Republican leaders rejected the advice of the radicals because they and their chief southern opponents saw the territorial issue as the crux of the political struggle against slavery.[33]

THE RELATIVE EFFICIENCY OF SLAVE LABOR

It was Benjamin Franklin who initiated efforts to measure the relative efficiency of slave and free labor. In an essay written in 1751, at a time when men such as Montesquieu and Hutcheson believed that slavery, at least in the context of the New World, was more efficient than free labor, Franklin set forth an accounting of the cost of slave labor that showed the opposite. Although his statement on this issue was extremely brief, and although the quantitative evidence he set forth was not sufficient to warrant his conclusion, Franklin's statement was highly influential in both France and England. In 1771 Pierre Samuel DuPont de Nemours, a prominent French abolitionist and a member of the Physiocratic school of French economists, set forth a lengthy elaboration of Franklin's theme. Adam Smith did not explicitly cite Franklin's essay, which had achieved considerable fame by the publication date of the *Wealth of Nations,* but he obviously had it in mind when he asserted that slave labor was more costly than free labor "even at Boston, New York, and Philadelphia where the wages of common labor are so high."[34]

Despite its limitations, Franklin's measure of efficiency was similar to those employed by economists today. Indexes of efficiency are ratios of output to input. One common measure is output per worker, which is usually referred to as an index of "labor productivity." A more comprehensive measure called "the index of total factor productivity" is the ratio of output per average unit of all the inputs (which in the case of agriculture are mainly land, labor, and capital).[35] Franklin used only labor in his denominator and he did not measure the output, but implicitly assumed that the output of a given number of slaves was less than, or equal to, that of a like number of free men. Consequently, if slave labor was more costly than free labor, as Franklin contended, it was also less efficient.

Although modern research on the problem of efficiency has been carried out along the lines suggested by Franklin, there have been significant advances of both a theoretical and empirical nature. The main theoretical advance involves the careful formulation of a distinction between profitability and "technical" efficiency, a distinction that has often been blurred. Technical efficiency refers to the effectiveness with which inputs are used in a productive process. One productive process is said to be technically more efficient than another if it yields more output from the same quantity of inputs.

Profitability does not necessarily imply technical efficiency, especially in the slave context, since even processes that were technically inefficient could have been profitable if masters expropriated some of the income that would have accrued to free labor. Profitability calculations can tell whether or not masters were efficient in the allocation of their resources among alternative investments, but not whether the productive techniques employed in each of these enterprises were technically efficient. The intense investigation of the profitability issue, which extended from the mid-1950s to the mid-1970s, revealed that the slave economy had a considerable degree of "allocative" efficiency, which means that masters were fairly efficient in shifting their resources from place to place, at least within agriculture, in order to exploit opportunities to increase their profits. But it still left open the possibility that slave agriculture was technically inefficient.

Frederick Law Olmsted, the great landscape architect and a critic of the economy and culture of the South, posed the problem of measuring the technical efficiency of slavery in a fairly clear way when he said that a comparison of the relative efficiency of slave and free labor should be made "man with man, with reference simply to the equality of muscular power and endurance."[36] To perform such a comparison it is necessary to take account of differences in the age and gender composition of the slave and free labor forces. About two-thirds of all slaves were in the labor force, which was about twice the proportion among free persons. Such a high proportion could be achieved only by pressing virtually everyone capable of any useful work at all into the labor force. As a consequence, nearly one-third of the slave laborers were untrained children and about an eighth were elderly, crippled, or disadvantaged in some way. Women represented a much larger proportion of field laborers among slaves than among free farmers.

In order to have a valid comparison of labor productivity on slave and free farms it is necessary to convert the labor of children, women, the aged, and the infirm into "equivalent prime hands." One way of doing this is to make use of the "hand" ratings that planters assigned to slaves in order to achieve a rational allocation of their laborers among the various tasks.[37] An even more refined and reliable set of ratings can be obtained from the abundant data on slave prices and on annual hire rates. Figure 13 shows that, on average, two women in their fifties did about as much work as one prime-aged male, and three boys in their late teens did about as much work as two prime-aged males.

When indexes of labor productivity (average output per equivalent prime hand) are used to compare technical efficiency, they give a marked advantage to slave plantations. By this measure the intermediate and large slave plantations of the cotton belt were nearly twice as efficient

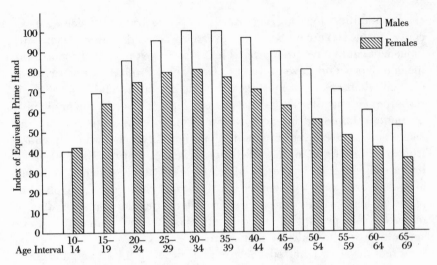

Figure 13. Work-capacity (hand) ratings of slaves, by age and gender (males aged 30–34 equal 100).

as the free farms of the same region in 1860. But indexes of labor productivity exaggerate the relative advantage of slave farms because they do not take account of the fact that the slaves usually worked on more fertile soils and had more work animals and other capital than did the free farmers of the region. The index of total factor productivity overcomes this problem because it takes account not only of the average amount of labor required to produce a given amount of output, but also of the quantity and quality of the land and capital that were employed.

Taking account of the superior land and capital with which slaves worked considerably reduces their edge over free farmers. The advantage of small plantations (1–15 slaves) over free farms that was indicated by the index of labor productivity is now almost completely wiped out, and the advantage of the two classes of gang-system farms (those with 16 or more slaves) is cut in half. Nevertheless, plantations with 16 or more slaves exhibit a considerable advantage over smaller farms, whether slave or free. The gang-system plantations produced, on average, about 39 percent more output from a given amount of input than either free farms or slave farms that were too small to employ the gang system.[38] A plantation with 16 slaves usually had about 10 slaves old enough to work in a gang, and 10 hands appears to have been the threshold number for the successful operation of a gang.

It is worth noting that most of the advantage made possible by the gang system was achieved by intermediate plantations (those with 16–50 slaves). They had an edge over free farms that was two-thirds of that enjoyed by the large plantations (those with 51 or more slaves). Part of the extra advantage of the large plantations was due to a degree of labor specialization that was higher than could be achieved elsewhere. On the large plantations, for example, plow hands were almost always men in the prime ages. But on intermediate plantations men in their teens or in their fifties, and sometimes the stronger women, were used for plowing. Part of the extra advantage also came from the much higher degree of regimentation than was typical of the large plantations, a regimentation that reflected itself not only in field work but in every other aspect of life, including the use of leisure time and the scope for personal choice that slaves were allowed in the selection of marital partners.

While the gang system gave cotton producers who skillfully employed it a clear edge over non-gang producers, it was no automatic guarantee of success. Not all masters were equally adept in the management of their slaves or in the techniques of growing cotton. Planters varied in their mastery of the special characteristics of their particular soils, in the art of combining the production of cotton with that of other crops in such a manner as to keep all hands as fully occupied as possible, and in those planting and cultivating skills that had such important effects on yields at harvest time. As a consequence, the efficiency of gang-system producers varied nearly as much as that of free farmers. This point is brought out by Figure 14, which shows that in both the free and large-farm slave cases, the top 10 percent of the farms were several times more efficient than the bottom 10 percent.[39]

Figure 14 also demonstrates the advantage that the gang system gave to large plantations. At every rank of the two distributions, except the tenth, large plantations were about 50 percent more efficient than free farms.[40] So considerable was the advantage of the gang system that only the top 20 percent of the free farms exceeded the efficiency of the plantation that was just of average efficiency among the large slaveholdings.

The average level of efficiency varied considerably from state to state, among both free and slave farms. The highest levels of efficiency among most classes of farms were generally in those states that attracted the bulk of the interstate slave traffic. Despite the scope of the traffic, the level of efficiency was still not equalized between the slave-importing (New South) and slave-exporting (Old South) regions as late as 1860. One possible explanation is that the planters and free farmers who responded to the opportunities in the New South were more efficient producers than those who remained behind.[41] Another possibility is that movement of slaves from the Old South to the New South simply was not large enough to bring the measured productivity of the two regions into line. The interregional gap in the annual hire or rental rate of slaves provides some support for the second hypothesis. During the last half of the 1850s the

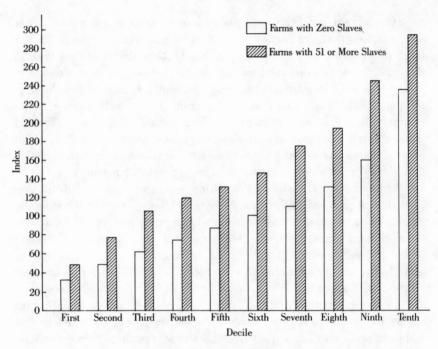

Figure 14. The distribution of efficiency scores of large slave farms compared with
that of free farms, the cotton belt, 1860 (average total factor productivity
on free farms = 100). Shown is the average efficiency score of farms
in each decile (each 10 percent) of the distributions of free and large
slave farms, when these farms are arranged according to their efficiency
scores. Notice that the top 10 percent of the free farms were more
efficient than most of the gang-system farms. Many of these very efficient
free farmers soon purchased slaves and some eventually accumulated
enough capital to rise into the ranks of gang-system planters. On the
other hand, the lowest deciles of the large slave plantations were so
inefficient that they could not compete with most of the free farms, let
alone with the majority of the other gang-system plantations. Some
owners of these inefficient plantations went bankrupt. Others sold out.
This process makes it likely that the gang-system plantations were run
by individuals with above-average ability in the production of southern
staples. Consequently, the superior efficiency of the big plantations was
due not merely to inherent advantages of the gang system but also to
the concentration of cotton farmers of above-average ability in the
ownership of such farms.

average hire rate in the New South exceeded that of the Old South by
38 percent, which would account for about two-thirds of the difference
in total factor productivity between the two regions.[42]

When the technical efficiencies of agriculture in the North and in all
farms in the South are compared, the South has an advantage of about
35 percent.[43] The superior performance of southern agriculture was not

due primarily to the high performance of its free farms. Free farms in the Old South were slightly less efficient than northern farms, while the free farms of the New South were somewhat more efficient than those in the North. These differences tended to net out so that, overall, only a small fraction of the edge enjoyed by southern agriculture was due to the superior performance of the free sector. The technical efficiency of the slave farms, particularly of the intermediate and large plantations, accounted for about 90 percent of the southern advantage.[44]

The cliometric debate on the validity of these findings began during the middle of 1974 and was carried on with such intensity that the convergence of views has proceeded more rapidly than it did on the issue of profitability. Critics of the efficiency computations questioned the way in which the measures of output and of each of the inputs were constructed. They also raised a series of issues regarding the proper interpretation of the findings. Although these issues at first appeared to be of a purely theoretical or statistical nature, they ultimately involved questions about the way that agricultural production was actually carried out in antebellum times.[45]

The effort to resolve these issues led to reconsideration of the working hours of both slaves and free farmers. Researchers turned to the business records of gang-system plantations, some of which kept schedules of what each slave on the plantation was doing on each day of the year. Independent studies of two different samples of these schedules produced quite similar results. Slaves on cotton plantations worked an average of about 2,800 hours per year. The number of days worked per year averaged 281, well below the potential maximum. This shortfall is explained primarily by the almost total absence of Sunday work. Occasionally, a few hands were used on Sundays for special tasks, but such incidents were rare. This nearly total absence of Sunday work is a unique feature of the intermediate and large slave plantations, and it bears on the special nature of the gang system. The balance of the shortfall is explained by other holidays and occasional half days on Saturdays (6 days), by illness (12 days), and by rain and inclement weather (15 days).[46]

Plantation records also revealed a surprisingly high degree of regularity in the length of the workweek over the seasons. The workweek averaged 5.4 days over the entire year, with only slight deviations from season to season. The regularity of the workweek is explained partly by the practice of requiring slaves to work a full day on Saturdays if rain forced a postponement of work on a weekday. When considered on an hourly basis, there was somewhat more variation in seasonal work patterns, due partly to variations in the number of daylight hours and partly to the natural demands of agricultural production. The spring, summer, and fall show roughly equal workweeks, ranging between 57 and 60 hours. Although the short period of daylight during the winter led to a significant reduction in the hourly length of the workweek, slaves still averaged about 40 hours per week during these months.

Comparable evidence on working conditions in the North revealed that although the length of the work year varied with the nature of the farm, free northern farmers averaged about 3,200 hours per year. The lowest subregional average, 3,006 hours, was found in the corn and general farming belt; the highest was 3,365 hours in the western dairy region. Thus, the average length of the southern slave workweek was not 10 percent longer than the average workweek in northern agriculture, as some cliometricians had conjectured, but 10 percent shorter.[47]

This finding seems paradoxical because of the widespread but incorrect assumption that the length of the growing season (the number of frost-free days) was the principal factor determining the length of the agricultural work year in antebellum times. Although the number of frost-free days determines which plants can be raised in a particular region, there is little relationship between the length of the growing season and the duration of the period from seedtime to harvest for particular crops. The growing season in South Dakota, for example, is about 150 days but the period from seedtime to harvest is 310 days for winter wheat and only 115 days for spring wheat.[48]

It was the overall mix of farm products, particularly the mix between field crops and animal products, that was the principal determinant of the hourly length of both the workweek and the work year. The length of the northern workweek was correlated with the degree of specialization in rearing livestock and dairying. Northern farmers specializing in these products generally worked an hour longer on weekdays and Saturdays than those who did not, and they also usually worked a half day on Sundays. So the paradox of the longer northern work year is resolved by the fact that dairying and livestock accounted for 38 percent of the output of northern farms, while the corresponding figure for the large slave plantations was hardly 5 percent.[49]

The discovery that the slave work year was shorter than the free work year does not contradict the proposition that slave labor was more intensely exploited than free labor, but only the proposition that such exploitation took the form of more hours per year. The available evidence indicates that greater intensity of labor per hour, rather than more hours of labor per day or more days of labor per year, is the reason the index of total factor productivity is 39 percent higher for gang-system plantations than for free farms. The principal function of the gang system was to speed up the pace of labor, to increase its intensity per hour. Slaves employed on the intermediate and large plantations worked about

76 percent more intensely per hour than did free southern farmers or slaves on small plantations. In other words, a slave working under the gang system produced, on average, as much output in roughly 35 minutes as a farmer using traditional methods, whether slave or free, did in a full hour.

Once it is recognized that the fundamental form of the exploitation of slave labor was through speeding up rather than through an increase in the number of clock-time hours per year, certain paradoxes resolve themselves. The longer rest breaks during the workday and the greater time off on Sundays for slaves than for free men appear not as boons that slaveholders granted to their chattel but as conditions for achieving the desired level of intensity. The finding that slaves earned 15 percent more income per clock-time hour is less surprising when it is realized that their income per equal-efficiency hour was 33 percent less than that of free farmers.[50]

Of the many issues raised by the investigation of working hours, perhaps the most intriguing and difficult is the meaning of "harder work" or "more intense labor." These terms are often loosely used, as though their meanings were perfectly obvious. Among the several possible definitions, two are most relevant. The first defines intensity of labor by caloric requirement. Thus, one person (of a standard weight and height) would be said to work more intensely than another if his (or her) caloric requirement per hour of labor was greater. But one person could work more intensely than another even if both required the same number of calories. Such a situation would exist if the amount of motion of the two workers was identical, but one "wasted" less motion than the other. The slave case probably involved both kinds of intense labor—that is, labor requiring more calories per man hour and labor with less wasted motion. Labor that eliminates wasted motion may result in psychic fatigue and alienation, and so be more obnoxious than labor that permits wasted motion. The unremitting, machine-like quality of gang laborers repelled mid-nineteenth century observers who valued traditional agrarian ways. And trade unions today frequently resist the introduction of practices aimed at eliminating wasted motion, even when workers are compensated by somewhat higher wages.[51]

Of course, the fact that blacks who toiled on large plantations were more efficient than free workers does not imply that blacks were inherently superior to whites as workers. It was the system that forced men to work at the pace of an assembly line (called the gang) that made slave laborers more efficient than free laborers. Moreover, the gang system, as already noted, appears to have raised productivity only on farms that specialized in certain crops.

After the demise of indigo production, only five U.S. crops appear to have lent themselves to the gang system. One of these, hemp, was quite minor and has yet to be analyzed. Of the other four, the advantage of the gang system appears to have been greatest in sugar, and nearly 100 percent of all cane sugar in the United States was produced on gang-system farms. In tobacco the advantages of the gang system appear to have been small because of the limited opportunities for division of labor, so it is not surprising that as much tobacco was produced by free or small slave farms as by gang-system farms. Although cotton and rice were intermediate cases, the advantage of gang-system plantations was so substantial that they accounted for the great bulk of the output of both crops.

CHAPTER FOUR

THE DEVELOPMENT OF THE SOUTHERN ECONOMY

Despite the convergence of views on the profitability and efficiency of slave agriculture, cliometricians remain divided about the effect of slavery on the development of the southern economy. Their investigations into this problem have turned on five issues: the effect of slavery on the distribution of wealth; the relative level and rate of growth of average (per capita) income in the South before the Civil War; the explanation for this growth rate; the explanation for the decline in southern per capita income after the Civil War; and the effect of slavery on the rate and pattern of southern industrialization and urbanization.[1]

Lurking behind most cliometric debates on the South is an "optimistic" assessment of the economic development of the North before the Civil War. Although this assessment has been shared by nearly all cliometricians, many social and political historians have been skeptical. They have argued that the conditions of northern labor were not only bad but deteriorated rapidly from the end of Andrew Jackson's presidency to the eve of the Civil War. Recently, a number of cliometricians (some investigating early industrialization and the role of women in that process; others investigating problems of health and mortality) have uncovered evidence more consistent with the "pessimistic" view than with the "optimistic" one. During the course of this chapter certain aspects of an emerging new synthesis on the northern economy will be brought out. However, the evidence on northern economic conditions is so deeply intertwined with the evidence on the social and political movements of the region that to separate the two questions would distort both. Consequently, the main analysis of the northern economy is set forth in Chapters 9 and 10.

THE DISTRIBUTION OF WEALTH

It is now clear that critics of the South were far off the mark when they said that the "majority of those who sell the cotton crop" were "poorer than the majority of our day-labourers at the North."[2] The average wealth among farmers of the cotton belt in 1860 was $13,124 (Figure

15). On the other hand, the average wealth of urban laborers in the major northern cities was less than $150, while the average for laborers in the rural areas of the North was hardly $400. The ordinary laborer, North or South, was too poor to purchase a single adult slave, let alone the land and other capital employed on the average farm of the cotton belt. Indeed, a Southerner "who owned two slaves and nothing else was as rich as the average man in the North."[3] In fact, the typical farmer of the cotton belt owned about eight slaves. However, slaves represented only about 50 percent of their total wealth.

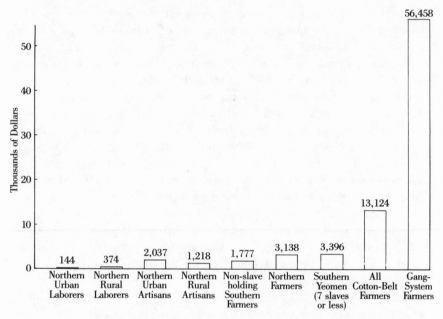

Figure 15. A comparison of average wealth per household head for various social groups in the North and South, 1860.

Nor were the non-slaveholding farmers of the cotton belt a "promiscuous horde"[4] living at the edge of subsistence, as some abolitionists charged. Their average wealth was about $1,800, which was several times greater than that of northern laborers. Far from being pushed out of the better lands, small-scale farmers in the New South actually increased their share of farmland between 1850 and 1860, except in the alluvial regions (the flood plains of the Mississippi).[5] It was not landholdings but slaveholdings that were becoming more concentrated over time. In other words, small-scale farmers were slowly being pushed out of slaveowning, but not out of landowning or out of farming. The fraction of southern households that owned slaves declined from 36 percent in 1830 to 25 percent in 1860.[6]

Scholars have been struggling with the problem of how to compare the relative prosperity of "yeomen" (small, independent farmers) in the North and South. One of the issues is where to draw the line on the definition of a southern "yeoman." To limit the term only to non-slaveholding farmers is to exclude the most enterprising of their number. As one German settler in Alabama in 1855 reported to Robert Russell, "nearly all his countrymen who emigrated with him were now slaveholders. They were poor on their arrival in the country; but no sooner did they realize a little money than they invested it in slaves." That, Russell said, was generally the way that those who "settle upon moderately fertile land in the Southern states, quickly come into a possession of considerable property."[7] Recent statistical analysis has confirmed Russell's generalization, revealing that in the South the accumulation of slaves was highly correlated with the accumulation of all other forms of wealth.

When the yeoman class of the South is defined to include both non-slaveholding farmers and farmers with seven or fewer slaves, their average wealth is nearly identical with that of northern farmers, although the distribution of wealth is somewhat more concentrated among southern yeomen.[8] On the other hand, the average wealth of gang-system farms exceeded $56,000, which is more than 15 times the average either for southern yeomen or for northern farmers. Thus, the distribution of wealth among northern farmers had "an upper limit which did not exist in the South."[9] It was not the pauperization of the small farmer but the existence of huge agribusinesses—the gang-system plantations—that made the rural wealth distribution of the South so much more unequal than that of the North.[10] Indeed, a more detailed analysis of the southern wealth distribution suggests that it is, in some respects, quite misleading to lump the wealth distributions of slaveowners and free farmers together.

Of course the North had large-scale enterprises also, but they were located mainly in the urban areas. The disparities of wealth in northern cities were so wide that they offset the relative egalitarianism of the countryside, leaving the overall distribution of wealth in the free North nearly as unequal as that in the slave South. In each region the top 1 percent of the propertied classes controlled more than one-quarter of all the wealth. By this measure, plutocracy was as well entrenched in the North as in the South.

Despite the similarity of their positions, the two plutocracies differed in certain important respects. In the North the top 1 percent of the wealth holders were mainly urban merchants and manufacturers whose businesses were based on wage labor, while in the South the top 1 percent were mainly rural planters whose businesses were based on slave labor. The southern plutocrats were considerably richer, on average, than their northern counterparts (by a factor of roughly 2 to 1). To put it another way, the very rich were more numerous in the South than in the North. Nearly two out of every three males with estates of $100,000 or more lived in the South in 1860.[11]

The big planters of the cotton belt were generally consolidating their economic positions during the late antebellum era. Between 1850 and 1860 the real wealth of the typical gang-system planter increased by 70 percent. Rather than gradually slipping from its economic dominance, this class was overthrown by the Civil War, which led to the destruction or loss of two-thirds of its wealth. By 1870 Southerners no longer predominated among the nation's super rich; four out of every five of the super rich were now Northerners. So it was not the vagaries of the market or other economic events but military defeat that moved the scepter of wealth from the agrarian South to the industrializing North.[12]

THE ECONOMIC PERFORMANCE OF THE SOUTH, 1840–1880

The principal measures of the overall economic performance of a nation used by economists today are "real national income" and "real national income per capita." National income is the dollar value of the goods and services produced by an economy during a given year. This index can be computed not only for nations, but also for given regions of a nation, or for given industries, to obtain such measures as "southern income," "New York income," "income originating in manufacturing," and "income originating in agriculture." When economists compare the productive performance of an economy, or of a sector of an economy, in two different years, they adjust their measures of income for changes in the price level —in effect, hold prices constant. An index of national income with prices held constant is called "real national income." This index measures the change in the real output of goods and services over time. "Real national income per capita" (or simply "real per capita income") is real national income in a given year divided by the population in that year.[13]

Regional income accounts constructed by cliometricians have made it possible to measure and compare the overall economic performance of the South between 1840 and 1860. The results of this work are summarized in Table 1, which displays two sets of estimates.[14] The first set gives the per capita income of the total population; the second gives the per capita income of only the free population. These two sets of estimates differ because slaves were exploited in the sense that their owners expropriated the difference between the value of their marginal product and

Table 1. Per Capita Income by Region, 1840 and 1860 (in 1860 Prices)

	Total Population		Free Population	
	1840	1860	1840	1860
National Average	$96	$128	$109	$144
North	109	141	110	142
Northeast	129	181	130	183
North Central	65	89	66	90
South	74	103	105	150
South Atlantic	66	84	96	124
East South Central	69	89	92	124
West South Central	151	184	238	274

their maintenance cost (the difference between what their wage would have been in a free market and what their implicit wage actually was under slavery).

Which of these sets of figures should one consider in judging the performance of the antebellum economy? The first set of figures treats slaves as consumers and implicitly assumes that their welfare was as important as that of free citizens. The second set implicitly treats slaves as "intermediate goods" used to produce the final products consumed by free persons—that is, it excludes the welfare of slaves as an ultimate objective of society.

Consequently, even though the measures of real income may be computed with scientific detachment, the evaluation of the performance of the southern economy cannot be neatly disentangled from moral issues. Abolitionists would have measured the performance of the southern economy by the per capita income of the total population.[15] These figures show that in both 1840 and 1860 the per capita income of the South fell short of the national average by more than 20 percent. A southern politician of the antebellum era, however, whose electorate included only free persons, would have given little attention to the income of the slaves. His evaluation of southern economic performance would have focused on the per capita income of free persons, which was nearly the same in the South as in the North. To some extent, then, antebellum disputes about economic performance reflected differences not in economic measurement, but in moral views as to which economic measures were most appropriate for comparing the performance of the two regions.[16]

From our viewpoint today, however, it is the figures on the per capita income of the total population that are obviously the relevant ones. These figures might appear to sustain Republican contentions that the South was a poverty-ridden, stagnant economy in the process of sinking into "comparative imbecility and obscurity," that under the burden of slavery the South had been reduced to the status of a colonial nation—"the dependency of a mother country." No such inference is warranted merely because of the gap between the North and the South in the level of per capita income in 1860. Before any conclusion can be drawn the sources of that gap must first be investigated.[17]

We begin this investigation by dividing the North into two subregions: the Northeast and the North Central subregions. Table 1 shows that the northern advantage over the South was due entirely to the extraordinarily high income of the Northeast. Per capita income in the North Central states was not only less than half as high as in the Northeast, it was 14 percent lower than per capita income in the South. If the South was a poverty-ridden "colonial dependency," how should one characterize the states that occupy the territory running from the western border of Pennsylvania to the western border of Nebraska— states usually thought of as examples of high prosperity and rapid growth during the antebellum era?

The dilemma arises in this instance from an important demographic fact which, if ignored, distorts comparisons between the economic performance of the Northeast and that of the rest of the nation: The fertility rate in the Northeast was lower than in the rest of the nation. Consequently, the proportion of the population that consisted of dependent children was lower in the Northeast than elsewhere. Adjustments for this and other demographic phenomena eliminate much of the apparent gap between the economic performance of the Northeast and that of the rest of the nation.

Even if these refinements in the measure of economic performance are set aside, it is evident that the South was quite advanced by the economic standard of the antebellum era. If we treat the North and South as separate nations and rank them among the countries of the world, the South would stand as the fourth most prosperous nation of the world in 1860. The South was more prosperous than France, Germany, Denmark, or any of the countries of Europe except England. The South was not only advanced by antebellum standards but also by relatively recent standards. Indeed, a country as advanced as Italy did not achieve the southern level of per capita income until the eve of World War II.

The last point underscores the dubious nature of attempts to classify the South as a "colonial dependency." The South's large purchases of manufactured goods from the North made it no more of a colonial dependency than did the North's heavy purchases of rails from Great Britain. The true colonial dependencies, countries such as India and Mexico, had less than one-tenth the per capita income of the South in 1860.

Much of the antislavery ammunition for the characterization of the South as a land of poverty was drawn from the debates on economic policy among southern leaders, especially during the economic crisis of the 1840s and during the political crises of the 1850s. As sectional tensions mounted Southerners became increasingly alarmed by federal policies that they thought were giving economic advantage to the North. They also became increasingly impatient with what they thought was an insufficiently active role by their state and local governments to promote internal improvements and to embrace other policies that would acceler-ate the southern rate of economic growth. To generate a sense of urgency, and to develop a spirit of unity against pro-northern economic policies, southern newspapers, journals, economic leaders, and politicians contin-ually emphasized every unrealized objective of the South. The region-wide economic conventions that were regularly organized to promote southern interests took on an increasingly nationalistic character, with "radical" politicians using economic arguments to promote support for a secessionist policy. By the mid-1850s southern discussions of economic issues were, if not the handmaiden of nationalistic politics, deeply entan-gled in it.[18]

Table 2 shows that far from stagnating, the per capita income of the South was growing at an average annual rate of 1.7 percent in the period

1840–1860. This rate of growth was not only a third higher than that enjoyed by the North, but was quite high by historical standards. Only a handful of countries have been able to sustain long-term growth rates substantially in excess of that achieved by the antebellum South between 1840 and 1860.[19]

Table 2. Average Annual Rates of Change in Real Per Capita Income, 1840–1860

National Average	1.4	South	1.7
North	1.3	South Alantic	1.2
Northeast	1.7	East South Central	1.3
North Central	1.6	West South Central	1.0

Note: The rates of growth of subregions do not necessarily add up to the growth rate of the region. The sum of the parts may be more or less than the whole, depending on population shifts among the subregions. For an explanation of this phenomenon, see the companion volume: *Evidence and Methods*, #40.

The impression that the economy of the antebellum South was thriving is further accentuated by the second set of figures in Table 1. Ignoring the income of slaves not only raises the per capita income of the South to near equality with the North, but it also gives a fillip to the southern growth rate. That growth rate becomes 1.8 percent, which exceeds the growth rate of the rest of the nation by more than a third.

Using "free" rather than "total" per capita income to assess the relative performance of the southern economy imparts a definite moral bias to the comparison. But that moral bias was, of course, the one that was embraced by the great majority of free Southerners in antebellum times.[20] Consequently, consideration of the difference between both the level and the rate of growth of "free" and "total" per capita incomes serves to emphasize the substantial stake of the free population in the continuation of the slave system. The exploitation of slaves raised the per capita income of the free southern population by 45 percent and the annual rate of growth of their per capita income by about 8 percent. Nor were slaveowners the only ones who appear to have benefited from slavery. For if it is true, as is frequently asserted, that slavery retarded the rate of growth of the South's free labor force, then free wage workers of the region also benefited from slavery. Whatever the merit of that argument, it is interesting to note that rate of increase in the average money wages of laborers between 1850 and 1860 was greater in the South than in the nation as a whole. Moreover, the 1860 money wage of southern farm laborers and domestics compared favorably with the national averages of these groups.[21] These considerations have some bearing on why the cause of the Confederacy enjoyed such strong support among non-slaveholding Southerners.[22]

The economic performance of the South deteriorated drastically dur-

ing the 1860s and 1870s. Some part of the decline was no doubt caused
by the devastation of the Civil War, which was more extensive in the
South than in the North, but other factors were probably also involved
and may have had a more depressing effect on the southern economy
than the physical destruction of men and capital. Table 3 shows how
dramatically the fortunes of the North and the South changed during
these two decades. Despite its heavy war losses, the northern economy
made a vigorous recovery. By 1880 per capita income in this region was
45 percent greater than it had been in 1860. The South did not experience a similar postwar boom. Economic conditions were better in 1880
than at the close of the war. But even after a decade and a half of
Reconstruction, southern per capita income was still 15 percent less than
it had been in 1860.[23]

Table 3. Per Capita Income by Region for 1860 and 1880 (in 1860 Prices)

	1860	1880	Average Annual Rate of Growth (+) or Decline (−) (%)
National Average	$128	$173	+1.5
North	141	205	+1.9
Northeast	181	244	+1.5
North Central	89	170	+3.3
South	103	88	−0.8
South Atlantic	84	78	−0.4
East South Central	89	88	−0.1
West South Central	184	104	−2.8

Because of the poor southern recovery from the war, the gap between
the per capita income of the South and the rest of the nation increased
dramatically. In 1880 southern per capita income fell short of the national average by nearly 50 percent.[24] This wide gap persisted until the
end of the century and then began to narrow. But the process of catching
up was so slow that it took the South more than a century to reduce the
income gap to the level at which it stood in 1860. Even today, southern
per capita income is still about 10 percent below the national average.

THE CAPACITY TO REALLOCATE RESOURCES BETWEEN REGIONS

Cliometricians have been grappling with two closely interrelated questions: Why was the southern rate of economic growth so high between
1840 and 1860, and why was the southern rate of economic growth so
low between 1860 and 1880? These questions are still unresolved,
despite more than a decade of work on them, but some definite progress

toward a resolution has occurred. The answers turn partly on the extent
to which the southern economy was able to reallocate its productive
resources in response to changes in demand for its products or to changes
in the technology of production.

The development of low-cost forms of transportation, which opened
the interior of the nation to commercial exploitation, was among the most
dramatic aspects of technological change during the antebellum era. It
has long been known that the South participated in the westward movement of population and production, but it was only recently that scholars
were able to demonstrate that this movement had a significant impact on
southern economic growth between 1840 and 1860. Its importance was
established when cliometricians examined the southern rate of growth by
subregions. As Table 2 shows, growth within each of the three subregions was less than the growth rate of the South as a whole. Approximately 30 percent of the South's growth was due to the redistribution
of the southern population from the older states to the newer ones,
particularly to the states of the West South Central subregion. It will be
noted that the West South Central subregion enjoyed an even higher
level of per capita income in 1860 than the Northeast (see Table 3). The
remaining 70 percent of southern growth was due to the rise of per capita
income within each of the subregions. Some scholars have argued that
only the growth within subregions is meaningful, that the proportion of
the growth rate attributed to the redistribution of the population from
east to west is a statistical illusion that ought to be exorcised.[25]

The capacity of an economy to grow, however, does not depend only
on the worldwide demand for its products, or only on its luck or its
technological creativity, but on its responsiveness to economic opportunity, whatever the source might be. The capacity of an economy to shift
resources from one geographic region (or one economic sector) to another, as circumstances may dictate, is always a major determinant of its
growth, because the various industrial sectors and geographic subregions
of a nation generally grow at uneven rates. The shifting demand for iron,
for example, led the U.S. iron industry to grow much more rapidly than
cotton textiles between 1842 and 1848, but much more slowly than
textiles between 1848 and 1858. The remarkable speed with which the
economy shifted resources into and out of iron and other manufacturing
industries in response to the ebb and flow of demand or to changes in
technology had much to do with the high U.S. rate of growth between
1840 and 1860. Cliometricians are still at an early stage of the effort to
measure the share of the growth rate that is due to such inter-industry
and interregional shifts. Current estimates indicate that more than half
of the northern growth rate between 1840 and 1860 was due to the

reallocation of labor and other resources between the agricultural, manufacturing, and service sectors.[26]

The belief that slavery impeded the reallocation of labor was one of
the main features of the economic indictment fashioned by the abolitionists. This is a matter on which cliometricians remain divided, despite the
fact that nearly one-third of the South's annual growth rate was due to
the westward migration.[27] Three points are at issue here. The first is the
possibility that in the absence of slavery the migration to the New South
would have been even more rapid than it actually was. There is also the
question of whether southern farmers shifted resources between cotton
and other crops in response to short-term movements in relative prices.
Perhaps the most difficult issue is whether the South redistributed its
labor force between rural and urban occupations in a manner that maximized the opportunities for economic growth.[28]

Given the scale of the westward movement of slaves, it might seem
unreasonable to question the adequacy of the South's response to economic opportunity in the West. There is, however, a piece of evidence
suggesting that westward movement of southern labor did not proceed
rapidly enough: the large and persistent gap in agricultural wages between the New South and Old South, a gap that ranged between 20 and
40 percent during the last three decades of the antebellum era. The
situation was quite different from the one prevailing in the North. Agricultural wages in the North Central states were quite similar to those in
the Northeast, especially in 1850 and 1860.

The East-West equalization of farm wages in the North was brought
about by the extraordinarily high migration rate into the North Central
states, due mainly to foreign immigration, which averaged 28 per thousand per year between 1850 and 1860. This means that over the course
of the decade, inward migration increased the agricultural labor force of
the Midwest by one-third. During the same period, migration added just
7 percent to the agricultural labor force of the New South, which was
far short of the level of migration needed to equalize wages across the
South. Rather than being overly aggressive in its westward expansion,
the South was moving far more slowly than the North.

It was not a hesitation to move slaves that was the source of the gap
between the northern and southern rates of western migration. The
westward migration rate of slaves was about the same as that of native-
born persons in the North. One problem was the difficulty of the New
South in attracting and holding native-born whites. The migration rate
for this class was negative, which means that during the 1850s more
native-born, free agriculturalists left the New South than arrived. But the
South was most deficient in its ability to attract the foreign-born, espe-

cially the new immigrants from Ireland and Germany who were surging into the country. The foreign born made up the majority of the farm laborers who entered the North Central states. But in the New South, foreign-born migrants were a relatively small number, hardly enough to offset the exodus of the native-born whites.

It should not be assumed that the East-West equalization of wages in the North implies that the North had a more optimal distribution of labor than the South. Since there was a cost to moving west, the absence of a wage gap between the North Central states and the Northeast states suggests that too much labor migrated to the West.[29]

These preliminary findings on the migration pattern raise a host of questions that require more detailed data than those now in hand, although the gathering of the required data is in progress. One of the more interesting questions is whether the slave movement rate should have been even higher than it was. The answer turns on whether the gap between eastern and western slave prices reflected the cost of transporting the slaves. If it did, the cost of relocating slaves may have been well above the cost of relocating native-born whites in the North.[30] There is also the question of why the New South was not able to hold on to more of its native-born whites, some of whom settled in the southern counties of Indiana, Illinois, and Missouri. Cliometricians are still divided on whether these migrants were pushed out by an aversion to slavery and an inability to compete with the big slaveholders or were pulled out by the prospect of higher earnings. However, political historians have called attention to the fact that the southern counties of the North Central states, where most migrants from the South resided, voted with the Democrats in the elections between 1852 and 1860.[31]

THE CAPACITY TO REALLOCATE RESOURCES BETWEEN CROPS

What abolitionists and later critics of slave agriculture had in mind when they criticized its allocative mechanism was not so much its failure to shift enough labor from the East to the West, but its apparently inflexible concentration on the production of a few staple crops, particularly cotton. Some of those who took up this issue offered an explanation for the presumed failure of southern farmers, particularly slaveowners, to change the mix of their crops in response to changes in prices. Slave labor, they said, was so inept that planters were "obliged to employ their negroes exclusively in the production of a few commodities and can only make their labor profitable by keeping up an invariable routine." Most of those who criticized the crop mix of the planters provided no explanation or suggested that the behavior was irrational. One historian, for example, simply asserted that because planters in the 1850s were so irresistibly drawn toward the overproduction of cotton, its price was bound to decline. Rather than defining the source of this irresistible tendency he was content to point to the doubling of cotton production between 1850 and 1860 as evidence that the tendency was real. He particularly emphasized the 57 percent increase in the crop between 1857 and 1860, because that rapid leap in output brought with it a decline in cotton prices. He was sure that, in the absence of the Civil War, overproduction and declining prices would have persisted throughout the sixties and would have guaranteed the peaceful destruction of slavery.[32]

The charge that the South was irrationally addicted to overproduction of cotton and other staples did not disappear with the Civil War, but was also a point of contention during the postbellum era. Some reformers attributed the depressed state of the southern economy between 1865 and 1880 and beyond to the failure of southern farmers to diversify the mix of their crops. Some attributed the rigidity to a hangover of bad habits developed during the antebellum era, and some emphasized the lack of experience of blacks in crops other than cotton. Others put the blame on merchants and landlords who forced tenants to grow excessive cotton in order to make these tenants buy food and other supplies from their stores at excessively high prices and (if purchased on credit) at usurious rates of interest. But perhaps the most common explanation for the overproduction of cotton was a presumed addiction to cash crops and an overemphasis on short-run profits. Reformers accused southern farmers of failing to appreciate the benefits of being self-sufficient, because self-sufficiency often meant a lowered average income. Critics who made these points often acknowledged that in good times concentration on cotton brought the highest profit, while stressing that such a policy not only left farmers extremely vulnerable when cotton prices were low, but bred the vain hope that prices "would rally again." "Multitudes of men" harbored this delusion "year after year" and "seemed utterly unable to tear themselves away from its constantly fastening power."[33]

Much of the cliometric work on the crop-mix problem has occurred at the theoretical level. Mathematical models have been constructed that restate the old criticisms of southern agriculture in a more precise way. Such models do not by themselves either confirm or contradict a theory, but they assist that process by identifying critical assumptions and by revealing measurable implications. These models have demonstrated that both the antebellum and the more recent criticisms of the southern crop mix depend on a single vital assumption—that the amount of land and labor that southern farmers devoted to cotton production was independent of fluctuations in the price of cotton.

That assumption has now been subjected to empirical tests. Using a statistical technique called "distributed lags," cliometricians have estimated the speed with which southern farmers changed the mix of crops in response to a change in the relative prices of these crops. Farmers in all regions of the United States, as well as in other countries, respond to changing prices with a lag; that is, they do not switch entirely into, or out of, a given crop in one year just because the price in the previous year was higher or lower than they expected it to be. Instead, farmers usually make only a partial adjustment in a single year, waiting for further evidence as to whether a previous change in price was just a chance fluctuation or a lasting change. A common measure of the responsiveness of farmers, then, is the number of years it takes for them to make a 90 percent adjustment to a lasting change in prices. It has now been shown that southern farmers in the postbellum era were just as responsive to lasting price changes as the wheat farmers in the North. In both instances farmers made a 90 percent adjustment in about five years.[34]

What about the slave era? The speed of adjustment was more rapid before the Civil War than after it. Slaveowners made a 90 percent adjustment in their output of cotton within just two years after a lasting price change. Far from lagging behind free farmers in responding to price changes, the big cotton planters appear to have responded with uncommon speed, perhaps because, as one cliometrician has suggested, their stronger financial position permitted them to take greater risks than a small farmer was willing to incur. In hindsight, this result does not seem so surprising. After all, the speed with which slaveholders reacted to the sudden change in the price of indigo after the Revolution came close to a controlled experiment on their sensitivity to market conditions. In that instance, slaveholders reduced their production of this slave-produced crop by 98 percent in just three years, and they never returned to indigo again, because the price of that crop never warranted a return.

What about the contention that the surge in cotton production during the 1850s, especially the leap in production between 1857 and 1860, was symptomatic of a long-term tendency toward the overproduction of cotton? There was nothing so unusual about the rate or manner in which cotton production increased during the 1850s that warrants such a conclusion. Similar booms were experienced during every decade of the nineteenth century except for the depression decade of the 1840s. Indeed, the annual rate of increase in cotton production between 1857 and 1860 was actually a bit below the average rate during other years in which cotton production increased.[35] Nor was it particularly unusual for output to have increased for three years in a row. There were four other long expansions, between 1806 and 1860, one of which lasted for ten years.

Those who advocated the overproduction thesis did not treat the 1857–1860 expansion as a fifth major cotton boom because of the slight decline in the price of cotton that occurred during these years. But there were comparable declines in the price of cotton during the booms of the 1810s, 1820s, and 1830s.[36] Moreover, the general trend of raw cotton prices was downward from 1802 on. Although there were fluctuations about this trend, the average annual rate of decrease was 0.7 percent. The basic cause of this long-term decline was the steady increase in productivity. Among the developments that made cotton farming increasingly more efficient were improvements in the varieties of cottonseeds, introduction of the cotton gin, reduction in transportation and other marketing costs, and relocation of cotton production to the more fertile lands of the New South.

It was, therefore, to be expected that increases in production would generally be associated with declining prices. Since advances in productivity caused costs to fall, profits of planters may have been rising despite declining cotton prices. What is crucial, then, is not the absolute level of prices, but the level of profits. An approximation of the movement of profits may be obtained by examining the deviation of cotton prices from their long-term trend. When cotton prices were above their long-term trend value, profits of planters were likely to have been above normal. When prices were below their trend values, profits on cotton were likely to have been below normal.

Figure 16 indicates that the 1850s constituted a period of sustained boom in profits for cotton planters.[37] Nearly every year of the decade was one of above-normal profit. What is more, profits remained high during the last four years of the decade, with prices averaging about 15 percent above their trend values. No wonder cotton production doubled between 1850 and 1860. It was clearly a rational economic response to increase cotton production by over 50 percent between 1857 and 1860. If planters erred, it was not in expanding cotton production by too much, but in being too conservative. Their expansion had not been adequate to bring prices down to their trend values and profits back to normal (equilibrium) levels.

What was responsible for making the 1850s so prosperous for cotton planters? An answer is provided by Figure 17.[38] It shows that the worldwide demand for southern cotton began to increase rapidly beginning in 1846. Over the next 15 years, the average annual rate of change in demand was about 7 percent per annum. Figure 17 also shows that changes in the supply of cotton generally lagged behind changes in

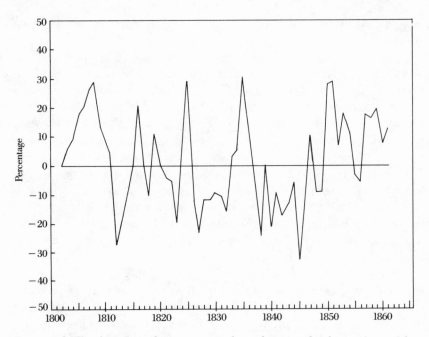

Figure 16. The deviation of cotton prices from their trend values, 1802–1861.

demand. As a consequence, prices and profits tended to be above normal in periods when demand was increasing, and below normal when demand was decreasing or stagnating. During most of the 1850s the supply of cotton lagged behind the demand, which caused the price of cotton to rise well above normal levels, creating unusually large profits for planters. While planters responded to this incentive, they did not increase output rapidly enough to return cotton prices and profits to a normal level by 1860.

THE ROLE OF THE COTTON BOOM

Some cliometricians have pushed the overproduction thesis in a novel direction. They agree that demand for American cotton boomed during the 1850s but contend that it was only this spurt in the world's demand for cotton that prevented the slave South from falling into economic decay. Since the growth of demand could not have continued indefinitely at the pace of the 1850s, southern prosperity was bound to come to an end at some point. According to this account, earlier advocates of the overproduction thesis were right in arguing that the slave South was teetering on the edge of a profound economic crisis. Their error was in attributing the impending crisis to overproduction rather than to an insufficiency of demand.[39]

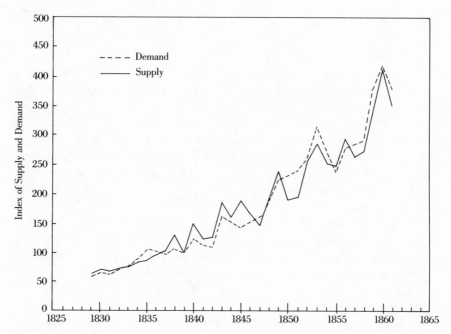

Figure 17. A comparison between indexes of cotton demanded and supplied, 1829–
    1861.

According to the new hypothesis, a crisis in demand had already
emerged by 1860 but was disguised by the Civil War, which abruptly
cut off shipments of American cotton to Europe. The temporary loss of
the American supply created so severe a shortage of cotton that many
textile firms were forced to close their doors and many laborers were laid
off. As a consequence of this "cotton famine," textile manufacturers
became too preoccupied with problems of supply to take note of the
weakening of the demand for their products. Stagnation in demand, by
itself, the argument concludes, could explain half of the fall in southern
per capita income between 1860 and 1880.

Some aspects of the hypothesis of insufficient demand have been
shown to be incorrect. The original effort to compute an index of the
demand for cotton was marred by computational errors. When these
errors are corrected, the index shows that demand increased quite rapidly between 1860 and 1870. Rather than declining by 45 percent, the
world demand for cotton was 69 percent higher in 1870 than in 1860.
The decade of the 1870s, however, ushered in general economic recessions in both the United States and Europe, and cotton textiles was
among the more severely affected industries. As a consequence, the
world demand for cotton, although still above the 1860 level, was about
10 percent less in 1880 than it had been in 1870. Vigorous growth in

cotton demand resumed in the 1880s, and by 1890 the world demand for cotton was more than twice as high as it had been on the eve of the Civil War.

Empirical research has also invalidated the contentions that "cotton goods were becoming 'an unmarketable burden' " in 1860 and that "the British textiles industry stood on the crest of a major crisis of overproduction, which would have ushered in this era of stagnation had it not been overshadowed by the Cotton Famine of the 1860s."[40] These contentions are based on the increasing inventories of raw cotton and of cotton cloth in Great Britain during 1859 and 1860. But rising inventories are not necessarily a sign of distress. Because manufacturers were unable to keep up with demand, inventories had fallen to an exceedingly low level in 1858. Although stocks were being replenished in 1859 and 1860, they were still below normal levels when the Civil War broke out.[41] If there had been severe overproduction of cotton goods, prices should have plummeted in 1859 and 1860, as they did during the textile recession of the 1840s. However, the price of cotton cloth held fairly steady and that of yarn increased slightly.

Correction of the measures of the demand for cotton textiles and for raw cotton weakens the argument of insufficient demand but does not dispose of it. Advocates of the hypothesis have also argued that all, or nearly all, of the increase in southern per capita income between 1840 and 1860 came from a single source: the growing share of cotton in total southern output. This argument is based on the assumption that labor productivity was so much higher in cotton than in all other agricultural products that the shift from other crops into cotton by itself was enough to explain the prewar growth of per capita income. The proposition implies that little, if any, of the prewar southern growth in per capita income was due to improvements in the method of producing cotton or other agricultural commodities. It also has a critical implication for the postwar period: If the changing share of cotton in southern output was the only source of rising productivity, the South could not have maintained its growth rate, even in the absence of a Civil War, because the demand for cotton did not increase as rapidly after 1860 as it had before that year.[42]

CHANGES IN THE PRODUCTIVITY OF SOUTHERN AGRICULTURE, 1840–1880

Cliometric hypotheses about insufficient demand have pointed up the need to measure changes in the productivity of southern agriculture between 1840 and 1880. The main sources of data for these measures are the decennial censuses of agriculture. The first such census was made

in 1840, but was not very complete. Since the 1860 census was the best
of those taken during the antebellum era, most of the work of measuring
productivity has concentrated on that year. For some purposes the data
in the published census volumes are adequate.

For other purposes, it has been necessary to draw from large samples
of data on the individual farms that can be found in the manuscript
schedules of the census, the original forms on which the census takers
set down the information supplied by each household or firm. The largest
and most perfected of these samples is the Parker-Gallman sample—
over 5,200 farms in the cotton South taken from the 1860 census.
Originally drawn in the mid-1960s, this sample has been intensively
analyzed by successive groups of cliometricians, each of which has built
upon the work of its predecessors.[43]

Perhaps the most important finding to date is that the labor productivity of southern farms declined sharply between 1860 and 1880. Indexes based on three different bodies of data yield the same basic result.
Although the magnitude of the decline varies from one index to another,
the range of the estimated decline is reasonably narrow—from 31 to 43
percent.[44] Since agriculture accounted for about three-quarters of all
southern output, this decline in the productivity of agricultural workers,
by itself, explains the entire decline in the South's per capita income
between 1860 and 1880 shown in Table 3. Present estimates indicate
that about two-thirds of the reduction in labor productivity was due to
a decrease in the efficiency of labor, which is measured by the index of
total factor productivity. The balance was due to a decline in the amount
of improved land, work animals, and other capital that was available to
each agricultural laborer.

These preliminary findings have a bearing on another issue that
cliometricians have been debating. Was there a significant reduction in
the supply of labor provided by blacks after emancipation, and if so
how large was it? Some cliometricians believe that the labor supply of
blacks decreased by a third after the Civil War, due partly to a withdrawal of women and children from the labor force and partly to a
reduction in the number of hours worked per day or per year by black
agriculturalists. There was, of course, a substantial disorganization of
the labor force during the first few years following emancipation, as
both freedmen and planters struggled to find new forms of organization
that were mutually acceptable. Freedmen were quite reluctant to return
to gangs, even when offered wage premiums to do so, and it took a
number of years for sharecropping to emerge as a substitute arrangement that was widely accepted by both sides. The process of transition
involved breaking the gangs into smaller units called "squads," and
these eventually gave way to the leasing of land to the families of the

ex-slaves, either for a cash rent or for a share of the crop.[45]

It is likely that there was a sharp reduction in the labor force participation rate (the share of the population that is in the labor force) during these years of transition, and the reduction could well have been in the neighborhood of a third, or even more. However, during the 1870s the labor situation began to stabilize and production of the principal staples began to exceed prewar levels. By 1880, the labor force participation rate of blacks was probably quite close to prewar levels. This conclusion is implied by the finding that virtually all of the decline in per capita income between 1860 and 1880 was due to the decline in labor productivity. The finding means that there is no room for a substantial labor withdrawal in 1880.[46]

Part of the progress toward an explanation for the postwar decline in productivity has involved the elimination of some of the early conjectures. The low productivity in 1880 was not due to a failure of demand to keep up with supply, since the real price of cotton in 1880 was about 10 percent higher than it had been in 1860. Nor was it due to a decline in the share of resources that southern farmers devoted to cotton, since the cotton share of the output of southern agriculture was slightly higher in 1880 than it had been in 1860. The conjecture that the decline in productivity was due to the rise of sharecropping also appears to be erroneous. Sharecroppers had a slightly lower labor productivity than cash renters, mainly because they had less capital and land per worker than did cash renters. In any case, the margin of difference between sharecroppers and cash renters was too small to explain more than a small portion of the postwar decline in labor productivity. Race has also been shown to have been an irrelevant factor, since black and white farmers, equally well endowed with capital and land, were equally productive in the 1880s and 1890s.[47]

The breakup of the gang system, with the loss of the productivity advantages associated with it, appears to be by far the largest factor in the postwar decline. The preliminary comparisons between productivity in 1860 and 1880 indicate that small white farms were about 5 percent less productive in 1880 than they had been in 1860 and that almost the entire decline is concentrated in the category of black farmers, who worked mainly on slave plantations before the war and on small farms after it. The labor productivity of black farmers was 60 percent lower in 1880 than it had been in 1860.[48] These findings do not mean that black farmers were much less efficient than white farmers in 1880, but that whether black or white, farmers who toiled on small farms after the war were considerably less productive than the gang-system laborers of prewar times.

Since the breakup of the gang-system farms was responsible for the decline in productivity, it might be thought that the price of cotton should have been higher than it actually was in 1880. Had the price of inputs remained constant, a 20 or 30 percent decline in total factor productivity would have led to a 20 or 30 percent rise in the price of cotton. However, the prices of the main inputs into cotton production— labor, land, and most other items of capital—fell by amounts that nearly offset all of the upward pressure on cotton prices caused by the change in productivity. Indeed, the ratio of input prices to the price of cotton is still another way of measuring total factor productivity, and this index indicates a 35 percent decline in the efficiency of cotton production—a figure that is quite consistent with the hypothesis that the breakup of the gang system caused the post–Civil War decline in productivity.[49]

So, although much work remains to be done on the collection and analysis of data, the preliminary findings based on three different sources of data point to the same conclusion: The shift of the majority of black agriculturalists from the large-scale farms of the antebellum era to family-sized farms of 1880 explains most of the postwar decline in the productivity of southern agriculture and thus in southern per capita income. This loss of productivity was a price that most black agriculturalists were willing to pay for the greater freedom and other benefits derived from family farming.[50]

Perhaps the most important finding of the studies of labor productivity before the Civil War is that the South, like the North, was experiencing a major boom in the nonagricultural sector of its economy. Over the period from 1840 to 1860, labor productivity in the service (commerce, banking, transportation, etc.) and manufacturing sectors was increasing more than twice as rapidly as in agriculture. This finding casts some doubt on the contention that the economic growth of the South before the Civil War rested purely on developments in the agricultural sector. Indeed, although the nonagricultural sector accounted for less than a quarter of southern output in 1840, it was the source of about 40 percent of all the increase in the region's per capita income during the last two decades of the antebellum era.[51]

These findings do not necessarily rule out the proposition that growth of the southern economy was dominated by the worldwide boom in the demand for cotton. However, that theory will, at a minimum, have to be revised so that the main developmental impact of the cotton boom is not on southern agriculture, as has heretofore been presumed, but on southern commerce and manufacturing. Such a reformulation should be based on a more detailed analysis of the antebellum sources of growth in southern commerce and manufacturing than has as yet been undertaken by cliometricians. It cannot yet be ruled out that the main factors affecting the rate of southern economic growth before 1860 were on the supply side rather than on the demand side.

THE LAG IN SOUTHERN INDUSTRIALIZATION AND URBANIZATION

At the end of the eighteenth century both the North and the South were overwhelmingly rural societies. Less than 10 percent of their respective populations lived in cities and about 80 percent of their workers were engaged in agricultural production. The manufacturing establishments of both regions (which produced such articles as hats, shoes, saddles, cloth, watches, beer, and metal products) were generally quite small. The typical establishment was the household of a farm family that "engaged in the production of simple manufactures during slack agricultural times and seasons."[52]

Both the North and the South lagged decades behind Great Britain, the world's economic leader, which began the Industrial Revolution in the middle of the eighteenth century. A quarter of Great Britain's population lived in cities as early as 1750, but that level of urbanization was not reached in the United States until 1869—a lag of more than a century. The lags in manufacturing were not as long. Nevertheless, in 1850 the United States trailed Great Britain in the production of cotton textiles by 17 years, while the lag in the production of pig iron was 23 years. The fact that the United States trailed in these respects does not mean that it was backward by the standards of the day. Quite the contrary—in its degree of urbanization and levels of production in most manufacturing industries, it stood second only to Great Britain. Moreover, the United States was industrializing rapidly enough to catch up with, and surpass, the leader. It surpassed Britain in the production of pig iron by 1890 and in cotton textiles by 1910.[53]

The American lunge toward industrialization began during the second decade of the nineteenth century. As late as 1810, the bulk of the cotton and woolen products were manufactured in households rather than in factories. During the next several decades hundreds of relatively large-scale cotton textile mills were constructed in the Northeast, with Massachusetts leading the way. By 1850 the typical cotton mill of the Northeast employed an average of about 150 workers, and the top 10 percent averaged more than 500 workers. These large, and by the standards of the time highly mechanized, factories symbolized the North's status as a leader of the Industrial Revolution. In heavy industry, it was Pennsylvania with its abundant deposits of coal and ore that led the way, accounting for nearly two-thirds of the nation's output of pig iron in

1860. The symbols of modernity in the American iron industry, the anthracite blast furnaces, were usually more heavily capitalized than the cotton textile mills. Paralleling the North's rise in manufacturing was the rapid growth of its cities. By 1860 the share of the northeastern population that was urban had increased to about 36 percent.[54]

The process of industrialization began in the South at about the same time that it began in the North, but proceeded at a slower rate. Between 1820 and 1860 the southern workers engaged in manufacturing increased by 72 percent, but the northern increase was 383 percent (see Figure 18).[55] By the eve of the Civil War one could foresee the emergence of a new society in the Northeast, in which the majority of the labor force would be engaged in manufacturing and commerce, rather than in farming, and in which a majority of the population lived in a few great cities. But the South, despite the growth of its commercial and manufacturing sectors, remained in 1860 much as it had been in 1820, a society based on a highly developed form of commercial agriculture, with the overwhelming majority of its population spread thinly across a vast rural territory. In an age when factories were often built in the countryside in order to exploit available resources, it was possible to industrialize without suffering the calamities of overrapid urbanization. Although the South retained its predominantly rural character, its manufacturing and trade were highly enough developed to place it among the forefront of nations in these respects. On a per capita basis it ranked second in the construction of railroads, sixth in cotton textile production, and eighth in the production of pig iron. Although behind Britain and the North, it had achieved a level comparable to those of such other relatively advanced nations as France, Germany, and Austria-Hungary.[56]

Attitudes toward the southern lag in industrialization were by no means uniform in either the South or the North. It was not clear to all who pondered the problem that the South was actually as far behind the North in the development of its industry as published data suggested. Census officials and other analysts did not make a sharp distinction between agriculture and manufacturing. The census of 1840, for example, employed a single schedule that combined these two sectors with mining and commerce. The censuses of 1850 and 1860 had separate schedules for agriculture and manufacturing, but most of what they classified as "manufacturing" involved the processing of agricultural products. Census officials do not appear to have been guided by a consistently applied principle, such as the scale of the productive unit, in dividing enterprises into sectors.[57] The typical sugar factory was larger than the typical factory in textiles, and the rice-cleaning mills were typically larger than flour and grain mills, yet the 1850 and 1860 censuses classified most sugar production and rice cleaning with agricul-

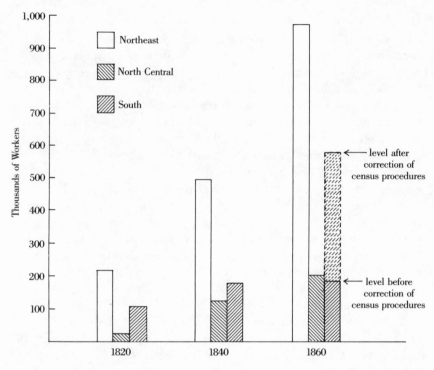

Figure 18. The growth of the labor force in U.S. manufacturing, 1820–1860, by
        region.

ture, while flour milling and textiles were classified with manufacturing.
Nor could the principle of division have been based on spatial location
since nearly all flour mills were located in rural areas, as was also the
case with cotton gins and sugar refineries. The census was also inconsistent in its treatment of such handicrafts as blacksmithing or coopering,
which were classified with manufacturing in the North, whether they
were in cities or in rural areas, but in the South blacksmith shops located
on plantations and run by slaves appear to have been classified with
agriculture. Figure 18 shows that when sugar factories and ginning mills
are classified with manufacturing, and when artisan crafts are treated
symmetrically in both regions, more than half of the apparent industrial
gap between the North and the South disappears. Although the revision
still leaves the share of the southern labor force in manufacturing below
that of the Northeast, it is higher than the manufacturing share of the
North Central states.

   Many Southerners could, and did, believe that their industrial and
commercial sectors were as prosperous, as dynamic, and as modern as
northern industry. They also believed that they were avoiding the corruption and degradation that had accompanied the factory, as well as the

overly rapid urbanization that outran adequate housing and public sanitation, raising mortality rates in New York, Philadelphia, and other large
northern cities far above those existing in the rural areas of either the
South or the North. According to George Fitzhugh, perhaps the most
articulate defender of the "peculiar institution," the South, which "has
been more usefully, more industriously, more energetically, and more
profitably employed than any people under the sun," had little reason
for "envying and wishing to imitate the little 'truck patches' [vegetable
farms], the filthy, crowded, licentious factories, the mercenary shopkeep-
ing, and the slavish commerce of the North."[58]

Those words were written during the boom years of the 1850s, when
virtually all economic interests in the South were prospering. During the
depression of the 1840s, however, when the European demand turned
simultaneously against cotton and tobacco and when the nominal prices
of slaves had declined from their previous peak to nearly half, envy of
the North and a desire to imitate her were widespread. The depression
led even so steadfast a defender of the southern way as James H.
Hammond, governor of South Carolina and one of the richest planters
in that state, to join the movement for the diversification of southern
industry, which he hoped to achieve through the promotion of manufacturing. Hammond and other southern leaders, fearing that European
markets had turned permanently against them, longed for a widely based
set of industries that would be impervious to fluctuations in European
demand.[59]

What made northern industry so attractive to Southerners during the
depression decade, then, was not the glamour or the dynamism of the
factory system, but the independence of northern industry from foreign
markets. Northern industry produced almost exclusively for the domestic
market, which to many Southerners during the 1840s seemed far more
stable than European markets. Moreover, northern politicians had succeeded in pushing through Congress new high tariffs that insulated
northern manufacturing from European competition. During the five
years following the passage of the tariff of 1842, five years of largely
stagnating demand for cotton and tobacco, both the price and the output
of such protected commodities as iron bounded upward. To Southerners
this protection of northern markets appeared to be obtained at their
expense, since it was southern consumers who had to foot the higher
costs of domestically produced iron.[60]

Southern concerns were much different during the boom times of the
1830s and the 1850s. When planters had to strain every resource at their
command to keep up with the surging European consumption of cotton
and tobacco, the South was rather content to let the North provide it with
manufactured goods and commercial services. Conservative newspapers,

such as the Montgomery *Daily Confederation*, which had been identified
with the movement for southern commercial independence, did not find
the South's reliance on northern manufactures and commerce quite as
alarming in 1858 as it had been in the mid-1840s:

> That the North does our trading and manufacturing mostly is true, and
> we are willing that they should. Ours is an agricultural people, and God
> grant that we may continue so. We never want to see it otherwise. It is
> the freest, happiest, most independent, and, with us, the most powerful
> condition on earth.[61]

The reference to power was not casual rhetoric. "Cotton Is King" was
one of the most frequent themes of southern politicians during the
1850s. With this slogan they asserted their belief that the whole of the
industrial world was controlled by the southern supply of cotton. Cotton
was the leading article of international trade, accounting for half of all
U.S. exports. It was the essential raw material for hundreds of thousands
of factory hands in the North and in Europe. It provided employment
for several million other workers in transportation, in handicrafts, and
in wholesale or retail trade. The South had a near monopoly of the
world's supply of cotton, they asserted, because their system of plantation slavery could produce a high-grade fiber far more cheaply than any
other actual or potential supplier. Many politicians believed that if deprived of southern cotton, not only "the industrial interests of our own
country, but also those of Great Britain and much of the continent
. . . would receive a shock that must retard their progress for years to
come."[62]

Southerners were far more concerned during the 1850s with how to
utilize their domination of the world's supply of cotton to the maximum
advantage of their region than with schemes to shift resources into other
occupations. This orientation led them to be deeply critical of federal
policies that seemed to sacrifice southern interests to northern ones.
Southern dissatisfaction fueled a drive to gain greater control of cotton
markets by trading directly with their European customers, bypassing
northern intermediaries. Some advocated secession to gain that end.
Southern politicians were groping for a mechanism similar to that used
by the OPEC nations during the 1970s, a mechanism that would enable
them to exploit to the fullest their domination of the raw material required by the largest, most-advanced manufacturing industry at that
time. It was in the manner of a Middle Eastern oil sheik that James H.
Hammond of South Carolina, while serving in the U.S. Senate in 1858,
issued a warning to his northern colleagues:

No, you dare not make war on cotton. No power on earth dares to make war upon it. Cotton is king. Until lately the Bank of England was king, but she tried to put her screws as usual, the fall before the last, upon the cotton crop, and was utterly vanquished. The last power has been conquered. Who can doubt, that has looked at recent events, that cotton is supreme?[63]

EXPLAINING THE LAG IN SOUTHERN INDUSTRIALIZATION AND URBANIZATION

Recent research by both cliometricians and traditional historians has clarified some of the issues surrounding the debate over the lag in southern industrialization. Robert S. Starobin and Charles B. Dew made the first big breakthroughs on this problem. Their independent studies of small samples of manufacturing firms that used slave labor led both scholars to reject the abolitionist charge that slaves could not perform "the difficult and delicate operations which most manufacturing and mechanical processes involve."[64] They found that slaves not only performed well in the routine aspects of factory production but equaled, and sometimes exceeded, the effectiveness of free men in engineering and supervisory posts. Many southern manufacturers preferred slaves because they were more reliable than free workers, and some firms mixed slaves and free men at all levels of production. These scholars also found that firms using slaves both as ordinary hands and in technical and supervisory posts were as profitable as those that relied exclusively on free labor (some firms were even more profitable). The sample on which the first of these two studies was based was not only small but confined primarily to firms engaged in the processing of such agricultural products as tobacco, cotton, and turpentine. The second study, which was based on a sample of firms in the iron industry, came to similar conclusions regarding the effectiveness of slaves in heavy industry, including their mastery of the "difficult and delicate" arts of the furnace masters, and of the profitability of firms that employed slaves in such occupations.

These findings have been buttressed by cliometric techniques. The factors most frequently cited to support the proposition that slavery was incompatible with urbanization—the increasing cost of control, the hostility of white workers, the fear of rebellion on the part of slaveowners—should all have worked to reduce the level of demand for slaves in the cities. Yet the measurement of the course of demand indicates no such downward trend, either for the urban South as a whole or for any of its leading cities.[65] Not only did the total urban demand for slaves rise in every decade between 1820 and 1860, but the demand for slaves actually increased more rapidly in the cities than in the countryside. Declines in the urban demand for slaves occurred only in isolated instances.[66]

Cliometricians have shown that the factors impinging on the urban demand for slaves were quite diverse. Some conditions, such as the increasing competition from white immigrant labor, served to reduce the urban demand for slaves as antislavery critics had stressed. But other forces worked in the opposite direction. Both the rapid rise in the free population of southern cities and the rise in income per capita swelled the urban demand for slaves in the crafts, in trade, and in domestic service. On balance, the factors that increased the demand for slaves in the cities proved to be substantially stronger than those that served to depress it.

Why then did the slave population of the cities decline between 1850 and 1860? Because the cities had to compete with the countryside for a supply of slaves whose growth was limited to the rate of natural increase. During decades in which the combined rural and urban demand was growing more rapidly than the supply of slaves, such as the decade of the 1850s, prices of slaves were forced up. Both the city and the countryside reacted to the rise in price, but in substantially different ways. In the rural areas there were no close substitutes for slave labor. In the cities, however, free labor, particularly immigrant labor, proved to be an effective substitute. Consequently, as the competition between the cities and the countryside forced the price of slaves up relative to the price of free labor, the cities shifted toward the relatively cheaper form of labor. In other words, slaves were shifted from the cities to the countryside not because the cities did not want slaves, but because as slave prices rose it was easier for the cities than for the countryside to find acceptable lower cost alternatives to slave labor.[67]

That the demand for slaves was much more inelastic in the country-side than in the cities is a discovery of major importance. This highly inelastic demand means that slavery provided masters with a special advantage in the countryside that could not be obtained with free labor. Moreover, the advantage was confined to large plantations based on the gang system, for, as we have seen, slaves working on small farms were neither more nor less efficient than free laborers.[68] The gang system was so obnoxious to free men that they could not be lured to work in gangs even when offered wage premiums to do so.[69]

The discovery of the inelastic rural demand for slaves has raised the possibility that the very advantage that slavery created for agricultural production simultaneously created a barrier to the industrialization of the South. This ironic possibility represents a significant departure from the traditional view of the question. Whereas abolitionists argued that the southern lag in industrialization was the consequence of the weakness of the southern economy, some cliometric theorists now argue that it was a consequence of the strength of its agricultural sector. Their approach implies that, at least for the short run, the policy of specializing in agriculture may indeed have maximized southern per capita income. But the new approach also suggests that slavery thwarted the long-run development of the South by restricting the rise of an entrepreneurial class and of a labor force that could capitalize on the many opportunities for economic growth thrown up by the succession of technological innovations that emanated from the nonagricultural sectors of the economy, particularly from manufacturing, during the century following 1860.

The critical aspect of the new approach is the emphasis placed on the scale of the units engaged in gang-system agriculture. Some cliometricians believe that the existence of these large-scale units kept the return to capital and to entrepreneurial ability much higher in southern than in northern agriculture. The northern devotion to family-sized farms, they argue, made it impossible to expand the size of northern farms, while maintaining the optimal ratio of capital to labor. The desire of farmers to restrict their hands to members of their families (or the unwillingness of hands to work for long on farms other than those managed by themselves or another family member) created an "obstacle to farm expansion and hence to the accumulation of a large absolute fortune within agriculture."[70] Northern farms thus tended to expand not by adding many workers to each unit, as happened in the South, but by adding capital to a farm with a limited number of workers. This practice led to a relatively high level of capital per worker, and so tended to lower the rate of return to capital within agriculture. Consequently, Northerners tended to search for more profitable outlets for their savings in manufacturing and in commerce.

The northern limitation on the size of farms might also have had a beneficial effect on the northern pool of entrepreneurial talent. Two aspects of this question have been stressed. Some believe that northern agriculture was unable to satisfy the ambition of the most talented entrepreneurs that it spawned. Although especially talented entrepreneurs in the South "could achieve and expand and use productively a large personal fortune within the agricultural sector,"[71] Northerners had to turn to manufacturing or commerce to satisfy their ambitions. It is also argued that the large number of small farms in the North permitted a larger proportion of individuals to acquire entrepreneurial skills than did the large agribusinesses of southern agriculture. The point here is that gang-system plantations were vertically integrated and so brought a variety of enterprises under a single management. In the North the typical farm was too small to support by itself a flour mill, a blacksmith shop, a textile shop, a carpentry shop, and a barrel-making shop. Consequently, the North gave rise to a large number of small firms in each of these crafts, the heads of which had to become adept not only in the techniques of their crafts but also in the arts of winning markets, acquiring raw materials, and managing capital.[72]

The plantations of the South, however, were often so large that they could, by themselves, fully support a rice-cleaning mill or a cotton gin (and sometimes both), a cloth house, a tailoring and dress shop, and a variety of handicraft shops. In such instances the craftsmen were not petty capitalists, forced to cope with the daily challenges of the market, but merely laborers trained in particular techniques, who worked at the direction of the planter (or his overseer) for an assured market and with an assured supply of raw materials. Indeed, these craftsmen could not usually even search for better-paying employers or quit the employment of the planter in order to establish their own businesses since, in most cases, they were slaves. Moreover, because of the central role of these agribusinesses, the typical manufacturing unit of the South remained small, and these small manufacturing and handicraft shops were widely dispersed in rural areas, rather than concentrated in towns. Consequently, towns and cities, which many argue were the source of structural change and modernization, were far less numerous in the South than in the West and the North.[73]

Initial tests of the South's performance in allocating resources between agricultural and nonagricultural activities suggest a higher degree of flexibility than many suspected, but the results are far from conclusive. An analysis of the scale of operation reveals that the optimum size of manufacturing firms at the end of the antebellum era was not very large. The South was as well represented in this optimum range of firm sizes (at which production costs are minimized) as were the North Central states.[74]

The most novel, and perhaps the most important, of the cliometric discoveries about the factors influencing the course of industrialization concerns the role of women. Analyses of the data in the manufacturing censuses indicate that the large-scale factories that characterized the Northeast were designed to make use of its relatively large, low-cost labor pool of women and children. The Northeast was unique not only because the top 5 percent of its manufacturing firms were far larger than the top 5 percent of any other region, but also because women comprised a much larger proportion of its manufacturing labor force. Women and young boys were particularly important during the 1820s and 1830s, when the Northeast pulled away from the South in the race for industrialization. The 1832 survey of manufacturing reveals that the majority of workers in northeastern factories with 16 or more employees were adult

women or children. For cotton textile firms, the figure was in excess of
80 percent. Moreover, the proportion of the manufacturing labor force
that was female was strongly influenced by the relative cheapness of
female labor. In the Northeast, females could be hired from farm
households at about 40 percent of the male wage. But in the South, where
women represented just 10 percent of the manufacturing labor force, the
hire rates for farm women were between 60 and 70 percent of those for
men. In other words, southern factory owners had to pay much higher
wages to women to lure them from the farms than did their northern
counterparts, because the nature of the crops in the respective regions
made the labor of females much more valuable on southern farms than
on northern ones.[75]

It thus appears that the rise of southern manufacturing was retarded
because women were much more effective in the production of cotton and
tobacco than in the production of wheat and other northern staples.
Cotton and tobacco were not only more labor-intensive crops than wheat,
but much of the labor required nimbleness rather than strength. In other
words, the labor characteristics of southern staples appear to have deprived the region of the pool of cheap female and child labor that was
so important in the early rise of the factory.[76]

Still another source of cheap labor promoted the rise of factories in
the Northeast. The large influx of Irish and German immigrants during
the late 1840s and early 1850s not only led to labor gluts, but caused
the wages of common laborers to fall more rapidly than those of skilled
artisans. This development increased the competitive advantage of factories in the marketplace over artisan shops, permitting a further penetration of factory-produced goods into markets once served by artisanal
products. Beginning in the late 1840s, large factories began substituting
the relatively cheap labor of foreign-born workers for that of native-born
workers, which led to substantial reductions in unit labor costs and to
increases in profits—developments that fueled the rapid expansion of
manufacturing during 1844–1854. In the long run, the rise of manufacturing was a great boon to northern labor, but during the last two decades
of the antebellum era the rise of manufacturing was associated with the
immiseration of substantial sections of the nonagricultural labor force.

RECENT CRITICISMS OF CLIOMETRIC APPROACHES TO THE QUESTION OF SOUTHERN ECONOMIC DEVELOPMENT

One strand of recent research is critical of the cliometric preoccupation
with mechanization and large-scale manufacturing in the antebellum

economy. Scholars engaged in this research place far greater emphasis on the dynamic role of artisan shops and of the trade and service sectors, arguing that large-scale manufacturing did not gain ascendancy until the end of the nineteenth century. They attribute the preoccupation with large-scale manufacturing partly to research undertaken during the first half of the twentieth century, when the influence of the "smokestack" industries was at its zenith.[77] To some extent this tendency reflected the abundance of data on manufacturing and the sparseness of data on services. Not only is the output of the service sector intangible, but with the exception of transportation, the firms in the service sector were typically small, so that their records have been difficult to recover. Some progress has been made in solving the problem of the recovery of data, and the new work suggests that the trade and service sectors were far more dynamic throughout the nineteenth century than has been appreciated. "Dynamic" does not mean that all of the changes in the economy associated with these sectors were desirable. We will return to this vexing issue in Chapters 9 and 10.

Historians of southern politics have triggered another, but complementary, set of criticisms of the cliometric approach to southern economic development. Their studies have revealed that white society was more deeply divided over changes in southern life wrought by the rapid penetration of the market economy than cliometricians have realized. These political historians depict "a southern version of a modernization crisis" that until now has been "identified too exclusively with the antebellum North."[78] Because the rapid development of southern commerce threatened the traditional or "precapitalist" structure of southern life, "banks, railroads, corporations, the expanding influence of distant merchants, and the rapid growth of state power" became "crucial issues"[79] in antebellum southern politics.

It was not the yeoman farmers (whom cliometricians, whatever their views of planters, have made bearers of modernity) but the wealthy slaveowners who led the drive for state-sponsored economic development. Because they were not merely landed aristocrats but railroad speculators, merchants, bankers, and corporate stockholders, when the wealthy slaveholders gained control over a state's legislature and judiciary, as they did in Alabama during the 1850s, for example, they used their power to expand greatly the role of the state in the promotion of economic development. It was this policy of statism that provoked the widespread political backlash of Alabama's yeomen, "especially those outside of the cotton belt."[80] Similar patterns have been described for North Carolina, Virginia, and Georgia. Taken as a group, these studies invert the traditional view not only of southern politics, but of the economic issues that defined much of the politics. This inversion does not undermine the principal technical results of the cliometricians, but it does place their economic findings in a different context than the cliometricians have generally presumed. It suggests that cliometricians may have exaggerated the role of manufacturing and romanticized the economic dynamism of the yeomen.[81]

CHAPTER FIVE

THE POPULATION QUESTION

The political skills of the abolitionists were demonstrated by the effectiveness with which they transformed mountains of demographic statistics into powerful images of the sexual exploitation of slave women and of the deadly overwork of slave men. These images roused the sympathy of citizens in every walk of life in both Great Britain and the United States and contributed to a political movement so powerful that it eventually brought down every slave system in the Western world.

DEMOGRAPHIC ISSUES IN THE POLITICS OF THE NEW NATIONAL STATES

As far back as recorded history can take us, there have been heads of state who were concerned with the question of population, a concern that finds reflection in the Old Testament. "In the multitude of people," says Proverbs (14:28), "is the king's glory; but in the want of people is the destruction of the prince." Although the tendency to identify numerousness with power and wealth has waxed and waned over the ages, it has remained a central theme, not only of those who govern, but of those who contemplate government. Pronatalist policies (policies designed to promote population growth) became an increasingly prominent aspect of politics between 1500 and 1800 as both statesmen and moral philosophers sought new ways of promoting population growth. These were the centuries during which powerful new national states were formed throughout Europe. The numerous and protracted wars that accompanied the emergence of national states pushed population policy toward the top of political agendas. Large populations were desired not only as a source of soldiers but as a source of revenue to finance wars. The desire to regulate the growth and distribution of population called attention to the need to have better information on population size and its determinants. In England, for example, William Petty (1623–1687), a founder of the Royal Society (for the advancement of science), campaigned for the establishment of a central statistical bureau that would carry out censuses in England and its overseas colonies and collect additional data on fertility, mortality, migration, religious affiliation, occupations, crime, commerce, and other matters bearing on government policy. Petty did not live to see his proposals put into practice in his homeland, since the first English census was not conducted until 1801. However, part of what he urged was instituted during the last quarter of the seventeenth century in England's American colonies.[1]

Stimulated by the wars over the colonies with Spain, the Netherlands, and France, and by continual wars with Indian tribes, Charles II and subsequent rulers instructed the governing body of the American colonies, the Council for Foreign Plantations (later called the Board of Trade and Plantations), to determine the number of able-bodied men in these colonies available for military duty. Between 1675 and 1775 more than 120 censuses were undertaken in various parts of the English empire. These censuses revealed that the white population of the American colonies was growing at an extraordinary rate, far exceeding plausible rates of population growth in England or elsewhere in Europe. Moreover, this increase was not due primarily to immigration but to natural increase, to the excess of births over deaths. By the middle of the eighteenth century leading American thinkers sought mathematical formulas that would summarize the process and provide a basis for predicting the future size of the American population. The most influential of those who took up the subject was Benjamin Franklin. His "Observations concerning the Increase of Mankind, Peopling of Countries, etc.," a short essay first published in 1755 and republished many times during the next two decades in England, in Scotland, on the Continent, and in the American colonies, had a far-reaching effect on economic and political thought.[2]

Franklin argued that the high rate of natural increase was partly due to the healthiness of the country, which kept the death rate in check. But the main cause of the rapid increase was the high fertility rate, which he attributed to the fact that the age of marriage was much earlier in America than in Europe. The early marriage age was, in turn, ascribed to the abundance of fertile land that was available for the support of new families. Because of the early age of marriage, American marriages yielded, on average, about eight live births (twice the number that he ascribed to European marriages) and half of these children lived to maturity. This line of reasoning provided Franklin's formula: The white American population, consisting mainly of transplanted Englishmen and their descendants, was doubling every 25 years.[3]

Those in and around government both in England and in the colonies were quick to draw the implications of Franklin's argument. Left unchecked, the American rate of natural increase meant that within a few generations there would be more Englishmen in the North American colonies than in England. "What then," asked one English writer, "will become of our Awe and Power over them . . . ?" Englishmen provided a variety of answers to the question. The majority of those in power sought to restrict the growth of the North American colonies by obstructing immigration and preventing the spread of the colonies beyond the Appalachian Mountains. They also sought to bring the colonies to heel, imposing taxes on them sufficient to pay for the maintenance of the troops required to protect the colonies from the French and the Indians. Critics of government policy called for an adjustment in Great Britain's relationship to the colonies, arguing "for an imperial policy which treated Americans as brothers rather than as subjects." To these critics "British policy and the plain facts of American population growth were leading inexorably to confrontation between the mother country and colonies that no longer felt dependent."[4]

Although the Revolution destroyed much of the information-gathering apparatus that the British had put in place, American political leaders soon constructed an even more extensive system. The Constitution of the new nation reflected the statistical orientation of its political leadership by tying the size of each state's delegation to the House of Representatives to the size of its population and by requiring Congress to institute regular censuses each decade for this purpose, thus making the United States the first nation committed to regular decennial censuses. The same clause of the Constitution that instituted federal censuses also sanctioned slavery by specifying that both for the purposes of taxes and for representation in the House, a slave was to be counted as three-fifths of a person. Given the strong connection between population and politics in the decades leading up to the Revolution and the way that population was tied to politics in the Constitution, particularly in the compromise in the counting of slaves for representation, it is not surprising that population issues were at the center of the struggle against slavery throughout the antebellum era.[5]

DEMOGRAPHIC ISSUES IN THE STRUGGLE AGAINST SLAVERY

Demographic issues were introduced into the struggle against slavery more or less simultaneously by David Hume and Benjamin Franklin. They both presented unfavorable population growth rates as proof of the system's inhumanity. Hume did so by arguing that it was a natural law that slave societies could not reproduce themselves. Franklin appealed to empirical evidence that showed that the death rate of slaves exceeded their birth rate. Both drew on the censuses and other statistical sources for the population of Britain's slave colonies, particularly her sugar islands, to argue that the population of slaves could be maintained or increased only by continual importations from Africa. Both were, at the time they wrote their respective essays, unaware that their characterizations of slave demography were no longer applicable to the situation in the Chesapeake region. By the middle of the eighteenth century the natural rate of increase of slaves on the North American mainland had not only become positive, but was well in excess of the rate of natural increase in Europe.[6]

The theories of Hume and Franklin were woven together in the work of Adam Smith. Smith criticized the proposition that employers of free labor did not have to bear a cost that hung heavy on slaveholders: the cost of reproducing their labor force. Employers of free labor, he argued, also bore that cost since the wages of free men had to be high enough to enable them to reproduce. The real difference was the frugality with which the fund allotted for reproduction was managed. In slave society it was "managed by a negligent master or careless overseer" but in free society it was "managed by the free man himself." The "strict frugality and parsimonious attention" that naturally affected the behavior of poor free men made the cost of their reproduction much less than that of slaves. And so in contrast to a declining slave population, the free population was increasing.[7]

To Smith, the negligence of slave masters was inherent in their position as owners of land and labor who received income without having to expend effort. Great proprietors, he argued, generally lacked both the inclination and the ability to improve their property or advance methods of cultivation: "The situation of such a person naturally disposes him to attend rather to ornament which pleases his fancy, than to profit for which he has so little occasion." The natural tendency of all land magnates to neglect the improvement of their property was magnified in the West Indian slaveholders who, in addition to natural indolence, loved "to domineer" and, because of the great profit from sugar, could afford to indulge themselves. In Smith's view slavery was so onerous that those who labored under it were worse off "than the poorest people either in Scotland or Ireland." This did not mean, he cautioned, that slaves "are worse fed, or that their consumption" of taxed articles (sugar, tea, and spirits) "is less than that even of the lower ranks of people in England. In order that they may work well, it is the interest of their master that they should be fed well and kept in good heart, in the same manner as it is his interest that his working cattle should be so."[8]

The contradictions in Smith's argument did not prevent it from becoming highly influential. Antislavery critics followed him in holding slaveowners responsible for the high rate of natural decrease in the West Indian slave population, but they dropped Smith's contention that it was to the interest of masters to see that their slaves were "fed well and kept in good heart." Stronger than the profit motive, they argued, was the other tendency that Smith delineated, the love to dominer, which so corrupted masters that they engaged in the most cruel and corrupt practices. Nowhere was this tendency more evident or more heinous than in the slave trade.

The general political campaign for the abolition of the international slave trade, which was launched in Great Britain in 1787, emphasized the shocking aspects of the slave trade in Africa and the inhuman conditions aboard the vessels transporting the slaves from Africa to the New World. Abolitionists not only pointed to the evil inherent in forcibly tearing men, women, and children from "relations and friends, and from all they considered valuable in life," but stressed the high mortality rate caused by this trade. These high rates were attributed to the cruelty of the African captors of the slaves, to the overcrowding of the vessels on which the "unhappy wretches were chained together hand and foot and 'crammed together like herrings in a barrel,' " and to the terrible sanitary conditions for slaves both on the anchored vessels and at dockside in port cities of the West Indies. In their investigation of the conditions of the slave trade the abolitionists discovered evidence indicating that the shipboard death rates were high not only for the Africans but also for the British sailors that transported them. A survey of slave ships that left Liverpool (the chief British port in this trade) in 1787 revealed that less than half of the embarking crews returned alive.[9]

After Parliament voted to outlaw slave trade in 1807, the British abolitionist movement became quiescent but revived again toward the end of the Napoleonic wars. The postwar movement set its sights not merely on suppressing the international trade, but on putting an end to slavery throughout the British empire. To promote their new objectives abolitionists pressed for the triennial registration of every slave in the British empire and for a law which provided that every unregistered slave was to be set free immediately. It was in data on death rates, fertility rates, and household composition culled from the slave registrations that the abolitionist found the proof that particular cases of overwork, torture, and sexual vice were not merely isolated incidents but a general pattern of inhumane treatment, so harsh and so deeply embedded in the slave system that emancipation was the only effective relief.[10]

The registration data revealed that slave death rates in most of the British colonies exceeded birth rates so as to produce natural decrease. Arraying the rates of natural increase or decrease in each colony with the amount of sugar produced in that colony, the abolitionists argued that the evidence in the registration data clearly established that natural decrease was tied to the extent of sugar production. They further argued that this was because the conditions of production of sugar were so harsh, the hours of labor so extended, the food so poor, and the punishment so severe that death rates were pushed to shocking levels. To support their contention the British abolitionists pointed to the high rates of natural increase among slaves in the United States revealed by the U.S. censuses from 1790 to 1820, and especially those between 1810 and 1820 which came after the close of American participation in the international slave trade. In 1825 the *Anti-Slavery Reporter* (the journal of the London Anti-Slavery Society) unhesitatingly attributed the difference in rates of natural increase to "the superiority of the United States in the physical treatment of their slaves."[11]

The West Indian slaveholders agreed with the abolitionist proposition that slaves were "naturally" prolific but denied the decline in their number was caused by a high death rate or by planter abuses. The cause of the decrease, they argued, was a low birth rate which they attributed to African preferences for polygamy rather than monogamy, to promiscuity among slaves, to slave-induced abortions, to the neglect of their infants by slave mothers, and to venereal diseases. Declaring they sought to encourage monogamous relationships and fertility within stable families, they claimed that they had had only limited success in winning their African slaves to these ideals. To support their case the planters cited plantation records on the food, clothing, fertility, morbidity, and mortality of slaves.[12]

After 1833 the demography of West Indian slavery largely disappeared from British politics because the emancipation of slaves throughout its empire made the question moot. In the United States, however, demographic issues that had previously played only a small role in abolitionist campaigns became increasingly important during the three decades preceeding the Civil War. Population issues were used in a new way in 1832 when antislavery representatives in the Virginia legislature introduced a bill for the gradual emancipation of slaves that nearly won (the last time that any southern legislature entertained such a measure). But it was the publication of Theodore Weld's pamphlet *American Slavery as It Is* in 1839 that pushed population issues to the center of the antislavery struggle in America and also provided the crucial link that unified the moral and the economic indictments of slavery.[13]

Since British abolitionists used the high rate of natural increase of U.S. slaves as the standard for measuring the harshness of West Indian slavery, it might appear that this issue provided little room for an attack on American slavery. Weld, however, articulated three lines of argument that converted the high rate of natural increase into evidence of the maltreatment of slaves. First, he attributed the high rate of natural increase to the deliberate practice of "slave breeding," by which he meant the application of practices employed in animal husbandry in order to obtain the greatest number of slaves for sale on the market. He supported the charge by quoting Southerners and others who said that slaveowners "keep a stock for the purpose of rearing slaves" for sale; who said that just as "the owner of *brood mares*" had "a reasonable right" to "their product," so "the owner of *female slaves*" had a right "to *their increase*"; who said that for many planters, "the only profit their masters derive from them [slaves] is, repulsive as the idea may justly seem, in breeding them like other live-stock"; and who said that some masters "took pains to breed from" their "best stock—the whiter the progeny the higher they would sell for house servants."

Second, Weld argued that it was "absurd" to say that a high rate of natural increase constituted "proof" that slaves were "well-clothed, well-housed, abundantly fed, and very *comfortable.*" He argued that "privations and inflictions," if carried far enough, as was the case in the West Indies and "in certain portions of the southern states," would cause natural decrease, but he also pointed out that the "Israelites multiplied with astonishing rapidity, under the task-masters and burdens of Egypt." Consequently, it was possible for U.S. slaves to "suffer much hardship and great cruelties without experiencing so great a derangement of the vital functions as to prevent childbearing." To prove that this was the case in the South, Weld cited page after page of testimony accusing masters of feeding slaves so poorly that they habitually suffered "the pain of hunger"; of supplying slaves with clothing "by day, and . . . covering by night" that was "inadequate, either for comfort or decency"; of treating slaves with "inhuman neglect when sick"; and of keeping slaves in wretched dwellings that were "a shelter from neither the wind, the rain, nor the snow."

Third, Weld cited evidence that showed not only that the internal slave trade "has become a large business" but that the continuation of that trade was essential to the continuation of slavery. The high rate of natural increase in the original slave states had made the pressure on land so great that "the value of slaves" depended "on the state of the market abroad," that is, on the market for slaves in the western states and territories. Consequently, slaveowners were "alarmed lest the markets of other states be closed against the introduction of our slaves" and pursued expansionist policies, such as the acquisition of Texas, so that the price of slaves "will rise again." The doctrine thus expounded was a direct extension of the population theory of Thomas Malthus, who held that the tendency of the growth of population to outstrip the supply of land was the ultimate source of the decline in the price of labor. Although it was far from a universally accepted doctrine in either the South or the North during the antebellum era, there were enough converts to Malthusian doctrine among slaveholders to make Weld's case credible.[14]

The demographic arguments adumbrated by Weld in 1839 were increasingly emphasized and elaborated by antislavery critics during the next two decades. One of the major aspects of the new approach was an increased emphasis on the destructive effects of slave trading on the integrity of slave families, an issue poignantly elaborated by Harriet Beecher Stowe in *Uncle Tom's Cabin*. Another thesis later developed with great effectiveness asserted that the rapid growth of the slave population reduced the rate of growth of the white population of the South, partly because the corrupting effects of slavery sapped the vigor of white masters, partly because non-slaveholding whites who were repelled by the system were migrating to the North, and partly because slavery was so distasteful to foreign immigrants that they shunned the South. Still another variation in argument, and ultimately perhaps the most politically effective of all the abolitionist arguments, was the contention that the growth of the slave population and its spread into non-slave states and territories constituted an imminent threat to the living standards of free workers and farmers.

Slaveholders replied to these charges in a variety of ways, sometimes exhibiting less unanimity than the abolitionists because of their differing views on Malthusian theory. On most points, however, they were virtually unanimous. They vigorously denied promoting promiscuity and practicing barnyard techniques to increase fertility. Although admitting that some masters abused their power, seducing or raping slave women, they argued that these were isolated cases and that such behavior was condemned by the generality of masters. They pictured themselves as devoted family men who promoted stable family lives among their slaves. Although they acknowledged their adherence to a pronatalist policy, they insisted that this was in keeping with church doctrine, both Catholic and Protestant, and that their means of implementing this policy among the slaves—bounties of various sorts for married couples, released time and special rations for nursing and pregnant women, bounties for parents of large numbers of children—were along lines sanctified by religion and long practiced by civilized states. They also acknowledged that the slave trade was an impediment to family life but contended that its deleterious effects were exaggerated. Masters forced to sell slaves for economic reasons, they insisted, sought either to sell slaves who were still single or to sell them in family groups.

As for food, clothing, shelter, and medical care, they argued that masters were at great pains to see that slaves were well taken care of in these respects because it was to their economic interests to do so. Far from being poorly treated, they claimed that slaves were better fed, clothed, and sheltered than free laborers in the cities of the North. To support their case they called attention to census and local registration data that showed that death rates were higher in northern cities than on slave plantations, turning the arguments that British abolitionists had used to condemn West Indian slavery into a critique of northern society.[15] They also denied that slaves were overworked, except in isolated cases, claiming that the daily hours on plantations were the normal ones for agriculture, that there was no work on the Sabbath, and that slaves also received part of a day, or all day, off on many Saturdays, on rainy days, and on various holidays.[16]

The principal demographic issues that divided slaveholders were whether the high rate of growth of the slave population constituted a long-run threat to the viability of the slave system, whether the interregional trade in slaves was essential for the continued economic health of the system, especially in the older slave states of the South Atlantic region, and whether slavery kept foreign immigrants from coming to the South. Positions on these issues turned to a large extent on whether one accepted or rejected Malthusian theory. The ambivalence of slaveowners on this question is well illustrated by the changing views of George Tucker, a Virginia congressman and professor of economics. Tucker was originally critical of Malthus, arguing not only that a large population was desired for military reasons, but that where population was most dense the use of natural resources was most efficient, productive arts were most developed, and culture was at its highest. He believed there was an optimum ratio of population to resources, and that if population advanced beyond that optimum welfare might decline, but he also believed that the growth of population beyond that point would "naturally stop" and leave society at "the golden mean." Other southern critics of Malthus placed less stress on birth control, emphasizing instead that "man's fertility as an inventor and improver" of the means of production would "at least equal his fertility as a progenitor." Many Southerners optimistically predicted continued high rates of population growth both for the South and for the nation as a whole.[17]

By the mid-1840s Tucker had reconsidered his earlier views and concluded that "Malthus' premises are in the main true," and that man's inability to regulate his impulses would lead population to increase, which would "elevate land rents, depress wage levels, and reduce the scale of living to a very low and mean level."[18] This process, he concluded, would render the ownership of slaves unprofitable; he went on to predict that slavery could not survive with population densities in excess of 60 persons per square mile. Not all masters, or even all those who accepted Malthus, shared this gloomy view of the future of slavery. Some argued that slavery could continue indefinitely even if the slave population should continue to double every 30 years and even if the slave system were "confined within present limits." All that would happen would be a shift of slaves from agriculture to manufacturing. Such a turn of events was welcomed, since then "the slave labor of the south will, instead of contributing to the wealth of the north, as it has heretofore done, become the successful competitor of northern white labor in those departments of industry of which the north has in times past enjoyed a monopoly."[19]

POPULATION TRENDS

The recent outpouring of research into the demography of slavery has rivaled, if not surpassed, the research into the more purely economic issues of profitability, distribution of wealth, productive efficiency, and economic growth.[20] The work on intercolony comparisons of population trends has generally confirmed the patterns noted by the abolitionists and other contemporary observers. Prior to 1700, slave populations in the gang-system colonies of the New World generally appear to have experienced rates of natural decrease so that growth in the population of all slave colonies was initially dependent on importations from Africa. Rates of natural decrease varied from colony to colony, and until 1700 ran as high as 5 percent per annum. Rates of natural decrease were particularly high in frontier colonies where the heavy influx of slaves was new and, as is illustrated by Jamaica in Figure 19, generally declined toward zero as the colonies became better established. But in most cases natural decrease did not give way to natural increase prior to emancipation. Rates of decrease were greater in tropical climates than in temperate ones, but within tropical colonies such as Jamaica, rates of decrease were significantly higher on large plantations than on small ones, especially on large sugar plantations, again confirming the observations of the abolitionists.[21]

Slave populations located in temperate climates, such as those of the United States and the British Bahamas, managed to achieve high rates of natural increase that generally eluded the tropical colonies (see Figure 19).[22] During the seventeenth century both the white and black populations of the southern colonies experienced natural decrease but the switch to natural increase took place about a half century earlier for southern whites than for blacks. Thus, the early frontier period in the American South, as in the Caribbean, appears to have been demographically severe. Settlers in the South, both white and black, appear to have required a minimum of two or three more generations to adapt economically and physically to their environment than settlers in the North, and the period of adaptation appears to have been even greater in the Caribbean. As Figure 19 shows, the white rate of natural increase in Britain's

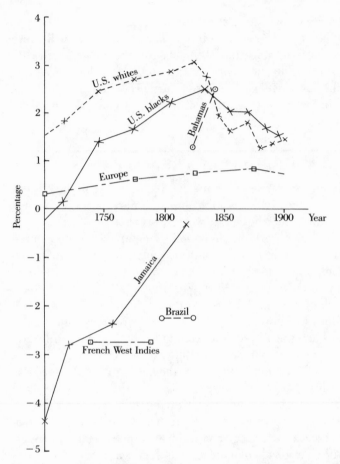

Figure 19. Approximate average annual rates of natural increase for various populations, 1700–1900. Negative percentages indicate rates of natural decrease and positive percentages indicate rates of natural increase. Thus
in 1700 Jamaica had a rate of natural decrease in excess of 4 percent
per year. The closer the line for Jamaica gets to zero, the lower its rate
of natural decrease. Since the rate of natural increase of U.S. blacks
became positive c.1710, the line representing its growth rate crosses
from the negative to the positive portion of the diagram at that point.

North American colonies had already substantially exceeded the European rate by 1700, and by the time Franklin was writing his famous
essay was close to the rate he set it at, doubling perhaps every 30 years.[23]
Though lagging behind that of whites, the natural increase of southern
slaves probably exceeded the European rate as early as 1725 and continued to accelerate throughout the eighteenth century and the early
nineteenth century. It was not until about 1840 that the slave rate of
natural increase surpassed that of whites. By then the rates of both U.S.

groups, although still greatly in excess of the European rates of increase, had begun to decline, and continued to do so for the next century. However, the black decline lagged the white decline by about two decades, so that after 1840 natural increase among U.S. blacks was somewhat greater than among the whites.[24]

Why was the rate of natural increase of U.S. slaves so much higher than that of slaves in the West Indies? Since the rate of natural increase is the difference between the birth rate and the death rate, the question can be reframed in terms of the differences in these rates: Did the U.S. slave population increase so much more rapidly than the West Indian slave population because the fertility rate was much higher in the United States than in the West Indies, or because the death rate was much higher in the West Indies than in the United States? Franklin and the British abolitionists, stressing the poor diets and overwork of the West Indian slaves, implied that the answer was the much higher death rate in the West Indies. American abolitionists of the late antebellum era, stressing the role of slave breeding in the South, implied that the answer was the much higher fertility rate in the United States.

At the present state of demographic research, it is possible to provide only a limited test of these answers. Intercolony comparisons can be made with reliability only for the second, third, or fourth decades of the nineteenth century, and only in those colonies where it has been possible to estimate and correct for the undercount of births and of deaths at early ages.[25] A comparison between the United States and Jamaica (see Figure 20) shows that while the mortality rate of U.S. slaves was about the same as that of Jamaican slaves, its fertility rate was more than 80 percent higher. Thus, the difference in mortality rates contributed little to the difference in their rates of natural increase; by far the most important factor was the difference in birth rates. The U.S. birth rate was exceptionally high by any historical standard, but the Jamaican birth rate, so often called low by both British abolitionists and West Indian planters, was actually at levels similar to those prevailing in Western Europe at the time. This observation should not be taken to imply that the factors that influenced the birth rates were the same in both regions since, as we shall see, the underlying determinants were quite different.[26]

A comparison of the United States with Trinidad or of Trinidad with Jamaica supports Weld's contention (although not quite in the way he intended) that one cannot necessarily infer differences in planter treatment of slaves merely from data on rates of natural increase. Trinidad's birth rate was slightly higher than Jamaica's but still well below that of the United States. Its death rate, however, exceeded those of the other two slave populations by a large margin. The death rate in Trinidad was so high that only an exceptionally high birth rate, such as that prevailing

Figure 20. A comparison of slave birth and death rates in the United States, Jamaica, and Trinidad during the first third of the nineteenth century. The birth rates shown here are the most common of the various birth measures employed by demographers. A relatively easy measure to construct, demographers refer to them as "crude birth rates." They are constructed by dividing the annual number of births in a population by the number of persons alive at the middle of the year. These rates are then multiplied by 100 (and presented as percentages) or by 1,000 (and presented as births per 1,000 persons). Similarly, the deaths displayed here are called "crude mortality rates." They are the annual number of deaths divided by the midyear population and then multiplied by 100 to put them in percentage form. Crude birth or death rates in several different years may be averaged, as they are done here for Jamaica over a 3-year period and for Trinidad over a 2-year period.

in the United States, could have prevented its population from suffering substantial natural decrease. It is ironic that this Crown colony, ruled directly by the British government, which under abolitionist pressure was at such pains to make the colony an example of the humane treatment of slaves, experienced death rates so much higher than did Jamaica, which was ruled by slave planters who stoutly resisted the pressures for reform emanating from London. It may be possible, however, to resolve the paradoxes raised by these comparisons by looking more carefully at what is now known about the causes of variations in mortality and fertility rates between and within the various slave societies.[27]

MORTALITY

Mortality rates among slaves in the British West Indies were far worse than indicated by the reports to Parliament during the emancipation campaign. Modern demographic analysis of the triennial registrations has revealed that the overall Jamaican death rate was understated by a quarter because planters usually reported only children who were alive at a given registration. Most of the children who were born after one registration and who died before the next one were never entered in the registry. Cliometric studies indicate that in the Jamaican case only 21 percent of the deaths under age 3 were counted. Analysis of the data for Trinidad indicates that the overall death rate was understated by about 31 percent. The registrations were reliable, however, in recording deaths at age 3 and over.[28]

Relating mortality rates to specific causes is difficult in the best of circumstances, and the data on slave mortality rates leave much to be desired in this respect. Nevertheless, cliometric studies of Jamaica, Trinidad, and the United States have made significant contributions toward unraveling this riddle. These studies are focused on the nineteenth century and so shed little light on earlier times, although the findings for Trinidad have some bearing on changes over time. Since it was still a frontier area in 1813, conditions in Trinidad suggest some factors that made the early death rates in the United States and Jamaica so high.

These studies reveal a significant association between certain crops and mortality rates. In Jamaica, for example, the death rate on sugar plantations was 50 percent higher than on coffee plantations, Jamaica's second most important crop. In Trinidad the death rate among adult males was nearly three times as high on sugar as on cotton plantations. In the United States the evidence on sugar plantations was inconclusive but mortality rates on rice plantations exceeded those on cotton plantations by levels comparable to the differences found in Jamaica and Trinidad. These provisional findings suggest that the differences in crop specialization may go much of the way toward explaining why the death rate in the United States was lower than in the West Indies.[29]

Yet such correlations by themselves do not reveal whether it was the location of sugar and rice plantations or the intensity with which slaves on these plantations were driven that made their death rates so much higher than those estimated for cotton and coffee plantations. Both sugar and rice were grown in low, swampy areas, while coffee and cotton were grown on high ground, so that environmental conditions (including the effect of population aggregation on the rate of spread of disease) could have played a role independent of the intensity of the work. Using value of output per slave as a measure of productivity, one study revealed that on Jamaican plantations specializing in sugar, labor productivity and mortality rates showed a weak positive correlation. On coffee plantations the correlation was also weak, but negative. Although the Jamaican evidence tends to suggest that the environmental influences had a greater effect on crop-specific mortality rates than differences in the pace at which laborers were driven, it does not exclude intensity of work, especially if it is considered in conjunction with such other influences as the level of nutrition.[30]

The Trinidad evidence supports the view that crop-specific mortality rates were heavily influenced by environment. To control for the effect of environment, one investigator looked at the difference in mortality between sugar and non-sugar plantations in those counties suitably located for the production of cotton. In the case of women, the differential previously attributed to the sugar crop was now explained by location, but in the case of men, location had little effect, suggesting that their conditions of work in sugar production were significant. This conclusion was further enhanced by the discovery that male artisans employed on sugar plantations, whether creole or African born, were less than half as likely to die during a given year as male field hands of the same age. Although this evidence strongly suggests that the nature of the work affected mortality it does not necessarily imply that intensity of labor was the critical factor, since artisans, especially during the harvest season, appear to have worked with an intensity that rivaled or exceeded the effort of field hands. Although intensity of labor is not ruled out, such other factors as inadequate sanitary conditions for field hands who worked with animal manure during the planting season may have been involved. Statistics on disease-specific causes of death are sparse, but those available for slaves of working ages indicate that dysentery and tetanus, which are promoted by poor sanitation and hygiene, were two of the leading causes of death.[31]

There has been some progress toward explaining trends in slave mortality over time. One of the more important discoveries is that the century-long decline in the mortality of U.S. slaves probably came to a halt during the 1810s or 1820s and then began to rise. A study of plantation records indicates that the death rates of infants rose by about 24 percent between the 1820s and the 1840s and that death rates among children aged 1–14 rose by half as much during the same period. The evidence on the course of mortality rates during the 1850s is more mixed, and mortality may have leveled off during that decade or even declined. It thus appears that even though the course of mortality rates after 1700 was mainly downward, it was not uniformly so, and may have risen significantly during the late antebellum era.

It is surprising to uncover evidence that death rates among U.S. slaves were increasing after 1820, although it is consistent with abolitionist charges that conditions were deteriorating, partly because of the prevalent view that the dominant force affecting the more enduring and more general decline in slave death rates was the adaptation of Africans to the American environment, which is thought to have taken place over successive generations. That view suggests that the closing of the African slave trade in 1807 should have contributed to a further decline in mortality, as the slave population became almost entirely American born. Since the decline in mortality rates between 1700 and 1820 was much greater than the subsequent rise, it may well be that other factors, including those that were raised by the abolitionists, were enough to offset the relatively small further increases in the proportion of slaves that were American born, a proportion that reached 90 percent early in the 1820s.

The recent work of demographic historians has also advanced our knowledge of the effect of intercontinental migration on mortality, revealing that death rates in the ocean crossing and during the first few years after arrival remained shockingly high, not only for African slaves, but also for Europeans, well into the nineteenth century. In the case of British migrants during the seventeenth century, it has been estimated that 1 out of every 10 persons who embarked from a British port died before reaching a port in the New World. Some of these deaths were due to vessels that were lost in storms at sea, but the great majority were due to outbreaks of disease which ravaged many of the vessels that made the Atlantic crossing. Of those who lived long enough to set foot on the soil of the New World, 15 percent died within a year. And so the first year in the colonies was referred to as a period of "seasoning." The term reflected prevailing beliefs that the high initial death rates were due to diseases, indigenous to the New World or brought over from Africa, for which the Europeans had little or no immunities. Some of these so-called seasoning deaths, however, especially those occurring early in the first year, were due to diseases contracted during the ocean crossing.[32]

Death rates on slave ships were higher than those on the ships embarking from England, running about one out of every seven or eight slaves sent from an African port. Studies that have probed abolitionist charges that overcrowding on both British and French slave ships caused slave death rates to exceed those of European immigrants have yielded mixed findings. The two principal factors that explain differential death rates are the length of the voyage and the port of embarkation. Ships embarking from African ports with especially virulent disease environments had higher death rates than those embarking from other ports. Death rates were especially high on ships that became becalmed or for other reasons took much longer than expected to reach their destinations. The protracted duration of voyages raised death rates partly because of the longer exposure to infections, and partly because food and water became spoiled or ran out. The evidence that favors the hypothesis of exposure to infection, rather than that of overcrowding, falls into two categories: the absence of a correlation between various measures of overcrowding and shipboard death rates and the statistically significant correlation between the death rates of slaves and those of their white crews. Indeed, the crew death rates generally ran about 30 percent above those of the slaves, probably because the crew lacked immunity to diseases brought aboard ship by their captives. However, a recent study of the trade during the late eighteenth century reveals that overcrowding affected mortality rates during loading (the period when ships were rounding up a full "cargo") but not during the voyage itself.[33]

The high crew death rates corroborate the abolitionist contention that the African slave trade took a heavy toll of the lives of those Englishmen who engaged in it. Here again, the actual situation was worse than the abolitionists realized. A study of English personnel sent to Africa by the Royal African Company, which had the English monopoly of the African trade, revealed that 63 percent of these men died within a year after setting foot in Africa.[34]

Death rates in the Atlantic crossing remained high throughout the seventeenth and eighteenth centuries but began to decline during the first half of the nineteenth century, rapidly for Europeans and more slowly and uncertainly for Africans. In the case of the Europeans the decline in death rates is closely tied to the increased speed of the vessels plying the North Atlantic. As late as 1816, the average voyage from England to the United States took over seven weeks. During the next quarter century rapid improvements in the design of sailing vessels, which led to the introduction of swift packets, steadily reduced the duration of the Atlantic crossing until, by the mid-1840s, it could normally be completed in about five weeks. Steamships were first introduced on the North Atlantic run in 1839 and increased in importance as their reliability and speed increased. By 1860 steamships were regularly completing the journey from England to New York in less than two weeks. As the speed of vessels increased, death rates of Europeans in the Atlantic crossing declined, reaching an average of between 1 and 2 percent per voyage by the late 1840s or early 1850s. Even so, the Atlantic crossing remained hazardous because the great variability of shipboard conditions could, and too often did, lead to shockingly high mortality rates. Thus, of 90,000 Irish immigrants to Canada in 1847, 6 percent died on board ship, 4 percent while in quarantine, and an additional 7 percent shortly thereafter—17 percent in all of those who started on the journey.[35]

After 1807 the African slave trade with the United States and the British West Indies came to an end, but it continued largely unabated with other slave colonies, especially Brazil and Cuba, past the middle of the century. Death rates on the ships in these trades did not continue the decline evident before 1800, but rose sharply after 1810, approaching or exceeding levels that prevailed in the late eighteenth century. The continued high level of mortality on slave ships after 1807 was due partly to the continued reliance of slave traders on sailing vessels of traditional design, which were relatively slow, and partly to an increase in the proportion of slaves coming from more distant parts of Africa.[36]

Evidence on the relative severity of seasoning on whites and slaves in the New World is mixed. In the Chesapeake region death rates for newly arrived Africans appear to have exceeded those of Europeans by about 10 percent, but in the West Indies the advantage seems to have gone the other way. Data carefully collected by A. M. Tulloch, one of the pioneers of English demography, indicate that the probability of dying within the first two years after arrival in Jamaica was about four times as high for Europeans as for Africans. Africans were far less likely to die from fevers (a term used to cover malaria and a variety of other diseases) than were Europeans, but were more vulnerable to tuberculosis and other diseases of the respiratory system, and to bowel complaints.[37]

The mortality attributable to the internal traffic in slaves was generally well below that attributable to intercontinental movements for a number of reasons. First, the main periods of internal trade came late in the slave era (after 1797 in the West Indies, and after 1820 in the United States) when conditions of travel were less hazardous than in earlier times. Second, the distances of movement were shorter and the speed of transit was more rapid than in the Atlantic crossing of the seventeenth and eighteenth centuries. Third, environmental conditions were generally more similar between the points of origins and destinations in the internal migrations than in those across the Atlantic. In the East-West migrations of the late antebellum United States, for example, fragmentary data suggest that death rates due to internal trade were less than a tenth of those attributable to the transit from Africa. Moreover, death rates after arrival in the western states were by then perhaps slightly higher, but still quite similar to those that the migrants would have experienced in the states that they left. On the other hand, the inter-island trade in the West Indies, while not as hazardous as the migration from Africa, appears to have been substantially more hazardous than interstate trade in the late antebellum South. The greatest increase in risk was probably encountered when creoles were moved from long-settled islands (such as Jamaica) to frontier islands (such as Trinidad). Jamaican-born male slaves of prime ages who were working in Trinidad in 1813 had annual mortality rates about 40 percent higher than those of Jamaican-born slaves who remained in Jamaica. This difference means that moving a 20-year-old Jamaican male to Trinidad probably reduced his life expectation by about seven years.[38]

ASSESSING THE AVERAGE DIETS OF SLAVES

There has been a good deal of progress in the estimation and evaluation of the adequacy of the average diets in slave societies. The questions under investigation vary in complexity and in the difficulties encountered in their resolution. Research initially focused on the questions posed by the abolitionists: Were slaves, as a rule, poorly fed by the standards of their day? Were slave diets generally poorer than those consumed at the time by ordinary laborers in England or in the northern United States? The abolitionist accusations were formulated with reference to specific foods, especially meat and fish, that masters were accused of stinting. Moreover, the abolitionist standard of adequacy turned not on modern nutritional concepts but on customary quantities that were assumed to be adequate and that, in the West Indies, were reflected in legislation dictating minimum quantities that masters were required to provide for slaves. It is quite possible that even diets that met these customary standards were inadequate for the rapid growth of young children and for the good health of the general population.[39]

Data required for estimating the nutritional content of the slave diet in the sugar colonies are scanty, but several estimates have been constructed for the years between 1830 and 1860 which indicate that the consumption of meat and fish, while low by current U.S. standards, was similar to standards prevailing in most European nations during the nineteenth century (see Figure 21)[40] and that the daily energy intake of adult slaves was probably in the neighborhood of 2,500 to 3,000 calories. Because of the intense pace of work on sugar plantations and because of their severe disease environment these diets appear to have been deficient in calories, protein, and other nutrients. It also appears that West Indian diets were substantially poorer before 1815 than in later years, because of a combination of hurricanes and embargos during the American Revolution and the Napoleonic wars that played havoc with West Indian food supplies.[41]

In the U.S. South, general food shortages were overcome by the end of the seventeenth century or the first quarter of the eighteenth century at the latest. That Virginia, Maryland, and South Carolina were substan-

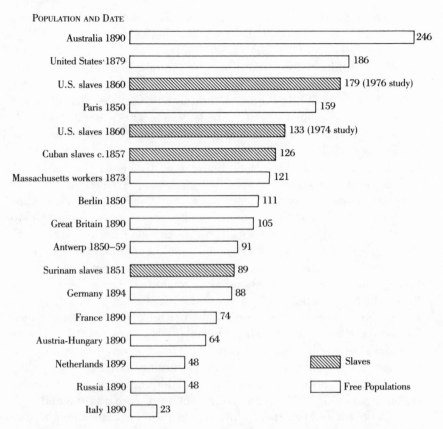

Figure 21. Average annual per capita consumption of meat in various populations during the nineteenth century (in pounds).

tial exporters of grains and meats on the eve of the Revolution gives indirect testimony to the relative abundance of food production in these colonies but does not necessarily imply that slaves were well fed. It was only after the drawing of a sample of slave plantations from the manuscript schedules of the 1860 census that the information needed to test abolitionist characterizations of slave diets on large plantations became available.

Two tests based on such a sample have been performed by different investigators, one reported in 1974, the other in 1976. Interestingly enough, despite numerous differences in estimating details, both studies report quite similar figures for the average daily energy value of the slave diet (4,185 calories in the 1974 study and 4,206 calories in the 1976 study). Perhaps the most notable difference between the two diets is in the consumption of meats. The estimate of the average annual consumption of meat per slave in the 1976 study exceeds the figure given in the

1974 study by 46 pounds, but a smaller share of the total is allocated to beef, and mutton is excluded from the diet entirely.[42]

Quite clearly, either diet (see Figure 22) was substantial by the standards of the day for workers, and so contradicts abolitionist contentions that "as a general thing" southern slaves "suffer extremely for the want of food."[43] While "there is no question that the slave diet was sufficient to maintain the slave's body weight and general health,"[44] research has shifted to issues that go beyond those raised by the abolitionists or considered in the 1974 study. Drawing on modern scientific knowledge about the relationship between nutrition and physical development, it can be argued that the diet of slaves prevented most women from becoming menarcheal before age 16, which implies an average degree of malnutrition that today is found in only the most impoverished populations of the underdeveloped world. Although the diet of the U.S. slaves might be adequate in calories, it could nevertheless be so badly lacking in variety as to produce general shortages of vitamin A, thiamin, and niacin. While slaves consumed large quantities of sweet potatoes and corn, which are usually rich in vitamin A, it is possible that they consumed only white corn and white-fleshed sweet potatoes, both of which are low in vitamin A. The slave diet may also have been deficient in thiamine, despite the fact that corn and pork are rich in this nutrient, because the procedures employed in preserving, storing, or preparing these foods in 1860 could have led to a deterioration of their thiamine content. And despite the high niacin content of corn and the ability of the body to convert protein into niacin, chemical imbalances might have prevented the niacin potentially available in corn from being converted into a useful form, and the protein content of the meat consumed by slaves might have been inadequate to make up the deficit.[45]

This array of new issues turns on intricate points of current research in nutritional science, some of which are not generally accepted by nutritionists, but which nevertheless require the close attention of those who wish to explain the levels and changes in the mortality rates of slaves. Unfortunately, neither of the previous exercises on the census data is sufficiently precise to permit resolution of this complex set of problems. The two previous estimates of the slave diet were limited to the 11 principal foods enumerated by the census (see Figure 22) not because these foods constituted the total extent of the slave diet, but because the simplifying assumption did not undermine a test of the relatively simple nutritional issues posed by the abolitionists. In other words, the previous tests implicitly assumed that all of the foods other than the 11 included in the exercises based on the 1860 census were so rarely consumed by slaves that they made only a negligible contribution to their nutritional status.

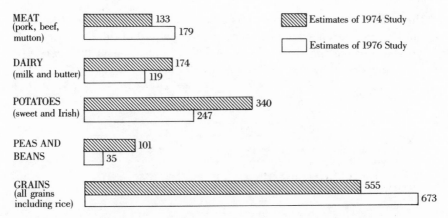

Figure 22. Two estimates based on the annual per capita consumption of meat, dairy, grains, potatoes, peas, and beans of U.S. slaves in 1860 (in pounds). These two estimates apply the procedures of the Department of Agriculture for estimating the available supply of food to data drawn from the manuscript schedules of the 1860 census.

It is possible to test this assumption with information on the food of slaves contained in nearly 2,000 interviews of ex-slaves collected during the 1920s and 1930s by researchers at Fisk University and in the Federal Writers' Project of the WPA. The information in these interviews permits the construction of an index that measures the proportion of interviewees in the sample who reported that as slaves they regularly consumed a particular food.[46] The ex-slave narratives do not provide a basis for estimating the quantity of a given food that was consumed but only for classifying foods into whether or not they were normally included in the diet on a particular plantation.

Figure 23 shows that various foods unenumerated by the census were widely consumed by the slave population. Vegetables not enumerated by the census—such as greens, turnips, collards, cabbages, onions, and tomatoes—were actually more widely consumed than the peas, beans, and potatoes that were included in the test diets. Other foods omitted from the census that bulked large in the slave diet include game (which was more widely consumed than potatoes or peas and beans), molasses, and fish (both of which were nearly as widely consumed as peas and beans).[47] Figure 23 indicates that game was a major source of animal protein, with nearly 60 persons eating game for every 100 who ate pork. To test the possibility that widespread consumption of game was limited to the frontier, separate indexes were computed for the New South and Old South states. While the diffusion index for game rose to slightly over 50 in the New South, the index for the Old South still remained above 40. Figure 23 also calls into question the contention that few slaves ate the meat of domesticated animals other than the pig. It shows that beef, mutton, and various domesticated fowl were a part of the slave diet, with 70 slaves reporting that they normally ate these meats for every 100 reporting that they normally ate pork.[48]

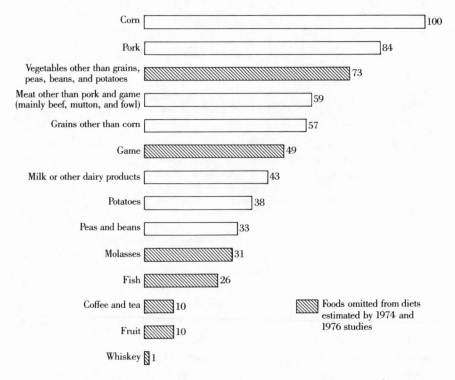

Figure 23. A diffusion index of food consumption: the extent of the regular consumption of various foods by slaves (corn = 100). The diffusion index measures the proportion of individuals who reported that they regularly consumed a given food, relative to the proportion who reported that they regularly consumed corn. It does not indicate how much of each food the slaves consumed.

The conclusion that the slave diet was more varied than suggested by the studies based on the 1860 census is supported by archaeological investigations of four plantations in Georgia and Florida. These excavations revealed that the remains of game and fish in the slave cabins were numerous (in one case more numerous than those of domestic animals) and that the bones of sheep, chicken, and cattle were also numerous. A comparison of the faunal remains in slave cabins with those in the planter's quarters revealed that slaves generally received the "less preferable cuts of meat" which came from the "forequarters, head, and feet," rather than the more "desirable upper hind quarters."

Beef, in fact, may have been more important in the diet than previously thought. The wild species are those which could have been captured in the nearby salt marshes or fields, possibly with clubs, nets, and traps, although some slaves did have guns as well. Slaves apparently did supplement their rations with resources obtained through their own efforts, concentrating on easily captured nocturnal mammals or fish. . . . Butchering techniques indicate maximum use was made of nutrients. . . .[49]

That the average diet of U.S. slaves was both high in calories and varied in nutrients does not necessarily imply that it was nutritionally adequate. The nutritional adequacy of a diet does not depend merely on the intake of nutrients but also on the claims made against these nutrients by work, disease, and other environmental conditions. Even if the average quantities of food consumed by U.S. slaves were greater than quantities consumed by most free working classes at the time, the nutritional status of U.S. slaves could have been far worse than that of most free working classes because of the greater intensity of their work or greater exposure to disease. Moreover, even if the *average* diet was sufficient to meet the varied claims on it and still provide for good health by the standards of the time, not all slaves received the average diet or experienced only average claims against their diets.

To resolve such issues various scholars have searched for evidence on the presence and extent of diseases now known to be directly caused or promoted by dietary deficiencies. Records have been uncovered that describe such maladies of slaves as aching and swollen muscles, night blindness, abdominal swelling, sore feet and legs, bowed legs, skin lesions, and convulsions. These maladies could have been produced by such nutrient deficiency diseases as beriberi (caused by a deficiency of thiamine), pellagra (caused by a deficiency of niacin), tetany (caused by deficiencies of calcium, magnesium, and vitamin D), rickets (also caused by a deficiency of vitamin D), and kwashiorkor (caused by severe protein deficiency). The difficulty with this line of analysis is that few of these nutritional diseases were actually identified as such in antebellum medical reports. The question that arises is whether the paucity of direct references to nutritional diseases means that they were uncommon in the antebellum South and the West Indies or that they were quite common but went undiagnosed because of the limits of medical science in the antebellum era. Most diseases that are today commonly diagnosed as caused by nutritional deficiencies were not scientifically identified until the twentieth century. Pellagra, for example, was not identified as a nutritional deficiency disease in the United States until about 1910, after which as many as 200,000 cases were diagnosed in a single year.[50]

Several of the historians who have examined the symptoms described

138

in antebellum records have argued that many of the cases could have
been caused by one or another dietary deficiency disease, although
symptoms described are usually too vague to permit a reliable resolution
of the issue. Even in the few instances where the symptoms are described
in sufficient detail to suggest beriberi or pellagra, the available information is too scanty to permit reliable estimates of the prevalence of these
diseases. The principal attempts to demonstrate that pellagra, beriberi,
tetany, and other nutritional deficiency diseases were widespread, particularly among children, ultimately rest on estimates of the average slave
diet suggesting that they were low in the nutrients that prevent these
diseases. Consequently, the debate over whether or not dietary deficiencies actually accounted for a large part of the mortality rate of slaves
leads back to the problem of measuring the average nutritional status of
slaves.

ANTHROPOMETRIC INDEXES OF MALNUTRITION

Anthropometric measures (measures of height, weight, and other physical characteristics) are now widely employed by the World Health Organization and similar agencies to assess the nutritional status of populations in the less developed nations. The use of height as an index of
nutritional status rests on a well-defined pattern of human growth between childhood and maturity. The average annual increase in height
(velocity) is greatest during infancy, falls sharply up to age 3, and then
falls more slowly through the remaining pre-adolescent years. During
adolescence velocity rises sharply to a peak that is approximately one-
half of the velocity during infancy, then falls sharply and reaches zero
at maturity. In girls the adolescent growth spurt begins about two years
earlier, and the magnitude of the spurt is smaller than in boys.

The relative importance of environmental and genetic factors in
explaining individual variations in height is still a matter of some debate.
Comparisons of many well-fed contemporary populations, however, indicate that systematic genetic influences appear to have very little impact
on the mean (average) heights. For example, the mean heights of well-fed
West Europeans, North American whites, and North American blacks
are nearly identical. There are, of course, some ethnic groups in which
mean final heights of well-fed persons today differ significantly from the
West European or North American standard. In these cases the deviation
from the European standard appears to be due to genetic factors. But
such ethnic groups have represented a minuscule proportion of the U.S.,
European, and West Indian populations. Consequently, they are irrelevant to an explanation of the observed trends in mean final heights in
the United States and in the various European nations since 1750; nor

can they account for the difference at various points of time between the means in the final heights of the U.S. population and the principal populations from which the U.S. population was drawn. In this connection, it should be noted that today the mean final heights of well-fed males in the main African nations from which the U.S. black population is derived also fall within the narrow band designated as the West European standard.

Biologists, epidemiologists, anthropologists, and nutritionists have charted the effect of nutritional deficiencies on the human growth profile. Nutritional insults in utero are reflected in birth length and birth weight. Short periods of malnutrition or prolonged periods of moderate malnutrition merely delay the adolescent growth spurt. Severe, prolonged malnutrition may diminish the typical growth-spurt pattern and contribute to permanent stunting, although most permanent stunting occurs at early ages. If malnutrition is prolonged and moderate, growth will continue beyond the age at which the growth of well-fed adolescents ceases. Hence, the average age at which the growth spurt peaks, the average age at which growth terminates, the mean height during adolescent ages, and the mean final height are all important indicators of mean nutritional status. Any one of them can be used to trace trends in nutrition within particular societies and to compare the nutritional status of different societies or of socioeconomic classes within a given society. The more of these measures that are available, the more precise the determination of the degree and the likely causes of the malnutrition that may afflict populations.[51]

Data on height-by-age for U.S. slaves are found in two main sources. The first are coastwise manifests covering the period from 1811 to 1862. They came into being as a result of the Act of March 2, 1807, which outlawed the slave trade with Africa and other foreign places. To guard against smuggling, Congress required coastwise vessels to prepare manifests of slaves taken on board, listing the name, age, sex, height, and other identifying characteristics of each slave. One copy of this manifest was kept by the customs office at the port of embarkation and the other was presented to the customs officer at the port of destination. The muster rolls of slaves recruited into the Union Army are another major source. For the British slave colonies, height, age, sex, place of birth, and tribal markings were recorded in the registrations of the four Crown colonies, and less completely for Guyana. Since tribal markings identify the ethnic group to which an African-born slave belonged, the registration data provide estimates of adult heights of various African ethnic populations. Records of slaves captured by British vessels engaged in the suppression of the African slave trade are another source of information on African heights. Between 1819 and 1845 about 57,000 slaves were taken by these cruisers and brought to Sierra Leone where they were officially registered by courts and then liberated. The registration information included age, sex, height, and the port from which the slaves embarked. Similar height data have been uncovered for Cuba and may exist for other slave colonies.[52]

Figure 24 compares the heights of various slave and free male populations during the nineteenth century.[53] It shows that slaves born in the United States as well as slaves born in the non-sugar colonies of the British West Indies were taller than French and Italian conscripts, British town artisans, and British Royal Marines, but about an inch shorter than U.S.-born whites in the Union Army. These heights indicate that the nutritional status of U.S. slaves and of creole slaves in the non-sugar islands was better than that of most European workers during the nineteenth century but not as good as that of native-born whites in the United States. Figure 24 also indicates that by modern standards all of the working classes of the nineteenth century probably experienced some degree of malnutrition. The average heights of U.S. slaves and of creole slaves of the non-sugar islands fall within the range currently considered normal, but they still suggest a significant degree of malnutrition during some part of their growing years. Although their malnutrition was not as severe as that experienced by the African-born slaves, the Italian conscripts, or the illiterate French conscripts, it could nevertheless have been concentrated in such a way that it had a substantial impact on mortality rates. It is to the investigation of this possibility that we now turn.[54]

When using height data to analyze the connection between nutrition and mortality, it is important to keep in mind that height is a net rather than a gross measure of nutrition. Height is not a measure of the intake of nutrients (which is gross nutrition) but of the balance between nutrient intake and the claims on that intake. Moreover, since changes in height during the growing ages reflect the nutritional status during these ages, mean *final* heights reflect the accumulated nutritional experience during childhood and adolescence. Mean final heights do not, however, indicate the course of nutrition after the attainment of maturity. Thus, when mean final heights are used to explain differences in adult mortality rates they reveal the effect not of adult levels of nutrition on adult mortality rates, but of nutritional levels during childhood and adolescence on adult mortality rates. Other factors that affect the body's ability to generate a surplus for growth include the climate, the nature of available food, clothing and shelter, the disease environment, the intensity of work, and the quality of public sanitation. In other words, the same nutritional input can have varying effects, depending on environmental conditions. While mean height measures the nutrients available after allowing for

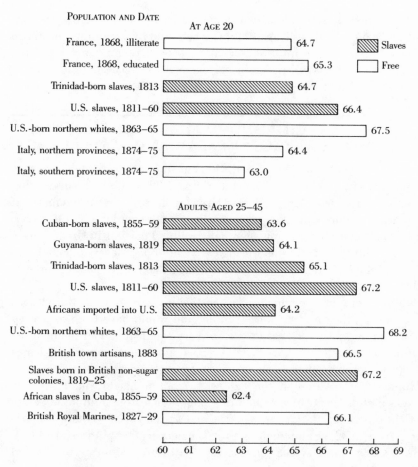

Figure 24. Heights of various slave and free male populations during the nineteenth century (in inches). The top part of the figure compares the
heights of French and Italian military conscripts (who were called up
when they reached their 20th birthday) with U.S. and Trinidad-born
slaves and with U.S.-born whites in the Union Army of the same age.
The bottom part of the figure compares the heights of adults who were
between 25 and 45 years of age. Before 1900, a male usually reached
about 99 percent of his final height by age 20. During the next five years
he may have grown another half an inch. The average adult male height
in Great Britain, which is often used as the modern standard, is currently 68.9 inches.

physical maintenance, for work, and for the impact of the man-made and
natural environment, it does not by itself indicate whether fluctuations in
net nutrition are due to changes in the diet or in the claims on the food
intake.[55]

How can one disentangle the influence of the factors that affected the net nutrition of slaves and determine which of them had the greatest influence on mortality rates? Clues can be found by examining the entire growth profile. Much information can be teased from an analysis of the extent to which slave heights at particular ages departed from modern standards. Figure 25 provides the basis for such an analysis.

FETAL AND CHILDHOOD MALNUTRITION AND THEIR AFFECT ON SLAVE MORTALITY

In this diagram the heights of both U.S. and Trinidad-born slaves, at ages from infancy to maturity, are superimposed on a set of curves that describe the current British standard for assessing the adequacy of physical development. The curve marked "50th centile" gives the average height at each age among generally well-fed persons in Great Britain today. Figure 25 shows that during early childhood slaves in both Trinidad and the United States were exceedingly small.[56] The figures for ages 0.5 and 1.5 are probably biased downward because the legs of the children were not stretched out when they were measured. But at ages 2.5 and 3.5 the children were walking and would have been measured in a standing position. Yet they were very small by modern standards, falling at or below the 0.1 centile. Such poor development indicates kwashiorkor and other diseases caused by severe protein-calorie malnutrition (PCM). Although the gap with modern height standards was reduced after age 3, it remained in a range suggesting mild to moderate PCM through age 8. Between ages 10 and 17 the growth patterns of U.S. and Trinidad slaves fluctuated in the range of moderate to severe PCM. By the mid-twenties, U.S. slaves were well into the normal range and Trinidad-born slaves were borderline normal.

In the U.S. case these findings tend to contradict the theory that male slaves were so overworked in the fields that their diets were inadequate and their health was consequently impaired. Figure 25 indicates that slaves were most deficient in height during early childhood, before they began work of any sort. Prior to puberty slave children were involved in light tasks, mainly around the master's house. The transition to childhood occupations began as early as age 5. The transition from childhood to adult jobs began with the early maturers at about age 11, and the last of the late maturers were generally switched into their adult jobs by age 16. Among adolescents aged 16–20, about five-sixths were employed in the fields. Yet as Figure 25 shows, far from retarding their growth, the ages of entry into field work and immediately thereafter were years of rapid growth. U.S. slaves experienced a delayed but vigorous adolescent growth spurt that extended into the late teens, and conse-

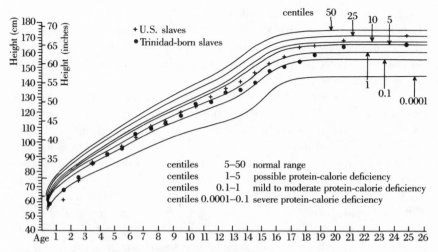

Figure 25. The extent to which mean heights of male slaves in the United States and Trinidad deviated from the modern height standard.

quently they made up three inches of the five-inch gap with modern standards that existed at age 10.[57]

It thus appears that the malnutrition of U.S. slaves was primarily a phenomenon of early life. The exceedingly small size of slaves at ages 2 and 3 suggests that they were also far below modern standards at birth. Many, perhaps most, babies were probably below 5.5 pounds at birth.[58] Babies that small would have been highly vulnerable to such infectious diseases as diarrhea, dysentery, whooping cough, and a variety of respiratory diseases, as well as to worms, which helped to push the infant and early childhood death rates of slaves to twice the levels experienced by the white infants and children in the United States. The small size of slaves at birth also bears on the explanation for the high rate of spontaneous abortions, stillbirths, and "mysterious" deaths shortly after birth. Many slave masters, and some scholars, attributed these events to induced abortions, maternal carelessness, or infanticide, but they were quite likely what demographers call "endogenous" deaths, deaths that are the natural outcome of malformed fetuses. The rate of fetal malformation, spontaneous abortion, and endogenous deaths is sharply increased by low weights caused by intrauterine malnutrition.[59]

The failure of small babies to exhibit much catch-up growth between birth and age 3 suggests chronic undernourishment during these ages. Breast feeding was quite common throughout the South, but its average duration is uncertain. On some of the larger plantations most of the infants may have been weaned within three or four months. Plantation records that describe the diets of weaned infants and young children suggest that even if it was sufficient in calories, it was low in protein. Gruels and porridges, usually made with cornmeal and often containing milk, were the most common fare. After age 3 these were supplemented to some extent by vegetable soups likely to contain more fat than meat, potatoes, molasses, grits, hominy, and cornbread.[60] These more balanced diets contributed to catch-up growth between ages 3 and 8, although even the 8-year-olds were still quite short by modern standards. Both the available descriptions of the diets of young children and the small stature of children, especially those under age 3, are consistent with the evidence on protein deficiency recently culled from the antebellum medical reports. The frequent descriptions of the "glistening fat ribs and corpulent paunches" of young children, the frequent listing of "dropsy" and "swelling" as a cause of death, and the concern of southern physicians with "the distention of slave children's stomachs," combined with the data on stature, suggest that kwashiorkor or pre-kwashiorkor was prevalent.[61]

Ironically, the entry of pubescent children into the adult labor force did not aggravate childhood malnutrition but led to its alleviation. Although subjected to the intense routine of the gang system, which was nutritionally far more demanding than the work or play of childhood, adolescents were switched from the porridges and gruels of children to the meaty diets of field hands. When working in the gang, young and old alike ate from the same kettles: no children's menu there. And so the entry into gangs permitted further catch-up growth in the late teens. That field-hand diets were rich enough to support intense labor and rapid physical growth is indicated not only by the growth in stature after age 11, shown in Figure 25, but also by data on weight per inch of height for slaves just before and after maturity. These data, which come from the records of slaves who were mustered into the Union Army, reveal that, on average, weight per inch of height was as high for male slaves in their late teens, twenties, and thirties as it is in the current standard for good health.[62]

That the nutritional deficiencies of early childhood, rather than the overwork or underfeeding of adults, were the main cause of the relatively high death rate of U.S. slaves is suggested by available data on mortality and morbidity rates. It was the excess death rates of children under 5 that accounted for nearly all of the difference between the overall death rates of U.S. slaves and of U.S. whites during the late antebellum era. If the diets of slaves before puberty had been as rich in proteins and other vital nutrients as were the diets of adult slaves, the overall slave death rate would probably have been reduced by 25 percent. That adult slaves in the United States enjoyed relatively good health is indicated by the fact that life expectations of slaves and whites were similar after age 20. The same conclusion is suggested by plantation records which indicate that the annual number of days lost from work by adults because of illness or disability was relatively low.[63]

If adult slaves were relatively well nourished and healthy, how could intrauterine malnutrition have been prevalent? Tiny, severely malnourished infants and relatively well-nourished parents seem to be incompatible phenomena. The resolution of the paradox appears to turn on the treatment of pregnant women. Some scholars have argued that pregnant women were generally released from field work for most or all of the last two trimesters of pregnancy, reassigned to such light tasks as sewing. No doubt that happened on occasion, but the currently available samples of the daily work registers maintained by overseers indicate few instances of women who were released from field work for extended periods during pregnancy. A recent analysis of the cotton-picking rates of pregnant women and nursing mothers indicates that there was no letup in the pace of work during the first two trimesters of pregnancy and very little in the third. Even during the last week before childbirth, pregnant women on average picked three-quarters or more of the amount that was normal for women of corresponding ages who were neither pregnant nor nursing. Only during the month following childbirth was there a sharp reduction in the amount of cotton picked.[64]

Continuing to employ pregnant women in the intense routine of the gang system down to the eve of childbirth may have severely restricted the amount of weight they gained during the pregnancy. Nor is there evidence of nutritional supplementation that might have compensated for such high levels of physical activity. The available evidence suggests that such supplementation was fairly common for nursing mothers, but rare for pregnant women engaged in normal field work before birth. In modern industrialized societies, where the physical activity of working women is moderate, the occurrence of intrauterine malnutrition is usually brought about by unduly low levels of nutrient intake rather than by unusually high levels of energy output. In some peasant societies, however, low weight gains have been caused not by deliberate restriction of consumption but by the especially heavy work loads undertaken by pregnant mothers.[65]

It thus appears that diets sufficient to maintain the health of non-pregnant women engaged in heavy labor were insufficient to produce average weight gains in pregnant women that would yield adequate average birth weights and forestall high infant death rates. Although the intense pace of labor of adult slaves does not appear to have added significantly to their own mortality rates, it may have doubled the death rate of their children during the first five years of life. It should not be assumed that the overwork and underfeeding of pregnant women means that the nutritional status of women was generally poorer than that of men. As with the males, females suffered the inadequate diets of early childhood. But they had, relative to the current female standard, as vigorous a growth spurt as adolescent boys, and their mean final height, 62.5 inches, was nearly as close to the modern standard as that of males.[66]

The analysis of the cotton-picking rates of pregnant women suggests that breast feeding might have been terminated quite early in many cases, since by the fourth month after the birth of a child the average cotton-picking rate of a mother returned to the level that was normal for women who were not nursing. The early weaning of children might also have contributed to the lack of "catch-up" growth in low-birth-weight babies during infancy and early childhood. Weaning to gruels and porridges could have prevented catch-up growth and promoted high death rates in two different ways. If the gruel was prepared mainly with water, then it was likely to have been *protein deficient.* If the gruel was prepared with raw cow's milk, infants and young children may have been exposed to increased risks of contracting tuberculosis, undulant fever, and salmonellosis, all of which may be transmitted by raw cow's milk. These diseases would have prevented catch-up growth by inducing loss of appetite (thereby reducing the nutrient intake of infants and children) or by promoting diarrhea (thereby preventing the body from utilizing the nutrients that were ingested). Descriptions of the causes of death for children under age 5 suggest that the incidence of these diseases in the antebellum South was quite high.[67]

The locus of malnutrition in Trinidad was in some respects similar to that of U.S. slaves, although the consumption of alcohol during pregnancy, which retards fetal development and induces a number of other abnormalities, may have been an additional complicating factor. On some sugar plantations liberal rations of rum were provided to slaves, especially during harvest time. Moreover, the weaker adolescent growth spurt and the lower final height of Trinidad slaves indicate that the nutrients available for adolescent growth were less in Trinidad than in the slave South. Not only was the nutrient intake of Trinidad slaves relatively low, but the more virulent disease environment of Trinidad undoubtedly exercised relatively greater claims against that intake.[68]

There is little doubt that the inferior nutritional status of Trinidad slaves contributed to their exceedingly high death rates. Analysis of the Trinidad registrations has revealed a strong relationship between height and mortality rates. Among males, those in the shortest fifth of the height distribution were more than twice as likely to die as those in the tallest fifth of the distribution. The relationship between height and mortality rates was not as marked for females but was still quite significant: The death rates of the shortest fifth of females exceeded those of the tallest fifth by nearly 50 percent. Even so, it was mainly the severity of the disease environment, rather than their inferior diets, that made the mortality rates of Trinidad slaves so much higher than those of U.S. slaves. If the diets of Trinidad slaves had been improved to allow as vigorous a growth spurt as that experienced by U.S. slaves, the death rates of prime-aged male hands could have been cut significantly, but three-quarters of the mortality gap between the prime hands in Trinidad and those in the South would have remained. This conclusion is supported by the fate of prime hands raised elsewhere in the West Indies before being brought to Trinidad; they died at rates that were 40 percent greater than the death rates of the cohorts they left behind.[69]

FERTILITY

The actual West Indian birth rates were closer to the birth rates of U.S. slaves than the British abolitionists thought they were. The undercounting of infants and children who were born and died between the triennial registrations led not only to an underestimation of death rates but also to an underestimation of birth rates. It would be a mistake to attribute the undercount primarily to the duplicity of West Indian planters. It was largely the consequence of a real and extremely important demographic phenomenon: the high proportion of endogenous deaths among infants—that is, deaths caused by malformed fetuses. This demographic phenomenon was complicated by a cultural one: Prior to the nineteenth century the churches of Europe and of the Americas, rather than civil authorities, usually undertook the task of keeping track of vital events (births, deaths, and marriages).

The churches generally kept quite accurate records of the marriages they performed, but instead of recording births they usually recorded only baptisms, and instead of recording deaths they usually recorded only burials in church grounds. Not every baby who was born was baptized, even in very religious societies, since quite often babies died so soon after birth that there was no opportunity to perform the ritual of baptism. Infants who died unbaptized were often excluded from both the baptism and burial records of churches. Infant deaths in these times were so common, and the tendency to withhold the recording of a birth until baptism was so deep in the prevailing culture, that even the private records of households, including those of slaveowners, frequently omitted the births of infants who died shortly after birth.

Demographers have developed techniques to correct for these undercounts by carefully analyzing the daily pattern of deaths during infancy. Their studies reveal that in high-risk societies, some 60 percent of all infant deaths occurred within the first month following birth, and that nearly half of these early deaths occurred within hours, or at most a few days, after birth. The available evidence indicates that in societies with very high infant death rates a large proportion, usually the majority, of these very early deaths are of babies suffering from intrauterine malnutrition or other impairments to fetal development. Such fetuses survived long enough to be born but, in the fierce disease environment and medical technology of the time, were doomed. Recognition of the relationship between fetal malformation and the level and temporal pattern of infant deaths provides the critical information needed to measure the undercount of births. When these techniques are applied to the slave populations of the New World they reveal that even the British West Indies were relatively high-fertility societies. The corrections show not only that fertility rates in these colonies exceeded those of Western Europe, but that much of the apparent gap between the fertility rates of U.S. and West Indian slaves was a statistical artifact, although even after the correction American fertility rates are well above the West Indian ones.[70]

Mortality contributed to the fertility gap between U.S. and West Indian slaves in another way: It reduced the average span of years during which West Indian women bore children. On average the childbearing span (the difference between the age at last birth and the age at first birth) of women in Trinidad was just 15 years, nearly 6 years shorter than that of slave women in the United States. Since women in both societies had their first child at about age 21, the shorter childbearing span in Trinidad was due to the young average age at which the Trinidad women bore their last child. For many Trinidad mothers childbearing came to an early end because of infertility. It is likely that, as in other nineteenth-century populations, about one-sixth of all mothers were infertile by age 35. But for an even larger proportion of mothers, childbearing was terminated because of the death of a husband. The death rate of males in Trinidad was so high that nearly 1 women out of every 3 who married at age 20 were widowed by age 35. The combined effect of infertility and widowhood ended the childbearing careers of half of all Trinidad mothers by their 35th birthday.[71]

Two other factors contributing to the fertility gap between West Indian and U.S. slaves have been investigated. One is the proportion of women who bore a child. In Trinidad only about 69 percent of women who lived to be 49 (that is, who lived through their entire childbearing span) ever bore a child, which was, and is still, far below the childbearing rate of women in the United States and Europe. The second is the average length of the interval between successive births (the birth interval). Early investigation of the registration data seemed to imply that the duration of birth intervals in the West Indies was exceedingly long, averaging about four years (50 to 100 percent longer than those estimated for U.S. slaves). More recent work, however, suggests that most of the difference in the apparent duration of birth intervals was another artifact of the failure to have adequately recorded the births of those babies who died in infancy.[72]

Table 4.[73] presents a summary of the various factors that accounted for the difference between the fertility rates of slaves in the United States and Trinidad. In this table fertility is measured by the "total fertility rate" rather than the measure presented in Figure 20, which was the "crude birth rate" (the number of babies born during a year per 100 persons in the population). The total fertility rate is defined as the total number of children born to a woman who lives through the childbearing ages (15–49) and who has the average fertility experience. Table 4 shows that on average a U.S. slave woman living to age 49 had about 9.2 children. By contrast, if the uncorrected registration data are used for the calculation, a Trinidad woman would appear to have averaged only 2.4 live births. However, correction of the registrations for the under-count of children who died before age 3 nearly doubles the number of live births. The corrected total fertility rate is somewhat above the fertility rate that prevailed in most of Western Europe at the time, but still below that of U.S. slaves.

Table 4. A Comparison of the Total Fertility Rates of Slaves in the United States (c.1830) and in Trinidad (c.1813), with an Explanation for the Difference in These Rates

Variable	U.S.	Trinidad	% of the Difference in the Fertility Rates Explained by Each Variable
	After Correcting the Undercount in Trinidad Registrations		
Total Fertility Rate (average number of children born to a woman living to age 49)	9.24	4.44	—
Average Childbearing Span (average number of years between first and last births)	20.1	14.5	39
Average Birth Interval (average number of years between successive births)	2.06	2.67	31
Proportion of Women Ever Bearing a Child	0.86	0.69	30
	Before Correcting the Undercount in Trinidad Registrations		
Total Fertility Rate	9.24	2.35	—
Average Childbearing Span	20.1	13.1	27
Average Birth Interval	2.06	3.83	38
Proportion of Women Ever Bearing a Child	0.86	0.53	35

The preceding discussion was cast in purely demographic terms. To many scholars the critical issues are the economic, social, and cultural forces that explain why the proportion of women ever bearing children, or the length of the childbearing span, varied so much from one slave society to another. The quest for answers at this level has led to comparisons of the organization of families and of households in different slave societies or in different kinds of plantations within a particular society. These investigations have revealed that most slaves in the United States and the Bahamas lived in "nuclear" households consisting of two parents and children, sometimes with grandparents also present (see Table 5). In Trinidad, however, half of the population lived in single-person households or in households of unrelated individuals. Moreover, mother-headed households were more numerous than two-parent households in both Trinidad and Jamaica. Studies of household structure have revealed important aspects of slave culture that will be explored in the next chapter. But first it is necessary to consider the connection between household structure and fertility rates.[74]

Table 5. The Distribution of Slaves by the Different Types of Households in which They Lived: A Comparison of Four Populations (in percent)

	Trinidad in 1813	Jamaica in 1825	The Bahamas in 1822	The United States c.1850
Nuclear Families (mainly two-parent families but also some childless couples)	24	37	72	64
One-Parent Families (mainly headed by the mother)	26	40	13	21
Non-Family Households (men alone or together, women alone or together, children living separately)	50	23	15	15
	100	100	100	100

The narratives of ex-slaves revealed that the two-parent households in the United States were about 60 percent more fertile than the mother-headed households, and study of Jamaican households yielded similar results. These findings suggest that much of the fertility gap between Trinidad (or Jamaica) and the United States (or the Bahamas) may have been due to the housing policies of planters—to a failure of planters in Trinidad and Jamaica to provide enough family cabins or to a deliberate policy of organizing slaves into barracks or other housing arrangements that were an insuperable barrier to the normal process of family formation.[75]

Much of the recent work, however, indicates that decisions about the types of houses in which slaves would live were not wholly under the control of the masters, who sometimes felt compelled to accede to strongly held preferences of their slaves. Moreover, small cabins appear to have predominated over barracks as the form of housing even for the unattached individuals in the societies described in Table 5 (although barracks may have been common in other times and places). The average number of persons per non-family household in a study of Jamaican plantations was about two, and in the sample of U.S. plantations covered by the ex-slave narratives the corresponding figure is six. In the case of Trinidad, part of the explanation for the large proportion of persons living in non-family households was the high male-to-female sex ratio in the prime childbearing years—a residue of the slave trade that made it impossible for many men to marry and form families. More important, however, was the large number of marriages ended by the ravages of mortality, which were twice as high for adult men as adult women. Out of every 1,000 marriages, more than half were dissolved by the death of one of the partners (usually the male), leaving as many single-parent households as two-parent households. In other words, much of the more than 2 to 1 margin by which the proportion of two-parent families in the United States exceeded that of Trinidad appears to have been due to an adult mortality rate (especially for males) that was much higher in Trinidad than in the United States, rather than to a resistance by West Indian planters (or indifference by their slaves) to the establishment of marital households.[76]

This is not to say that policies adopted by planters did not affect fertility rates. Whether the demand for family-sized cabins stemmed from the planters or the slaves, the decision to build such houses did more to promote high fertility rates than any other policy that might have been contemplated by planters. The evidence that has been developed to date by historical demographers shows that marital households in a culture of natural fertility were all that was needed to achieve high fertility rates and, provided that mortality rates were kept in check, high rates of natural increase.[77]

Abolitionist suggestions that the high U.S. fertility rate was the consequence of the efforts of planters to manipulate the breeding of slaves as they did their cattle and to take advantage of changing market conditions, including the closing of the slave trade, cannot account either for trends in fertility within the United States or for the fertility differentials between the United States and the West Indies. The large differences in the U.S. and West Indian fertility rates existed while the international slave trade was open and after it closed. Efforts to relate changes in U.S. fertility rates to cotton and tobacco prices, to slave prices, or to the ratio between slave prices and slave hire rates have shown that these assumed correlations were absent.[78]

It would, however, be incorrect to conclude that the economic policies of planters had no influence on fertility rates. Quite often family life and fertility rates were sacrificed to gain profit, but in these instances changes in family organization and fertility rates were incidental to the thrust of economic policy rather than its central objective. One study, for example, revealed that the proportion of women who bore children was substantially lower on plantations with 100 or more slaves than on those with just a few slaves. Although encouraging marriage, the masters of these large plantations also insisted on maintaining the rigid labor discipline characteristic of the gang system. Consequently, they discouraged or even prohibited unmarried slaves from searching for partners outside of the plantation itself. But slaves on plantations too small to sustain a gang system were allowed to fraternize with slaves on other farms and to marry slaves belonging to other owners. As a consequence, slave women on small farms typically married younger, had longer childbearing periods, and were less likely to remain childless than the women on the big gang-system farms.[79]

In general, it may be said that when economic considerations led U.S. planters to interfere with the normal family lives of slaves, it usually served to reduce fertility rather than to increase it. By far the most common form of interference, besides limiting marriages to partners available on the plantation, was the destruction of marriages through the internal slave trade. The ex-slave narratives reveal that in a third of the slave households headed by a single parent the marriage was destroyed because either the mother or the father was sold or given away.[80]

Much remains to be learned about changes in patterns of slave fertility, particularly before 1800. The two principal studies of the demography of U.S. slaves during the eighteenth century thus far are for the Chesapeake region and the Carolinas. Although these studies are based on relatively small samples, they both indicate that fertility rates of the magnitude discovered for the 1850s were achieved as early as the mid-eighteenth century. The Chesapeake study also found that the average age of females at first birth in the 1730s was about 19, which is about two years younger than the age at first birth in the 1830s. This rise in the age of first birth appears to have been offset by a rise in the average age of mothers at last birth, probably because of reduced mortality, so that the total fertility rate remained fairly constant, or increased slightly, during this century-long period.[81]

It appears that two main factors were involved in the decline of the fertility rates of U.S. slaves after 1830. One was the increase in the proportion of slaves living on large plantations. The other was the shift of slaves from tobacco production to the production of cotton and other crops. A larger proportion of female slaves on tobacco plantations married than did those on cotton, rice, or sugar plantations. Women on tobacco plantations also married earlier and continued childbearing to a later age than did those on other plantations. These findings raise intriguing issues about the way that slave culture differed from one type of plantation to another.[82]

What have two decades of intensive research revealed about the demographic issues that were so highly politicized during the struggle to end slavery? With hindsight it is obvious that the issues were far more complicated than either side realized. Mortality rates were actually worse than abolitionists charged. These high rates were often caused not by the malice of masters but by the backfiring of well-intentioned practices, as when masters fed raw milk to weaned infants or rewarded field hands with liberal allotments of rum. Masters were not generally guilty of working field hands to death but they were guilty of so overworking pregnant women that infant death rates were pushed to extraordinary levels. Fertility rates were high not because masters manipulated the sexual behavior of slaves as they did their cattle, but because they housed slaves in family cabins rather than barracks. When economic motives led masters to interfere with the sexual lives of slaves, such interference did not usually raise fertility but reduced it, as when husbands were sold from wives or when young adults were prohibited from seeking marital partners beyond the boundaries of their plantations. Nor is it likely that a cooler, more objective approach to the causes of high mortality and low fertility among slaves could have sorted out the determinants of their vital rates. The underlying factors were obscured by misreporting as well as by the state of medical science, of nutritional science, and of demographic techniques. Under the circumstances, it was probably inevitable that political arguments would take precedence over scientific ones.

CHAPTER SIX

CHANGING INTERPRETATIONS OF SLAVE CULTURE

The images of slave culture conveyed by history books written between World War I and the late 1960s were largely creations of the ideological warfare of the late antebellum era and of the justifications for the system of political disfranchisement and social segregation that reigned from the 1890s to the 1960s.[1] A counterview of slave culture, fashioned mainly by black scholars, began to emerge after the turn of the twentieth century but was largely ignored by the mainstream of writers on slavery until World War II. The anti-racist themes in the struggle against fascism suggested two metaphors that drastically reoriented the main thrust of research on slave culture. One metaphor compared slave plantations with concentration camps; the other compared slaves with the members of the underground resistance movements during World War II.[2] Although both metaphors eventually broke down, the debate over them stimulated an enormous wave of research aimed at unearthing the true nature of slave culture. Searching deeply into long-neglected bodies of evidence such as the letters of slaves, slave songs and folk tales, the autobiographies of runaway slaves, and the remembrances of ex-slaves three-quarters of a century after the close of the slave era, historians have gone a long way toward reconstructing various aspects of that culture. Influenced by the principles of modern anthropology, they have sought to recreate not only the music and art of slaves but all of the conditions that affected the quality of slave life as well as the conceptions that slaves had of themselves and of the world around them.

The debate over slave culture began in antebellum times with attempts to characterize the work patterns and work attitudes of slaves. Historians who subsequently took up these questions sought to understand the way that the slave system of labor operated, the relationship of slaves to each other in the work process, and the relationship of slaves to their masters. Characterizations of the work patterns and the work ethic of slaves have been among the most critical points in the interpretation of slave culture, deeply influencing views of other aspects of slave life including family mores, religion, music, folk tales, art, and the nature and extent of slave resistance to oppression.[3]

THE WORK ETHIC OF SLAVES AND THEIR MODES OF RESISTANCE

The myth of black incompetence, which permeated debates between the abolitionist and proslavery camps before the Civil War, was given a stamp of authority in the papers and books that constituted the mainstream of historical scholarship after the war. James Ford Rhodes, a Northerner and the most influential American historian at the turn of the twentieth century, found nothing that was admirable either in the personal character of slaves or in the quality of their labor. He described slaves as "indolent and filthy"; on their "brute-like countenances . . . were painted stupidity, indolence, duplicity, and sensuality"; their labor was "stupid, plodding, machine-like." In Rhodes's view the error of southern apologists was not in the claim that blacks were inferior, but in the manner in which they sought to cope with the problem created by this inferiority. "So long as Southern reasoners maintained that the Negro race was inferior to the Caucasian, their basis was scientific truth, although their inference that this fact justified slavery was cruel as well as illogical."[4]

When U. B. Phillips claimed that he was revolutionizing the interpretation of the antebellum era, he was not referring to the myth of black incompetence, but to the harsh judgments by Rhodes and other northern historians about the character of slaveholders. In *American Negro Slavery*, published in 1918, Phillips provided numerous examples intended to demonstrate the inherent laziness, docility, and incompetence of blacks, whether enslaved or free.

Of the principal reviewers of that book, only two attacked its portrait of slaves. W. E. B. DuBois, the director of publicity and research for the NAACP and the editor of its journal, *Crisis*, found *American Negro Slavery* "curiously incomplete and unfortunately biased." Nowhere in the entire book was there an "adequate conception of 'darkies,' 'niggers' and 'negroes' (words liberally used throughout the book) as making a living mass of humanity with all the usual human reactions."[5] The other critic, also black, was Carter Woodson, who founded the Association for the Study of Negro Life and History in 1915 and served as its director until his death in 1950. While giving Phillips due credit for his analysis of the business aspects of plantations, Woodson criticized Phillips for dealing with slaves "as property in the cold-blooded fashion that southerners usually bartered them away," and for his "inability to fathom the Negro mind."[6]

To fill the void, Woodson wrote or edited 18 books dealing with such diverse questions as the education of the Negro during the antebellum era, the development of the Negro church, and the history of the Negro wage earner. Perhaps his most important book was *The Negro in Our History*, first published in 1922, which aimed "to present to the average reader in succinct form the history of the United States as it has been influenced by the presence of the Negro in this country." An energetic and effective entrepreneur, as well as a scholar, Woodson gathered around himself a number of young black and white scholars who pioneered in writing history from "the bottom up." These scholars were decades ahead of the rest of the profession in identifying and exploiting new sources of evidence on the lives and times of ordinary people, sources that have, in recent years, become the standard materials of what is now called the "new social history." Woodson also founded the *Journal of Negro History*, which published a number of landmark papers that pointed the way toward a new view of slave culture.[7]

The work of the Woodson school was focused more on the lives of free Negroes than on the lives of slaves. This emphasis was partly the consequence of the availability of evidence. Materials that contained information on the aspirations and accomplishments of free blacks were more numerous, or at least more accessible at the time, than those which contained information on the culture of slaves. But their research strategy also reflected a belief that they would uncover more praiseworthy accomplishments by studying the lives of men who were free rather than of those whose opportunities for achievement were severely restricted by slavery. Although members of the Woodson school accepted much of the economic indictment of slavery, they did not accept the conclusion that the oppression was so complete that it was "impossible for a slave to develop intellectual power."[8] It was their view that in most times and places slaves were left with room to maneuver, with room to find effective (sometimes even heroic) methods of resisting the worst features of the slave system. Consequently, the Woodson school allocated a significant and, as the years wore on, increasing share of its resources to searching for evidence that would reveal the record of slave achievement under extremely adverse conditions.

One accomplishment brought to light by this search was the persistent drive of slaves to acquire education and vocational skills. Toward the end of the eighteenth century, said Woodson, "Negroes were serving as salesmen, keeping accounts, managing plantations, teaching and preaching, and had intellectually advanced to the extent that 15 or 20 percent of their adults could then at least read." The striving for education and vocational training continued, according to Woodson, even after 1830 when the reactionary movement directed at repressing all resistance to slavery took command. Woodson estimated that even after 30 years of reactionary onslaught some "10 percent of the adult Negroes (slave and free) had the rudiments of education in 1860, but the proportion was much less than it was near the close of the era of better beginnings about 1825."[9] The Woodson school also called attention to the large proportion of "skilled and semi-skilled" slaves engaged in the "mechanical pursuits of the plantations and of the towns,"[10] and estimated that slaves and free blacks made up over 80 percent of the artisan class of the South.

Woodson and his colleagues provided evidence that slaves also engaged in forms of resistance that were more radical than the struggle for formal education and vocational skills. In *The Negro in Our History,* Woodson described the bold attempts of a number of Negroes at insurrection, attempts which proved that submissiveness was not an inborn characteristic of blacks. These incidents revealed that under sufficient provocation slaves would defy the odds and seek relief from their oppression "by refreshing the tree of liberty with the blood of their oppressors."[11] The significance of these revolutionary forms of resistance was underscored by Herbert A. Aptheker who, in a book published during World War II, argued that slave insurrections and conspiracies were not only more numerous than previous scholars had assumed but were increasing so rapidly toward the end of the antebellum era that "acute fear" of "militant concerted slave action"[12] pervaded the ruling circles of the South.

The image of slave resistance was radically transformed during World War II by Melville J. Herskovits, an anthropologist at Northwestern University, and two of his students. They argued that slave resistance was manifested chiefly through shirking, destruction of tools, stealing, malingering, spoiling of crops, slowdowns, and other deliberate forms of sabotaging production. Thus, a new image of slave resistance was created, one far less heroic than Aptheker's image of widespread revolutionary assaults, but to many scholars also more credible. And, in contrast to Woodson's vision of slaves pressing for general education and for the acquisition of vocational skills, the new view of covert or "day-to-day" resistance was quite consistent with the standard characterizations of the quality of slave labor.[13]

Indeed, the case for day-to-day resistance rested on two propositions accepted by both antislavery critics and southern romantic historians: first, that slave plantations were relatively unproductive and, second, that slave labor was quite inefficient. Herskovits sought to turn these propositions against southern apologists by challenging not the alleged poor performance of slaves, but the explanation for this performance. Rejecting contentions that slaves were descended from "the poorer stock of Africa" or from "savage" cultures "low in the scale of human civilization," he asserted that the low quality of slave labor was really an expression of indirect protest. While acknowledging that rarely had the poor work performances of slaves previously "been recognized as modes of slave protest," he nevertheless insisted that they were acts of sabotage. The evidence that Herskovits invoked to support this thesis consisted of seven quotations from Frederick Law Olmsted recounting either the dissatisfaction of masters with the work of slaves or Olmsted's own view of the low quality of slave labor.[14]

The image of day-to-day resistance was elaborated and extended by Kenneth Stampp in *The Peculiar Institution*. Published in 1956, that book finally succeeded in pushing the question of slave culture into the mainstream of historiographic debate. Stampp acknowledged the symbolic significance of revolutionary conspiracies and insurrections, but he did not view them as the principal form through which slaves expressed their discontent because the generality of slaves believed that "the odds against success" were "too overwhelming." Running away was a more common act of resistance than insurrection but still involved only a relatively small proportion of slaves. Although much less spectacular than either of these overt forms of rebellion, day-to-day resistance was, in his view, both effective and widespread. Stampp also argued against the necessity of linking extensive covert sabotage to the proposition that slave plantations were unprofitable. They were in fact quite profitable, Stampp held, since the inefficiency of slave labor was offset by longer hours of work, more complete exploitation of women and children, and lower real wages for slaves than for free men. Stampp described a wide array of devices invoked by slaves to frustrate the production goals of planters, citing not only more instances of the poor work performance of slaves than were found by Herskovits but even more than were documented by Phillips for quite a different purpose.[15]

Stampp's most important amendment of day-to-day resistance lay in his elaboration of the work ethic of slaves. Herskovits and his students had treated planter complaints about laziness and irresponsibility as evidence for inchoate forms of slave resistance. Stampp made this behavior the consequence of an articulated morality, attributing to slaves a political consciousness that Frederick Douglass, the leading black abolitionist, had not found among his fellow bondsmen. Within this moral code, evasion, deception, and sabotage represented the highest level of achievement. Most slaves, according to Stampp, "believed that he who knew how to trick or deceive the master had an enviable talent, and they regarded the committing of petit larceny as both thrilling and praiseworthy." And what of the minority of slaves who sought "personal gratification and the esteem of their fellows" by "doing their work uncommonly well"? They "lacked the qualities which produce rebels," said Stampp. Resistance was thus the linchpin of a work ethic that was well defined, politically motivated, and predominant.[16]

The difficulties created for this view of the slave work performance and ethic by the new findings on the productivity of slave labor are immediately apparent. Slave plantations and laborers were not less efficient than free farms and free farmers. Slaves on small plantations who, like ordinary hired hands, worked in the fields alongside their masters were just as productive as free farmers. But those who toiled in the gangs of the intermediate and large plantations were on average over 70 percent more productive than either free farmers or slaves on small plantations. These gang laborers, who in 1860 constituted about half of the adult slave population, worked so intensely that they produced as much output in roughly 35 minutes as did free farmers in a full hour.[17]

That gang laborers were harder working and more productive than their free counterparts does not, of course, rule out the type of behavior that has been called day-to-day resistance. But it does raise questions as to the extent of this behavior and its location. Not all large plantations were as successful as the average and it may be that the types of sabotage of production described by Herskovits and Stampp were heavily concentrated on these less successful plantations. Plantations run on the gang system might have been sabotaged, even though they were more productive than free farms, if they fell well below the standard for the gang system. Eugene D. Genovese has suggested that masters who practiced paternalism were more successful than those who used their power ruthlessly. Some support for this conjecture comes from Stephen C. Crawford's quantitative study of the ex-slave narratives. He finds that stealing was over eight times as frequent on the plantations of masters who provided meager rations as on those with masters who provided ample rations.[18]

But even if day-to-day resistance was rife on these more brutal and presumably less successful plantations, one should not blithely translate resistance into low labor performance. Resistance could reduce but not cancel out the greater intensity of gang labor. Resisters who were able to deprive masters of half the extra product to be expected from the gang system (it would be a rare plantation on which sabotage was that effective) would still have found themselves compelled to produce as much output in roughly 45 minutes as did free men in a full hour. In other words, while sabotage could deprive the master of some of his gain, it could not free the slaves from the burden of intense labor. And there was a heavy price to be paid for this type of resistance. On plantations where stealing was most frequent, masters made heavier use of the lash, provided coarser diets, and imposed greater restrictions on freedom than were typical of paternalistic plantations.[19]

An alternative way of reconciling the resistance work ethic with the new findings in slave productivity was set forth by Genovese in *Roll,*

Jordan, Roll. He propounded what might be called a modified resistance
ethic. On the one hand, he acknowledged that large slave plantations
represented "a halfway house between peasant and factory cultures" and
that planters sought to impose a factory-like discipline on their labor
force. On the other hand, he insisted that while slaves were willing to
work extremely hard, so hard that they could "astonish the whites by
their worktime elan and expenditure of energy," they would do so only
sporadically and they resisted efforts to subjugate them to the tyranny of
regularity, to transform them into "clock-punchers." "The actual work
rhythm of the slaves, then," was "hammered out as a compromise between themselves and their masters." Stressing the extraordinary exertion at certain points of the year, especially at harvest, required by plantation crops, Genovese believes that planters settled for measures that
would "capitalize on the slaves' willingness to work in spurts rather than
steadily." In accepting this compromise planters responded both to the
resistance of the bondsmen and to the realities of the "preindustrial
side" of the plantations. Although their economic organization promoted
a quasi-industrial discipline, said Genovese, plantations also generated
countervailing pressures and embodied inescapable internal contradictions. Planters had come to terms with the fact that the setting was rural
and the rhythm of work varied with the seasons.[20]

This modified view of resistance overcomes several of the difficulties
of the thesis it seeks to replace. The perpetual sabotage movement
embodied in the concept of day-to-day resistance is, as a general phenomenon, incompatible with the new findings on productivity. The high level
of productivity implies either that such resistance failed dismally, over
and over again, or that it was so limited in extent and localized that it
left aggregate production largely unaffected. Genovese replaces the
image of slaves in a perpetually unsuccessful campaign of sabotage with
one in which slaves strove to modify the most distasteful aspects of the
system in ways that would ameliorate their oppression. Slaves worked
hard but extracted concessions. Masters attempted to exploit these
concessions for their own purposes but, under slave pressure, ended up
making "far greater concessions to the value system and collective sensi-
bility of the quarters than they intended."[21] In this world in which
frontal assaults are suicidal but successful struggles for amelioration of
the worst abuses are possible, an ethic which embraces hard work and
which is responsive to economic inducements is not necessarily an act
of collaboration or a sign of weakness of character. While reformist
rather than revolutionary, such behavior nevertheless emerges as a limited form of struggle for the interest of the slaves. Genovese's thesis
preserves the notion of slave resistance, and even allows for substantial
success of limited goals, while at the same time making slave behavior

consistent with high levels of productivity.

Perhaps the most questionable aspect of the Genovese thesis is his insistence that slaves successfully avoided adhering to a system of regularity. He views the slave attitude toward regularity as a special case of the agrarian, pre-industrial work pattern found widely among those who immigrated to the United States from the farms of Europe. But whereas the Europeans became part of an industrial system that transformed them into suitable industrial workers, "the Africans found themselves drawn into a plantation system, that despite certain similarities to an industrial setting, immensely reinforced traditional values. . . ."[22] This sharp distinction between the regularity of factory production and the seasonality of plantation production is overdrawn, especially for the antebellum era. Many blast furnaces, for example, especially those using charcoal, operated for only part of the year. And textile production, milling, transportation, meat packing, and various other industries tracked by economic historians exhibited sharp variations in level of production over the seasons.[23]

Nor was the seasonality of labor demand as uneven on plantations as Genovese suggests. His insistence that heavy labor requirements were limited largely to a short period at harvest time draws too heavily on the experience of American wheat farms and sugar plantations. In the United States both these crops had relatively short harvest seasons, and thus required a relatively brief period of exceptional exertion. But cotton was a different case. The harvest generally began in late August and usually lasted until late December or early January. While one peak of activity was reached in October, daily cotton-picking records indicate that most of the five-month harvest period was marked by a relatively steady level of work. Nor was the harvest season the only, or even the most demanding, period of pressure on labor. The heaviest demand for labor actually came during the season of cultivation, which extended from mid or late May through mid or late July. The planting season, running from late March to late April, was still another period of heavy labor demand in cotton.[24]

But it is misleading to concentrate exclusively on the labor requirements of cotton in order to ascertain the seasonal work rhythm of slaves, for the planters chose their secondary crops with the aim of smoothing out the seasonal labor requirements of cotton. Corn was so frequently produced in combination with cotton because it could be planted before cotton and harvested either early or late, depending on other pressures. Masters also smoothed the seasonal pattern of labor utilization by scheduling maintenance, new construction, and various indoor tasks during periods when work on crops was slack. As a consequence of such measures the number of days worked showed little variation from season to season. Even when one takes account of seasonal differences in daylight hours, the spring, summer, and fall show roughly equal workweeks ranging between 57 and 60 hours. Although the short period of daylight during the winter led to a significant reduction of the workweek, slaves still averaged about 40 hours per week during these months.[25]

And so masters did succeed in subjugating slaves to the regime of regularity, in transforming them into metaphoric clock punchers. That was one of the features of slavery that made it so repulsive to free men. Masters might celebrate the beauty of assembly lines in the fields, but to free men who valued the independence and flexibility of traditional agrarian ways, nothing could be uglier. In their eyes the rhythm of the gangs was not steady but "plodding," and the men and women who labored in them were not disciplined and efficient but "machine-like" and "stupid."[26]

The critical element of Genovese's thesis, then, is the proposition that struggle for improvement of conditions within the slave system rather than revolutionary assault on the system was the chief form of slave resistance to their oppression. Some scholars have argued that diligence by slaves implies that they must have accepted the morality and objectives of the master class. This view, according to Genovese, over-looks the contradictory forces that influenced the behavior of both slaves and masters. Whatever the motives of the master class, slaves had good reasons of their own to be diligent and to acquire skills. The level of the material conditions that slaves could obtain for themselves and for their children, the capacity to resist encroachments on the integrity of their families, and the opportunity to enlarge the scope for freedom of choice were all related to their effectiveness as workers. On the matter of diet, for example, statistical analysis of the Fisk University and WPA narra-tives of ex-slaves reveals that slaves who relied purely on the rations provided by masters had less varied diets than those who cultivated their own plots or engaged in hunting and fishing. Analysis of the notarial records in New Orleans reveals that slave artisans and craftsmen, at every age, were less than half as likely to have been sold as were ordinary field hands. For slaves, as for most industrial workers of the antebellum era, then, struggle with the system was not political in the usual sense of the term; it was focused, rather, on the protection of the family and on the amelioration of conditions of life for slaves and their children.[27]

THE SEXUAL MORES AND FAMILY NORMS OF SLAVES

Before World War II mainstream histories that described the sexual mores and family norms of slaves generally projected degrading images.[28] Rhodes believed not only that licentiousness was "a natural inclination of the African race," but that slave women, because of their "entire lack of chastity," yielded "without objection, except in isolated cases, to the passion of their master." To Phillips, the family and sexual mores of slaves merited only a few passing references that occupied a small fraction of the space in *American Negro Slavery* allocated to the chapter on slave crime—a chapter that dwelt on the rape of white women by slaves.[29]

These racist stereotypes were anathema to black scholars such as DuBois and E. Franklin Frazier, who set out to discover the true nature of the sexual mores and family norms of slaves. The problem was that most of the readily available commentaries on black life that had survived from the slave period were written by whites who, in one degree or another, shared the view that Africans were licentious and submissive. In circumventing this obstacle, DuBois and Frazier pursued somewhat different strategies, but the conclusions they reached were quite compatible. They, together with Stampp, are the principal authors of the paradigm on the slave family that reigned from the eve of World War II until the early 1970s.

DuBois critically reread such traditional white sources as Olmsted and Weld, selectively abstracting from them those elements which he thought reflected the reality of slave conditions. The central feature of his reinterpretation, as published in his 1908 monograph *The Negro American Family,* was a sharp dichotomy between the family patterns attributed to slaves who were servants and to those who were field hands. Among the house servants, he wrote, "religion and marriage rites received more attention and the Negro monogamic family rose as a dependent offshoot of the feudal slave regime." But among the field hands, especially those who lived under the ruthless regime of the overseer, "there was no family life, no meals, no marriages, no decency, only an endless round of toil and a wild debauch at Christmas time." DuBois emphasized the crippling effect of slavery on the position of the slave father who, he said, lacked "authority . . . to govern or protect his family. His wife could be made his master's concubine, his daughter could be outraged, his son whipped, or he himself sold away without his being able to protest or lift a preventing finger." The position of the mother, DuBois argued, was also deeply undermined. Whether field hand or house servant she could "spend little or no time" in her own home, so "her children had little care or attention." Not only was she "often the concubine of the master or his sons" but she "could at any time be parted" from her husband by the "master's command or by his death or debts." "Such a family . . . ," DuBois concluded, "was a fortuitous agglomeration of atoms."[30]

DuBois's main concern in *The Negro American Family* was not to explain the slave experience but to comment on what he believed to be the disorganization of the Negro family at the turn of the twentieth century—a disorganization that was symbolized, above all, by a black illegitimacy rate that he placed in the neighborhood of 25 percent. Turning to the slave experience to find an explanation for this family disorganization, he concluded that slavery left Negroes with mixed mores. The majority had adopted "the monogamic sex *mores,*" but a substantial minority had not.[31]

In *The Negro Family in the United States,* published in 1939, Frazier returned to the point at which DuBois had ended—the extremely high illegitimacy rate among blacks, which averaged between 10 and 15 percent during the period from World War I to 1930. While DuBois had merely attributed this phenomenon to the incomplete acceptance of the monogamic sex mores, Frazier argued that there was a dual family structure among blacks. The male-headed nuclear family that typified white life was also found among blacks, but this form coexisted with a female-headed family that "continued on a fairly large scale" and that was "tied up with . . . widespread illegitimacy."[32]

Frazier rejected the possibility that this dual structure was a carryover of African life. It was, he contended, a product of the slave experience and subsequent developments. The sexual mores of slaves as well as their notion of family were affected by "the disproportionate number of males in the slave population" and by the "casualness" of sexual contacts. "There were masters who, without any regard for the preferences of their slaves, mated their human chattel as they did their stock." On the other hand the "plantation economy, which was more or less self sufficient, gave numerous opportunities for the expression of individual talent." Thus, there arose "a division of labor that became the basis of social distinctions among the slaves." Following DuBois, Frazier drew a sharp distinction between house servants (who he assumed were preponderantly mulattos) and the field hands, holding that it was the house servants who were the bearers of the nuclear norm and monogamy. He also placed great emphasis on the crucial role of mothers who, despite (or because of) the exigencies of the slave trade, were, unlike slave fathers, rarely torn apart from their children.[33]

The view of slave family life and mores projected by Stampp in *The Peculiar Institution* was consistent with Frazier's but gloomier. He gave only passing mention to those elements of strength on which Frazier dwelt, emphasizing instead the demoralizing factors. First, the masters destroyed the strictly regulated family life and rigid moral code that had prevailed in Africa; then they "more or less encouraged" slaves to live as families and to accept white standards of morality. The family that emerged from this "cultural chaos" lacked "most of the centripetal forces that gave the white family its cohesiveness." The slave woman was "only incidentally a wife, mother, and home-maker," and "the male slave's only crucial function within the family was that of siring off-spring." The consequences were manifold. The typical slave family was matriarchal and "had about it an air of impermanence." "Most fathers and even some mothers regarded their children" with indifference, and sexual promiscuity was widespread.[34]

Discontent with the reigning paradigm on slave family and sexual mores surfaced during the late 1960s. From 1968 through 1972 Herbert Gutman, in a series of papers, most of which are unpublished, began to argue that the black family emerged from bondage with a high degree of stability.[35] John Blassingame, in his study *The Slave Community* published in 1972, wrote that however "frequently the family was broken, it was primarily responsible for the slave's ability to survive on the plantation without becoming totally dependent on and submissive to his master."[36] And Genovese, in *Roll, Jordan, Roll,* published in 1974, held that historians and sociologists had misunderstood the nature of the slave family because "they have read the story of the twentieth century black ghettos backward in time and have assumed a historical continuity with slavery days." The record of evidence, he contended, showed that "slaves created impressive norms of family life, including as much of a nuclear family norm as conditions permitted, and that they entered the postwar social system with a remarkably stable base."[37]

Despite this broad agreement on the need to fashion a new paradigm for slave family life, social and cultural historians struggling with the problem have been divided on certain issues. One of the most important of these is whether the family norms and sexual mores of slaves should be called mixed, as in the judgments of DuBois and Frazier, or whether slaves produced unique norms and mores of their own. Gutman argued passionately against the mixed-mores thesis. While in 1971 Gutman was prepared to counter Frazier's dual-family model merely by insisting that the "black family that emerged from slavery already had a distinct and quite simple nuclear structure,"[38] by 1975 he saw the slave family as embodying a blend of African and indigenous features that could not be described as merely nuclear. In his book *The Black Family in Slavery and Freedom* he argued that slaves had developed unique sexual mores that, although different from the norms of white society, were coherent and conformed to the group's own rules. Under these well-defined mores a girl typically had intercourse fairly early and bore a child, but then settled down with one man and had the rest of her children by him.[39]

Blassingame's initial description of the slave family reflected the influence of Frazier's dual-family and dual-mores model. He did not follow Frazier in limiting the development of the male-headed nuclear family primarily to house slaves, but found instead respect for the monogamous family among all occupational groups. He called attention to striking evidence of the strength of the monogamous family in the autobiographies of ex-slaves, contending that in "no class of American autobiographies is more stress laid upon the importance of stable family life"[40] than in these.

Genovese propounded sexual mores that included elements to be found in the interpretations of DuBois, Frazier, Blassingame, and Gutman. What emerged from his crucible was a distinctive and rather modern blend of sexual freedom for single slaves and Victorian standards for married slaves, especially women. Slaves resisted European "denigration of sex as sinful, dirty, or anything other than delightfully human and pleasurable." Under their flexible standards of sexual morality, "virginity at marriage carried only small prestige" and parents "did not get hysterical if their unmarried daughters got pregnant." On the other hand, Genovese found that "Victorianism made surprising progress in the quarters, especially among slave mothers who worried about their daughter's happiness. . . ." Not only married women but also married men considered marital fidelity a personal and social responsibility. Although lapses of women from a white-inspired standard of premarital sexual morality were treated liberally, postmarital philandering and adultery were considered a serious breach of their own standard of decency.[41]

Blassingame, Genovese, and Gutman differed again on the role of external factors, particularly the role of the masters, in shaping the family norms and sexual mores of the slaves. Blassingame recognized the influence of masters but emphasized the role of the white church in attempting to restrain masters from breaking up families and in promoting fidelity among married slaves. Genovese also recognized the coexistence of destructive and stabilizing factors in the policies of the masters, but in his portrait the stabilizing factors were more conspicuous. "The masters," he said, "understood the strength of the marital and family ties among their slaves well enough to see in them a powerful means of social control," and their desire to exploit the family for this conservative purpose tended to constrain the more destructive impulses of the system. Families were broken by the slave trade, but such sales "might be delayed or avoided because it would cause resentment among . . . normally good workers." Even in a regime in which masters took account of the resistance offered by slaves, slave women still "fell victims to white lust, but many escaped because the whites knew they had black men who would rather die than stand idly by." So strong was the resistance that it curbed "white sexual aggression" against married women. Genovese allowed masters to have a stronger imprint on the content of family life than did Blassingame. Slaveowners, he said, sought to promote order in slave households, fearing "that domestic abuse would undermine the morale of the labor force." But they were wise enough to limit their personal intervention, often allowing drivers and slave preachers to usurp "the role of *paterfamilias.*" Sensible masters even "encouraged a limited sexual division of labor among their slaves and saw some advantage in strengthening the power of the male in the household." Plantation policy was thus designed to deal with the powerful forces welling up from within the slave quarter. The end product was a new set of family norms.[42]

Gutman largely bypassed the role of masters and of white clergy in the development of the slave family. The family was cast by slaves according to their own design and almost completely from their own resources. The issue was not the interaction between masters and slaves but the interactions between the experiences of slaves born in the New World and the African culture from which their parents and grandparents were torn. The aims and actions of the planters with respect to the slave family were reduced to the level of background noise.

Another disputed question is the extent to which marriages were destroyed by the slave trade. Gutman's examination of the birth and death lists of six plantations indicated that among slaves who survived into their forties most unions were long lasting, broken usually by the death of one of the partners, although he also emphasized the destructive role of the slave trade in separating children and other kin from the family. Genovese argued that the extent to which marriages were destroyed by that trade is less than has been supposed, emphasizing instead the "painful uncertainty" created by "the potential for forced separation—whatever the ultimate measure of its realization."[43] Blassingame, on the other hand, believed that the slave trade was so extensive and masters were so willing to subordinate marriage bonds to profits that roughly one-third of the unions "were dissolved by masters" and he suggested that this estimate, which he derived from records of the Freedmen's Bureau, may be understated.[44]

These unresolved issues call attention to the critical importance of quantitative consideration in the effort to construct a new paradigm on the slave family. Quantitative considerations insinuate themselves not only into the debate over broken marriages but into every other major point at issue. Whether the division is between Stampp and Genovese, between Blassingame and Gutman, or any other combination, what is invariably at issue is the frequency distribution of one or another attribute of the family. When Stampp, for example, said that the slave family was matriarchal in form, he did not contend that the mother's role was always more important than the father's. And when Genovese responded that husbands easily dominated their wives, he did not rule out the opposite situation. Differences over the definition of family norms turn primarily on disagreements over what was typical and what was exceptional behavior.[45]

THE AUTONOMY AND UNIFORMITY OF
SLAVE CULTURE

Underlying the debate over the slave family are two fundamental issues that permeate every aspect of the discussion of slave culture. Whether the topic is the work and resistance ethic, the slave family, slave religion, or slave perceptions of themselves and their oppressors, the discussions of historians are beset by unresolved differences of opinion regarding the autonomy and the uniformity of slave culture. In this context "autonomy" refers to the degree to which slaves produced a distinctive slave culture that was independent of white influence; "uniformity" refers to the degree to which slaves shared common views and responded in similar ways to the various aspects of their lives, their circumstances, and their physical and spiritual futures. Before probing further into the nature of these disagreements, however, it is important to define their boundaries.

All of the current investigators of slave culture believe that the culture that arose among slaves was an adaptive response to their circumstances. Since their circumstances were, to a considerable degree, shaped by white masters and overseers, all the scholars acknowledge at least the indirect influence of whites on this culture. The disagreements on autonomy turn on the extent to which slaves were able to choose which aspects of white-imposed technology, skills, attitudes, and values they would accept. Disagreements on autonomy also involve the extent to which slave culture incorporated elements that were drawn from sources other than the European heritage of whites—from either their African heritage or those spontaneously invented by slaves from the circumstances under which they lived.

Similarly, historians of slave culture generally agree that regardless of the idiosyncrasies of individual masters, local customs, and local laws, most slaves shared some elements of an African heritage, accepted various elements of Christianity, valued kinship, and sought varying degrees of independence from their ubiquitous and powerful oppressors. They also agree that the common experiences of oppression and African heritage were not by themselves sufficient to provide all slaves in the New World with a common culture. The material and social circumstances that served to shape slave culture varied over both space and time.

Household organization, language, planter policies, policies of religious and secular authorities, demographic rates, conditions of labor, slave social structure, the extent of contact with whites, and the extent of direct contact with Africans were so different from one slave colony to another that they produced quite different slave cultures in the various colonies despite the common African heritage and the common oppression experienced by all slaves in the New World.

Disagreements about the uniformity of slave culture include such issues as the intensity of carryovers of African culture and whether African heritage, except in a highly attenuated sense, could have provided slaves with a unifying cultural outlook since the ethnic groups of Africa from which the slaves were drawn were differentiated from each other by a myriad of languages, religions, and customs as well as by a variety of political and economic institutions. In the case of U.S. slaves, a central issue which is more often implicit than explicit is the extent to which cultural norms that were common on plantations with large numbers of slaves who lived out their lives mainly in a black world (having little contact with their white masters) and who were (within certain sharply defined limits) largely self-governing could have been transmitted to the majority of slaves who lived on relatively small plantations, which usually had fewer than five slave households and in which slaves were usually under the constant supervision and regulation of their masters.

Throughout *The Peculiar Institution* Stampp emphasized the markedly different circumstances and conditions of life for slaves on small (or medium) and large plantations. On small plantations masters and slaves usually worked alongside each other in the fields without a rigid division of labor and without excessive emphasis on profits. They often ate in the same room (if not at the same table), shared the same food, belonged to the same churches, and were exposed to the same health risks. Management was a matter "of direct personal relationships between individuals" who knew one another, undistorted by the intervention of overseers, and "hard driving" (work so intense it was injurious to health) "seldom occurred on smaller plantations and farms." But closeness had its burdens, since the relationship between masters and slaves could never be one of equality. A slave would warrant his master's affection only if he conformed constantly to "the subtle etiquette that governed his relations with his master," if he carefully observed "the fine line between friskiness and insubordination, between cuteness and insolence." To be the recipient of his master's paternalism, said Stampp, a slave had to adopt the pose of "a fawning dependent," a relationship that robbed slaves of their confidence and promoted a "process of infantilization."[46]

On large plantations, however, relationships between masters and slaves were generally quite distant and, with the exception of house servants, were nearly always mediated by overseers who were typically poorly educated, poorly motivated, and inadequate to their tasks. The division of labor among slaves was rigid, with slaves assigned to specialized occupations, some of which required fairly complex craft skills. Rarely content with the bare subsistence that satisfied many smaller planters, masters of large slaveholdings "had the businessman's interest in maximum production without injury to their capital" and so required their overseers, on pain of discharge if they failed, to have slaves "labor vigorously as many hours as there was daylight." On such plantations, "excessively heavy labor routines" were tolerated, if not sanctioned, by masters, and "slaves were more frequently overworked by calloused tyrants than overindulged by mellow patriarchs."[47]

Large plantations had another aspect. They permitted slaves to live together in close-knit communities—the slave quarters—where they could develop a life of their own, relatively free of "humiliating contacts with the whites," and where "they could express their thoughts and feelings . . . amid a wide circle of friends." In such communities slaves produced "their own internal class structure" and "social hierarchy." This stratification was not merely the product of the occupational hierarchy created by the masters, but "resulted from an impelling force within the slaves themselves," from their "quest for personal prestige" and for "recognition of their worth as individuals." Stampp stressed the loyalty of slaves in the quarters to one another and their solidarity in finding ways to outwit masters, to resist the encroachments on their lives, and to turn the balance between labor and compensation as far in their direction as was feasible.[48]

This latitude associated with a relatively large slave quarter and the sense of solidarity among those in the quarter stimulated a notion of leadership among slaves that departed significantly from the occupational and social hierarchy promoted by masters. Stampp argued that the "management of whites" was as central to these slaves as the management of Negroes was to the masters. Early in life children learned from their parents "how to behave around the master and other whites," while adult newcomers to the quarter were "immediately initiated" into its rites and advised on how to outwit the master while avoiding the lash. Sometimes those who provided this sort of leadership were artisans, drivers, or domestics who, because of their status, were both better off materially than the majority of slaves and better positioned to learn how to deal with masters and other whites, and who could, from time to time, assist runaways and other rebels. But others were men and women who won their distinction in the quarter because of their success in challeng-

ing the master's discipline or because of their "practical wisdom," or
their apparently "mystical powers." Masters of large plantations were
aware, Stampp said, of slave preachers and other leaders who had a
"magical sway over the minds and opinions of the rest." Some masters
even allowed unsupervised religious meetings, even though it was in
violation of the law, but in other cases such meetings were covertly
organized by slaves. These unsupervised observances were vastly preferred by slaves to services at regular churches because they allowed slaves
to "express themselves freely and interpret the Christian faith to their
own satisfaction."[49]

Masters were often content to permit such meetings and to leave
slaves in the quarters to their own devices in other respects as well, so
long as they did not become troublesome. This latitude allowed slaves
to develop certain distinctive views and cultural characteristics. On plantations that were not only large but located in regions where blacks were
the predominant population, especially if they were relatively isolated (as
on the sea islands off South Carolina and Georgia), slaves retained more
of their African heritage and wove it in novel ways into their folklore,
their music, and their religion. Their folklore combined legends from
Africa with their "new experiences in America" and often reflected "with
charming symbolism the story of the endless warfare between black and
white men." These tales "made virtues of such qualities as wit, strategy,
and deceit—the weapons of the weak in their battles with the strong."
The songs of slaves expressed their sorrows and their aspirations, revealing "the yearnings which they dared not, or could not, more than half
express." They were a "unique blend of 'Africanisms,' of Protestant
hymns and revival songs, and of the feelings and emotions" of slaves
about their lot.[50]

Despite the distinctive aspects of life in these large slave quarters,
Stampp did not believe that slaves were able to produce a truly independent and articulated Afro-American culture that was embraced by the
generality of U.S. slaves. To be left alone in some places and at some
times was, in his view, not enough for such a transformation. Not only
was the degree of slave autonomy highly circumscribed, even on fairly
large plantations, but there was little connection between slaves across
these large plantations. Even when a plantation provided the residents
with a world of their own, that world was limited to the few square miles
surrounding their cabins—to an "island beyond which were strange
places"[51] that the slaves heard about but rarely encountered.

It was not just the absence of contact, Stampp stressed, but the
absence of power that circumscribed the cultural opportunities of slaves.
Bondage deprived them of the institutions needed to fully develop and
propagate a new culture, including "the authority to apply vigorous

sanctions against those who violated or repudiated their own traditions."
Slaves were able to fashion only certain limited institutions and cultural
forms, which varied greatly from one plantation to another depending
on the personalities and policies of masters, the size of the slave community, and the personalities and skill of its leaders; but bondsmen did not
give rise to anything that might be described as "cultural nationalism."
Under the exceedingly unequal power relationships, what the generality
of slaves could develop, Stampp concluded, was far less than a new
culture. As long as they remained in bondage blacks were caught in a
"twilight zone between two ways of life."[52]

Stampp's depiction of slave culture stimulated divergent responses.
Some scholars, building on his description of the awesome repressive
power of the masters, went on to compare plantations to concentration
camps, prisons, and insane asylums. As in all such institutions, they
argued, the extreme power brought to bear against the inmates precluded
the type of self-conscious, essentially political resistance movement described by Stampp. The repressive power was so great, argued Stanley
Elkins, that it not only precluded political resistance, but actually reduced the typical slave to infantile dependence. Thus, what Stampp
described as one of the tendencies of the slave system Elkins made the
predominant personality trait of adult slaves generally.[53]

Most scholars believed that Elkins's view was too extreme, but his
critics were divided on the degree of his exaggeration. George Fredrickson and Christopher Lasch argued that although the comparison of
plantations with concentration camps was overdrawn, a comparison with
prisons or insane asylums was appropriate. Plantations were not institutions aimed at the destruction of slaves but at the strict control of their
behavior. What developed on plantations, then, was something between
infantilization and politicized resistance. Like prison inmates, slaves
responded to the severe repression on the plantations by seeking personal strategies for survival. That strategy allowed for episodes of non-
cooperation, but the main thrust of the strategy was to beat the system
at its own game by adopting an "institutional personality" and seeking
favors from masters whenever they could. The real horror of slavery,
they concluded, was that "slaves (even in their intransigence) mentally
identified themselves with the system that bound and confined them."[54]

Other scholars have criticized Stampp for deeply underestimating the
extent to which slaves were able to shape their own culture. Far from
living "in a twilight zone between two ways of life," said Thomas L.
Webber, American slaves

> fashioned a new culture from both the culture fountain of the African
> past and the crucible of their experiences under slavery in the South.

Slave culture had at its heart a set of cultural themes, forms of artistic expression, a religion, a family pattern, and a community structure which set blacks apart from whites and enabled them to form and control a world of their own values and definitions.[55]

Webber agreed with Stampp's contention that masters used all of the instruments of power at their command to shape slaves into their image of an appropriate slave. Their primary objective was to train slaves in all the jobs related to the running of a plantation, ranging from the most technical artisanal crafts to field labor. However, masters realized that to run a profitable plantation they also had to motivate slaves to use their skills effectively. To accomplish this end masters did not rely on a system of reward and punishment alone, but sought every means of inculcating slaves in "a carefully constructed set of attitudes."[56] To pave the way for effective indoctrination, masters cut off all access to written materials, strictly limited direct contact with persons off the plantation, and tried to prevent secret or unsupervised meetings among slaves belonging to their plantation. The message of planters to their slaves from early childhood on was that Negroes were innately inferior to whites and that without the benevolent protection of their powerful masters they would become the prey of hostile whites or fall into the extreme poverty that afflicted free labor, especially free blacks. They were also told that it was their good luck to belong to a kindly master and not to a cruel one—a point that always carried an implicit threat. In addition to their own exhortations masters made use of religious instruction to convince slaves of the inevitability of their condition and the benevolence of the masters.

It is at this point that the interpretations of Stampp and Webber diverge sharply. For while Stampp granted the masters substantial successes, Webber stressed the wide difference between what masters preached and what slaves learned. In Webber's portrait few slaves were misled by white propaganda. The majority clearly recognized that the interests of whites, especially the interests of the masters, were not those of the quarter. They held masters "responsible for most of the sorrow that blacks experienced under slavery." They believed that masters and their ministers misrepresented Christian principles, that slavery was not God's design but a sin, which could be corrected only by emancipation. Slaves also believed that God was on their side and that God showed His anger with masters by "sending suffering and sickness to plague the unrepentant" South. While accepting Christianity slaves consciously modified it in ways that suited them, allowing for "a spirit world which played an active role in the earthly world," influencing day-to-day life in direct and immediate ways. They "felt a special kinship towards Jesus," because He "had experienced pain and grief."[57]

Webber did not see among slaves the awe of planter power that impressed Stampp. While Stampp found few slaves who "could free themselves altogether from the notion that their masters were 'invested with a sort of sacredness,' "[58] Webber argued that "members of the quarter . . . thought of themselves not only as morally superior to whites but as superior" in work, energy, discipline, and style. Nevertheless, they were willing to take from white culture anything that would advance their own interest. Despite the many impediments placed in their way, slaves yearned to learn to read and write, and by "impressive efforts . . . on their own behalf,"[59] some were able to do so. But most of all slaves yearned for freedom—not just freedom in heaven but on earth.

How could slaves develop a culture that ran so counter to the one that masters sought to impose on them? How could they succeed in transmitting to others a culture so subversive to the designs of the master class? The key to this success, said Webber, was the ability of slaves to turn the quarter into "a society within a society."[60] The institutions that nurtured and protected the counterculture, that gave it cohesiveness and stability, were the family, the peer group, the clandestine congregation, and folk music and stories. The family preserved elements of African culture by transmitting stories from grandparents and parents to their young; it promoted responsibility by teaching older children to care for the younger ones; it transmitted skills needed for household tasks, for hunting and fishing, for artisanal crafts, and for reading and writing; and it interpreted scripture for the young. Through their peer group young slaves formed lasting relationships outside of the family. With the greater freedom allowed to them, children could explore the neighborhood beyond the plantation and exchange information. The mutual experiences of childhood produced strong bonds that promoted solidarity in adulthood.

"Nearly all quarter communities organized their own clandestine congregations without the sanction or participation of plantation authorities." These congregations, said Webber, served to "perpetuate" not only the community's "religious ideals and beliefs but crucial secular understandings, values, and attitudes." The heads of these congregations were usually slave preachers who had earned leadership through their great faith, their "knowledge of the Bible and true Christianity," and their "demonstrated commitment to the welfare of the community." Such meetings were usually held at night out in the fields after the master and overseer had completed their rounds. Because several communities sometimes participated, these congregations provided slaves with a means of exchanging information as well as a vehicle for worship in their own way. By placing them "within the arms of the black church," clandestine congregations allowed blacks, "while still legally slaves under the white man's political system," to "experience moments of peace, ecstasy, fellowship, and Freedom."[61]

The songs and stories of slaves were, according to Webber, a medium by which slave values were transmitted, and they also served to kindle these values. "Story telling often took the form of a community happening" that gave slaves, especially children, "a sense of communal spirit and camaraderie" and an "identification with the larger community of American slaves." No matter how far slaves might be sent "from their home quarter, these feelings of communality and kinship would be always rekindled"[62] by the singing of a song or the telling of a story which, although differing in detail from region to region, embodied similar values throughout the antebellum South.

SOURCES AND PERCEPTIONS

The leading scholars of slave culture have stressed the many difficulties that arise from the types of evidence with which they are forced to work. The publications, the private letters, and the other papers of slaveholders "can hardly be accepted as 'objective,' " writes Genovese, "especially when they purport to describe slave attitudes." He also notes the limitation of such other white sources as the accounts of travelers to the South which, even when they were not written by persons with axes to grind, "varied considerably" with the "talent, length of stay, and social attitudes" of the writers. Nevertheless, Genovese and the other scholars in the forefront of research on slave culture continue to make use of these sources (just as DuBois and Frazier did) because, as Genovese put it, "no comprehensive treatment can afford to ignore them."[63]

Perhaps the greatest advance in the reconstruction of slave culture has been the systematic utilization of black testimony, which until recent years had been largely neglected. Blassingame has favored the published autobiographies of runaway slaves because they represent "the largest body of life histories dealing with the intimate details" of slave life, and because they reveal "what went on in the minds of black men."[64] Genovese is more skeptical of this source than Blassingame. He argues that even when these autobiographies were not strongly influenced by the abolitionists who edited them, they remain "the accounts of highly exceptional men and women and can be as misleading in their honesty and accuracy of detail as in the fabrications."[65]

Although Genovese has made use of the fugitive autobiographies, he favors the interviews of thousands of ex-slaves conducted in the 1920s and 1930s, first by scholars at Fisk University and at Southern University and later by the Federal Writers Project of the Works Project Administration (WPA). He and some other scholars believe these inter-

views are a better source of information about slave life than the autobiographies of the runaways, not only because they are more numerous,
but because they represent the broader slave population. Whatever their
advantages, the interviews are less than a perfect source of evidence. In
the edition of over 2,300 interviews published by the Greenwood Publishing Company in 1972, for example, residents of the state of Arkansas
provided nearly 30 percent of the interviews, although that state had less
than 2 percent of the slave population in 1850.[66]

The preponderance of whites among the interviewers also troubles
some scholars. Blassingame suspects that the ex-slaves were more reserved in speaking to white interviewers and may even have given
misleading replies to some questions. The age of the ex-slaves at the time
of the interviews is another possible source of bias. With two-thirds over
age 80 when interviewed, it is possible that time had dimmed memories
of the harshness of their experiences. Blassingame suggests that ex-
slaves who managed to live to such ripe ages might have been better off
than the majority of slaves. Some have argued that superannuated slaves
who were interviewed during the depression of the 1930s would have
looked back favorably on the security of slavery. Others believe that the
narratives may confuse the memories of slave and post-emancipation
experiences.[67]

Spirituals and folklore are a third major source of black testimony
about life under slavery. According to Sterling Stuckey, the study of folk
materials provides an effective way of getting " 'inside' slaves to discover
what bondsmen thought about their condition."[68] A similar point was
made by Lawrence W. Levine, who argued that folk materials refuted the
view that slaves were "inarticulate intellectual ciphers." Folk materials,
he continued, showed that they were "actors in their own right who not
only responded to their situation but often affected it in crucial ways."
Levine, who worked his way through thousands of Negro songs, folktales, proverbs, aphorisms, jokes, verbal games, and narrative oral
poems, was keenly aware of their limitations as a historical source: Dates,
locations, and creators of folk materials were hard if not impossible to
determine. Some folklore was censored by editors while other offending
material was banished completely, neither published nor preserved; and
the black narrators "were often extremely selective and circumspect in
choosing the songs and stories they related to the dignified whites" who
came to collect them.[69]

Whatever the category of slave testimony, two points are commonly
emphasized by the scholars who have worked on these documents: One
is the potential pitfalls of this type of evidence; the other is a confidence
in their ability to cope "with altered documents, with consciously or
unconsciously biased firsthand accounts," and "with manuscript collec-

tions that were deposited in archives only after being filtered through
. . . overprotective hands."[70] According to Genovese, an experienced
investigator can tell "what is and what is not typical—what does and
does not ring true."[71] Webber argues that "although it would be extremely difficult to make an adequate analysis of the life or character of
any individual slave" from the material in his or her autobiography or
interview, "a satisfactory analysis" of the culture of the slave quarter "as
a whole can be achieved when the sources are studied in their en-
tirety."[72] Virtually all scholars of slave culture agree, as Genovese put
it, on the need to "weigh different kinds of testimony against each other"
and they "feel safest" in their conclusions "when various kinds of
sources" tend "to agree on what, how, and where, even if they disagree
on interpretation and value judgment."[73]

More recently cliometricians have sought to utilize quantitative evidence, much of it circumstantial, to contribute to the debate over slave
culture.[74] Coding, quantifying, and analyzing data from such sources as
the probate records of southern courts, the birth and death lists included
in the surviving business records of large plantations, and the ex-slave
interviews, cliometricians have been able to construct distributions of
attributes relevant to a number of the points now at issue.[75] Crawford,
for example, was able to evaluate some of the biases thought to be
present in the ex-slave interviews contained in the edition published by
Greenwood in 1972. To test the hypothesis that the experience of the
Great Depression led ex-slaves to look back favorably on the security of
slavery, Crawford compared the responses of slaves interviewed by scholars at Fisk University in 1929 with those interviewed by the WPA in
the 1930s and found that the views of the two groups were quite similar.[76]

Crawford also searched for evidence that the responses of ex-slaves
were affected by the race of the interviewers. He found suspicious differences in the responses to several questions, but these differences disappeared or became slight when Crawford took account of the characteristics of the ex-slaves who were interviewed by each group. The difference
in the characterization of the diet reported by black and white interviewers is a case in point. Among ex-slaves interviewed by blacks, 23.5
percent reported an inadequate diet, but among those interviewed by
whites, the proportion reporting inadequate diets was only 14.3 percent—a gap of 9.2 points. When Crawford controlled for plantation size,
black interviewers still reported a higher percentage of inadequate diets
on large plantations, but the margin of difference between black and
white interviewers had declined to 5.5 percent and was no longer statistically significant. Moreover, among ex-slaves from small plantations the
relationship ran in the opposite direction, with white interviewers actu-

ally reporting a higher percentage of inadequate diets than black interviewers. Crawford concluded that what initially appeared to be an interviewer bias "was largely due to the failure to standardize for the distribution of plantation sizes within the black and white interviewer
samples."[77]

More generally, Crawford's statistical analysis of the interviews confirmed the basic assessment of other scholars: Taken as a whole, the
Greenwood edition represents "an important source of information about
slave experiences" but it "does not always replicate the proportions in
which various attributes existed in the overall slave population."[78] He
also found that when the investigator paid proper attention to such
matters as the plantation size, the location of the plantation, the principal
crop, and the occupation that the ex-slave or his or her parents had held,
it was possible to define subsamples of attributes that were representative
of the overall slave population as well as of particular subgroups.

A point that emerges over and over again from Crawford's analysis
is that the size of the plantation was a major determinant of the quality
of slave life. On such matters as the severity of punishment, the supply
of clothing, the occupation of the slave, the stability of the family, and
the uses of leisure time, the experiences of slaves living on small plantations differed significantly from those living on large ones. Crawford's
analysis also suggests that the overrepresentation of large plantations in
the sources that particular scholars have favored may have affected their
generalizations about the nature of slave culture. This point can be
illustrated by considering in somewhat greater depth Crawford's findings
on the connection between the structure of slave families and plantation
size.

Using the Greenwood sample of interviews, Crawford was able to
construct a distribution of the households in which 742 slaves under age
13 were raised. He found that 66 percent lived in two-parent families,
24 percent in single-parent families (nearly all of which were headed by
mothers), and the rest (about 10 percent) either in the master's house
or alone in the quarters. The large share of children raised in two-parent
households tends to sustain the belief of Gutman and Genovese that the
black family emerged from slavery with a "remarkably stable base." It
was, at least, a more stable base than most slavery scholars had realized
before the early 1970s. On the other hand, one-third of slaves under age
13 were living in households from which one or both parents were
absent. Crawford's analysis of the reasons for the large proportion of
single-parent households revealed that in about 60 percent of the cases,
the families were broken by the slave trade or by other features of the
slave system.[79] So Frazier appears to have been correct when he called
attention to a dual family structure, although he underestimated the

prevalence of two-parent families and he incorrectly assumed that such families were much more likely to be found among house servants and artisans than among field hands.

Size of plantation was far more important than occupation in determining household structure. Mother-headed families were 50 percent more frequent on plantations with 15 or fewer slaves than on large ones. These smaller units also had a disproportionately large share of the divided-residence households (families in which the father and mother lived on different plantations for most of the week). Although plantations with 15 or fewer slaves contained 43 percent of the slave population in 1850, they accounted for nearly two-thirds of all slaves living in divided residences and for over 60 percent of the slaves in one-parent residences. These figures suggest that the conventional family structure was under greater pressure on small than on large units. As Crawford points out, on plantations with 15 or fewer slaves, just one out of three children lived in "fully formed" or conventional households; on plantations of 50 or more slaves, the proportion was reversed.

These proportions pointed out by Crawford help to explain why Gutman found so much more stability and uniformity in the slave family than did Blassingame, Genovese or Stampp. Gutman's portrait of the slave family was based primarily on his intensive study of the records of six large slaveholdings, located mainly in preponderantly black counties. He chose these particular plantation records because they had exceptional birth registers that permitted him to investigate the marriage patterns of successive generations, to compare the names of children with those of parents and other kin, and to study the evolution of slave families over time. The best of these record sets for his purposes was that of the Good Hope plantation in South Carolina, which toward the end of the antebellum era had about 175 slaves. From its birth register Gutman was able to reconstruct the genealogies of slaves for up to five generations, and to observe the extent of intermarriage among kin, the stability of marital relations, and evolving patterns of naming children. It was on the basis of this set of records that Gutman originally developed the thesis that over time U.S. slaves had evolved a distinctive set of marital and sexual mores which involved prenuptial conceptions, relatively long-lasting marriages, a taboo against first-cousin marriages, and a marked tendency to name sons after fathers. In these records Gutman saw evidence that dramatically affirmed the important cultural role of slave fathers and the independence of slave traditions from their white masters, evidence that slave culture of the late antebellum era had its "roots in adaptive slave practices that had begun much earlier."[80]

Records fit to study the intergenerational patterns that so concerned Gutman were not likely to be generated on small plantations. All but one

of the six plantations in his sample had over 100 slaves, and the sixth
had 47 slaves. A sample composed of such large plantations was quite
likely to give much more of an impression of family stability than a
representative sample of the entire slave population. The plantations in
Gutman's sample were exceptional even among the large plantations
because they were growing so rapidly. Between 1838 and 1857, the
Good Hope plantation grew twice as fast as the overall slave population,
and between 1842 and 1861 the Watson plantation (another of his six)
grew nearly three times as fast as the overall slave population. Such
rapidly growing, successful plantations were less likely to suffer the
disruptions to families that stemmed from declining or disbanded plantations. Rapidly growing plantations, because of their exceptional vital
rates and age structures, tend to give a misleadingly low impression of
the average age of mothers at their first birth. Gutman put that age at
about 18, which, as James Trussell and Richard H. Steckel pointed out,
was biased downward by about three years.[81]

The last point is important because it affected Gutman's generalizations about the sexual mores of adolescent slaves. Assuming that 18 was
the typical age of mothers at first birth and that the average age of
menarche (the onset of reproductive capacity) came relatively late for
slave women (about 16 or 17), Gutman inferred that slave women generally began their sexual lives at extremely young ages and, unlike white
women who were beset by "Victorian" values, seldom refrained from
having sexual intercourse prior to wedlock. Slave women, he concluded,
generally had a child as soon as they were physically capable of having
one and not necessarily by the man that they would eventually marry.[82]

Richard H. Steckel, working with a larger and more representative
sample of data, found evidence of significant variation in the sexual
practices on plantations of different sizes and in different regions, including evidence that there was more abstention from sexual intercourse
among slave women than suggested by Gutman.[83] His data revealed that
the proportion of slave women living through their childbearing years
without ever bearing a child was higher on large plantations (19 percent)
than on small plantations (about 10 percent), and higher on the cotton
farms of Georgia and Louisiana (16 percent) than on the tobacco and
wheat farms of Virginia (8 percent). Such high rates of childlessness
cannot be explained by physiological sterility. For populations as fecund
as the U.S. slave population had been, sterility rates are generally less
than 5 percent. It thus appears that roughly 10 percent of slave women
either largely abstained from sexual intercourse until they reached the
end of their childbearing lives or else practiced contraception so effectively that they avoided births throughout these years.

That systematic, sustained practice of contraception was a characteristic of slave society is not sustained by the data in Steckel's samples. His sources show that the average age of women at the birth of their last child was close to 40. Moreover, for women whose children died within three months of birth, the average interval to the next birth was just 19 months. Both of these statistics are characteristic of non-contraceptive societies. An analysis of living arrangements also argues against contraception. Steckel's study of plantation registers indicated that few of the women who remained childless throughout the childbearing ages lived with a man. The proportion of couples who were childless was at a level that can be explained by physiological sterility. In other words, infertility was primarily a characteristic of women who did not cohabit with men.

There is also evidence that a large proportion of women who eventually bore children abstained from sexual intercourse for a substantial period after they became fecund. This possibility is suggested by the finding that the average age of women at the birth of their first child was about 21 while the average age of menarche was about 14.5.[84] The relatively early age of puberty implies that if slave women had been having sexual intercourse regularly from menarche on, they would typically have had a child by age 16 or 17. It follows that there was an average interval of adolescent abstention from sexual intercourse lasting at least three years. All told, the sexual mores of slave women appear to have resulted in not making use of roughly one-fifth of their childbearing potential.

Steckel's findings do not necessarily preclude regular sexual intercourse before marriage, but they do indicate that such behavior was far from universal. A substantial proportion of slave women must have abstained from sexual intercourse during much of their adolescent years. Further evidence that marriage triggered the beginning of sexual intercourse for many adolescents and young adults is provided by the marked seasonal pattern in the first births. Steckel shows that the first-birth pattern was correlated with the seasonal pattern of marriages, which were concentrated after the harvest and also in the slack period between the end of cultivation and the beginning of harvest. The correlation implies that for many adolescent women sexual intercourse began either with marriage or in immediate anticipation of marriage.

Both Crawford and Steckel call attention to several factors that were more likely to destabilize family life on small plantations than on large ones. Sexual relationships between whites (mainly men) and blacks (mainly women) was one of the most disruptive of these factors. The point here is not only that the rape of black women by white men was both deeply traumatic and destructive of family life, but that even when interracial unions were spawned by mutual affection, they could not lead to conventional family life because southern laws generally prohibited such unions.[85] Crawford's study of the ex-slave interviews revealed that in one out of every six mother-headed families, the father was white. He also discovered that the probability of having a white father was considerably higher on small than on large plantations. It was also higher if the mother worked in the master's house than in the fields. Very similar findings emerged from Steckel's analysis of data in the manuscript schedules of the 1860 census, which indicated that, on average, 1 out of every 10 slave children was a mulatto. Using a larger sample than could be obtained from the ex-slave interviews and a more powerful statistical technique, Steckel was able to relate a number of variables to the proportion of mulatto children reported on a given slaveholding. He found that this proportion was seven times as high on a farm of 10 slaves engaged in mixed farming in a border state than it was on a cotton plantation of 75 slaves in the deep South. Two other factors that strongly affected the probability of having a mulatto child were the ratio of whites to blacks in the area of the plantation and residence in a city. The proportion of mulatto children was highest on small slave units in large cities (which were predominantly white); it was lowest on large plantations in the rice-growing regions (where the density of white settlement was low).[86]

The failure to take adequate account of the differences between slave experiences and culture on large and small plantations is neither a new problem nor one confined to the characterization of the slave family, nor one which entraps only unwary or inexperienced scholars. It is more than three decades since Stampp called this problem to the attention of slavery specialists and virtually every scholar who has been concerned with slave culture, including myself, has on one issue or another fallen victim to it. Part of the problem is that for many issues of slave culture the best, often the only, documents that have survived are those of large plantations. Moreover, the extent to which various bodies of evidence are dominated by experiences of slaves from large plantations is not always obvious. Nor is it necessarily obvious which cultural characteristics will vary with plantation size. Sometimes the true relationship is obscured by other, poorly understood variables which are, for that reason, inadequately controlled. The numerous mistakes that have been made in estimating the average age of mothers at the birth of their first child is a case in point. When Engerman and I originally calculated this statistic in the early 1970s, we found that age at first birth was lower on large than on small plantations. It was only several years later, after James Trussell called our attention to a powerful statistical technique (the singulate mean) that would control for the age structure of plantations, for their rates of growth, for their mortality rates, and for other variables that were obscuring the true underlying relationship, that we discovered that women on small plantations actually had lower ages at first birth than women on large plantations.[87]

This correction was not merely a technical flourish. It was one of a series of discoveries that served to reveal that the freedom of slaves to search for marital partners was more circumscribed on large plantations than on small ones. Masters on large plantations generally placed strict limits on marriages across plantations or completely prohibited them. The banning of cross-plantation marriages made family life more stable on large plantations since such marriages were vulnerable to unpredictable circumstances that might affect the owner of either slave. If requiring slaves to marry within the plantation increased family stability, that boon was achieved at a heavy cost to the slaves. A significant proportion of adults who could not find mates on their own plantation were forced to remain single for large parts, if not all, of their lives. Thus, slavery tended to destabilize slave marriages in a variety of ways, some of which were inherent in the system.

I have emphasized the differences in the stability of slave families and of variations in sexual mores on large and small plantations in order to demonstrate that this aspect of slave culture was far from uniform. The families of slaves varied in significant ways because of objective differences in the circumstances of slaves. One should not, however, exaggerate the differences. Despite the prevalence of single-parent and divided-residence families, the majority of slave children on plantations with 15 or fewer slaves were still raised in households presided over by both parents. And although slave women on small plantations generally bore their first child a year earlier than women on large plantations, the average period of adolescent abstention from sexual intercourse was still about two years.

Disagreements among scholars of slave culture regarding the nature of the sexual and family mores of slaves thus appear to be related in part to the bodies of evidence on which they have focused. The varied sources employed by Blassingame and Genovese suggested greater pressures on the slave family, a larger degree of white influence, and greater vulnerability to the economic forces that affected the cotton, sugar, rice, and tobacco kingdoms than Gutman inferred from his sources. While Blassingame and Genovese saw more strength and autonomy in slave families than did Stampp, there was a clear line of continuity between their studies and his. Most of the pressures tending to undermine the integrity of the slave family that Stampp saw also appear in their studies, but Blassingame and Genovese differ from Stampp in their emphasis on the drive of slaves to counter these destructive tendencies and their degrees of success in doing so. Here again the much greater use of ex-slave narratives by Blassingame and Genovese, while not the only factor, appears to have contributed significantly to their more optimistic views.

Implicit assumptions about plantation size are also deeply embedded in current characterizations of the culture of the slave quarter and of the relative autonomy of that culture from white influence. The point at issue here is not whether substantial and largely autonomous slave quarters existed, but where they were located and how wide a cross section of the slave population they embraced. Most current descriptions of the slave quarters are so vague on this point that they raise a series of issues which need to be addressed before the debate over the autonomy of slave culture can be adequately resolved. How numerous did the slaves of a plantation have to be before they constituted a "substantial" community? How large did the slave community have to be before it could produce its "own internal class structure"[88] filled with domestics, artisans, and foremen as well as such customary leaders as preachers, midwives, slave doctors, and conjurers? How many plantations had quarters consisting of two rows of slave cabins that formed a street that was "several hundred yards away from the 'great house' " of the master and also far enough away from the overseer's house to be "out of sight and hearing?"[89] How many plantations had so many adults that they had to reassemble in fields, woods, or other remote sections of the plantation to hold their covert meetings?

Webber suggests that a plantation as small as 20 slaves might have been large enough to form a "slave quarter" and produce "a society within a society."[90] That is a surprisingly small number for communities that were as isolated from whites and that had as elaborate a social structure as he and some other scholars have suggested. On the typical plantation of 20 slaves, only eight or nine would have been adults, with perhaps one woman working in the master's house as a cook or maid and possibly one part-time carpenter or other artisan among the males— hardly enough to produce "an internal class structure."[91] A private conversation among eight or nine adults would not normally have required a clandestine meeting in the woods but could easily have been conducted around the outdoor fire at which many evening meals were cooked without unduly arousing the suspicions of the master. Even on a plantation of 50 slaves, just five adults would normally have been regularly engaged in non-field occupations, and the typical slave quarter would have consisted of six to eight cabins—hardly enough to form a street.

When Leslie H. Owens characterized a slave quarter as "a village-like setting" with a "physically tight community animated by the life within,"[92] he pointed to a much larger plantation. In that case the slave quarter consisted of "some forty or fifty . . . two room cabins facing each other across an open space for a street."[93] A plantation with that many cabins would typically have had at least 250 slaves, of whom perhaps 130 were adults. On a plantation of that size the house servants, artisans, and drivers might have numbered 30 to 40, more than enough to provide several layers of elites. With just six or seven whites in residence such a plantation would, indeed, have been a largely black world in which few slaves had regular contact with the master. It is not difficult to envision a hierarchy of black leaders in such a community, and if they had planned a clandestine congregation of the adults, they might well have held it in a remote, wooded section of the plantation.

Plantations that large did exist in the United States but they were relatively rare. In 1850 there were just 125 plantations with over 250 slaves and less than 2 percent of U.S. slaves lived on them. Plantations that large were relatively common in Jamaica and nearly one out of every four Jamaican slaves belonged to such a plantation. But the distributions of slaves were much different in Jamaica and the United States. The overwhelming majority of U.S. slaves lived on plantations of small or modest size, while the overwhelming majority of Jamaican slaves lived on large plantations.[94]

Thus, only a small fraction of southern slaves lived in the quarter, if that term is intended to designate a "society within a society." There were cases where slaves living on small units could develop an autonomous life, particularly in cities where slaves could easily mingle with each other. Control over urban slaves was loosened by the widespread practice of hiring slaves out on a daily or weekly basis. Some slaves were even allowed to hire out on their own account, paying their owners a fixed percentage of their income. Such independence was fairly common among urban craftsmen but field hands who lived in this way were few and far between. Whether their plantation was large or small, most field hands worked under the constant surveillance of their master or his agent.[95]

Under normal circumstances slaves could develop a degree of cultural autonomy only if there was a community in which they could interact with one another, a community that they could shape in some significant way. Plantations consisting of just two or three families might have provided some aspects of community life, but they could not have produced the complex, multilayered societies depicted by some scholars. In contrast, grand plantations such as Butler's Island in Georgia, the Acland estate in Tennessee, and the Houmas estate in Louisiana were not only large but complicated organizations engaged in the production of diverse commodities and services. Slaves on grand plantations possessed a wide variety of skills and did, indeed, live in villages of their own making, in both a physical and a psychological sense. The house staff, by itself, was sometimes a larger organization than many modest plantations. There was often a hospital staff of nurses, a midwife or two, and perhaps even a "medicine man" who assisted the resident white doctor. The stable staff consisted of coachmen, teamsters, hostlers, and stableboys, some of whom made frequent trips into town, alone or with a member of the master's family. The highest ranking slave among the field hands was the head driver, who had several assistants, each of whom headed up one of the gangs. The corps of craftsmen included carpenters, blacksmiths, masons, coopers, millers, and shoemakers. And there was frequently a spinning and weaving house in which a number of the older women and the lame men were at work. In such communities there was plenty of room for conjurers, preachers, elders, musicians, storytellers, and other native leaders not in the master's table of organization.[96]

Even if slave communities approaching such complexity could have come into being on plantations with 100 or even 50 slaves, hardly 20 percent of the slave population in 1850 would have lived in these communities. While the culture (or cultures) of the other 80 percent of the slave population has not been neglected, so far we have only shadowy sketches of the quality and content of their lives. The trauma of broken families, the opportunity to move more freely in the neighborhood, the discomfort of always being at the beck and call of the master or his wife have been adumbrated, but not much more. Here again, the problem is related to the nature of the sources. Abolitionist editors seem generally to have found the stories of fugitives from large plantations more newsworthy than those from small plantations. The interviewers of ex-slaves in the 1920s and 1930s also found the stories of big plantations more compelling than those of small ones, for it is the experiences on the big plantations that predominated in the Greenwood collection.[97]

THE BALANCE OF POWER

The different views of slave culture arise not merely from the different sources favored by particular scholars but from different views of the balance of power between masters and slaves. Some scholars have emphasized the great power of the masters and the extreme weakness of the slaves. The power of the masters arose from the fact that the state invested them with virtually unconstrained authority to deal with slaves and provided the judicial backing and physical force required to maintain that authority. American slaveholders demonstrated their determination and their capacity to exercise control by the way they responded to challenges, bringing to bear as much force as was necessary to crush the challenge. Few cultural historians have portrayed a balance that typically precluded resistance by slaves; a more common view is that the

balance was so one-sided that slaves typically responded "with the weapons of the weak," with forms of resistance so subtle that they were
frequently undetected by masters, although they provided a means of
self-expression that helped to preserve the humanity of the slaves.

There are no scholars who argue that the balance of power was
actually in favor of slaves, but some skirt that position. In such assess-
ments the weapons of the masters are made ineffective, or largely so, by
their arrogance, self-deception, and stupidity. The slaves, on the other
hand, deprived not only of the control of the state or even its protection,
but of the political organizations that are normally necessary to establish
a base with which to contest power, are nevertheless able to outwit
masters so completely as to create an autonomous society of their own
design dedicated to goals that directly contradict the goals of masters.

Arguments that make the balance of power turn on the ineptness of
masters and the cleverness of slaves, despite their romantic attractions,
are difficult to sustain. How inept could the masters have been if they
were, as a class, able to multiply their wealth rapidly, extend their
domain widely, fend off external threats to their hegemony, and dominate national politics for more than half a century? How strong could
the slaves have been if they were forced to endure a trade that destroyed
10 to 20 percent of their marriages, yield a product that was a third
higher than that of free laborers, submit to a division of the product that
was less favorable than that accorded free labor, and endure forms of
coercion that by the middle of the nineteenth century were more severe
than any that could legally have been applied to free men? If during the
late 1950s and early 1960s there was a noticeable tendency for some
scholars to exaggerate the power of the masters, during the mid and late
1970s there was an equally noticeable tendency to exaggerate the power
of the slaves.[98]

The considerable scholarly energy expended on the exploration of
extreme positions was useful in these cases because it produced evidence
that contradicted exaggerations in either direction, evidence that has
been leading toward a more tenable view of the balance of power between
masters and slaves. Although the principal scholars who have contributed to this potential consensus differ with each other on a variety of
important points, they agree that the purposes for which slaves were used
created practical constraints on the power of the masters. These constraints led to significant differences between the legal status of slaves
and their actual conditions of life, and affected the degree to which slaves
could develop an autonomous culture.

The most critical proposition in this analysis is that southern slavery
was, above all, an economic system in the sense that masters valued
slaves principally as producers of the commodities upon which their

wealth, honor, and status depended. U.S. masters were not unique in this respect since the masters of all the gang-system economies of the New World were usually profit oriented. However, in many other slave societies, such as those of the Islamic world, slaves were not valued because they produced an economic surplus and were in fact often an economic drain. They were "luxuries," maintained by masters at considerable expense to themselves for the honor, pleasure, and advantage they gained from sheer domination. Such slaves, as Orlando Patterson has pointed out, were not only generally exempt from arduous labor but often lived in considerable material comfort as long as they remained completely loyal and subservient to their masters.[99]

There may have been some southern masters who, like Islamic lords, valued slaves as luxuries, but they were rare. Cliometric studies of the U.S. markets for slaves have demonstrated that slave prices are fully explained by the value of the commodities that they produced. Such a test does not imply that masters did not derive honor or status from the sheer domination of slaves but that the independent value they placed on this aspect of slave ownership was too small in the aggregate to have a measurable effect on the observed price of slaves. In contrast to societies where slaves were demanded principally as "luxuries," as a form of "conspicuous consumption," in the United States even the house slaves were expected to work hard at a variety of arduous tasks and were often also sent into the field at periods of peak demand for field labor. With the exception of the lame or slaves otherwise incapacitated and occasional favorites, the life-cycle pattern of labor usually guaranteed that slaves who served in the master's house during their youth or old age labored in the fields during their prime ages.

It is now nearly two decades since Genovese called attention to the connection between the culture of U.S. slaves and the purposes for which masters used slaves on plantations. The analogy between inmates of concentration camps and other "total" institutions, he argued, was misleading because plantations were organized for a fundamentally different purpose than concentration camps (which were used to exterminate people), prisons (which are used to isolate criminals from the general population), and asylums (which are used to control the mentally deficient).[100] Plantations were places that used slaves to produce staples for sale on world markets. Because masters were principally concerned with getting work out of slaves, said Genovese, they were forced into "a whole series of adjustments" to the desires of slaves. Thus, the economic objectives of masters "set limits" on what "could be done to" slaves, "including the degree of cruelty that could be imposed on them."[101] The Nazis did not need the cooperation of the inmates of concentration camps to exterminate them, but masters of gang-system plantations needed at least the passive cooperation of slaves to make their plantations profitable. Had these masters been content merely to exercise power for its own sake, plantations might have been transformed into something approaching "total institutions." Had slaves been determined to sabotage production regardless of the cost to themselves and their families, they undoubtedly could have frustrated the economic goals of the planters.

Genovese's analysis called attention to the practical limits that usually governed each class. Masters could not push the exercise of power so far that they lost even the passive cooperation of slaves in the profitable production of staples. Slaves could not push resistance so far that masters had nothing to lose from the unrestrained exercise of their overwhelming power. There was a wide range of feasible "compromises" between these limits, so that the balance of power between slaves and their masters varied greatly from plantation to plantation depending on such matters as plantation traditions; the personality of the master, his paternalistic tendencies, and his financial condition; the size and solidarity of the slave community; the skill of the leaders of that community; and the desires of individual slaves, including their willingness to run risks.

The variety of positive incentives that masters developed to elicit the cooperation of slaves in their productive enterprises are evidence that naked force, indispensable as it was for the effective functioning of gang-system slavery, was not enough. Masters were compelled to recognize the humanity of slaves, taking into account what their particular slaves would or would not endure in the drive to shape their plantations into more and more effective places of production. Consequently, positive incentives were not merely or (despite the intentions of masters) necessarily methods of leading slaves to act against their own interests but were often concessions to the desires of slaves that compromised the position of masters more than they realized. The "imperfect or partial 'solutions' " of masters to the "key" problem of expanding the production of agricultural staples, as Sidney Mintz has pointed out, sometimes gave rise to institutions within gang-system slavery that "challenged it and, eventually, destroyed or obviated it."[102]

In the Caribbean, one of the institutions introduced by planters that was ultimately most lethal to their interests was the "provision grounds." Provision grounds were sections of land that planters allocated to their slaves. Although they were intended to encourage slaves to produce a major part of the supply of food that they consumed, slaves were also allowed to sell the product of these grounds on the open market for cash or trade it for whatever other products they desired. The use of provision grounds was apparently widespread in the British and French colonies, but the best studies of its operation pertain to Jamaica.

The origins of the provision-grounds system of slave production and marketing in Jamaica have been traced back to the 1680s and the institution appears to have been widespread by the middle of the eighteenth century. Under the pinch of a shortage of hard currency, provision grounds were introduced by Jamaican planters as a means of easing the shortage of food that existed when planters depended primarily on imports. The grounds allotted for these purposes were usually on the hilly lands of the plantations, lands too poor to use for sugar or one of the other export crops and commonly far from the eyes of the overseers. Slaves were allowed to work these lands during their "time off"—on Sundays, usually a half day on Saturdays, and on holidays. The marketing of the food that they did not themselves consume was done on Sundays. From the point of view of the master the provision-grounds system had a variety of economic and political benefits. By providing the slave "with a better diet, a small source of income, and a feeling of proprietorship in the land," he became "less discontented, less likely to run away, and less dangerous as a potential rebel." Provision grounds were, as one planter put it, "a happy coalition of interests between the master and slave."[103]

Without denying the short-run benefits to masters, Mintz pointed to several aspects of the system that were ultimately inimical to slavery. Because work on provision grounds was conducted without the strict supervision characteristic of the gang system, such work was "counter to the whole conception of how the slave mode of production was supposed to operate." It nourished independence because it permitted slaves to make their own decisions about what and how much to grow, about how to dispose of their product, and about what to buy with the money earned from their sale. The provision-grounds system was thus a " 'radical breach' in the slave mode of production" that transformed a gang slave into, as Mintz put it, a "proto-peasant."[104]

By the turn of the nineteenth century provision grounds, and the system of internal marketing to which they gave rise, were central features of Jamaica and other West Indian colonies. In Jamaica slaves eventually gained a "virtual monopoly" on "internal marketing." Collectively they possessed 20 percent of the colony's circulating currency. On the eve of emancipation the value of the output of their grounds was equal to about 40 percent of the value of exported sugar, which gave slaves a central role in town markets, not only as suppliers of food but also as purchasers of "large quantities of imported goods." Individually, slaves accumulated substantial sums of capital in cash and commodities, which sometimes exceeded their value as slaves and which they were able to bequeath. They even acquired the right "to bequeath their provision grounds," a right "so fully recognized" by planters "that they

offered compensation" to slaves "whenever it became necessary to convert an area of slave cultivation to estate purposes." Eventually Jamaican
law not only required planters to set aside some of their estate lands for
provision grounds but also recognized that slaves could travel to town
or from place to place without a pass from the planter or his overseer
if they were going "to market" or "returning therefrom."[105]

Proto-peasant institutions both stimulated the desire for land and
freedom among West Indian slaves and allowed them a degree of interaction that eventually contributed to the downfall of slavery. Proto-peasant
experiences played a role in the Jamaican slave revolts of 1831 which,
ironically, were promoted by planter denunciation of the efforts of British
abolitionists to push an act of emancipation through the House of Commons.[106] The "panic" that these efforts induced among the planters
could not be hidden from slaves who moved about so freely, some of
whom became "convinced . . . that their masters were conspiring to
thwart an imminent emancipation."[107] Although the revolts of 1831
were crushed, the influence of the proto-peasant experience again became apparent a few years later when slaves refused to accept the
diminished form of slavery called "apprenticeship" that Parliament established in its act on gradual emancipation.[108]

U.S. masters also designed a wide array of positive incentives to
promote the productivity of slaves, but they generally did so in a manner
calculated to reinforce the gang system. They sought rewards that motivated slaves without encouraging what some described as a "dangerous"
loosening of control such as occurred in the Caribbean. A favorite device
was the awarding of prizes to the individual or the gang with the best
cotton-picking record on a given day or during a given week. Year-end
bonuses, often distributed at Christmas, were another common device
and could be quite substantial. One Louisiana planter, for example,
distributed gifts averaging between $15 and $20 per slave family in
1839 and 1840, with the amount of the gift made proportional to the
planter's view of the performance of each of his slaves. Not all gifts were
this large ($20 in 1840 was about one-fifth of per capita income; a bonus
of the same relative magnitude today would be about $3,000), but $20
was by no means an upper bound.[109]

Indeed, many large-scale planters had elaborate systems for reward-
ing exceptional work that not only recognized outstanding performances
by field hands but generally led to substantial income differentials between ordinary field hands on the one hand and exceptional workers,
especially drivers or artisans, on the other. Fragmentary evidence suggests that the ratio of the income of the more highly rewarded field hands
to basic income (the value of the food, shelter, clothing, and medical care
ordinarily furnished by the master) was about 2.5. This ratio becomes

larger when the income of craftsmen is taken into account. The income of top craftsmen was probably four or five times that of basic income, and in some exceptional cases craftsmen appear to have earned as much as ten times basic income.[110]

Like their West Indian counterparts, southern planters found that the encouragement of occupational and income differentials among their slaves paid off in both output and social stability, but they were uneasy about reward systems that increased the independence of slaves. Consequently, southern counterparts to provision grounds were less widespread than in the West Indies and when undertaken were usually restricted in numerous ways. Most U.S. planters allowed slaves to supplement rations with vegetables raised in gardens or by rearing small livestock and often purchased eggs, chickens, and vegetables raised by slaves for use on their own tables. There were also masters who rewarded top hands by allowing them plots of up to a few acres to grow cotton or other staples on their own time, with the proceeds of the sales of these crops accruing to the hands. On the Texas plantation of Julian S. Devereux, for example, some of the slaves who received such plots earned in excess of $100 per annum per family. Devereux did not, however, permit the slaves to market the cotton from the plots independently; he sold their cotton along with his own. Nor did Devereux pay his slaves in cash. Instead, he set up accounts for each slave family to which he credited the proceeds of the sales. The slaves drew on these accounts when they wanted to purchase pots, clothing, tobacco, or other items. More often than not Devereux procured these items for them from his suppliers, although he sometimes gave the slaves cash, allowing them to purchase the items directly.[111]

The majority of planters appear to have shared Devereux's reluctance to allow slaves to act as "proto-peasants." Crawford's analysis of the ex-slave interviews revealed that only 30 percent of the heads of slave households ever received cash, although about 60 percent of these households were allowed to have their own patch of land, raise livestock, hunt, or engage in other income-producing activities (such as splitting rails, weaving baskets, and making charcoal). Southern masters not only restricted the manner in which slaves could dispose of their products but often restricted the commodities a slave could produce on his plot of land. Some planters prohibited the allotments from being used to grow the staple in which the plantation specialized for fear that slaves would steal some of the planter's crop and pass it off as their own. Sometimes planters allowed rice or cotton to be grown on the allotments only if the slaves used a variety of seeds different from those used by the planter.[112]

Planters who depended on the task system were more inclined to allow the rise of proto-peasant institutions than those who relied primarily on the gang system. A recent study by Philip D. Morgan of the practices of planters in the low country of South Carolina, where the task system predominated, revealed that despite legal injunctions prohibiting slaves from producing and marketing on their own account, the practice was widespread. An industrious slave could sometimes finish his daily task by 2 P.M. Such slaves accumulated property at a high rate. Morgan estimates that in one county the average recorded accumulation of mature males was over $300, which is similar to the estimates of the wealth of industrious slaves in Jamaica. Some slaves claimed to have amassed over $2,000. In one of these cases (that of Alexander Steele) the assets accumulated over 30 years included a silver watch, four horses, a mule, two cows, a wagon, "and large quantities of fodder, hay, and corn." Three white planters verified that Steele's claim was true, with one of them testifying that he had made "an unsuccessful offer of $300 for one of Steele's colts."[113]

Southern planters were ambivalent about such "success" stories. During the late antebellum era these stories provided effective propaganda against abolitionist charges, but many masters complained that the task system gave slaves too much liberty and promoted idleness that threatened to become "the parent of mischief."[114] Others felt that the time of slaves that they lost under this system (often several hours a day) was inefficient and costly. Differences of opinion among masters about the virtues of the task system were never resolved, but the task system was never used as extensively in the South as the gang system. Its principal domain was in the low country of South Carolina, although it was sometimes used as a supplement to the gang-system methods nearly everywhere. Gray and Morgan have argued that tasking was effective in crops and operations that did not lend themselves to the regimentation of an assembly line because they required individualized attention. The critical issue was whether the individualized work could be inexpensively monitored. These two conditions were most often satisfied in the production of rice and sea-island cotton (a long-staple variety of cotton that accounted for about 10 percent of the annual cotton crop).

The general uneasiness about the task method among masters of medium and large plantations reveals their consciousness of the limits of their power. Masters feared that a task, once established, was more easily lowered than raised since the definition of the task hardened into a custom buttressed by such strong sentiment that masters found it prudent to respect the custom. A part of the arrangement, as Morgan points out, was that the time of the slave once he finished his task was sacred in the sense that the slave could not be asked by the master for further work that day. This "right" of the slaves "was duly acknowledged by lowcountry masters,"[115] to the point that masters would hire their own slaves, or someone else's slaves, if special circumstances required an additional labor call. Nevertheless, the power of the slaves under the task system should not be exaggerated. The custom that limited the master was recognized only by him, not by law. If the master was constrained to accept the limitation, it was because his judgment dictated that the cost of failing to do so exceeded the benefit. The cost of violating the custom, said Olmsted, was the possibility that a slave would run off "to the 'swamp'—a danger a slave could always hold before his master's cupidity."[116]

If "concessions" and rewards now appear to have been a more important part of the system of controlling slaves than was appreciated by scholars in the past, the fact remains that they were just that: part of a system of controlling slaves rather than of liberating them.[117] Masters were aware that rewards and concessions were two-edged swords and they were careful, as we have seen, to use these weapons in a manner that advanced their interests (even if they were not always successful). Some concessions may have contributed ultimately to the negation of slavery, but in most places and times, for periods of up to several centuries, these concessions generally served the interests of masters (although, at a different level, they may have served the interests of slaves in either the long or the short run). Even manumissions, which may seem to be the negation of slavery, were sometimes actually part of the system of control. Manumission, as Patterson has pointed out, was not used only as an instrument to elicit cooperation from slaves by holding it up as a reward that might ultimately be gained. It also could serve as a powerful instrument of domination since it emphasized the completeness of the slave's dependency on his master. Even so, southern masters rarely made use of this instrument. The available evidence indicates that most manumissions during the late antebellum era were due to free blacks who first purchased their relatives and then freed them.[118]

It is also important to keep in mind what the masters of the South and the West Indies did not concede. They did not concede their right to destroy slave marriages when that served their economic interests or to invoke force when rewards failed to produce a desired result. Nor did they concede to slaves the full measure of the extra product that their intense labor produced. Cliometricians have been engaged in a debate over the rate of the expropriation of slaves, a debate that turns not on whether slaves received a smaller share of their product than free laborers but only on the size of the gap. That debate is considered more fully in the companion volume *Evidence and Methods,* since the points at issue are quite technical.[119] What is relevant here, however, is that all of the cliometricians who have worked on the problem agree that the rewards masters gave to their slaves never became so large that they obliterated the extra margin of expropriation.

"In all government," said the "Instructions to Managers" of a widely used plantation account book, "rewards and encouragements are as necessary as punishment." Which instrument of "government" a given master chose at any moment in time depended on many considerations, some rational, some irrational; some well thought out, some impulsively settled in a moment of passion. The mix of controls varied greatly from plantation to plantation, turning in large measure on the personalities of the planters. No doubt economic considerations played a large part in these decisions, and such considerations did not elude the author of "Instructions to Managers" who emphasized that rewards "are often more effective" than punishment. Yet, since different masters read their economic interests in different ways, it would be a mistake to assume that economic interests were so constraining that they necessarily over-whelmed personality or other noneconomic considerations.[120]

That masters had widely different views of what was in their best interest is pointed up by the recent research into the slave diet. Linear programming revealed that the average diet fed to slaves on large south-ern plantations was about twice as expensive as it had to be in order to satisfy modern nutritional standards.[121] The principal reason for the relatively high cost is the large quantity of pork included in this diet. Given the relative prices of various foods in the antebellum South, masters could have saved money by substituting vegetables, beef, or fish for pork without sacrificing nutritional requirements. Indeed, modern nutritional standards could have been met with a diet consisting of corn, cowpeas, sweet potatoes, and milk.

Southern slaveowners did not know about the modern recommended daily allowances of the principal nutrients but many of them knew that the diets they fed to slaves were more expensive than they had to be to meet the nutritional standards of their time. If a cotton planter who purchased expensive pork for his slaves was asked why he did not reduce his costs by feeding his slaves on his own beef, it was "Simply because it would raise a revolt, sooner than all the whiplashes ever braided in Massachusetts. Fat pork and corn bread is the natural aliment of a negro. Deprive him of these and he is miserable."[122] Yet not all masters felt compelled to cater to this dietary preference and those who deviated from it were not necessarily less humane or less rational than the majority who adhered to it. Thomas Jefferson, among the more humane of the Virginia slaveholders and as rational as any, was one of the planters who often deviated from the dietary preferences of his slaves. Noting on one occa-sion that "a barrel of fish" (which sold for $7) "goes as far with laborers as 200 pounds of pork" (which sold for $16), Jefferson switched to fish as an economy measure. Another Virginia planter, Landon Carter, seems to have discovered the linear programming solution to the slave diet, or something quite close to it, without the aid of high-speed computers. The basic diet of his slaves consisted of cornmeal, cowpeas, seasonal vegetables, and offal (brains, sweetbreads, hearts, liver). He served meat other than offal "only to reward favored slaves, to induce slaves to work, or to treat his slaves at irregular times during the year."[123]

Although the available evidence indicates that most southern planters considered the extra cost of conceding to their slaves' dietary preferences was worth the price, even in the South this view was far from universal among planters. And in the West Indies the majority of planters made the opposite decision. As far as is known, there were no food riots among the slaves of Jefferson or of Carter or in the West Indies. Thus, although slaves were often able to influence the content of their diets, there were many plantations on which they could not do so. Had slaves been able to dictate their diets, the proportion of slave households in the South with garden plots or hunting and fishing privileges would probably have exceeded 60 percent and West Indian slaves would have eaten more meat than they did.

Some scholars have argued that the current "pursuit of culture" by slavery historians is "full of logical traps." The problem, according to Elkins, is that research focused "almost wholly upon resistance" has diverted attention from how damaging chattel slavery was "to every man, woman, and child, white or black, who was in any way touched by it." What has been overlooked, he continues, is that "culture, under such conditions as those of slavery, is not acquired without a price; the social and individual experience of any group with as little power, and enduring such insistent assaults (of cruelty, contempt, and, not least, uncertainty), is bound to contain more than the normal residue of pathology."[124]

Those who emphasize the autonomy of slave culture raise a disturbing question that did not need to be confronted by Stampp, Elkins, and other scholars who had emphasized "the enormous and pervasive power of the masters." That question is why there was not more resistance from the slaves. Scholars "who see slaves as shaping their own lives to a significant degree seem to be nagged by the charge that because there were not more rebellions and runaways, Negroes were somehow reconciled to bondage." Acknowledging that cultural historians have wrestled with the issue, Carl N. Degler finds their answers unconvincing. He suggests that if the issue has been handled in a fruitless way, it is partly because of the tendency to portray "slaves as solely responsible for whatever autonomy they may have enjoyed," neglecting that plantation institutions were "the result of" an "interaction between master and slave."[125]

These are important caveats. Unbalanced and sometimes superficial discussions of planter concessions and of their reward systems tend not only to give an overly favorable view of life under the gang system but to exaggerate the power of slaves in their contests with masters. Although there were issues and circumstances that masters met with concessions, they are only part of the story. Since it was under such circumstances that slave autonomy and culture were most likely to flourish, the recent scholarly concentration on slave culture has tended to convey an exaggerated impression of the ability of slaves to affect their circumstances. Keenly aware of these pitfalls, Mintz, Genovese, and Blassingame, among others, have repeatedly called attention to the dual nature of planter concessions as well as to the naked force that stood ready to take over when rewards and concessions failed to produce the desired results. Genovese suggests that the ultimate contradiction of gang-system slavery, and perhaps the ultimate measure of the autonomy of slave culture, is that so often the leadership for slave rebellions came from the craftsmen, drivers, and other elite slaves who received the most favored treatment under the system.[126] "Being most exposed to assimilation by the dominant culture and its superior technology," he argues, the privileged slaves were "least likely to equivocate on political issues." Either they identified "with their oppressors," seeking "individual advance," or they identified "with their people," placing "their sophistication at the disposal of the rebellion." Whether or not one agrees with this assessment, Genovese calls attention to the fact that even the most generous concessions of masters failed to extinguish the desire for freedom by slaves.[127]

Historians of slave culture have now provided abundant evidence that the passion for freedom was deep among slaves in every society for which information is available. After studying the evidence of scores of these societies from antiquity to modern times, Patterson concluded that there was "absolutely no evidence from the long and dismal annals of slavery to suggest that any group of slaves ever internalized the conception of degradation held by their masters. To be dishonored—and to sense, however acutely, such dishonor—is not to lose the quintessential human urge to participate and to want a place."[128]

Why then were reformist activities rather than revolutionary ones the predominant form of resistance by slaves, especially in the South? The short answer is that "revolution grows out of the barrel of a gun," and slaves rarely had the necessary firepower. The problem is poignantly illustrated by the revolts in Jamaica during 1831. About 150 slaves

organized themselves into a Black Regiment which had several successful actions; but having only 50 guns among them, they were easily
defeated by British troops.[129]

If such revolutionary activities never became the predominant form
of resistance in the South, it is because the objective conditions for
successful rebellion never emerged. As that master of revolutionary
strategy and tactics V. I. Lenin pointed out some seven decades ago, a
revolution cannot be made at will. It requires a crisis within the ruling
class that prevents it from ruling in the old way. While such a crisis
threatened to erupt at certain points prior to the Civil War, it never
matured. Revolution also requires an organized movement capable of
channeling inchoate resentment against the system and its ruling class
into purposeful and effective acts of revolution. U.S. slaves were, of
course, almost completely deprived of the mobility and means of communication needed to create such an organization. The capacity of the
slaveowners to preclude these opportunities is a measure of the distance
that had to be traversed before revolution became a practical possibility.
In the only place (Haiti) in the Western Hemisphere where slaveowners
became too divided to rule effectively, slaves did seize the moment and
overthrew their ruling class. In all other instances the power needed to
destroy slavery, as we shall see, came from the intervention of forces
outside the system.[130]

PART TWO

THE IDEOLOGICAL AND POLITICAL CAMPAIGN AGAINST SLAVERY

CHAPTER SEVEN

THE BRITISH CAMPAIGN

For 3,000 years—from the time of Moses to the end of the seventeenth century—virtually every major statesman, philosopher, theologian, writer, and critic accepted the existence and legitimacy of slavery. The word "accepted" is chosen deliberately for these men of affairs and molders of thought neither excused, condoned, pardoned, nor forgave the institution. They did not have to; they were not burdened by the view that slavery was wrong. Slavery was considered to be part of the natural scheme of things. "From the hour of their birth," said Aristotle, "some are marked out for subjection, others for rule."[1]

It is true that some theologians were troubled by the possible dichotomy between servitude and the "divine law of human brotherhood." But this apparent contradiction was neatly resolved in Christian theology by treating slavery as a condition of the body rather than of the spirit. In the spiritual realm, "all men were brothers in union with God," but in the temporal realm slavery was "a necessary part of the world of sin." Thus, "the bondsman was inwardly free and spiritually equal to his master, but in things external he was a mere chattel."[2]

The Catholic Church not only rationalized the possession of slaves by others but was itself a major owner of slaves. Even before the Jesuits began to encourage the importation of Africans into the New World, the Church actively promoted slavery. In 1375, Pope Gregory XI, viewing bondage as a just punishment for those who resisted the papacy, ordered the enslavement of excommunicated Florentines whenever they were captured. And in 1488 Pope Innocent VIII accepted a gift of a hundred Moorish slaves from Ferdinand of Spain and then distributed them to various cardinals and nobles.[3] Nor was it merely the conservative members of the hierarchy who countenanced human bondage. No less a humanist than Thomas More held slavery to be an appropriate state for the "vyle drudge," the "poor laborer,"[4] and the criminal. He therefore included slavery in his vision of *Utopia*.

Differences on the legitimacy of servitude were not among the issues that motivated the Protestant Reformation. "When Swabian serfs appealed for emancipation in 1525, holding that Christ had died to set men free, Martin Luther was as horrified as any orthodox Catholic." He considered that demand to be a distortion of scripture which, if permitted, would confuse Christ's spiritual kingdom with the world of affairs. He reaffirmed Saint Paul's dictum that "masters and slaves must accept their present stations, for the earthly kingdom could not survive unless some men were free and some were slaves."[5]

Acceptance of slavery was not less common in the secular than in the religious world. As prominent a champion of the "inalienable rights of man" as John Locke wrote a provision for slavery into his draft of the "Fundamental Constitution of Carolina," and also became an investor in the Royal African Company, the organization that enjoyed the British monopoly of the African slave trade. Thus, the man who formulated the theory of natural liberty, and whose thesis that men had the moral obligation to take up arms in defense of liberty later inspired many revolutionaries and abolitionists, was, nevertheless, a defender of slavery. This paradox stemmed from Locke's belief that

> the origin of slavery, like the origin of liberty and property, was entirely outside the social contract. When any man, by fault or act, forfeited his life to another, he could not complain of injustice if his punishment was postponed by his being enslaved. If the hardships of bondage should at any time outweigh the value of life, he could commit suicide by resisting his master and receiving the death which he had all along deserved.[6]

THE RISE OF THE ANTISLAVERY MOVEMENT AND THE CENTURY OF EMANCIPATION

By the beginning of the eighteenth century the latent contradictions between slavery and evolving religious and political ideals began to emerge in a limited way. Although Western Europeans had come to abhor the thought of enslaving other Western Europeans, they continued to sanction the enslavement of Muslims and black Africans. During the next six decades some thinkers in England, Scotland, France, and America expressed strong misgivings about the legitimacy of enslaving Africans, but their views had little practical effect. Rationalizations for the transatlantic slave trade combined age-old sentiments on slavery with a new emphasis on race that justified white dominion over blacks. Although the sources and the degree of the intensity of early racism remain a matter of debate, it is agreed that the degradation of color was increased by servility. Racism was also spurred by the anxiety of slaveowners and by resistance to slavery, first by slaves and later by the rising abolitionist movement. During the eighteenth and nineteenth centuries it was reinforced by anthropological theories that ordered the races of man into a ladder of inherent capabilities and related these to differences in color and other physical characteristics.[7]

The greatest obstacle to the rise of an antislavery ideology was the belief that slavery promoted material improvement. To the modern mind it seems ludicrous to hinge major aspects of human progress on so backward and immoral a system. Yet it was commonplace for 2,000 years to connect vaunted achievements with slavery. Athenians, for example, identified the enslavement of foreign captives as a turning point that ushered in freedom and prosperity for their citizens and that permitted science and technology to flourish. "From Plato onward even the visions of a utopian society toward which humans might evolve assumed the continuing existence of slaves," and Cynic, Stoic, and Epicurean critics of corruption in Greek society accepted the legitimacy of slavery.[8]

Slavery was more explicitly coupled with material improvement by those who spread the system during the Middle Ages, especially after Europe regained partial control of the Mediterranean from the Arabs and European commerce revived. During the twelfth and thirteenth centuries Venice, Genoa, and Pisa dominated Mediterranean trade routes, and the sale of Moorish slaves to Muslims and slaves from the Balkans and the Black Sea to Western Europe became one of their most lucrative lines of commerce. To promote the trade, the Italians built colonies in the Levant and Black Sea that were "virtual laboratories" for "testing and developing the techniques of commercial companies, colonial administration and finance, and long-distance trade and plantation agriculture." By the thirteenth century Venetian entrepreneurs had established large sugar plantations on the island of Cyprus that they ran "by 'capitalist' methods, importing expensive copper boilers from Italy, using hydraulic mills to press the cane, and employing a mixed labor force of local serfs and Muslim slaves."[9] Even the switch from Muslim to African slaves during the fifteenth century was viewed as progress, partly because it was authorized by Papal Briefs as a blow against the economy of Muslim infidels and enemies of Christ, and partly because each captured African represented the "salvation" of a lost soul.

The rise of sugar production in the New World, the innovative methods of labor organization, and the technological advances on which the large sugar plantations were based further reinforced the identification of slavery with material improvement. The American North-South split that later produced the Civil War was not yet evident at the turn of the eighteenth century. Far from shunning slaves, the northern colonies eagerly imported them. In 1703 some 42 percent of the households in New York owned slaves. Indeed, during the early decades of the eighteenth century the slave share of the population in New York and

New Jersey was larger than in North Carolina and only a little less than in Maryland. "These comparisons simply underscore the willingness of every colony to turn to black slaves, despite universal fears of insurrection, complaints from white artisans and servants, and desires for racial and ethnic homogeneity, when the demand for cheap labor could not otherwise be met."[10]

The religious radicals of the late seventeenth and early eighteenth centuries denounced slavery as "a filthy sin" not because it was an economic failure but because its economic successes were abhorrent to them. They saw slavery as the worst symbol of a creed that identified human progress with economic progress and that extolled the virtue of this union. They called on their brethren to renounce the ethos of their age, to renounce material gain as a motivating force for human behavior, to seek a purified life, and to devote themselves to benevolence. These beliefs merged with an evangelical movement that emphasized the responsibility of each Christian to accept the burden of fighting evil and to seek God's blessing by struggling to change the hearts of men. The struggle against slavery was thus only the starting point of a crusade for a general moral reform. Slavery was singled out not as the only sin but as the "greatest" of the many sins of a corrupt society.[11]

The last quarter of the seventeenth century and the first three quarters of the eighteenth century were a watershed between the routine acceptance of slavery and the onset of a concerted, successful movement for the abolition of human bondage. The early outspoken critics of slavery were easily ignored. Such men as Judge Samuel Sewall, a Puritan from Massachusetts who published an antislavery tract in 1700 entitled *The Selling of Joseph,* were viewed by most of their contemporaries not as prophets, but as men of questionable integrity, if not sanity, who for inexplicable reasons had set out to controvert both the scripture and natural order. Even within the Society of Friends, where the doctrinal considerations made the minds of its members more open to abolitionist arguments than in other circles, the opponents of slavery were rebuffed for three quarters of a century—from 1688, when a small circle of Germantown Quakers issued their condemnation of human bondage as a violation of the Golden Rule, until the 1758 Yearly Meeting of Quakers in Philadelphia which, for the first time, condemned not only the slave trade but slavery itself and threatened to exclude any members who participated in that trade from positions of responsibility within the society.[12]

It is remarkable how rapidly, by historical standards, the institution of slavery gave way before the abolitionist onslaught, once the ideological campaign gained momentum. The moment at which abolitionism passed over from apparently ineffectual harangues by isolated zealots to a significant political movement cannot be dated with precision. Nevertheless, 1787, the year a handful of English Friends and evangelicals launched a public campaign against the slave trade, seems to be a reasonable, although not unique, occasion to mark the onset of concerted political action to end slavery. Slavery was abolished in its last American bastion—Brazil—in 1888. And so, within the span of a little more than a century, a system that had stood above criticism for 3,000 years was outlawed everywhere in the Western world (Table 6).[13]

It is important to emphasize that although religious radicals provided the spark for the antislavery movement, they did not usually lead (sometimes they even resisted) the transformation of their moral crusade into a political movement capable of defeating the entrenched proslavery coalitions that governed Great Britain, the United States, and other slave-based societies. The circumstances under which these transformations took place varied from society to society, but in many cases political ascendancy involved the fusion of the antislavery movement with other political movements aimed at seizing power from the governing coalitions.

While the struggle to end slavery was often associated with violence, it was only in the United States that slaveowners resorted to full-scale warfare to halt the abolitionist trend. And only in Haiti did a whole colony of slaves obtain liberation through bloody revolution. Much of the violence elsewhere was not the consequence of emancipation per se but of nationalist revolutions. In countries such as Colombia and Venezuela the emancipation of slaves became an instrument of the revolutionaries who sought state power. With many of the nationalist leaders of these movements drawn from the wealthy landholding and slaveholding classes, abolition was generally a protracted process. Indeed, the majority of slaves—those in the northern United States, the British colonies, Puerto Rico, Cuba, and Brazil, among others—were emancipated under more or less peaceful conditions and with at least the begrudging acquiescence of substantial parts of the slaveowning classes. This is not to say that slavery merely faded away, but to emphasize that its demise resulted from the cumulative impact of the ideological and political, rather than military, pressure of the abolitionists.[14]

In this connection it should be noted that many, perhaps most, of the slaves outside of the southern United States were freed under programs of gradual emancipation. These schemes usually involved the freeing not of adults but of children born on some date after the emancipation law was enacted. Moreover, the freeing of slave children was delayed beyond their eighteenth birthday. Under such arrangements, slaveholders suffered no losses on existing male slaves or on female slaves who were already past their childbearing years. Having control over the services

Table 6. A Chronology of Emancipation, 1772–1888

1772	Lord Chief Justice Mansfield rules that slavery is not supported by English law, thus laying the legal basis for the freeing of England's 15,000 slaves.
1774	The English Society of Friends votes the expulsion of any member engaged in the slave trade.
1775	Slavery abolished in Madeira.
1776	The Societies of Friends in England and Pennsylvania require members to free their slaves or face expulsion.
1777	The Vermont Constitution prohibits slavery.
1780	The Massachusetts Constitution declares that all men are free and equal by birth; a judicial decision in 1783 interprets this clause as having the force of abolishing slavery.
	Pennsylvania adopts a policy of gradual emancipation, freeing the children of all slaves born after November 1, 1780, at their 28th birthday.
1784	Rhode Island and Connecticut pass gradual emancipation laws.
1787	Formation in England of the "Society for the Abolition of the Slave Trade."
1794	The French National Convention abolishes slavery in all French territories. This law is repealed by Napoleon in 1802.
1799	New York passes a gradual emancipation law.
1800	U.S. citizens barred from exporting slaves.
1804	Slavery abolished in Haiti. New Jersey adopts a policy of gradual emancipation.
1807	England and the United States prohibit engagement in the international slave trade.
1813	Gradual emancipation adopted in Argentina.

of a newly born child until his or her 21st or 28th birthday meant that most, if not all, of the costs of rearing such slaves would be covered by the income they earned between the onset of their productive years and the date of their emancipation. In other words, gradual emancipation usually limited the economic losses suffered by slaveholders to a relatively small fraction of the value of their slaves. Thus, in countries where the slaveholding classes were too weak to repel the onslaught of the abolitionists, which was the usual case, they begrudgingly acquiesced to schemes for gradual emancipation.[15]

In the United States, southern slaveholders viewed the successes of the antislavery movement in Great Britain and elsewhere with alarm. By 1830, more than a third of the blacks in the Western Hemisphere were free. The greatest inroads were made in Spanish and French America. Only 25 percent of blacks in the colonies or former colonies of Spain

Table 6 (*continued*)

1814	Gradual emancipation begins in Colombia.
1819	England establishes a naval squadron on the west coast of Africa to suppress the slave trade.
1823	Formation of the London Anti-Slavery Committee. Slavery abolished in Chile.
1824	Slavery abolished in Central America.
1829	Slavery abolished in Mexico.
1831	Slavery abolished in Bolivia.
1838	Slavery abolished in all British colonies.
1841	The Quintuple Treaty is signed under which England, France, Russia, Prussia, and Austria agree to mutual search of vessels on the high seas in order to suppress the slave trade.
1842	Slavery abolished in Uruguay.
1848	Slavery abolished in all French and Danish colonies.
1851	Slavery abolished in Ecuador. Slave trade ended in Brazil.
1854	Slavery abolished in Peru and Venezuela.
1863	Slavery abolished in all Dutch colonies.
1865	Slavery abolished in the United States as a result of the passage of the thirteenth amendment of the Constitution and the end of the Civil War.
1867	Slave trade ended in Cuba.
1871	Gradual emancipation initiated in Brazil.
1873	Slavery abolished in Puerto Rico.
1886	Slavery abolished in Cuba.
1888	Slavery abolished in Brazil.

were still slaves. And the revolution in Haiti had freed 80 percent of the slaves under French rule. Before the decade of the thirties was over, all the black slaves in the British colonies were freed.[16] Southern slaveholders were determined to prevent the abolitionist tide from sweeping across the South. They formulated and effectively executed programs to protect their region from abolitionism and to resist the antislavery forces in every political arena of the nation. In their resolve, their vigor, and their effectiveness in repelling encroachments on their system, southern slaveholders were more successful than any other slaveholding class in the Western Hemisphere. Ironically, in the end this strength became an instrument of their undoing, as antislavery politicians found ways of converting southern successes in defending their system into assets for the antislavery cause.

BACKGROUND OF THE ANTISLAVERY MOVEMENT

The political struggle to end slavery in the British empire began in 1787, initiated by a relatively small religious sect, the Quakers, whose members were then excluded from political power. Yet within 25 years (by 1807) the coalition that they initiated won a lopsided parliamentary majority for the abolition of the international slave trade. Within 50 years (by 1833) this coalition had become so powerful that they not only commanded a sizable majority for the emancipation of all black slaves in the British colonies, but forced the majority of the West Indian bloc in Parliament to vote in favor of the scheme to dismantle the slave system. Still not satisfied, this coalition then demanded that Britain serve as the world's policeman in a campaign to root out slavery wherever else it might exist and in whatever subtle form it might be disguised. That demand became British policy for the balance of the nineteenth century. Whatever disagreements they might have had on other points, the succession of British governments remained committed to using their diplomatic influence, and the navy and army when necessary, to abolish slavery in lands not only under their own jurisdiction but often under other jurisdictions that protected or encouraged so evil a system.

How could the policies initially embraced by so small and isolated a sect, one that was initially widely despised and severely persecuted by the Anglican majority, become so influential that these policies became embedded in a new orthodoxy and became a central feature of the prevailing political ethos? The answer to that question has been brilliantly illuminated by the cumulative research of intellectual and political historians, some concerned directly with the antislavery struggle, others focused on the more general processes of ideological and political transformation in Great Britain during the eighteenth and nineteenth centuries. Indeed, it is with these more general processes that an explanation must begin because the Quakers and their allies in other religious sects could never have succeeded if their policies had not been consonant with the political drift of the times.

It was the gradual broadening of the British "civility" (not just the electorate but all of the population directly influencing the political process) that opened the way for the abolitionist crusade to be successful.[17] This transformation traces back at least to the early sixteenth century when Henry VIII utilized Parliament to legitimize his struggle against the Catholic Church. Although Henry's elevation of Parliament initially strengthened the Crown's grip on power, in the long run it facilitated the formation of coalitions powerful enough to challenge the Crown. The shift in the balance of power between the Crown and other great households stretched out over the next three centuries, punctuated by the English Civil War (1642–1646) and the Glorious Revolution of 1688, which brought William III, prince of Orange, to the English throne.

By the end of the third quarter of the eighteenth century such "party" politics had become a feature of English life, but these parties were largely a phenomenon of Parliament and the executive institutions that centered on the king. Parties increasingly became the instruments through which particular noblemen, bishops, and heads of a handful of other exceedingly rich households vied for power. This sort of party politics amounted to a struggle within this narrow circle of a few hundred families ("The Establishment") to form dominant coalitions.[18]

Historians of eighteenth-century England still debate the relative importance of ideological motivations and pure political expendiency in the formation of these coalitions. During the reign of George III (1760–1810), however, party politics changed in a manner that transformed the ideological element. The growth of cities, the spread of literacy, the development of newspapers, and improvements in transportation led to the involvement of sections of the middle classes in political conflicts that heretofore had been limited to a few hundred powerful households. The change became manifest during the early 1760s when John Wilkes, a Member of Parliament and a newspaper editor, launched a personal attack on the king's prime minister. Wilkes's arrest on grounds of seditious libel touched off demonstrations for "Wilkes and Liberty" among the literate public in London and other cities across Great Britain. The coffeehouses of the middle classes emerged as a new political arena in which the issues of the Establishment were debated. This new public, which was substantial enough to strike down the warrant against Wilkes, release him from prison, and return him to Parliament, thus emerged as a political force with which the Establishment had to reckon.

In what sense did the Wilkes affair change politics and the ideological component of politics? Certainly not in the sense that it introduced ideological issues into the struggle for power. From the Reformation on, charges of "papist plot" and "heresy" were calls to political (and military) battle that, when properly played, could override virtually any other issue. What was novel about the Wilkes affair was not that it had a strong ideological component, but that there was a new civility to which the ideological campaign was addressed, a new set of issues on which the ideological struggle raged (religion lost its capacity to eclipse all other matters in the drawing of party lines), and new forms through which the struggle was conducted. The Wilkes affair demonstrated that politics was no longer confined to Parliament and that campaigns mounted outside of Parliament could influence the course of struggles within it.[19]

Although the Quakers launched the political struggle to abolish slavery, it is doubtful that their efforts would have been successful if they had not formed alliances with the Methodists and other dissenting denominations as well as with the evangelicals of the Anglican Church. The alliance with the Methodists was strategic because they were deeply rooted among the laboring and artisanal classes of the big cities of Britain, which made them an important counterweight to the lower-class radicalism feared by the centrists in Parliament, especially after they observed the consequences of a radical politics based on lower classes during the French Revolution. The alliance with the evangelicals of the Anglican Church was even more strategic: Their number included an influential bloc in Parliament which, while primarily Tory, cut across party lines. Here, then, was a combination of parliamentary and extra-parliamentary forces that could appeal to centrist politicians striving to gain the reins of power or to maintain them. It was not a safe road to extra-parliamentary politics, since no form of such politics was safe in a revolutionary age, but it was the safest of the available roads. To some politicians the rise of extra-parliamentary politics was deplorable, but it became an important feature of the struggle for power in Britain during the late eighteenth century. Opposition politicians within the Establishment had used it to come to power in the 1760s and early 1780s. By then it was clear that no government could stay in power if this form of politics was abandoned to the opposition.[20]

If the rise of extra-parliamentary politics and the threat of lower-class radicalism were the tinder for a political crusade against slavery, dissenting theology, particularly that of the Quakers, provided the spark. Led by George Fox, the Quakers were one of the numerous Protestant sects spawned in England during the civil wars of the seventeenth century. The aim of Fox and his followers was to liberate men "from enslaving creeds and institutions," and to bring them into a personal union with Christ. Their doctrine stressed the perfectability of man in the face of the corrupting forces of the world through personal struggle against these forces. They refused to pay certain taxes, swear oaths to the state, bear arms, or "bow or doff their hats to superiors."[21]

Despite their doctrinal views and their relatively extreme positions on individual liberty, Quakers were not political revolutionaries. They "respected the authority of government and the inviolability of private property," "they viewed labor at once as a duty and a necessary discipline," and they initially accepted slavery as part of the natural order of things. Fox sought converts among the slaveholders in the West Indies, the Quaker-dominated assembly of Pennsylvania passed a harsh slave code, and some Quaker merchants in the northern colonies and in England prospered through the slave trade and by supplying provisions to slaveowners throughout the Caribbean. Although a few Quakers began to question the compatability of slavery with their fundamental beliefs as early as the 1670s, such doubts were distinctly minority views until the mid-1750s.[22]

An earthquake in Philadelphia in 1754 followed by fierce Indian raids on Quaker households along the Pennsylvania frontier, which presaged the outbreak of the French and Indian War, created alarm and precipitated a moral crisis among Quakers. Their collective trauma was exacerbated by the persecution they experienced when they refused to vote for war taxes or to pay them. Interpreting the Pennsylvania events as divine retribution for sin, Quakers began a searching reconsideration of their entire record in the colony. Seeking inward spiritual resurrection, they launched a campaign to purify themselves that soon focused on slavery. The decision of the Philadelphia Yearly Meeting in 1758 to ban anyone participating in the slave trade from membership was the initial step of a quiet but successful drive that occupied the next quarter century, eventually disassociating Quakers on both sides of the Atlantic from every aspect of slavery.[23]

THE CAMPAIGN TO ABOLISH THE SLAVE TRADE

The transition from self-purification to public action against slavery did not come easily for British Quakers. The question of public action, which was forced upon them by their American brethren, remained contentious for nearly two decades. Finally in 1783 the London Yearly Meeting established an ad hoc committee to draft a petition calling on the House of Commons to forbid the slave trade and took other steps to lobby for that end, including the wide distribution of antislavery pamphlets through a system of provincial correspondents. In 1787, the Quakers established a non-sectarian committee that could widen the abolitionist campaign. Although they persuaded Granville Sharp, an Anglican evangelist with close ties to members of Parliament, to become the chairman of the London Abolition Committee, all but three of the 12 original members were Quakers, and none of the three Anglicans was in Parliament. However, the Committee rapidly won the covert support of William Wilberforce, the leading figure in the influential Clapham sect of Anglican evangelicals, a member of Parliament, and a close friend of the prime minister, William Pitt. By 1791 the membership of the London Abolition Committee was expanded to include Wilberforce (a "closet" member until that year) and several other members of Parliament including Charles James Fox, a leader of the Whig party, who was in power or at its edge for three decades.[24]

From 1787 to 1792, the London Abolition Committee concentrated on extra-parliamentary activities against the slave trade. To rouse the moral conscience of the nation they launched elaborate propaganda campaigns, distributing antislavery literature both through cooperating provincial committees and through the network of cooperating churches. John Wesley, for example, offered to cooperate with the Committee by preaching against the slave trade and by republishing and distributing through all Methodist chapels a new edition of his tract *Thoughts Upon Slavery*, in which he condemned the trade as a "pagan abomination," as "murder . . . by thousands," and as the most reprehensible practice in all English history. Wesley's support was important because he was one of the earliest religious leaders of first rank to speak out against slavery, because Methodist churches provided an effective instrument for conducting the extra-parliamentary campaign among the lower classes of the cities, and because his support represented an impeccable auspice for the campaign. The political orientation of the Methodists was initially conservative. Wesley opposed the extension of the franchise because the greater the role the people had in government, the less liberty the nation would enjoy. Viewing the French Revolution as the work of Satan, Wesley believed that the proper way to reform society was by transforming the will of the individual. To the lower classes Methodists preached that abstinence, hard work, and thrift were the essential qualities of those seeking salvation and of those saved. In Methodism the Puritan ideal was reborn without its political radicalism. What safer channel for extra-parliamentary politics in the cities could leaders of the Establishment find?[25]

Pamphlets and preaching were two ways in which abolitionists sought to rouse "the general moral feeling of the nation." A third and more novel method was the mass petition campaign aimed at the House of Commons and the House of Lords. Initiated by advocates of limited parliamentary reform and then employed by merchants and manufacturers of Manchester in their campaign against a tax on cloth, the abolitionists transformed petitioning into the central instrument of extra-parliamentry politics. For many subsequent decades the petition campaign became the pivot for rallying popular support not only for abolitionist aims, but for all middle- and lower-class reforms and radical movements that sought to alter the course of Parliament. The abolitionist petition campaign reached an apex during 1791–1792 when an unprecedented 519 abolitionist petitions, coming from all over Britain, were delivered to Parliament. Some 400,000 persons signed these petitions (1 out of every 11 adults), with Manchester alone contributing 20,000 names from an adult population of about 30,000.[26]

The enormous success of this drive was due in large measure to its auspices. "Unlike the political radicals of the 1790s" who had to use the "tavern, pub, or public place for their meetings" and petition campaigns, in city after city the abolitionists enlisted the official support of local governments, churches, and respectable private and public societies. If the local petition was not made available in the local city hall, it could usually be found in the churches or on the premises of some other officially recognized institution. Despite the degree to which the abolitionists "won over the formal structure of local governments and seduced a wide range of corporate institutions," their popular tactics had to be abandoned after the outbreak of war with France in 1793. The widespread revulsion against the excesses of the French Revolution and the patriotic fervor tended to tar all public campaigns. Even Wilberforce, staunch conservative, defender of private property, and close friend of the prime minister, was accused of Jacobin sympathies. Popular politics ceased to be a central factor in the struggle to close the slave trade during the next two decades, although awareness of the wide popular support for the measure influenced the debates in Parliament.[27]

How did the extra-parliamentary activities come to be translated into votes for abolition within Parliament? The connection was by no means automatic. As late as 1792 Edmund Burke, a Whig leader who later switched to Pitt's side and the leading theorist of the new brand of party politics, noted the great difficulty in developing as much support for abolition of the slave trade within Parliament as existed on the outside. The years before 1792, when the extra-parliamentary campaign was most intense, saw relatively little progress within Parliament. Despite persistent efforts by Wilberforce beginning in early 1788 to bring a bill up for debate in the Commons, it took three full years to achieve that end. The issue was delayed first by the establishment of a government committee to gather evidence on the issue, and later by a second investigation by a committee of Commons. The issue had to wait until April 1791 to be brought to a vote, and then it lost by nearly 2 to 1 (163 to 88). It was not until 1792 that the Commons voted in favor of gradual abolition of the slave trade, but that bill was put aside by the House of Lords in favor of their own investigation of the issue. It was not until 1795 that Wilberforce was again able to force a vote on a bill for abolition of the trade, which lost 78 to 26. A similar bill lost in 1796 by 74 to 70. Bills introduced by Wilberforce in 1797, 1798, 1799, and 1802 suffered similar fates. In no vote during these years did the support for abolition exceed 83 votes—which was less than 15 percent of the membership of the Commons.[28]

In May and June of 1804, shortly after the start of Pitt's second administration, the Commons again approved an abolition bill. Although the vote in favor of the bill rose to 124 (mainly because of strong support from Irish MPs newly admitted to Parliament by the Act of Union between Ireland and Britain) and the vote against fell to half its previous level, the measure died before it could be taken up in the House of Lords. In 1805, however, the bill was again defeated in the Commons, this time with the defection of Irish MPs who had become convinced by the West Indian lobby that the abolition of the slave trade was a threat to property.[29]

At this point Wilberforce changed tactics. Stating that "if we cannot stop the whole of this accursed traffic, it is much to stop half of it," Wilberforce called on Pitt to ban further sales of slaves to Dutch Guiana and to the French islands, which the British had captured in 1803. It was a critical maneuver in two respects. First, such a ban could be accomplished by administrative decree, since it fell within Pitt's powers to regulate the trade of captured territory without consulting Parliament. Pitt issued the decree on August 15, 1805, defending his action as a necessary expediency of war. Second, more than any other maneuver of the abolitionists, this approach tended to divide their potential opponents. Since the captured Dutch colonies were receiving a large share of the slave trade, and threatened to produce an increasing share of the sugar entering the English market, it could be, and was, asserted that English policy was an aid to the enemy. The claim was credible since at the Peace of Amiens in 1802 England returned nearly all of the Caribbean colonies it had captured during the first phase of the Napoleonic wars. Even though Pitt could quite reasonably base his decree on grounds of economic and military expediency, rather than on moral principles, he vacillated on the matter for more than a year and at one point presented a draft of the decree that was unacceptable to Wilberforce and his allies before taking the promised action.[30]

Pitt died five months after this decree and a coalition cabinet representative of most of the factions in Parliament took office, with Lord Grenville as prime minister and Charles Fox as leader in the Commons. The new ministry represented a precarious balance, with Grenville and Lord Sidmouth seeking to restrain the reformist instincts of Fox's friends, and with Fox under fire for betrayal of principle by the more radical wing of his faction. However, for the first time, a majority of the cabinet favored abolition of the slave trade and the two co-leaders of the cabinet, despite their differences on other issues, had long been identified with the abolitionist cause. Thus, abolition of the slave trade emerged as one of the few reform issues that could bind the coalition, the so-called "Ministry of all the Talents," together. The new ministry quickly passed a bill that ratified Pitt's decree banning the sale of slaves to Dutch Guiana and extended the ban to all foreign colonies, which brought an end to three-quarters of the British slave trade. Six months later, after a vigorous campaign to line up votes, especially by Grenville, both Houses passed a bill closing off the balance of the British slave trade.[31]

The British abolition of the slave trade was hailed by supporters of the measure and by subsequent commentators as "the most humane and merciful Act which was ever passed by any Legislature in the world"[32] and as one of "three or four perfectly virtuous pages comprised in the history of nations."[33] Even if one accepts the purity of the motives of those who engineered the campaign, such statements exaggerate the degree of British self-denial. The economic cost of the act to the British, or even to the West Indian planters, was small. The only clear economic losers were the merchants directly engaged in the African slave trade (located mainly in Bristol and Liverpool) who were forced to switch their capital to other enterprises. It is not at all clear that the West Indian planters were made *economically* worse off by this act per se. Indeed, during the 1760s and 1770s, the Jamaican legislature had moved to suspend the slave trade as a means of restricting the production (and raising the price) of sugar, but were prevented from doing so by the British government on the ground that the colonies could not be allowed to "check or discourage in any degree a traffic so beneficial to the nation."[34] As late as 1804 some members of the West Indian lobby in Parliament let it be known that they still favored a self-imposed suspension of the slave trade, although they vigorously opposed one forced upon them for moral reasons by Parliament. It should not be forgotten that the slaveowners of Virginia and the Carolinas were also refused permission to close the slave trade while under British rule, but did so after they won their independence—not because of moral scruples, but, as with the Jamaicans, out of a sense of economic self-interest. Recent cliometric estimates have sustained their view, revealing that a restriction of sugar production would have raised West Indian profits.[35]

There is still the question of the motivation of Parliament. In 1944 Eric Williams vigorously challenged the belief that those who abolished the slave trade were purely altruistic. Their professions of humanitarianism, he argued, merely cloaked the selfishness of a rising capitalist class that sought to sweep aside the outworn slavery interests that barred its way. There were sound grounds for disputing the saintly disinterest of the politicians who combined to close the slave trade. Surely there was enough virtue in that crusade to warrant its celebration without overlooking its self-serving aspects. But Williams sought the selfish aspect in the wrong place, emphasizing economic rather than political expediency. Recent studies of the economics of slavery (see Chapter 3 of this volume), especially the analysis of the economic position of the West Indian colonies before and immediately after the passage of the Act of 1807, have demonstrated that slavery in the West Indies and in its other main bastions in the New World was a vital, profitable, and expanding system that enhanced rather than diminished the wealth of the new commercial and industrial classes of Great Britain. The closing of the slave trade was a political move, not an economic one. The ending of British participation in the African trade, by itself, had relatively little effect on the economic life of the West Indies or the rest of the slave world.[36] The cost to the losers was mainly political: The ban revealed the political weakness of the West Indian bloc and so laid the basis for later moves that had a far more devastating impact on the economic position of West Indian interests. The benefits to the winners of the issue were also mainly political. Although a concession to the rising tide of reform sentiment, the ban was not as great a blow to the status quo as full legal equality for Protestant dissenters (which was delayed for another two decades) or parliamentary reform (which had to wait until 1832, and even then was of a limited nature). The ban satisfied some of the popular passion for reform and it clothed some of those politicians who supported it in an ethical garb. It was the only solid accomplishment of the "Ministry of all the Talents," yet it could not save that ministry, which was turned out of office on the Catholic issue just as the king gave his assent to the Act of Abolition.[37]

With the passage of the Act of 1807, the British abolitionist movement became relatively quiescent. Some of the former crusaders believed that the closing of the international trade would force West Indian planters to ameliorate the condition of their slaves so that, like the American planters, they could enlarge their labor force through natural increase. Others felt that the closing of the trade by itself would be sufficient to gradually strangle the slave system. Moreover, after 1807 cabinet ministers and key officials in the Colonial Office were sympathetic to the abolitionist cause. James Stephen, son of one of the militant leaders of the London Abolition Committee, became the legal counsel to the Colonial Office in 1813 and rose to the post of undersecretary. George Canning, one of Wilberforce's most vigorous allies before 1807, later became foreign secretary, the leader of the House of Commons, and, during the last few months of his life (he died in 1827), prime minister. Other foreign secretaries and prime ministers who cooperated with Wilberforce and later abolitionists included Viscount Castlereagh ("peacemaker of Europe" in 1815), the Duke of Wellington, Lord Liverpool (prime minister from 1812 to 1827), and Lord Palmerston (foreign secretary during 1830–1841 and 1846–1851 and prime minister during 1855–1857 and 1859–1865).[38]

The London Abolition Committee was disbanded in 1807, its place taken by an organization called the African Institution which worked through regular government channels to pressure other nations to follow the British example. Sweden agreed to abolish its slave trade in 1813, and a year later Holland made the same pledge. The restored Bourbon government of France signed a treaty in early 1814 agreeing to abolish the trade within five years, and at the Congress of Vienna held in late 1814 it joined in a general condemnation of the trade. But the declarations were easier to obtain than effective action. France did not legislate against the trade until 1818, and then did little to enforce its ban. Spain outlawed the trade in 1820, but like France, took no measures to enforce the ban. Consequently, the international traffic in slaves was nearly as large in the 1820s as it had been two decades earlier. As opponents of the Act of 1807 had predicted, the vacuum in the slave trade left by Britain's withdrawal was filled by its competitors, mainly Spain, France, and Portugal.[39]

Between 1807 and 1823 Wilberforce and other abolitionist leaders generally preferred to rely on their personal influence with cabinet members rather than on public campaigns. The one major exception took place in 1814 when Viscount Castlereagh seemed ready to let France resume the slave trade in order to win other concessions from Louis XVIII at the Congress of Vienna. On short notice the abolitionists launched a nationwide petition campaign to press for articles against the trade at the peace negotiations. In a little over a month some 800 petitions with about 750,000 names were gathered. It was a public campaign of unprecedented magnitude. About one out of every eight adults had aligned themselves with the demand for international agreements to end the slave trade. Although "irritated by this abolitionist pressure," Castlereagh felt "compelled"[40] to make the slave trade an issue and "to use both threats and bribes"[41] to obtain an agreement.

The British government moved to put teeth into declarations against the slave trade by pressing for treaties that permitted the mutual right of the parties to intercept and search ships on the high seas suspected of transporting slaves. Since Britain alone had the warships needed to patrol the coast of Africa, other nations feared that such treaties were devices through which Britain sought to continue the high-handed policy of interfering with merchant shipping that she practiced during the Napoleonic wars. Nevertheless, through a combination of pressure and indemnifications, agreements were signed with Portugal, Spain, and the Netherlands which authorized mutual search and which established "prize" commissions in Freetown, Sierra Leone, for the adjudication of the cases of captured slave ships. These commissions were empowered to decide—without the right of appeal—whether a captured ship was to be confiscated and the slaves liberated, but the crew and owners were to be tried in the courts according to the laws of the nations to which they belonged. In 1819 the British established a separate Slave Trade

Department in its Foreign Office to oversee its antislavery program and the admiralty established a separate naval squadron, initially consisting of six warships, to patrol the west coast of Africa. The African Squadron continued to operate for half a century, with the number of ships eventually increased to over 20.[42]

Between 1820 and 1870 the British Navy captured nearly 1,600 slave ships and liberated over 150,000 slaves. However, these figures reflect only a part of the British impact on the slave trade.[43] According to recent estimates, the risk of capture raised the cost of the slave trade so much that the importation of slaves from the regions of Africa patrolled by the navy was reduced to about 75 percent of the level that would have prevailed in the absence of the Squadron. Moreover, because of heavy British pressure, Brazil agreed to abandon the slave trade in 1851. Although Cuba formally acceded to British pressure in 1862, slaves continued to be imported until 1867, when the Atlantic slave trade finally closed.[44] Cliometric estimates indicate that the direct cost of the policy of suppression to Britain was about £12.5 million, with the maintenance of the African Squadron accounting for about 60 percent of the total. Indirect costs, including lost profits from sales of manufacturers in African markets, higher sugar prices at home, and red tape, may have added as much as £16 million, which would make the total cost of suppression nearly as large as the entire domestic expenditure on poor relief during the first seven years of the reign of Queen Victoria.[45]

THE CAMPAIGN FOR EMANCIPATION

During the last several years of the Napoleonic wars, abolitionists began pressing for the registration of all slaves in the British colonies, ostensibly to prevent smuggling. The idea was originally advanced by the elder James Stephen (the father of the legal counsel to the Colonial Office). Such a measure, he argued, could be justified as "a supplementary enforcement of a parliamentary act regulating imperial trade," but he expected it to be a powerful lever for amelioration and emancipation. He believed that an "accurate registration system" would provide "irrefutable evidence" of the abominable treatment of slaves, and either force the colonial legislatures to institute effective steps to ameliorate their conditions or provide a basis for the intervention of the British government. In 1812 the prime minister, Spencer Perceval, agreed to introduce such a system in Trinidad, where an administrative decree was sufficient (as a Crown colony Trinidad was governed directly by the Colonial Office). Shortly thereafter registration was extended to four more Crown colonies. The other colonies, established under charters, had self-governing legislatures that vigorously resisted registration, but eventually acquiesced under the threat of parliamentary action. Although not as complete as the Trinidad scheme, the registration acts of the colonial legislatures still provided much of the ammunition for the subsequent campaign for emancipation.[46]

The missionary work of dissenting churches among West Indian slaves, especially the work of the Methodists and Baptists, may have been the most important stimulus to the popular campaign for emancipation which began in 1823. Missionary work by the Methodists in the West Indies traced back to the 1780s but did not become widespread until the mid-1810s when an organization with a central secretariat was established. By 1823, about one out of seven slaves in the West Indies had been converted, four-fifths of them to Methodism.[47]

The official directions to Methodist missionaries warned that their "only business" was "to promote the moral and religious improvement of the slaves . . . without in the least degree, in public or in private, interfering with their civil condition."[48] Yet this stance did not clear Methodist missionaries from the suspicions harbored by West Indian planters. Although some planters saw the efforts of the Methodists as a means of promoting obedience, sobriety, and hard work among their slaves, those who remembered Wesley's antislavery tract and Methodist promotion of antislavery campaigns in England vigorously opposed their presence. Reports that missionaries sent back to England described the threats and harassments they suffered at the hands of planters and lent authenticity to the growing view not only among the Methodists but throughout the evangelical churches that West Indian planters were a corrupt class who were determined to keep slaves ignorant, to continue the oppressive gang system, and to resist all pleas for amelioration.

Aroused by these reports and frustrated by the constitutional scruples that led Lord Liverpool and his cabinet to resist parliamentary legislation that would override the colonial legislatures, the evangelical community again turned to extra-parliamentary politics to achieve their goals. The new campaign was led by the Society for the Mitigation and Gradual Abolition of Slavery throughout the British Dominions, popularly known as the London Antislavery Committee, which was established in 1823. Its personnel included the remnants of the old London Abolition Committee together with many younger foes of slavery, including Thomas Fowell Buxton who, like Wilberforce, was an Anglican evangelical and a member of Parliament. It was to Buxton that Wilberforce relinquished the leadership of the parliamentary fight against slavery. The new Committee was far more broadly based than the London Abolition Committee of 1787. Although Quakers were part of the new committee, they were a minority. Not only were Anglicans well represented, but Jabez Bunting, the leading figure in the Methodist movement

during the first half of the nineteenth century, was also an active supporter. This time the president of the Committee was not a former
linen-draper, but Prince William Frederick, Duke of Gloucester. The
vice-presidents included 14 members of the House of Commons and 5
peers of the realm. Although the ultimate aim of the Committee was the
gradual emancipation of all slaves, its immediate objective was the amelioration of their condition through judicial regulation of corporal punishment, the prohibition of labor on Sundays (which extended to the
right of slaves to market produce from their private plots), legal redress
for slaves, opportunity for manumission through self-purchase, and the
removal of all impediments to the religious instruction of slaves.[49]

As soon as Buxton introduced this program into Commons, George
Canning, as leader of the House of Commons, proposed a government
resolution incorporating the specific articles on amelioration and vaguely
committing the government to gradual emancipation but leaving it to the
colonial legislatures to give the force of law to the proposed program of
amelioration. Canning's motion was adopted without opposition because
the administrative measures he proposed were just strong enough to
sustain the hopes of the abolitionists while giving the West Indian lobby
the impression that they were a political expedient aimed at keeping the
humanitarians at bay. The government, which actually expected these
measures to be ratified in some form by the colonial legislatures, immediately instituted them in Trinidad, going even further than Wilberforce
and other abolitionists thought wise by making it illegal for drivers to
carry whips. Removal of that emblem of authority, said Wilberforce,
invited chaos.[50]

Despite government attempts to cajole and pressure them into adopting similar measures, the legislatures of the other colonies remained
defiant. And despite repeated mobilizations of British popular opinion
during the decade of the 1820s, the Antislavery Committee was unable
to rouse Parliament to enforce its previous call for amelioration. Parliament was so unmoved by these extraordinary extra-parliamentary displays that by early 1830 the leaders of the Antislavery Committee were
discouraged and their public campaign had ground to a virtual halt. Yet
within a year the tide turned dramatically and by the end of 1832
parliamentary leaders of both the Whig and Tory parties were eager to
ally themselves with the abolitionists in drafting the long-sought Act of
Emancipation.

These gyrations can only be understood by considering the more
general political currents within which the antislavery movement ebbed
and flowed. The new antislavery movement of the 1820s and 1830s, like
the earlier movement, was only of secondary importance in the rapidly
changing structure of British politics. Its fate was determined largely by

the way it intersected with more fundamental aspects of the struggle for power. The dominant issue that confronted contending political factions was how to control an expanding, increasingly complicated, and highly volatile civility.

The tight governmental controls, the heavy taxes, and the repression of popular liberties introduced during the Napoleonic wars were continued and, in some respects, intensified during the immediate postwar years. The 1820s, however, ushered in a series of liberal reforms that were supported by both Tories and Whigs. Taxes and tariffs were lowered, other restrictions on international trade were eased, the Combination Acts (which prevented the formation of trade unions) were repealed, criminal law was reformed, and "many capital offenses were swept away." The most fundamental reforms of the decade, in the sense that they rocked the foundations of the Establishment, involved encroachments on the supremacy of the Anglican Church. With the rapid growth of cities, the membership of the dissenting Protestant churches had grown much more rapidly than the Anglican majority, and were particularly strong around London and in such industrial and commercial cities as Manchester, Liverpool, and Leeds. By 1820 Protestant dissenters represented about 30 percent of the population. In 1828, after many years of pressure, culminating in mass campaigns led by a United Committee of all the dissenting churches, Parliament repealed the Test and Corporation Acts which had denied public office to Nonconforming Protestants. Although the growing urban civility made that decision expedient, it was not popular with the Anglican majority. The following year Parliament confronted an even more divisive issue.[51]

In order to forestall a revolutionary rupture of the union between Britain and Ireland, or at the very least a political crisis in which "the electoral influence of the landed gentry would suffer irreparable damage," Parliament passed the Catholic Emancipation Act. This was an exceedingly unpopular measure among Protestants, Anglicans, and dissenters alike. The price of that decision was the defection of many traditional supporters of the Establishment. The callousness of the leaders to the opinion of the public led conservative defectors "to the conclusion that there was more to be said for a reform of Parliament than they had so far been prepared to admit." Not only was the Tory party driven from office at the end of 1830, but when the Ultra-Protestant Tories joined the radicals in demanding a reform of Parliament, the Establishment was plunged into the deepest and most destabilizing split since 1688. This time, however, the issue was not which faction of the Establishment would rule, but the political fate of the Establishment as a whole.[52]

The various reforms of the 1820s, including Catholic emancipation, were forced to a considerable degree by the politicization of the lower classes. Food riots and industrial strikes, which had previously been aimed at specific grievances, began to take on a political character after 1815. In both Britain and Ireland the politicization of lower-class protests was due partly to the efforts of radical leaders of the movement for parliamentary reform who established political organizations in working-class districts. At the end of 1830 it was quite clear both to the outgoing Tory government and to the incoming Whig government that some sort of political reform was necessary if the Establishment was to retain its control of the nation. The parliamentary Reform Act sponsored by the new government of Lord Grey aimed at meeting the threat of lower-class radicalism by forging a coalition between the middle and aristocratic classes.

The revolutionary threat was created by a conjunction of events that split the Establishment and simultaneously propelled sections of the lower and middle classes excluded from the political process into increasingly more radical attacks on the Establishment. The rapid growth of trade unionism after the repeal of the Combination Acts in 1824 was one of the main ingredients in the crisis. Local underground labor organizations not only emerged into the open, but began to cooperate with one another.[53]

The downward movement in the business cycle of 1829–1832, although characterized as "minor" by some economic historians, appears to have had severe effects on the lower classes, and so added another ingredient to the crisis. Data on heights of poor London boys indicate that the period of rapid improvement in lower-class nutrition which began toward the end of the Napoleonic wars appears to have come to a halt in the late 1820s and that the nutrition of the London lower classes may even have declined for about half a decade. There was also widespread distress among rural laborers, especially in southern England during 1828–1830, brought about by rising unemployment, by declining income for small farmers, by declining wages for rural laborers, and by reduced funds for poor relief. These conditions led to a spontaneous series of rural riots in late 1830, with widespread destruction of farm machinery and the burning of stores of grain belonging to rich farmers, which spread from the southern counties to the Midlands. The attack was extended to the English church when middle-class farmers called for a repeal of the tithe and egged laborers into riots against the local churches. The rural uprising was finally brought to a halt when the new Whig government called in the army. Military action was followed by justice: Over a thousand protesters were imprisoned or exiled to Australia and 19 were executed, one for the crime of "knocking off the hat of a member of the Baring family."[54]

The crisis was further exacerbated by the spread of political radicalism, once largely a middle-class movement, to the lower classes, and by the danger that these two anti-Establishment movements, which were often divided on issues of deference and property, would coalesce. Lower-class radicalism was spurred during 1829–1832 by a succession of defeats for the unions, including the lost struggle over wages by the textile workers and the rout of the coal miners in pitched battles in the north of England and in Wales. The defeats led workers to entertain political solutions to their grievances, such as those offered by the movements for a new Factory Act and a 10-hour workday, movements promoted by the National Political Union and the more radical National Union of the Working Class. By early 1831 these competitive movements were being drawn together by the growing belief that the unreformed Parliament no longer acted for the nation. Despite deep mutual suspicions these extra-parliamentary factions joined in an "uneasy alliance" aimed at winning popular support for a radical reform of Parliament. The possibility that this radical coalition would pass from agitating for reform to fomenting revolution intensified in the fall of 1831 when the rejection of the Reform Act by the House of Lords touched off riots in Nottingham, Bristol, and Derby that ushered in a half year of continuing peril for the Establishment.[55]

The Reform Act was finally passed and became law in June 1832. It ended the revolutionary threat by splitting the middle-class radicals from the working-class radicals (the outcome that the authors of the Act had intended), despite the modest nature of the reform. Some "pocket" boroughs completely controlled by rich gentry were abolished, some large cities received greater representation in the House of Commons, and the property qualification for voting in boroughs (pegged to the ratable rental value of a house) was set at £10, which opened the franchise to some of the richer artisans. Perhaps the greatest change was the increase in the number of contested constituencies, which doubled, reaching two-thirds of the total in the election of December 1832, although in subsequent elections the number of contested seats declined.[56]

Despite the gentry's continued dominance in Parliament, the Reform Act of 1832 represented a fundamental concession to popular sovereignty, which became increasingly important over the subsequent decades. The immediate result of the reform, however, was to restore the alliance between the aristocracy and the middle classes by conceding to the latter a carefully measured role in the political process, "the least that would satisfy . . . the bulk of informed and influential opinion." The size of the electorate, which was increased from 500,000 to 813,000, still represented just one out of every seven adult males but now embraced "the entire urban middle class and the main body of farmers."[57]

How did the antislavery movement intersect with the main line of British politics? The critical element in the answer to this question is timing. During most of the period after 1823 the abolitionist movement was largely independent of the radical movement and was, to some extent, an alternative which served to deprive the radical cause of potential recruits. Whether this characterization is true or false (the issue is still in dispute among scholars), the abolitionist movement was perceived in this way both by radical leaders such as William Cobbett (who argued that black slaves in the West Indies were better treated than England's white "wage slaves") and by many members of the Establishment. However, a particular set of circumstances, culminating in 1832, greatly increased the militancy of the antislavery forces, threatening to alienate some of those sections of the population that Lord Grey called indispensable to the continuing rule of the gentry. The critical role of timing becomes clear when one considers the sequence of events that increased the political problem posed to the government by the abolitionist movement.[58]

Since the antislavery movement clearly identified itself with the Establishment, just as the West Indian lobby did, the principal problem for government leaders was to find a formula that would placate two loyal groups that were on a collision course. All of the government ministers who had to deal with the conflict between 1823 and 1832, both Whigs and Tories, sought to mediate between the two groups, conceding to some of the demands of the abolitionists but protecting the most critical interests of the West Indians on procedural grounds: The desired reforms had to be achieved constitutionally, which meant acting through the colonial legislatures.

Until 1830, the abolitionists within Parliament made the task of the government leaders relatively easy. Although they wanted a commitment to gradual emancipation, they were prepared to hold that demand in abeyance if there was genuine progress toward amelioration. They were persuaded that such progress was possible partly because the government pledged itself to that goal and moved vigorously in the Crown colonies, where it had the administrative power to do so. Moreover, the largest and most influential bloc of West Indian planters, investors, and merchants begrudgingly committed themselves to the full program of amelioration. These were the men who lived in Great Britain (many were in the Commons or were peers) and exercised their combined political influence through the Society of West India Planters and Merchants (the West Indian lobby) which in 1823 agreed to press the colonial legislatures for action on amelioration.[59]

A program that depended on action from these legislatures was bound to involve delays; it took half a decade before they all knuckled under to diluted versions of slave registration. Wilberforce, Buxton, and other parliamentary abolitionists were prepared to accept such a tortured route, provided there was clear evidence of progress. To prod the government into a policy of maximum pressure on the legislatures, the abolitionists organized massive extra-parliamentary campaigns, inundating Parliament with petitions for both amelioration and gradual emancipation. Meanwhile, they sought to pressure the West Indian legislatures by organizing boycotts of West Indian sugar and they campaigned for a reduction in the tariff on sugar from competing regions.[60]

In all their efforts to create an irresistible movement for amelioration and gradual emancipation, the abolitionists were careful not to antagonize their friends within the government or to encourage the growth of lower-class radicalism, which, like the Cabinet ministers and the great majority of Parliament, they considered an ever-present danger. Consequently, especially after the sharp rise in radical activity beginning in 1825, abolitionist leaders often felt compelled to restrain the popular antislavery campaign when it seemed to be in danger of encouraging radicalism and to relax their pressure on government leaders when they were obviously preoccupied with internal issues that threatened the entire Establishment. In 1825, for example, the London Antislavery Committee turned down a proposal to hire a corps of paid agents who would organize meetings across the nation aimed at rousing "public feeling" on the ground that such meetings might promote the already dangerous unrest among laborers. In 1826 Buxton and other abolitionists in Parliament deferred to Canning when he called on them to withdraw a motion censuring the colonial governments for the brutal treatment of missionaries and for the mass executions of rebellious slaves. Between 1827 and 1829 parliamentary and extra-parliamentary campaigns were subordinated to the struggles over the repeal of the Test and Corporation Acts and the Act of Catholic Emancipation. Even the Methodists, who became the main driving force in the campaign for amelioration and emancipation, were deeply distracted by the struggle over the religious issues. From 1826 to mid-1829 they paid so little attention to the antislavery campaign that discussion of it nearly disappeared from their publications. After passage of the Catholic Emancipation Act, the parliamentary abolitionists still hesitated to renew their pressure on the Cabinet because of the problems created by the "acute industrial depression"[61] and attendant disorders.

The call for renewal of the antislavery campaign came from the Methodists, first in July of 1829 and again in 1830. Drawing strength from their newly won political liberties at home, and deeply resentful of their persecution in the West Indies, the Methodists launched a series of antislavery activities more militant than ever previously undertaken.

The annual Wesleyan Conference of 1830 not only called on its members to support the petition campaign, but also enjoined each congregation to undertake a petition as a religious obligation, thus putting the petition "on a confessional basis."[62] The same conference urged its members to "give their influence and votes" only to those candidates for Parliament "who pledge themselves" to effective measures for the immediate and total abolition of slavery.[63] Such a patently political program was a "radical step" by the governing body of a church that had traditionally been firmly conservative.[64]

In May 1830, following the strong stand of the Methodists and pushed by the militancy of younger members, the Antislavery Committee voted in favor of immediate emancipation, thus abandoning the gradualist approach adopted in 1823. Although the new position was announced to Parliament in July 1830, no motion on the matter was introduced until April 1831. That motion was not pressed, however, when the new Whig government announced it "would have nothing to do with immediate emancipation" but agreed to take sterner measures to compel the colonial legislatures to adopt the program for amelioration. The government also adopted more stringent restrictions on the use of slave labor in the Crown colonies, including a reduction in the workday to nine hours during the crop season—a concession not yet granted to free laborers in Great Britain. Incensed at being forced to limit the workday of "a full-grown negro" to nine hours when "the Lancashire cotton manufacturers could legally exact twelve hours of labor from persons under sixteen," the planters in St. Lucia shut their sugar mills. Public meetings were held in parishes throughout Jamaica that repeatedly called for secession from the British empire and threatened to seek "the protection of the United States."[65] From May 1830 until the end of 1831, the majority of the Antislavery Committee, including its parliamentary representatives, much to the consternation of its young militants, hesitated to press the Whig government to go beyond its commitment to work vigorously for amelioration.

The campaign for immediate emancipation became much more militant in 1832. The change was precipitated by the slave uprising in Jamaica, which began during the Christmas season of 1831. Starting in St. James parish it rapidly spread to other parts of the island. Mansions, sugar works, and cane fields were burned, rum stores were pillaged, several whites were killed, and the local militia was at first unable to control the violence. However, the rebels were quickly subdued by a detachment of British troops. Within two weeks order was largely restored and by February 8 martial law was ended. Vengeance followed quickly and was meted out by the courts-martial conducted by the local militias, which shot, hanged, or flogged to death hundreds of slaves. The orgy of retribution turned from the slaves to the missionaries because Sam Sharpe, the slave who led the uprising, was a Baptist convert and a lay preacher in the church of Reverend William Knibb. Led by the Colonial Church Union (an organization dedicated to the protection of slavery and to the supremacy of the English church), a reign of terror was unleashed during which 14 Baptist and 6 Methodist chapels were destroyed. Knibb and four other Baptist missionaries were arrested on charges of sedition. While Jamaican newspapers called for the execution of the incarcerated preachers, missionaries of other sects, including several Methodists, were attacked; one of them was tarred and nearly killed by a mob.[66]

The terror against the missionaries inflamed public opinion in Great Britain and pushed the Methodists and other dissenters to new levels of militancy. The hatred for the dissenting missionaries displayed by the Anglican Colonial Church Union had the effect of fusing the struggle for religious freedom with antislavery. The combination was explosive. The Methodists, said Zachary Macaulay, member of the Clapham sect, "have not only caught fire themselves but have succeeded in igniting the whole country."[67] By May 1832 the new militancy had gone so far that it alarmed the parliamentary abolitionists. During this period the centrist politicians had largely lost control of the extra-parliamentary campaign, which was now in the hands of the younger and more radical abolitionists who, under the aegis of the newly formed "Agency Committee," had established within a matter of months several hundred new antislavery organizations throughout Britain. During the last half of 1832 the Agency Committee, the National Political Union, and the dissenting churches turned their attention to the parliamentary elections of mid-December, the first to be held under the Reform Act. Every candidate standing for election was asked to pledge himself to the abolition of slavery and about 200 did so. Early in 1833 the Antislavery Committee and the dissenting churches inundated Parliament with petitions. About one out of every seven adults, nearly twice the number of voters in December elections, had joined in the call for emancipation.[68]

The Grey government did not wait for the outcome of the December elections to decide that it was time to change its position to immediate emancipation, although the outcome of the elections reinforced its resolve to move along a new course. Having narrowly avoided a radical explosion in May over the Reform Act, the government recognized that the growing militancy and impatience of the abolitionists could undermine what stability had been achieved by the Act. In November 1832 Buxton was privately asked to draw up "a specific plan"[69] for emancipation that could guide the government. A few weeks later Viscount Howick, son of Lord Grey and a leading figure in the Colonial Office, held a private meeting with the West Indian lobby in which he warned that unless abolition could be put through by an "amicable arrangement."[70] between the government and the lobby, abolition would be forced upon the planters by Parliament. The next several months were occupied with intense negotiations between the government (under the direction of a special committee of the Cabinet which for a time met almost daily), the West Indian lobby, the parliamentary abolitionists, and the leaders of the Tories in the House of Lords. It was necessary to obtain a bill that would satisfy both the abolitionists and the West Indian lobby since Wellington had let it be known that the Lords would block any bill "which the West Indians, as an important interest group, would not accept." It was only after Wellington gave his assent to the government plan ("because the West Indians were satisfied") that it was announced to the Commons on May 14, 1833.[71] Debates in Parliament combined with behind-the-scenes maneuvering led to the introduction of a new compromise on July 5. Several attempts to amend the new plan were defeated. With one minor change, the bill was signed by the king on August 28, 1833, and the new law became operative on August 1, 1834.[72]

Under the Emancipation Act, the planters were to be compensated for the loss of their property. About half of the compensation would be in the form of a cash payment (£20 million) to the planters at the direct expense of British taxpayers. Most of the balance of the market value of the slaves would be recovered by permitting the planters to continue working the blacks for six more years under a regulated form of slavery euphemistically called "apprenticeship." The idea was to introduce immediately the reforms that had been set forth in the government's earlier program for amelioration. The next six years would thus provide an additional measure of compensation to the masters, borne by the slaves rather than by British taxpayers. The government argued that this period of time was also needed to inculcate slaves into the culture of wage labor, a task in which the churches would assist.[73]

The emancipation of British slaves, like the abolition of the slave trade, was caused by the "defection of the capitalists from the ranks of slaveowners," according to Eric Williams. Capitalists turned against slavery because they were "eager to lower wages" and the sugar monopoly that the West Indies held in the British market was a barrier to that goal. Yet the effect of the Act of Emancipation was not to lower the price of sugar to the British public, but to raise it. The increased price was due partly to higher sugar duties which were used to help finance the compensation of the planters. The main reason for the rise in sugar prices, however, was the fall in the productivity of the West Indian plantations. Not only did labor discipline on the sugar estates decline, but once free, the ex-slaves fled these estates in droves, moving onto vacant land where they produced foodstuffs (either for self-subsistence or for sale in the local markets) instead of sugar. West Indian exports of sugar declined and the price of sugar rose sharply in Britain. British consumers paid 48 percent more for sugar during the first four years of freedom than they had to pay during the last four years of slavery. Indeed, between 1835 and 1842 the extra cost of sugar to the British was about £21 million, thus raising the British outlay for emancipation to over £40 million. No wonder Cobbett and other radical leaders were so hostile to the antislavery campaign. Distributed to the urban poor, that sum could have doubled their income for a decade.[74]

It was neither capitalists nor their representatives in Parliament who passed the Emancipation Act, but the landed gentry, since the reformed Parliament was as fully dominated by the gentry as the unreformed Parliament had been.[75] The votes in Commons for the overall Emancipation Act were not produced by a tiny minority of special interests that somehow got the upper hand; support for the Act was so overwhelming that it passed by voice vote.

It has been possible to test the hypothesis that representatives of the rising capitalist class or other special interests played a critical role in the passage of the Emancipation Act. One cliometrician recently constructed several indexes of the degree of the pro-emancipation sentiment of individual MPs, using such information as their votes on key amendments, their parliamentary speeches, the ratings they received on emancipation by the Agency Committee, and a similar rating in *Dod's Parliamentary Companion,* an annual that reported on events in Parliament. These indexes were then related to characteristics of the individual MPs (occupations, sources of income, religion, ties to the West Indian lobby) and to the characteristics of their constituencies (region, urban or rural, whether the constituency benefited by the Reform Act of 1832, and the dominant economic interest of the district).[76]

This analysis revealed that religion and economic interests did influence voting behavior. Nevertheless, the various characteristics that denote "special interests" explain only 15 percent of the variation in the support for emancipation. In other words, whether considered singly or in combination, the "special interests" that have been advanced to explain the passage of the Act in the House of Commons were of minor consequence. Neither the domestic capitalists nor the members of the West Indian lobby voted consistently for or against the "pro-emancipation" position, although both tended to favor emancipation. The passage of the Reform Act appears to have strengthened support for emancipation but the effect was too weak to alter the final outcome. The strongest and most consistent influence was religious affiliation: Membership in a dissenting church added significantly to the likelihood that an MP would support emancipation. But the number of MPs belonging to dissenting churches was too small to make a difference in the outcome of any of the important votes.

It was the general political interests of the aristocratic class that accounted for the overwhelming vote in Commons for emancipation. To Lord Grey and the other centrist leaders of the Establishment the fundamental problem posed by the emancipation issue was precisely the same as that posed by the reform issue: doing just enough to ensure that the Establishment enjoyed the allegiance of the middle classes and the upper strata of the laboring class. Until mid-1832 the Grey government interpreted "just enough" to be more stringent about rules for the protection of slave labor in the Crown colonies, including a drastic reduction in the hours of labor and the right of representatives of the Crown to enter slave huts, inspect medical records, and otherwise monitor the treatment of slaves. In the legislative colonies, "just enough" meant new threats to penalize the islands economically if they did not adopt stringent measures for amelioration.

The Grey government shifted its policy to immediate abolition because the pressure to do so sharply escalated during a year of grave crisis. It was an issue that had galvanized all of the dissenting churches, particularly the Methodists, to new levels of political action. The government felt obliged to conciliate that large and potentially decisive political bloc on the issue of emancipation in order to ensure its support on other, more vital issues. By 1832, according to recent estimates, religious dissenters represented about 21 percent of the English electorate. The Methodists were especially important not only because they were the largest part of this bloc, but because they were becoming a swing vote; their new militancy on the slavery issue was pulling them from the conservative to the liberal side. When Grey spoke of needing to cement an alliance with "the real and efficient mass of public opinion," he was referring above all to the nonconformists, especially the Methodists, who formed the main counterweight to the radicals. In parts of England such as the textile region of Yorkshire, the Midlands, and East Anglia where the Methodists were very strong, radicalism had made little headway. Even in cities such as Manchester, where the radicals were strong, the Methodists could also claim the allegiance of a substantial part of the upper strata of the working class.[77]

Although the political activism of the nonconforming churches increased noticeably in 1832, the process of change had been under way for some time. The repeal of the Test and Corporation Acts set the process in motion by moving the leaders of the dissenting churches beyond the demand for toleration and toward an insistence that religious pluralism should be the official position of the state. The parliamentary campaign of 1831 in Leeds was a harbinger of what was to come. Richard Watson, second only to Jabez Bunting as a figure in the Methodist movement, boldly intervened in that election, supporting the Whig (Thomas Babington Macaulay) and denouncing the Tory-Radical (Michael Sadler). The ostensible reason for this intervention was Sadler's failure to sign a pledge committing himself to immediate emancipation, but beneath that veneer was a deep hostility to Sadler's radicalism and Anglican prejudice. "Ambition," said Watson, had made Sadler "court the high church and despise us."[78]

The attack on Sadler was one of many signs that the dissenting churches were intent on winning a wider role for themselves in civil affairs, signs that multiplied in 1832 as new demands for the rights of the dissenters and even proposals for the disestablishment of the Anglican Church began to surface. Although the dissenters were not yet strong enough to undertake a full-scale attack on the Anglican monopoly, they could, and did, raise the question obliquely by pushing the antislavery issue with unprecedented vigor. The Anglican Colonial Church Union conveniently provided a link between antislavery and the attack on the Anglican monopoly when they unleashed their religious war on the dissenting missionaries in Jamaica. The new intensity of the nonconformist campaign for immediate abolition was reflected in many ways: numerous public meetings, mass distribution of pamphlets, a new boycott of slave-grown sugar, and redoubled efforts to amass petitions. The scope of the movement became evident to every MP when the antislavery petitions deposited with Parliament reached 1.5 million signatures, which was more than double the number presented to Parliament at the height of the campaign on the Reform Act.[79]

The government's switch to immediate abolition thus appears to have been a timely response to the roaring demand of the "public . . . without whom the power of the gentry is nothing."[80] The switch not only enhanced the Whig position among the dissenters, but had the further effect of driving a wedge between liberal reformers and radicals. The radicals viewed the abolitionist campaign with deep suspicion, denouncing it as an instrument intended to divert attention from the plight of the English workers. They also denounced the dissenting churches, particularly the Methodists, contending that they sought to enslave "men's minds so that they could neither perceive the nature of their wage slavery nor rebel against it."[81] Few issues would give the centrist leaders of the Establishment a better weapon with which to isolate the radicals from the middle class and the more well-to-do workers.

Despite the claims of some abolitionists, the Emancipation Act brought no real economic advantages to domestic interests, and it is unlikely that many of those who voted for the Act placed much weight on hopes of economic gain. It is true that both Whig and Tory leaders vigorously defended the property rights of the West Indians, but the motivation was more political than economic. Since the protection of property rights was one of the most ancient and fundamental principles of the Establishment, emancipation could not become politically viable until the majority of Parliament was satisfied that the general rights of property holders would be unimpaired. To calm fears on this matter the government stressed that only one highly specialized and narrowly held form of property was being proscribed. Not only was the amount of property at issue relatively small (it represented less than 2 percent of the total wealth of all British property holders), but its proscription was handled in such a way as to reinforce the rights of property in general. This was accomplished by offering to compensate slaveowners fully for the value of their slaves, as well as by promising to continue commercial preferences to West Indian planters in the English market. Far from using emancipation to enhance the economic position of domestic interests, Parliament made domestic interests pay a heavy price in order to protect the "legitimate" property rights of the West Indians.[82]

What about the upper-class Anglican evangelicals who provided so much of the leadership and the money for the antislavery campaign, some of whom thought that slavery should be abolished without compensation to the planters, and who were so widely hailed as saints for their generosity? Were they not altruistically motivated? If by altruism one means a concern for the welfare of others, then the "saints" were without doubt among the most altruistic men of their age, for they zealously pursued that concern, often to the point of being meddlesome. If by altruism one means philanthropic, then the "saints" were certainly altruistic since they shunned the goal of economic self-enhancement and willingly expended their lives and wealth in benevolent enterprises. Lord Teignmouth and Charles Grant, for example, refused to follow the "conventional practice" of using their positions as high officials in India "to enrich themselves." Zachary Macaulay, to cite another example, sacrificed not only his health but almost his entire fortune in behalf of the antislavery movement, causing his son, Thomas Babington Macaulay, to sell gold medals won as a student in order to support himself. It is when one comes to other such connotations of altruism as "leniency or mercifulness in one's judgment of others," "absence of selfishness," and "indifference to one's own welfare or interests" that difficulties arise. The "saints" were neither democrats nor egalitarians, but thoroughly patrician gentlemen. They believed that it was the pious obligation of their class to be charitable to the "worthy" poor, but they were equally dedicated to suppressing "the mob," "revolution," "industrial conspiracy," "radicalism," and everything else that threatened the established order. They were convinced that poverty for the masses was inevitable and that only demagogues would preach otherwise. In their view attempts to agitate the lower classes on this question were a threat to the established order that justified repression by the sternest measures.[83]

In all of their various campaigns, including the struggle against slavery, the "saints" strove to strengthen the aristocratic order, to protect the rights of property holders, and to ensure the preeminence of the Anglican Church. To the extent that their endeavors were intended to serve and preserve the institutions that they cherished, the "saints" were driven by something less than pure altruism. Neither by word nor by deed did they indicate their willingness to sacrifice cherished institutions in order to enhance the welfare of those who hated these institutions or sought to replace them. They had the fortunate capacity to see mercy in the sternest measures of repression when they were exercised against the enemies of the aristocratic order and the Anglican Church. Zachary Macaulay, for example, staunchly defended the authorities responsible for the "Peterloo Massacre," the forceful attack on a radical meeting in Manchester during which 11 people died and hundreds were wounded, blaming the incident on "seditious publications"[84] that had inflamed the lower classes. Antislavery, in the view of the "saints," was not an assault on the aristocratic order but a step that was essential to purify and preserve it. Their altruism resided in the personal sacrifices they were prepared to endure in order to improve and protect their way of life, rather than in a willingness to assist those who wanted to institute another way of life.

THE STRUGGLE TO ABOLISH SLAVERY "THROUGHOUT THE WORLD"

Buxton and his colleagues closely monitored the application of the Emancipation Act in the West Indies and soon mounted a new campaign against the efforts of planters to sabotage its implementation. Although Buxton threatened to take parliamentary action to terminate the period of "apprenticeship" and bring about the immediate and total abolition of slavery, such action was not necessary. Harassed by abolitionists, missionaries, and Crown officials, encountering increasing difficulties in maintaining the labor discipline of "apprentices," and fearful of possible slave uprisings, the various colonies voluntarily voted to end slavery in 1838, two years ahead of the statutory deadline. Abolitionists developed an extensive program to help the freedmen adjust to their new circumstances, but their attention after 1838 increasingly turned to the problem of eradicating the slave trade and ending all slavery.

The question naturally arose, even in abolitionist circles, as to whether Britain had the right to interfere in the internal affairs of other nations. But such qualms were generally overridden by both pragmatic and moral arguments. The pragmatic argument was that "no change of principle" was involved "since Britain was already committed to interfering in the affairs of other nations in seeking to put down the slave trade." The moral argument was that slavery was such a cruel and sinful system that "the nationality of the slaveholder became a matter of secondary importance as compared with the obligation to act." Citizens of other countries, including those hostile to slavery, did not look kindly on British intrusions into their domestic affairs. To other nationals this moral "obligation to act" raised suspicion and resentment when the meddlers were private citizens, and it led to a rise in international tension when the Foreign Office did the meddling.[85]

Consider France, for example. In the early 1840s the prime minister was François Guizot, a former professor of modern history at the Sorbonne, a leader of the Revolution of 1830 which ushered in the constitutional monarchy of Louis Philippe, and a supporter of the antislavery cause. Guizot and his cabinet were reluctant to act quickly on the report of a Royal Commission which recommended the compensated emancipation of French slaves. One sticking point was the high cost of such action and the taxes required to cover the cost. Confronted with a movement for reform of the French Assembly and with the threat of renewed lower-class radicalism, the Guizot government was reluctant to risk the prevailing balance on a secondary issue. When a delegation of British abolitionists arrived in Paris in 1842 to stir popular sentiment for emancipation, Guizot invited their leader to dine with him, but his minister of the interior issued a decree canceling the public meetings at which they were to speak. French abolitionists did not adopt the recommendations of their British colleagues that they launch a nationwide campaign to pressure Guizot's ministry into immediate action. Having no provincial affiliates, nor desiring any, the aristocratic leaders of the Société pour l'Abolition de l'Esclavage preferred to use their influence quietly among high government officials in Paris. That approach bore little fruit. It was not until the Revolution of 1848 swept out the monarchy and proclaimed a republic that emancipation was enacted.[86]

By the mid-1830s, the U.S. South was the main bastion of slavery and the biggest challenge to British abolitionists. They sought to help rouse public sentiment in America by writing and distributing pamphlets aimed at winning support for immediate emancipation from the American branches of the Protestant churches with which they were affiliated, by sending speakers to tour American cities, by raising tens of thousands of pounds from British citizens to support the campaigns of American abolitionists, and by calling on the British Foreign Office to bring pres-

sure to bear on the American government. Although American abolitionists largely embraced this support, it raised a storm of protest throughout
the nation, North as well as South. In his address to Congress in 1835
Andrew Jackson called attention to the recent lecture tour of British
abolitionist George Thompson, labeling him a "foreign emissary." Well
before Jackson's address, Thompson had been threatened by mobs in
Boston and Lowell which denounced him as a "racial amalgamist" and
newspapers had branded him as a "foreign incendiary" who was sent by
the British to "subvert American institutions." The annexation of Texas
provides another example of the way that the good intentions of British
abolitionists backfired. Treaty negotiations had been stalled by Northerners who feared that the entry of Texas would tip the political balance
in favor of the South when word leaked out that the British foreign
secretary, under pressure from the abolitionists, was attempting to use
loan guarantees to get Texas to agree to abolish slavery. That news was
used by the administration to kindle nationalism in Congress and helped
to build support for annexation.[87]

British abolitionists were able to find other countries where their
exertions could be effective. One of these places was India, where slavery
of various forms flourished on a vast scale. The estimates of the number
who were enslaved ran as high as 16 million souls. Indian slavery was
not proscribed by the Emancipation Act of 1833 because it was an
indigenous institution. British policy in India, while promoting trade,
had developed on the basis of "nonintervention in the affairs of the
native states."[88] Moreover, unlike the profit-driven gang system of the
West Indies, the slavery that flourished in India was of the domestic
variety. Most slaves in India "were kept for purposes which had no
immediate connection with pecuniary profit." They worked typically as
"hereditary domestics" in the houses of rich landowners for whom a
"large retinue" was "a sign of affluence and station." It was widely held
that "much Indian slavery was relatively benign," and that "there was
no conscious desire for freedom on the part of the slaves, who were well
aware of the advantages of their condition as compared with that of the
landless freemen."[89] Among the starving freemen, the sale of children
by parents, of wives by husbands, and self sale were common.

There were enough harsh characteristics of Indian slavery, however,
such as the extensive trade in concubines, including girls as young as 8
or 9 years of age, to arouse abolitionists to action when they were no
longer preoccupied with the West Indies. Their public campaign to end
Indian slavery was launched in 1839. Under the threat of action in
Parliament, the British governors of India removed the legal sanction for
slavery in 1843. Implementation of the antislavery policy, which frequently brought the British into conflict with local rulers, was difficult

and many decades passed before Indian slavery was finally ended. The struggle against slavery was part of a wider movement (initiated by Wilberforce, Zachary Macaulay, and other members of the Clapham sect) to impose English culture on India, which included opening India to British missionaries and the substitution of English for Persian as the official language.

The last great victory of the British abolitionists was the suppression of the Islamic slave trade. Since it had little to do with the West Indies, the British at first paid scant attention to the trade of African slaves across the Sahara and along the east coast of Africa, bound for the Islamic world. Larger and more ancient than the Atlantic trade, it originated in the early Middle Ages. According to recent estimates, the cumulated trade to Islamic countries in Northern Africa and the Near East probably exceeded 4 million persons before the New World was even discovered, and it doubled by 1800. Although the Atlantic trade went into decline after 1830, the trade to the Islamic regions continued to expand. The total for the nineteenth century appears to have been about 3 million—considerably larger than the trade to Cuba and Brazil, the main targets of the African Squadron.[90]

The struggle to suppress the Islamic slave trade did not move to center stage until the 1860s. The principal figure in rousing the British public on that issue was David Livingstone. A medical missionary in Africa from the early 1840s, he became a national hero in Great Britain during the early 1850s when accounts of his trek up the length of South Africa and then across central Africa, from the west to the east coast, won him an award from the Royal Geographical Society. On his return to Africa in 1858, this time at the head of an expedition financed by the British government, Livingstone set out to explore the territory surrounding the Zambezi River and its tributaries. On this expedition, which lasted six years, he saw for the first time how the Islamic slave trade operated. Shocked at "the bloodshed, the burning villages, the deserted corn, the corpses floating down the river, the panic-stricken fugitives," and "the chained slave gangs on their way to the coast," he appealed to the foreign minister, Lord John Russell, to allow him to take possession of the territories he had discovered in the name of the Crown "as the only means of saving the unhappy people."[91] In the mid-1860s, however, the Foreign Office was not willing to expend its resources on such an enterprise. Recalled to England by Lord Russell, Livingstone campaigned vigorously for a change in English policy, arguing that the interception of Islamic slave ships on the high seas was not enough. The slave trade would not be suppressed unless England accepted the obligation of bringing "Christianity, commerce, and 'civilization' to the source of the evil, the heart of Africa from which the slaves came."[92]

By the 1870s missionaries began pouring into the hinterland of Portuguese Mozambique, the source of the Islamic trade, to the annoyance of officials in the Foreign Office who had to deal with Portuguese protests against the intrusion. In the late 1870s the Foreign Office negotiated a treaty with Portugal for the cooperation of the two governments in opening the interior of Africa to European commerce and in suppressing the slave trade, but before it could take effect the Portuguese government collapsed because of opposition to the treaty. An effort to revive the treaty in 1884 failed when British abolitionists and missionaries (who doubted that Portugal would actually suppress the slave trade and feared that it would discriminate against Protestant missions) campaigned against it. Another attempt was made to find some agreement among the European powers for a cooperative approach to the development of Africa at the Conference of Berlin, held during 1884–1885. But its resolutions were largely ignored. The scramble of the European nations for African territory had begun. The British antislavery movement continued to press for British intervention in Africa, calling on the Foreign Office to promote humanitarian objectives including the abolition of the slave trade, the control of the arms and liquor traffic, the protection of missionaries, and the encouragement of legitimate commerce—all of which would bring "civilization" to Africa.[93]

CHAPTER EIGHT

THE AMERICAN CAMPAIGN: From the Revolution to the Abolitionist Crusade

British abolitionists who toured the United States in the 1830s and 1840s found it a difficult, sometimes dangerous, but most often frustrating experience. "It is," wrote Harriet Martineau, British author and social critic, after returning from such a tour, "a totally different thing to be an abolitionist on a soil actually trodden by slaves, and in a far off country, where opinion is already on the side of emancipation."[1] What made the American struggle against slavery so different from the British one, and politically so much more difficult, was not so much that American soil was trodden by slaves but that it was also trodden by their owners. Slaveowners did more than merely walk on American soil. They had been instrumental in defining American polity and in shaping American culture; from the beginning of the United States to the time that Martineau ended her American tour (1836), they had controlled the politics of the nation. Not only were five of the first seven presidents slaveholders, but the slaveowning members of Congress had had a far-reaching influence over national legislation for nearly half a century, and there was no end in sight.

It was not merely the overarching power of the slaveholders that differentiated the American and British cases. There was also a different constitutional situation and a different political process in America. The Constitution not only recognized slavery and made it lawful, but also guaranteed that the power of the federal government would be employed to protect the master's right to his human property. Nowhere in the Constitution was there a word regarding the rights of slaves or of the duties of masters to treat them humanely. Such matters would continue to be regulated by state and local governments and courts, as they had been in the colonial era, and hence were beyond federal jurisdiction. Since Congress was deprived of the power to ameliorate the conditions of servitude, a whole range of humanitarian issues that were so critical in building Parliamentary support for emancipation in Great Britain were removed from the congressional arena.[2]

The Revolution and the Constitution greatly accelerated the process of popular democracy, making it impossible to insulate congressional

238

politics from popular politics. Although developments in Great Britain were also pushing that nation toward popular politics, the pace in Britain was much slower than in America. As has been shown, the main victories in the British struggle against slavery took place during an era in which British politics were, despite the increasing influence of popular movements, still substantially controlled by a few hundred families and their supporters in Parliament.

American abolitionists, by contrast, could not expect to achieve their goals by persuading a few powerful figures in Congress. Although they did find American counterparts to Wilberforce and Buxton in such congressmen as John Quincy Adams of Massachusetts and Joshua R. Giddings of Ohio and in such senators as Salmon P. Chase of Ohio and Charles Sumner of Massachusetts, there were no American counterparts to William Pitt, Lord Grey, and Lord Palmerston: political figures in whom power was so concentrated, and who were sufficiently insulated from popular pressures that they might use their office, even when it was politically questionable, to restrict slavery or to abolish some major aspect of it. From the beginning, American political leaders had to heed their electorate. The struggle over policy was a complicated mixture of congressional and popular politics in which the popular aspect predominated. The struggle for power and for control of policy in America rapidly became a struggle to shape or to anticipate the changing views of an electorate that was rapidly growing wider and more diverse in economic interest, religion, ethnicity, and political culture.

Despite the exceedingly difficult constitutional and political situation, a powerful antislavery movement eventually emerged in America, and it prevailed. Recent research in three overlapping fields (intellectual, religious, and political) of American history has greatly illuminated this process.[3] Although some of this work has focused on the antislavery struggle per se and has been stimulated by the same currents that have prompted black history, much of it has not. The flowering of religious history, for example, is related to developments after World War II in American theology. The new work in political history, on the other hand, reflects a number of technical advances in this field including a more thorough analysis of the documents of the Revolutionary and the early national era, intensive studies of hitherto neglected documents bearing on state and local politics (especially after 1820), and the use of quantitative methods to analyze voting patterns and their changes in legislatures and in popular elections. Whatever the impetus, the new work has produced massive amounts of new evidence bearing on the evolution of the antislavery movement and has stimulated numerous reinterpretations of that movement and its place in the transformation of American society.

A marked feature of all three fields is the attempt to uncover the "social forces" that brought about changes in religious institutions, in ideology, and in political life. The influence of the sociological approach may, to some extent, explain the recent convergences in the interpretation of the antislavery movement among scholars whose fields have led them to approach the subject from quite different perspectives. Yet the influence of the sociological approach should not be exaggerated. Among historians of religion and intellectual historians specializing in the antislavery movements there has been a determined effort to resist "obtuse secularism"[4] and to accurately recreate the role of religious inspiration, of mysticism rather than secular materialism, in the shaping of the American antislavery movement. Despite their seeming inconsistency, interpretations that stress mysticism have dovetailed rather than clashed with interpretations spawned by secular materialism.

Before considering this synthesis it is necessary to define two terms that were used interchangeably in the discussion of the British case but which need to be distinguished in the American case. In this chapter the term *abolitionist movement* will refer to organizations or societies that were avowedly dedicated to the emancipation of slaves in America regardless of the method by which they sought to achieve that objective. The term *antislavery movement* or *coalition* will refer to organizations or societies that were prepared to oppose some aspect of slavery even if they also opposed the emancipation of slaves. Although abolitionists were part of the antislavery movement, most of the participants in the broader movement were not abolitionists and many were hostile to abolitionists and their goals. Two subgroups of the abolitionist movement also need to be recognized. The term *abolitionist crusaders* will designate the most radical wing of the movement, evangelicals who believed that slavery was a sin. The term *political abolitionists* will designate those professional politicians and their advisers who sought complete emancipation but realized that their goal could be achieved only by building a coalition that was capable of embracing every opponent of slavery, no matter how limited the basis for that opposition. The political abolitionists were also often crusaders, but they did not usually advertise that fact to the public and sometimes even denied it, especially if they were elected to their office by a diverse constituency, representing themselves instead merely as consistent antislavery men.

THE REVOLUTION AND THE DESPIRITUALIZATION OF ANTISLAVERY

The American Revolution gave an enormous impetus to the struggle against slavery, but it also profoundly affected the course of that struggle.

The Revolution changed the ideological basis for the opposition to slavery; it shifted the initiative in the definition of the issues from mystics to rationalists, from saints to politicians, and it plunged the question of slavery into the center of the struggle for power. These changes had much to do with the profound differences in the character and the effects of the British and American struggles against slavery: with the peaceful outcome of the British movement and its fratricidal course in America, with the relatively conservative role of the movement in British politics and its promotion of radical politics in America.

In both America and Great Britain the struggle against slavery arose as a religious movement rather than as a political one. In both countries the issues eventually entered politics, but the circumstances of that entry were much different. In Great Britain the movement from a purely theological issue to a political one came gradually and the issue was introduced to political life by men who felt that the struggle against slavery was an indispensable part of their religious testimony, of their struggle against sin. They sought first to convince evangelicals in other denominations who shared their belief in the possibility of achieving personal salvation through the struggle against inner and outer sin. Thus, the struggle to win Parliament to antislavery was in content a simple extension of their religious witness, although the method of the exercising of this witness was more complicated since they had to win the support of men who, although Christians, did not share their theology and often held theological views contrary to their own. They met this obstacle both by seeking to convert those in power to their views, in whole or in part, and by finding new arguments against slavery that would not only bridge theological and philosophical gaps but make antislavery politically expedient. Toward that end they sought to convince men engrossed in secular affairs that parliamentary action against slavery, even if limited, was an appropriate matter for the state and politically feasible, perhaps even advantageous. Throughout the long struggle against British slavery, "saints" were always forcing the issue on reluctant, or at least cautious, politicians who would rather have neglected the issue; they never had to compete with these politicians for moral leadership of the issue.

In America the issue of slavery was brought into politics before the "saints" were really prepared to carry it there and, ironically, some of the men who made it a political issue were interested in protecting their property rights in slaves rather than in abolishing slavery. During the 1760s and 1770s the Quakers were still mainly concerned with purging their own ranks of slaveowners, although their antislavery message spread beyond their own circles and influenced Benjamin Franklin and other Revolutionary leaders in Pennsylvania and New England. A few

of these leaders began to question slavery, not on the religious grounds
of the Quakers, but on the grounds that it was uneconomical and that
it clashed with the political doctrine of natural rights that formed the
basis for Revolutionary agitation.

The linking of slavery with the doctrine of natural rights also arose
in Virginia, quite independently of Quaker or evangelical theology.
During the 1760s and 1770s the Virginia legislature, dominated by
slaveholders, passed acts encumbering or prohibiting the external slave
trade, not as a step toward emancipation, but to prevent a glut from
depreciating the economic value of their slaves. These acts were eventually "vetoed by authorities in London"[5] and the failure of the English
government to permit slaveholders to act in their own self-interest became part of the Revolutionary indictment. In 1772 Virginia directly
presented its grievances on this point to the king, complaining that
English insistence that slave trade into Virginia should continue unabated was a sacrifice of colonial interests in order to enhance the
position of English merchants. And in the Continental Congress, ironically, the most insistent demands for action against the African slave
trade came not from the delegates of Pennsylvania or New England, but
from Virginia.[6]

So it was the leaders of the South as well as the North who made
slavery a central issue of the Revolution. That southern slaveholders
could join with non-slaveholding Northerners in opposing slavery, and
could do so in good conscience, is explained by the particular way the
issue was articulated during the Revolution. Revolutionary leaders not
only politicized the issue of slavery but transformed it from a spiritual
question to a rational one. This transformation deprived slavery of the
keen moral edge that Quakers and evangelicals gave it and subordinated
the slavery imposed on blacks to the overall goals of the Revolution.[7]

Two aspects of Revolutionary ideology, common to both Northerners
and Southerners, were involved in the transformation. First, the leaders
of the Revolution were deists—rational religionists who shunned mysticism and revelation. Indeed, 52 of the 56 signers of the Declaration of
Independence belonged to the Freemasons, the principal organization
promoting deism in America, which held that "reason and scientific
knowledge could supply all the necessary elements of religion and ethics." Deists were not necessarily anticlerical, and the majority of the
Revolutionary leaders, although in favor of the disestablishment of the
Anglican Church and in favor also of the separation of church and state
generally, wanted to maintain and expand the influence of the various
denominations on a voluntary basis. As John Adams put it, "Christian
Religion" was the most effective instrument in spreading "the great
Principle of the Law of Nature and Nations, Love your Neighbor as

yourself." Thus, Christian churches advanced rationalism because "no other Institution for Education, no kind of political Discipline, could diffuse this kind of necessary Information, so universally among all Ranks and Descriptions of Citizens." Deism also produced a radical position, most eloquently articulated by Thomas Paine, which attacked the Bible and organized religion, stigmatized the clergy as a "priest-craft," and offered instead a totally secular democracy. But it was Thomas Jefferson, "the St. Paul of American democracy," who was by far the most influential of the rationalists. A central figure in working out the solution to the problem of the relationship between church and state, his particular blend of religious philosophy and political theory, and his sometimes blunt anticlericalism, did much to make deism ascend-ant over mysticism during the Revolution and the early years of the new republic.[8]

The despiritualization of the slavery issue was also promoted by the tendency of Revolutionary leaders to view all political issues through the prism of natural rights. That doctrine emphasized that government was a social contract voluntarily accepted by free men. To the northern and southern rebels the most heinous form of slavery was the imposition on a free people of a government that acted against their will. Revolutionary leaders thus saw their struggle for independence as a struggle to free America from enslavement by England. "Slavery" became "the most frequent" word "in the Revolutionary vocabulary." But the outrage inherent in this use of the term was directed not at what American masters were doing to their chattel but at what the king and Parliament were doing to their colonists. Although Revolutionary leaders saw a connection between the two forms of slavery, the nature of the connec-tion was not beyond debate. Moreover, the appropriate remedy for chat-tel slavery was far less clear than the remedy for the political slavery forced on the colonists by the English.[9]

The usurpation of the slavery issue by politicians had a mixed effect on the abolitionist movement. By despiritualizing the problem of chattel slavery the moral urgency of the issue was blunted. Chattel slavery was not a sin, a horrible violation of God's commandments, but at worst the breach of a contract among men. Moreover, it was not at all clear that a contract was actually breached since Locke, among others, had specifi-cally excluded chattel slaves from the social compact. Even if it was conceded that slaves were included within the compact, the precise nature of their rights had to be carefully considered, as did the rights of their masters. Revolutionary leaders generally agreed that black slaves were, in most respects, inferior to whites and that, whatever the arguments in favor of emancipation, its implementation posed numerous problems and dangers to the community.[10]

One of the dilemmas created by the switch from divine revelation to natural rights as the basis for opposing slavery related to the rights of the masters. The natural rights doctrine closely linked freedom and justice with the inviolability of private property. The threat to the liberty of the colonists created by Parliament's attempt to confiscate a part of their property by arbitrary taxes was one of the central issues of the Revolution. Since life, liberty, and property were an inseparable trinity in the natural rights doctrine, compulsory manumission of slaves "would violate the right of masters to their own property" including their right to dispose of their property as they wished. "A revolution carried forward in the name of this right" thus created "a serious and enduring impediment to compulsory abolition."[11] Adherence to the natural rights doctrine embarrassed those southern politicians who were prepared to concede that slavery was a violation of the natural rights of the enslaved. Adherence to the doctrine also embarrassed northern politicians who, although they despised slavery, felt compelled to concede that the doctrine protected masters who would not voluntarily manumit their slaves.

The quandary between the natural rights of masters and of slaves made it difficult to turn rhetorical declarations against slavery into concrete action, even in the northern states. The isolation of the Quakers during the Revolution, because of their refusal to endorse the war, also undermined the movement. The Pennsylvania antislavery society that Quakers organized in 1775 soon became inactive and did not revive until 1784. Quiet efforts by Quakers and antislavery evangelicals in other denominations nevertheless continued, but required a shift in rhetoric. At least in their public expressions, their spiritual objections were often couched in the secular language of the Revolution. Thus, appeals to natural rights tended to replace the former emphasis on the sinful avarice of the master, on the violation of "the spiritual brotherhood of all men," and on the sin of condemning slaves to perdition by preventing them from exercising their free will.[12]

THE PROSLAVERY OFFENSIVE AND THE DECLINE OF THE FIRST ABOLITIONIST MOVEMENT

The Constitutional Convention also served to weaken the antislavery movement. Although there were numerous antislavery speeches, the overriding problem before the delegates was the development of a structure for national government strong enough to fulfill the millennial aspirations of the Revolutionary leaders and flexible enough to win the support of the contentious interests in the different states. To achieve that goal it was necessary to overcome not only divisions over slavery, but rivalries between large and small states, between agricultural and commercial interests, and between those who wanted a strong federal government and those who feared that a strong federal government would lead to despotism. The determination of most Southerners to protect their sectional interests meant that slavery had to be accommodated if the overriding goals of the Convention were to be attained.[13]

Because the deep-South bloc was "demanding where their opponents were more tepid and ambivalent, and because they knew just what they wanted, where their opponents had no particular program concerning slavery," the Constitution that emerged from the Convention contained "no less than ten clauses . . . that directly or indirectly accommodated the peculiar institution." In the compromise on counting slaves as three-fifths of a person both for purposes of representation in Congress and for direct taxes by the federal government, in empowering Congress to provide the military force to quell slave rebellions, and in requiring states to return fugitive slaves to their lawful masters, the Constitution clearly legitimized slavery, although the "scruples" of the delegates, as James Madison put it, kept them from actually using the word "slavery" in these clauses.[14]

Indeed, the power of the national government to trespass on the interests of slaveholders was explicit only in giving Congress the authority to prohibit the international slave trade. Yet even this authority was not necessarily perceived as an antislavery measure since Virginia slave-holders favored such a ban. As a concession to the newer slave states, the implementation of the ban was postponed for at least 20 years, but an immediate ban on the international slave trade was imposed on the Northwest Territories.[15] That provision did not arouse the opposition of any of the slaveholding interests at the Convention, although it introduced an ambiguity upon which antislavery forces later seized. Neither Article IV, Section 3 (which gave Congress the power to "make all needful rules respecting the territory or other property belonging to the United States"), nor Article I, Section 9 (which deferred the abolition of the international slave trade until at least 1808), explicitly acknowledged the right of slaveowners to migrate into the territories with their slaves. Slaveowners did not push for such an explicit guarantee because, as Madison later put it, not even the most "farfetched interpretations ever hinted" that Congress had the power "to prohibit an interior migration of any sort."[16]

Yet after the loophole became apparent, its usefulness as an instrument for the emancipation of slaves was far from obvious. Even if Congress voted to prohibit slavery as a condition for the establishment of a new state, slaves elsewhere would not be emancipated. Moreover, the implementation of this limited encumbrance on slavery was beset by political barriers far greater than those faced by British abolitionists.

When the Constitution was ratified slavery was legal not just in the South
but in all but two of the northern states, although three others had passed
acts of gradual emancipation. To win a majority in Congress against the
extension of slavery into the territories there had to be a majority of
Congress committed to such a policy. Yet the first two western territories
admitted to the Union after the ratification of the Constitution were
slaveholding territories that became Kentucky and Tennessee, and no
group in Congress sought the abolition of slavery in these territories as
a condition for their admission to statehood. Their senators and representatives were seated "without protest" in either house.[17]

The positive influence of the Revolutionary doctrine on the abolitionist movement was most evident in New England and Pennsylvania. The
Vermont Constitutional Convention of 1777 outlawed slavery in its first
article. In New Hampshire and in Massachusetts slavery was outlawed
as a result of judicial interpretations of the new constitutions of these
states, although in New Hampshire the issue remained somewhat ambiguous until 1857. Abolition advanced in Pennsylvania, despite the attack
on the Quakers, when "a new coalition, composed of Philadelphia radicals and their Scotch-Irish backcountry allies, assumed the reins of
power under the new and radical constitution of 1776." By 1780 the
Pennsylvania legislature passed the new nation's first act of gradual
emancipation which freed the unborn children of slaves on their 28th
birthday. Similar legislation soon followed in Rhode Island and Connecticut, but it was not until 1799 that New York followed suit, and New
Jersey delayed enacting gradual emancipation until 1804.[18]

On the other hand, the negative influence of the Revolution on the
abolitionist movement began to reveal itself even before the Constitutional Convention. The sudden concentration of power into the hands of
committed rationalists, the tendency for Quakers, Anglicans, and Methodists to be identified as loyalists, and the perils besetting devout mystics
in other denominations who failed to embrace fully the Revolutionary
spirit all combined to repress evangelical fervor. For most denominations
the Revolutionary era and the early years of the new nation were a period
of decline. "The churches reached a lower ebb of vitality during the two
decades after the end of hostilities than at any other time in the country's
religious history." Under these circumstances much of the energy that
evangelicals might otherwise have devoted to abolitionist activities was
spent on protecting their churches and on struggles within their churches
over theological issues.[19]

Nevertheless, the religiously inspired antislavery movement was
never entirely snuffed out. Quakers cautiously continued their antislavery witness during the war years and when hostilities ceased they reorganized an antislavery society in Pennsylvania, with Benjamin Franklin

as its titular head. Between 1784 and 1791 abolitionist societies were organized in all of the states except for North Carolina, South Carolina, and Georgia. The inhospitality of these states to any sort of antislavery activity was prefigured by the large number of slaves they continued to import and by the militant, implacable defense of slavery that the delegates of these states made at the Constitutional Convention.[20]

The new abolitionist societies were directed primarily toward local issues, especially the prevention of the deportation of slaves from states that had instituted gradual emancipation, the execution of the provisions of emancipation acts, the prevention of the kidnapping of free blacks, and "the improvement of the condition of the free blacks by mental and moral training and by teaching and helping them to support themselves." In New York and New Jersey, which had not yet instituted gradual emancipation, the societies also pressed for the passage of such legislation. The main thrust of the societies was not toward mobilizing popular protest but toward defending the legal rights of blacks, enslaved and free, and organizing programs for self-improvement of free blacks.[21]

After the adoption of the Constitution, abolitionist societies cautiously sought a more political role, focusing on the power of Congress to control the international slave trade. The lead was taken by the Quakers and by the Pennsylvania Abolition Society, which in February of 1790 (less than two weeks after the Constitution became operative) presented Congress with its first three antislavery petitions. Over the signature of Benjamin Franklin, the petition of the Pennsylvania Society urged Congress "to countenance the restoration of liberty"[22] to slaves, while the two Quaker petitions, in language that reflected a deeply religious hostility to slavery, denounced the "licentious wickedness"[23] of the international trade and called on Congress to take immediate action to abolish it. The petitions were referred to a committee which soon reported that the Constitution prevented Congress "from passing an act of emancipation," from prohibiting "the slave trade until 1808,"[24] from interfering in the management or sales of slaves, and even from stopping the reinslavement of free blacks. However, Congress did have authority to regulate immediately the conditions of the African trade and to prohibit foreigners from outfitting slave ships in U.S. ports. After a bitter debate, and by a margin of one vote, Congress voted to accept a version of this report that was stripped of the clauses that were most offensive to slaveowners.[25]

Even these small concessions helped to stimulate a more political orientation on the part of the abolition societies. Memorials urging Congress to take those actions against the slave trade that were available to it were submitted in 1791 and 1793. In 1794 a conference of nine abolition societies met in Philadelphia to plan concerted activities aimed at inducing congressional action. They constituted themselves as the American Convention for Promoting the Abolition of Slavery and Improving the Conditions of the African Race. This convention met annually until 1806, and then biennially or triennially until its demise in 1832. However, the activities of the abolition societies produced only one clear-cut victory against the proslavery bloc in Congress during the next quarter century. That was the Act of 1794 (strengthened somewhat in 1800) which "forbade any person in the United States, citizen or foreigner, to engage in the carrying of slaves from Africa to countries other than the United States." In 1803 Congress rejected Indiana's request that the ban on the importation of slaves into that territory be suspended, but that position was supported by slaveowners who feared that any revision of constitutional provisions on slavery might set a dangerous precedent.[26]

Nor can the enactment of a ban on the international slave trade in 1807 be viewed as a defeat for the proslavery forces. By 1798 all of the slave states had enacted laws prohibiting the importation of foreign slaves. Although these laws were ineffective (slave importations reached an all-time peak between 1790 and 1808), they reflected the belief of many slaveholders that further importations were harmful to their economic interests. Although the majority of representatives from the slave states appear to have regretted the ineffectiveness of state laws, they resisted early action by Congress as a dangerous breach of the constitutional safeguards of slavery.[27]

By 1807 the end of the constitutional delay on congressional action against the external slave trade was at hand, and slaveholders joined with Northerners in enacting a law with teeth in it. When the critical vote came up in the House, the bill passed by 113 to 5, three of the dissenters coming from the South and two from the North. The insertion of additional provisions by the Senate aimed at providing a further safeguard against smuggling raised alarm among proslavery forces in the House that a precedent might be implied for regulating the internal slave trade. Although fear of the effects of this provision led to a substantial deflection of southern support, enough remained for the amended bill to pass. A threat that disaffected southern congressmen would "march to the White House and demand that Jefferson veto the act" never materialized. On March 3, 1807, Jefferson signed the Act which, although it effectively ended the external slave trade, nevertheless reconfirmed the legitimacy of slavery and the control of the institution by the governments of the states in which it flourished.[28]

Indeed, during the first 20 years of the operation of the Constitution, abolitionist attempts to impair the effectiveness of slavery through congressional action had come to naught. Quite the contrary, the proslavery bloc in Congress won decisive victories in every major confrontation with the antislavery bloc. Successive attempts to push forward the date of effective actions against the slave trade were defeated, as were attempts to prevent the extension of slavery beyond the original thirteen states. Moreover, Congress overwhelmingly enacted a stringent Fugitive Slave Act in 1793; it refused to act against the kidnapping of free blacks by slave traders in 1796; it refused to prevent the reenslavement of manumitted slaves in 1797; and it nearly passed a bill in 1801 that would have compelled an employer who hired a black anywhere in the country to publish a description of him in two newspapers and would have put the burden of proving that he was actually a free man on the black and his employer. But even on so aggressive a bill, the setback to the proslavery forces was temporary. In 1817 Congress enacted a law that directed "the seizure of any black suspected of being a fugitive and ordered his removal to the state granting the warrant for his arrest."[29]

The string of victories by the proslavery bloc in Congress, which indicated their increasing domination of federal policy, served to dishearten and demoralize many abolitionists. Moreover, in New England the local victories against slavery, together with the dwindling of the black population in these states, reduced the opportunity for antislavery suits or benevolent activities in behalf of free blacks. In the eastern border states, especially Virginia, the antislavery movement was undermined not only by the decisive legislative rejections of gradual emancipation and by the encumbrance of voluntary manumission, but also by the general unwillingness of Jefferson, Monroe, and other heroes of the Revolution to lend public support to even attenuated forms of opposition to slavery. The proslavery forces within these states, preying on the public's fear that freed slaves would become a burden if not a threat to society, "vented their spleen upon the abolition societies" which sponsored "court suits" for the freedom of slaves. Not only were the antislavery societies infiltrated by opponents of such tactics, but in 1795 the Virginia legislature passed an act that penalized "all those who assisted Negroes in unsuccessful freedom suits."[30]

That act, which seemed to be aimed at abolishing all antislavery activity, together with the hysteria promoted by the attempted slave insurrection organized by Gabriel Prosser in 1800, led to the demise of the Alexandria Anti-Slavery Society. This society was not the only casualty of the proslavery offensive. Harassment in the South and weariness in the North led to the collapse of most of the antislavery societies. Toward the end of the first decade of the nineteenth century, only the abolition societies of New York, New Jersey, Pennsylvania, and Delaware were still active, and they were "weak and discouraged." Even the "mainstay of the movement," the Pennsylvania Society, could ask the meeting of the American Convention in 1806 "whether any material injury would arise from a temporary suspension of its functions."[31]

Underlying the weakness of the abolition societies was the disheartening of the antislavery forces within the evangelical churches that had previously vitalized the antislavery movement by providing both moral fervor and personnel. Among the Methodists, for example, the retreat from their strong antislavery position of 1784 became apparent at their General Conference in 1796 when the rule requiring expulsion of a church member who bought or sold a slave was modified to apply only to members who sold slaves. In 1804, members of churches in the Carolinas and Georgia were made entirely exempt from the rule about slave trading, and Methodist preachers were, for the first time, required to "admonish and exhort all slaves to render due respect and obedience to the commands and interests of their respective masters." In 1816, a report of the General Conference concluded that political circumstances rendered "emancipation impracticable" in the South and admitted that it was "not in the power of the General Conference" to "bring about such a change in the civil code as would favor the cause of liberty."[32]

Ironically, the revival of religious enthusiasm at the beginning of the nineteenth century also contributed to the decline of the first abolitionist movement. The process is illustrated by the experience of Samuel Hopkins, a congressional minister and a leading theologian of the New Divinity school which gradually succeeded in coping with rationalism without subordinating mysticism; they did so by creating an evangelical movement for spiritual and social reform that was based on divinely inspired benevolence. Moved by such a spirit, Hopkins became one of the first non-Quakers to denounce slavery as "a very great and public sin." He also called on the Continental Congress to go beyond merely condemning the slave trade and to free "all those who have been reduced to a state of slavery by that trade."[33] By 1787, however, Hopkins began to express disappointment at the failure of the Revolution to produce a "unified, purified society." He interpreted this failure "as evidence of God's displeasure with America for the continued existence of slavery."[34] His dismay deepened when he discovered that the Constitution had delayed the abolition of the slave trade for 20 years.[35]

By the mid-1790s disappointment had deepened into resignation. Viewing the abolition of slavery as an event that would follow rather than precede the millennium, Hopkins counseled the faithful and benevolent to concentrate not on social but on spiritual reform, to "preach the gospel and thereby subdue the pride and greed that caused slavery in the first place." The successes of the religious revival that began at the turn of the nineteenth century, together with the series of defeats at the hands of the proslavery forces, channeled the evangelical impulse for reform into the spread of the gospel at home, the conversion of heathens at home and abroad (especially in Africa), the distribution of the Bible and of Christian tracts, the reform of manners, the care of the handicapped, the suppression of drinking, and the honoring of the Sabbath. Many evangelicals, especially in the South, sought to overcome worldly corruption and to achieve salvation through the quest for "personal holiness" and by promoting "revivalism rather than by direct attacks on social evil."[36]

Despite the succession of defeats and the dwindling of supporters, abolitionists continued to fight against slavery, seeking new forums, new forms, and new issues that could reverse the proslavery trend. Many evangelicals continued to press their denominations to speak out against slavery. Some congregations took such stands even when they expected to be overruled by higher councils, and some churches withdrew from their denominations when the majority "turned a deaf ear to their antislavery proposals,"[37] prefiguring the sectional schisms of the 1830s and the 1840s. Quakers were especially active in finding new ways to promote antislavery activity. Between 1811 and 1823, Elias Hicks, a leading Quaker minister, published pamphlets denouncing the use of slave-produced products as a sin and called on his brethren to desist from dealing in such products. In 1826, Benjamin Lundy, the editor of a Quaker newspaper called the *Genius of Universal Emancipation*, began to publicize and establish "free-produce stores."[38] Others concentrated on freeing slaves, some legally by promoting private manumission or using the courts to free slaves who had been kidnapped, others illegally by giving refuge to runaway slaves and organizing "stations" for the "Underground Railroad."

One of the persistent schemes of abolitionists was to organize colonization programs for manumitted slaves. "The colonization idea, in one form or another, went back almost as far as the Quaker antislavery testimony itself." Such American abolitionists as Benjamin Lay, Anthony Benezet, Hopkins, and Lundy and such British abolitionists as Granville Sharp, Zachary Macaulay, and Wilberforce endorsed black colonization. Some proposals called for the organization of settlements west of the Alleghenies, others singled out Africa, but Haiti, Louisiana, and Mexico were also suggested as feasible sites. The motivations for colonization among sincere abolitionists varied. Some proponents believed that "Negroes were incapable of assimilation into the American body politic," others feared that whites would never treat blacks as equals.[39]

Evangelism was also a powerful motivation. Hopkins believed that God "had allowed the slave trade so that blacks could embrace the gospel in the New World and then bear the glad tidings back to Africa."[40] A similar spirit moved Sharp, Macaulay, Wilberforce, and other members of the Clapham sect when they established the Sierra Leone Company

to resettle freed slaves in that land. For more than two decades the
Clapham sect "cherished this Company as one of their most important
and significant projects" because "it offered a means of demonstrating
how Africa could develop under civilization and Christianity."[41] During
the early years of the nineteenth century, "northern religious magazines
popularized the idea that the Christianization of Africa would atone for
the accumulated sins of slavery and the slave trade"[42] but it was not until
1817 that a nationwide organization was established to implement that
objective.

The establishment of the American Colonization Society not only
stimulated a renewal of antislavery activity but it represented the last
major effort to develop an intersectional movement against slavery. The
principal initiative for the formation of the organization came from
Robert Finley, a Presbyterian cleric in New Jersey. The organization was
widely supported by abolitionists who advocated gradual emancipation
but was viewed with suspicion by the more radical abolitionists in the
older societies. Nevertheless, it was overwhelmingly supported by the
evangelical establishment and by the 1820s many northern ministers,
especially Congregationalists and Presbyterians, commonly gave Independence Day sermons endorsing African colonization. The organization
was also widely supported by prominent leaders of the Federalist party,
many of whom (in keeping with their desire to reverse the loosening of
the traditional social hierarchy and to bring "order and decorum" into
cities rocked by growing crime, drunkenness, and indigence) were also
active in a wide array of benevolent organizations.[43]

It was in the South, especially the border states, that the American
Colonization Society did the most to revive antislavery activity. The state
legislatures of Maryland, Virginia, Kentucky, Tennessee, and Georgia
initially endorsed the activities of the Society. Local auxiliaries were
established in most of the southern states, and men of great distinction
served as its officers. Bushrod Washington, nephew of the father of the
country, was its first president. He was succeeded by Charles Carroll of
Carrollton, James Madison, and Henry Clay. The southern renewal of
support for moderate antislavery activity was made possible by the care
with which the Colonization Society defined its position. Nowhere did it
challenge the legality of slavery, and to calm the alarm of the proslavery
forces it disclaimed "any intention of interfering" with the legal right
"of slaveholders to control their human chattels and dispose of them as
they saw fit." Its constitution declared that its direct activities were
aimed solely at "the removal of free Negroes." However, in its official
journal the Society admitted that it hoped these activities would have the
indirect effect of increasing voluntary manumission and that it would
ultimately lead to "the total elimination of black servitude in the United

States" by convincing "the Southern people that emancipation might be safe, practicable, replete with blessings, and full of honor."[44]

Resolute abolitionists like Lundy thought that this approach might work, and in any case the colonization movement created a favorable atmosphere for the promotion of abolition societies that openly advocated and promoted gradual emancipation. During the decade of the 1820s both colonization societies and more openly abolitionist societies greatly increased in number and membership. By 1832 there were 306 local colonization societies, 70 percent of which were in slave states. The abolitionist societies experienced a similar expansion. According to Lundy, by 1827 there were 106 abolitionist societies with 5,150 members in slave states, and 24 societies with 1,475 members in free states.[45]

Despite the willingness of the Colonization Society to proclaim the legality of slavery, despite its promise not to infringe on the property rights of slaveholders, and despite the many slaveholders who felt that clearing free Negroes from the South would reduce the danger of insurrections, militant leaders of the proslavery bloc, especially in the deep South, viewed the Colonization Society with alarm.[46] To them "colonization was a front for northern 'fanatics,' " a Trojan horse peopled by men eager to open the gates to the legions of their enemies. The issue came to a boil in 1827, when the Society petitioned Congress for support. Having difficulties in finding free blacks who were willing to go to Africa and in raising funds to support their settlement in Liberia (where the Society had purchased a large tract of land), the Society appealed for funds to be set aside from the sale of federal lands for this purpose.[47]

Proslavery militants in Congress responded with fierce hostility. This petition was a subterfuge, an "entering wedge" to reopen the slavery question and to establish a "constitutional precedent" that was "vital" to the antislavery forces. If it was admitted that "Congress could promote the general welfare by colonizing free Negroes, it could also promote the general welfare by freeing Negro slaves." South Carolina's senator Robert Y. Hayne demanded that the petition be tabled without further discussion. "The only safety of the Southern States," he argued, "is to be found in the want of power on the part of the Federal Government to touch the subject at all."[48] Congress complied with the demand, and it did so again in 1830 when the petition was reintroduced. The reaction of the deep-South bloc made it clear that it would not consider any scheme, no matter how mild or how remote, that in any way threatened to end slavery. In 1827 the Georgia legislature repudiated its earlier support of colonization and condemned the request for federal support with "self-righteous scorn." The "selfishness" and "zeal," it declared, with which "citizens in other states" attempted to interfere "with our local concerns" was "totally unwarranted by either humanity or constitu-

tional right" and the result of such continued interference would be
"awful and inevitable."[49]

By the beginning of the 1830s the failures of the colonization movement and gradual emancipation in the South were becoming increasingly
evident. Abolitionists who had once agreed that cautious, indirect approaches had their virtues were now having doubts. After more than a
decade of effort, under 1,500 blacks had been settled in Liberia, and very
few of them were manumitted slaves. The proposition that the colonization movement would weaken southern resistance to gradual emancipation had been disproved. In 1830 William Lloyd Garrison, who had
supported colonization just two years earlier, had come to view it as "a
proslavery plot, designed to rid the South of the troubling presence of
free Negroes." The most dangerous aspect of such indirect approaches
was that they diverted the energies of humanitarians who despised
slavery from effective action into impractical schemes that promoted
racism and undermined abolition.[50]

THE RELIGIOUS SOURCES OF THE NEW ABOLITIONIST MOVEMENT

Beginning about 1831 a new abolitionist movement came into being. To
be sure, the old and the new movements were related, but as cousins
rather than as father and son. There was relatively little overlap among
the leaders of the two movements, although William Lloyd Garrison, the
editor of the *Liberator*, began his antislavery career as an aide to Lundy.
The most important difference between the new and the old movements
was in their religious inspirations. Although Quakers participated in the
new movement, the driving leadership came from men identified with the
transformed Calvinism that took root especially in the Congregational,
Presbyterian, and Unitarian denominations. Although the new movement had a highly rational aspect, it was the rationalism of New England
theology rather than of deism; it was rationalism used as a weapon to
fight infidelism, to justify divine revelation, to convert nonbelievers to
revealed truth, and to infuse society with religious zeal. To understand
the origins of the new abolitionist movement, the divisions within it, and
its contribution to the emergence of an antislavery movement so successful that it prevailed over the proslavery forces, it is necessary to understand the religious movements of the first half of the nineteenth century.[51]

THE SECOND GREAT AWAKENING
The new wave of religiosity, which historians of religion call the "Second
Great Awakening," began toward the end of the 1790s in New England

but rapidly spread to the rest of the nation, and gained momentum after the close of the War of 1812. The movement surged in the 1820s and 1830s and then continued with some ups and downs to the end of the 1850s. During this half century the revival movement spread west; first into upstate New York, along the Mohawk Valley, then into Ohio, especially in the area known as the Western Reserve which had once belonged to Connecticut, then into northern Indiana, Michigan, northern Illinois, Wisconsin, and Iowa. The New England churches belonged predominantly to the Congregational and Presbyterian denominations in which Calvinist theology predominated. However, the Second Great Awakening was spurred by a significant modification in the Calvinist doctrines of New England theologians. While retaining and even intensifying their mysticism and their piety, the disciples of the modified Calvinism (called the "New Divinity") began to emphasize the capacity of sinners to achieve salvation through personal struggle against inner and outer corruption.[52]

The new theological movements of the Northeast coincided with two other developments that in combination transformed religious life in America so profoundly that it produced what one theologian has called a "righteous empire."[53] The first was the rise of the Methodist Church. Although it had no independent existence in America at the close of the Revolution, by the middle of the nineteenth century it had become by far the nation's largest Protestant denomination. The Methodist Episcopal Church was organized in Baltimore in December 1784, with a creed derived from the Church of England, as modified by Wesley. It also adopted Wesley's modified version of the Anglican Book of Common Prayer. From its initial footing in the Middle Atlantic states, the denomination spread West, North, and South, establishing itself in every region of the nation. By 1790, the church membership had increased to nearly 58,000. Inspired by Wesley's condemnation of slavery, the Methodists were the first church in America that "exhorted" its "preachers to proclaim the gospel to slaves,"[54] and it indirectly gave birth to the first black denomination when some free black Methodists withdrew to form the African Methodist Episcopal Church in 1816.

The proselytizing zeal of the Methodists led to an eightfold increase in its membership during the 1780s. Although schisms slowed its growth during the 1790s, the rapid expansion of the denomination resumed in the new century. During the first three decades of the nineteenth century its membership again increased eightfold, reaching over a half million by 1830. During the next two decades, the membership more than doubled, so that by 1850 the Methodists, with one and a quarter million members, far overshadowed the Baptists, who had become the second-largest Protestant denomination.[55]

The rapid rise of Methodism was a major factor in the emergence of an "evangelical empire" in America. The theology of Wesleyan Methodism accepted a man's sinful state but, unlike Calvinism, emphasized the possibility of achieving grace by faith. Rejecting the doctrines of predestination to damnation of all but a few elect and the irresistibility of grace to those on whom it was bestowed, Wesleyans declared both "that men could resist the Spirit and fall from grace"[56] and that sincere Christians could, by appropriately ordering their lives, achieve not just salvation but perfection; that is, they could become "perfected in the love of God and man and wholly delivered from sin."[57] Thus, the life of every committed Methodist became a search for sanctification or sinlessness. That ultimate objective was available to everyone and could be achieved through the dynamic interaction between divine grace and human will. The quest for perfection required piety, austerity, and benevolence—not just self-examination, but the promotion of an enthusiasm for holiness among others.

Another significant development was the emergence of the Baptists as a popular denomination. One of the three original Puritan denominations, the Baptists grew slowly after the establishment of their first church in Rhode Island in 1639. A century later there were still just 96 Baptist churches with about 100,000 members, which was less than a quarter of the Congregational membership. Then two Baptist missionaries fired by the First Great Awakening (the New England revivalist movement of 1730–1760) undertook the immense task of evangelizing the stream of migrants to the southern frontier. They achieved great success in the Piedmont section of North Carolina during the 1760s, and then in Virginia in the early 1770s, despite fierce repression by the government. The influence of the Baptists continued to increase during the Revolutionary era. Commended by Jefferson and Washington for contributing to freedom of conscience, and inspired by Calvinist zeal, Baptist churches grew rapidly, especially in New England and Virginia.[58]

With the pushing of the frontier beyond the Allegheny Mountains, Baptist influence accelerated. Their membership increased more than tenfold in 60 years, reaching over 750,000 at mid-century. Baptist success was due in large measure to the vigor with which they organized revival meetings, their appeal to emotions rather than intricate theological arguments, and their widespread use of ministers who traveled westward with their flocks. Although often unlearned, these Baptist preachers exuded zeal and warmth that moved their hearers to "overpowering emotions" and that often led to "seizures, convulsions, and uncontrollable weeping."[59]

The revivalist movement among the Congregationalists and Presbyterians of New England differed significantly from that led by Methodists and Baptists. Although both denominations reflected a modified Calvinism which offered sinners the possibility of salvation through struggle against worldly corruption, the New England movement was more sedate and intellectual, less personal, less emotional, and less inwardly oriented. To be sure, the "New Divinity" stressed the need for an inner conversion but it also sought to make contact with rationalistic Scottish philosophy, and to recognize the human capacity to act virtuously. The aim of this theology was not to demysticize religion but to make mystical experience relevant to the needs of the time. One of the central tenets of the New Divinity was that self-love was sinful and that "true virtue consists in 'disinterested benevolence,' even unto complete willingness to be damned if it be for the greater glory of God." This emphasis led in two directions. It helped to promote "a benign, optimistic, and utterly respectable Christian rationalism" which eventually emerged as the Unitarian schism. But it also served to turn reformed Calvinism in the direction of fighting inner corruption by engaging in movements for "moral reform and social benevolence." In so doing they inspired an army of "missionaries and humanitarians" who created an array of new organizations to facilitate such work and so brought into being "the benevolent empire."[60]

The revivalist efforts of the Congregational and Presbyterian churches accelerated when the two denominations formally agreed to join forces under a "Plan of Union" drawn up in 1801. Spurred by "the threat of deism and Unitarianism," by competition from Baptists and Methodists, and by the shortage of "adequately trained clergymen to maintain doctrinal standards"[61] in the rapidly expanding frontier areas of western New England and upstate New York, the plan allowed the two denominations to cooperate in missionary work. Under this agreement, Congregational and Presbyterian clergymen could minister to congregations of either denomination, depending on the availability of clergymen and the desires of the congregation, although west of the New York–New England border, the churches would fall under Presbyterian administration, while to the east of this border administrative authority would be in the hands of the Congregationalists.

In agreeing to the Plan of Union, the two churches were responding to a remarkable exodus of New Englanders. This exodus was brought about not by a catastrophe but by a situation far more favorable to the natural increase of population than existed anywhere else on the continent or in the world, for that matter. Not only were birth rates very high in New England, but during the seven decades between 1750 and 1820 mortality rates were exceedingly low by the standards of the time, due in part to the high protein diet and the low density of the population.

The life expectation that prevailed in New England during this half
century would not again be achieved until the 1930s. The consequence
was a rate of natural increase so rapid that in the absence of outmigra-
tion, New England's population would have multiplied by about twelve-
fold during these seven decades. The crowding of New England and the
rise in land values spurred the exodus that prevented New England's
garden from being turned into a Malthusian hell. Yankees swarmed into
the western frontiers at the call of land companies set up in the northern
portions of New York, Pennsylvania, and Ohio.[62] Lying along the "natural line of advance for migrants from New England's rock-strewn fields,"
the "society and institutions" of these areas "took on a strong Yankee
tincture." The exact proportion of Yankees in the eight northern states
that formed New England's diaspora cannot be known with certainty. It
seems likely, however, that by 1820 about three-quarters of the people
in the territory north of the Ohio River, stretching from the New England
border to the Missouri River, were either Yankees or their descendants.[63]

It was not only natural for the Congregational and Presbyterian
churches to follow their flock, but urgent to do so. The available evidence
indicated that in the absence of an adequate ministry, more than half of
all families had become "lapsed Christians," baptized but no longer "in
the habit of either attending church or practicing religion at home."[64]
The Plan of Union cleared the way for an effective ministerial response
to this grave situation. Clergy were recruited to go forth as itinerant
ministers serving far-flung congregations in the frontier areas, and missionary societies were established in Connecticut, Massachusetts, New
York, and elsewhere in the East to raise the funds needed to promote
a revival.

The work of the missionaries was initially focused on Vermont and
upstate New York, but soon spread across the northern tier of Pennsylvania, into the Western Reserve of Ohio, and into the northern portions
of Indiana and Illinois. By 1826 the various local missionary societies
amalgamated into the American Home Missionary Society (AHMS),
whose first report indicated that it was supporting a total of 169 Congregational and Presbyterian missionaries, more than two-thirds of whom
were working in upstate New York. By 1835 the total number of missionaries had increased to 719, and the main focus of activity was now in
Ohio and other parts of the "Old West," although the number of missionaries at work in upstate New York had increased by nearly 50 percent.
During the nine years of operation in western New York, the Society had
provided "four hundred years of missionary labor" which "nurtured and
strengthened more than two hundred different Presbyterian and Congregational churches," and which turned the region into "a delightful resi-

dence for the Christian, and for the lover of order."[65]

The overarching figure in this phase of the movement who, more than any other evangelical, "incarnated the aspiration and the philosophy of the revival" was Charles Grandison Finney. He was a successful lawyer in Adams, a town of upstate New York, until "his violent conversion" in 1821. After seeing "a vision of Christ in the main street of Adams," he went "into the woods" to "wrestle with the Lord" and he "could feel the impression, like a wave of electricity going through" him. He "immediately gave up his lucrative law practice,"[66] studied theology under the tutelage of a local but prominent Presbyterian minister, was ordained in 1824, and embarked on his spectacularly successful career as an itinerant home missionary. Tall, "graceful in motion, skilled in vocal music, with a voice of extraordinary clarity, tone, ranges of power and pitch,"[67] Finney rode from town to town on horseback across western New York for the next decade, and with "passionate conviction" called on those who came to hear him "to give themselves to God," as he had done. His hearers by the thousands, "so thoroughly wrought up that they literally fell off their seats in a state of shock and ecstasy,"[68] repented their sins and joined the church.

Finney was more than a charismatic figure. He projected a new conception of revivals, denying their miraculous nature, contending that success in conversions depended purely on the use of proper methods and that anyone using them could obtain the desired results. His new methods included directions for sermons that cultivated a taste for the sensational. Prayer ran all day and sometimes through the night. Women and men prayed in small circles for the conversion of particular individuals, unrepentant sinners were singled out, "prayers became high leverage presses for enforcing community opinion upon stubbornly impenitent consciences," and an "anxious bench" was set up in front of the congregation on which seekers of faith were seated. These were all the devices for producing a community-wide anxiety over the spiritual state of its inhabitants with the aim of developing a new conviction.[69]

MORAL REFORM AND EVANGELICAL ZEAL

To Finney, salvation required "that the reborn became totally unselfish or totally altruistic." Sin, in his view, consisted of selfishness and "all holiness or virtue" resided in "disinterested benevolence." Reformed sinners should strive to be "useful in the highest degree possible," to "make the world a fit place for the imminent return of Christ." Their spirit had to be that of the reformer; they were "committed" to "the universal reformation of the world," to the "complete and final overthrow" of "war, slavery, licentiousness, and all such evils and abominations."[70] Finney was far from a radical in either religion or politics, but

one of the consequences of his campaigns was the emergence of "increasingly radical religious beliefs" that became known as "religious ultraism" and which spread throughout the western regions that Finney and
his "holy band"[71] evangelized.

Rooted in a passionate devotion to American democracy and a belief
in the possibility of the ultimate perfection of society, ultraism was also
nourished by a fear derived from Calvinism that unless these goals were
continually promoted, the natural tendency was toward degeneracy. Religious ultraism was propagated not only by radicals but by some of the
most conservative men in religious life. To nearly all the evangelical
leaders, conservatives and liberals alike, revivalism was a fight not only
for the spiritual regeneration of a naturally sinful people but against
powerful satanic forces that promoted corruption and vice in American
life. The enemies of Christ came in many guises, but to many religious
leaders of New England between 1790 and 1815, the secular, anticlerical
doctrines advocated by French *philosophes* and put into practice by fanatical leaders of the French Revolution were the main threat. They could
see that American society was menaced by these doctrines since they
were openly embraced by Jefferson and his pro-French faction, but the
threat went far beyond that which was plainly visible. There was a plot,
an "international conspiracy," organized by a secret European society
called the *Illuminati,* that was being promoted in America by Jacobin
agents with the aim of overthrowing the government and abolishing religious freedom.[72]

While "the pulpits of New England were ringing with denunciations
of the *Illuminati,* as though the country were swarming with them,"[73]
the Federalist party, with the consent of its principal leaders, President
John Adams and Alexander Hamilton, pushed the Alien and Sedition
Acts through Congress and began to enforce them. Modeled after the
British Treasonable Practices Act, the American Sedition Act placed
"drastic restrictions" on "the press and the right of assemblage, and
even legitimate forms of party activity were proscribed."[74]

The split of the Federalist party into two factions (one headed by
Adams, the other headed by Alexander Hamilton) and the loss of the
presidency to Thomas Jefferson in the election of 1800 caused New
England clerics to retreat from direct political involvement. The next 20
years brought an unbroken Republican rule under the leadership of
Virginia planters who were not only deists and pro-French in their
international policy and general outlook, but who were on guard against
overrapid expansion of urban industries. The political adjustments of
New England Calvinists to the ascendancy of the Jeffersonian party were
begrudging and as limited as circumstances permitted them to be. Both
the "Old Calvinists" and the more liberal "New Divinity" men remained

steadfast in their notions of "moral stewardship" and in their belief that the struggle for Christian morality was a duty of the state.[75] To a greater or lesser degree, they continued to be politically active both in New England and in the Yankee diaspora throughout the rule of the Virginia dynasty, but direct participation in politics was more restricted than it had been before 1800 or it would become after 1830. During the interim, however, internal reform of their theological establishment, the rebuilding of their congregations, and intensification of religious zeal among communicants and potential communicants became the overriding objectives. It was the success in these objectives that permitted the evangelicals to reassert forcefully their influence on political life after 1830.

There were three aspects to the counteroffensive of New England evangelicals. The first step was a concerted campaign, based on a coalition of the "Old Calvinists" and the "New Divinity" men, against the deistic theology that had infiltrated the New England churches. Toward that end, Jedidiah Morse and others founded a new theological seminary in Andover, Massachusetts, which "immediately became a major rallying point for orthodoxy." With a "brilliant and aggressive faculty," it attracted a "large and enthusiastic" student body, and its graduates soon joined in the far-flung movement to restore Calvinist zeal in the Congregational and Presbyterian churches.[76]

The second step was the rallying of the resources of the entire evangelical establishment for a joint effort to extend the religious revival into every corner of the nation. This was a new undertaking which called for the radical reworking of old forms and the creation of new ones— forms that would permit leaders of rival denominations to subordinate theological differences to common evangelical goals and to shared articles of faith and values. The rapid growth of the population and its relatively sudden leap across the Appalachian barrier not only made potential communicants more numerous, but also harder to reach. Despite the establishment of new seminaries at Andover and Princeton, which accelerated the training of ordained clergy, the clergy alone could not solve the problems of ministering to the needs of stalwart communicants who were streaming out to the frontiers, let alone reaching lapsed church members, unbelievers, and victims of vice and idolatry.[77]

The solution to this problem was found in a new form of voluntary society, administratively independent of the churches, but manned by both clergy and devout lay members of churches. Shortly after the turn of the nineteenth century a variety of organizations "for the promotion of Christian knowledge and education" came into being under the inspiration or prodding of English evangelicals. "Bible societies modeled on the English organization of 1804" were established in Philadelphia in 1808, and in Connecticut, Massachusetts, Maine, and New York in

1809. By 1815 the number of these societies had grown to 108, with
at least one in every state in the Union, and amalgamation into an
interdenominational national organization (the American Bible Society)
followed a year later. While the Bible societies spread the word of God,
a related group of societies, beginning with the New England Tract
Society of 1814, was set up to publish and distribute brief pamphlets that
defined a code for the daily behavior of devout Christians. Still another
set of organizations, the Sunday schools, was created to teach Christian
values to children. The Sunday school movement was initiated in England during the late eighteenth century by the Wesleyans, and was later
taken up by the Clapham sect, which pressed the idea on their American
friends.[78]

Although the benevolent empire was a united front of all the major
evangelical churches, the main drive and the bulk of the personnel came
from the ministers and laity of the Congregational and the Presbyterian
churches. Faculty members at Andover Seminary were behind the formation of several of the major societies. Ebenezer Porter, who taught
homiletics and was later president of the Seminary, organized a group
that sought to emulate the Clapham sect. Their weekly meetings in
Porter's study, which included a few devout outsiders, devised "plans of
doing good, and advancing the Redeemer's kingdom, at home and
abroad, in every practical way." Their fingers extended into most benevolent projects around Boston and they were instrumental in forming the
American Board of Commissioners for Foreign Missions (the first of the
national benevolent organizations), the American Tract Society, the
American Education Society (which provided scholarships for seminary
students), the American Temperance Society, and the Association for the
Better Observance of the Sabbath.[79]

The vigor of the Congregational and Presbyterian clergy in promoting benevolent organizations was matched by their laity. A few rich,
devout families provided much of the money for these societies and were
highly influential in their management. Especially prominent were Arthur Tappan and his brothers (rich merchants in New York City and
Boston), Gerrit Smith (a land magnate in upstate New York), Thomas
Smith Grimké (son of a prominent judge and slaveowner in South Carolina), and William Jay (son of the first Chief Justice of the Supreme
Court).[80]

The enormous success of the united front of missionary and educational organizations in reviving religious zeal led evangelicals to return
to their broader goal of shaping the moral and political character of the
American nation. Initially concentrating on issues and methods relatively remote from politics (such as persuading individuals to refrain
from intoxicating liquors or persuading prostitutes to accept self-reform),

the evangelicals gradually reasserted their influence in the political arena. Beginning in 1817, they began to expand the societies of the benevolent empire beyond the original bounds of missionary work and religious education by forming a series of single-issue organizations concerned with moral and institutional reform. The first of these was the American Colonization Society which, as we have seen, was initially so limited in its goals, and so cautious in its intrusions on the political process, that it won significant support from slaveholders. By 1827, however, it had passed from its focus on private philanthropy and appeals for support from state and local legislatures to more contentious appeals for congressional financing of colonization and a more open advocacy of gradual emancipation. Aggressive campaigns were also organized on such issues as a congressional ban on the delivery of mail on Sundays, the licensing or the prohibition of the sale of intoxicating liquors, the introduction of Bibles and sectarian books into public schools, and U.S. sponsorship of an international congress on disarmament.[81]

By the early 1830s the evangelical churches had not only regained most of the political influence they lost when the Jeffersonians took command of the federal government, but in some respects they were politically more powerful than they had ever been. "Christianity and liberty" had become "so completely mingled," said Tocqueville, that Americans could not "conceive of the one without the other." Despite the absence of a national church, despite the fact that priests "held no public appointments" and were "at pains to keep out of affairs and not mix in the combination of parties," Christian religion had the "greatest real power over men's souls" in America than in any other nation. So although one could not say that American religion influenced "the laws or political opinions in detail," the religious establishment did "direct mores, and by regulating domestic life" it served "to regulate the state." Tocqueville was particularly impressed with the freedom accorded to different denominations, pointing to the astounding success of the Roman Catholic Church.[82]

In this instance Tocqueville's fascination with American society prevented him from anticipating the ferocious anti-Catholic and nativist campaigns that would soon erupt or the political parties that they would spawn.[83] In the late 1820s, evangelical concern about the growth of the Catholic Church manifested itself mainly as a vague uneasiness over Catholic competition. But as reports from the West began describing the large numbers of Protestants who were attending Catholic schools, contributing to Catholic causes, and converting to Catholicism, uneasiness became transformed into apprehension, and then rapidly escalated into alarm that the liberty of the nation was menaced by a foreign conspiracy.

During the 1830s, evangelical newspapers began charging that the sudden rise in Catholic immigration was the result of a papal plot, backed by the power of the Austrian monarchy, with the aim of taking control of America by means of Catholic infiltration.[84]

Numerous nativist, anti-Catholic periodicals came into existence and soon books and pamphlets, "which often had a strong salacious appeal,"[85] began pouring out to create a literature of Catholic horrors. Sometimes written by disaffected Catholics, sometimes concocted by anti-Catholic propagandists, these exposés described the terrors endured by escaped nuns, the crimes of priests, and the murders of infants who were buried beneath convent grounds. The most famous of these revelations, Maria Monk's *Awful Disclosures of the Hotel Dieu Nunnery of Montreal* (which was actually written by a group of lay and clerical anti-Catholics from New York), sold over 300,000 copies, and achieved such influence that one historian called it the "Uncle Tom's Cabin of Know-Nothingism."[86] The accumulated impact of the anti-Catholic, nativist literature on popular thought led to the formation of the American (or Know-Nothing) party, which became powerful throughout New England, the Yankee diaspora, and the South, and which did much to pave the way for the Republican victory in 1860. It is ironic that so ignoble a movement as anti-Catholic nativism should have played so large a role in the ultimate victory of the crusade to abolish slavery.[87]

THE ABOLITIONIST CRUSADE

The abolitionist crusade began about 1831 and, despite internal dissention and some defections, it continued with unabated intensity until the outbreak of the Civil War. The new abolitionist movement was a crusade in several senses. It was a militant and uncompromising war against slavery; it was a holy war, inspired by the deep religious convictions of its leaders; and although it did not seek recovery of holy land, it sought the immediate and complete recovery of the holy souls of the enslaved. It was a crusade also in the sense that revivalist campaigns were crusades. The abolitionists wanted to save the souls of free people, the souls of their hearers, by bringing them to the realization that slavery was the vilest of all American sins, which corrupted not only the slaveholders but all those who countenanced the continuation of slavery, no matter how innocent their reason for doing so. Using all of the methods of revivalism developed during the Second Great Awakening, the leaders of the new abolitionist movement sought to save Christians who failed to realize that no matter how pious they were in other respects, their immortal souls were stained and jeopardized by their complicity with slavery. They sought to reach especially the masses of Northerners who accepted the legitimacy of slavery or were indifferent to it, and to convert them, in the religious sense. They called on them to confess their sins and to atone by joining in the struggle against slavery through which they would not only achieve saving grace but hasten the arrival of the millennium.[88]

THE ORGANIZATION OF THE CRUSADE

The new movement was formed by a coalition of three abolitionist groups into the American Anti-Slavery Society (AASS) at the end of 1833. The largest centered around two wealthy New York merchants and philanthropists, Arthur and Lewis Tappan, who had been pivotal figures in the rise of the benevolent empire. Closely associated with them were Theodore Weld (a member of Finney's "holy band") and a number of well-to-do professionals and activists in the benevolent organizations of New York City, especially in the temperance movement. Almost all of the members of the Tappan group came from Congregational families in the Northeast, especially New England, and their parents had generally been supporters of the Federalist party.

The second, and ultimately the most influential group in the new movement, was centered around the youthful William Lloyd Garrison, who in 1831 founded the most famous of the abolitionist newspapers, the *Liberator,* and in 1832 founded the New England Anti-Slavery Society. The Garrison group, drawn mainly from the Boston area, was less uniform in religious background. Some were Quaker while others came from orthodox Congregational families but lacked the Finneyite evangelical orientation that was prominent in the Tappan group. It appears that most of the group reflected the cultural milieu of sophisticated Boston Unitarianism and Transcendentalism, which made them liberal in religious outlook but not necessarily deistic, since the predominant Unitarian strain at the time was mystical; and recently converted Calvinists, even if Unitarian, could be a fiery lot. The Garrisonians also had strong ties to black abolitionists who provided a significant share of their early financing and served as agents in promoting the sale of the *Liberator.* Black abolitionists spurred the break of the Garrisonians with the colonization movement and influenced their commitment to the struggle for the civil rights of blacks in the North.[89]

The third group centered around Gerrit Smith, a wealthy landholder in upstate New York. A Presbyterian who was active in temperance, Sabbatarian, and peace movements, he also contributed generously to theological schools and colleges. Preoccupied with other benevolent activities and initially cautious about the program of the new abolitionists, Smith did not join AASS until November 1835. Thereafter, he was one of the most influential figures in the movement and a leader of the effort to project abolitionism into the political arena. At first, Smith proposed modest lobbying to win support for abolitionism within regular parties, but by 1838 he favored an even deeper involvement in politics. A year later he advocated the formation of a new national party, based on strict antislavery principles, that would turn the 1840 election campaign into an exercise "in Bible politics" and that would join "religious truth" with "political life" in such a way that politics would become the vehicle for an "evangelical moral revolution."[90]

The principal slogan of the new abolitionist crusade was "immediate emancipation." Designed to be a repudiation of "earlier, ineffective abolition" and a denunciation of moderation toward slavery as a compromise with sin, this slogan gave the new abolitionist movement its distinctive identity. By raising the banner of immediate emancipation, the new leaders announced their intention to cleanse the movement of all those who temporized with slavery, including troubled slaveholders who (despite bad consciences) remained slaveholders, spineless politicians who feared that overt action against slavery would cost them their offices, and vacillating ministers who recognized that slavery was sinful but admitted slaveholders into Christian fellowship. The new slogan was, above all, a repudiation of "gradual emancipation," which had been emblazoned on abolitionist banners since the Revolution. To the new leaders, the demand for "gradual emancipation" was not only outworn but pernicious. Rather than a weapon against slavery "gradual emancipation" was its shield. Whatever its merits during the Revolutionary era, by the late 1820s the old slogan had become a device for the indefinite postponement of emancipation, for the infinite toleration of sin. The times demanded a zealous denunciation of slavery and an inflexible insistence on immediate emancipation. No other program could work; anything less would tranquilize the Christian conscience and justify endless procrastination.[91]

The abruptness of the switch from gradual emancipation to immediate emancipation reflected the influence of the British abolitionist movement. As discussed in Chapter 7, British abolitionists turned "their eyes to America and to the goal of 'universal emancipation,' " using letters and personal contacts to urge their American brethren to follow their lead. These direct contacts no doubt accelerated the rise of an immediatist movement in America, but they may not have been necessary. Garrison had already embraced the idea of immediatism in a speech delivered on July 4, 1829, drawing his inspiration not from English sources but from a pamphlet by George Bourne, a Presbyterian minister in Virginia, published 13 years earlier. Moreover, the new slogan and the new tactics of the British abolitionists were widely reported in the American press. Garrison and other reformers were deeply moved by the long reports of the passionate speeches in Parliament for the immediate emancipation of West Indian slaves. As the slaveholders of the deep South brooded over the dangers posed to them by an imminent abolition of slaves in the British colonies, Garrison and others were heartened by the apparent inability of West Indian slaveholders to stem a righteous moral tide.[92]

Although England provided the spark for a new American crusade, the fire would neither have been lit nor sustained without kindling and a large reserve of fuel. The kindling was domestic, manufactured by militant leaders of the benevolent empire, most of whom were only tangentially involved in antislavery activities before 1830, but who led the ultraist temperance and Sabbatarian campaigns. The fuel was the vast supply of religious zeal created by the Second Great Awakening in New England and in the Yankee diaspora. Even the reemergence of theological rivalries in the evangelical churches favored the new abolitionist crusade. Both the revival of orthodox Calvinism and the spread of theological liberalism, including its Unitarian manifestation, abetted the crusade. The orthodox strain of reformed Calvinism made the struggle against sin urgent and exceedingly intense; liberalism made both capitulation to sin and the struggle against it a matter of free will. Thus, if sin persisted it was a human failure—not only the failure of the sinner to repent but also the failure of the missionary to fulfill his divine appointment. Failure to extirpate sin no longer was proof of preordination but of an inadequate zealousness by the faithful, of an inadequate will to root out corruption totally and immediately. The doctrine of immediacy was thus inherent in the "new means" and "new ideas" of the revivalism ushered in by Finney, especially in his belief that "perfect holiness"[93] was an attainable goal for those who sought it.

While Finney's type of revivalism served to promote a belief in the imminency of the millennium and in the need to struggle for immediate perfection, the quest for perfection took numerous directions. Many (perhaps the majority of) evangelical Protestants, especially in the South, believed, as Finney did, that Christian perfection was sought above all in personal holiness. Inward perfection could be achieved only through a "constant," "relentless" self-scrutiny in which "all available energy" was used to restrain "the dangerous passions" to which human frailty was constantly exposed.[94] Others believed that perfection could be achieved only by completely withdrawing from a corrupt society and building new communities of individuals steadfast in their dedication to virtue. During the Great Awakening, such communities were initiated not only by inspired mystics such as Joseph Smith (who founded the

Mormon Church) and Richard McNeimar (who was instrumental in the spread of Shaker communities), but by rationalists such as Robert Owen (whose New Harmony community in Indiana sought to create a socialist system of production) and mystico-rationalists such as John Humphrey Noyes (whose community in Oneida, New York, sought to reconstruct the family on scientific principles that involved new types of "complex" marriages and new methods of raising children).[95]

To some seekers of immediate perfection, withdrawal from contact with a corrupt society, whether to the inner recesses of one's soul or to an artificial community, was capitulation to sin. In their view the struggle for inward perfection and a Christian order required exactly the opposite course: an immediate, uncompromising assault on the moral corruption of existing society. This course was particularly appealing to the legion of religious radicals precipitated by Finney and his "holy band," many of whom moved from one cause to another in hope of finding a "single panacea for the ills of their age."[96]

The temperance movement that began in New England after the War of 1812 was one of the first benevolent movements to be transformed under the impact of religious ultraists. At first, the movement aimed only at restraining "the intemperate use of intoxicating liquor,"[97] which involved restrictions on the sale of liquor through licensing and campaigns for personal pledges of abstinence. These pledges of abstinence did not initially include hard cider or wine and they also allowed for the use of distilled liquor "for medicinal purposes." As Finney and his "holy band" moved across the Yankee diaspora intensifying zeal everywhere, the "use of intoxicants became a sin instead of a mere departure from decency,"[98] a sin that required immediate and total abstinence. The ultraist leaders of the movement called on the churches to cast out unrepentant drunkards, launched political campaigns to ban "ardent spirits from the list of lawful articles of commerce,"[99] and organized boycotts of stores that sold liquor.

The earlier involvement of the principal leaders of the new abolitionist movement—including Garrison, Arthur and Lewis Tappan, Weld, and Smith—in revivalism and in the temperance movement during their ultraist phases not only influenced their willingness to join in a crusade for the immediate emancipation of all American slaves; these experiences also shaped their rhetoric, their conception of what had to be done, their view of what could realistically be achieved, and their strategy for achieving it. The evangelical call for "immediate repentance" and the temperance call for "immediate abstinence" could easily be translated into a call for "immediate emancipation."[100]

Immediate emancipation of slaves was not a new idea when it burst forth in America during the early 1830s. Such a course had been advocated in America long before it became popular in England, but there was not a public ready to rally behind so radical a banner. Samuel Hopkins had "hinted at immediatism" in 1774; and in 1780 a New Jersey abolitionist used the ideology of the Revolution to justify "a secular plea for immediatism."[101] An even more powerful cry was raised by George Bourne in 1816, but his demand for "total and immediate emancipation" led only to his expulsion from the Presbyterian ministry and his radical antislavery tract was largely ignored until Garrison, more than a decade later, took up Bourne's argument. Nor did Senator Rufus King of New York touch off a movement for immediate emancipation in 1820 when he attacked the Missouri Compromise and maintained that "all laws or compacts" that protected slavery were "absolutely void" because they "were contrary to the law of nature" and "the law of God,"[102] which superseded civil law. If religious radicalism had been as widespread in the second decade of the century as it was by the middle of the fourth decade, the appeals of Bourne and King might have had a different effect. The emergence of an abolitionist crusade required not just an idea, and not just a corps of missionaries ready to spread the idea, but a public ready to receive it. By the mid-1830s such a public existed in the evangelical churches of New England and of the Yankee diaspora.

ABOLITIONIST THEOLOGY AND DENOMINATIONAL SCHISMS

These churches and their communicants were the principal target of the crusade. Those who had been touched by the Great Awakening understood the meaning of sin and many among them already recognized that slavery was a violation of sacred rights and a blight on American society. They would be receptive to abolitionist testimony on the sinfulness of slavery, and on its threat both to personal holiness and to America's holy destiny. The new testimony was spiritual rather than secular. Garrison, Weld, the Tappans, and others labored diligently to undo the damage done to the abolitionist movement when the Revolution secularized it. Slavery was evil, they argued, not because it was a violation of the Constitution or of the Declaration of Independence, not because it was a threat to public safety, not because it was a blight on the economy, but because it was "a sin—always, everywhere, and only a sin."[103] In condemning slavery as a "sin," the new abolitionists were using the word in its theological sense: as "the purposeful disobedience" of "the known will of God."[104] This distinction between the secular and the theological meaning of the word is exceedingly important since evangelical theology required sinners to repent as soon as they became aware of their sin and to seek atonement immediately. As Garrison put it, "no plan was needed to stop sinning."[105]

In asserting that slavery was inherently sinful, sinful regardless of the intention of the slaveowner or the benevolence exhibited toward slaves, the abolitionists were proclaiming a theological proposition. The implication of their position was that opposition to slavery was a fundamental point of doctrine, a question of the nature of the evangelical creed, rather than a mere matter of church policy on a public issue. In other words, they were calling for a reformation of the evangelical churches on the basis of an abolitionist creed. Under this creed slavery was not just *a* sin, but an extraordinary sin, a sin so corrupting that persistence in it, or complicity with it, overrode and degraded all other efforts to achieve salvation. "No man," said Garrison, "can love God who enslaves another," nor could "man-stealing and Christianity . . . co-exist in the same character."[106]

Acknowledgment that slaveowning was a sin was the most essential point in abolitionist theology, but not the whole of it. If slaveowning was a sin, then those who persisted in it had to be cast out of the church. Given the original premise, the call for the enforcement of church discipline against slaveholders was not radical theology, or extreme liberalism, but a legacy of Calvinist orthodoxy. In evangelical churches the expulsion of "unrepentant sinners" was the final step of "strictly defined disciplinary procedures." Expulsion followed when admonishment failed to move the sinner to repentance and atonement. Moreover, if slavery was a sin, "the only acceptable atonement" was "immediate emancipation" because evangelical theology "required sinners to repent and cease wrongdoing *at once.*" Expulsion of unrepentant slaveowners by evangelical churches was necessary "to avoid contamination from fellowship with sinners" and to prevent the corruption of the evangelical creed, which prohibited compromising with sin or temporizing with sinners. Moreover, if slaveowning was a sin, the churches not only had to cast out unrepentant slaveholders, they also had to warn their members, clergy and laity alike, that it was their Christian duty to promote immediate emancipation. The teaching of emancipation had to be as vital an aspect of the Christian testimony of evangelical churches as any of God's other commandments.[107]

Those who came together to launch the American Anti-Slavery Society in 1833 did not view themselves in conflict with church and pulpit. They were all solid church members who, although tenacious in their particular theological views, were full of veneration for the organized church and ministry, and they were confident that they could win both clergy and laity to their views. Opposition to slavery was still a part of the Methodist creed in 1830, even if honored only in the breach. The declaration by the Presbyterian General Assembly in 1818 that slavery was "utterly inconsistent with the law of God" remained in effect, although the clergy and church elders were increasingly treating slavery as a social evil for which particular individuals "could not be held morally accountable." The Congregational Church had a strong antislavery tradition, initiated by Hopkins and Ezra Stiles (president of Yale) before the Revolution, and reasserted by Lyman Beecher and Finney in the 1820s and 1830s. The task of the abolitionist was to revive the antislavery tradition. The crusaders expected not only a positive but a quick response, especially from the evangelical churches of New England and the Yankee diaspora. The leaders of the new movement, most of whom were either clergy or lay leaders in these churches, expected support not only at the local level but at the top; they expected that the major denominations would officially rally behind the abolitionist banner in America, as they had in Great Britain.[108]

The accomplishments of the abolitionist crusade during its early years were considerable, even when compared with the British movement. By 1838 the American Anti-Slavery Society had 1,346 auxiliaries with about 100,000 members, which matched or exceeded the strength of the British movement at its peak. As opposed to the British movement, which could support only six paid antislavery agents, there were 70 paid agents in the enthusiastic band organized by Weld. The scope of the petition campaigns was still another measure of the success of the abolitionists. So numerous were the petitions demanding congressional action against slavery in the District of Columbia (and on other issues that Congress "clearly had the constitutional power" to act) that they overwhelmed the congressional machinery. The decision of the House first to table all such petitions and later not even to receive them merged the struggle against slavery with the compelling issues of freedom of speech and of the right to petition, which were guaranteed by the First Amendment of the Constitution.[109]

The scope that the abolitionist crusade achieved was all the more remarkable in light of the deep and widespread hostility to it, not only in the South but throughout the North, even in New England and in the heartland of the Yankee diaspora. In contrast to Great Britain, where antislavery agents were usually warmly welcomed, American abolitionists had to face the angry mobs that roamed American cities in the 1830s, destroying printing presses, burning meeting halls, and physically assaulting speakers. In 1833 a mob rioted outside the hall in which the Tappans were founding the New York City Anti-Slavery Society. Another New York mob gutted the home of Lewis Tappan in 1834; during the same year and in 1835 Weld was pelted with eggs and stoned in upstate New York and Ohio; Garrison was beaten by a Boston mob in

1835, dragged through the streets at the end of a rope amidst shouts of "Lynch him," and then rescued by police who arrested him for "disturbing the peace"; and in 1837 Elijah Lovejoy, editor of an abolitionist newspaper in Alton, Illinois, was murdered by the mob that stormed and burned his press.[110]

The outrage that these attacks aroused and the courage with which the abolitionists endured them rallied support from people of property and standing who had remained aloof from abolitionist organizations. Wendell Phillips, the young Boston patrician and lawyer, saw the mob dragging Garrison through the streets and decided to join his cause. It was the dispersal of the state antislavery convention by mobs in Utica, New York, that led Gerrit Smith to actively commit himself to abolitionism. When John Quincy Adams began his campaign in support of abolitionist petitions, he told a friend that he supported abolition because of a sense of duty to governmental process rather than because of sympathy with antislavery. Even such limited support was risky business in the mid-1830s. Adams worried that his defense of the right to petition could cost him reelection since many voters opposed aiding antislavery men for any reason. Yet Adams was reelected and he enhanced his reputation because of the widespread American commitment to freedom of speech. Many persons joined the abolitionist movement during the 1830s, said Catherine Beecher, Lyman's daughter and the older sister of Harriet Beecher Stowe, not because of the arguments of the abolitionists "but because the violence of opposers had identified that cause with the question of freedom of speech, freedom of the press, and civil liberty."[111]

The most significant achievement of the abolitionists was also the cause of their keenest disappointment. Although the movement to convert the evangelical churches to an abolitionist theology had many successes, it did not move forward as quickly as its leaders had hoped and it failed to achieve as complete a success as they had originally expected. In 1829, when Garrison called for a Christian united front in a "great enterprise" against slavery, he was "certain that once Christian opinion was brought to bear on slavery it would not survive another day." He retained his belief in the imminency and invincibility of such a united front through much of the 1830s, and these beliefs were shared by the co-founders of the AASS. So certain were the leaders of the new movement in 1834 and 1835 that the churches would rally to their call that they planned to proselytize the South as well as the North. The northern campaign rested on the spoken word, the southern campaign on the written word.[112]

In 1835 the AASS launched "the greatest pamphlet campaign in evangelical history." With the South as its particular target, more than a million pieces of antislavery literature were printed. By July 175,000 pamphlets were brought to the New York City post office for delivery to southern clergy and prominent laymen thought to be open to an antislavery appeal. This literature was expected to rouse the latent antislavery spirit of the South and to precipitate a new movement in the region. The new movement was expected to exert an irresistible moral pressure on slaveholders who would either repent and voluntarily free their slaves, or else be forced to bow to the will of an antislavery majority that was prepared to abolish slavery by law. English churchmen, sharing this optimistic prophecy, supported the "great postal campaign" by sending letters to their American co-religionists.[113]

Rather than rousing an antislavery majority in the South, the postal campaign roused a fierce proslavery backlash. In South Carolina, a mob broke into the Charleston post office and burned the mail sacks containing the abolitionist literature; organizations and individuals in Virginia, South Carolina, Georgia, and Louisiana offered rewards for "the heads of Garrison, Tappan, & Co."; newspaper editors and governmental officials demanded the extradition of leaders of the AASS for trial in the South on the ground of inciting slaves to rebellion. The threats of assassination caused the mayor of Brooklyn to patrol the house of Arthur Tappan, "stationing a relay of men at the Brooklyn Navy Yard in case military force became necessary." The threat of private assassins from New Orleans created such a panic that Lydia Maria Child, a novelist and ardent abolitionist, compared their situation with "the times of the French Revolution when no man dared trust his neighbor."[114]

The reaction to the abolitionist crusade was much more favorable in the North. To many churchmen, the attempts to muzzle free speech and the threats made on the lives of the abolitionists were proof that slavery had corrupted southern society. The smaller northern sects were the first to embrace the abolitionist theology. The Freewill Baptists declared slavery sinful at their General Conference in 1835, while the Reformed Presbyterians repudiated their earlier endorsement of colonization and switched to immediate emancipation. There was also substantial support for immediatism in the northern churches of the major denominations. Among the Baptists, the churches of Maine led the way with more than 80 percent of the Baptist clergy in that state reported as "decided abolitionists."[115] The pro-abolitionist line up among Baptists was similar in New Hampshire and Vermont, and there was another strong abolitionist bloc in Massachusetts. There was also a large bloc of abolitionists among the Presbyterians of Ohio and upstate New York. According to Weld, "a quarter of the delegates" to the Presbyterian General Assembly of 1835, "including several from the border states,"[116] were "avowed immediate abolitionists."[117] Abolitionists were in "control of several Methodist annual conferences in New England," and "several thousand Congregationalists from the rural regions of New England joined the antislavery society."[118]

These developments were not enough to satisfy the leaders of the abolitionist movement, but they did frighten proslavery clergy and laity in three of the major denominations. Between 1837 and 1845, the rise of immediatism led to sectional schisms in the Presbyterian, Methodist, and Baptist denominations. The first split occurred in the Presbyterian Church. At the General Assembly of 1837 two factions emerged, one called "Old School," the other called "New School." The split was not strictly sectional although the New School churches were mainly in the North while the Old School churches were mainly in the South. Nor was slavery the only basis for the split. Old School leaders charged that the "evangelical united front" promoted by the New Schoolmen had undermined the Presbyterian Church organization and had perverted Presbyterian doctrine by "propagating unorthodox theories of original sin, regeneration, justification, and human ability." This doctrinal split was mainly a northern phenomenon until the Old School leaders identified the general corruption of doctrine with the influence of the abolitionists, charging that "nearly the whole of the New school" were in the abolitionist camp.[119]

The Methodist split, which occurred in 1844, was initiated by the southern churches of the denomination despite the denomination's policy of accommodation to slavery. Although the governing body of the denomination, the General Assembly, which met every four years, had never rescinded its long-standing resolution that slavery was "the great evil" or its prohibition against slaveholders occupying church office in those states where laws "will admit of emancipation," it had overwhelmingly rebuffed the demands of the abolitionists. At its 1836 meeting the General Assembly disclaimed "any right, wish, or intention" by its denomination "to interfere in the civil and political relation between master and slave." Moreover, "Methodists everywhere" were admonished "to abstain from all abolition movements and associations, and to refrain from patronizing any of their publications."[120]

During the next four years northern bishops vigorously enforced that proscription, suspending clergy who would not cease antislavery agitation. With hardly 10 percent of the Methodist membership committed to abolitionism, abolitionist memorials were again summarily dismissed at the 1840 General Conference, and shortly thereafter much of the northern abolitionist strength was diminished when the principal clerical spokesmen for abolition seceded and formed the Wesleyan Methodist

Connection of America, ultimately taking some 20,000 members (about 3 percent of the church) with them. Despite these concessions to its southern membership, the General Assembly refused to rescind its resolution that slavery was morally evil, as many southern preachers were demanding, and the 1844 meeting voted to censure a bishop for having acquired slaves, the mildest action that could have been taken "without producing disastrous division within northern Methodism." Southern delegates "fiercely resented" the censure, and a year later they organized the Methodist Episcopal Church, South, with some 500,000 members, leaving somewhat over 600,000 members in the northern denomination.[121]

The Baptist churches were the most democratic of the schismatic denominations with an ecclesiastical polity that rested on the independence and autonomy of each local church. Since there was no organization with the power to enforce an antislavery policy on the entire denomination, abolitionists concentrated their efforts on the local churches and on Baptist voluntary organizations, especially the missionary organizations. The "Baptist crisis" came to a head in 1845 at the Baptist Triennial Convention, which supervised the foreign missionary work of the denomination. In an attempt to stave off a schism, that convention disclaimed "all sanction, either express or implied, whether of slavery or antislavery." Not satisfied with that declaration, Alabama Baptists asked the Board of Foreign Missions in 1845 whether "it would appoint slaveholding missionaries." When the Board declined to do so on the ground that such an appointment "would imply approbation of slavery,"[122] southern Baptist churches from nine states proceeded to establish the "Southern Baptist Convention,"[123] which declared its support for slavery. The northern churches responded by organizing the American Baptist Missionary Union, headed by Francis Wayland, president of Brown University, under a constitution that was "equally free from slavery and antislavery."[124]

Even after the southern churches bolted, the majority of the northern clergy of the three schismatic denominations continued to resist abolitionist theology. Although they agreed that slavery was a moral and social evil, they refused to agree that slaveowning per se was sinful or that slaveowners (some of whom, especially in the border states, remained in the northern denominations) should be cast out of the church. The more conservative northern clergy argued that slaveowning could not be inherently sinful since slavery was acknowledged in two of the Ten Commandments, and since St. Paul had admitted slaveowners into the church. The more liberal resisters of abolitionist theology admitted that slavery was a sin, but argued that it was a social rather than an individual sin, and therefore a civil rather than an ecclesiastical matter.

Wayland's position probably came closest to articulating the predominant sentiment of the northern clergy in the 1830s and 1840s. "Whether slavery be good or bad," he said, "we wash our hands of it, inasmuch as it is a matter which the providence of God has never placed within our jurisdiction."[125]

To such moderate antislavery clergymen, slaveowning became a matter of church jurisdiction only if "the master misused his power over the bondsman." The physical or material abuse of slaves was a sin because it violated the Golden Rule, and masters guilty of such behavior were subject to church discipline. Beyond such special cases, the obligation of the church was "to preach the gospel to master and slave alike and to inculcate the duties of each according to the Pauline epistles." The majority of northern churchmen who opposed slavery believed that such a course would "ameliorate the condition of the slave" and "eventually result in his freedom with the full consent of his master."[126] Under the circumstances of the time, in which slavery was a civil issue within each state, so guaranteed by the Constitution, agitation for immediate emancipation was not only reckless for the church, disruptive of civil order, and harmful to the slave, but doomed to fail. So in the 1830s and 1840s moderate church leaders such as Wayland denounced the abolitionists as "lawless persons" and "tools of third rate politicians" whose agitation had "rivetted, indefinitely the bonds of the slave, in those very States in which they were" just "a few years" ago "falling off."[127]

DISARRAY AND NEW DIRECTIONS

The inability to win the majority of the clergy and devout laity to abolitionist theology, even in the North, caused dismay and disarray in abolitionist ranks. There was a growing conviction that new appeals were needed, but fierce disagreements broke out on both the content and the form of the new appeals. To Garrison and his circle, the failure of the postal campaign in the South and the rejection of abolitionist principles by the majority of northern clergy showed that the corruption of American life and institutions, even of religious institutions, was deeper and more widespread than they had originally imagined. Their solution was to extend the attack against corruption, revealing its penetration into the church, the Bible, and the Constitution and virtually every civil institution in American life.

This course led Garrisonians into an uncompromising struggle for equal civil rights for free blacks in the North. They initiated campaigns to end discrimination against blacks in the courts, at the ballot box, and in churches (many of which excluded blacks from membership altogether or segregated them). The Garrisonians also pointed to the marked similarities between discrimination against blacks and against women, which extended even into abolitionist societies. Garrison demanded the right for women to share leadership of the abolitionist societies with men and opened the pages of the *Liberator* to debates over whether women had a right to vote. The willingness of northern churchmen to temporize with slavery and their use of the Bible to justify their actions led Garrison to denounce corruption of the clergy and to repudiate certain biblical passages "as contrary to God's true intent."[128] The Methodist General Assembly was "a cage of unclean birds and a synagogue of Satan"; the Baptist clergy behaved as "sophistical bigots" and refused to see "self-evident sin"; the Congregational Church was led by "clerical despots" and bedfellows "of the most implacable foes of God and men."[129]

Abolitionist clergy were encouraged to withdraw from the established denominations and form new churches and new denominations on anti-slavery principles because the established denominations had to "be regarded and treated" not "as the Church of Christ, but as the foe of freedom, humanity, and pure religion."[130] Their desire to quarantine both slaveholders and the vacillators who protected them eventually led the Garrisonians to call the Constitution "a covenant with death" and a "corrupt bargain" that was "conceived in sin." Protection of Christian principles, therefore, required northern secession from the Union. The same logic that led Garrison to declare that there could not be Christian fellowship with slaveowners also led him to declare that there could not be a Christian political union with slaveholders. These attacks on the clergy and the Constitution were not a retreat to atheism and anarchy, but the logical progression of Garrison's mystical inspiration and his refusal to compromise with his theological principles on grounds of political expediency. He remained convinced that "moral suasion" in the "apostolic mode" was the only certain way of "changing corrupt institutions," the only "mode appointed by God to conquer error, and destroy the works of darkness."[131] In piling one corruption upon another, Garrison sought to increase the moral anxiety of Northerners, to create a region-wide concern about their spiritual state so intense that it would shake listeners off their seats and open their spirits to conversion, as Finney had done throughout the Yankee diaspora.

Abolitionists outside of Garrison's circle were more willing than Garrison to jettison, or at least attenuate, the original conception of abolitionism as an evangelical campaign in the style of the Great Awakening. Even Weld, Finney's disciple, moved gradually away from his original belief that the antislavery appeal had to be rooted in spiritual sensation. "If it is not FELT in the very *vital tissues of the spirit,* " he had argued, "all the reasoning in the world is a feather thrown against the wind." In the mid-1830s Weld had also insisted the antislavery appeal had to turn on the inherent sinfulness of slavery rather than on "horror

stories." " '*Instances of cruelty*' he wrote, could not carry the day because
they would be criticized as unbelievable or exceptional and, more important, because 'treatment, however bad, [was] but an appendage of slavery.' " The sin was "slavery itself" which "with or without the lash" was
" 'a death-stab into the soul of the slave.' "[132]

By the end of the 1830s, however, it was apparent that the conservative northern clergy could not be won to the crusade on the basis of so
pristine an argument. Although Weld held to his belief that slavery was
inherently sinful, that contention was rejected by conservative clergy
who insisted that sinfulness adhered not in the mere ownership of slaves
but in the mistreatment of slaves. That proposition, together with the
contention that cruel treatment was exceptional, had become the chief
excuse for allowing slaveowners to remain within the church. Weld set
out to undermine "benevolent treatment" as an effective defense of
slavery. Together with his wife and sister-in-law (Angelina and Sarah
Grimké) he turned clippings culled from more than 20,000 southern
newspapers into a powerful refutation of the benevolence of slaveholders, into a demonstration that slaveholders were inevitably corrupted by
their power.[133]

The pamphlet was entitled *American Slavery as It Is: Testimony of a
Thousand Witnesses.* Except for *Uncle Tom's Cabin,* which it inspired, it
was probably the most influential antislavery tract of the antebellum era.
Called "a book of horrors" and the "most crushing indictment of any
institution ever written,"[134] Weld used his collection of clippings to
"prove that the slaves in the United States" were "treated with barbarous inhumanity," that they were "overworked, underfed, wretchedly
clad, and lodged," that they were chained in "iron collars," forced to
"wear yokes," kept in "stocks day and night for weeks," "stripped
naked" and "flogged with terrible severity," as well as "cut with
knives," "torn in pieces by dogs," "branded with red hot irons," "muti-
lated," and "burned to death over slow fires." Far from being "exceedingly rare" exceptions to the "kind" and "merciful" care claimed by
"slaveholders and their apologists," the evidence clearly demonstrated
that "barbarous" practices were the normal condition. These crimes
were "not perpetrated by brutal overseers and drivers merely, but by
magistrates, by legislators, by professors of religion, by preachers of the
gospel, by governors of states, by gentlemen of property and standing,
and by delicate females moving in the highest circles of society." According to Weld such degeneracy was far from unique to Southerners but was
the curse of anyone entrusted with unlimited power. Unlimited, "arbitrary power," he said, "is to the mind what alcohol is to the body; it
intoxicates."[135]

In 1839 Weld's compromise with the original conception of the antislavery crusade was minor compared with the compromises proposed by others. He had previously used "material illustrative of abuse" to add "an emotional dimension" to an appeal that was "based on principle." The new approach was initially more of a shift in emphasis or an adjustment in style rather than a change in the character of the enterprise. Weld still viewed abolitionism as an evangelical campaign aimed at conversion, at the spiritual rebirth of sinners. Within a few years he would abandon both antislavery activism and much of his earlier religious beliefs, but as the 1840s began he was still in transition.[136]

Other abolitionists searching for a way out of the impasse welcomed Weld's pamphlet but doubted that intensifying revivalism along Garrisonian lines would be helpful. Lewis Tappan, while still committed to revivalism, believed that Garrison's mixing of causes would lose adherents rather than attract new ones. Yet he had no well-defined alternative program for revamping the abolitionist appeal. The most active men outside of Garrison's circle had become convinced that the next phase in the abolitionist struggle had to take place in the political arena rather than in the churches. The lead was taken by men in Gerrit Smith's circle, although it was strongly supported by some of the leading figures in the Tappan circle. After several false starts, the Liberty party was organized in April 1840 with James G. Birney and Thomas Earle chosen to run for president and vice-president of the United States on a platform limited to one point: a pledge "to oppose slavery to the full extent of legislative power under the Constitution." This was to be a Christian party, uncompromising in its opposition to slavery, yet capable of reaching far beyond the circles reached by the evangelical crusade.[137]

To Garrison the effort was a "farce," both "ludicrous and melancholy,"[138] and sure to fail. Not only were the men who formed the party political amateurs, but the exigencies of politics were bound to force them into compromises of Christian principles. Their appeal would inevitably turn away from conscience and "to the pocketbook," "to the love of political preferment, rather than the duty of Christian reformation."[139] Lewis Tappan shared Garrison's concern that even men who were as dedicated as those who founded the Liberty party could not resist the pressures of politics and remain "true to their principles."[140] Nevertheless, along with most of the other abolitionist crusaders, he joined the party in the hope that it would bring morality into politics. The Liberty party contributed significantly to the ultimate emergence of a powerful political coalition. Yet in many respects, Garrison's jeremiad proved prophetic. The more that abolitionists became involved in the machinery of politics, the more they conceded principle to expediency. Nor were their compromises of principle a sacrifice that purchased control of the antislavery coalition. As the coalition increased in strength, control rapidly passed to professional politicians of questionable commitment to abolitionism. Nevertheless, this impure and, in the Garrisonian sense, highly corrupt coalition succeeded in doing, more by accident than by premeditation, what moral purity could not: Overthrow the "Slave Power."

CHAPTER NINE

THE AMERICAN CAMPAIGN: Breaching the Barriers to Antislavery Politics

When they plunged into the political arena, the abolitionist crusaders became immersed in the struggle for power. It was exceedingly difficult at first to project the abolitionist program into that struggle. In the presidential election of 1840, the Liberty party received fewer than 1 out of every 300 votes. In 1844 its share of the vote increased, but it still drew just 3 percent of the total, and it did not capture a single congressional seat.[1] During the next decade, however, antislavery issues were propelled to the center of the electoral struggle for power. A new antislavery coalition, within the Republican party, came into being between 1854 and 1856; it established a powerful antislavery bloc in Congress in 1856 and 1858; and it won control of the executive branch of government in 1860. Why was it so difficult for the abolitionists to make antislavery a viable political issue in the 1830s and the 1840s? And what were the changing conditions that facilitated the breakthrough of the 1850s?

BARRIERS TO ANTISLAVERY POLITICS

The answer to the first question is simpler than the answer to the second one. Politicians were initially unwilling to make the abolition of slavery an issue of national politics because they believed that the Constitution enjoined them from doing so. That interpretation of the Constitution was reaffirmed by Congress so often during the first half century after its ratification that it became a "federal consensus,"[2] a consensus as prevalent among politicians of the North as of the South. According to this consensus the Constitution had unequivocally sanctioned slavery in the states where it existed and guaranteed that Congress would not abolish or regulate its operation in those states. This consensus was so deeply embedded in American political thought by the early 1830s that it was accepted without question even by the abolitionist crusaders.

The constitution of the American Anti-Slavery Society (AASS), which (together with its Declaration of Sentiments) announced the aims and goals of the new movement, flatly stated "that each State, in which

281

slavery exists, has, by the Constitution of the United States, the exclusive right to legislate in regard to its abolition in said State." That is one of the reasons the crusaders initially saw moral suasion as their principal weapon, a weapon intended to circumvent the constitutional safeguard either by convincing each slaveholder immediately to relinquish his unrighteous claim or by making slaveholders so loathsome within their own communities that the rest of the local citizenry would act to abolish slavery. When it was clear that this campaign had failed, some leaders of the AASS sought to reinterpret the Constitution in such a way as to give the federal government the power to abolish slavery. But to Garrison this stratagem was hopeless; his "textual exegesis" led him to conclude that the "Constitution was a bulwark of slavery in at least four particulars"; moreover, James Madison's detailed descriptions of the debates at the Constitutional Convention confirmed his belief that "the framers consciously wrote guarantees for slavery into the Constitution."[3]

Moderate northern antislavery men who refused to join the abolitionist crusade often did so not because they were content to see slavery continue but because they could see no practical way under the Constitution of extirpating this evil. Moreover, to most evangelicals and other moralists slavery was but one of many evils that affected American society. In their view, exclusive preoccupation with this one evil would permit other corruptions to fester, making the possibility of the eventual abolition of slavery less, rather than more, likely. All that the abolitionist crusaders could show at the end of a decade of intense activity was a mountain of northern petitions and resolutions that had not impaired the operation of the slave system by one iota or reduced the total number of persons in bondage. Some moderates, such as Wayland, felt that by encouraging a proslavery backlash, the crusaders had actually delayed eventual emancipation. Even as long-standing a critic of slavery as Finney warned against excessive preoccupation with abolitionism and urged his followers "to subordinate abolition to revivalism."[4] Denunciation of slavery, he said, would serve Christian goals only if "uttered in a spirit of loving reproof," only if abolition was "an appendage" to the overall struggle for salvation. Otherwise, abolitionist agitation would abet worldly corruption and embroil people in an "infernal squabble" that would "roll a wave of blood over the land."[5]

Professional politicians in the North, even if devout evangelicals and hostile to slavery, were generally far more skeptical than Finney about the wisdom of focusing on abolitionism. They not only doubted the constitutionality of the political demands of the abolitionists, but were convinced that these demands were an invitation to political suicide. To the leaders of the two great national parties of the 1830s and the 1840s, the Democrats and Whigs, the issues that exercised the public and that determined victory or success in electoral contests were, as Garrison had said, matters of the pocketbook rather than of Christian principles. Each party was an interregional coalition of diverse constituencies. Each party included both pro- and antislavery men who, because they accepted the federal consensus, originally kept the direct question of slavery out of the internal struggles for control of their party and out of the competition between the parties for control of Congress and the presidency. Between 1836 and 1852 both parties were well represented in each of the three main sections of the nation, although the Whigs tended to be stronger than the Democrats in the Northeast, while the reverse tended to be true in the South and in the North Central states. Yet the margins were close enough so that the plurality of votes within each section shifted between the parties from one election to another.[6]

The two parties were distinct in political culture and philosophy, although both embraced the democratic creed of the nation, and they sometimes exchanged positions on particular issues as the political winds shifted.[7] In general, the Democrats tended to be both more republican and more laissez-faire than the Whigs. Constructed mainly from the remnants of Jefferson's party, and led initially by Andrew Jackson, who was politically educated in Tennessee (one of the first states to adopt universal manhood suffrage), the Democratic party called itself "a let-alone party" and denounced the Whigs as "a meddling party." Blaming "nine-tenths of all the evil" on misguided legislative enactments, Democrats argued that "spontaneous action and self-regulation" would produce a better society than one which was directed by the state or restricted by legislative fiat. To the extent that government was unavoidable it should be "light and simple," carried out as far as possible on the state and local levels, rather than on the national level.[8]

With respect to the franchise the Democrats championed popular government based on universal male suffrage, with one conspicuous exception, and they favored a shift in the selection of governors and judges from state legislatures to the public arena. Whigs, on the other hand, tended to be distrustful of "the city rabble, the backwoodsmen, and the illiterates in general." They lamented the extension of the franchise to the "ignorant and the vicious" and they denied that such people had a right to vote, but they could not reverse the growth of populism. In the end they were forced to acknowledge that they could not find a "remedy that was not worse than the disease."[9] The one conspicuous exception for the Democrats pertained to the extension of the franchise to free blacks in the North, which "the Democrats strenuously opposed and the Whigs, somewhat less strenuously, supported." With the exception of four states "blacks either had to meet higher qualifications than whites" in order to vote, "or were disfranchised

altogether." During the Jacksonian years, the Democrats led campaigns
that "succeeded in disfranchising blacks" in New York, Connecticut, and
Pennsylvania.[10] Opposition to these restrictions was not the only ground
on which Whigs could defend the claim that they were the more genuine
champions of republicanism. They denounced Jackson's patronage system as a corruptor of government at every level and they fiercely resisted
Jackson's far-reaching extension of executive prerogatives.[11]

Although the Whigs denounced the laissez-faire policies of the Democrats and declared their belief in the obligation of the government to
promote economic progress and the welfare of the population, they were,
by their own designation, the "conservative" party, the party of "law and
order," the party dedicated "to the defense of property," the party which
celebrated the "Puritan ethic of hard work and self-reliance," and the
party which said that it was "the duty of every man to be a prosperous
man." The Whigs did not believe it was the duty of the government to
protect the free working man from his employer or the farmer from the
merchant. They compared the different groups in society to the different
parts of the body and saw a fundamental "harmony of interests" between
the parts, an "interdependence of different classes," and an "organic
unity of society."[12] Whigs deplored the demogogic attempts of the Democrats to win votes by setting class against class—by depicting the Whigs
as the instrument of "a concentrated money power,"[13] "a monopoly of
the old aristocracy,"[14] and the "enemies" of the common people, and
by depicting themselves as the defenders of "the laboring classes," as
the defenders of the "producers" from the aggression of "the nonproduc-
ers," and as the defenders of the "house of want" against the aggression
of "the house of have."[15] To the Whigs the "laboring classes" meant
"every working male, whether employed or self-employed," whether
"mule spinner or factory owner."[16] Senator Daniel Webster, the most
celebrated Whig orator, accused the Democrats of seeking to "inflame
the poor against the rich,"[17] and he warned that if Americans fell victim
to such demagogy they would "cease to be men, thinking men, intelligent
men" and be turned into "slaves to their own passions."[18] The Whigs
would not concede the egalitarian impulse to the Democrats, and they
claimed that they also sought "to establish perfect equality," but they
would do so by leveling "upwards, not downwards, by education and
benignant legislation, not by subverting established laws or institutions."[19]

The Democratic and Whig parties were divided not only on economic
philosophy but along religious and ethnic lines. Evangelical Protesta-
nism was so strong in the Whig party that a leading historian of the party
called it "the evangelical united front in the polling place." The Whig
party in the North was formed largely out of the remnants of the Federal-

ist party, in which New England divines had been so influential, and out of the Antimasonic party, an overtly Christian party that became powerful in New England and the Yankee diaspora during the late 1820s and early 1830s. The Antimasonic party sought to exclude all Masons from public office on the ground that they were part of a national conspiracy of deists which aimed to subvert the liberty of the people. It was as Antimasonic candidates that northern politicians who later became as influential in the Whig party as Thurlow Weed, William Henry Seward, and Thaddeus Stevens were first swept into public office. The Whigs were not an overtly evangelical party, but Whig political leaders such as Henry Clay and Daniel Webster "cultivated good public and private relations with clerical opinion-shapers," and they promoted various causes of the benevolent united front at national, state, and local levels, including temperance reform, legal observance of the Sabbath, and anti-Catholicism. While the Whigs sought to promote an alliance between church and state, the Democrats opposed it. Jackson opposed Whig proposals to end the Sunday delivery of mail and blocked a congressional resolution introduced by Clay for a national day of prayer for the victims of a cholera epidemic, arguing that both actions would have violated the separation of church and state.[20]

Democratic insistence on the secular nature of the state offended the New Divinity men and their lay associates in the benevolent empire. According to Lyman Beecher, the Democratic party was a coalition of "Sabbath-breakers, rum-selling tippling folk, infidels, and ruff-scuff generally." However, the Democrats had strong support from religious groups Beecher classed with the "infidels" and "minor" denominations: Catholics, Lutherans, Baptists, Old School Presbyterians, Episcopalians, religious liberals, and various groups of free thinkers. Members of liturgical denominations as well as evangelicals to whom personal holiness was more critical than public reforms resented both the "moral absolutism" of the evangelical reformers and their attempts to use the Whig party as a means of imposing their creed on others. The Democratic party won large pluralities among voters who harbored such resentments, many of whom were foreign born. In the New York elections of 1844, for example, it has been estimated that 95 percent of the Catholic Irish, 80 percent of the Germans (mainly Catholics and Lutherans), 90 percent of the French Catholics, and 95 percent of the French Canadians voted for the Democrats.[21]

The sharpest clashes between the Whigs and the Democrats during the 1830s were on economic issues that were pushed to the center of the political stage by a succession of crises. The recession of 1819–1821 was particularly sharp in the North and led to widespread unemployment in the newly established cotton and woolen textile industries. The recession of 1826–1832, which affected southern agriculture more deeply than northern manufacturing, was followed by a sharp inflation in the mid-1830s and a bank panic in 1837 that ushered in a decade of declining prices and a sharp contraction of production in both manufacturing and agriculture. The Democrats, who blamed these cycles on "monster banks" that were polluting the money supply by the promiscuous issue of unsound paper money, instituted a series of measures aimed at reducing the growth of powerful banks and restricting their control over the money supply. The Whigs proposed to deal with the economic difficulties of the time by passing legislation aimed at stimulating rapid economic growth. Toward that end they proposed to subsidize railroad and canal construction by huge grants of federal lands and federal loans, to increase the tariffs on foreign goods that were competing with American manufacturing (especially textiles and iron) and agricultural products (especially sugar and wool), and to provide federal relief to those devastated by the recession of the 1840s. The Democrats countered with proposals to distribute federal lands to ordinary settlers in farm-sized parcels at modest prices, and to use the proceeds of such sales to reduce the national debt.[22]

The differences between the parties on these issues in the first half of the 1840s were quite sharp. Between 85 and 100 percent of the Democrats in both the House and Senate voted against the banks, against relief, and against tariffs, while between 70 and 96 percent of the Whigs voted in their favor. These were not sectional issues but party issues. On the banking legislation, for example, where the partisan lines were sharp, the divisions within sections were very similar: "whether North, South, and Northwest" or "East and West," votes for and against the banks "were scattered almost evenly."[23]

Not even the slavery issue was able to dissolve party solidarity during this period. Even during the divisive debates over the gag rule on antislavery petitions, partisan considerations served to mute sectional differences. Despite their strong pro-slavery position, 9 of 31 southern Whigs refrained from joining the attack on the antislavery measures and either sided with the northern Whigs or remained neutral, on the ground that the real issue was not slavery but "freedom of speech." Similarly, 33 of the 38 northern Democrats sided with the southern Democrats, claiming that Whigs were pushing these issues for partisan reasons, with the aim of driving "a wedge between the Northern and Southern wings of the Democratic party." Down through the end of the 1840s, the political parties of the United States remained national rather than sectional. Despite "their local differences and viewpoints," sectional considerations were subordinated to "the shrine of party," because the dominant issues of national politics were economic issues that cut across sectional boundaries, and strong national parties were needed to build winning coalitions on these issues. Until the end of the 1840s, most politicians thought of slavery as a moral and constitutional issue which, except in the South, was not really an issue that excited the mass of the voters in the way that they were excited by economic issues. Consequently, most leaders in both parties considered these economic issues as the fulcrum of the partisan struggle for power.[24]

There were minorities in each party who disagreed with the political agendas defined by their party leaders. In the Whig party a tiny northern group, initially led by John Quincy Adams, believed that it was possible to project the antislavery issue to the top of the political agenda and use it as the basis for a partisan realignment along sectional lines that was capable of capturing control of the federal government. Adams groped for a strategy that could effect such a realignment in the 1830s and early 1840s. Although he made progress in that direction, he did not find the key issue on which to base such a strategy before he died in 1848. Yet he edged very close to his goal and he laid much of the groundwork needed to capitalize on the issue when it finally emerged shortly before his death. Adams's diary reveals how prescient he was in describing a sectional realignment that was capable of winning control of the federal government, in suggesting the idea of a "general slave-power conspiracy" (although he did not imbue that slogan with the ideological content it later acquired), in foreseeing the likelihood that the victory of the antislavery coalition might well lead to a civil war, and in indicating how the war-power clauses of the Constitution could be employed to effect emancipation.[25]

THE ORIGINS OF THE TERRITORIAL ISSUE

The critical issue in the transformation of the political agenda was the exclusion of slavery from the territories of the United States. John Quincy Adams, Thomas Jefferson, and many other leaders had been aware of the potentialities of that issue, but it was removed from the political agenda by general consent in 1820 and did not reappear until the 1840s. Moreover, even a politician as skillful as Adams could not have pushed that issue to the top of the political agenda without the inadvertent aid of his most dedicated adversaries: the faction of southern Democrats that sought a political realignment along sectional lines in order to remove forever the threat that slavery would be undermined by hostile northern politicians. Led by John C. Calhoun in the 1830s and 1840s, this group sought a sectional realignment based on an increase in southern political strength through the extension of U.S. territory to the west of the Mississippi River and to the south of the Arkansas River,

with possible additional support coming from conservative business interests in the North. Although the program of territorial expansion
advocated by the Calhoun faction "was defensive in intent," it appeared
to be "exhorbitantly aggressive."[26] Joshua Giddings in the House and
Salmon P. Chase in the Senate, who succeeded Adams in leading the
campaign for political realignment based on antislavery, saw the opportunity created by the appearance of an "exhorbitantly aggressive" southern political faction and brilliantly worked out the ideological content of
a campaign to rally the North against "The Slave Power." To understand
the constitutional issues and the political history that allowed their
strategy to work, it is necessary to consider a major oversight of the
founding fathers and its political consequences.

The Constitutional Convention took great pains to ensure a balance
of power between the sections, such that neither the North nor the South
could impose its values on the other. This struggle for sectional balance
reflected not only the southern desire to protect slavery, but also deep
differences in regional culture that transcended slavery and made the
North, especially New England, as leary of southern domination as the
South was of northern domination. Although some of these cultural
differences reflected the different religious and ethnic origins of the
original settlers in the several colonies, much of it was due to the relative
isolation of the colonies from each other during more than five generations. Such a long separation in environments that were physically,
economically, and socially quite different allowed for independent cultural developments even among people who shared a common, but increasingly remote, ethnic and religious heritage. These cultural differences continued to evolve during the two generations following the
ratification of the Constitution, but aspects of the cultural differentiation
were already manifest in 1789, and others that were latent, some perhaps
merely incipient, were nonetheless influential in creating a sense of
sectional differences among political leaders in Congress under the Articles of Confederation, at the Constitutional Convention, and in the new
nation.[27]

One of the issues most vexing to the stability of the sectional compromise struck in the Constitution was the treatment of territories that might
form future states, since a disproportionate increase in states more partial to the values of one region than the other could upset the fragile
balance. This problem arose immediately after the Revolutionary War
was concluded and was an issue of contention from early 1784 until it
was resolved by the passage of the Northwest Ordinance in 1787 (which
prohibited slavery in the territories north of the Ohio River) and the
Southwest Ordinance of 1790 (which allowed slavery in the territories
south of the Ohio).[28] The compromise extended a metaphoric Mason-

Dixon line to the Mississippi River, which at the time formed the nation's western boundary. Despite occasional antislavery sorties, this compromise was not seriously challenged for three decades. In 1798, for example, a New England Federalist sought to prohibit slavery in the Mississippi Territory, but his amendment was decisively rejected in the House, not only by southern representatives but by the overwhelming majority of northern ones. The dominant view among Northerners, Federalists and Jeffersonians alike, was that slavery in the South was the business of Southerners. Politicians in both sections reaffirmed that "just as the Northwest Territory 'belonged' rightfully to men from New England and the mid-Atlantic states, so Mississippi 'belonged' to Southerners," and that to abrogate this agreement violated the compact between the states embodied in the Constitution.[29]

The careful balancing of political power in a way that protected the cultural integrity of each section removed the issue of cultural autonomy from the political arena and brought to the fore issues of economic and foreign policy that cut across sections. This is not to say that cultural values were removed from national politics. The Federalists were stronger in the North than in the South, and the opposite was true of the Jeffersonian party. The cultural values of the North made such programs as government promotion of mercantile and manufacturing enterprise, a sound currency, and a British orientation in foreign policy popular in that section, and so these positions were embodied in the program of the Federalist party; but since these positions also had significant support among Southerners, the Federalists were a national rather than purely a sectional party. Similarly, southern cultural values shaped the program of the Jeffersonian party, but the central planks of its program (minimal governmental intervention in the economy and a French orientation in foreign policy) also had substantial northern support, especially in the non–New England states.

In 1803 the carefully contrived balance of sectional interests was endangered by an event unforeseen by the founding fathers, the territorial expansion of the nation beyond the Mississippi River. This potential breach in the sectional balance was precipitated by Napoleon's "startling decision" to "dismantle France's American Empire." His offer to sell the Louisiana territory to America not only presented an opportunity to double the size of the nation, but it also revealed that "nowhere in the Constitution was the power to acquire or receive territory" granted to either the president or Congress. As an agrarian expansionist, Jefferson wanted to move quickly to seize the opportunity to make America "a continental nation" before Napoleon changed his mind. But as a "strict constructionist" of the Constitution, he feared that "enlargement of the power" of the federal government by mere reinterpretation, by "a construction," would undermine the South's security, which rested in "a written Constitution." To avoid turning the Constitution into "a blank paper," he initially wanted to fill the gap in federal authority by a constitutional amendment.[30]

In the end, however, Jefferson decided to incorporate the territory under the Constitution's treaty-making power, rather than risk a change of French policy during the lengthy amendment process. The Senate overwhelmingly ratified the treaty and both houses overwhelmingly voted in favor of appropriating the funds for the purchase, but the majority of New Englanders in both the House and the Senate opposed the purchase. New Englanders feared not only that too large a nation was inconsistent with their vision of a good society, a society of "tidy villages, each gathered around a scrubbed Congregational church," but also that the new territory "would seal the triumph" of the Jeffersonians over the Federalists "forever." Indeed, some "High Federalists" who believed that their influence "in the union had been dealt a mortal wound" began "to broach publicly the idea of a Northern secession." Several attempts were made to limit slavery in the southern tip of the new territory, but all failed except those banning a trade in foreign slaves and an ineffective limitation on a domestic trade.[31]

Interestingly, John Quincy Adams, then senator from Massachusetts, voted against even these mild limitations on slavery as unconstitutional, and the New England delegation was split down the middle on stronger antislavery restrictions. The fact that no one proposed to exclude "slavery from the northern part of the Louisiana Purchase" revealed "the desultory, uncrystallized nature of the antislavery sentiment" in the North when it did not seem to threaten the balance of power between the regions. In 1804 Adams not only defended his unwillingness to disturb the sectional compromise established by the Constitution but added that although slavery was "evil" in "a moral sense," it had "important uses" when "connected with commerce." In 1803 and 1804 it was the addition of a vast, sparsely settled territory with unknown consequences for the shape of the national character, rather than the small population of slaves at its southern tip, that most disturbed New Englanders. Yet the failure to pass legislation restricting slavery in the territory to its southern foothold opened "the whole west bank of the Mississippi" to the spread of slavery and that oversight later emerged as a serious menace to the sectional balance.[32]

The crisis inherent in the Louisiana Purchase finally erupted in 1819 when the Missouri territory applied for admission as a slave state. The prospect that this territory, stretching far north of the Ohio River, might undermine the long-standing sectional balance suddenly aroused northern congressmen. Jeffersonians and Federalists alike "awakened suddenly to the realization that the national prospect had somehow become weighted in favor of slavery." Earlier hopes that prohibition of the international slave trade in 1808 would sound the death knell of slavery had failed to materialize. During the decade that followed, slavery grew more rapidly than ever, and two new slave states, Louisiana and Mississippi, had been added to the Union. Although the admission of the slave states had ostensibly been offset by the admission of Illinois and Indiana, both of these "free" states "were in fact tainted with slavery." Some French and English slaveholders who had crossed the Ohio River before the passage of the Northwest Ordinance were exempt from its antislavery provisions. Other slaveholders were lured into Illinois and Indiana by an indenture system that gave de facto protection to slaveholders. Although this security for their property was deemed insufficient by many out-of-state slaveholders who might otherwise have migrated, the governor and other high officials in Illinois were proslavery men. There were heavy pressures for a change in the Illinois constitution that would fully legalize slavery because slaves were in demand not only for tobacco and hemp farming but for the lead and salt mines that were then major industries in the state.[33]

The move to ban slavery in Missouri as a condition of statehood erupted in the House in February 1819 and was led by two New Yorkers, James Tallmadge and John W. Taylor. The Tallmadge amendment to the statehood bill prohibited all further introduction of slaves into Missouri and provided for the gradual emancipation of all children of slaves born after the date of statehood. The voting on the amendment broke party lines, with Northerners voting overwhelmingly for it and Southerners unified against it. Since the Northerners outnumbered the Southerners in the House, the amendment passed, only to be defeated in the Senate when northern senators split their vote while the Southerners were unified in opposing the amendment. The issue carried over into the next session of Congress and became the occasion for renewed abolitionist campaigns in the North. Nevertheless, the continued deadlock between the House and the Senate led to compromise in 1820. Missouri was admitted as a slave state and Maine as a free one, but slavery was prohibited from all remaining "territory north of 36° 30' (Missouri's southern border)."[34]

At one level, the Missouri Compromise restored the sectional balance that had been disturbed by the Louisiana Purchase. It did so by extending metaphorically the Mason-Dixon line westward to the Rocky Mountains. Since this territorial restriction calmed the fears of northern politicians that Southerners were seeking the domination of their region, the Missouri Compromise removed antislavery as a serious issue in national politics for a quarter of a century. Despite the inflamed rhetoric of some northern congressmen, the majority of northern politicians accepted the federal consensus. Moreover, the times were not ripe for making anti-slavery an issue of popular politics. Although the congressional debates helped to revive abolitionist activities in northern states, where the movement had become virtually moribund, antislavery was far from the top of the list in the concerns of politicians, newspapers, or voters. Numerous northern newspapers and local politicians expressed conster-nation that Congress had become "inflamed" and distracted by an issue that was considered "a waste of time" at home, while they neglected the acute, widespread distress created by the bank panic of 1819, which had by 1820 turned into the nation's first major depression. The popular cry was for congressional action to relieve economic misfortune by raising tariffs, enacting a national bankruptcy law, and postponing payments on land purchased from the federal government. The same preoccupation with economic issues pervaded popular thought in the South.[35]

The majority of southern leaders, like those of the North, wanted to put the acrimony of the Missouri debates aside and get on to more urgent business. In that spirit, Calhoun sought to assure fellow South Carolini-ans that they need not fear a northern "conspiracy either against our property or just weight in the Union."[36] He probably reflected the majority opinion of the leadership of South Carolina when he hailed the Compromise as having settled "forever" the threat to southern interests. Yet within two years South Carolina's political opinion reversed itself. The passionate antislavery speeches during the Missouri Compromise began to be viewed as a northern program for the eventual overthrow of slavery. Calhoun, secretary of war in Monroe's administration and committed to Monroe's broad nationalist policies, bucked the trend to-ward sectionalism for a while, but after 1822 he became as "unbend-ing"[37] on the slavery issue as the most fervent sectionalists in his state, and after 1827 he became a principal leader of southern sectionalism.

The Missouri debates had a jarring effect on the politics of the South. To a number of prominent leaders these debates revealed a grave threat to southern interests that was only temporarily put to rest by the Compro-mise. The sense of danger was most widespread in Virginia, but it was shared by many political leaders in Georgia, and by a smaller group in South Carolina. The Virginia delegation to Congress, which opposed the prohibition of slavery above 36°30′ by a margin of 4 to 1, saw the Missouri Compromise as a major defeat for the South. Since that provi-sion excluded slavery from all but a small proportion of the Louisiana Purchase, it raised the specter that the South would be overwhelmed by the admission of numerous antislavery states to the north of the 36°30′ line. Moreover, the treaty with Spain negotiated by John Quincy Adams and signed in 1819 renounced all U.S. claims to Texas, thus apparently closing off the possibility that the addition of new slave states to the south of the 36°30′ line could offset the new antislavery states to the north of it.[38]

To many Virginians, including Jefferson, the Missouri debates were ominous for another reason, which turned out to be more prophetic than the belief that a series of antislavery states would soon be established in the northern part of the Louisiana Purchase. What alarmed Jefferson was not only the bitter antislavery speeches of the Federalists, but the fact that they had been joined, indeed led, by a large faction of northern Jeffersonians. Tallmadge and Taylor were both part of a wing of northern Jeffersonians who were spontaneously breaking away from the domination of the Virginia dynasty, and many of them would find their way into the Whig party. Jefferson saw this combination of dissident Jeffersonians and Federalists as an incipient coalition striving to gain power on an antislavery program. It was, he said, an evil conspiracy prepared to sacrifice all that was gained "by the generation of 1776" and to commit "treason against the hopes of the world" in order to gain power.[39]

Although his view of the motives of those who joined together in the temporary antislavery coalition of 1819–1820 may have been jaundiced, Jefferson was not exaggerating the threat that such a coalition would ultimately pose to slavery. He was correct in describing it as the "knell of the Union" and in recognizing that the Compromise had merely postponed, not eliminated, a concerted northern attack on southern interests. It was not a mystical revelation that made Jefferson prophetic, but a shrewd politician's reading of congressional debates which had laid out, however prematurely and disjointedly, a thorough reinterpretation of the Constitution as an antislavery compact and which projected a program for the abolition of slavery.[40]

Some of the antislavery speakers argued that the "new-states clause" of the Constitution gave Congress the power to "impose any condition it wished on a state's admission"[41] and hence the power to prohibit slavery in any state outside of those in which it was extant when the Constitution was ratified. Others latched on to the slave importation clause, contending that since Congress was only enjoined from barring the *international* slave trade for a specified time, it was by implication fully empowered to regulate the interstate slave trade or abolish it altogether. Others went further still, arguing that the slave trade provision implied that Congress had the power to abolish slavery even in states where it had existed at the time of the Constitutional Convention by abolishing the interstate slave trade entirely, which would undermine the internal population adjustments required for slavery to survive. More openly abolitionist was the contention that slavery was made illegitimate by the Declaration of Independence, the Preamble of the Constitution, and the clause guaranteeing a republican form of government to every state of the Union. It was the speech of Senator Rufus King, however, that came closest to enunciating the basic creed of the later abolitionist crusaders when he declared that "no human law, compact or compromise can establish or continue slavery"[42] and that laws which attempted to do so were "absolutely void" because they were "contrary to the law of nature, which is the law of God." King's speeches were published in pamphlet form and a copy was read by Denmark Vesey, a free black who sought to organize a slave revolt in Charleston in 1822. Vesey's admission that his conspiracy had been inspired partly by the speeches in Congress was a major factor in turning South Carolina on the path toward nullification and secession.[43]

THE SECTIONALIST MOVEMENT IN THE SOUTH

Led by such Virginians as Jefferson and John Randolph of Roanoke, a new sectional strain of thought began to emerge among southern political leaders. Convinced that the Missouri debates foretold an onslaught against slavery and southern values generally, and fearful of the increasing concentration of power in the federal government (they called it the "consolidationist" tendency) promoted by both presidential and judicial reinterpretations of federal powers, these leaders called on the South to unite in defense of its democratic principles, its economic interests, and its southern values. The question was how to bring about sectional unity, especially when some of the most prominent younger figures in southern political life, including John Calhoun and Henry Clay of Kentucky, were ardent nationalists who were calling for a stronger and more active federal government with powers, particularly in the economic realm, not enumerated in the Constitution. These younger southern leaders constituted a major barrier to southern sectionalism since they favored a "broad" or "loose" interpretation of the Constitution, which increased the dominion of the federal government over the states, an approach abetted by the Supreme Court which under Chief Justice John Marshall claimed for itself the power to review the constitutionality of both federal and state legislation and its supremacy in the interpretation of the Constitution.[44]

Jefferson and other southern leaders of the Revolutionary generation promoted the sectional movement not only by raising the alarm of a concerted northern attack on the South, but by proposing programs on which Southerners could unite. One of Jefferson's proposals was to train the South's elite in southern universities, and toward that end he founded the University of Virginia.[45] He also called on the South to resist the consolidationalist tendency that was being promoted by the executive branch of the federal government, and he disputed Marshall's claim that the "judiciary was the ultimate arbiter of all constitutional questions," including the extent of federal power over the states. As founders of the nation Jefferson, Madison, and Charles Pinckney wielded immense authority on the constitutional issues that they raised. Consequently, the sectional movement initially gained strength not on the question of slavery per se, but on a constitutional question that was critical to its defense: Did the Congress have the right to extend its sway over the domestic economy of the states by passing legislation directed at shaping the course of economic affairs? Since no such right was enumerated in the Constitution, southern sectionalists charged that every such attempt, regardless of its economic substance, was an unwarranted extension of federal power over state rights.[46]

Even a bill as remote from the rights of slaveholders as one that merely authorized "the President to have surveys made for such roads and canals as he regarded as of national importance for commercial, military, or postal purposes" drew the fire of southern sectionalists. John Randolph, putting aside the virtues of a program for internal improvements, decried the "dangers of loose construction" of the Constitution on which the bill rested. To Randolph, the fundamental point at issue in this bill was the protection of state's rights through the strict construction of the Constitution. By hooking a program for internal improvements "upon the first loop they find in the Constitution," Congress was establishing a "most dangerous doctrine," a doctrine that could eventually lead them to "emancipate every slave in the United States" on the basis of "the war making power" or some other clause reinterpreted to suit their purpose.[47]

The principal economic issue on which the southern struggle against the federal usurpation of powers turned during the 1820s and 1830s, however, was not internal improvements, but the tariff. The point at issue was whether the federal government had the right to turn the tariff from an instrument designed merely to raise federal revenue into an instrument by which the government could shape the course of economic growth and act to favor the interests of one section of the nation over another. Ironically, Calhoun, who became the chief opponent of that power in the late 1820s, was one of its most ardent advocates when, as a member of Congress in 1816 and later as secretary of war, he defended the protective tariff along with a national bank and internal improvements as being within the scope of the Constitution and justified by "the exigencies of national defense."[48] By 1820 Calhoun, without denying its constitutionality, nevertheless opposed a further increase in the tariff along with William Lownes and Robert Y. Hayne, two other South

Carolinians who had previously favored policies that strengthened the federal government. By 1828 Lownes was dead, and both Hayne and Calhoun had become ardent sectionalists, with Calhoun (although still vice-president) the secret author of a pamphlet attacking the tariff of 1828 as a "Tariff of Abominations" and setting forth the doctrine of "nullification." The sectionalist's declaration of independence, the nullification doctrine declared that "the people of a state, being sovereign, had the right to nullify an unconstitutional law, such as the tariff; and the law would then be null and void in that state" unless "the Constitution should be amended so as to give Congress the power in dispute,"[49] in which case a state had the right to secede.

Calhoun, along with other one-time nationalists, justified the change in his position by charging that the tariff and other economic measures which were used in the national interests before 1820 were subsequently perverted by a "corrupt" Congress to promote the sectional interests of the North. They were quite right in complaining that the nature of the tariff had changed. Duties set at between 20 and 25 percent in the tariff of 1816 were raised so high under the Tariff of Abominations that average duties reached 61 percent of the value of imports in 1830. Although the tariff of 1828 was tilted in favor of northern manufacturing interests, the tariff was never a purely sectional issue. It had strong support from slaveholders in sugar, raw wool, and hemp production who benefited from tariffs on these items, at the expense of Northerners.[50]

However, hostility toward the protective tariff was deep in areas where cotton and tobacco were the chief crops. Jefferson had always viewed the economic program of protective tariffs and big banks as a scheme to promote the interests of the North against those of the South. The economic downturn of 1825–1830 hit the South much harder than the North, with the markets for both cotton and tobacco deeply depressed until the early 1830s. Even if the Tariff of Abominations had some bones for slaveholders in the western states, to the cotton and tobacco growers of the Old South it was a clear case of taxing them to build up northern industry. Calhoun and other Southerners developed sophisticated arguments, which prefigured modern economic theory, to demonstrate that a protective tariff was actually a tax on cotton producers. Recent cliometric studies have confirmed that contention. High protective tariffs reduced the price of cotton and effectively imposed a tax of between 10 and 20 percent on the profits of slaveholders, while they raised the income of northern labor and the profits of northern manufacturers.[51]

Southern anger at a federal policy that sought to solve northern economic problems at the expense of the South was most intense in South Carolina. In November 1832, a state convention passed an ordinance that declared the tariff of 1828 and a new tariff law enacted in 1832 null and void within the borders of South Carolina and authorized the state government to resist federal attempts to collect duties in its ports by force of arms. The nullification crisis was resolved by quick congressional passage of a new law which reduced tariffs and provided the excuse for South Carolina to rescind its act of nullification. Although Calhoun's hope that other southern states would join the nullification movement failed to materialize, the congressional retreat on the tariff partially offset the defeat for southern sectionalism in two respects. It demonstrated that southern militancy could win victories in Congress. It also forced Jackson and the Democrats to commit themselves fully "to the state's rights, strict-construction economic policies" demanded by the sectionalists, even as rumors flew that Jackson had threatened to hang Calhoun if he did not desist in his treasonable policies.[52]

The burden of the depression of 1825–1830 on slaveholders appears to have been more severe in South Carolina than in other states, and the belief that the tariff imposed a heavy tax on their economy appears to have been more deeply held in South Carolina than elsewhere in the South. Nevertheless, it was politics more than economics that led the nullifiers to challenge the authority of the federal government—not partisan politics, although men scampered for partisan advantage during the crisis, but class and cultural politics. On balance, nullifiers probably weakened their position in the Democratic party (Calhoun may have sacrificed his chances of election to the presidency, which he coveted) and they were willing to do so because they believed that they were fighting to preserve their class and their society. The tariff, Calhoun frankly stated, was "the occasion, rather than the real cause" of the crisis. The real danger was that an oppressive majority in Congress would use its power of "taxation and appropriation" against "the peculiar domestick institutions of the Southern States."[53] The nullifiers deemed this indirect approach as a more effective way of uniting the South against an abolitionist danger, because the rest of the South did not yet realize how great that danger was and did not appreciate how determined the enemies of slavery were and how quickly the tide could turn against slavery if the South was not united in a militant defense of its interests and values.

The militancy of South Carolina in defense of slavery after 1830 was consistent with its history before that date. At the Constitutional Convention the Carolina delegates led the fight for a series of clauses ensuring that the federal government could not emancipate slaves or impair their property rights in slaves, warning that they would never agree to a union without such guarantees. Unlike Jefferson or other Virginians, the founding fathers from South Carolina did not suffer from a bad conscience over the existence of slavery, nor did they express the hope that their state would someday be freed of the evil. They unselfconsciously declared that their economy was dependent on slaves, that without them "South Carolina would soon be a desert waste,"[54] and that the system of slavery was "justified by the example of all the world."[55] When they urged ratification of the Constitution, the Convention delegates assured their fellow Carolinians that the Constitution guaranteed that slavery was "strictly a local matter forever beyond the reach of the national authority."[56] During the first four decades after ratification, South Carolina, which benefited more from the invention of the cotton gin than any other state, was ever on the alert against attempts of the national authority to impinge on the exclusive control of the states over slavery, always insistent that it was purely a "municipal issue." South Carolina also led the way in developing the ideology that slavery was a positive good, an argument set forth in pamphlets published in Charleston as early as 1803.[57]

This long history of vigilance against the foes of slavery made South Carolina's leaders especially sensitive to the new menace to slavery at home and abroad in the 1820s. They closely followed the campaign of British abolitionists and, as early as 1827, concluded that Wilberforce and company had gained the upper hand in Parliament. They heard the loud complaints of West Indian planters about the damage done to their economy by the red tape and legal expenses imposed on them by the Colonial Office, by the meddling of antislavery ministers in plantation affairs, and especially by the restriction of the inter-island slave trade. They warned the rest of the South not to be lulled into complacency by the mildness of the antislavery men in the Colonization Society, pointing out that when Wilberforce first proposed the abolition of the slave trade he "took especial care" to hide that this "was but the *first* step towards an object which he then most deeply had at heart": the total abolition of slavery.[58]

By the mid-1830s, such Carolinians were no longer engaged merely in speculation about the international conspiracy against slavery. Emancipation in the West Indies was a fact and a new, exceedingly zealous movement had come into being in the North demanding that America follow the British example by immediate emancipation of all southern slaves. The British experience was proof that "incendiary" campaigns, such as the "great postal campaign" of the AASS, "could provoke successful slave revolts, and abolitionist movements could gain sweeping legislative victories." To those who ridiculed such arguments as gross overreactions to a fanatical movement devoid of political support, the Carolinians replied that in the 1790s "Mr. Wilberforce was repeatedly mobbed in the Streets of London for his fanatical doctrines," yet within his lifetime these doctrines prevailed.[59]

Moreover, it was argued that these fanatics could undermine slavery economically well before they gained enough power in Congress to pass enactments of emancipation. Since "public confidence in slavery" was a crucial aspect of the economic viability of their system, merely warding off unconstitutional attempts to promote emancipation was not an adequate defense. Slaveholders also had to be protected from the continual agitation and threats of the abolitionists. Otherwise, "apprehensions" about the "safety" and "permanency of the institution would cause many planters to sell their slaves"; such a "wave of sales" would cause "a sharp drop of slave prices" that could "bankrupt . . . many planters," "erode" the "shaken morale of the South," and "reduce the South" to a condition "of *consenting* almost to any terms that may be prescribed."[60]

Such economic arguments had appeal during the 1820s and the early 1840s when times were hard and slave prices were declining, but during the mid-1830s as well as the late 1840s and early 1850s, when slave prices were rising rapidly, prophecies of economic catastrophe seemed contrived and unrealistic.[61] Yet the scenario written by the South Carolinians is precisely the one that later came to pass in Brazil. The campaign of Brazilian abolitionists eroded 80 percent of the value of slaves and forced Brazilian slaveholders to accept immediate emancipation without compensation in order to protect what remained of their investment in land. The negative effect of abolitionist pressures between 1823 and 1832 on the profits of Jamaican planters, although not as extreme as in the Brazilian case, also influenced the willingness of the Jamaicans to accept compensated emancipation, even though some feared that the disorganization of the labor force and the decline in land values following emancipation would offset much of the compensation package offered by Parliament.[62]

During the 1830s and early 1840s, the Calhoun faction in South Carolina and the southern-rights minorities in other states, although far more powerful politically than the abolitionists were in the North, failed in their attempts to create a South-wide coalition against the antislavery menace. Calhoun and other sectionalists clearly saw the menace of northern antislavery and prophesized that its relentless advance would soon threaten the foundations of southern civilization. However, to most political leaders in the South the menace was quite remote and the prophecy was quite unlikely to materialize. Distasteful as they found the antislavery crusade, it represented only a handful of fanatics who, as mob attacks on them showed, were as despised in the North as they were in the South. Abolitionist attempts to stir discord among Southerners were doomed to fail and their fanatical appeals for slave revolts could be managed by the vigilance of local authorities. The political failure of the abolitionist movement in the North was evident in the isolation of the handful of

Whig congressmen who promoted their antislavery petitions and in the utter failure of the Liberty party at the polls. Moreover, the tariff, which southern-rights men had earlier called the chief instrument of southern economic exploitation, was moving downward, and the "Monster Bank" was slaughtered.

Thus, appeals for a sectional realignment that would abandon prevailing party arrangements initially had little attraction for most southern politicians. During the late 1830s and most of the 1840s conventional southern politicians resisted sectionalism as the call of the Sirens, and stubbornly clung to their Democratic or Whig affiliations. The alarms raised by Calhoun and his supporters were perceived as the partisan maneuvers of a faction intent on displacing the conventional politicians who controlled the southern wings of their respective parties and propelling Calhoun into the presidency. The sectional appeal was also undermined by the Panic of 1837 and the long depression that followed it. Declining prices of both southern staples and northern manufacturers as well as widespread bankruptcies once again propelled economic issues to the center of national politics. The resurgence of the monetary issues, of debt relief, and of land policy reinforced the Whig and Democratic parties as the principal vehicles in the struggle for power and cemented political alliances across the Mason-Dixon line rather than within the sections.

A new issue came to the fore during the late 1830s and early 1840s that would eventually help to undermine the existing two parties: the annexation of Texas and absorption of the Oregon territory into the United States. Although the annexation of Texas helped to stir sectionalism in the second half of the 1840s, prior to that time expansion was primarily a party issue. In a series of votes on territorial expansion in the 28th Congress (1843–1845), between 75 and 96 percent of the Democrats were strongly pro-expansionist while between 88 and 93 percent of the Whigs opposed it. Both North and South had anti-expansionist pluralities, with only the West voting strongly pro-expansionist. Calhoun and various southern sectionalists were for the annexation of Texas along with most of the more conventional Democrats, both northern and southern. But the southern Whigs, including some of the biggest planters in Louisiana and Mississippi, were opposed to annexation, not because they were opposed to expansion of slavery in principle (as were northern Whigs) but because they feared that their economic interests would be harmed by a war with Mexico and that new territory would only lower the already badly depressed price of cotton. As late as June 1844, 9 out of 20 southern senators voted against the annexation of Texas.[63]

However, the victory of James K. Polk, the Democratic candidate for president, in the election of 1844 on an expansionist platform that included Texas annexation helped to change the tide of congressional sentiment. Both the Senate and House now voted in favor of annexation, but the new alignments in each branch of Congress remained "more partisan than sectional." The divisions on the issue "reflected sharp differences of opinion about expansion per se"[64] in all sections. Among northern Whigs, however, antislavery feeling merged with anti-expansionism in such a way as to heighten northern hostility to the Slave Power. Adams led the struggle to interpret the annexation of Texas as a "conspiracy" of the "slaveholding aristocracy" to control the Union. Texas was "but a stepping-stone to all of Mexico"; then "Canada would follow," for the "oligarchy of slave-traders" was "hell-bent" on the "military conquest"[65] of the entire continent. Hardly a year after Polk (a slaveholder from Tennessee) assumed the presidency, the United States was at war with Mexico, thus appearing to verify the dire progression of events forecast by Adams and many other Whigs. Polk's aim was to acquire Mexican territories reaching from the Rio Grande to the north of San Francisco, a vast expanse that together with Texas would add more to American territory than the Louisiana Purchase.

Oddly, in light of Adams's interpretation of events, war with Mexico was strenuously opposed by Calhoun. Such a war, he argued, would produce an antislavery backlash in the North, while in no way benefiting the South, since arid Mexican lands were entirely unsuited to a cotton culture. Calling Mexico "forbidden fruit," he warned that "the penalty of eating it would be to subject our institutions to political death."[66] That prediction was perhaps the most prophetic of Calhoun's many warnings to his fellow southern politicians.

THE DESTABILIZATION OF THE SECOND AMERICAN PARTY SYSTEM

The war with Mexico, and the vast new territories it was expected to yield, precipitated a new constitutional crisis. Once again territorial expansion threatened to upset the fragile balance between the states that had been so carefully established at the Constitutional Convention. The crisis of 1846–1850 was more extended and far more destabilizing politically than the Missouri crisis, partly because of changes that had occurred in the political cultures of the North and the South during the intervening decades, and partly because of changes in the political balance between the regions. Both types of changes undermined the political equilibrium that prevailed during what political historians call the era of the "second American party system"—the decades during which the struggle for power was channeled through, and moderated by, the Whig party and the Democratic party shaped by Andrew Jackson. Political equilibrium was also undermined by major changes in economic conditions and in social circumstances, as well as by perceptions of these circumstances.[67]

DESTABILIZING EFFECTS OF ECONOMIC GROWTH

Economic changes led to political destabilization, though oddly enough, not because general economic conditions were much worse after 1844 than they had been before it. In some respects they were much better. In both the North and the South economic growth was more vigorous and stable between 1844 and 1860 than it had been during the preceding quarter century. Indeed, the economic issues of the Jacksonian era were pushed to the top of the political agenda partly by the exigencies of the War of 1812 but mainly by the series of recessions that burst into American life for the first time in 1819 and rocked the stability of the economy. It was the different solutions of the Whig and Democratic parties to these crises that turned the struggle for power into a contest between parties structured on national rather than on sectional lines. Ironically, the strong surge in the growth of both the northern and southern economies after 1844 did much to diminish the urgency of such older economic issues as monetary and banking policy, tariff policy, and internal improvements, and thus weakened the national coalitions that were embodied in the Whig and Democratic parties.

The main economic issues of the Jacksonian era still had some force during Polk's administration, but they rapidly dwindled in their political importance. By the mid-1840s it was clear that the "Monster Bank" was forever slain, and that other issues connected with the money supply were being pushed toward the bottom of the national political agenda—first by international factors that led to an adequate flow of specie from abroad, and later by both the success of the state systems of free banking and the discovery of gold in California. These factors combined to increase the money supply at a rate that was sufficient to support the long period of rapid economic expansion, although there was a minor bank panic in 1854 and a sharp but brief panic in 1857–1858.[68]

Rapid growth of the economy also transformed the tariff issue from a burning national question into a relatively local issue affecting particular groups of producers, especially in the iron region of Pennsylvania. By 1841 the average tax on imports had become so low that it was inadequate to meet the ordinary revenue needs of the federal government. Although the increase in the tariff voted in 1842 built some protective elements into what was basically a revenue measure, and the tariff of 1846 removed them, the average tax on imports ranged between 15 and 30 percent from 1840 to 1860. Such a level of taxation was too low to incite the agrarian interests, while the general boom in manufacturing calmed most northern manufacturing interests, with the notable exception of the producers of iron.[69]

The long boom also changed political positions on the question of internal improvements. Entrepreneurs discovered that most of the capital needed for the rapid expansion of the railroad network could be obtained from either the New York or London capital markets. Where private markets for capital were inadequate, state and local governments, too impatient for the federal process to work its way out, extended their credit to railroad and canal companies. That these measures were sufficient is clear from the fact that the size of the railroad network increased by more than threefold between 1840 and 1850 without direct federal financing. It also tripled during the 1850s, mainly on the basis of private capital, although Congress did vote a grant of land to aid in the construction of the Illinois Central Railroad, a grant that proved to be unnecessary to make that enterprise commercially feasible. However, the success of Illinois Central demonstrated that land grants to railroads could actually increase federal revenue by raising the value of government-owned land in the neighborhood of the railroads, and that land-rich railroads relieved economic distress in the East by extending credit to potential migrants for purchases of land and even for the cost of moving to the West. From the late 1840s on, the most important issues of internal improvements before Congress related to the construction of a transcontinental railroad and the improvement of such interstate waterways as the Mississippi River. These measures were strongly supported by Democrats as well as Whigs. Indeed, the major obstacle to a large federal grant of land in support of a transcontinental railroad was no longer the issue of constitutional scruples but the latitude at which such a road would be constructed. And that issue split both Whigs and Democrats along sectional lines.[70]

The building of the railroad and internal waterway networks, the greatest technological achievements of the antebellum era, was also politically destabilizing. The development of the steamboat turned the Ohio River and the lower Mississippi River systems into great arteries of commerce. Consequently, such slave states as Kentucky, Tennessee, Missouri, and Louisiana grew more rapidly between 1810 and 1820 than most of the states of the North Central region. Moreover, much of the population in Ohio, Indiana, and Illinois in 1820 consisted of Southerners who migrated into the region up the Mississippi or who came over from Virginia, Kentucky, or Tennessee along tributaries of the Ohio River. By 1830, the three main midwestern cities were Cincinnati, St. Louis, and Louisville, whose principal commercial connections were with the South rather than with the Northeast. Of the four cities that later became the great midwestern ports of the Great Lakes, neither Chicago

nor Milwaukee was yet on the map, and Detroit and Cleveland were still
too small to meet the census definition of cities. The population of the
slaveholding states in 1820 was nearly as large as that of the free states
and two of the free states, Indiana and Illinois, were teetering on the
brink of legalizing slavery.[71]

The completion of the Erie Canal in 1825 drastically changed the
political balance between the North and the South. This canal not only
brought hundreds of thousands of acres in upstate New York into the
commercial orbit but also turned the counties of Ohio, Indiana, Michigan, Illinois, and Wisconsin that bordered on the Great Lakes into prime
farming areas. Between 1825 and 1840 hundreds of thousands of people
from New England, upstate New York, and northern Pennsylvania began
pouring into the midwestern counties above the 41st parallel, which cuts
off roughly the northern quarter of Pennsylvania, Ohio, Indiana, and
Illinois and runs close to the southern border of Iowa (see Figure 26).
The building of canals in Ohio, Indiana, and Illinois during the 1830s
and 1840s, and of canals that permitted boats to pass from Lake Erie
to Lake Ontario and from Lake Superior to Lake Huron, not only turned
the counties of the Great Lakes basin into the granary of the nation, but
drastically altered commercial relations between the Midwest, the South,
and the Northeast. Until the beginning of the 1830s the states of the
Midwest shipped nearly all of their agricultural surpluses to the South
and supplied much of their wants from merchants in New Orleans. The
new canals changed the direction of trade. By 1840 more of the West's
surplus was moving eastward along the Great Lakes and the Erie Canal
then was moving southward along the Ohio and Mississippi rivers. At
the same time eastern merchants replaced those of New Orleans as the
principal suppliers of the goods required by the West.[72]

The enormous surge of railroad building in the Midwest during the
1840s and 1850s completed the task of reorienting that region's commercial relations from the South to the Northeast. Although there were
barely 200 miles of railroad track in the region in 1840, by 1850 the
Midwest was laced with 1,300 miles of track and by 1860 the figure had
increased to over 10,000 miles. By the eve of the Civil War the great
railroad trunk lines connecting the cities of the Midwest and the East
were completed, but there were still no railroad links between the Midwest and the South.[73]

The shift in trading patterns from a North-South to an East-West axis
coincided with an increasing cultural differentiation between the North
and the South. In the 1820s both sections were agrarian societies with
a white population overwhelmingly of British origin, and they were in
the midst of an evangelical religious revival. North and South celebrated
the countryside, preferring a society of farmers and merchants organized

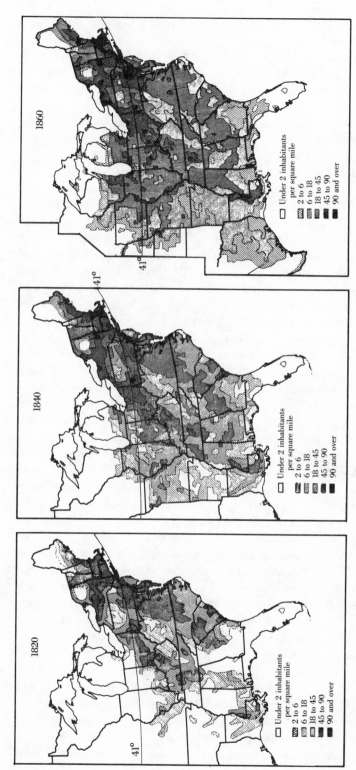

Figure 26. U.S. population density in 1820, 1840, and 1860. In 1820 the main settlements of Ohio, Indiana, and Illinois were along the Ohio and Mississippi rivers and their tributaries. The northern parts of these states were still largely unsettled, although a thin population ringed the western end of Lake Erie. After the completion of the Erie Canal, hundreds of thousands of Easterners began pouring into the Great Lakes basin, filling up land above the 41st parallel that was within easy access of the lake. The building of canals during the 1830s and 1840s and of railroads during the 1850s promoted rapid settlement of the interior regions of these states.

around villages and towns to a society based on manufacturing industries and organized around large cities. It was commonly argued that the countryside with its yeoman class "guaranteed the safety of property" and propagated "a due sense of independence, liberty, and justice." But large cities of "the European pattern" polarized society, creating both extreme "wealth and luxury" and extreme "misery and vice." Such cities bred an "alienated poor" who could be turned into mobs bent on the destruction of liberty and "well balanced government."[74]

Neither a class of prosperous merchants nor one of prosperous planters was perceived as a threat as long as merchants dutifully served the needs of market-oriented agriculturalists and as long as plantation society remained an open elite into which any yeoman might enter by virtue of economic success and cultivation of manners. Manufacturing was still more a rural than an urban pursuit since textile mills, grist mills, and ironworks were located next to the waterfalls that provided their power. Substantial enough to be noticed by 1820, the new factories were not yet viewed either as a source of urban corruption or as a threat to the agrarian ideal. In 1820 it was still thought that in a country like America, where every man "can have a piece of land of his own," manufacturing was bound to occupy a small role in economic life, useful mainly because it gave employment to women, children, and "redundant" males. Experience had shown that few free men would willingly give up agriculture, where they were independent, and look to manufacturing for their livelihood, where they had to "work for a master."[75]

Even the two largest American cities in 1820, New York and Philadelphia, each with over 100,000 inhabitants, fitted comfortably into the vision of America as an agrarian nation. They were large because their excellent harbors and access to the rural hinterland made them the best centers for the export of America's agricultural surpluses and the import of the foreign merchandise craved by American farmers. Altogether there were only 61 cities, and barely 7 percent of the entire population lived in them. Since the urban share of the population was slightly less in 1820 than in 1810, unchecked urban growth did not appear to be a menace. There were only six large cities in America at the time, if one defines "large" as 25,000 or more inhabitants, and half of these were in the South. Thus, all but a few cities in 1820 were little more than overgrown villages, small enough to be managed without resorting to a professional police force and light enough in density to permit most families to own livestock and produce their own vegetables. All except the largest three or four cities were tightly knit communities, not yet divided into class and ethnic neighborhoods, and they were walking towns, in the sense that all parts could easily be reached by foot.[76]

Economic growth after 1820 did not change the fundamental relationship between the cities and the countryside in the South. As late as 1860 barely 10 percent of the southern population lived in the cities. Only Baltimore, New Orleans, and St. Louis had more than 100,000 inhabitants, while the next seven cities had populations between 68,000 and 15,000. Even the large cities remained almost exclusively commercial in character, servicing the "traditional agricultural economy." The medium and small cities remained tightly knit, prosperous communities, with relatively even distributions of wealth among free white males.[77]

The change in the northern cities was, by contrast, a veritable revolution in culture. Not only did the urban population of the Northeast expand at an unprecedented rate during the last four decades of the antebellum era, but nearly half that population was concentrated in just two cities. By 1860 Philadelphia's population exceeded a half million and New York's was close to a million. Such large cities made possible or promoted certain elements of high culture—music, literature, and theater. They were also showcases for some of the most spectacular aspects of the new technology of the age, especially in transportation, communication, and commerce. Yet it was not the achievements of these and other large cities but the severe new problems they posed which were foremost in American thought at the time. Philadelphia, New York, and other large cities were perceived as threats to social order; as breeders of disease, crime, violence, and moral decay; and as threats to American religious freedom and to popular democracy.[78]

The big cities of the 1840s and 1850s were not only incubators of crime and vice but negations of the cultural vision of the founding fathers and of their children. The principal leaders of these two generations, whether northern or southern, had firmly believed that "those who labor in the earth are the chosen people of God" and the repository of a "substantial and genuine virtue." They feared the manners and conditions that would be spawned by urban industries, warning that the great cities, like sores on a body, would destroy the vigor of the republic. By the late antebellum era the prophetic metaphor had become a gruesome physical reality. Between 1790 and 1850 northern life expectations declined by 25 percent, and the decline in New York, Philadelphia, and other large cities was twice as great. Life expectation at birth in New York and Philadelphia during the 1830s and 1840s averaged just 24 years, six years less than that of southern slaves. In some of the working-class districts mortality rates were as high as in Trinidad during 1813–1815.[79]

This transformation of cities into death traps was due partly to a growth in population far more rapid than the housing stock, and partly to the inability of urban sanitation and water services to cope with either the rate of growth or the sheer mass of the population in large cities.

Thousands of lower-class families were crowded into flimsy shacks and shanties. Many small, older houses originally intended for a single family were partitioned to hold three or more families. Thousands more moved into windowless underground cellars where they had to share space with their own lifestock—pigs and fowl—as well as with carnivorous rats.[80]

By the 1830s the deep poverty and class conflicts of urban life appeared as threatening to the stability of American society as to those of Europe. "I regard the size of some American cities," said Tocqueville, "and especially the nature of their inhabitants as a real danger threatening the future" of American democracy. Pointing to the "serious riots" that had recently occurred in Philadelphia and New York, he characterized the lower classes of "these vast cities" as "a rabble more dangerous even than that of European towns" and warned that the "passions that agitate" them would destroy America unless the "government succeeds in creating an armed force" that is "capable of suppressing their excesses." Such an armed force, the uniformed police, was of course created, first in New York and soon after in Philadelphia, Jersey City, Baltimore, Chicago, Boston, and Cincinnati.[81]

Thus, the vast new cities of the nation were plunged into a new kind of urban politics, which not only attracted professional politicians but created large new bureaucracies, required huge budgets, and provided new opportunities for personal enrichment. The struggle for control of these governments transformed local politics, bringing to the fore parties intent on repressing "the rabble," while other parties became the champions of "the rabble." The cities also became a focus of radical politics, both of the left and the right, with new ideas of socialism introduced into American life by foreign immigrants, especially those from Great Britain and Germany.[82]

It was not socialism, however, but ethnicity and religion that became the principal basis for urban politics in the late antebellum era. During the late 1830s and early 1840s nativist parties became powerful enough to contend for political control in the major cities of the Northeast. From the mid-1840s on in Philadelphia, Boston, and New York, ethnic politics became the foremost basis for the formation of coalitions and the center of the struggle for power. In the elections of 1844, the explicit campaigns against Catholic Irish, native Protestants, Negroes, and abolitionists, repugnant as they were to a democratic society, nevertheless brought "professional boss control, and therefore institutionalization, of the expression of conflicts which formerly could seek only fragmentary, irregular, and violent expression."[83] Leaders of the Whigs and the Democrats were often reluctant to turn away from the Merchants vs. Mechanics issues on which their parties had been structured, and their hesitations led to the emergence of nativist third parties such as the American

Republican party which seized control of New York City's government in the spring elections of 1844, taking "about 60 percent" of their vote "from the Whigs and about 40 percent from Democrats." In the mid-1840s, the principal leaders of the Whig and Democratic parties, at the national level as well as at local levels, sought to keep ethnic issues out of national politics, just as they sought to avoid the slavery issue, but they were ultimately unsuccessful. In both cases the issues bubbled up from below, and the failure of the leaders to adapt to them quickly enough ultimately led to the destruction of the second American party system.[84]

DESTABILIZING EFFECTS OF IMMIGRATION

Since American economic growth was both a cause and a consequence of the huge influx of immigrants between 1835 and 1860, it is difficult to neatly disentangle the separate contributions of these two factors to the political destabilization of the late antebellum era. No doubt many of the dislocations, social imbalances, and regional realignments promoted by rapid economic growth would have taken place even if immigration had been kept down to a trickle by federal law. However, under the Constitution as it existed between 1840 and 1860, the politics of the era would have been quite different both because of the particular ideological twists wrought by massive immigration and because control of the federal government by a purely sectional party would have been impossible. Immigration provided political ingredients that not only shaped the ideological and programmatic content of the political realignment that was eventually embodied in the Republican party, but it made such a realignment practical politics.

The sudden, massive increase in immigration would have been disruptive to the economy and would have promoted social conflict even if the new immigrants, like those of the past, had been predominantly British and Protestant. Between 1790 and 1820 annual immigration into the United States had averaged about 10,000 persons per year. The rate suddenly escalated after 1825, rising to more than five times the pre-1820 rate during the decade of the 1830s. The tide of immigration rose still higher during the next decade. Indeed, the total number of immigrants entering the country during the 10 years beginning in 1841 exceeded the number that arrived during America's entire previous history of more than two centuries. The immigration rate continued to rise in the 1850s, reaching a peak in 1854. The total arrivals between 1846 and 1854, the nine years of heaviest migration before the Civil War, exceeded the combined 1850 population of 9 of the North's 16 states.[85]

Impressive as they are, even these figures fail to convey the disruptive effects of the massive immigration on labor markets, since they do not reveal the uneven pattern of the settlement of the immigrants. Only 14 percent of the foreign-born population of 1850 lived in the 16 slave states and 60 percent lived in just four northern states: New York, Pennsylvania, Ohio, and Massachusetts. Despite their largely peasant origins, the majority of immigrants who settled in the North crowded into the cities. About 37 percent of the population of northern cities with more than 10,000 inhabitants in 1860 was foreign born, while the corresponding figure for the rural areas was hardly 10 percent. Yet figures on the proportion of foreign-born individuals in the urban population give a misleading impression of the foreign-born pressure on urban labor markets since the labor force participation rate (the percentage of a population in the labor force) of the foreign born was more than twice as high as that of the native born. This differential was due partly to a statistical artifact (the antebellum censuses classified native-born children with native-born adults, regardless of the ethnicity of their parents) and partly to the proclivity of foreign-born women and children to work for wages. Consequently, although the foreign born accounted for only 48 percent of New York City's population, they made up about 69 percent of its labor force.[86]

So it was the urban labor markets of the North that were put under the heaviest pressure by the influx of immigrants. This pressure was detrimental to native-born workers in several respects. Prior to 1820 the typical urban worker was a skilled craftsman and usually self-employed. Of those not self-employed, most were either apprentices (youngsters still learning the craft under the supervision of an artisan) or journeymen (young men beyond apprenticeship who had not yet accumulated enough experience or capital to set up an independent business but who, in the normal course of events, would do so). In a sample of free adult males living in Philadelphia on the eve of the Revolution, 25 percent were professionals or merchants, 58 percent were artisans or craftsmen, and only 17 percent worked as laborers or in other low-skilled occupations. By the late antebellum era, however, the majority of the labor force in New York City consisted of day laborers and other low-skilled occupations. This mass of low-skilled laborers (including a reserve army of unemployed), 90 percent of whom were either immigrants or blacks, exercised a depressing effect on the wages and employment opportunities of native workers.[87]

Although native factory hands, especially in textiles, were displaced by immigrants, it was the native artisans, craftsmen, and small shopkeepers (who in the 1830s and 1840s were still the largest segment of the urban labor force) that suffered most from this competition.[88] Immigration undermined their position in two ways. First, the rapid growth in the pool of unskilled labor in the Northeast put heavy downward pressure on the wages of unskilled workers, and thus encouraged the growth of the factory system of production, which substituted machines operated by relatively unskilled labor for the hand production of skilled labor. The low prices of factory-produced cotton and woolen textiles, carpets, shoes, and ready-made clothing reduced demand both for the custom-produced commodities of these industries and for the craftsmen who made them.[89]

Second, although most of the immigrants became relatively unskilled laborers in cities such as New York, Philadelphia, and Boston, immigrants were such a large portion of the urban labor force that they still probably accounted for most of the increase in the number of artisan and craft workers in northern cities between 1830 and 1860. In New York City in 1855, for example, artisans and craftsmen who were foreign born outnumbered those who were native born by a ratio of more than 2 to 1 (see Figure 27).[90]

Native-born workers sought to defend their economic interests both through trade unions and through the political process. Efforts to form trade unions increased significantly during the late 1820s and the early 1830s, a period that coincided with the first wave of increased immigration. The first joint meeting of various crafts took place in Philadelphia in 1827, and a year later the Mechanics' Union of Trade Association was formed, but it survived for only a year. However, in Philadelphia, New York, and other cities particular craft unions grew in strength between 1825 and 1837 around demands for improving wages and working conditions. Strikes for higher wages or against reductions in wages became increasingly common, and the effectiveness of these actions in addressing worker grievances stimulated the trade union movement. A high point was reached in 1834 when delegates from six cities representing over 20,000 craftsmen from a number of crafts formed the first National Trades' Union. At the same time national organizations of workers or other intercity forms of cooperation within particular crafts developed among cordwainers (leather workers), carpenters, handloom weavers, and printers. However, this early phase of aggressive trade union organization was brought to an end by the depression of 1837–1844, which snuffed out many businesses and produced the most severe unemployment in the North during the antebellum era, with perhaps a quarter of the northern urban labor force unemployed during the worst years.[91]

The depression not only destroyed the incipient trade union movement but split workers along ethnic lines. During the affluent part of the 1830s, the emerging trade unions embraced workers of every skill and every ethnic background (except the blacks), a point demonstrated in Philadelphia during 1835 when the General Trades' Union of that city called a general strike in support of Irish dockworkers. "Even the

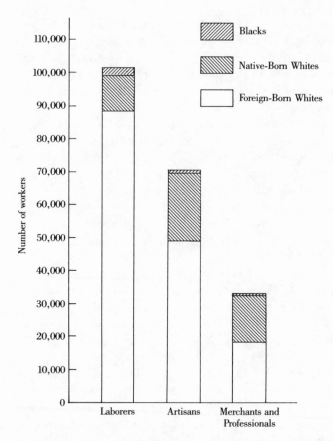

Figure 27. The occupational structure of the labor force of New York City by
          ethnicity in 1855. Despite the occupational stratification of ethnic
          groups, the foreign born were such a large proportion of the adult
          population of New York City in 1855 that they were not only a majority
          of the laborers but of the artisans and of the merchants and profession-
          als. However, foreign-born "merchants" were heavily concentrated
          among storeowners and peddlers in the foreign-born communities. Na-
          tive-born persons still accounted for 90 percent of the lawyers, 93
          percent of the financiers, and 79 percent of the government employees
          other than policemen.

cordwainers, who a decade later were to prove themselves implacable
foes of the Irish," vowed in 1835 to support the demand of the Irish
dockworkers for shorter hours and steady pay. However, the combined
effects of the depression and the rising tide of immigration discouraged
native workers who had sought to better themselves through trade union
organization. When they turned to the political arena for relief, they
focused on the competition from immigrants as the principal source of
their difficulties.[92]

THE EMERGENCE OF A NATIVIST
POLITICAL PARTY

It was the native-born artisans of both Philadelphia and New York City who became the leaders and the principal supporters of the nativist American Republican party in the 1844 elections. Neither the upper-class merchant princes associated with the benevolent empire nor the important industrialists of these cities were active in the party. Some lawyers and other professionals were active, but in Philadelphia less than 4 percent of the leaders were lawyers or other professionals, and the lawyers were with few exceptions marginal members of their profession. The largest bloc of the leadership, 55 percent, were craftsmen, mainly artisans who ran their own shops with a few journeymen and apprentices. As petty proprietors they "were particularly susceptible to the Jacksonian siren song of upward mobility through capital accumulation," and the narrowing of such opportunity became a cause for resentment that drew the "frustrated native artisans into a scapegoating anti-immigrant movement." The next largest bloc of leaders consisted of small shopkeepers with a "modicium of prestige that proprietorship offered them in working-class neighborhoods, and their extension of credit to many of their customers afforded them influence and made their premises convenient political headquarters."[93]

The American Republican party was not the first working-class party to have entered the American political lists. During the late 1820s Working Men's parties came into being in Philadelphia, New York, Boston, and several smaller cities. Dedicated to the support of candidates who would promote "the interests and enlightenment of the working classes," they put forward a program which included a 10-hour day, the public provision of free, high-quality education for children of working-class families, the abolition of imprisonment for debt, and "a mechanics' lein law to assure workers first claim to their employers' payroll." The Working Men's party had its most notable success in the New York City election of 1829 in which it garnered about a quarter of the vote city-wide, and close to half the vote "in the five poorest wards." However, internal feuding soon splintered the party, with "the largest splinter" absorbed into the Locofoco or left wing of the Democratic party. The Locofocos were soon coopted by the Democratic regulars they sought to oppose and so "paradoxically helped fasten an egalitarian reputation on that party both nationally and in New York," a reputation that gave the Democrats considerable strength among urban workers for the balance of the antebellum era.[94]

Unlike the Locofocos, who basically strengthened the second-party system by appearing to give the lower classes an option within that system, the American Republican party and its successor in the 1850s (the Know-Nothings) were politically destabilizing. By the early 1840s the foreign-born vote in New York and Philadelphia had become substantial enough so that it was worth vying for. In that competition the Democrats had a clear edge, both because of their egalitarian reputation and because of the close Whig association with evangelical Protestants. Nevertheless, after William H. Seward was elected governor of New York on the Whig ticket in 1838 he made a determined effort to win the foreign-born vote by calling for public support for Catholic schools.[95]

Despite the antipathy of Seward and Thurlow Weed (the kingmaker of the Whig party in New York State) to the nativist movement, local Whig leaders formed alliances with the nativists. In both New York City and Philadelphia the "*quid pro quo* was clear and simple: the Americans would vote for the Whig gubernatorial and presidential tickets, the Whigs would vote for the American congressional and local tickets." The outcome of the elections was striking victories for the nativists who won the New York City mayoral election and swept the city council. In Philadelphia they gained three out of four congressional seats. However, the alliance proved costly for the Whigs, since enough of the nativists reneged on their agreement to support Clay, permitting Polk to win the state in the presidential contest and thus obtain the slender electoral majority with which he captured the presidency.[96]

The year 1844 was a high-water mark for the nativist political movement.[97] Its rapid decline during the next three years was due partly to the boom of the last half of the 1840s which, although uneven, was particularly vigorous in northern manufacturing, construction, and commerce. The iron industry was one of the first to experience the beneficial effects of the boom. Disastrously depressed in the early 1840s, the recovery got under way in 1843 and proceeded vigorously until 1847, with output tripling in just five years. In cotton textiles the boom of the 1840s did not begin until 1844 but continued on until 1849 with output increasing by 41 percent from trough to peak. The most spectacular aspect of the 1840s boom, however, took place in construction. Residential, railroad, and other industrial construction expanded at unprecedented rates in the North, with the Northeast leading the way during the last half of the 1840s after which the scepter passed to the Midwest for half a decade. The increased demand for common and craft labor in construction between 1844 and 1848 was more than enough to offset the influx of immigrants. Finally, the huge expansion of the army for the Mexican War, with recruits coming disproportionately from men in the northern cities, also promoted a strong northern labor market. Consequently, the downward pressure on native wages before 1845 brought about by immigrant competition for jobs was relieved during much of the last half of the 1840s.[98]

It was not merely the economic boom that promoted the eclipse of the nativist movement. Many of the most prominent leaders of the Whig party—including Seward and Horace Greeley (publisher of the New York *Tribune*)—were deeply hostile to nativism for ideological and political as well as for economic reasons. Although native craftsmen and common laborers suffered from the competition of immigrants in the labor market, native landowners, farmers, manufacturers, and merchants generally profited from the influx of immigrants. The surging population greatly increased the demand for housing, land, and agricultural products. Seward, Greeley, and other leading Whig politicians speculated in western lands and hence were beneficiaries of the foreign influx. Big-city landlords were also among the chief beneficiaries of immigration, especially in the 1840s and 1850s, when rent gouging was the order of the day, with single rooms just 12 feet square renting for as much as 50 percent of the average monthly income of a laborer.[99]

Whig opposition to working-class nativism does not appear to have been motivated purely, or even primarily, by the economic self-interests of the upper-class leaders who dominated the party. Upper- and lower-class native Protestants were also divided by issues of manners, individual rights, and democratic principles. Although many upper-class Yankees had "an activist religious orientation" that led them to seek a restructuring of society according to "divine will," as they perceived it, they did not equate the promotion of evangelical doctrine with hostility to immigrants. Lyman Beecher sought to unite American Protestants against Catholic theology, not against immigrants per se. He and other Whig leaders were appalled by the lower-class Protestant mobs that burned Catholic convents in Boston and rioted against Irish communities in Philadelphia. They defended "the civil and religious rights of the Catholics" including their "rights to proselyte the nation to their faith if they are able to do it." Their objective was to defeat the Catholics ideologically and politically by creating a Protestant united front so powerful that it would overwhelm opponents of the evangelical crusade in ways consistent with the nation's democratic principles.[100]

The political spokesmen of these Protestant crusaders in the Whig party emphasized that they were not opposed to the immigrant, but only "to the immigrant as he was."[101] Their objective was not to exclude the immigrant but to assimilate him into the dominant British-American culture. "All we desire" of the immigrants, said Daniel Webster, "is that they will Americanize themselves; that forgetting the things that are behind, they will look forward" and become "worthy and respectable citizens."[102] Evangelicals who sought both to protect individual rights

and "to keep the United States a Protestant nation" saw the Whigs
rather than American Republicans as the most effective instrument for
mobilizing the public to resist the political "assaults of Romanism" and
to save America from "the traditional alliance between Roman Catholicism and political reaction."[103]

THE SEARCH FOR NEW ISSUES AND NEW ALIGNMENTS AMONG THE WHIGS

Party leaders opposed the nativist movement not only because of its
manners and methods but because they viewed it as a serious threat to
the Whig hold on an important section of its electorate. The strong
expression of working-class discontent in the nativist movement made
some Whig leaders aware of the need to recast their party's program in
a way that permitted it to recapture the support of lower-class native
Protestants without alienating its supporters in the propertied classes.[104]

The attempt to reorient party policies was led by the liberal triumvi-
rate of New York Whiggery: Seward, Weed, and Greeley. Badly shaken
by the Whig losses in New York in 1844, Weed became convinced that
the times required a program of "mild" reform that "professed sympathy
for the antirenters and for labor," that vigorously opposed nativism and
defended the civil rights of immigrants, and that advocated the cleanup
of local government as well as the democratization of state and local
elections. He also supported high tariffs as a means of protecting American working men from foreign competition and he took a stand against
the extension of slave power. Greeley used the pages of his newspaper,
the New York *Tribune*, to popularize that program. Beginning in the
summer of 1845 the *Tribune* carried a series of articles exposing "the
miserable conditions of the workers in the city's sweated trades" and
urging "that the city should find remunerative labor for the unemployed,
with honest workers paid at least the means of subsistence until they
found better jobs and with shirking paupers contracted out to the lowest
bidder for ten-year periods." Greeley lashed out at the tariff of 1846,
which sharply lowered duties on iron and textiles, predicting that thousands of honest men "would be thrown out of work." When the expected
economic collapse failed to materialize in late 1846 or 1847, Greeley
shifted his priorities. He downplayed tariffs and championed a policy
that hitherto had been anathema to Whigs, the free distribution of government lands, calling it the key issue in the defense of working men.[105]

From the late 1820s through the early 1840s southern and western
Democrats had been the chief advocates of the liberal distribution of
public lands at low prices. Whigs fought that policy tooth and nail. They
proposed to sell lands at higher prices and to distribute the revenue to
the states for support of internal improvements and education. "Too

rapid settlement of the West," they argued, "would outrun the transportation network, draw the work force away from manufacturing, and keep the country at a more primitive economic stage." As late as the 29th Congress (1845–1847) the Whigs voted 4 to 1 against a liberal land policy while the Democrats favored it by 3 to 1.[106]

Greeley's campaign for land reform made little headway among Whig leaders. His "wild-eyed" reform policies became the target of conservative forces within the Whig party of New York who wanted to regain control from the Seward-Weed-Greeley alliance. Although Weed generally supported "Greeley's attempt to identify the Whig party with progress and the Democratic party with depravity and obscurantism," he looked askance at his ally's penchant for extreme reforms, including land reform, because they exacerbated divisions within the Whig fold. So devisive had Greeley's position become within party circles that Weed and Seward "had formed the habit of disclaiming it, sometimes openly and sometimes by indirection."[107] Conservative opposition fed on the fact that Greeley's pet reform originated with the left wing of the Democratic party. Greeley was converted to the belief that land reform was the best way to relieve urban poverty by George Henry Evans, the editor of the *Working Man's Advocate* and a leader of the Locofocos. Evans argued that granting free, inalienable homesteads to settlers "would cause the fall of land prices throughout the country" and so would not only make land accessible to wage earners, but also strengthen the "bargaining position" of those workers who remained in cities. "Free, inalienable homesteads" would reverse the polarization of classes that was taking place in America because land monopolies had thwarted the tendency of competition to promote equality. Free land would also put an end to wars (since "there would be no land to fight about") and to slavery (since "slaveholders would have no interest in keeping slaves if they had no large estates"). However, in the absence of a free-land policy northern workers "should vigorously oppose emancipation," said Evans, because without free land "emancipation would merely increase the number of laborers" competing for northern jobs "and depress wages." These arguments made sense not only to Greeley but to immigrant German Communists, refugees from the revolutions of 1848 who, "with Karl Marx's blessing," supported the demand for free homesteads "as a step toward the goal of communism."[108]

To those who were shocked by his strange bedfellows, Greeley replied that the reforms he advocated "combined good politics with social and economic progress."[109] Farms built on virgin prairies or carved from forests would create markets for eastern manufacturers. "Every smoke that rises" in the "Great West," he wrote, "marks a new customer to the counting rooms and warehouses of New York." Nor did employers need to worry about losing their labor reserve, since free homesteads would drain off only a portion of the surplus. Greeley estimated that there were 30,000 unemployed "heads of families" during the winter of 1845–1846, which was in other respects a boom period, because the declining cost of ocean transportation was bringing immigrants into the East quicker than they could be "drained off by the West."[110] A shift in program was timely, Greeley argued, for still another reason. The splits in both the Whig and the Democratic parties on the eve of the 1848 elections indicated that both parties "were on the verge of breaking up, and that new ones would form along radical and conservative lines." A new, winning party "could be rallied in plenty of time for 1852,"[111] he told a friend, on a program of land and labor reform, without becoming ensnared in the issue of slavery expansion.

Subsequent events substantiated Greeley's belief that new political alignments were in the making and that land reform was a realigning issue. The solidarity of southern and western Democrats on liberal land policies, which had persisted for more than a quarter of a century, suddenly began to crumble in the early 1850s. Party lines on this question had been established in the late 1820s when such Democrats as Thomas Hart Benton of Missouri and Robert Y. Hayne of South Carolina led the fight for cheap land, while such Whigs as John Quincy Adams and Samuel A. Foot (of Connecticut) denounced the Democratic policy as a plot to injure "the real estate and manufacturing interests of the East." Democratic unity on the question remained intact down through the 30th Congress (1847–1849), but during the 31st Congress (1849–1851) some Southerners began to equivocate and during the 32nd Congress (1851–1853) Democrats from Virginia, the Carolinas, and Georgia abruptly turned against their long-standing policy and formed a phalanx against the homestead bills sponsored by their colleagues in the Northwest and by some in the Southwest.[112]

To many Southerners it seemed clear that policies which had once served their interests were in 1853 better designed to aid the North in its struggle for hegemony over the South. The good farming land that remained in the public domain was located almost exclusively in the North, since the arid lands acquired from Mexico were unsuitable for cotton and of dubious value for other crops. The free distribution of land located in the North not only would promote competition with southern agriculture and undermine southern land values but would lure foreigners from "the poorhouses of Europe and pour upon the United States a population unskilled and untutored in American institutions."[113]

In addition to these economic and cultural issues there was a deep fear of the purely political implications of hordes of foreigners pouring into the North, a fear that on the surface might seem paranoid. Since the foreign born were generally anti-abolitionists and voted overwhelmingly for the Democrats, why did southern Democrats suddenly swing against policies that enhanced the strength of their northern allies? By 1853 many southerner leaders, deeply alarmed by the ideological drift in the North and the concomitant growth of anti-southern agitation, believed that the influx of foreigners was doing more to hurt their cause than to help it. One reason for concern was a new wave of defections among native northern Democrats. Although the native bolters in the election of 1852 were not as great as in 1844, and smaller in number than the foreign additions to Democratic strength, the relative decline of Democratic strength in the native precincts was large enough to be noticed.[114]

The effect of the foreign influx on the electoral balance between the two regions was more obvious and more threatening. Whether voters or not, the foreign-born population and their underage children added to the congressional contingent and to the electoral count in the North, since it was purely the body count (not the number of legal voters) that affected the distribution both of House seats and of electoral votes. It was the huge influx of foreigners into the North after 1820, rather than the northern rate of natural increase, that gave the North its increasing predominance in the struggle for power and made it possible for a party based exclusively in the North to gain control of the federal government. If the northern population of 1820 had grown only at the rate of natural increase a purely northern party such as the Republican party could have neither controlled Congress nor captured the presidency, as it did in 1860. Without immigration a northern antislavery coalition would have been a much less attractive instrument than it actually was to those practical politicians whose principal concern was the control of the federal government.[115]

CHAPTER TEN

THE AMERICAN CAMPAIGN: Forging a Victorious Antislavery Coalition

During the decade between 1844 and 1854 changes in economic and social conditions outran the capacity of the second American party system to cope with them. Both the extent and the suddenness of the collapse of the coalitions embodied in the Whig and Democratic parties are evident in the shift of congressional voting patterns between the 29th Congress (1845–1847) and the 32nd Congress (1851–1853). Although the 29th Congress was rocked by dissension over the Mexican War and the possible impact of any territories that would be acquired from Mexico on the political balance between the North and the South, the Whig and Democratic parties effectively continued to represent the major political divisions in American life. The differences on the Mexican War found expression within the existing party structure, with the Democrats overwhelmingly supporting the war effort and the Whigs opposing it by equally one-sided margins. It was only on the question of the Wilmot Proviso (the attempt to prohibit the extension of slavery into any newly acquired territories) that sectional interests proved to be stronger than party commitments, although it was only in the South that sectional unity completely overrode partisan alignments. Among Northerners partisan consideration continued to affect voting alignments even on the Wilmot Proviso. Northern Whigs voted 100 percent for the antislavery position, but only a quarter of the northern Democrats were willing to do so. A core of northern Democrats argued that the issue had been raised to divide the Democratic party and so put preservation of party unity above sectional considerations.[1]

The weakening of party lines over the Wilmot Proviso did not carry over to the traditional set of economic issues which originally gave rise to the Whig and Democratic coalitions. Cohesion remained high within each party during the 29th Congress on an array of bills dealing with economic policy, and the division between the parties on these issues was sharp. In the House, for example, 99 percent of the Whigs voted for high tariffs while 83 percent of the Democrats voted for low or moderate tariffs. Traditional partisan alignments also dominated the voting on bills

320

concerned with the distribution of public lands and on federal support for internal improvements.

By the 32nd Congress, however, party cohesion had largely disappeared. The disintegration of the old alliances was not due primarily to the divisive effects of the struggle over the extension of slavery. That issue had been pushed to the background by the Compromise of 1850, which ended the stalemate on the organization of the territories ceded by Mexico.[2] There was a limited rear-guard action over the antislavery resolutions in the 32nd Congress, but sectional solidarity on such resolutions prevailed over partisan solidarity again only in the South, where the majority of Whigs and Democrats staunchly opposed a continuation of the agitation. In the North, however, it was partisan solidarity that prevailed; the Democrats voted fairly solidly against continuing antislavery agitation, while Whigs were equally unified in their desire to perpetuate it.

Oddly enough, it was on the economic and social issues that once had been the cement of the Whig and Democratic parties in Congress that cohesion disappeared, with members of each party scattered over the scale of attitudes. On monetary policy, internal improvements, and tariffs, "different factors influenced congressmen at different times." Nor was it that sectional alignments had generally come to dominate partisan alignments on these issues. Quite the contrary, it was often purely local considerations and individual decision making that was predominant. More than ever before the Congress of 1851–1853 was split into "a multiplicity of factional groupings" and it was only occasionally that these numerous small factions coalesced "into large-scale partisan or sectional" alignments.[3]

Intense factional struggle rather than coalition making dominated the congressional scene in 1853 both because the political agenda of the 1830s and the 1840s had become obsolete and because a new national agenda that could form the basis for new national coalitions had not yet appeared. The absence of such an agenda did not imply that political harmony had finally been achieved. Quite the contrary—at the local level political discontent was reaching the boiling point. The principal arena for these conflicts in 1853, however, was not the federal government but state and local governments. The issues of the early 1850s that assumed such explosive potential traditionally fell into the purview of city councils and state legislatures rather than that of Congress. They were such issues as unemployment, maintenance of wage rates, reduction in the length of the workday, protection of labor monopolies, improvement of housing conditions, reduction of rents, prevention of strikes, control of public schools, prohibition of liquor sales, improvement of sanitation and public health, control of crime and violence, political and ideological containment of the Catholic Church, and control of mob violence. The new issues were more urban than rural, more northern than national. Although the seething conflict on these issues clearly had the potential to erupt into an exceedingly dangerous national crisis, it was difficult for old-line leaders of the two main parties to find a way to nationalize issues that had traditionally been considered outside of the federal domain, or to find a way of fitting the new movements these issues touched off into the framework of the prevailing national party system.

It was largely in political formations outside of the two main parties and from political leaders who were either outside of these parties or largely excluded from their top councils that the new national coalitions based on new national agendas were projected. Two rival movements for a national political realignment emerged in 1854. Neither of these alternatives was structured along the radical-conservative axis envisioned by Greeley in 1847. One of the movements aimed to establish a new national coalition on an anti-Catholic, anti–foreign-born program. The other movement sought the formation of a purely northern coalition on an antislavery program. During the political chaos that prevailed between 1854 and 1856, it was impossible to predict which of these rival movements would gain the upper hand.

The eventual victory of the antislavery movement required, above all, the subtle but far-reaching change in northern attitudes wrought during the two preceding decades by the abolitionist crusaders. It also required the persistence of a handful of professional politicians, converts of the crusaders, who were dedicated to the abolition of slavery. Their devotion to the antislavery cause led them to take risky political positions that were abjured by ordinary politicians and to persist in their objectives in the face of political defeats that would have daunted less zealous men. Political courage and zealous devotion to principles were necessary but not sufficient conditions for their triumph. They also needed an ingenious political strategy, plenty of good luck, and a fair bit of unintended help from their proslavery adversaries. The overarching role of contingent circumstances in their ultimate victory needs to be emphasized. There never was a moment between 1854 and 1860 in which the triumph of the antislavery coalition was assured. Before considering the politics that brought victory to the antislavery coalition, it is first necessary to understand the changes in the antislavery appeal that made such politics viable.

THE BROADENING OF THE ANTISLAVERY APPEAL

Although even the most devout abolitionists never relied exclusively on theological arguments, during the better part of the 1830s the religious content of the appeal overwhelmed all of its other aspects. The publication of Weld's *American Slavery as It Is* in 1839 was the most visible manifestation of a general shift to an appeal that was much more secular and political. This shift was quite gradual at first, partly because Garrison and other deeply mystical leaders hesitated to rely on tactics which, however effective they might have been in attracting nonbelievers, would inevitably have corrupted and subverted the moral principles on which the movement was based. Ever alert to proposals that subordinated principle to expediency, Garrison continually warned his fellow abolitionists not to lose sight of their fundamental objective. Their cause turned not on "laws to be passed or steps to be taken" but on *"error* to be rooted out and *repentance* to be exacted." It was not "simply the freedom of the Negro" that was at stake but the salvation of America, which could be achieved only by a penitence profound and sweeping enough to let the nation "escape sin and death by destroying evil."[4]

The struggle to broaden the antislavery appeal was, therefore, first and foremost a struggle within the abolitionist movement over the balance to be struck between moral purity and effectiveness. The victors in this painful conflict were the men who believed that good works for the many took precedence over purity for the few and that principles without votes to make them stick were of no use whatever. Their victory, however, was not without heavy cost. Each step in the dilution of the religious zeal that initially animated the crusade alienated some of the original leaders of the movement. The Garrisonians were the first but not the last major defection. By the late 1840s many of those who had led the way into the political phase of the struggle, such as the group around Gerrit Smith, felt that the effort to broaden the antislavery appeal had passed beyond acceptable limits, because expediency had become the master rather than the servant of fundamental principles.[5]

Although the broadening of the antislavery appeal was largely a process of secularization, the new secular arguments never entirely crowded out the religious ones. The religious strain persisted partly because the principal architects of the secular appeal—including John Quincy Adams, Joshua R. Giddings, and Salmon P. Chase—were deeply religious men and partly because the evangelical movement was a major political constituency that could not be won to the antislavery banner by purely secular appeals. The broadening of the antislavery appeal thus involved adding new arguments rather than abandoning old ones. Indeed, the four principal aspects of the secular appeal—the indictment of southern morality and culture, the development of constitutional rationalizations for federal action against slavery, the call for resistance to the political conspiracies of the Slave Power, and ultimately the call for resistance to the economic conspiracies of the Slave Power—were generally consonant with the religious appeal. Even the Garrisonians made use of secular arguments that dramatized the corruption which inevitably followed from temporizing with sin, but they were highly critical of an antislavery appeal that permitted economic arguments to overwhelm and trivialize the fundamental moral issues, that allowed selfish material considerations to supplant Christian duty, as largely occurred during the last half of the 1850s.

THE INDICTMENT OF SOUTHERN MORALITY AND CULTURE

The development of an indictment of southern morality and culture was the only aspect of the reformulation of the antislavery appeal that did not lead to deep divisions among the crusaders. Since it arose out of the debate within theological circles, and was initially intended to demonstrate the impossibility of drawing a line between the inherent sinfulness of slavery and corrupt behavior by slaveholders, it was fully consonant with abolitionist theology. Indeed, the indictment of southern culture merely spelled out one implication of abolitionist theology—that the failure to exorcise the sin of slavery would lead inevitably to the corruption of every other aspect of life.

Abolitionists had from the outset of the new crusade portrayed slavery as the chief manifestation of the antichrist in American life. As long as they thought that the South could be won to the antislavery crusade, however, they placed as much emphasis on the salvation of the South as on its damnation. But when their efforts to enlist southern support ended so disastrously in the mid-1830s, abolitionists became disheartened over immediate prospects in that region and began to focus almost exclusively on the North. If the sin of slavery could not be extirpated immediately from the South, the North was in imminent danger of moral contamination, since the evangelical concept of sin made slavery not only a malignant disease of the soul, but a highly contagious one.[6]

The danger of contamination was imminent not only because of the natural tendency of moral disease to spread, but because of the determined proslavery counteroffensive launched by Calhoun and other southern leaders in 1836. The southern campaign went beyond the mere exclusion of abolitionists from the South; it was aimed at destroying their influence in the North as well. In pursuing these goals, southern political leaders found many supporters among highly placed northern leaders, including President Martin Van Buren. Under the circumstances of the late 1830s, northern complicity in the sin of slavery was an obvious fact of life. As Garrison saw it, the southern disease had penetrated deeply into every northern institution, including the churches, so that even "the religious forces on which they had relied were all arrayed on the side of the oppressor." By the end of the 1830s it was clear "that the spirit of slavery was omnipresent, invading every sanctuary, infecting every pulpit, controlling every press, corrupting every household, and blinding every vision." The goal of promoting a popular movement against slavery within the South thus gave way to the more urgent need to defend northern values and institutions from the aggrandizement of an unholy alliance between Godless northern and southern leaders. They had "no other alternative," according to Garrison, "except to wage war with 'principalities, and powers, and spiritual wickedness in high places.' "[7]

It was self-defense, then, that required the crusaders to bend every effort to rouse Northerners to the nature of the moral, cultural, and political menace emanating from the South. To quarantine slavery Northerners had to be made aware both of the horror and virulence of the southern disease and of northern complicity in its spread. "If the South depends on you to protect slavery," Garrison warned his fellow Northerners, "then who but you are the real slaveholders." The theme that Northerners who failed to bend every effort to struggle against slavery were guilty of sin by association became the foundation of the abolitionist appeal during the 1840s. Garrison went so far as to insist that the struggle for moral purity required the North to secede from the Union. Shocking as this contention was in 1842 even to New England abolitionists, it soon became the majority position of his followers.[8]

Indeed, by the mid-1840s anger in New England and in the Yankee diaspora over the annexation of Texas and the war with Mexico became so widespread that talk of disunion and civil disobedience became almost fashionable, especially among those sections of the elite in which the traditions of the old Federalist party were still strong. Adams and 12 other congressmen openly threatened it; as conservative an evangelical as Francis Wayland, still reticent and cautious in his antislavery statements, hinted at it; and federal judge William Jay, son of John Jay, provided a constitutional justification for it. The compact between the states embodied in the Constitution was destroyed by the South, said Jay, when Texas was admitted by a simple majority of both Houses rather than by a two-thirds vote of the Senate, as required for transactions with a foreign power. Although not every violation of the Constitution warranted dissolution, this one did because "it enabled slavery to burst the bounds within which it had been confined and ensured a permanent proslavery majority in the Senate." The prospect was not only for an "indefinite extension of the southern boundary" and a perpetual "slaveholding control of the federal government," but it was now "more likely" that "continuance of the Union" would "enslave the North rather than free the South." Under the circumstances the "morals and happiness of the children of Northerners" deserved "more weight than the vain hope of freeing the slaves who would populate Texas and the territories to its south."[9]

As the belief that they could touch the consciences of slaveholders faded, so did abolitionist restraint on the language and imagery that might be employed against southern masters and southern society. There were exceptions to this trend. During the 1840s and 1850s Lewis Tappan urged fellow abolitionists not to dismiss the importance of "missionary work" among southern leaders, which "required subtlety, restraint, and diplomatic skill," and he pursued that mission through personal contacts and correspondence with southern congressmen, governors, and clergy. By the beginning of the 1840s, however, Garrison and most other abolitionists had concluded that such efforts were "a useless waste of time."[10] The urgent task was to "abolitionize the North" by exposing the corruption of southern society. Northerners had to understand the depths of corruption that slavery had imposed on the South and to join not only in ostracizing Southerners, but in proclaiming "their iniquity throughout the World."[11]

By the early 1840s abolitionists widely agreed that this northern strategy offered the best hope for eventual moral reform in the South. Since the backlash of the late 1830s had made proselytizing within the South virtually impossible, resistance to moral reform could only be cracked from the outside. Southerners had to feel the contempt in which their institutions, beliefs, and habits were held by all Christians outside their own region. The indictment of southern society in the North was, therefore, essential not only to save the North but, as contradictory as it might seem, to awaken and save the South. By exposing southern depravity, abolitionists expected to do for the abolitionist cause what Finney's "new measures" had done for revivalism: produce converts by creating "a state of anxiety." The abolitionist's descriptions of the horrors of southern culture were analogous to the revivalist's descriptions of the pain and torture suffered at death by unrepentant sinners. The South was the hell on earth that would befall all those who did not struggle against the sin of slavery.

As the indictment of southern culture became more pronounced, the appeal to altruism began to diminish. Rather than calling on Christians to act purely out of a spirit of benevolence toward blacks, they were called upon to save themselves from the inevitable moral corruption visited upon slaveowners and their retainers. The increasing emphasis on spiritual peril was a more subtle appeal to self-interest than later economic arguments, but still a departure from an appeal that rested on justice and righteousness. The indictment described the price that Southerners were paying for permitting avarice to overcome Christian duty, and it warned Northerners that they would have to pay as great a price if they allowed themselves to be implicated in the sin of slavery.[12]

The overarching count in the abolitionist indictment of southern culture and morality dealt with the lust for power that permeated southern society and on the way that this lust corroded southern personalities and character. Slavery bred in the master class a "love of power and rule" that was nurtured from infancy onward. Educated, as Jefferson had lamented, and "daily exercised in tyranny," the mature Southerner entered the world of affairs "with miserable notions of self-importance, and under the government of an unbridled temper." The absence of restraint on their power made those who exercised it "invariably capricious, unreasonable, and oppressive." These character traits not only led Southerners to treat their slaves brutally—beating, branding, and maiming them at the slightest provocation and often without any provocation at all—but also predisposed them toward violence in their dealings with each other. Consequently, "pistols, dirks, bowie knives, or other instruments of death, are generally carried throughout the slave states" and "deadly affrays with them, in the streets of their cities and villages, are matters of daily occurrence." This passion for violence infused the entire society, so that even "among the most distinguished governors of slave states, among their most celebrated judges, senators, and representatives in Congress, there is hardly *one*, who has not either killed, or tried to kill, or aided and abetted his friends in trying to kill, one or more individuals."[13]

Nearly as abhorrent as the Southerner's lust for power and violence was his lust for pagan pleasures. The consequences of the Southerner's compact with Satan were to be seen in his wholesale subordination of spiritual matters to earthly ones and in his unbridled pursuit of sensual gratification. To be sure, abolitionists viewed debauchery as a national problem, but "the South led the way." As George Bourne put it, the South was "an erotic society" in which whites "have been indulged in all the vicious gratifications which lawless power and unrestrained lust, can amalgamate." Although drunkenness was a national vice, it was many times greater in the South than in the North, and far more resistant to change. In the South drunkenness was so often combined with a penchant for violence that wife-beating became a common occurrence. If prostitution was a problem in northern cities, it was far worse in the South where men brought the corruption of the bordello into their own bedrooms by their "unnatural and monstrous expenditure of the sexual element, for mere sensual gratification." In the South sexual passions were bounded neither by the bedroom nor by the bordello since on plantations the temptation of illicit sex was "always at hand." There was no constraint that prevented the master from turning the slave quarter into a harem. His "legal authority" was "absolute," his "actual power" was "complete," and "the vice" was "a profitable one." So rampant was dissolution that the southern states had become "one great Sodom," so deep was the depravity that by comparison "a Turkish harem" was "a cradle of virgin purity."[14]

The third major count was the degradation of labor in the South. The slave South was also a "lazy South," which celebrated idleness rather than work, and which promoted sloth rather than diligence. Slavery was the root cause of the problem because it identified work with servility. The poor quality of slave labor was inherent, some thought, in the character of the slaves, while others placed the blame on the nature of the system. For whatever reason, it was agreed that slave labor was of low quality and unproductive because it was given reluctantly, because it was unskilled, and because it was wanting in versatility. The labor of whites was degraded by the identity between labor and servility. Demoralized by their low estate, white workers were "driven to indolence, carelessness, indifference to the results of skill, heedlessness, inconstancy of purpose, improvidence, and extravagance."[15] Crowning this edifice of indolence were the planters who, with their aristocratic pretensions, believed that labor was fit only for the "mud-sill" of society.[16] Their lives were dedicated to pleasures of the flesh, dancing, drinking, gambling, martial arts, and other entertainments.

The indictment of southern culture and morality was carried to the northern public by scores of abolitionist newspapers; in books, tracts, pamphlets, and magazines whose titles numbered into thousands; in almanacs, circulars, leaflets, and wafers (sheets of detachable coupons with antislavery quotations that could be used as seals) which first numbered into tens of thousands and then into hundreds of thousands; through posters, cartoons, lithographs, and paintings; in songs, poems, stories, novels, and plays; by sermons delivered from hundreds of pulpits, week in and week out; and at meetings organized throughout the length and breadth of the North. It was the most massive ideological campaign of the age, far exceeding the campaigns of the British abolitionists against the West Indian planters. During the 12 months ending in May 1838, for example, the AASS published more than 600,000 books, tracts, pamphlets, and other pieces of literature. By 1840 the output of tracts and pamphlets had increased fivefold.[17]

At the center of this literary barrage was a corps of 20 or 30 newspaper editors and other publicists whose skill and effectiveness were begrudgingly acknowledged by southern adversaries who called them "zealous, able, and efficient,"[18] and who charged them with endangering the future of the Union. If allowed to continue, Calhoun declared in 1838, these publicists will "in the course of a few years" teach Northerners "to hate the people and institutions of nearly one half of this Union, with a hatred more deadly than one hostile nation ever entertained towards another."[19] Although it took more than "a few years" for Calhoun's prophecy to be fulfilled, by the 1850s northern attitudes toward the South had changed so much that many northern politicians eagerly sought to pin the label of "southern lackey" on their rivals, and temporizing with southern morals and sensibilities became anathema. The indictment of southern culture was no longer confined to abolitionist tracts but was routinely published in conventional magazines and in literary journals. The authors of the indictment were no longer just publicists of AASS or the Liberty party but included such towering figures of *belles lettres* as Henry Wadsworth Longfellow, Ralph Waldo Emerson, and James Russell Lowell. By the 1850s the indictment often emerged not as a direct critique of Southerners (whose moral infamy was by then taken for granted) but as a searing critique of those Northerners who privately professed hostility to southern institutions and culture but failed to speak out against them—as when Lowell excoriated those northern Christians who publicly condemned "a dance or a Sunday drive" in their own communities but were "blandly silent" about Southerners engaged in "the separation of families" and in "selling Christian girls for Christian harems."[20]

CONSTITUTIONAL RATIONALIZATIONS FOR FEDERAL ACTION AGAINST SLAVERY

As long as moral suasion was perceived as the principal means of ending slavery, abolitionists accepted the federal consensus which held that under the Constitution "the federal government had no power over slavery in the states." Once it became obvious that slaveowners were unwilling to yield to patient pleading, to stern admonitions, or to various forms of castigation, abolitionists were increasingly pushed to political action at the federal level as the most effective remedy. Toward the end of the 1830s abolitionists began a wide-ranging reconsideration of their previous position that "only the states could abolish or in any way regulate slavery within their jurisdictions."[21] This review led to three principal interpretations of the constitutional status of slavery.

By far the gloomiest of these interpretations, and probably the most accurate description of the intentions of the founding fathers, was the one developed by Garrison and Wendell Phillips. They concluded that the "Constitution was a bulwark of slavery in at least four particulars" and "that the framers consciously wrote guarantees for slavery into the Constitution." Because "our fathers were intent on securing liberty to themselves," and because they were not "very scrupulous as to the means they used to accomplish their purpose," they "did not blush to enslave a portion of their fellow men." Consequently, they institutionalized slavery in the clause that counted a bondsman as three-fifths of a free person, and in the clause that prohibited federal legislation against the importation of slaves for at least 20 years. The Constitution not only institutionalized the system but obligated the federal government to defend it in the fugitive slave clause and in the clause requiring the federal government to suppress "insurrections and domestic violence," which clearly covered "uprisings of slaves." It was the publication in 1840 of the Madison papers which described the deliberations of the Constitutional Convention that clinched the issue for the Garrisonians. Even John Quincy Adams had to concede that the Constitution was so saturated "with the infection of slavery" that "no fumigation could purify" it.[22]

To Garrison and Wendell Phillips, the logical conclusion of this analysis was disunion—"not merely a moral, token or symbolic act, but . . . actual secession from the Union by the free states." In supporting their position Garrison and Phillips developed a theory of the Constitution and of the U.S. legal system that was grounded in mysticism. They drew a distinction between "divine government" and "human government." Human institutions were corrupt and imperfect in varying degrees and, regardless of the intentions of their architects, inevitably became obstructions that thwarted the "divine goal of perfection." Unlike "divine government" which required a society free from sin and which was ordered only by a universal obedience to Christ, human governments required prisons, police, armies, and other means of force to sustain control and power. It followed that law was merely "a rule prescribed" by civil authorities, which "may be immoral," violating the natural law implanted by God, but "still be of binding authority, as far as the judicial agents of the state were concerned." Since statutory law "merely codified what custom had created" and since the framers of the Constitution regarded slaves as "a very inferior portion of the human race," "it was impossible, of course, for those who framed the Constitution to concede to them any of its privileges." Under these circumstances it was not merely the state governments of the South but also the national government, including all of its branches, that was dedicated to "the preservation, propagation, and perpetuation of slavery."[23]

Although Garrison's constitutional position emanated from the perfectionist, millennial theology that he embraced, it was also sustained by a long New England religious tradition of "exclusiveness" that was carried into political life through the Federalist party and later through the Whig party. At the core of this tradition "was the conviction that the people of New England, and none more so than those of Massachusetts, were somehow set apart from the rest of the nation." Belief in their moral, ethnic, social, economic, and political superiority was widespread among the New England elite during the early years of the republic. Not only had the "God of nature, in his infinite goodness made the people of New England to excel every other people that ever existed," but the "fathers of Massachusetts" had created a society that was homogeneous in its "habits, manners, language, government, and religion," and which over time "had become the special home of liberty."[24]

The New England elite prized this accomplishment and, as long as the Federalist party was in the majority, eagerly supported nationalizing endeavors. However, the long reign of the Virginia dynasty in national government not only frustrated their missionary aims but threatened to overwhelm and corrupt their own society. Fearful that their culture might be made politically subordinate to the inferior cultures of an expanding South and West, New England leaders began to toy with the possibility of secession. The idea that expansionism might make disunion inevitable was a factor in the convening of the Hartford Convention of 1814–1815, which was organized by New England Federalists with the declared objective of mounting a campaign to revise the Constitution. Although the Hartford Convention contributed to the disaster which befell the Federalist party in the election of 1816, the notion that New England culture was imperiled by the expansion of the nation lingered on in elite circles, as did the possibility that New Englanders might eventually be forced to secession as their only remedy.[25]

By the mid-1830s the thought of a New England secession had receded into the background, but it was revived during the 1840s by the annexation of Texas and the war with Mexico. In the neosecessionist atmosphere provoked by these events, Garrison's views of the Constitution, while extreme, were nevertheless viewed with a certain sympathy among prominent members of New England's elite. William E. Channing, for example, a leading spokesman for Unitarianism and a distinguished man of letters, while unwilling to accept Garrison's attack on the Constitution, nevertheless joined him in calling for a "moral blockade" of the South. Despite such expressions of sympathy few men outside of Garrison's circle embraced his view of the Constitution. The Constitution was too sacred a symbol to be profaned by anyone who seriously aspired to public office and by most of those who hoped to influence the course of government.[26]

The second interpretation of the constitutional status of slavery was in its own way as radical as that advanced by the Garrisonians and was, like the Garrison position, an invitation to political oblivion. Although its advocates were motivated by as intense a hatred of slavery as that which impelled the Garrisonians, their position on the Constitution was diametrically opposed to his. Far from being "a bulwark of slavery," the Constitution, they argued, was an antislavery document because it was based on natural law and common law, both of which made slavery illegitimate. Moreover, the Constitution explicitly contained three major clauses and several minor clauses which were inimicable to slavery. They denied that any clause of the Constitution legitimated slavery, arguing that the four clauses singled out by the Garrisonians as "bulwarks of slavery" either did not apply to slaves or "could easily and legitimately be evaded."[27]

This optimistic view of the Constitution, which one legal historian has called "radical constitutional antislavery," did not emerge as a major position within abolitionist circles until the mid-1840s. Down to the end of the 1830s the principal abolitionist leaders accepted the federal consensus that held that under the Constitution only the states could abolish or in any way regulate slavery. When Alvan Stewart, a member of the circle around Gerrit Smith, sought to remove the clause affirming this position from the constitution of the AASS in 1838, he was condemned by William Jay, among others, for a "vile heresy."[28]

The principles of radical constitutional antislavery were not systematically set forth until 1844–1845 when three tracts on the theme were published—one by Stewart, the second by William Goodell (also a member of the Smith circle), and the third by Lysander Spooner (a Massachusetts lawyer). All three men rooted their arguments "on the legally binding force of natural law," which mystics such as Stewart and Goodell believed was the law given to mankind by the Creator, and which could be discovered both by reason and by revelation. It followed that no human laws that contradicted natural law were valid. Natural law was, in this formulation, not only superior to man-made laws, but the "source of individual human rights" so that "any governmental act infringing human liberty was ipso facto void, of no obligation, and incapable of being legitimized."[29] Unlike Goodell and Stewart, Spooner did not believe in mystical knowledge. As a deist he believed that "man's proper goal" was "to understand the laws of nature instead of chasing after supernatural substitutes."[30] To Spooner, natural law was inherent in "the nature of men, and their relations to each other." Declaring that the nature of men was as unalterable as "the laws of motion" or "the laws of gravitation," he said that any man-made law which was inconsistent with natural law was "of no obligation at all, when the two come in collision." Consequently, statute law could not "lawfully authorize government to destroy or take from men their natural rights" to acquire "property, privilege, &c. . . . by labor and contract."[31]

Although Spooner's definition of natural law was in its own way as mystical as that of Stewart and Goodell, in the sense that it required belief in a moral code beyond the control of men, his skepticism and his legal training led him to focus on the ambiguities in the Constitution. By insisting that every ambiguity "must be construed 'strictly' in favor of natural right," he developed a powerful argument for negating those clauses of the Constitution that directly or indirectly protected slavery. In this connection, he held that external evidence about the intentions of the founding fathers with respect to slavery was irrelevant since "the only authentic evidence" of such intentions was whether the Constitution explicitly sanctioned slavery: "The legal meaning of the words" in the Constitution was the "only guide to its intention" and "no terms, except those that are plenary, express, explicit, distinct, unequivocal, *and to which no other meaning can be given, are legally competent* to authorize or sanction anything contrary to natural right."[32] Since the Constitution did not explicitly use the word "slaves" or explicitly acknowledge the right of property in men (because, as Madison put it, of "scruples against admitting the term 'slaves' into the Instrument"[33]), slavery could be deemed constitutional only by accepting the proposition that the sanction is conveyed by "enigmatical words, by unnecessary implication and inference, by innuendo and double entendre, and under a name that entirely fails of describing the thing."[34]

Reasonable as Spooner's arguments appear to a modern reader, they were strained in the extreme to those who lived in a world in which the congressional, judicial, and executive branches of government repeatedly reaffirmed both the constitutionality of slavery and the exclusive right of the states to regulate slavery where it existed. Wendell Phillips saw no basis whatsoever for the claim that the proslavery clauses of the Constitution were ambiguous. That the three-fifths clause applied to slaves rather than to "resident aliens" (Spooner asserted the latter) was perfectly evident from the way in which the elections to Congress were carried out immediately after the Constitution became effective. "Now *there never yet was a State,*" said Phillips, *"which took any special account of aliens in fixing its basis of representation."* Further, in apportioning representation for the first congressional election, the allocations made in the Constitution to the free and slave states (35 and 30) are exactly the figures obtained "on the basis of reckoning *three-fifths of the slaves.*"[35]

Similarly, Spooner's attempt to interpret the fugitive slave clause as applying only to apprentices was, said Phillips, based on the strained contention that the words used in that clause (a person "held to service or labor") did not define a slave. He demonstrated (by reference to various dictionaries in use at the time the Constitution was drafted, as well as by the usage contained in such contemporaneous legal documents as the Northwest Ordinance of 1787 and the Connecticut Emancipation Act of 1784) that "the term 'held to service or labor' does aptly describe the condition of a slave, and was the phraseology usually employed for that purpose."[36]

It was not merely to Garrisonians that Spooner's arguments appeared so strained, but to the public at large. When most of the leaders of the Liberty party decided in 1848 to merge with factions of the Democrats and the Whigs to form the Free Soil party, the radical antislavery constitutionalists formed the "Liberty Party Abolitionists." This new party, which nominated Gerrit Smith for president, ran on a free Constitution program but could garner only an insignificant vote (less than 1/10th of 1 percent of the total cast for president). Similar trials in 1852, 1856, and 1860 led to results that were even more dismal. Whatever the moral virtue of their program, the Free Constitutionalists (as these radicals called themselves in 1860) were devoid of political support.[37]

The third theory of the constitutional status of slavery was developed by the most politically oriented of the abolitionists, and was constrained by their sense of what was politically feasible. Those who promoted "moderate constitutional antislavery" acknowledged the various clauses of the Constitution that legitimated and protected slavery. Recognizing the reverence in which the Constitution was held by the electorate, these abolitionists trimmed their real objectives and affirmed their acceptance of all aspects of the Constitution, including those provisions that guaranteed the regulation of slavery to the states. Their objective, they said, was not to denounce the Constitution or to change it, but to uphold it. The threat to the Constitution came not from the abolitionists but from the slaveowners who sought to pervert the Constitution by turning it into an instrument for the establishment of slavery in places where it did not and had not existed. The real issue of aggression was not an abolitionist aggression against the rights of slaveholders, but an aggression against the Constitution and the rights of free men by slaveholders who sought to undermine liberties guaranteed by the Constitution. The real constitutional issue was the defense of the federal government against unconstitutional schemes to bring the entire nation under the political domination of the slaveholding class.[38]

The principal figures in the development of the moderate antislavery theory of the Constitution—John Quincy Adams, Joshua R. Giddings, and Salmon P. Chase—were also the principal architects of the campaign to develop a political realignment on an antislavery program.[39] Their theory of antislavery constitutionalism was developed in close synchronization with their assessment of the type of antislavery politics that was feasible within Congress and among their electorates. In the late 1830s and early 1840s, when Congress was overwhelmingly committed to the view that the Constitution sanctioned slavery, direct legislative assaults were impossible. The issue could be raised, if at all, only obliquely. In 1836 and 1837 Adams pushed the issue purely on the basis of free speech, abjuring any desire to violate the federal consensus but defend-

ing the right of citizens, no matter how misguided, to have their antislavery petitions received in Congress. In 1837, 1838, and 1839 he used the
congressional debate over the annexation of Texas to insinuate attacks
on slavery. Exploiting widespread fear that such an annexation would
lead to a war with Mexico, Adams charged that the slavocracy was
engaged in a nefarious plot aimed at increasing its political stranglehold
over the federal government, a plot which involved the perversion of the
Constitution and the risk of a war with Mexico. Since Texas was a foreign
state, he argued, any attempt to annex it was "unconstitutional, null, and
void, because it would be a violation of the rights reserved to the people,"
unless the Constitution was amended to give Congress such a right.[40]

By his adroit manipulation of the petition and annexation issues,
Adams kept antislavery demands steadily before Congress from 1836 to
early 1842. Using his mastery of parliamentary procedure, he repeatedly
forced an "unwilling majority" in the House to give him a platform.
Although he knew that in the end he would be voted down, he repeatedly
lured southern supporters of slavery in the House to attack him for
insinuating the forbidden issue of Congress's power to regulate slavery.
In so doing he was able to cast congressional defenders of slavery into
the role of enemies of free speech who repeatedly violated the Constitution in order to protect and extend an onerous system.[41]

The elections of 1838 and 1840 brought several additional antislavery Whigs into the House, including Joshua Giddings and Sherlock J.
Andrews of Ohio, William Slade of Vermont, and Seth M. Gates of New
York—all of whom were products of the revivalist campaigns led by
Finney and others in the Yankee diaspora.[42] In the words of Weld, they
were all "revival men," "professors of religion," and five out of perhaps
a dozen were elders in the Presbyterian Church. Three of them—Giddings, Gates, and Andrews—had been "Weld's own converts to abolition, and others without doubt had felt his inspiration in some degree."
Under the leadership of Giddings, with Weld and Joshua Leavitt (another
member of the Tappen circle) as "staff" men, this group of congressmen
formed themselves into an antislavery bloc (which they called a "Select
Committee on Slavery"). They took out rooms in Giddings's boarding
house (which were converted into a staff center) and planned a concerted
offensive against slavery, in defiance of the Whig House leadership.
Toward this end they devised ways of openly introducing antislavery
bills and resolutions on such issues as the interstate slave trade and the
annexation of Texas while still avoiding "political annihilation." Adams
had doubts about this new strategy, but he worked closely with the
"Select Committee." Fearful of too open an assault at this time, he
counseled the bloc to stick to the strategy of obliquely raising the slavery
issue in the course of an aggressive defense of the freedom of citizens

to petition Congress on their grievances, of the freedom of debate in Congress, of the freedom of speech, and of the freedom of the press.[43]

Early in 1842 the members of the bloc concluded that the *Creole* case provided a good opportunity to introduce openly a series of antislavery resolutions. The *Creole* was a vessel engaged in coastwise trade that was captured by its "cargo": slaves who were being transported from Hampton Roads, Virginia, to New Orleans. The mutineers diverted the ship to the Bahamas, where they expected to be freed. The case roused a great storm in the southern press, which demanded the return of the mutineers and murderers. In anticipation of a resolution in the House to that effect (such a resolution was passed by the Senate), Giddings and other members of the bloc prepared a series of counterresolutions. These resolutions were aimed at converting the federal consensus from a shield for slavery into a weapon against it. The problem for Giddings and his collaborators was how to develop a position that would have to be recognized within Congress and among the electorate as one that was constitutionally plausible or at least arguable. The strategy they hit upon was to concede unhesitatingly to all of the clauses in the Constitution that legitimated slavery, and then to put the narrowest possible interpretation on these clauses. It further involved accepting the southern position that under the Constitution slavery was purely a municipal issue and beyond the power of Congress. By carrying this point to its logical conclusion, said Giddings, it was possible to turn their own weapon against them. For if "the Federal Government has no Constitutional right to interfere" with slavery "in any way," then it followed that the federal government "had no constitutional right to support it."[44]

In applying this principle to the *Creole* case, Giddings argued that since the slave laws of Virginia applied only to its territory, once on the high seas only federal law pertained. Moreover, since the Constitution prohibited the federal government from legislating either to prohibit or to establish slavery, reserving that right exclusively to the states, once the *Creole* was at sea the slaves who reclaimed "their natural right to liberty violated no law of the United States, incurred no legal penalties, and are justly liable to no punishment." He contended not only that using the federal government "to regain possession of or to re-enslave" this group of persons was unlawful but that any federal intervention "in favor of the coastwise slave-trade" was "subversive of the rights" and "interests of the people of the Free States," and "unauthorized by the Constitution."[45]

The shrewdness of Giddings's logic and its threat to slavery was immediately apparent. Southern leaders pushed through a motion to censure Giddings for violating House Rule 21, which prohibited members from introducing antislavery resolutions. Giddings immediately resigned his seat and ran for reelection. Despite the opposition of Whig leaders in Ohio, Giddings was swept back into office. This outcome effectively nullified the House gag on antislavery speeches, and demonstrated that moderate antislavery was politically viable, at least in the northern constituencies in which the influence of the Second Great Awakening was strong.[46]

During the balance of the 1840s and into the 1850s Giddings and other antislavery members of Congress continued to develop the theme that every action of the federal government in support of slavery was a violation of the Constitution. The principle was extended to the issue of fugitive slaves. Although the Constitution called upon the states to return fugitive slaves to their owners, it did not authorize the federal government to expend its resources to retrieve them. The states were obligated to deliver up fugitive slaves, but the federal government had no right to require them to do so because Article IV, Section 2, of the Constitution (which contains the fugitive slave clause) failed "to delegate to Congress power to enforce it by appropriate legislation." Consequently, the fugitive slave laws enacted by Congress in 1793 and thereafter were all unconstitutional. Similarly, it was unconstitutional for Congress to have legalized slavery and the slave trade in Washington, D.C., as it did in 1801. Other unconstitutional enactments and actions by the federal government included the regulation of the coastwise slave trade, the Florida War (which represented intervention in favor of slavery), and the establishment of slavery and the slave trade in Florida and other territories. In other words, anything whatsoever that the federal government did to support slavery outside of the original slave states was unconstitutional because it put the federal government in the position of promoting the interests of the slave states against those of the free states.[47]

Giddings's maneuver was adroit. It enabled him to challenge the widely held belief that the Constitution required the federal government to pass legislation and to take action to implement the slavery clauses of the Constitution. He did so neither by denying that there was a series of proslavery clauses in the Constitution nor by challenging the southern view that the Constitution prohibited the federal government from acting against slavery. He argued instead that the Constitution required the federal government to be neutral with respect to slavery. He also defined neutrality in such a way that it barred the federal government from any behavior that facilitated the operation of the slave system or its extension beyond the states in which it existed at the time of the ratification of the Constitution.[48]

This line of argument permitted the moderates to shift the onus for violating the Constitution from the abolitionists to the slaveholders. The slaveholders had, from the beginning, violated the Constitution by using their control of Congress and the federal government to pass proslavery resolutions adverse to the interest of the free states. It was the South that had violated the Constitution by making the federal government the tool of a section instead of the instrument of the entire nation. Moreover, every new demand made by the South to protect or extend slavery beyond the original slave states, including the annexation of Texas, the passage of new fugitive slave laws, and the legitimizing of slavery in territories, represented further aggression against the Constitution and against the constitutional rights of the free states. The antislavery moderates, on the other hand, sought only to defend the Constitution and restore its integrity, which required "the absolute and unqualified divorce of the General Government from Slavery."[49]

RESISTING THE POLITICAL CONSPIRACIES OF THE "SLAVE POWER"

The thesis that the North was the victim of a "Slave Power" conspiracy was inherent in the moderate antislavery theory of the Constitution, but it went beyond the purely constitutional issues. The "Slave Power" slogan implied not just the unconstitutional use of the federal government to protect and promote the interests of the slaveowners, but a more far-reaching plot against American freedom, a plot aimed ultimately at the complete subjugation of free people. The plot was unfolding in a series of steps which began with the seizure of the federal government by slaveowners immediately after the ratification of the Constitution. It then progressed toward the suppression of the democratic rights of Northerners to free speech, free assembly, free press, and free elections. The final stage, some argued, would be the reduction of free whites to slavery—not a metaphoric slavery but a literal one.[50]

The concept of the political conspiracy by the Slave Power traces back to the split between the Federalists and the Jeffersonian party. At that time it found reflection not in a hostility to slavery per se but in resentment by Federalist politicians, particularly the New Englanders, at being frozen out of power by the Virginia dynasty. With such a conception of the issue, the political power of the slaveholders stirred resentment mainly among politicians and those who aspired to national political influence. When this resentment broke into the open, as it did at the time of the Hartford Convention and again during the Missouri crisis, it aroused only limited sympathy among an electorate whose chief concerns were about issues that affected them more directly.[51] Although the hostility of many northern politicians to southern control of all branches of the federal government became quiescent after the Missouri Compromise, it was never obliterated. It remained a latent factor in intraparty struggles that became evident as factions jockeyed for position, but during the early years of the second-party system it was kept in tight reign by the demands of interparty competition.

This reservoir of resentment over southern domination began to be exploited by the abolitionists in the late 1830s and became the political counterpart of their indictment of southern culture. William Jay and Joshua Leavitt were important figures in designing the early phases of the appeal against the political conspiracy of the Slave Power. The basis for the conspiracy was the three-fifths clause of the Constitution which gave slaveholders political power far beyond their number. If only free persons were counted in establishing representation in Congress then the slave states would not have been entitled to the 100 members of the House that they had in the late 1830s but only to 75. It was these extra 25 seats in the House, said Leavitt, which gave the South control of Congress and tipped the balance in the struggle for the presidency to the South (since the three-fifths clause gave the South, according to Leavitt's calculations, 25 extra electoral votes).[52]

Not all abolitionists accepted the logic behind these calculations. Wendell Phillips found it strange for abolitionists to advocate an electoral procedure that treated slaves not as three-fifths of a person but as a zero person. Others who were disfranchised in both the North and the South, such as free Negroes, immigrants, and women, were treated as whole persons when apportioning House seats and electoral votes. To recognize fully the humanity of slaves in apportionment, however, would only increase the power of slaveholders in the House and in the contest for the presidency. Whatever the merit of Phillips's logic, it was bad antislavery politics and so was dismissed by those who designed the theory of the Slave Power conspiracy.[53]

The architects of the theory maintained that the three-fifths clause was unjust to Northerners because it permitted slaveholders to make the federal government the instruments of their will. The slaveholders had packed federal offices with their men, beginning with the presidency. For 40 out of 52 years they had installed Southerners in that office and in 8 of the remaining 12 years the Northerners who held the office were beholden to slaveowners, especially "Mr. Van Buren, who glories in the cognomen of 'the northern man with southern principles.' " Southerners also were installed as Speaker of the House in 28 of the preceding 35 years; they were a majority of the Supreme Court and of the Cabinet; and every Senate president *pro tem* since the ratification of the Constitution had been a slaveholder. The South also used the 25 extra House seats to control the legislation of Congress since "very few debatable measures" had been carried during the preceding "30 years by a greater majority than 25." As a result the North had been reduced to the position of a "conquered province."[54]

The conspiracy of the slaveholders was aimed not merely at usurping power and at freezing the North out of its rightful share of offices, but at using that power and those offices to advance southern interests at northern expense. When the Treasury surplus was distributed to the states it was done not on the basis of the free population but according to electoral votes, thus transferring revenues "derived chiefly from the industry and enterprise of the North"[55] to the slave states. Northerners were made to pay an even higher price when the Slave Power used the federal government to seize Texas and other Mexican territories. The Mexican War, denounced as the most crass example of the Slave Power conspiracy to date, forced Northerners to pay for southern adventures not only with money, but with the blood of their sons. Moreover, the seizure of Mexican territories, out of which a dozen or more states could be carved, threatened to maintain the Slave Power's grip on the federal government and to ensure its domination in perpetuity.

The attractiveness of the "Slave Power conspiracy" as a political slogan became apparent almost as soon as it was launched. Not only did it mesh well with the indictment of southern culture but it also meshed with other popular political slogans of the age. It aroused fear that the democratic liberties of ordinary people were threatened by invisible but malevolent minorities who secretly wielded catastrophic political influence, just as such fears had been aroused by Jackson's alarms about the conspiracies of the "Money Power," the Federalist alarms about the Illuminati and the Freemasons, and the Protestant alarms about the "papal conspiracy." As early as 1842 a friend of Giddings pointed out that although many Northerners "still regarded themselves as friends of the South, and the uncompromising enemies of the abolitionists," if you agitate them on "the question of Southern dictation," their "eyes flash and their faces burn."[56] By 1848 Leavitt could write that the Slave Power slogan had became so "indissolubly incorporated in the political nomenclature of the country" that it was widely used by northern politicians of both major parties. The abolitionists would markedly advance their cause, he continued, by promoting "the incessant use of the term" without demanding "that they who use it should ever know who taught it to them. . . . Let it appear that it is the *Slave Power* which we wish to restrict and curtail; that it is the *Slave Power* whose demands we resist, whose growth we will put down."[57]

The ideological achievements of the 1840s made it possible to transform the content of the Slave Power slogan from a grab for office and control of legislation to a direct and immediate attack on the personal liberties of free men. It was on the issue of political liberty that Adams first raised the banner of antislavery in Congress. When he railed against the "Slave Power," his reference was to the coalition of southern and northern House members who overwhelming voted against receiving petitions for the abolition of slavery: *They* were the Slave Power in the House. Adams made the case that in voting to lay antislavery petitions on the table, without further consideration of them in the House, the Slave Power had violated the freedom to petition and the freedom of speech. That argument was quite effective in the sense that it won a sympathetic hearing among many Northerners who were otherwise hostile to abolitionism.[58]

But no matter how visceral a reaction it produced among Southerners, for Northerners the argument was over an abstract and remote issue that appealed more to the mind than the heart, more to the politician or the intellectual than the common man. Although the "gag" rule had limited the speech of Adams and other antislavery representatives within the House, they could and did speak without constraint in other forums. Although the House had voted to lay antislavery petitions on the table, that vote did not prevent the abolitionists from collecting hundreds of thousands of signatures and delivering their petitions to Congress. Since the indictment of southern culture had not yet unfolded, the impact of Adams's attack on the Slave Power was not amplified by the widespread aversion to the South that existed among Northerners at the beginning of the 1850s, but it laid the basis for much of what followed.

Ironically, a set of bills known as the Compromise of 1850, intended to defuse the constitutional crisis brought on by the acquisition of Mexican lands, became the vehicle for raising northern fears of a Slave Power conspiracy to a pitch never previously attained. Clay, Webster, and Senator Stephen A. Douglas, the principal architects of the Compromise, were preoccupied with settling the territorial issues in a manner that preserved the prevailing political balance between the sections. The crux of the compromise was the admission of California with an antislavery constitution and the establishments of territorial governments in the rest of the Mexican cession "without any condition regarding slavery." The establishment or exclusion of slavery in the territories was thus to be left to the people that inhabited them—a doctrine called "popular sovereignty." To complete the Compromise, the slave trade (but not slavery) was abolished in the District of Columbia and a stringent fugitive slave law was enacted.[59]

Although the Compromise of 1850 effectively removed the slavery question from the 1852 elections (the vote for the Free Soil party fell to barely half its total in 1848), the fugitive slave law turned out to be "a firebrand vastly more inflammatory than the Wilmot Proviso." Unlike the Proviso, which sought to bar "hypothetical" slaves from a "hypothetical" migration, the attempt to implement the fugitive slave act focused northern attenton on "hundreds of flesh-and-blood people who had risked their lives to gain their liberty, and who might now be tracked down by slave-catchers." One could clearly see the disregard of the Slave Power for the rudiments of personal liberty in this act which denied not only fugitives, but also free Negroes accused of being runaways the right of a jury trial. They "were seized and carried off forcibly without any judicial process," condemned to a life of slavery merely on the word of a slave catcher.[60]

One could clearly see the designs of the Slave Power on the personal liberties of free whites in the North when those who sought to rescue blacks from slave catchers were threatened with incarceration or actually prosecuted under the law. Even those who merely sat idly by ran the risk of prosecution since the act empowered "federal marshals to summon all citizens to aid in enforcement of the Act." So the Slave Power had not only put the federal government "into the business of man-hunting," bringing to bear the power of federal marshals and of the army, but it "also required every freeborn American to become a manhunter." A new and wider circle of voices from the press, pulpit, and rostrum now joined in the denunciation of this evil, but the most devastating critique of slavery and slave catching was *Uncle Tom's Cabin* by Harriet Beecher Stowe. It was published first in 1851 as a series of weekly installments in the *National Era*, an antislavery newspaper. In March 1852 it was republished as a book and became an instant best seller with over 300,000 copies sold in the first year (about one copy for every eight northern families). The U.S. sales eventually reached 3 million and 3.5 million books were sold abroad. A few months after the book was published, the story of Uncle Tom began its long career as America's most popular play.[61]

The Kansas-Nebraska Act of 1854 (which repealed the Missouri Compromise for those territories), the drive of the proslavery minority in Kansas to impose a state constitution that legalized slavery (the Lecompton constitution), and the Supreme Court's ruling on the Dred Scott case (which gratuitously declared that all attempts to bar slavery in the territories were unconstitutional) provided irrefutable evidence that a drive to subvert northern freedom was under way and would not end until the Slave Power achieved complete domination over the North. The note for the new phase of ideological struggle against the Slave Power was sounded in the "Appeal of the Independent Democrats in Congress," which was written largely by Chase, but in which Giddings, Gerrit Smith, and Charles Sumner had a hand. The Kansas-Nebraska Act, they charged, brought into the open the "monstrous plot" of the Slave Power to "permanently subjugate the whole country to the yoke of a slaveholding despotism."[62]

By 1858 the antislavery forces, now coalesced in the Republican party, could assert that the objectives of the Slave Power and the manner of their conspiracy were fully visible.[63] The conspiracy was centered in the Democratic party and had as its objective nothing less than national-ization of slavery. The leading conspirators, according to Lincoln, were Senator Stephen A. Douglas, Presidents Franklin Pierce and James Buchanan, and Chief Justice of the Supreme Court Roger B. Taney. Although the elements that formed the plot were produced at different times and places, they fitted together so perfectly that there could be no doubt about it. Douglas rammed the Kansas-Nebraska Act through Con-gress, Pierce signed it, Buchanan implemented it as the slaveholders desired, and Taney reinforced the whole edifice by declaring that neither Congress nor a territorial legislature could exclude slavery from any territory. All but one piece was missing from this conspiracy to national-ize slavery, said Lincoln. That was a Supreme Court decision "declaring that the Constitution of the United States does not permit a *state* to exclude slavery from its limits." And such a decision "will soon be upon us," he warned, "unless the power of the present political dynasty shall be met and overthrown." Otherwise "We shall *lie down* pleasantly dreaming that the people of *Missouri* are on the verge of making their state *free;* and we shall *awake* to the *reality,* instead, that the *Supreme* Court has made *Illinois* a *slave* state."[64]

In such an atmosphere, it was easy to go a step further and charge that what the Slave Power wanted was not just political domination of the North, not just the restriction of some cherished liberties, but out-right enslavement of all white labor—a slavery for the free whites of the North that was as real and as complete as the black slavery of the South. It was not difficult to defend this charge since by the mid-1850s southern writers, newspapers, and politicians were widely proclaiming the superi-ority of slave labor and commending it to the elite of the North. They announced that slavery was "the natural and normal condition of the laboring man, white or black"[65]; that free society was a disastrous "little experiment," originally designed "in a corner of Western Europe," which had "failed dismally" both there and in the North; that the free society of the North was a "self-destroying"[66] and unstable form of social organization which alternated between famine and insurrection; that the North was an insufferable "conglomeration of greasy mechanics, filthy operatives, and small-fisted farmers"[67]; that if the "laboring man" of the North became "the slave of one man instead of the slave" of the eco-nomic system, "he would be far better off"; that northern employers "should become the owners of their laborers and as such be compelled to clothe and feed them decently"; and that "in the West the public lands should be parcelled out in great estates and tilled by the landless poor bound in perpetuity to the soil."[68] The struggle against the Slave Power conspiracy was thus nothing less than the struggle to prevent the free workers of the North from becoming white slaves.

RESISTING THE ECONOMIC CONSPIRACIES OF THE "SLAVE POWER"

Economic issues were not entirely absent from the antislavery appeal during the 1830s and 1840s, but prior to the emergence of the Republican party they were little more than afterthoughts.[69] During the panic of 1837 and again during the more severe depression of 1840–1843, abolitionist leaders sought to connect their moral critique of slavery with burning economic issues, but these attempts were haphazard and unimaginative. In 1837 the AASS put the blame for the devastating economic panic on the South, charging slaveowners with attempting to save their "failing fortunes" by resorting to the "necromancy of banking" and with reneging on their debts to northern merchants. Since southern banks were few in number and generally much smaller than the banks of the Northeast, and since 1837 was an average year for cotton producers, neither charge carried conviction. They made no contact whatsoever with the economic issues that agitated most merchants, laborers, and farmers, and which were at the center of the struggle for power between the Democrats and the Whigs. To the extent that banks were held responsible for the panic, as the Jacksonians said they were, the blame was placed not on the minor banks of the South but on the Bank of the United States, which was located in Philadelphia, and on the other great banks in New York and Boston. To the Whigs, both North and South, it was Jackson's destruction of the Second Bank of the United States, his pandering to his own "pet" banks, and his Specie Circular that triggered the orgy of wildcat banking and then brought on the panic.[70]

Leaders of the Liberty party also sought to enhance their antislavery appeal by linking it to economic issues. During the worst months of the depression of 1840–1843 Joshua Leavitt produced a pamphlet attacking the "Financial Power of Slavery." Once again the attack centered on the claim that the crisis in the North was due to the drain of its capital, which "flows to the South as water runs down hill." Leavitt never provided evidence to substantiate the contention that the South actually was a net debtor to the North and, although cliometricians have yet to address this issue squarely, some of the work on southern probate records suggests that northern securities (especially railroad bonds) held by Southerners may have exceeded their debts to Northerners. Even less convincing, in light of the eagerness of northern merchants to continue lending to the South, was Leavitt's claim that Southerners had reneged on over $100 million in notes to the North between 1836 and 1841.[71]

Even if Northerners were sympathetic to the abolitionist charge that the South was "a bottomless gulf of extravagance and thriftlessness" (in contrast to the "economical, self-denying, heaven-blessed industry"[72] of the North), nothing in these denunciations mitigated the specific economic grievances raised in the complaints of specific northern constituencies during the 1840s. The native-born mechanics generally complained about the downward pressure on wages caused by the glutted labor markets and the competition for jobs from the foreign born. The foreign-born workers complained about the labor monopolies of the native workers and the high price of housing. Northeastern farmers complained about the falling prices of agricultural commodities caused by western competition and by the low shipping rates that both railroads and water carriers gave to western merchants. Workers and capitalists in iron and cotton textiles complained about the competition from British imports. Western farmers complained about the high price of land sold from the public domain and the inadequacies of the transportation system. Virtually everyone complained about the shocking growth of urban slums; the riots, crimes, and vices that rocked the cities of the North; the terrible increase in urban morbidity and mortality rates; and the epidemics that spread from the slum districts of the foreign born to the better urban communities and then to the surrounding rural areas.[73]

Abolitionist Whigs, such as Giddings, were far more skillful than the leaders of the Liberty party in developing economic positions that appealed to northern voters. In a series of articles published late in 1842 he argued that "protective tariffs, national roads, and homestead bills were as much antislavery measures as the abolition of servitude in the District of Columbia." But the men in the Liberty party reacted suspiciously to what they viewed as Gidding's attempt to divert antislavery votes from them to the Whigs. Even when they cautiously took up such measures as protective tariffs the Liberty leaders were inept in their development of the theme, coupling their condemnation of slaveholders for having failed to protect northern manufacturers from foreign competition with the bizarre claim that slaveholders had used the tariff to exclude cheap foreign-grown cotton from American markets. Since American cotton had vanquished West Indian cotton in European markets, despite the heavy British and French tariffs levied against the American product, it was hardly likely that foreigners could undersell American planters in markets where they had numerous natural advantages. It was especially bizarre to float this claim in a year that U.S. cotton prices were close to an all-time low and after five years of a general depression in cotton prices, during which southern Democrats continued to demand the lowering of tariffs.[74]

Abolitionists also neglected the economic arguments developed by such southern foes of slavery as Cassius Marcellus Clay. A Whig from

Kentucky, Clay's arguments were designed to appeal to the self-interests of free farmers and small slaveholders in tobacco farms who, during the early 1840s, were suffering the most severe economic depression of their history. Slavery was inefficient, he argued, because "it impoverishes the soil"; because, in comparison with whites, slaves were "not so skilful, so energetic, and above all, have not the stimulus of self-interest"; because 3 million slaves performed "only about one-half of the effective work of the same number of whites in the North"; because slaves not only "produce less than freemen" but also "consume more"; because slavery was "the source of indolence, and destructive of all industry"; and because slavery caused the "poor" to "despise labor" by "degrading" it, while simultaneously turning the "mass of slaveholders" into "idlers." Slavery induced national poverty and thwarted economic development, he continued, by restricting education, by diverting capital into the purchase of slaves where it became "a dead loss," by discouraging the development of "mechanical" skills, and by retarding the growth of manufacturing. Clay also introduced an argument that would become one of the bulwarks of the Republican appeal in the late 1850s. He declared that slavery was "an evil to the free laborer" because "by the laws of competition, supply, and demand," he was forced "to work for the wages of the slave—food and shelter. The poor in the slave states are the most destitute native population in the United States." Despite the publicity that Horace Greeley gave them, Clay's arguments did not catch on in 1843 and 1844—perhaps because of the improvement in the northern economy in 1844 and in the southern economy a year later; perhaps because in 1843 and 1844 most labor leaders attributed the falling wages and devastating unemployment of the North to competition from Irish immigrants rather than from slaves.[75]

Some progress toward integrating economic issues into the antislavery appeal was made after the Liberty party merged with "Conscience" Whigs and "Barnburner" Democrats in 1848 to form the Free Soil party. More secular in its orientation, and led by more sophisticated politicians than the party it supplanted, the emphasis of the Free Soil party was more on the political than on the economic threat of slaveholders to northern interests. The principal plank of the new party was the barring of slavery from all territories. Unlike the Liberty party, the principal rationale for the plank was not concern for the blacks but defense of northern political interests against the political aggrandizement of the Slave Power. A new party was needed, said the Free Soilers, because both of the old parties had been captured by the South and had nominated candidates for president who, "under Slaveholding dictation," were committed to using the federal government to advance the interests of the Slave Power over that of "Free Labor."[76]

By making the contest one between *free labor* and the Slave Power, the program of the new party suggested a deeper and more fundamental economic conflict than had hitherto been embodied in the antislavery appeal. Horace Greeley, who toyed with the possibility of supporting the new party, sought to accentuate the economic content of its program by committing the party to free (or very cheap) land for actual settlers. However, in 1848 the free land or homestead issue remained highly controversial in antislavery circles. Since the "Barnburner" faction of the Democratic party had sided with New York landlords during the anti-rent rebellion of tenant farmers in 1844–1845, Van Buren (the leader of the Barnburners and the presidential candidate of the Free Soil party) was ambivalent on the homestead issue. Northeastern Conscience Whigs were also ambivalent because many still embraced the Whig doctrine that all cheap land schemes were aimed at undermining northeastern manufacturing, commercial, and landholding interests. Moreover, despite Giddings's contention that a homestead act was an antislavery measure, his claim was far from obvious in 1848 when such southern Democrats and slaveholders as Andrew Johnson of Tennessee, Sam Houston of Texas, W.R.W. Cobb of Alabama, Robert J. Walker of Mississippi, and Felix G. McConnell of Alabama had been in the vanguard of the homestead movement. Consequently, the Free Soil party "hedged on the issue of free land," alienating Greeley. Its plank on homesteads was not only equivocal but subordinate to its planks on cheap postage and federal improvement of rivers and harbors. Gerritt Smith's splinter Liberty League was the only party that fully committed itself to a policy of free land in 1848.[77]

It was not until Douglas introduced the Kansas-Nebraska Act in 1854 that economic issues assumed a central position in the antislavery appeal. The backlash from that bill led to a sudden expansion of the antislavery movement and precipitated the political realignment that became embodied in the Republican party. Many factors led the Republican party to place far greater emphasis on economic issues than had either the Liberty or Free Soil party, not least of which was the bitter struggle between political abolitionists and nativists for control of the realignment. The nativist upsurge of the early 1850s, like that of the early 1840s, was led by native mechanics and shopkeepers who were suffering economic distress as a result of competition from immigrants. Although the emergence of the Know-Nothing movement forced the antislavery men to come to grips with economic issues in a new and urgent way, it was Horace Greeley who provided the intellectual leadership needed to convert these issues into a compelling aspect of the antislavery appeal.[78]

Greeley's whole life prepared him for this task. Born on a small farm in Amherst, New Hampshire, he was apprenticed to a printer and news-paper editor in upstate New York at age 15. His "religious faith devel-oped early" and he imbibed the piety and moral convictions of New Englanders. From his parents and neighbors he learned that slavery was wrong and he was drawn into the temperance movement at an early age. A few weeks before his 13th birthday, he pledged "never to drink distilled liquors" and shortly afterward, he helped form a local temper-ance society. Since his parents and most of his neighbors were Federal-ists, it is not surprising that Greeley became a "juvenile Federalist," a supporter of John Quincy Adams, an opponent of the Masonic order, an advocate of tariffs, and a critic of Jacksonian Democracy. Protection was more than an abstract issue to him. His parents lost the family farm during the panic of 1819, as young Horace saw it, partly because British dumping of cotton goods ruined the market for the "cloth that his mother wove."[79]

In 1831, at age 20, Greeley moved to New York City to pursue his career as a printer. By 1833 he had accumulated enough money to start a printing firm in partnership with a fellow workman. A year later he began to publish and edit the *New Yorker*, "a family weekly devoted to current literature and politics, one designed to reach the masses, inform them, and elevate their taste." Greeley's success as an editor made him prominent, and his forceful exposition of Whig economic policies made him an important asset to the new party. In 1838 Greeley began editing the *Jeffersonian*, the principal Whig paper for the gubernatorial cam-paign in New York, and in 1840 he became the editor of the *Log Cabin*, an enormously successful campaign paper for the presidential election of that year. The experience gained in these ventures enabled him to launch the New York *Tribune* in 1841. The *Tribune* was a "political paper," a "family paper," and a paper "built with an eye to profit" but "dedicated to reform." Its causes included: "Anti-Slavery, Anti-War, Anti-Rum, Anti-Tobacco, Anti-Seduction, Anti-Grogshops, Brothels, Gambling."[80]

But it was relief for the conditions of northern urban laborers that Greeley saw as the most urgent of all the social reforms. The economic devastation caused by the panic of 1837 had a traumatic effect on him. He was appalled by the thousands of persons living "in damp, narrow cellars, or rickety, wretched tenements, unfit for cleanly brutes." The "filth and disease," the "children wasting away from hunger," the "able-bodied and ambitious pleading in vain for work"—all this convinced Greeley that the nation had succumbed to a "terrible sickness" and he "began to look about for remedies." An "exodus from city to country" attracted him as a possible solution during the early 1840s, but since the very poor lacked the money to transport themselves to the West, he did not take up that remedy until later in the decade.[81]

Greeley's search for solutions led him to embrace the socialist doctrines of the French writer Charles Fourier, which were brought to America by Albert Brisbane. Brisbane preached a socialism of class harmony which was to be realized through the establishment of communities in which both laborers and capitalists bought shares. These communities would raise productivity far above the level of ordinary shops or factories because they would be organized on principles of cooperation rather than on competition and because laborers would be spared the indignities associated with the wage system. Greeley gave considerable publicity to Brisbane's movement, but few workers or capitalists were attracted to it. He continued to lend his name to Brisbane's "Associations" but after 1846 land reform became his central preoccupation.

Despite his opposition to slavery, Greeley kept his distance from the abolitionist movement during the 1840s. Although the *Tribune* published articles on the iniquities of slavery and criticized the political aggrandizement of southern slaveholders, Greeley was opposed to making slavery a "political question." He attacked the Liberty party as "a sectionalizing influence, disruptive of the Whig party" and of "our great national interests,"[82] and he held the abolitionists responsible for Polk's victory over Clay in the election of 1844. In the following year he told an antislavery convention in Cincinnati that he could not join with them because his first responsibility was to alleviate the suffering of labor in New York. He agreed that southern slavery was "hideous," but he saw many similarities between the condition of urban laborers in the North and that of southern slaves. "How can I devote myself to a crusade against distant servitude," he asked, "when I discern its essence pervading my immediate community and neighborhood?"[83]

The Mexican War and the Wilmot Proviso aroused Greeley's natural antipathy to slavery and to the menace of an emerging southern nationalism, but he continued to work within the Whig party, opposing appeals for a purely sectional approach to the struggle for power. He also continued to back the efforts of Democrats to promote a homestead bill. Indeed, given the congressional alignment on cheap land, as late as 1851 it was impossible to form a coalition that would allow Greeley to satisfy both his economic goals and his antipathy to slavery. His hope for a political realignment that would encompass both issues gained some strength when a few antislavery Whigs in the Northeast began to shift their position on the land issue. By 1852 Seward and Weed were committed to vigorous promotion of a cheap-land policy, but Greeley could not induce the majority of northeastern Whigs to take a similar position. The barriers to integrating the free land and antislavery (free soil) movements were revealed by the vote in March 1854 on the Homestead Act, which passed the House by 107 to 72. About 30 percent of the affirmative votes came from the slave states, while more than a third of the opposition came from New England, New York, and Pennsylvania. "With very few exceptions, the New England" and other northeastern "representatives who voted against homestead also opposed the Kansas-Nebraska bill." Two of the four Free Soilers also voted against the homestead bill.[84]

Nevertheless, the Kansas-Nebraska Act marked a turning point in the struggle to make economic issues central to the antislavery appeal. This bill was a turning point partly because of the outspoken way that some southern Democrats linked the change in their position on a homestead bill to the struggle to shore up the proslavery vote in Congress. As Representative John Letcher of Virginia put it, he would oppose a homestead act as long as the consequence was "the propagation of northern sentiment and the multiplication of northern representatives here and in the Senate."[85] It was a turning point also because it drew into direct conflict with the Slave Power the northern working-class leaders who had previously remained aloof from the antislavery movement.

Until 1854 labor leaders believed that the antislavery movement was diverting attention from the issues most pressing to workers such as higher wages, a 10-hour day, free grants of land to actual settlers, free public education, housing, and mechanics' lien laws. George Henry Evans, the intellectual father of the land reform movement, for example, criticized the abolitionists for neglecting "the slavery of poverty." It was "most proper," he said, for the abolitionists to deal with "that form of slavery that is nearest home"[86] before seeking to deal with the more distant slavery. Similar views were expressed by Hermann Kriege and Wilhelm Weitling, early Communists and leaders of German-American labor organizations. They argued that "under the conditions prevailing in modern society" emancipation of slaves would intensify the competition of " 'free workingmen' beyond all measure" and "depress labor itself to the last extremity." Consequently, without solving the prior issue of wage slavery "we could not improve the lot of our 'black brothers' by abolition" but only "make infinitely worse the lot of our 'white brothers.' "[87] Despite Greeley's effort to win such men to the Whigs, both Kriege and Weitling joined the Democratic party through which they fought for land reform and free soil.

Between 1845 and early 1852 land reformers, such as Evans and Kriege, went a long way toward making land reform the chief political demand of the revitalized labor movement and toward tying many urban workers, both native and foreign born, to the Democrats. Land reform was endorsed at the annual meetings of the National Industrial Congress from 1845 to 1853 as well as by state and city industrial congresses throughout the North. These meetings initiated numerous mass petitions to local governments calling for relief on rents and to Congress calling for land reform. They also sought to control elections by supporting candidates of either major party who endorsed land reform and by opposing those who did not. Tammany Hall responded in 1851 by adopting the entire land reform program and endorsing Senator Isaac A. Walker, Democrat of Wisconsin and a leading advocate of a homestead act, as its favorite for the presidential race in 1852.[88]

Disillusionment with the Democrats among the land reformers became evident in the presidential elections of 1852. Holding Democrats in the Senate responsible for the failure to pass a land reform bill, some leaders of the movement called on their supporters to vote for Winfield Scott, the Whig candidate (because he had declared in favor of the distribution of the public domain only to actual occupants), and to punish Pierce (because he was "the candidate of a party responsible for the defeat of the homestead bill"). By linking the fate of the homestead bill with the struggle to make Kansas a slave state, as many southern congressmen did in 1854, virtually the whole of the northern labor movement was brought into a head-on clash with the Slave Power. Men who had been passive or hostile to the antislavery appeal suddenly became convinced that there really was a conspiracy by the Slave Power to seize control of northern land. They also became convinced that the party on which they counted to promote their interests against rich capitalists and land monopolists had become the vehicle for a slaveholders' plot to seize the public domain.[89]

Leading land reformers, disillusioned with the corruption of both parties, moved to the forefront of the "anti-Nebraska" struggle. In Wisconsin, for example, Alvan E. Bovay, long one of Evans's chief lieutenants in the land reform movement, became a leader in that state's anti-Nebraska movement and a founder of the Republican party. The Cincinnati *Daily Unionist*, the paper of journeymen printers, averring that they were "no abolitionists," felt compelled to "oppose slavery's extension over new lands." That was in March of 1854, before the passage of the Kansas-Nebraska Act, before proslavery men from Missouri started pouring over the border to preempt the best Kansas lands, and before the New England Emigrant Aid Company pushed its campaign to bring settlers from the Northeast to Kansas. The form of the struggle for political control of Kansas could hardly have been better designed to turn the anger of northern labor against the Slave Power, to prove that the Slave Power was the main obstacle to realizing labor's demand for free land. No one recognized the opportunity more clearly than Greeley. Through the pages of the *Tribune* he promoted the emerging Republican party and he utilized every opportunity to expose the treacherous campaign of the Slave Power to seize the best Kansas lands, thus denying them to free labor.[90]

Greeley and his allies were not the only politicians struggling to use the anti-Nebraska movement as the basis for a political realignment. The most serious challenge came from the Know-Nothings who had launched a struggle for a political realignment on a nativist program more than a year before the emergence of the anti-Nebraska movement and hence were quick to capitalize on it. Their victories in the state and local elections of 1853, 1854, and 1855 were so large that Greeley feared that they might emerge as the dominant party in 1856. Working class in their origins, the northern Know-Nothings raised political demands that coincided closely with those of the labor movement. They supported universal free education, they favored free homesteads but only for native Americans, and they favored a voter registry law that would reduce the "alien influence" in state elections.[91]

To deflect the votes of native workers from the Know-Nothings, and to win over the Protestant German workers, Greeley pressed fellow Republicans to emphasize the homestead principle. That point was not easily won because of the opposition to homesteads by the more conservative Whigs who had joined the Republican party. Greeley also promoted the campaign to settle northeastern mechanics and farmers in Kansas, not merely because it dramatized that it was the Slave Power rather than immigrants who threatened the living standards of northern workers, but because it increased the chances of getting an antislavery constitution in that state. It was slavery, Greeley told his readers over and over again, that thwarted the economic development of the West and also of the South.[92]

After the election of 1856 Greeley increasingly emphasized the inherent economic backwardness of a South based on slave labor. To develop this line of argument he turned to the writings of southern abolitionists who had, for decades, based their antislavery appeal on the self-interest of slaveholders. An anti-southern strategy could hardly have been effective below the Mason-Dixon line where the great slaveholders were widely regarded as honorable men and admired for their culture and refinement. Antislavery men in the South, therefore, hinged their appeal on the backwardness and inefficiency of slaves as workers, on their tendency to butcher the soil, on the inflexibility of slaves (and hence the inability to shift them from one occupation to another as changing market conditions demanded), and on the diversion of southern capital from factories and land improvement to the purchase of labor. Of the antislavery Southerners whose writings Greeley promoted in the *Tribune*, none had a greater impact on northern sentiment than Hilton Rowan Helper.

The son of a poor white farmer from the Yadkin Valley of western North Carolina, Helper was a minor author before 1857 when he wrote the volume that brought him fame, *The Impending Crisis of the South*. An eight-column review of the book in Greeley's New York *Tribune* contributed to a first-year sale of 13,000 copies. In 1859 the Republican party converted Helper's book into a major ideological weapon of its presidential campaign. Condensed editions were published and 100,000 copies were distributed by the Republican party. *The Impending Crisis* became the center of a series of bitter political battles, including a congressional debate that delayed the election of the Speaker of the House for two months.

Helper portrayed the South as a stagnant society in which not only free farmers but even slaveowners were reduced to shocking levels of poverty and economic distress. The "causes which have impeded the progress and prosperity of the South," he wrote, "may all be traced to one common source . . . Slavery!" Slavery had failed as an economic system because it was based on the labor of an inferior race, a race bereft of the qualities required for efficient production. Moreover, because of the competition from slaves, free laborers in the South were degraded and impoverished. Helper found evidence of the inefficiency of slavery in the low rates of return which planters earned on their capital, citing a South Carolinian who reported that many cotton planters were earning less than 1 percent on their investment. Further proof was to be found in the low value of southern land relative to northern land. Helper put the average value of an acre of northern land in 1850 at $28.07, while the average value of a southern acre was $5.34. What explained the difference of $22.73? Since southern land was equal to, or better than, northern land in "greater mildness of climate, richness of soil, deposits of precious metals, abundance and spaciousness of harbors, and super excellence of waterpower," he contended that "had it not been for slavery, the average value of land in all the Southern and Southwestern states would have been at least equal to the average value of the same in the Northern states." If slaves were emancipated "on Wednesday morning," predicted Helper, then "on Thursday following" southern lands "will have increased to an average of at least $28.07 per acre."[93] From this point Helper drew the further conclusion that even uncompensated emancipation of slaves would improve the economic position of slaveholders, for the capital gain on their lands would be twice as great as the loss on the capital value of slaves.[94]

By publicizing the testimony of Southerners on the economic backwardness of the South, Greeley was able to advance the political objectives of the Republicans in three ways. First, he diverted attention from the immigrants to the Slave Power, making it the principal threat to the living standards of all northern working men—not just urban mechanics but farmers as well. If planters were able to send their slaves en masse into Kansas and other territories of the North, not only would free homesteads for the northeastern mechanics be foreclosed but, through the competitive forces of the market, the income of northern farmers would be driven down to the level of slaves and the value of northern farm land would decline sharply, as had already happened for the free farmers of the South. Second, by featuring the antislavery tracts of Southerners, Greeley hoped to demonstrate that the mission of the Republican party was national, not sectional. Thousands of whites in the South already "prayed for Republican success," he wrote, and as the rest became enlightened to "the precise objects of the Republican party, they would rise en masse, wrest control of those states out of the hands of the Negro Aristocracy, and give their electoral votes to our candidate." Third, the economic arguments enabled Republicans to present a peaceful, long-run solution to the problem of slavery: Since it was economic forces that impelled the South into its expansionist policies, if slaveholders were bottled up in their own region, slavery would gradually die.[95]

THE "HIDDEN" DEPRESSION AND THE POLITICAL REVOLT OF THE NORTHERN WORKERS

What were the conditions that permitted the economic arguments against slavery to become so much more effective in the mid-1850s than they had been in the 1830s or 1840s?[96] The question is puzzling since the period 1843–1857, during which the economic critique of slavery rose to preeminence, is often portrayed as one of vigorous economic expansion and general prosperity. There were, of course, economic slowdowns during 1847–1848 and 1853–1855 but they were apparently so mild or so localized that many economic and social historians of the antebellum era have had little to say about them, and some recent economic histories do not even mention them. The emphasis is instead on the 14 years of phenomenal economic growth which began in 1843 and during which the economy rode a tremendous wave of expansion. These were the years of the rapid settlement of the Mississippi Valley, of the gold rush in California, of the accelerated expansion of the merchant marine and foreign trade, of the emergence of the factory system as a major sector of the economy, of the spread of the banking system, and of the era of tremendous construction in railroads.[97]

Indeed, it was railroad construction that became the symbol of the era. The railroad network expanded from a mere 4,200 miles in 1843 to nearly 25,000 in 1857, and most of this increase was concentrated in the North, especially in the North Central states. With fully half of the world's mileage of track located in the United States, railroads were the most spectacular but by no means the only aspect of the great construction boom of 1843–1857. Between 1843 and 1855 the annual gross tonnage of merchant vessels built and documented rose by more than ninefold, with shipyards in New England accounting for about two-thirds of the increase and with most of the rest of the increase handled by northern yards along the North Atlantic coast, the Great Lakes, or the midwestern rivers. Although not as impressive as either railroads or vessel construction, the building of houses, factories, stores and offices, and urban public works also boomed, with annual production increasing by about threefold between 1844 and 1854.[98]

There can be little doubt that 1843–1857 was an era during which nearly all of the major economic interests of the nation prospered. It was a particularly good period for the agricultural interests. For northern farmers, especially those in the North Central states, it came close to a golden age. Not only were the harvests of the major crops generally increasing rapidly, but despite the vast expansion in supply, agricultural prices generally bounded upward so rapidly that the rise in the prices of most agricultural products exceeded the rise in the general price level by wide margins. With such a large share of the nation's capital and labor force in agriculture, it is little wonder that the recession of 1853–1855 did not attract a great deal of attention from either the nation's commercial press or its established political leaders. Nor was it only farmers who shared in this economic golden age. The vast increase in foreign trade triggered by short harvests in Europe and the Crimean War made 1853–1855 a boom period for merchants. Landholders, both speculators in the rural lands of the interior states and the urban landlords, petty and great, prospered as rural land values and urban rents shot upward.[99]

THE TRIPLE CRISIS FOR NATIVE, NON-FARM WORKERS IN THE NORTH, 1848–1855

One part of the free U.S. population failed to share in this prosperity. These were the non-farm manual workers, especially those in the North, and especially the native-born skilled males. Petty merchants who served this class in the cities probably also suffered. Together the native-born craftsmen, tradesmen, and petty merchants probably made up less than a sixth of the free U.S. labor force, although in the North they probably represented about a quarter of the region's electorate. Their repeated cries of distress were carried into one city council after another all across the land. In southern cities they aimed their pleas against slave craftsmen who were their chief competitors. In northern cities they sought protection against the foreign-born Irish and German workers. Everywhere their pleas were repelled, or at best paid lip service, by the prosperous classes that controlled local governments: by the slaveholders in such cities as Charleston and Savannah; by a combination of rich merchants, landlords, manufacturers, and well-to-do professionals in Boston, New York, Philadelphia, Pittsburgh, and other large northern cities. Both individual and collective efforts to improve their lot were of little avail. Amidst the phenomenal economic growth, amidst the tremendous wave of expansion, this relatively small but important sector of the northern population suffered one of the most severe and protracted economic and social catastrophes of American history. Largely, but never entirely, lost from sight by scholars of the period, the full scope of this "hidden" economic depression and social catastrophe, as well as its political significance, has only recently been analyzed and its various aspects are still under investigation. Nevertheless, the main outline of what occurred now seems to be fairly well established.[100]

The root cause of the depression that engulfed native workers during 1848–1855, as during 1840–1844, was the high level of immigration, which once again surged upward after 1846, fed by the refugees of the Irish famine and of Continental revolutions. Immigration rose sharply from 1846 to 1854, reaching five times the level of the first half of the 1840s. Once again the migration was heavily concentrated in northern cities. As a consequence, the growth of the labor force in many cities was double or triple the natural rate of labor force growth. So large a rate of increase not only put heavy downward pressure on wages and upward pressure on rents, but greatly outstripped the capacity of local politicians to deal with the mounting problems of public health and crime.[101]

Indeed, the whole period from 1840 to 1858 was one of hard times for native-born manual workers, broken only by three interludes. The longest of these extended from 1844 to 1846 or 1847; the other two (1851–1852 and 1856) were much weaker and briefer. During 1844–1846, the downward pressure on the earnings of native workers eased partly because of a brief interruption in the rapid climb of immigration, but mainly because of the strong recovery from the depression that bottomed out in most industries in 1843. During the recovery phase of the cycle, which lasted through 1846 or 1847, the northern economy expanded so rapidly that the rise in the demand for labor exceeded the rate of growth of the labor supply, despite levels of immigration that began exceeding earlier peaks in 1845. Consequently, the squeeze on urban workers that occurred during the early 1840s gave way to several years of improved conditions. It is not entirely clear whether the rise in money (nominal) earnings during these years exceeded the rise in the prices of the goods and services purchased by workers since the available price indexes for the antebellum era inadequately measure the urban cost of living, but it appears likely that the real earnings (money earnings divided by an index of the cost of living) rose moderately in most northern cities for both skilled and unskilled workers.[102]

The brief mid-decade interlude in the squeeze on native craftsmen came to a halt during 1847 or 1848. Not only did the immigration rate leap upward in these years, but food prices shot upward in 1847–1848 and the mild recession of 1848 had some locally severe pockets of declining labor demand. Iron workers probably suffered more than any other industrial group. The drop in the tariff on iron, combined with a brief slackening of the construction boom, had disastrous consequences in most phases of the iron industry. In Pennsylvania, half of all the furnaces that were in production in 1847 closed during the next three years, when many firms plunged into bankruptcy. Nationally, pig iron production declined by nearly 50 percent between 1847 and 1851 and did not again return to the 1847 peak until 1856. The widespread unemployment in the industry put heavy downward pressure on the wages of those still working. Strikes by foundry workers in Cincinnati, Pittsburgh, and other cities against wage cuts failed as employers imported immigrants to take the places of their former employees.[103]

Since the depression in the iron industry was more severe than in other industries, the decline in the wages of iron workers was probably greater than among those of other crafts. However, even workers in the booming construction industries suffered from the excess supply of labor created by the successive waves of Irish and German immigration. The combined effects of immigration and the business cycle on the wages of building craftsmen are illustrated by the experiences of carpenters in upstate New York. Between 1842 and 1844 when the labor supply surged and the demand for labor declined, the daily wage rates of carpenters fell by a third, a decline that was only partially offset by the decline in the cost of living. During the strong recovery of 1845–1846, however, the pattern reversed and wages rose toward earlier highs, only to decline again after 1849.[104]

Declining daily wage rates, however, were not the only reason for the plight of the native workers. They were also afflicted by reductions in the number of days worked per year, by the reclassification of their jobs from higher to lower skill categories, by various charges imposed on them by their employers (which were an indirect method of cutting wages), and by the permanent loss of jobs that occurred when foreign workers were hired in their place, a process that appears to have greatly accelerated during the early 1850s. This process of displacement has been most fully documented for weavers in one of the leading textile mills of Lowell. There the proportion of native-born workers declined from about 90 percent in 1849 to about 35 percent in 1855. Lowell weavers were mainly women but similar displacements occurred in such predominantly male occupations as carpentry, iron casting, shoemaking, tailoring, and cabinetmaking.[105]

Not only was the decline in the real income of native workers large, but it persisted for nearly a decade. The worst phase of their depression came during 1853–1855. These were years of substantial decline in the nonagricultural demand for labor, with sagging wages and widespread layoffs in construction, iron, and lumber. Distress was particularly acute in the Midwest because of the large number of immigrants who migrated to the region during the early years of the 1850s, many of them responding to the heavy demand for labor in the construction of railroads. Railroad construction surged to unprecedented levels in Michigan, Ohio, Indiana, and Illinois during 1850–1854, requiring about 180,000 workers at the peak of the boom, which was about a third of the nonagricultural male labor force in these states. When railroad construction declined sharply, first in Michigan in 1850, then Indiana in 1853, and then Ohio and Illinois in 1854, the railroad workers, overwhelmingly foreign born, were thrown onto the general labor market where they competed with previously established native workers in urban labor markets, especially in the building trades. The flood of labor released from railroads created downward pressure on the wages of the established workers and led to heavy unemployment throughout the Midwest.[106]

Although established workers sought to protect their jobs by forming labor organizations and striking, either to prevent wage cuts or to obtain wage raises to offset the sharply escalating prices of food and housing, these efforts usually came to naught. In the face of the excess supply of labor, employers had little difficulty in finding unemployed men, usually foreign born, who were eager to take their places at lower wages.[107]

Indeed, a characteristic of the period was the general degradation of skill premiums by the downgrading of once highly skilled operations. Typical of the process was the so-called "Berkshire system," which was widely introduced in iron foundries during the 1850s. Prior to the introduction of this system, iron casting was performed by highly skilled journeymen. Afterward, journeymen were required to hire unskilled helpers (called bucks), each journeyman working in teams with from one to five bucks. Although the bucks were supposed to be purely helpers, the high-priced journeymen were often replaced by low-priced bucks who, if given the opportunity, soon learned enough of the trade to be given a rammer (the tool used to pack sand around a mold pattern). Under these circumstances, employers were also able to find new ways of reducing the wages of those journeymen who were retained, such as compelling them to buy rammers, shovels, sieves, dustbags, bellows, and other tools, as well as requiring them to pay rent for their floor room. To hold journeymen to these unfavorable contracts, one-third of their wages were withheld until the end of the year (in a period of rapidly rising prices such a delay was the equivalent of a real pay cut of several percent) and they were also compelled to accept their wages in store pay (usable only at the company stores) rather than in cash.[108]

At the very time that the demand for native craftsmen was at its lowest, the price of wheat, corn, and meats soared, due partly to short crops in Europe, which greatly increased the foreign demand for American food products, and partly to short wheat crops at home caused by poor weather or infestations of insects. In general, the upward surge in food prices was sharpest in the Midwest, rising nearly twice as much between 1848 and 1855 in the Ohio Valley as in New York City. The distress suffered by workers who were squeezed between the excess supply of labor and sharply rising prices found reflection in the rash of strikes during 1853 and 1854 which broke out in nearly every craft in at least 20 cities of the northeastern and midwestern states. The distress of urban workers did not spill over to northern farmers, however, since the downward pressures on the aggregate demand for food in urban markets of the North were slight even in 1853–1854 and were more than offset by the surge in the foreign demand.[109]

Although precise measurement of the combined effects of the various infringements on the real income of native-born craftsmen must await the completion of research still in progress, the average decline between 1848 and 1855 was probably in the range of 25 to 50 percent. In other words, native-born mechanics and tradesmen suffered one of the most severe economic disasters in American history, rivaling, if not exceeding, the economic blow suffered by urban labor during the Great Depression of the 1930s.[110] In one respect the "hidden" depression of the antebellum era was far worse than the visible depression of the 1930s. The economic disaster of the antebellum era coincided with a wave of devastating epidemics, which were particularly severe in the North. These epidemics are the third facet in the triple crisis that beset northern native workers. Epidemics are usually treated as natural disasters, but these antebellum epidemics had a substantial economic component, related in part to the same circumstances that led to a glut in the markets for manual labor in the North.

The deterioration in the health and longevity of native-born Northerners was closely related to the surge in immigration and the accelerated pace of urbanization that began in the 1820s. These factors brought to an end a century-long improvement in health that made the northern states of the new nation the healthiest place in the world. Diseases that had plagued the North at the beginning of the eighteenth century, such as diphtheria, malaria, smallpox, and yellow fever, were greatly diminished or had disappeared from the North altogether by the end of that century. Such other diseases as cholera, tuberculosis, dysentery, and typhoid—among the greatest killers of the second and third quarters of

the nineteenth century—were still unknown in America or had not yet
reached alarming proportions.[111]

The exceptional health of native-born Northerners during the late
eighteenth century is revealed by new time series on stature and life
expectation recently constructed by cliometricians (see Figure 28).[112]
They show that by the end of Washington's administration, native-born
American white males were more than 68 inches tall (which was 2 to 4
inches taller than the typical Englishman) and had average life expectations at age 10 of close to 57 years (about 10 years longer than the
English). However, both life expectations and stature began to decline
early in the nineteenth century. The most rapid period of deterioration
was between 1830 and 1860. By the eve of the Civil War life expectation
was 10 years less than it had been just before the turn of the century
and males born in 1860 reached final heights that were about 1.5 inches
less than those born in the early 1830s.

Northerners were aware that rapid urbanization and heavy immigration were undermining the health and the moral fiber of their society.
Many of those who sounded the alarm reaffirmed their fidelity to the
Revolutionary vision of America as a refuge for the oppressed of Europe,
but declared that "the founding fathers could never have foreseen that
the deserving poor" of their age would "become the degraded and
criminal refuse that polluted American shores" in the 1840s and 1850s.
Whatever doubts there might have been that cities were the incubators
of killer epidemics and that it was immigrants who spread them from one
community to another were dispelled by the experiences of the cholera
epidemic of 1848–1850.[113]

This epidemic was brought to American shores in December 1848
by two ships carrying German immigrants, one bound for New York, the
other for New Orleans. Although New York–bound passengers who were
sick with cholera when the ship arrived were kept in quarantine, others
were allowed to enter the city. Within a few days cholera broke out in
the immigrant districts of New York; later it spread to the predominantly
native-born, lower-class districts nearby and eventually to upper-class
districts. In the case of the ship bound for New Orleans, public health
officials were able not only to tie the spread of disease to New Orleans
with the disembarkation of the immigrants there, but to follow the
movement of cholera up the Mississippi and its tributaries. As immigrants from the infected ship boarded river steamers, cholera broke out
aboard these ships and then in the cities at which the steamers called,
including Memphis, Nashville, Louisville, Cincinnati, Wheeling (now
West Virginia), Pittsburgh, and St. Louis. Soon after it reached these
cities, cholera broke out in the surrounding countryside.

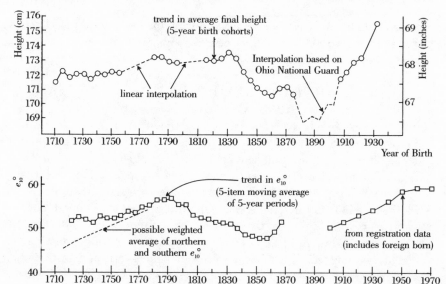

Figure 28. A comparison between the trend in mean final height of native-born white males and the trend in their life expectation at age 10 ($e_{10}°$). The top part of this diagram shows the height of native-born white males at maturity by the year of their birth, from 1710 to 1930. The bottom part shows life expectation (the expected number of additional years of life) at age 10, the symbol for which is $e_{10}°$. Both parts of the diagram reveal that during the eighteenth century the northern United States was an extraordinarily healthy region compared with other parts of the world. At the time of the American Revolution native-born white males were 68.1 inches tall, about 3 inches taller than the British men they were fighting. The rising waves of immigration and the overrapid urbanization of the nineteenth century, especially in the North, set off waves of infectious diseases that led to a deterioration in physical development and a sharp increase in mortality rates. By the eve of the Civil War health and life expectation in the North had declined to their lowest levels since the seventeenth century. The cities had become reservoirs of disease that spread into the countryside. It was not until World War II that public health officials were able to raise conditions of health in cities to a level that matched the countryside, and it was not until then that stature or life expectations returned to the levels that had been achieved at the time of Washington's presidency.

Cholera was the most dramatic disease of the antebellum era because it struck the nation suddenly, spread quickly, had a high fatality rate, and its victims often succumbed within 24 hours after they became sick. But such other killer diseases as typhoid, typhus, tuberculosis, and dysentery were also thought to be incubated in urban slums and immigrants were often singled out as their principal carriers. Cholera re-

mained endemic in most northern cities during the first half of the 1850s
and the crisis in public health associated with immigration and rapid
urbanization went unabated.[114]

THE POLITICAL REVOLT OF NORTHERN
NATIVE WORKERS

Native workers fought back against their immiseration in a variety of
ways. One response was to organize strikes to protect their wages and
to stave off the de-skilling maneuvers of their employers. Strikes broke
out in different cities at different times. Puddlers and boilers in Pittsburgh struck in early 1850 after iron manufacturers cut their wages.
With the iron industry in the midst of a depression and with foreign-born
workers clamoring to replace the strikers, the outcome of the contest was
foredoomed. As despair turned to anger, infuriated wives of the puddlers
rioted on two successive days, beat up the strikebreakers, and destroyed
some of the furnaces—but to no avail. The mills were soon filled with
imported help working at reduced pay.[115]

Between 1850 and 1855 a wave of strikes, sometimes combined with
violence, swept across trade after trade in city after city. The new militancy of labor was both cause and consequence of an upsurge in trade
union organization. Rising prices and glutted labor markets during the
early years of the 1850s renewed efforts to establish citywide, regional,
and nationwide trade unions. The result was a far larger and more
aggressive northern trade union offensive than had ever been mounted
in the past. Instead of conducting strikes on a shop-by-shop basis at the
initiative of employees of individual firms, organizations came into being
aimed at coordinating the efforts of all the men in the trade of a particular
city. Beginning in 1850 new unions were formed among such trades as
the bootmakers, bricklayers and plasterers, carpenters, cordwainers,
printers, jewelers, and cigarmakers in New York, Philadelphia, and most
other large cities. The new unions not only led strikes for higher wages,
they also established labor exchanges to get new jobs for strikers fired
by their employers, regulated the length of service of apprentices, tried
to set the ratio of apprentices to journeymen (in order to prevent employers from using apprentices to undermine the bargaining power of the
unions), and tried to establish union shops.[116]

The peak of strike activity came during 1853–1854 when about 400
strikes were initiated, covering most of the major trades in the major
cities of the North. The heightened militancy was promoted not only by
rising prices and unemployment but also by the more aggressive strike-
breaking tactics of employers. These tactics included advertising for
strikebreakers in other cities, using police and troops against strikes

under anticonspiracy statutes, more aggressive hiring of immigrants to replace native workers, and forming employers' associations to coordinate resistance to unions.[117]

Trade union militancy spilled over into the political arena. One form of political action was the formation of single-issue organizations that pressed for relief from city councils and state legislatures. In New England the campaign to limit the working day to 10 hours became very influential. The first New England convention on this issue was held in 1844 and the campaign it launched gathered considerable force. New Hampshire passed a 10-hour law in 1847 after a successful mass petition campaign, and a similar law was passed in Pennsylvania in 1848. However, the movement declined temporarily at the end of the decade after legislative defeats in New York and Massachusetts. It was revived in 1851, led not by humanitarians as it had been earlier, but by trade unionists who wanted a more effective law than that passed by New Hampshire. The thrust of the new movement was also quite different from the older one. Pointing out that nonpartisan petitions to legislatures had failed, the new leaders set out upon a course of organized political action aimed at electing the friends of the 10-hour day and defeating its enemies. In the mill towns of Massachusetts the 1852 elections pivoted on the 10-hour issue and 10-hour men claimed control of a tenth of the lower house.[118]

An even more influential political movement of workers took shape around the land reform issue. Since the demands of the land reformers required the action of Congress and the president, this movement developed a strong political orientation from its outset. Under the aegis of the National Reform Association, which was established in 1844, land reformers organized to defeat any candidate "for any legislative office, who will not pledge himself, in writing, to use all the influence of his station, if elected, to prevent all further traffic in the Public Lands of the states and of the United States, and to cause them to be laid out in Farms and Lots for the free and exclusive use of actual settlers." The influence of the movement rose steadily and by 1850, according to one estimate, more than a quarter of all the newspapers supported free land to actual settlers. During the early 1850s free homesteads emerged as one of the most popular cries of northern labor. It was adopted by the 10-hour organizations, and it became the central demand of the organizations and newspapers of German workers which were strong not only in New York and Philadelphia, but also in such midwestern cities as Cincinnati, Chicago, Milwaukee, and St. Louis. Land reform was as naturally supported by the new trade union movement of the 1850s as it was opposed by their foes—the manufacturers, capitalists, and landowners of the East. The completeness with which Tammany Hall embraced land reform in 1851 and again in 1853 testifies to its popularity among northern urban workers.[119]

Free primary education was another issue that mobilized workers. Although tax-supported schools in Massachusetts antedated the rise of the labor movement, labor was a driving force behind the establishment of public schools in the Middle Atlantic states and Rhode Island during the 1830s and early 1840s, and somewhat later in the 1840s and in the 1850s in the Midwest. To many of the Protestant workers who campaigned for public education, the Catholic Church was the arch foe. The strong Protestant religious orientation in the public schools, especially their use of the King James version of the Bible, led New York bishop John Hughes in 1840 to demand "their just proportion" of public funds for church-controlled schools so that Catholic children could be educated in their own religion. During the 1840s and early 1850s the split between Protestants and Catholics on the school issue smoldered, igniting from time to time in one city or another, and became inextricably intertwined with labor's demand for the expansion of free primary education.[120]

The benevolent and fraternal organizations of workers were instrumental in bringing the labor movement of the early 1850s into being. They were the principal organizations behind both the upsurge in trade unions and the mobilization of workers for political action. While some of these organizations traced back to the Revolutionary era, most of them were established during the years of the second-party system. Some included both masters and journeymen, but "on the whole the journeymen established separate mutual aid societies." Their principal function, aside from fellowship, was to provide for workers in time of need by paying benefits to mechanics who became disabled due to sickness or accident and to their widows and orphans when a mechanic died. They also paid funeral expenses and sometimes established schools for apprentices in their trades. Many of these benevolent and fraternal organizations were organized along craft lines, and some crafts had more than one.[121]

Some of the benevolent and fraternal organizations cut across trade lines, and these often had an ethnic and religious orientation. This was true of the Order of United Americans, formed in New York in 1844, and the Order of United American Mechanics, formed in Philadelphia in 1845. Both, reflecting the nativist upsurge of the mid-1840s, limited membership to "American-born laborers." Although nonpolitical in the sense that they disavowed "all association with party politics," they nevertheless reserved the right to use "all lawful means to counteract" those "foreign interests, political or religious," that operated "in any manner injurious to our country." Foreign-born workers also established fraternal and benevolent organizations that cut across craft lines and some embraced radical political philosophies. Whether formed on craft or more general lines, the benevolent organizations of labor were often secret orders having passwords, grips, and so on.[122]

Secrecy was not purely a matter of ritual but also of necessity in an era of anticonspiracy statutes which made it a crime for workers to combine for the purpose of compelling employers to raise wages or institute any other reform. To circumvent the possibility that they might spawn illegal activities, some societies were even required by their charters "to file annually with the county clerk" a "sworn affidavit" that the society had undertaken no activities other than "extending the right hand of fellowship to each other when in distress, sickness, or in the hour of death." Despite such restraints it was the benevolent societies that gave organized form to the upsurge of labor militancy in the early 1850s. Some of the benevolent societies reorganized themselves into trade unions, while others retained their separate identity but sponsored parallel independent organizations for the purpose of conducting strikes.[123]

The benevolent organizations were also the principal vehicles through which labor sought to rally workers into action on political issues. These benevolent organizations provided the bulk of the delegates to the first industrial congress in New York City in June 1850, which launched a campaign to commit candidates to land reform during the elections of the following October. The delegates believed that by eschewing "partyism of every description" they could command "the balance of power through reliable men of either or both of the old parties."[124] Evans believed that the tactic of supporting labor's friends and punishing its enemies in the old parties was more likely to succeed than an attempt to gain power through a workers' party, which had been tried in the 1830s and 1840s and had failed. Widely embraced by the labor movement during the early years of the 1850s, the new tactic had the effect of weakening the grip of the Democrats over the vote of labor. For Evans and other radicals in the Democratic fold, the rhetoric of class struggle embraced by the left wing of the party, and often reflected in the language of its national leaders, was no longer enough.

The rapidly growing, increasingly aggressive, and increasingly politicized movement of skilled workers gradually produced a grass-roots political movement for control of local and state governments. At the beginning, the movement was basically uncoordinated, propelled not so much by the unions or the single-issue labor organizations as by the benevolent societies, although each movement helped to reinforce the other. The skilled native workers, aided by allies both above and below them in the social order, were in rebellion against incumbent local politicians who were seen as indifferent or even hostile to the interests of their class. They were no longer willing to trust the fate of their communities to mayors and councilmen who came overwhelmingly from the ranks of the wealthy merchants, the bankers, the manufacturers, and their lawyers. They were tired of cities that "were governed largely by the propertied for the propertied" and in which "social inequities and pervasive misery were not simply" ignored but were "treated as the wages of sin and of individual fault." They had lost faith in the antimonopoly rhetoric of the Democrats since it was increasingly evident that "class attachments counted for more than party differences in determining the political . . . behavior of rich men."[125]

Although the role of the benevolent societies in this rebellion has not yet received as much study as it deserves, certain important points seem to be fairly clear. One is that during 1844–1851, when many of these societies were established, they were genuinely nonpolitical. This is true even of the Order of United Americans, which later became the principal organizational foundation for the American (Know-Nothing) party. Like other benevolent societies, their main business during the 1840s was health insurance and other forms of aid to members in distress.[126]

Initially, the O.U.A.'s nativist propaganda was designed to promote solidarity among American-born workers in cities such as New York and Boston where immigrants had already become the majority of the labor force and were also threatening to become the majority of the voters.[127] The O.U.A. praised the Revolutionary heritage of America, denounced the international Catholic conspiracy to subvert American values, and organized patriotic celebrations on Washington's birthday and on July 4th. It also sought to promote a spirit of economic solidarity, urging those who were employers to hire native Americans and urging everyone to buy from native Americans. This combination of benevolent services, patriotism, and appeals for solidarity turned out to be so popular that the O.U.A. grew from a score of members in a single lodge in New York City in 1844 to thousands of members in numerous lodges in at least six states (New York, Pennsylvania, New Jersey, Connecticut, Massachusetts, and California) by the beginning of the 1850s.[128]

The scruples of their members and leaders against becoming organizationally involved in politics kept the O.U.A. on the political sidelines during these years. Its first tentative move toward political action came in February 1850 when it called upon its members to participate in a "nonpartisan" meeting in New York City in support of Henry Clay's plan for a compromise on the territorial issue. However, it was a local issue—Bishop John Hughes's campaign to repeal the New York law providing support to public schools—that led the O.U.A. to plunge into politics. During 1851 the Order set up a new machinery for effective political intervention in defense of the public schools. The machinery was not designed to transform the Order into a political party or to abandon its functions as a beneficial organization for workers, but to give it an added dimension: the capacity to mobilize its members secretly for the defeat of politicians who catered to the "Romanists" and for the victory of candidates who would defend the interests of native Americans.[129]

The issues taken up by nativists varied from city to city and so did the organizational apparatus that they utilized. However, it was the perceived indifference or hostility of local and state politicians to their material interests that initially galvanized them to action. Although some of the nativist organizations endorsed a presidential candidate in 1852, such actions were perfunctory. Their efforts were overwhelmingly centered on local issues, including the defense of public schools; establishment of police systems capable of controlling prostitution, drunkenness, and rioting; passage of mechanics' lien laws (laws that put pressure on employers to pay wages before settling other debts); abolition of imprisonment for debt; and the curbing of corruption in the distribution of licenses for businesses and of patronage appointments. If any single idea united these disparate issues it was that the politicians of both major parties were corrupt, concerned primarily with lining their own pockets and with maintaining their grip on offices. To many workers the most blatant aspect of this corruption was the way that both Democrats and Whigs toadied to immigrants to obtain their votes, often by illegal means.[130]

The nativist presence in New York City politics became evident during the 1853 elections. Various nativist organizations mobilized to defeat the reelection bid of the Whig district attorney because of "his lack of zeal" in prosecuting immigrants engaged in riots. Greeley soon discovered that there was a plot by a "mysterious society," which he called the "Know-Nothing organization," and he exposed its O.U.A. auspices. It was, he said, "a new dodge of protean nativism," "especially anti-Irish and anti-Catholic," and its objective was to "control the elections of our city for the benefit of its leaders." Although Greeley's attack, and the last-minute defection of one of the nativist organizations, narrowly saved the Whig incumbent from defeat, the 1853 elections publicized the emergence of a powerful new force in the politics of New York.[131]

Nativist campaigns reaped greater success elsewhere. In the Detroit election of 1853, the central issue was the defense of the schools. The year before this election the bishop of Detroit, Peter Paul Lefevre, launched a campaign to divert part of the state's school funds to Catholic schools or else to prohibit the reading of Protestant Bibles in public schools. His intense lobbying before the state legislature, and the mass

petition campaign organized to bring pressure on the legislators, provoked a Protestant backlash that split the Democratic party. The breakaway Democrats formed an "Independent" slate, with considerable Whig
support, that ran against the Catholic "plot" to subvert the government.
Raising aloft the banner of "Protestantism against Popery," the Inde-
pendents "won a sweeping victory," carrying all but one of the eight
wards. News of the outcome of the Detroit election promoted nativist
tickets in other towns of Michigan and loosened attachments to both the
Whig and Democratic parties.[132]

Between 1850 and 1854 nativists also won victories in other major
cities or came close to doing so. In Pittsburgh nativist victories began
in 1850 when Joe Barker, "a jobless street-corner orator renowned only
for his venomous anti-Catholicism," became an independent candidate
for mayor. Although he was in jail at the time of the election (for inciting
a riot in a working-class area packed with Germans, Irishmen, and bars),
Barker won, trouncing both the Democratic and Whig candidates. His
antics in office, particularly his unwillingness to enforce the liquor laws,
cost Barker reelection in 1851, but he received enough votes from
Protestant workers to erode the usual Whig majority and give the election to the Democrats. In Philadelphia a nativist-backed slate of candidates for the state legislature won in 1853, and in December of the same
year a nativist slate nearly won the city elections in Boston. In 1854
Cincinnati nativists, backed by anti-Catholic Germans, crushed the usually dominant Democratic party in the local elections. The nativist upsurge also produced a new epidemic of anti-Catholic violence and coun-
terviolence in northern cities—much of it centered in working-class
communities—that contributed to the growing cry for governments that
could enforce law and order.[133]

By 1854 the basis had been laid for a nationwide campaign for the
reform of local and state governments. The victories or near-victories in
a score of cities demonstrated that the sentiment for reform was there,
that the majority of voters were repelled by the corruption of Democratic
and Whig officeholders, and that they were prepared to elect new men,
ordinary men, who were dedicated to the type of "people's government"
envisioned by the founding fathers. Much of the machinery for such a
campaign was set in place when the O.U.A. and other benevolent societies began to mobilize their members for political action. In order to
extend their organizational capacity beyond the journeymen, who were
the primary constituency of the benevolent societies, the O.U.A. promoted a new, more directly political society that would appeal to all
patriotic, reform-minded voters, regardless of class.[134]

The new vehicle was the Order of the Star-Spangled Banner. Although founded in 1849, it had only 43 members when it was taken over

by the O.U.A. in 1852 and transformed into a powerful political machine. Because it was purely a political organization it did not require the heavy fees and dues of a beneficial society. Anyone could join if he pledged to advance the goals of the organization, at no cost whatsoever, provided that he also agreed to abide by the pledges of secrecy entailed in membership. Financial contributions to the organization were purely voluntary. Initially, the Know-Nothings worked through the established parties since their objective was "the *control* rather than the *making* of nominations." Meanwhile, they built up organizations on a ward basis in the cities and on a county basis in the rural areas.[135]

When they began to sponsor independent tickets, the names varied from place to place, but during 1855 they increasingly called themselves the "American party." The congressional elections of 1854 brought 70 or more Know-Nothings into the House. They also swept all the state offices in Massachusetts and took all but two of the seats in the state legislature. In 1855 they won victories in nine other states and made strong showings in another eight. And so a year before the election of 1856 "the Know-Nothings confidently expected to place their candidate in the White House" and that expectation "was reluctantly shared by many impartial observers and even by the party's avowed enemies."[136]

THE STRUGGLE FOR CONTROL OF THE POLITICAL BREAKAWAY

The antislavery forces were not especially well positioned to take control of the political breakaway at the end of 1853. The vote for the antislavery ticket in races of that year was at its lowest point since the 1848 elections. In New Hampshire, John P. Hale was defeated in his bid for reelection to the U.S. Senate, and in Massachusetts the coalition ticket of Free Soilers and Free Democrats was trounced by the "Cotton" Whigs. In state after state in which they had shown such strength in 1848, their votes were down sharply. They were reduced to just three seats in the House, and they were practically without representation in state legislatures, unable to exert pressure on either major party. However, the Free Soilers drew heart from the gubernatorial campaign in Wisconsin where they were able to form a joint ticket with the antislavery Whigs, even though their candidate was defeated by the Democrats.[137]

Another handicap of the Free Soil party was its weak relationship with the mushrooming labor movement. Although the party's platform in the 1852 election contained a stronger land reform plank than in 1848, Greeley again spurned them, choosing to stay with the Whigs. The party program did not contain planks on other issues of burning importance to the labor movement such as the 10-hour day, the right to strike, and rent gouging. It was not so much that the Free Soilers were opposed to labor's position on these issues. As individuals many of them were also active in the temperance movement, in the free schools movement, and in various anti-Catholic campaigns. However, with a few exceptions, prior to 1854 the state organizations of the Free Soil party showed little skill in linking their antislavery demands, which centered on the question of who would control the federal government, with the class issues that raged at the local level.[138]

The introduction of the Kansas-Nebraska bill and the congressional debate on it, which dragged on for five months, transformed the struggle for power in the North. The potential of this act for promoting major political realignments, North and South, was signaled by the vote in Congress. Southern Whigs broke with the northern members of their party and voted almost unanimously with the southern Democrats for the bill. However, nearly half of the northern Democrats voted against the bill, despite President Pierce's insistence that support for the bill was an issue of party discipline. The heavy congressional defections of northern Democrats reflected the serious difficulties that beset many leaders of the party. Some of their safest constituencies were crumbling because working-class supporters of the Democrats were repelled by the corruption of the party in toadying to Catholic immigrants. The outcome of the struggle over the Kansas-Nebraska bill merely reinforced the image of northern Democrats as pusillanimous and corrupt. Now they were giving way on one of labor's most passionate demands—free land for the poor. This time they were prostrating themselves before the Slave Power rather than before Catholic power, but it was all part of the same pattern of corruption.[139]

Opposition to the Kansas-Nebraska Act did, of course, revive the abolitionist-led antislavery movement. The outcries against the Act, which Pierce signed in late May of 1854, spread far beyond the usual antislavery circles. One of the most notable events was the fierce attack on the Slave Power suddenly launched by the land reformers.[140] Although they had long criticized the antislavery movement because of its disdain for the suffering of free labor, radical labor leaders now found that the struggle against wage slavery and chattel slavery was fused in a way that they had not anticipated. No longer were the Democrats the champions of free land for free labor. They were now seen increasingly as champions of northern lands for slaveholders. As early as February, New York land reformers called a mass rally protesting the Kansas-Nebraska Act. The more than 4,000 workers who attended this meeting bitterly denounced the attempt to repeal "the Missouri Compromise, in order to introduce Slavery into *our* free territory of Nebraska and Kansas." They called the bill "a crime, a breach of plighted faith," and "a violation not only of our just rights but of the rights of man."[141]

Huge rallies of workers were also held in the cities of nine other states. Although the land reformers and other labor leaders were careful to put distance between themselves and "fanatic abolitionism," they nevertheless began to adopt the language and imagery of the abolitionists. The workers' rally at Newark, for example, did not call for emancipation but it admitted to jealousy and suspicion of the bold attempts that the Slave Power was now making to degrade northern workers by introducing chattel labor in the free territories of the West. They pledged to repel all efforts to introduce the black slaves into their workshops or to substitute slave labor for free and independent labor. At the Ninth National Industrial Congress, which met in August 1854, delegates voted down a minority that objected to a departure from its focus on land reform and pure labor issues, and they passed resolutions demanding repeal of the Kansas-Nebraska Act and the fugitive slave law. They also called for the ouster of those politicians who had "sold the priceless principle of freedom to the slave power" and urged both native "workers and foreign immigrants to . . . thwart the machinations of the slave power"[142] by moving to Nebraska. Organizations of German workers also moved into conflict with the Slave Power for the first time. The *Arbeiterbund,* for example, condemned the Nebraska bill because it favored "capitalism and land speculation" at "the expense of the mass of the people" by authorizing "the further extension of slavery." Anyone who lent support to the bill was "a traitor against the people and their welfare."[143]

The defections from the Democratic party, together with the crumbling of the Whig party, created opportunities for a northern realignment on an antislavery program. However, the obstacles to realizing such opportunities in mid-1854 were enormous. To be successful, the Free Soilers would have to attract not only the bulk of the northern Whigs but some northern Democrats. Since the Democratic defections were mainly among workers, the antislavery coalition would have to win a sizable number of either native workers or anti-Catholic Germans. Radicals alienated from the Democrats were not, however, the natural allies of Whigs who preached class harmony and opposed a homestead act. Nor were the Free Soilers the ideal brokers for such a marriage. Because of the prominence of abolitionists in their leadership Free Soilers were often seen as allies of fanatics who were more concerned with the emancipation of slaves than with the improvement of the conditions of northern workers.[144]

During most of 1854 and 1855 it was the Know-Nothings rather than the Free Soilers who were generally in command of the political realign-

WITHOUT CONSENT OR CONTRACT

ment. The anti-Nebraska issue did not give the Free Soilers an immediate edge since the Know-Nothings were also vigorous in condemning attempts by slaveholders to seize northern territories, and they pledged to protect northern labor markets from competition by slaves. Moreover, the Free Soilers were far less effective than the Know-Nothings in dealing with the array of local and state issues that so agitated northern workers. The Know-Nothings responded unambiguously to the strong nativist sentiments harbored by Whigs and by many Democrats, and they initiated numerous campaigns for the defense of public schools, for the enforcement of law and order, and for the prevention of election fraud. They were also able to form coalitions on the anti-corruption issues with the anti-Catholic Germans, as they did in Cincinnati during the municipal elections of 1854, by emphasizing the anti-Romanist rather than the anti-immigrant aspect of the nativist appeal.[145]

The most striking victory of the Know-Nothings over the Free Soilers took place in the Massachusetts elections for local and state offices in 1854. There the Free Soilers, seeking a clear victory over the Know-Nothings, established a ticket under the Republican name on a program focused exclusively on the restriction of slavery. The Know-Nothings also took an anti-Nebraska stand, but they ran primarily on a program of local reform that emphasized the removal and punishment of city and town officials found guilty of embezzlement, the withdrawal of state funds for sectarian schools coupled with increased funds for public schools, the establishment of a mechanic's lien law, the abolition of imprisonment for debt, and enforcement of the state's anti-liquor law. The contest resulted in a thumping defeat for the Republicans, who were unable to win a single seat, and virtually a clean sweep for the Know-Nothings.[146]

In most other northern states the Free Soilers joined forces with ex-Whigs, Know-Nothings, anti-Catholic Germans, land reformers, other anti-Nebraska Democrats, and temperance men to form anti-Democratic fusion tickets that were generally called "Independent," "Fusion," "People's ticket," or "Republican." The Know-Nothings were by far the best organized of these various factions. Invigorated by the young voters who responded to their "powerful reform appeal,"[147] drawing on fresh candidates from the ranks of artisans, clerks, and rural clergymen rather than from the wealthy businessmen and professionals, it was the Know-Nothings who dominated these coalitions in the elections of 1854 and 1855. Although some Free Soilers were aghast at the crude nativism of the Know-Nothings, others saw the campaign against the Catholic Church as a legitimate part of the antislavery struggle since the church was everywhere allied with the proslavery Democrats. Free Soilers who were anti-liquor men also found much in common with the Know-Nothings, since they believed that the Catholic Church always used its political influence "directly in favor of drunkenness."[148]

Despite these points of commonality, many Free Soilers were deeply suspicious of the antislavery credentials of Know-Nothing leaders, and they deplored the tendency of the antislavery issue to be subordinated to anti-Romanism in coalitions led by Know-Nothings.[149] "But for this ill-timed and distracting crusade against the Pope and the foreigners," said George Julian, son-in-law of Giddings, it would be possible for a coalition led by Free Soilers to win control of the federal government at the close of the "execrable administration" of Pierce. Many of the abolitionists within the Free Soil party condemned nativism not merely because it was inexpedient but as a matter of principle. Nativism was inconsistent with "the fundamental principles of civil and religious liberty,"[150] and it impeded the struggle for a purified society, which required the reform and conversion of Catholic immigrants rather than their exclusion.

During 1855 Free Soilers tried to end Know-Nothing hegemony over the fusion movement. In Vermont, Massachusetts, and New York they established separate tickets, which they called Republican, aimed at defeating the Know-Nothings' ticket in head-on contests. Despite the more militant, more highly focused antislavery stand of the Republicans, and despite their condemnation of the "absurdity" and "bigotry" of crude nativist attacks on Catholics and immigrants, the Know-Nothings won decisive victories in Massachusetts and New York. Much of the appeal of the Know-Nothings was due to their capacity to deal with both the nativist and the antislavery issues in the context of local reform. They opposed the Catholic Church, not for theological reasons, but because it had become a political machine, a party, determined to undermine public education and to repeal the anti-liquor laws. They opposed the Irish, not because they were Irish, but because they were the political pawns of the hierarchy of the Catholic Church, the instruments of Democratic election frauds, and the reservoir of support for the pro-southern policies of the Cotton Whigs and the Democrats—and, under the protection of corrupt Democrats and Whigs, the Irish accounted for most of the drunkenness, crime, and pauperism in the cities.[151]

Free Soilers also sought to establish separate tickets under a Republican or People's party label in other key states, but were overwhelmed by the nativists who participated in the organizing conventions. In Pennsylvania, for example, Free Soilers were involved in organizing the founding convention of a Republican party in that state, but could not gain control of the party apparatus. The state chairman and most of the members of both the state central committee and the state ticket were Know-Nothings. The would-be antislavery coalition went down to defeat before the Democrats in 1855 because of the divisive infighting between the Know-Nothings and the committed antislavery men. "The long and short of the matter," said one of the antislavery leaders in a letter to Chase after the election, "is that, as things are now, I have no hope" for Pennsylvania, since "I cannot see how all parties can cooperate here without a sacrifice of principle or loss of votes sufficient to insure defeat."[152]

Pennsylvania was by no means the most difficult state in the struggle to gain control of the political breakaway. Know-Nothings continued to control the Republican party in Indiana down through the 1856 election and beyond. Although it supported the Frémont ticket, the state convention continued to refer to itself as the People's party, carefully avoiding the name Republican for fear of alienating some of the factions within the coalition. During the campaign for state offices, which ended in October, the managers of the People's party resisted accepting the services of George W. Julian, the most successful Free Soiler in the coalition, on the ground that he was an abolitionist. Such maneuvers did not prevent the coalition from a disastrous loss to the Democrats in the October contest. Afterward, Julian said they lost because "Know-Nothingism was petted," because "we were willing to sell our principles for office," and because "neither the moral or economic bearing of slavery was discussed."[153]

Despite such difficulties the Free Soilers did gain predominance in the fusion movement, and they did so with a suddenness that was dazzling. The turnabout came in fewer than six months. At the end of 1855 the Know-Nothings seemed to have the upper hand in the struggle for the control of the breakaway in all of the key northern states, with the Free Soilers dominant only in Vermont, Iowa, Wisconsin, and Michigan. Six months later, the Republican party had jelled as a national political party under the influence of the Free Soilers. The Know-Nothings, on the other hand, were split. The antislavery faction, representing the bulk of the northern Know-Nothings, was absorbed by the Republicans, while the rest joined with southern Know-Nothings to form the American party that nominated Millard Fillmore (conservative Whig and ex-president) to oppose the Republican candidate, John C. Frémont. Although Republican leaders had to maneuver adroitly to placate their Know-Nothing constituency, the control of the party remained with the men who were committed to antislavery policy as the overriding principle of the Republican coalition.[154]

Ironically, this sudden turn in events was due to the spectacular successes of the Know-Nothings during 1853, 1854, and early 1855. Their startling electoral victories transformed the coalition from a grassroots movement led by amateurs, mainly journeymen, artisans, petty shopkeepers, and some second-rank professionals, to a powerful political machine that threatened to take command not only of local and state governments but of the national government. Professional politicians of all the parties ran for cover by joining the Order. Typical of these was Nathaniel P. Banks, an antislavery Democrat from Massachusetts. Elected to Congress in 1852 on a joint Democratic and Free Soil ticket, he had played for the support of foreign voters and, as late as May 1854, had denounced religious tests for voting. When news reached him in Washington about the smashing Know-Nothing victory in his home district of Waltham, Banks hastily joined a Know-Nothing lodge in the District of Columbia and then returned home to seek the endorsement of the Know-Nothings in his bid for reelection. So Banks returned to Congress in 1855 as a full-fledged Know-Nothing, portraying the party as a labor uprising that would put opposition to the Kansas-Nebraska Act at the center of its platform.[155]

Professional politicians in the South, particularly Whigs, also rushed into the Know-Nothing party. As their constituents, outraged by the stand of northern Whigs on Kansas-Nebraska, deserted the party in droves, southern Whigs seized on the Know-Nothings as a vehicle for regrouping in a new national party. The nativism of the Know-Nothings fitted with the widely held view of Southerners that the bulk of the immigrants arriving in this country during the mid-1850s were antislavery inclined. "Their aversion to our institutions," said a Whig paper in Alabama, "is manifested by their choice of homes, in the nonslaveholding states."[156] Limitations on immigration also made good political sense since they would slow down northern growth and "preserve southern political power in the national government."[157] By the mid-1850s virtually the entire southern Whig party was regrouped into Know-Nothing organizations and was prepared to join with their northern allies to contest for the presidency in 1856.

In June 1855, the National Council of the Know-Nothings met in Philadelphia to draw up a platform on which the Order could mount a presidential campaign. After a long struggle between northern and southern delegates, the council adopted a plank that placated the Southerners. The 12th section of the platform "accepted as final the existing legislation on slavery (i.e., the Fugitive Slave and Kansas-Nebraska Acts), recommended against congressional interference in the territories, and condemned further agitation of the slavery question." Many northern delegates were outraged and bolted. Some reconvened at a conference in Cleveland where they formed a Know-Something party on a program that endorsed both antislavery and anti-Catholicism. Most northern state councils deplored the pro-southern action of the National Council but waited to see what action would be taken at the national convention called for Philadelphia in February 1856. When that convention reaffirmed the 12th section of the platform and nominated Millard Fillmore, a Cotton Whig, as its candidate for president, most of the remaining northern leaders bolted and, together with the Know-Somethings, formed the North American party, determined to field a northern nativist candidate committed to antislavery.[158]

Although the split of the Know-Nothings provided the opportunity for Free Soilers to take command of the political breakaway, it was the tactical brilliance of such dedicated foes of slavery as Henry Wilson and Salmon P. Chase that realized the opportunity. Wilson correctly assessed the power of the nativist appeal in Massachusetts and led many of the state's Free Soilers into the Know-Nothing party. Once there, they worked assiduously to elevate the antislavery militancy of Know-Nothings. Wilson united the Massachusetts delegation to the 1855 meeting of the National Council behind the proposition that unless the party committed itself to a moderate antislavery stand, it would be better to split the party. When the Council refused to call for the restoration of the Missouri Compromise, Wilson organized a meeting of the antislavery delegates who agreed "that the time had arrived . . . for the formation of a new party, not only in Massachusetts, but throughout the country," on the basis of antislavery principles. Most of these delegates were not yet ready to follow Wilson into the Republican party, but his tactical skill at Philadelphia was a major factor in promoting the Know-Something and North American parties, which became stepping stones into the Republican party.[159]

Chase was the most brilliant of the Free Soil tacticians. By late 1854 he recognized that the Know-Nothings had developed a powerful hold on the constituencies that the Free Soilers had to win. Despite the opposition of close antislavery colleagues in Ohio, he urged the formation of a Republican party for the 1855 state election that "would combine the Free Soilers, Whigs, anti-Nebraska Democrats, Protestant Germans, and those he termed 'liberal Americans.' " Chase managed to persuade reluctant Free Soilers that "without significant nativist backing" the Republican party would be defeated by the Democrats. At the same time he resisted the Know-Nothing demand that he join one of their lodges and accept a minor place on the Republican ticket. His patient maneuvering finally produced a coalition based on a firm antislavery program that was devoid of explicit nativist planks. The Know-Nothings also agreed to make him the gubernatorial candidate of the party, but he had to accept nativists in the other eight slots of the state ticket.[160]

The Republican victory in Ohio was the only bright spot in the otherwise dismal election results for Free Soilers in 1855, since they lost in every other major northern state.[161] Capitalizing on the Ohio victory, Chase, together with leaders of four other states in which the Free Soilers

had won or made credible showings, issued a call for a preliminary
national Republican convention on February 22, 1856, in Pittsburgh.
The timing could hardly have been better since the convention came just
after Republicans and Know-Nothings had combined to elect Nathaniel
Banks (by then a covert Republican) as Speaker of the House and it
coincided with the second split of the Know-Nothings in less than a year
(at the American national convention in Philadelphia).

The contest for the Speaker of the House, which extended from
December 3, 1855, to February 2, 1856, was a critical aspect of the
campaign to organize a national, or at least a North-wide, Republican
party. It was apparent at the beginning of the 34th Congress that pro-
administration Democrats could be denied the Speakership because of
the defection of perhaps nine Democrats on the Kansas-Nebraska issue
and because of the large number of Know-Nothings in the House.[162] The
problem for Republican strategists was twofold: to organize the diverse
anti-administration men behind a single candidate and to keep control
of that coalition in the hands of the Republicans. To accomplish the
second objective it was necessary to split the Know-Nothings into pro-
and anti-southern factions, for otherwise the anti-administration forces
in the House would be united around a national nativist party. By
adroitly playing the antislavery issue and by putting forth Banks, a
former Democrat and a popular Know-Nothing, the Republicans were
able to rally enough anti-administration Democrats and northern Know-
Nothings to beat the candidate of the Pierce Democrats and southern
Know-Nothings by three votes.[163]

It was in the course of that protracted battle for the Speakership that
a potential coalition for an antislavery party was initially formed at the
congressional level. At the outset the group committed to the formation
of the Republican party and without allegiance to the Know-Nothings
represented just 30 to 35 members in a House of 234. However, congressional promoters of the Republican party were able to win support of
about 75 northern Know-Nothings, nearly half of whom were persuaded
to join in the formation of a new national party on an anti-Nebraska
program. The protracted contest over the Speakership called public
attention to the sectional struggle for power and pushed the conflict
between the North and South to the center of congressional politics.
Moreover, the split in the ranks of the Know-Nothings prevented the
American party from organizing the House, putting control instead in the
hands of the Republican party which, through Banks, occupied key
committee posts. So the Republicans, rather than the Know-Nothings,
were able to set the political agenda for the 34th Congress.[164]

It was on the foundation of the newly forged congressional coalition
that the preliminary Republican convention in Pittsburgh established a

national party machinery and issued a party platform that focused on the principle that the territories were to be forever free. Making their political objective the overthrow of the Democrats, the delegates set June as the date for the main national convention (which nominated John C. Frémont to head their ticket), and they appealed for the support of all those of antislavery sentiment, including Whigs, Democrats, and Know-Nothings. By the end of the June convention, it was clear that the Republican party had jelled. The great antislavery coalition, long sought by the political abolitionists, was finally a reality.[165]

The split in the Know-Nothing movement and the tactical brilliance of key Free Soil leaders were two of the four elements that permitted the Republican party to emerge triumphant in the struggle for control of the political breakaway. The third was a set of favorable developments that greatly improved labor market conditions in the North and thus reduced the conflicts over jobs between natives and immigrants, reduced the pressure on urban housing, and reduced the heavy burden of foreign pauperism. The most critical of these developments was the sharp drop in annual immigration, from a peak of 427,000 in 1854 to less than half that figure in 1856 (by 1858 the number was down to less than a third of the peak). The sharpest drop was among the Irish, who were the principal nemesis of the nativists. By 1858 Irish immigration had declined to levels below those of the early 1840s. At the same time the northern economy recovered from the long recession of 1853–1855. The recovery was especially strong in northern manufacturing. The iron industry, for example, rebounded from the devastating bankruptcies of the early 1850s and reached an all-time peak production in 1856. Still another fortunate turn took place in consumer prices, especially food, which declined sharply in 1856, ending a decade-long inflation. The economic relief provided by this combination of events permitted northeastern and midwestern workers to focus their minds on the significance of the bloody civil war in Kansas provoked by the efforts of slaveowners to seize lands that rightfully belonged to free labor.[166]

Acts of southern violence against Northerners, especially those in May 1856, were the fourth element in the compound that gave the Republicans control over the political breakaway. One of the acts took place in Kansas where the pro- and antislavery forces had been engaged in a bitter struggle for control of the state since the middle of 1854. That struggle, which involved electoral frauds on both sides, intermittent violence, and the parading of arms, began to tilt sharply in favor of the antislavery forces as the stream of migrants from the North exceeded the trickle from Missouri and other slave states. By early 1856 two rival governments had been established, each passing its own laws and claiming to be the legitimate authority in the territory. Since only the proslavery government had federal sanction, a U.S. grand jury issued indictments charging "high treason" against members of the antislavery government. A U.S. marshal with a large body of men marched on Lawrence, the political and military stronghold of the antislavery forces, to arrest those named in the indictments. On May 21 the marshal made his arrests, without any resistance, and disbanded his posse. However, a sheriff who had proprietary interests in a rival town not far from Lawrence, and who was an impulsive extremist, took unauthorized command of the posse. The mob that he led burned the hotel that served as the headquarters for the New England Emigrant Aid Society, as well as the house of its head, destroyed the presses of two antislavery newspapers, and pillaged several shops and houses. The one death during the course of the raid occurred when a wall of the burning hotel collapsed on one of the members of the proslavery mob. Two days later, in retaliation for the "sack of Lawrence," John Brown and his sons killed "five helpless and unprepared pro-slavery settlers."[167]

As the posse moved toward Lawrence, Senator Charles Sumner (R, MA) delivered a searing indictment of Democratic policies in Kansas. Called "The Crime against Kansas," this speech, which stretched over two days, was filled with personal invectives against leading Democratic members of the Senate, including Stephan A. Douglas (D, IL) and Andrew P. Butler (D, SC). Butler was absent from the chamber during Sumner's speech but Preston S. Brooks, a relative and a member of the House from South Carolina, brooded over the insults to his aged kinsman and to his state. Determined to teach Sumner a lesson, Brooks entered the Senate chamber after it adjourned on May 22 and delivered a series of blows to Sumner's head and shoulders with his cane. The assault, which lasted for nearly a minute, left the Massachusetts Republican "unconscious and bleeding profusely."[168]

These two events traumatized the nation. The southern Democrats and their northern allies, however, interpreted the events in a much different way than the Free Soilers, the antislavery Whigs, the anti-Nebraska Democrats, and the North Americans. To the Democrats it was the Emigrant Aid Society and other abolitionists who were the aggressors. These radicals sought to thwart "the natural laws of increase and immigration" by sending antislavery forces armed with Beecher's Bibles (Sharp rifles donated by Henry Ward Beecher) into Kansas in order to deprive Southerners of their right to settle in the territory and to establish institutions of their choice. As for Sumner, although Democratic papers regretted "the mode and measure of redress" used by Brooks, they thought that Sumner's speech was so provocative that he had only himself to blame and they deplored the hysterical exaggerations of the superficial wounds inflicted on him, exaggerations aimed at inflaming

northern opinion against the South. The northern opponents of the
Pierce administration were certainly inflamed. To them the outrages in
Kansas and the caning of Sumner were proof beyond doubt of the
South's determination to use violence in order to suppress free speech
and to impose its will on the North. Whatever the uncertainty about the
facts in Kansas, the facts about the caning of Sumner were beyond
dispute and they showed that not even a U.S. senator was safe from
southern aggression.[169]

Although the May violence cost the Democrats some of their northern support, its most important political effect was on the struggle between the Know-Nothings and the Republicans for control of the political
breakaway. As late as February 1856 that control still seemed to rest
with the Know-Nothings. But the May violence decisively shifted the
balance to the Republicans by turning the attention of Northerners from
the key Know-Nothing issue (the papal conspiracy to subvert American
institutions) to the key Republican issue (the Slave Power conspiracy to
subvert northern liberties and economic welfare)—from a foreign menace to a southern menace. By mid-June it seemed that the Republicans
had gained the upper hand. Writing to Lincoln, Senator Lyman Trumbull
(R, IL) expressed a new confidence over Republican chances of taking
such complete command of the breakaway that they could beat the
Democrats. "The outrage upon Sumner & the occurrences in Kansas
have helped us vastly," he reported.[170] Greeley, even more exuberant,
appealed to the farmers and working men who were the main supporters
of the Know-Nothings in a language they could understand: Those who
wished their children to be free and economically independent had to
join the Republican crusade against the conspiracy by the "great capitalists" of the North and the planters of the South "to exclude white
laborers from the Territories and hand them over to the sole occupancy
of slaves and slave-breeders."[171]

Despite the enormous inroads of the Republicans into the Know-
Nothing constituency, Frémont lost in 1856. Nevertheless, his vote was
so large that the Republican party had emerged as the leading party in
the North, although its northern margin was not yet large enough to
offset the Democratic majority in the South. The Republicans also were
in a strong position in the House, despite the fact the Democrats elected
118 members to the Republicans' 92. By forming a coalition with the
American party, they could block Democratic legislation. The election
also devastated the Know-Nothing party in the North, with Frémont
drawing three votes for every one received by Fillmore. The Republican
party was clearly in control of the northern political breakaway.

THE PRECARIOUS VICTORY OF THE ANTISLAVERY COALITION

The outcome of the 1856 election was both encouraging and disappointing to the Republicans. It was disappointing because they had lost the campaign for the presidency; it was encouraging because the Democrats were now a minority party in the North. Thus, by winning over the remaining Know-Nothing voters in key northern states, the Republicans could in 1860 obtain an electoral majority in the North alone, and it could win a clear majority of the House as early as 1858. Moreover, with the admission of some new northern states and sufficient inroads in one or two border states, they could also control the Senate. The victory was particularly sweet to the Free Soilers. The outcome of the 1856 elections completely vindicated their strategy. There was now a party poised to take power that was alert to the threat of southern ideology and determined to restrict slavery's political and economic domination and to guarantee that the federal government promoted northern interests and principles. The Republican party had jelled within a few months after the call for a national convention. It survived the chaos of the fusion era and Free Soilers were now an influential force in a powerful party. The antislavery coalition was poised to conquer the last defense of the Slave Power—the northern Democrats, the "Dough Faces."

Victory in the next presidential race was a practical goal, but by no means an easy one. The Democrats were down in 1856, but far from out. Despite their weakness they still controlled the presidency and the Senate, and they had the capacity to form winning coalitions in the House. Moreover, the Democrats were a remarkably resilient party, as the elections of 1855 had demonstrated. It was by no means assured that the Republicans would beat the Democrats in the contest for the remaining Know-Nothing votes, or that they would prove more popular among new voters.

Consolidating Republican ranks also posed considerable problems. It would be difficult to hold both the North American Know-Nothings (who deserted the Fillmore Know-Nothings because they wanted to fight both the pope and the Slave Power) and the Germans (who were willing to belong to an anti-papist party and an anti-Irish party but not to an anti-German party or a temperance party). There was also the problem of how to hold prosperous ex-Whigs (who believed in the harmony of interests of all classes and opposed free land to settlers) within their ranks without alienating the land reformers and other class-conscious labor leaders (some of whom still had strong Locofoco proclivities). Finally, there were the divisive internal struggles for control of the

Republican party, in which the Free Soilers frequently found themselves in battle with the more conservative ex-Whigs, the ex-Know-Nothings, and the ex-Locofocos—all of whom sought to increase their hold in the party and its patronage, as well as to push the party in different directions than those desired by the Free Soilers, especially by the closet abolitionists in their faction.

That the Republicans managed to surmount all of these difficulties is evident by their victory in 1860. The antislavery coalition had finally gained control of the presidency, but its grasp on power was precarious. Although Lincoln's 180 electoral votes exceeded the 152 needed for election, he received less than 40 percent of the popular vote. A shift of just 25,069 New York votes from Lincoln to Douglas would have reduced Lincoln's electoral count to 145. An even smaller shift of popular votes (18,239) in four other states (California, Illinois, Indiana, and New Jersey) would also have wiped out his electoral majority. In such an event, the election of the president would have been thrown into the House where each state has one vote. Republicans controlled only 15 of the 34 state delegations in the House (with 18 needed for election). Of the remaining 19 delegations the Democrats controlled 14 and needed 1 Know-Nothing vote in four others to control those delegations. In the remaining delegation (Tennessee), the Know-Nothings were a majority, but were unlikely to have voted for Lincoln. If the House had failed to elect a president, the decision would have passed to the Senate, where each senator had one vote and where there were 38 Democrats, 26 Republicans, and 2 Know-Nothings. So the Republican victory in 1860 and the consequent abolition of slavery turned on less than 1/2 of 1 percent of the northern ballots cast in the popular contest.[172]

Further insights into the nature of the Republican victory are provided by Table 7, which relates the Republican vote in 1860 to the principal northern political constituencies in the election of 1852, the last national election preceding the political breakaway. It shows that the Republican victory turned on the party's capacity to draw both the Free Soil and Whig constituencies into its fold. Together they accounted for 89 percent of Lincoln's northern vote. About 9 percent of northern ex-Whigs voted for Lincoln's opponents, nearly all of them for Bell, the presidential candidate of the Constitutional Unionists. In place of these conservative Whigs, the Republicans gained about 12 percent of the northern constituency of the Democrats (about 210,000 voters).[173] The net effect of the Whig defections and the Democratic additions was to raise the Republican share of the northern presidential vote by about 1.7 percent: from a combined Free Soil plus Whig share of 50.2 percent in 1852 to a Republican share of 51.9 percent in 1860. Given the closeness of Lincoln's victory, even this small numerical gain was important.

Table 7. The Northern Vote for Lincoln[a] in 1860 Distributed with Respect to
the Probable Political Allegiances of These Voters in 1852

Region[b]	Free Soil	Whigs	Democrats	Total Vote[c]
	Part A			
	Lincoln's Vote (in Thousands) by Political Allegiance in 1852[d]			
New England	68	171	58	297
Middle Atlantic	44	568	77	689
Midwest	118	634	75	827
Far West	—	45	—	45
The North	230	1,418	210	1,858
	Part B			
	Percentage Distribution of the Vote in Each Region and for the North by Political Allegiance in 1852[c]			
New England	23	58	20	100
Middle Atlantic	6	82	11	100
Midwest	14	77	9	100
Far West	—	100	—	100
The North	12	76	11	100

[a]Does not include Lincoln's vote in DE, MD, KY, and VA.
[b]Regions are defined as follows: New England: ME, NH, VT, MA, RI, CT; Middle Atlantic: NY,
NJ, PA; Midwest: OH, MI, IN, IL, WI, IA, MO, MN; Far West: CA, OR.
[c]Components may not sum to line and column totals because of rounding.
[d]New voters are distributed among the 1852 constituencies. See *EM*, #69.

However, the main aspect of the Republican realignment of northern
voters, most of whom were already opposed to the Slave Power in 1852,
is that they were radicalized in the process. Two events prepared the way
and were probably necessary conditions for the radicalization. First, the
Whigs had to be destroyed as a national party. That condition was largely
fulfilled between 1853 and 1855 when, under the pressure of growing
southern nationalism, the majority of southern Whigs left the party,
seeking a more viable vehicle in which to continue the struggle for power
within their home states. Second, the Whig party machinery in the
North, still largely in the hands of a minority of conservatives (who had
placed the accommodation of their southern allies above antislavery
principles), had to be disrupted. That condition was satisfied by the
political successes of the Know-Nothings during 1853, 1854, and 1855,
which reduced the Whig party to a shambles in nearly all of the northern
states.[174]

Whether it was under the Know-Nothing label (as in Massachusetts),
under the Republican label (as in Michigan), or under the fusionist label
(as in Ohio and Indiana), disgruntled Whigs and Democrats were separated from the "protective" shields of the old party machines. Whatever

the intention of the nativists, this dissolution, or at least temporary attenuation, of traditional political ties made large numbers of Whigs and Democrats far more accessible to the arguments of Free Soilers. The Know-Nothing party thus created a pool of detached voters in which Free Soilers could fish for support in the struggle to build a militant antislavery coalition that was far broader than any previously achieved.

Analysis of election data suggests that they were much more successful in catching ex-Whigs than ex-Democrats. In the Massachusetts and New York elections of 1854, for example, the Know-Nothings drew their support from Whigs and Democrats in roughly equal numbers. However, by 1860 ex-Whig supporters within the Republican party outnumbered the ex-Democrats by roughly 7 to 1. It thus appears that the Republicans were able to capture about half of the Democrats but virtually all of the Whigs who strayed into the Know-Nothing party. Indeed, since many Whigs remained loyal to their party in 1854 and 1855, the eventual Whig "catch" of the Republicans considerably exceeded the number who passed through the Know-Nothing movement. The bulk of the Whig voters were farmers, and it was farmers who constituted the bulk of the Republican vote. Moreover, the richer the farmers, the more likely they were to vote Republican.[175]

We do not yet know which of the Democrats returned to their original political home. It may have been those who were more attracted by the class rhetoric of the Know-Nothings and their militancy on labor issues than by their anti-Catholic rhetoric. To such voters Republican hostility to strikes and their emphasis on the "harmony of interests" between labor and capital may have been too reminiscent of the Whig party. Some of the Germans who cautiously backed the Know-Nothings and also joined the attack on the Slave Power in 1854 may not have found the Republican appeal as beguiling later on. In this connection it is worth noting that when the *Arbeiterbund* issued a new platform in 1857 slavery was not even mentioned in it.[176]

Since a large proportion (about two-fifths) of Republican voters were former Know-Nothings, it is no surprise that Republican appeals often linked Catholicism and slavery as twin despotisms. During the 1858 campaign for the Senate, for example, the organ of the Republican party in Illinois maintained that "the Catholic church was in league with the proslavery Democratic party to destroy the principles of free government." Other Republican journals pointed out that "Douglas's wife and children were Catholics," and charged that he "was a secret convert to Catholicism and the candidate of Catholic bishops." Despite such rhetoric, the Republican party did not embrace nativism or anti-Catholicism in their official platforms since to do so would have alienated not only some of their Democratic supporters but also ex-Whigs within the party who had remained aloof from the Know-Nothings and who shunned crude appeals to bigotry.[177]

Party leaders were divided on the policies needed to placate both constituencies. In 1858 Greeley pushed hard in New York for fusion with those Know-Nothings still outside of the party, fearful that without their support the Republicans might lose the state election to the Democrats, as they had in 1857. To appease the Know-Nothings, he sought to commit the New York Republican party to "a rigid registry law [a list of eligible voters, which was widely considered a measure to harass foreign-born voters] and an interval of one year between naturalization and the right to vote." Thurlow Weed condemned fusion as an act that would "lower the Republican standard" and he blocked such a move, but the planks proposed by Greeley were added to the state platform.[178]

Party leaders were also divided on how to deal with the divergent economic beliefs of Republican constituencies. Old-line Whigs within the party firmly favored protective tariffs and firmly opposed a homestead bill. The ex-Democrats, however, were land reformers who believed that free trade was "beneficial to the consumer." There was also a rift between the mill hands, who demanded enactment of a 10-hour day, and the farmers, who derisively opposed such a law because it would prevent them from milking cows in the mornings. Differences on economic issues became acute under the impact of the devastating panic of 1857. For a time leaders of the Republican party became almost as badly divided on the causes and cures of the panic as the Whigs and Democrats had been on the same issues during the 1830s and 1840s. Fearful that the party was not strong enough to withstand internal dissensions on these issues, Greeley, who had advocated a return to traditional Whig economic policies, apologized for his provocative statements on protection and banking.[179]

The Republican party was not wrecked by the panic of 1857 and by 1860 it had lured most of the former Know-Nothings into its ranks. However, neither outcome was inevitable. The party was able to maintain its hold on its diverse constituencies partly because of fortunate events over which it had no control. One of the most critical of these was the sharp drop in immigration after the middle of 1854 which remained at low levels throughout the balance of the decade. Another was the swift, powerful recovery from the panic. If 400,000 extra immigrants had piled into the North during 1857–1858, urban unemployment rates would have gone up by about 10 percentage points, on top of the unemployment that the panic had already precipitated. It is doubtful that party leaders could have continued to suppress the nativist impulses of so many of its members if immigration had returned to the 1854 rate, or if the panic of 1857 had produced an extended depression. If, under such circumstances, the party would have resisted pressures for a more militant stand on nativist issues, some of the former Know-Nothings would surely have bolted. If the party would have conceded these demands, some of the Germans and the more conservative Whigs would have been alienated. Only relatively small defections were needed to deny power to the antislavery coalition in 1860. Even under the favorable conditions that preceded the 1860 election, the Republicans were barely able to eke out a victory.[180]

Whether or not the antislavery coalition could have maintained its weak grip on the federal government in the absence of the Civil War, secession made the issue academic. When the Confederates fired on Fort Sumter they sent a surge of patriotic sentiment through the North that temporarily made the coalition invincible. Of course, that surge dissipated as the burdens of the war increased and victory began to seem illusive. Had the chances of war gone the other way (better southern management at Antietam, for example), England might have intervened on the side of the Confederacy and the northern peace movement might have gained the upper hand. But they did not. The North won the war and abolished slavery.[181]

That victory, and its exploitation by the Republicans after the war, obscured the weakness of the antislavery coalition. Despite being the party that won the war and saved the Union, the Republicans found that the Democrats retained considerable strength in the North. With control over Congress almost evenly divided between the two parties throughout the postwar years, "Republicans relied in part on waving the 'bloody shirt,' appealing to the large army of Union veterans as the party which kept the country united, while denouncing the Democrats as the party of secession."[182] The myth of an invincible antislavery coalition was not a prewar product. It was cast in the flames of the postwar struggle for power.

Although the antislavery coalition was fragile in 1860, it might have grown stronger even in the absence of the Civil War. The evangelicals who were at the heart of the movement would not have abandoned their struggle for moral purification merely because of political setbacks that might have occurred in the early 1860s. Their dedication to the abolitionist cause allowed them to overcome the discouraging setbacks of the late 1830s, of the first half of the 1840s, and of the early 1850s. However, in attempting to assess the opportunities for a peaceful victory over slavery one must consider the stamina not only of the abolitionists but of the proslavery forces and of the accommodationists. Nor should one ignore the deeply racist prejudices of the majority of Republican voters and of many of the party's leaders. Prior to the 1860 election and well into the war years neither Lincoln nor the Republican party was committed to freeing the slaves or to granting political and social equality to the free blacks of the North. Quite the contrary, when the Democrats sought to portray them as the advocates of black rights, many Republican leaders, including Lincoln, emphasized their commitment to maintaining "the superior position assigned to the white race."[183] I will return to these matters in the Afterword since they need to be addressed within the context of a broader set of issues that I call "the moral problem of slavery."

THE MORAL PROBLEM OF SLAVERY

Alexander Pope, in his *Essay on Criticism,* said that a little knowledge is dangerous.[1] Perhaps he should have added that it is also often comforting. Intellectual comfort has been one of the main casualties of the past quarter century of slavery research. The new knowledge about the nature of the slave system and the struggle to destroy it has revealed agonizing dilemmas and paradoxes that did not arise in the historical glosses that most of us learned in school. The heroes of the antislavery struggle are generally still heroes, but they are somehow less perfect than one would like heroes to be. The alternative to slavery generally embraced by the abolitionists, while morally better than slavery, is to the modern mind still brutal and exploitative. That the abolition of slavery often led to extended periods of economic decline is an unsettling discovery to scholars living in an age when technological advance and rising incomes have been viewed by so many as moral imperatives, and even more widely viewed as political imperatives. It is distressing to learn of the central role of the British antislavery movement in the rise of imperialism, an experience that still hangs heavy on hundreds of millions of people in the less developed nations of the world and still contributes to the suspicions these nations have of the industrialized world. Equally distressing is the discovery that the leaders of the struggle to improve the conditions of free labor were often aligned with the slaveholders, while the abolitionists were often aligned with the foes of the free labor movement.

It is easy to invent an antislavery policy that would be far more congenial to the predominant moral standards of our own age than the policies actually put forward by any of the major historical players. To censure the abolitionists for not fully anticipating our values, however, would be foolish. A policy congenial to us could not have built the political coalition needed to destroy slavery. Even policies that now seem conservative were too radical to succeed in 1860. Here then is a dilemma posed not only by the antislavery struggle but by most other moral movements: It is difficult in a democracy, if not impossible, to transform a moral movement into a winning political coalition without deeply compromising its moral integrity; it is also difficult to pursue one moral goal without compromising or even sacrificing other important moral goals.

This chapter does not attempt to describe an emerging scholarly consensus on the moral paradoxes and dilemmas posed by the history of slavery and of the movement that destroyed that system. No such consensus has arisen, nor does one appear to be imminent. I could pick and choose among current scholarly views but that would merely be another way of presenting my personal assessment of the problem. Under the circumstances, I believe that the best way to illuminate the issue is to describe how the slavery research of the past three decades has changed my own views. An autobiographical approach not only emphasizes the personal nature of the statement, but provides a relevant historical context.

It was in 1958, while a graduate student in economics at Johns Hopkins University, that I first became seriously interested in the history of slavery. The views that I held on the subject at that time had been formed by two experiences. One was my conventional education in the schools of New York City during the 1930s and early 1940s and at Cornell University during the middle and late 1940s. During these years, especially after the outbreak of World War II, formal education in New York began to incorporate the anti-racist propositions of modern anthropology as popularized by Ruth Benedict and Gene Weltfish in their famous pamphlet, *The Races of Mankind.* In my teens their views were taught not only in the classroom but even in the New York subways. Slogans from *The Races of Mankind* were repeated on advertising placards that rimmed the ceilings of the trains. As an undergraduate at Cornell, I was introduced to Gunnar Myrdal's penetrating critique of the history of race relations in the United States, *An American Dilemma.* Equally impressive was the experience of participating in the popular student protest movements of the 1940s and early 1950s, which in New York were generally anti-capitalistic, anti-fascist, and anti-racist. Anti-racist meant opposition both to the racial policies of Nazi Germany and to discrimination against minorities, especially blacks, at home.[2]

My youthful experiences did not give me a very clear picture of the slave system or how it operated but I had read about the barbarities of the international slave trade and accepted the proposition that slavery was a primitive form of the accumulation of capital. I also believed that slaves who grew cotton and sugar on large plantations were cruelly treated; that slavery kept the South economically and socially backward; that the Civil War was fought to free slaves; that after the Union Army withdrew from the South a combination of carpetbaggers and ex-slave-holders seized control of state and local governments; that this coalition

deprived blacks of the right to vote and developed systems of segregation
in education, jobs, housing, and public facilities; that segregation and
slavery had been justified by false racist theories; and that these same
theories were promoted in the North by businessmen who wanted a
cheap source of labor and who sought to keep workers from uniting to
defend their interests.

These were the views I held when the publication of the paper by
Conrad and Meyer in 1958 drew me into the debate on the profitability
of slavery. Although an old and recurrent issue, it had been reopened
by Stampp two years earlier with the publication of *The Peculiar Institution*. Conrad and Meyer argued that they could resolve this hoary question scientifically by applying the analytical and quantitative methods of
economists to the evidence that Phillips, Stampp, and other traditional
historians had uncovered. It was the methodological challenge, rather
than the substance of the issue, that initially caught the attention of most
of the cliometricians. The central problem posed by Conrad and Meyer
was one of logic, not ethics: It concerned the inferences about profitability that could be validly drawn from the data needed to compute a rate of
return. When the debate pushed beyond the bounds of economic logic, it
initially went no further than questioning the empirical validity of the
estimates of the economic and demographic variables employed by Conrad and Meyer. During the early 1960s the investigation of the economics of slavery was extended to include two additional issues: the economic
viability of slavery and the rate of economic growth in the antebellum
South.[3]

Some scholars found the cliometric analysis of the economics of
slavery morally offensive. Yet far from distracting attention from the
immorality of slavery the cliometric debate had underscored it, although
sometimes indirectly.[4] By itself the *size* of the profit reaped by masters
was irrelevant to the moral indictment of slavery. Whether the profit was
large or small, it was extracted by cruel exploitation. Conrad and Meyer
had, however, added to the moral indictment when their computations
revealed that fully a third of the profits of planters in the older regions of
the South were derived from breeding slaves for sale in the interstate
trade.[5] Moreover, the demonstration that the slave system was economically viable, and that the excess profit or the economic "rent" was increasing during the 1850s, punctured the claim that the Civil War was a
tragic blunder because slavery was about to expire from economic causes.
The discovery that the South had a high rate of economic growth between
1840 and 1860 was surprising. It seemed to contradict the proposition
that slavery retarded the economic development of the South. Yet no
essential moral belief was undermined by this finding. The propositions
that planters as a class squandered their income on high living and were

irrationally attached to agriculture now seemed dubious, but the view
that planters were profit-oriented, premeditated, and coldly rational ex-
ploiters of their laborers was reinforced. "The case for abolition of slavery," I wrote in 1966, "thus appears to turn on issues of morality and
equity rather than on the inability of a slave system to yield a high rate of
economic growth."[6]

Despite these words, I had not thought very deeply about the substance of the moral issues because they seemed so obvious. The brutali-
ties of the slave trade, slave breeding, and the extremely hard conditions
of labor spoke for themselves. In 1966 I no longer believed that masters
deliberately worked slaves to death in seven years (Conrad and Meyer
estimated a life expectation of 30 years at age 20),[7] but I still believed
that competitive pressures led masters to work slaves until they reached
the outer limits of their endurance and to stint on their food, clothing,
and shelter. The root of the evil was the unconstrained power over the
lives of slaves exercised by the masters. "Absolute power corrupts absolutely",[8] and the master class was the most corrupt of all the ruling
classes in modern history.

Between 1968 and 1972 my view of the moral problem of slavery
changed considerably. The discovery that slave plantations were more
efficient than free farms challenged my beliefs about the moral problem
of slavery in a way that previous cliometric discoveries had not. The
notion of efficient plantations created a dilemma because it was difficult
to see how individuals so deeply oppressed, without incentive, many
demoralized, others determined rebels, could nevertheless produce more
output per worker than free farmers. It was not only inconsistent with
my vision of slaves as semi-starved, listless workers who barely had the
energy to pull themselves through the day, but it seemed to imply a far
greater level of labor discipline and a far greater degree of, if not
cooperation, at least acquiescence to the objectives of the planters than
I was prepared to entertain. I realized that the dilemma might be more
apparent than real—the artifact of errors in our conceptualization of
efficiency, of errors in our measurement procedures, or of the poor
quality of the data employed in the computations. Engerman and I
delayed publication of our preliminary findings for nearly two years as
we investigated these possibilities and searched for new data that might
reverse the computation.

The results of these searches did not relieve me of the dilemma.
Quite the contrary, the new evidence further eroded my confidence in
conventional views of the moral problems of slavery. The food, clothing,
and shelter provided to slaves were far better than I had imagined—not
good by twentieth-century standards but better than what was typically
available to free urban laborers at the time.[9] I was also startled to

discover the numerous ways in which masters relied on rewards to elicit labor—a device I had assumed was almost entirely absent since David Hume, Adam Smith, John E. Cairnes, and most of the other classical writers had identified this lack as the fatal flaw in slavery as an economic system. Whipping, which I had assumed was so common that demoralization among slaves was widespread ("they stood in fear" was not a metaphor but a literal description), was certainly there and was indispensable to the operation of the gang system. But its use was more premeditated and selective than I had imagined. Planters did not abandon rewards because they had the power to use the whip but as a general policy sought to utilize both weapons to fashion a highly disciplined labor force.[10] The most jarring discovery was that slave breeding, as Weld had originally used the term, was neither a general policy nor a major source of profit.[11] To my mind nothing had symbolized the inhumanity of American slaveholders more completely than their attempt to reduce people to the level of animals. The collapse of this charge was unsettling for another reason: It contradicted a finding that I had welcomed as one of the main contributions of the first decade of cliometric research on slavery. The research by social, political, and cultural historians also eroded my confidence in the conventional view of the moral problem of slavery. Cultural historians, for example, found more scope for the development of slave family life, occupational skills, and a more distinct culture than convention dictated. Mistreatment was not excluded from the new histories of slave culture, but its role was considerably diminished.

By the middle of 1973 the view of the moral problem of slavery that gained ascendancy after World War II no longer seemed adequate. It was increasingly difficult to defend it, and this was not merely because the new evidence contradicted, or at least severely qualified, many of the factual assumptions on which that view was based. The weakness in an indictment resting primarily on mistreatment is easier to recognize after some of its main props have crumbled than it was beforehand. Suppose that they had all crumbled; suppose every claim of planters regarding the benevolent treatment of their slaves was confirmed; suppose slaves were better clothed, fed, and housed than proletarians. Would that be enough to quash the moral indictment, to relieve masters from the charge of profound injustice? The question begs the answer. Obviously the indictment would stand even if slaves were treated as well as the favorite Arabian steed of a very rich man, because people are not horses.[12] While physical abuse compounded the immorality of slaveholders, good treatment is insufficient to free them from condemnation.

What then is the fundamental basis for the moral indictment of slavery? Engerman and I grappled with that problem as we wrote *Time on the Cross.* [13] Observations were scattered through both volumes, but they did not add up to an adequate statement of the problem.[14] An additional decade of research into the economics, politics, and ideology of both the slaveholders and the abolitionists encourages me to make a new assault, not only on the nature of the moral indictment, but on a somewhat broader range of issues that collectively represent what might be called "the moral problem of slavery."

TOWARD A MODERN INDICTMENT

I believe that we should no longer interpret the moral problem of slavery within the framework of the indictment fashioned by the winners of the antislavery struggle. The contention that we need a new indictment does not mean that all continuity with past views need be broken. Quite the contrary, a new indictment could restore continuity with the earlier and more frankly ethical aspects of the attack, which leaders of the popular movement abandoned, or at least attenuated, because it was politically expedient to do so. Such an indictment, then, would be more closely bound to the radical position on slavery than to the later and more politically successful one. The successful position was carried into our time by virtue of processes that make winning ideologies valuable political capital, and by historians of the antebellum era who, until recent years, did more to popularize the winning attack on slavery than the more radical and more frankly ethical position. Yet ethical propositions that were highly factious in the antebellum era are now so deeply embedded in the modern democratic thought that virtually every organized political force in American life accepts them, often without realizing their origin.

I believe that the new indictment should turn on four counts. Each of these counts has to some degree been set forth previously by one or another scholar. My goal is not novelty per se but the construction of a concise, coherent statement of the main counts against slavery that is free from the factual errors that have misdirected the moral debate and weakened the case against slavery. It is the indictment as a whole—the way in which the particular points are developed, what is included and what is left out, and how the individual points are related to each other—that imparts whatever novelty may reside in it. I offer the indictment not only as a highly personal view of the fundamental basis for condemning slavery, but also as a tentative view. My beliefs about slavery have been changing continually for more than a quarter of a century and I have no reason to assume that the process has come to an end. I anticipate that new evidence and further reflection will lead me to modify some of the beliefs set forth here, although I shall be surprised if the future changes are as marked as those of the past.

The first, and overarching, count in the new indictment is that slavery permitted one group of people to exercise unrestrained personal domination over another group of people. The proposition that such power was by itself profoundly evil and corrupting was the original basis for the condemnation of slavery by the religious radicals who initiated the campaign and (no matter how overlaid by political expediency it became) that proposition continued to impel the antislavery crusade throughout its history. The proposition was the logical outcome of the theologies of both Quakers and evangelicals. Believing that "all men were equal before God," associating "moral evil with institutions of the external world,"[15] holding that it was within the capacity of men to achieve salvation by unselfish acts and unremitting struggle against inward and outward evil, slavery loomed not only as a corrupter of the masters but as a barrier to the exercise of the free will through which slaves could obtain salvation. Personal domination was condemned as a sin and those who sought it were denounced as usurpers of powers that belonged only to God.

Despite the religious origins of this view and the religious zeal that animated the antislavery crusaders who brought it into political life, the expediency of politics secularized the attack on personal domination and made freedom from such domination a central feature of the modern democratic creed. Personal freedom became a necessary condition not only for heavenly salvation but for the earthly perpetuation of popular democracy. The process of secularizing the demand for personal freedom has been intensified in recent decades by psychological theories that have made freedom from personal domination an essential condition for the development of a normal, healthy personality. As Elkins put it, the culture of any group forced to submit completely to the power of others and forced perpetually into fawning dependency "is bound to contain more than the normal residue of pathology."[16]

Slavery thus became a capital offense on both religious and secular grounds because, regardless of the benevolence or cruelty of particular owners, the system transformed each slave into "the mere extension of his master's physical nature"[17] and will. The extreme degree of domination required by the system, and not percentages of masters who were cruel or benevolent in their operation of the system, was and is the essential crime.[18] Cruelty was bound to be one of the consequences of unlimited domination because sooner or later it was necessary to sustain domination. The tendency to generate physical cruelty condemns the system, even if many masters struggled against that tendency. Nevertheless, physical cruelty is but one of many necessary consequences of unlimited personal domination, some of which are more profoundly evil, although perhaps more subtle, than physical abuses.

Denial of economic opportunity is the second count of the new indictment of slavery. In some slave societies and among some masters in every slave society, the material conditions of slaves were worse than those of free laborers. Nevertheless, preoccupation with the relative standard of living of slaves and free laborers during the antebellum era had served as a diversion from the basic moral issue inherent in the denial of economic opportunity. A quarter century of intensive research into the standard of living both of urban industrial workers (especially in Great Britain) and of American and West Indian slaves has not demonstrated a clear-cut moral advantage for the performance of either system on these purely material matters, at least not for the first six decades of the nineteenth century. Evidence recently collected on the heights of British and other European workers confirms the opinion of radical leaders such as William Cobbett that British "wage slaves" of the early part of the century were generally more poorly nourished than chattel slaves in the New World. The comparison between the nutrition of urban wage earners in the United States with that of American slaves is closer, yet here too the slaves appear to have had an advantage, although only a slight one. The same studies clearly reveal that the nutrition of native-born American farmers surpassed that of slaves in every period and region for which evidence is available. Heartening as that discovery may be, it is too special to the American case to be converted into a general moral advantage for free labor systems during the nineteenth century, since such a general nutritional advantage did not exist, even if we confine ourselves to farmers. It is now clear that during most of the nineteenth century typical European peasants were as poorly nourished as the typical native-born slaves in the West Indies.[19]

The decisive economic advantage of free labor systems was not what had been achieved but what was unfolding: the opportunity for laboring classes to improve their lot as a consequence of rapid technological progress.[20] Free labor systems provided two routes to such improvement. One was individual economic and social mobility, the opportunity of individuals to rise on the economic ladder by acquiring land, labor skills, and other forms of capital. A critical aspect of the upward movement was geographic mobility, the freedom of individuals to migrate to those places where their opportunities were greatest. Millions of impoverished Europeans were able to escape from the rigid class structures and poverty of their homelands to find opportunity in the New World. Recent cliometric studies have demonstrated that both international and interstate migrants generally improved their economic positions rapidly after entering new communities. There was also upward economic mobility among those who stayed put. Over their lifetimes persons from lower classes tended to rise in the occupational hierarchy and to improve their standing in the distribution of wealth. Moreover, whether their parents were native born or foreign born, sons from lower-class families were generally better off than their fathers, having not only more wealth but generally standing higher in the hierarchy of occupations than their fathers had stood.[21]

Opportunity for individual advancement was much more restricted among slaves. Although the incentive systems developed by masters created more economic differentiation among slaves than I once thought, and although the proportion of slaves in the skilled crafts appears to have increased over time, slaves could not seek to improve their lot by changing masters or by moving from one region to another in pursuit of economic opportunity. Even though a master might increase his wealth by moving his slaves from the East to the West, it does not appear that the slaves shared in the master's windfall. Opportunities for acquiring land, becoming independent entrepreneurs, or rising into the professions were exceedingly rare. Small items of movable property, clothing, some garden crops, limited quantities of staple crops, small livestock, and occasionally horses and cattle were generally the only assets that slaves could trade and these only by the leave of their masters.

Nor were slaves permitted to improve their lot by collective action. The whole range of organizations and activities through which free laborers successfully combined to advance their economic interests was forbidden among slaves. Collective action by slaves was insurrection, talk of it was conspiracy, and both brought swift, ruthless suppression. Slaves were prohibited from any explicit role in designing the rules of the economic game.

Consequently, there was no mechanism through which slaves could link their incomes to the prosperity of the industries in which they labored. Indeed, although American slave prices and hire rates rose quite sharply during the 1840s and 1850s, there is no evidence that this led to an improvement in the standard of living of slaves. Quite the contrary, the available evidence indicates that, at least with respect to nutrition, the average condition of slaves was declining during these years. The long-term economic opportunities of slaves as a class were nil.[22]

Denial of citizenship to slaves is the third count of the new indictment. Even the word "alien" is too weak to describe the utter exclusion of slaves from civil and political rights. Free persons, even if aliens, were entitled to the protection of the state against attacks on their person, against violations of their family, and for security of their property. In this respect it is necessary to emphasize a curious anomaly in the treatment of slaves in different nations. Although the American and British systems of slavery often provided better material conditions of life than slaves experienced in the French and Spanish colonies, the civil control that masters exercised over their slaves was often more complete in the Protestant nations than in the Catholic ones. The Catholic Church, as the guardian of the souls of Christian slaves, proclaimed that it had the authority to review the practices of masters, and so it established ecclesiastical courts which in a number of countries recognized that slaves had certain civil rights. These courts sought to protect slave families and they made it possible for large numbers of slaves to buy their freedom and thus enter the realm of free labor in Spanish and French colonies. However, the effectiveness of the Catholic Church varied from country to country and from one time to another, according to the strength of the slaveholding class and the will of local church leaders. In the United States the Catholic churches of the North generally refused to speak out on the slavery issue, while those of the South openly accepted slavery as it was practiced. In Cuba the church was unable to prevent slaveholders from greatly intensifying the oppressiveness of the system which, during 1841–1886, produced mortality rates among slaves far in excess of those prevailing in the United States toward the end of the antebellum era. In some periods and places, as in nineteenth-century Cuba, slaveowners could easily ignore the injunctions of the church.[23]

Whatever the problems of the Catholic Church in its role as protector of slaves, the Protestant churches initially lagged behind them. It was not until the last two decades before emancipation that the missionary work in the West Indies became extensive or that amelioration of the lot of slaves became a principal objective. In the South, the Protestant clergy made some efforts to ameliorate the worst abuses of slavery, especially after 1830. But since their churches were generally dominated by slaveowners, such intervention was exceedingly cautious and not always effective. The Quakers, long in the vanguard of the antislavery struggle, were severely circumscribed in their ability to improve the lot of southern slaves. Even when they directed their appeal to the consciences of the slaveholders, they could not interpose themselves between the masters and the slaves, although they were able to establish schools and contribute to the spread of literacy among slaves. After 1830, when they joined in the campaign to rouse the moral conscience of the North, they lost whatever previous ability they had had to minister directly to slaves.[24]

After 1830 the forces in the South that stood for total abrogation of even the most elementary civil rights of slaves were in the ascendancy. They pressed the view that slaves were a special form of property to its fullest extent and developed novel attacks on the humanity of blacks. They also pressed for the vigorous enforcement of the slave codes, which

entailed a rollback of whatever loosening in the civil isolation of slaves
had occurred: Schools were closed; teaching of literacy even by masters
was made a crime; white overseers were imposed over slave drivers on
plantations where none had operated previously; and uncontrolled movements of slaves in both rural and urban areas were curtailed. As the civil
rights of slaves diminished some southern courts intervened to protect
slaves from the worst excesses of unbridled power. But given the context,
such intervention did more to support the increased assault on the civil
rights of slaves than to restore them.

Although slaves were deprived of the vote, that is not the main point
in this count. Virtually all laboring classes of Europe were similarly
denied and so were most free blacks in the North. Even after the "Great
Reform" of 1832, all but the most prosperous tenth of the British
laboring classes were still denied the right to vote. Only in America were
masses of free workers allowed to join in the electoral processes. To the
political leaders of Europe, including the abolitionists, such extreme
republicanism was considered revolutionary and destabilizing. Nevertheless, from the mid-eighteenth century on, laboring classes in Europe
were gradually permitted to enter the civility, to influence the course of
government. Even though disfranchised, they were permitted to form
organizations that advanced their interests, to agitate for change, and to
demonstrate. Despite their official proscription between 1795 and 1815,
British urban and rural laborers engaged in food strikes and other illegal
forms of action. Although never officially sanctioned, these protests were
nevertheless accepted, especially at the local level, as forms of expression
to which governments had to respond. The slave South, however, never
closed its eyes to any form of collective action by slaves but treated even
rumors of impending protests as occasions for brutal repression. Southern ruling circles never had any intention of allowing slaves to have the
slightest role in the civility. Quite the contrary, after 1830 changes in
state and local laws as well as new judicial decisions were directed toward
buttressing the principle that slaves were utterly and permanently de-
barred in every manner possible from a role in law and government.
American slaves had none of the common-law rights of the disfranchised
free workers in Europe, or even rights of the type enjoyed by slaves in
the ecclesiastical courts of the Spanish colonies. As far as citizenship was
concerned, they had not even a shadow of it. They were merely a peculiar
form of property.[25]

Denial of cultural self-identification is the fourth count in the new
indictment. It might seem odd to include this point as a major count when
some slavery historians are currently emphasizing the cultural autonomy
of slaves. Yet it would be unfortunate and misleading if current research
aimed at defining slave culture and at revealing the role of slaves in

shaping that culture served to mitigate the condemnation of southern and West Indian masters for their ceaseless attempts to achieve cultural domination. The demonstration that slaves were able to retain certain African customs, to modify the content of the European religions that they embraced, to exercise some independence in the use of their leisure time, and to produce songs and folktales that embodied their views and aspirations should not be interpreted to mean that masters conceded cultural independence to their slaves. Nor does it mean that masters failed in their cultural objectives.

The central cultural objective of the masters was the creation of a new kind of worker, well suited to serve as a cog in the large-scale systems of production (the agribusinesses) that they were building. This objective required neither the extinction of every African carryover nor the extinction of every cultural expression that sprang from the experiences of native-born slaves. It was not prudent for masters to repress every aspect of slave culture but only those aspects that masters viewed as inimical to their grand designs. In this respect masters were similar to the men who developed the factory system; manufacturers also sought to transform the individualistic culture of rural laborers into a new culture of collective discipline. However, the cultural domination of the masters went far beyond that of the factory owners. Factory owners focused primarily on the workplace, leaving considerable latitude for workers to develop their own religious organizations, fraternal organizations, educational institutions, publications, and eventually unions and their own political organizations. Opportunities for the development of an independent group culture were far greater for free laborers than for slaves. Even the free blacks of the antebellum era, so deeply victimized by racism, were able to establish their own churches and benevolent organizations, to initiate a literature, to establish a press, and to become independent factors in the struggle against slavery and discrimination.[26]

The work of cultural historians in delineating the areas in which slaves were able to influence their culture has indirectly emphasized the extent to which the masters were successful in their incessant campaigns for cultural domination, especially in the United States. Thus, although it has been shown that southern slaves were able to influence the style of their religious rituals and to infuse them with greater elements of magic than their masters probably preferred, the degree of cultural autonomy implied by these findings should not be exaggerated. Especially after 1830 many masters supervised the religious activities of slaves, hiring preachers to instruct them or bringing their slaves to the churches to which they were affiliated. Such slaves were not free to abandon Christianity in favor of infidel religions or even to subscribe to Christian churches of a denomination different from that of the master.

Similarly, the emergence of an Afro-American sexual and family ethic does not imply that slaves fully controlled their family structure or their sexual lives. Not only were some slaves prevented from forming families altogether, but some forms of family organization that slaves sought to carry over from their native cultures were condemned by masters and missionaries alike.[27]

Perhaps the most important point that has emerged from the work of cultural historians is the intimate connection between political power and culture. As long as slaves were subjected to virtually unrestrained personal domination, were denied citizenship, and were highly constrained in economic opportunity, they were unlikely to achieve a large degree of cultural self-identification. The relative speed with which independent class cultures emerged among free urban workers, and the more or less rapid politicization of these cultures, is a measure of the moral advantage of free labor systems over slavery. The explosive growth of black churches, businesses, political clubs, and fraternal organizations after the Civil War mirrored working-class experiences in Europe and underscores the immense importance of freedom (even the "half" freedom of a thwarted Reconstruction) for the development of black cultural self-identification.

How does the new indictment compare with the one fashioned by the leaders of the antislavery movement? In the introduction I suggested one difference: The new indictment is more consistent with the known facts about slavery than is the abolitionist indictment. Another difference is the consistency of the four counts in the new indictment with each other; in the abolitionist indictment many of the counts were mutually inconsistent because they were the product of competing factions. Consider, for example, the moral assessment of the profitability of slavery. Some abolitionists condemned the system because the men who ran it earned large profits through the cruel exploitation of its laborers. Others condemned the system because the men who ran it were willing to sacrifice profits in order to feed their passion for domination. Similarly, some antislavery leaders condemned the system because the cost of slave labor (in maintenance, etc.) was far greater than that of free labor; but others condemned slavery because the food, clothing, and shelter provided to slaves were greatly inferior to those free laborers enjoyed.[28]

These inconsistencies imply that the new indictment would not have been universally hailed by antislavery leaders. Nevertheless, I believe that the first count, unlimited personal domination, would have been embraced by virtually every leader of the antislavery struggle: by evangelical abolitionists and by the political ones; by British abolitionists and by the Americans; by the radical abolitionists who believed that free blacks should have all the civil rights of free whites and by those racist abolitionists who believed that every black should be exported to Africa. It is on the other three counts that deep divisions would have arisen among antislavery leaders.

The second count of the new indictment, denial of economic opportunity for slaves, would have been rejected by most of the British antislavery leaders and would have divided the Americans. To the generality of British abolitionists, economic opportunity for the lower classes, slave or free, had no real meaning. They believed that the inability of the poor to curb their sexual passions caused population growth to outrun the food supply so that wages always sank toward the level of subsistence. Poverty was the inevitable fate of the lower classes, their misery caused by their own improvidence. To most British abolitionists, therefore, economic opportunity for the laboring classes, free or slave, was a demagogic cry raised only by radicals who sought to overthrow the established order.[29]

The majority of American antislavery leaders would also have rejected the second count, but their reason for doing so would have been quite different. Americans did not accept the pessimistic theory that an iron law of wages foreclosed economic opportunity to the common man. Quite the contrary, they celebrated the free labor system as one that richly rewarded "honest industry and toil"[30] and that gave the working man a wide range of opportunities for economic and social advancement. Every northern working man had it within his power to become a person of property and standing, to become, in the words of James G. Birney, a member of an "honest yeomanry."[31] The bright future was guaranteed by the rich virgin lands of the West which constituted "a mighty theater for enterprise" and a "vast empire in the process of rapid development."[32]

The main threat to the economic independence and comfort of northern free labor did not come from uncontrolled sexual passions, although abolitionists worried about that too, but from southern masters and their slaves. Southern masters coveted western lands and, if they had their way, it would be slaves rather than free men who occupied them. Antislavery candidates promised to thwart the designs of the Slave Power. They promised their white electorate that they would preserve the public domain for whites alone. This position was not purely expedient. Many Republican candidates, including some of the most radical leaders of the party, detested blacks. They were quite sincere when they assured voters that as "true Republicans" they "cared nothing for the nigger" and that the aim of the Republican party was to "make 'white labor respectable and honorable' by keeping Negroes, free and slave, out of the West."[33] Since the Republican party was a coalition it also had leaders who resisted popular prejudices and who sought to align the party with the struggle to widen the civil rights of free blacks. They campaigned against

northern laws that excluded out-of-state blacks and for the right of blacks
to education in public schools. But only a minority of antislavery leaders,
some of whom refused to join the Republican party, such as William
Garrison and Gerrit Smith, stood for full racial equality and vigorously
advocated full economic opportunity for blacks, including equal voting
rights and equal access to jobs and lands.[34]

The third count, denial of citizenship, would also have divided antislavery leaders. Certainly the pro-colonization men in the Republican
party would have had no truck with it. As late as March 1862 the
majority of Republicans in the Senate voted to subsidize the colonization
of freedmen. Five months later Lincoln called a group of black leaders
to the White House to enlist their support for colonization. Arguing that
racial differences created insuperable barriers to citizenship for blacks,
and noting the terrible injustices that blacks had suffered at white hands
and the white blood being shed in the Civil War on their behalf, Lincoln
called on the black leaders "to make clear to their people that removal
was the only solution." Those who refused to leave the country, he
continued, were taking "an extremely selfish view of the case." This
speech led Frederick Douglass to criticize the president for "his inconsistencies, his pride of race and blood, his contempt for negroes and his
canting hypocrisy."[35] Even Republicans who deemphasized colonization
argued vigorously for the sharp restriction of the civil rights of free
blacks. During the election campaign of 1858 David Davis, friend of
Lincoln and one of his advisers, urged Republican candidates to "em-
phatically disavow *negro suffrage,* negroes holding office, serving on ju-
ries and the like."[36]

It was only the more radical antislavery leaders such as the followers
of Garrison, Birney, and Gerrit Smith who staunchly demanded full
citizenship for free blacks. "If the professed friends of the colored people
avoid social intercourse" with blacks, said Birney in the early 1840s,
"only because they are colored disregarding their individual intelligence
and moral worth—their professions will be suspected—their sincerity
will not be trusted in, and all hold on their confidence for good will be
lost." Such views led Birney to join with Garrison in denouncing the
program of the American Colonization Society. But the poor showing of
the Liberty party and the need to forge a broader antislavery coalition
eventually led some, but not all, of the more radical abolitionists of the
1840s to retreat in the 1850s. While continuing to reject the racist
principles of the Colonization Society, Birney reluctantly concluded in
1850 that the white electorate harbored such deep and violent prejudices
"that exodus to Liberia might prove after all the wisest course for American Negroes."[37] Only such radicals as Garrison, Smith, and Lydia Maria

Child remained adamant defenders of the civil rights of free blacks. As Smith put it, the continued repression of the rights of free blacks in the North gave "the greatest efficiency to the main argument for justifying slavery." Consequently, the struggle for the civil rights of northern blacks had to be "an integral part of the antislavery movement."[38] Such views found reflection within the Republican party, and had an influence on party policies in those constituencies in which abolitionist theology was most influential, but the negrophobic position remained predominant.

The position of British abolitionists on the civil rights of freedmen was more liberal than that of the pro-colonization wing of the Republican party but less liberal than the position of the Garrisonians. They could not subscribe to the Garrisonian view because it implied a degree of republicanism that nearly the entire British gentry viewed as an invitation to chaos. Indeed, many British liberals believed that America was courting disaster by giving suffrage to the laboring masses. "The time will come," said Thomas Babington Macaulay in the mid-1850s, when "New England will be as thickly peopled as Old England," when "wages will be as low, and will fluctuate as much with you as with us," and "hundreds of thousands of artisans" will be "out of work." Then, he warned, Americans would finally realize that they needed agencies that could "suppress the rancorous, unemployed mechanics" and they would regret their decision to extend "the ballot" and "political power" to "the unwashed multitude." When that day came, "the American nation would fall into anarchy or into despotism, but freedom would not survive." With such fearful visions of the consequences that would flow from an extension of full citizenship to free laborers, British abolitionists could hardly have endorsed full citizenship for ex-slaves. On the other hand, they were insistent that ex-slaves should have the same common-law rights that free laborers had long enjoyed in England. So they carefully monitored the conditions of freedmen in the colonies, demanding justice for them in the courts and campaigning against novel efforts by planters to use vagrancy laws and other devices that whittled away at their citizenship.[39]

The fourth count, denial of cultural self-identification, would have found few supporters even among the radical abolitionists. Despite their revulsion over personal domination, which was at the heart of their hatred of slavery, they were not pure libertarians. As we have seen, both British and American abolitionists could countenance, and in the British case could collaborate in, repressing the freedom of those who attacked institutions and principles they valued. They were cultural elitists and religious crusaders who believed that they had not only the right but the duty to bring their culture and their religion to the "backward" masses in order to save them from damnation.

Although the leaders of the American abolitionist societies wanted people to be free and to act as their own moral agents, their concepts of freedom had anti-individualistic strains and often countenanced compulsion to achieve moral ends. Many drew a distinction between "liberty" and "license," supporting liberty but crusading against license. To them freedom meant the opportunity to "exercise the virtuous part of their nature: it allowed no latitude for evil conduct—it was not freedom to sin." In this view liberty required the "suppression of ungodly passions." The suppression of sin "was a precondition to genuine social order, to a state in which humans could come together out of love and sympathy rather than out of force and base motives."[40] Although they were "zealous advocate[s] of moral suasion," they also believed in using legislation to compel rectitude from "incorrigible transgressors."[41]

These generalizations, of course, need to be modified to take account of the differences that existed among even the most pious abolitionists. The pacifism of the British Quakers led them to break with the majority of British abolitionists who supported the use of force to suppress the slave trade. The Quakers also objected to the lifting of tariffs on sugar because it would stimulate slavery in Cuba and Brazil. Garrison estranged himself from many fellow abolitionists by embracing a "Christian anarchism" that led him to denounce both formal church organizations and civil government on the grounds that human beings should be ruled only "by God's law and not by earthly legislators." Yet Garrisonians compromised their pacifism in the 1850s, supporting John Brown's raid and justifying slave insurrections "against their tyrant masters" as a legitimate means of achieving "complete enfranchisement." Although initially appalled by the carnage that would be unleashed by a civil war, the Garrisonians eventually rallied to "the Union cause, especially after the Emancipation Proclamation turned the war (however begrudgingly) into a struggle against slavery."[42]

Despite their denunciation of institutional power, and even war, Garrison and his followers were prepared to use both when the end was just. Ultimately, it was an inner sense of justice that governed abolitionist behavior and fired their zeal. No individual who violated their inner sense of righteousness was immune from their wrath, no institution that stood in the way of the deliverance from their definition of evil was sacrosanct. It was that deep conviction that they alone knew the true road to righteousness that led Garrisonians to excoriate abolitionists who differed from them in either tactics or ultimate objectives. Garrison's bitter denunciation of his erstwhile protégé and ally, Frederick Douglass, led Harriet Beecher Stowe to despair. "Is there but one true anti-slavery church," she asked Garrison, "and all others infidels?"[43]

British and American abolitionists were not only zealous evangelicals; they were also enthnocentrics who viewed Anglo-Saxon culture (in their British and northern versions) as the pinnacle of civilization. Wilberforce and his fellow "saints" took it as a duty to bring their civilization to the "backward" peoples of the world. They criticized West Indian planters, not because they were cultural imperialists who sought to impose English values on Africans, but because of their failure to do so. They did not want to preserve African languages and religions, but wanted to replace them with the English language and with the Protestant religions. They believed that cultures that differed significantly from theirs were backward and in need of reform. In this respect the "saints" were as intolerant of ancient Hindu society as of the slave societies in the New World, and they used their influence in high government circles to press for anglicization of the Indian subcontinent. They promoted the English missionary movement worldwide, not merely to save souls, but to carry English values to "less civilized" peoples everywhere.[44] American abolitionists did not canvass the entire world but they, too, felt the obligation of bringing Anglo-Saxon culture to "the unenlightened blacks." Even as keen an advocate of racial toleration as Gerrit Smith, who gloried in the charge that he was "a colored man," felt called upon "to fund missionary ventures to supervise 'dwarfed' blacks so that their 'undisciplined' qualities might be eradicated."[45]

Some antislavery leaders would have objected to the new indictment as much for what it excludes as for what it includes. Some would have deplored the lack of emphasis on the physical mistreatment of slaves and would have been aghast at my contention that with respect to food, clothing, and shelter free labor systems had no clear-cut moral advantage prior to 1860, and perhaps for the whole nineteenth century. They would have decried my failure to emphasize the sexual abuses of slaves and the destructive effects of the slave trade on the integrity of slave families.[46]

I recognize that there is a case for stressing such charges, but in light of the recent scholarship on servile and free laborers during the eighteenth and nineteenth centuries, I doubt that a factual account of these matters would lead to a stronger moral indictment of slavery than has already been set forth. The indictment is not advanced by insisting that the food, clothing, and shelter of slaves must have been worse than those of free laborers when so much recent scholarship indicates that northern economic growth during the 1840s and 1850s was purchased at a shocking cost to the health and welfare of urban labor. To become engaged in a debate over the degree of exaggeration in abolitionist charges of

abuse, to dwell on whether more blacks starved under slavery than
during their first several decades of freedom, to become engaged in a
debate over whether illegitimacy rates were higher on southern plantations than in European cities, or to search for measures that can reveal
whether more marriages were thwarted and broken by the personal
decisions of masters or by the impersonal operation of glutted labor
markets is to diminish rather than to emphasize the special horrors of
slavery. Even worse, exaggerations of the severity of slavery divert
attention from the novel forms of exploitation that replaced it, from the
long period during which the occupational opportunities, the real income, and the life expectations of freed blacks deteriorated, and from
injustices of our own time which are often more a product of recent
policies than a legacy of slavery.[47]

A DILEMMA AND A PARADOX

The antislavery struggle was marked by numerous dilemmas and paradoxes that strained the unity of the movement and frequently led to
conflicts between highly moral men and women who chose different
solutions. I want to describe briefly two of these problems: one a dilemma, the other a paradox. The dilemma arose out of the exigencies of
politics that led leaders of a just cause to compromise principles, join
arms with opportunists, accept immoral propositions, misrepresent their
ideals, disguise their real goals, and deliberately mislead, not for career-
ist advancement or financial gain—although some fell victim to these
temptations—but to strike down an exceedingly evil foe. Time and again
moral crusaders found that they could vanquish sin only by sinning and
thus were repeatedly faced with anguished choices. Some could cope with
this moral stress; others were broken by it.

Impatience was the root of many dilemmas. Moral purity could have
been maintained if the crusaders had been willing to remain a movement
of moral suasion, never compromising principle but doggedly affirming
and broadcasting views they knew to be wholly moral. Yet such a course
was painfully slow. Converts could be won in this way but not rapidly
enough or in sufficient numbers to threaten the continued political sway
of the proslavery coalition. For most antislavery crusaders the impulse
to accelerate the pace of their movement was irresistible. To speed
persuasion they sought to dramatize the evils of slavery and to win
converts on grounds requiring less than full commitment to the abolitionist creed. Although dramatization led not only to exaggeration but also
to deception, the cause was moral and the intention was virtuous. It was
deception that harmed only the slaveholders.[48]

To build coalitions that were wider than their ideological base leaders of the crusade were sometimes forced to disguise their ultimate aims and misrepresent their true beliefs. In 1805 Wilberforce, for example, repudiated the claim that the abolition of the slave trade would harm the economic interests of West Indian planters. Quite the contrary, he argued, it would actually enhance planter profits by forcing them to make timely economic reforms. Yet he later acknowledged that he had hoped and believed that the closing of the trade would serve to destroy slavery. It is ironic that a deceptive claim intended to disarm the proslavery opposition turned out to be true, while the suppressed belief actually held by Wilberforce turned out to be false. Wilberforce voted against a bill to outlaw slavery itself in order to demonstrate that he was not opposed to slavery per se, although he later acknowledged that the total abolition of slavery had been his goal all along.[49]

Deception was usually forced upon abolitionists by turns of events that threatened to undermine support for the antislavery movement. Investigations of economic conditions in the West Indies during the 1840s and 1850s, for example, revealed a withdrawal of labor and sharp declines in the production of sugar following emancipation. This unfortunate news was seized upon by southern propagandists. The West Indian experience, they claimed, showed that emancipation in the United States would have disastrous economic repercussions. Both Northerners and Southerners would suffer when the output of cotton declined, factory hands would be thrown out of work, and consumers would be forced to pay higher prices for clothes. How could this proslavery offensive be met? In Great Britain abolitionists acknowledged that sugar production had declined to just two-thirds of the pre-1833 level (the figures that came from official inquiries could hardly have been denied by abolitionist MPs) but they argued that it was the inability of the planters to cope with free labor markets rather than emancipation that was to blame. Although neither the planters nor the officials of the Colonial Office found this argument persuasive, the abolitionists remained adamant. They were unwilling to concede that a properly run free labor system could be less productive than a slave system.

In America the abolitionists avoided the issues of causes by flatly denying that there had been declines in productivity. Such claims, according to Lewis Tappan, were based on "fabricated and false information" concocted by the United States Consul in Jamaica in order to misrepresent the progress of emancipation in the British West Indies. Ralph Waldo Emerson simply ignored the statistics and managed to see an "unparalleled increase in prosperity that had come to the West Indies since emancipation," so much so that in his mind the West Indies had begun to resemble the North. He could almost hear "the throb of the factory" and "the whistle of the railroad." Even Garrison succumbed to the deception, citing figures on just one West Indian island in which sugar production was greater in 1854 than it had been in 1833 (there were a total of two such islands), in order to claim that "emancipation had universally proven a great success."[50]

Few issues were more troublesome or more deeply divisive in abolitionist circles than the decision to build an antislavery coalition solely on opposition to the extension of slavery into the territories. This was the one issue that appeared capable of corralling enough northern votes to wrest control of the federal government from the proslavery coalition. The strategy had the great advantage of shifting the onus of aggression from the abolitionists to the slaveholders. It was not abolitionists who sought to destroy slavery in the South, but slaveholders coveting northern land who sought to destroy the freedom of northern farmers by reducing them to levels of poverty worse than slavery, just as they had done to southern whites. To radical abolitionists such as Gerrit Smith this strategy represented a betrayal of principle. It made the main issue not the emancipation of slaves, but the protection of the rights of whites. Not only did it explicitly concede the constitutional right of slaveholders to maintain their system where it already existed, but it fed the negrophobic passions of the great majority of northern whites.[51]

Few radical abolitionists took seriously the contention that the North was on the brink of invasion by slaveholders. Nor did they accept the view that slavery could be destroyed merely by banning it from the territories, that it would wither and die unless it could expand beyond its existing borders. None of the principal leaders of the South had advocated the extension of slavery into the northwestern territories; such leaders as Jefferson Davis rejected the claim as "absurd"; and the failure of many slaveowners to move beyond the 40th parallel in Missouri, even though it had been legal since 1820 to do so, clearly indicated that slaves were too valuable in the South to be sent in any significant numbers into regions unsuited for the gang system. During the 1850s the large-scale migration into Missouri was purely a white phenomenon. Far from moving into the border states, slaves were leaving them for the deep South.[52]

To some radical abolitionists, then, the Republican call to resistance of the Slave Power in the territories smacked of sheer opportunism. It was a cry to oppose slavery "where it is not" instead of "where it is."[53] They suspected that those who called only for resistance in the territories were more interested in preventing free blacks from competing with whites for western lands than in striking a death blow at slavery. The nonextension rhetoric seemed far more likely to feed the popular prejudices against blacks than to promote their civil rights. Critics like Lydia Maria Child believed that without a concurrent campaign for the civil rights of blacks in the North, emancipation would be a sham: "Every-thing *must* go wrong, if there is no heart or conscience on the subject."[54] She was right, of course. Yet without pandering to northern negrophobia, the antislavery coalition would surely have lost the 1860 election. As it was, Lincoln just barely squeezed through. The antislavery forces were caught on the horns of a genuine dilemma. Although the negrophobic strategy undoubtedly contributed to patterns of discrimination that still plague the nation, the alternative—an indefinite continuation of slav-ery—was far more evil.[55] The radical program was unattainable. Under the conditions of 1860, rigid adherence to the purest abolitionist princi-ples, unwillingness to join hands with opportunists, and squeamishness over deceptive tactics would have led the antislavery forces to certain defeat.

The paradox turns on the relationship between economic or techno-logical progress and ethical goals. It came to light shortly after the emancipation of British slaves but was studiously avoided by antislavery leaders and has not yet been adequately confronted. It plagued the movement for moral reform in antebellum times and it still haunts moral movements today. Abolitionist leaders in both the United States and Great Britain, as we have seen, refused to admit that the gang system could be technically more efficient than a free labor system, or that emancipation led to a decline in labor productivity. Their refusal to acknowledge the abundant evidence on this decline, their evasive re-sponses to the charge, and their sometimes transparent deceptions un-dermined their claims to moral integrity and provided their foes with powerful propaganda against the antislavery cause.[56]

Why were abolitionists so reluctant to admit that productivity had deteriorated after emancipation? Several considerations were undoubt-edly involved. The free market principles to which they subscribed led them to expect emancipation to improve economic conditions. Since this expectation had been raised to the level of a certainty during the public and parliamentary campaigns for emancipation, an admission of error could have undermined their political credibility and interfered with efforts to promote emancipation in other slave societies. Many abolition-ists no doubt believed that matters would eventually turn around. Yet as year after year passed without a return to prosperity, some reassess-ment was surely in order. The attempt to place the blame on planter incompetence also wore thin with time. Convincing as that argument might originally have been, it could not have remained convincing to those who studied the findings of the parliamentary investigation, the reports of the Colonial Office, or the speeches of abolitionists who visited the colonies and criticized the freedmen for their idleness. If it were merely the ineptness of the planters, more experienced capitalists should have rushed in to take over plantations that could have been purchased for a fraction of their former price. Yet British capitalists were unwilling to pour their money into either plantations or the various railroad schemes that colonial legislatures tried to promote. Political cynicism? Deception as the lesser evil? Perhaps for a time, perhaps by some. Yet the belief that emancipation was bringing, or bound to bring, prosperity was held with too much conviction by too many righteous people to make cynicism or expediency a sufficient explanation.

The tenacity with which abolitionists clung to the contention that emancipation was bringing prosperity, despite all the contrary evidence, strongly suggests that they were swayed by a theory which told them that their expectation of prosperity had to be correct, a theory to which they were so deeply committed that their theoretical knowledge swept aside all empirical evidence to the contrary. There was, of course, such a theory, or more appropriately, a theological proposition, in the evangelical creed. That was the proposition that divine Providence rewarded virtue and punished evil. The proposition continues to be widely accepted today not only among Protestant evangelicals, but also among individuals with highly secular philosophies. The secular version is embodied in a nontheistic optimism that "events" reward virtue and punish evil. Whether theological or secular in origin this optimistic theory implies that immoral economic systems cannot be productive, for that would reward evil, and moral systems cannot be unproductive, for that would punish virtue. The theory operates in two directions. If something is known to be evil, it cannot work well (slavery must have been inefficient; capitalism is bound to die of its internal economic contradictions; totalitarian societies must be less productive than democratic societies). Alternatively, systems that fail must be evil (the French Revolution proves that the ancien régime was economically corrupt; the overthrow of slave systems proves their economic backwardness; the incidents at Three Mile Island and at Chernobyl prove not only the danger but the immorality of nuclear energy programs).

The time has come to resolve the paradox, to cut the tie between economic success (or failure) and moral virtue (or evil). A quarter century of research on the economics of slavery has demonstrated that no such connection exists. Slavery was profitable, efficient, and economically viable in both the United States and the West Indies when it was destroyed, but it was never morally good. Slavery did not die because either divine Providence or "events" ensure that evil systems cannot work. Its death was an act of "econocide," a political execution of an immoral system at its peak of economic success, incited by men ablaze with moral fervor. Slavery deserved to die despite its profitability and efficiency because it served an immoral end. Efficiency is not a synonym for good and it is a disservice to the struggle for a moral society to make it a synonym. During the early years of World War II there was no more perfect example of human efficiency, or a more perfect symbol of evil, than the Nazi Wehrmacht that swept across Europe like a flawless machine.

In and of itself, economic or technological efficiency is neither moral nor immoral. The virtue of an efficient technique depends exclusively on its moral nature or the moral purposes that it serves. One need not be an evangelical Protestant or a pious believer of any other formal religion to agree that moral values, rather than economic, political, or scientific achievements, are the supreme guides for human behavior. When we celebrate such technological advances as the blast furnace, electricity, and medical surgery it is not because they are intrinsically good but because they have usually served well the great ethical goals of human-kind. Nevertheless, each of these innovations has been used at various times for demonic ends. Slavery was a somewhat different case. It was intrinsically evil because its productive efficiency arose directly out of the oppression of its laborers. The efficiency of slavery seemed paradoxical not because an intrinsically good or a morally neutral technology was made to serve an evil purpose, but because an intrinsically evil technol-ogy was so productive. Discarding the assumption that productivity is necessarily virtuous resolves the paradox.

THE MORAL PROBLEM OF THE CIVIL WAR

For more than a century historians have been engaged in an intense debate about the causes of the Civil War. Although some scholars have held that slavery was *the* cause, others have developed complex analyses that draw distinctions between immediate and ultimate causes and that explore a variety of ways other than war that could have settled or at least contained the issue of slavery. They have also analyzed a wide range of economic, political, and cultural issues between the sections other than slavery that promoted antagonisms and that rival slavery (some believe they dominate it) as an explanation for the war. Among the most nagging of the moral questions to emerge from these debates is the one posed by David M. Potter, who, until his death in 1971, was one of the most respected historians of his generation.

In totaling up the balance sheet of the Civil War, Potter concluded: "Slavery was dead; secession was dead; and six hundred thousand men were dead."[57] So one soldier died for six slaves who were freed and for ten white Southerners who were kept in the Union. In the face of so bloody a war, a "person is entitled to wonder," said Potter, "whether the Southerners could have been held and the slaves could not have been

freed at a smaller per-capita cost."[58] When he posed this problem it was
still widely believed that slavery was an economically moribund system
and the proposition that economic forces would eventually have solved
the problem of slavery was tenable. Even so, there was a question of how
soon. And if not, there was a question of when, if ever, southern slaveholders would have peacefully acceded to any scheme for emancipation,
no matter how gradual, no matter how full the proffered compensation.

Whatever the opportunity for a peaceful abolition of slavery along
British lines before 1845, it surely was nonexistent after that date. To
southern slaveholders, West Indian emancipation was a complete failure.
It provided undeniable proof, if any was needed, of the malevolent
designs that the abolitionists and their allies harbored for their class.
They could plainly see that the economy of the West Indies was in
shambles, that the personal fortunes of the West Indian planters had
collapsed, and that the assurances made to these planters in 1833 to
obtain their acquiescence to compensated emancipation were violated as
soon as the planters were reduced to political impotency. Given such an
assessment of the consequences of compensated emancipation, a peaceful end to slavery could only have been achieved if economic forces made
slaves worthless or, more compelling, an absolute drain on the income
of their owners.[59]

From the mid-1840s on, however, the slave economy of the South
was vigorous and growing rapidly. Whatever the pessimism of masters
during the economic crises of 1826–1831 and 1840–1845, during the
last half of the 1840s and most of the 1850s they foresaw a continuation
of their prosperity and, save for the political threat from the North,
numerous opportunities for its expansion. The main thrust of cliometric
research has demonstrated that this economic optimism was well-
founded; it has also undermined the competing thesis that slavery was
gradually expiring of its own internal economic contradictions. Although
he presented it in a political rather than an economic context, Stampp's
rejoinder to Potter is equally germane here. A "person is also entitled
to ask," he said, "how many more generations of black men should have
been forced to endure life in bondage in order to avoid its costly and
violent end."[60]

After the election of Lincoln the choices open to northern foes of
slavery no longer included the moderate strategy—which was to restrict
and gradually undermine the slave economy as the British abolitionists
had done between 1812 and 1833, and as the Brazilian abolitionists were
able to do in the 1880s. Once the cotton states of the South moved on
to the secessionist path, peaceful restoration of the Union was no longer
possible merely by returning to the status quo of c. 1850, even if the
rights of slaveholders everywhere below 36°30' and of their property

rights in fugitives were embodied in new, irrevocable amendments to the Constitution, as was proposed in the Crittenden Resolutions. The majority of the Senate and House members from these states rejected all such compromises. They were convinced that northern hostility to slavery precluded a union that would promote the economic, political, and international objectives that had become predominant among politicians of the cotton South. As the votes for the delegates to the state convention indicated, by early 1861 majority opinion in the deep South held that a future in the Union "promised nothing but increasingly galling economic exploitation by the dominant section and the rapid reduction of the South to political impotence."[61]

So the central moral problem of the Civil War is not the one posed by Potter but the one posed in Stampp's response to him. By early 1861 maintenance of peace required not merely northern acquiescence to the status quo of c.1850, but acquiescence to the existence of an independent confederacy dedicated to the promotion of slavery. It follows that assessment of the dilemma posed by Stampp requires more than weighing the sin of slavery against the sin of war. It requires also a consideration of the likely chain of events that would have unfolded if the South had been unshackled from northern restraint and allowed to become a worldwide champion of slavery and of aristocratic republicanism.

Consideration of what might have happened if the Confederate states had been allowed to secede peacefully is an excursion into beliefs about a world that never existed. Even if these beliefs are based on patterns of behavior during the years leading up to the war, patterns of behavior that provide a reasonable basis for prediction, the best predictions are necessarily shrouded in uncertainty and open to debate. Yet there is no way of dealing with the moral issues of the Civil War that avoids these "counterfactual propositions" (as philosophers call them). Every historian who has set out to deal with the causes of the Civil War (certainly all those who have debated its necessity or avoidability) has implicitly or explicitly presumed what would have happened to slavery if some events had unfolded in a way that was different from the actual course. Indeed, much of the voluminous literature on the causes of the Civil War is nothing more or less than a marshaling of evidence on the events leading up to the Civil War that is dictated by different visions of this counterfactual world.

Peaceful secession, I believe, would not only have indefinitely delayed the freeing of U.S. slaves but would have thwarted the antislavery movement everywhere else in the world. It would also very likely have slowed down the struggle to extend suffrage and other democratic rights to the lower classes in Europe, and it might have eroded whatever rights had already been granted to them in both Europe and North

America. Since the forces of reaction everywhere would have been greatly encouraged, and those of democracy and reform demoralized, it is likely that the momentum for liberal reform would have been replaced by a drive for aristocratic privilege under the flags of paternalism and the preservation of order.

Such a vision of events may seem fantastic to those accustomed to the rhetoric and conventions of modern (plebeian) democracy. We live in a world in which the underprivileged regularly contend for power: abroad, through labor and socialist parties; at home, through such influential organizations as the AFL-CIO, NOW, and the Rainbow Coalition. However, during the 1850s and 1860s democracy as we now know it, and lower-class rights generally, hung in the balance throughout the Western world. In Great Britain the great majority of workers were disfranchised, trade unions were illegal, strikes were criminal acts, and quitting a job without an employer's permission was a breach of contract punishable by stiff fines and years of imprisonment. The legacy of serfdom was heavy in Portugal, Spain, Italy, eastern Prussia, Russia, Hungary, the Balkans, Turkey, and much of South America, while slavery flourished in Cuba, Brazil, Surinam, Africa, the Middle East, and numerous other places. Even in the North, strikes were proscribed, property qualifications for voting were widespread until the 1820s (and were still enforced against free blacks in New York and other states in the 1860s), and vagrancy laws were a powerful club against workers. The movement for the disfranchisement of the foreign born was partially successful in some northern states during the 1850s, and in Virginia a referendum to reinstitute a property qualification for voters was approved on the eve of the Civil War.[62]

The fact that the liberals who dominated politics in the North and in Britain rejected slavery as a solution to the menace posed by an unconstrained lower-class "rabble" does not mean that they were oblivious to the menace. Reformers such as Lord Macaulay remained adamant in the opinion that the franchise had to be restricted to men of property and that a large police force and army were needed to keep the lower classes in check. Even such a celebrated champion of the propertyless masses as Horace Greeley supported the use of military force to put down strikes.[63]

If the Confederacy had been allowed to establish itself peacefully, to work out economic and diplomatic policies, and to develop international alliances, it would have emerged as a major international power. Although its population was relatively small, its great wealth would have made it a force to be reckoned with. The Confederacy would probably have used its wealth and military power to establish itself as the dominant nation in Latin America, perhaps annexing Cuba and Puerto Rico,

Yucatan, and Nicaragua as well as countering Britain's antislavery pressures on Brazil.[64] Whether the Confederacy would have sought to counter British antislavery policies in Africa or to form alliances with the principal slave-trading nations of the Middle East is more uncertain, but these would have been options.

The Confederacy could have financed its expansionist, proslavery policies by exploiting the southern monopoly of cotton production. A 5¢ sales tax on cotton not only would have put most of the burden of such policies on foreign consumers, but would have yielded about $100 million annually during the 1860s—50 percent more than the entire federal budget on the eve of the Civil War. With such a revenue the Confederacy could have emerged as one of the world's strongest military powers, maintaining a standing army several times as large as the North's, rapidly developing a major navy, and conducting an aggressive foreign policy. Such revenues would also have permitted it to covertly or overtly finance aristocratic forces in Europe who were vying with democratic ones for power across the Continent.

Shrewd manipulation of its monopoly of raw cotton would have permitted the Confederacy to reward its international friends and punish its enemies. Embargoes or other restrictions on the sale of raw cotton could have delivered punishing blows to the economies of England and the Northeast, where close to 20 percent of the nonagricultural labor force was directly or indirectly engaged in the manufacture and sale of cotton textiles. The resulting unemployment and losses of wealth would have disrupted both the labor and capital markets in these regions, and probably speeded up the emergence of a large textile industry in the South. The West would also have been destabilized economically, since the decline of the Northeast would have severely contracted the market for western agricultural products. As the Confederacy shifted more of its labor into manufacturing, trade, and the military, it would probably have developed an increasing deficit in food, making it again a major market for the grain, dairy, and meat surpluses of the Northwest.

Such economic developments would have generated strong political pressures in the North for a modus vivendi with the Confederacy. Northern politics would have been further complicated by any border states, such as Maryland, Kentucky, and Missouri, that might have remained inside the Union. Attempts to appropriate their slave property would have run a high risk of further secessions. The Republicans not only would have borne the responsibility for the economic crisis created by the rise of the Confederacy, but would have lost the plank on which the party had risen to power. With the bulk of slaveowners prohibited from entry into northern territories because of secession, the claim that the victory by the Republican party was the only way of saving these lands

for free labor would have been an empty slogan to farmers and nonagricultural workers who were suffering from the effects of a severe and
extended depression. Moreover, the failure of the North to act against
the slaveholders who remained within the Union would have undermined
its credibility with democratic forces abroad. Such developments would
probably have delivered both a lasting blow to antislavery politics and
an enormous fillip to nativist politics.[65]

I do not maintain that the preceding sketch of what might have
happened in the absence of a civil war is the only plausible one. However, it is a credible sketch of the likely train of events, one that is
consistent with what we now know about the capacity of the slave
economy of the South as well as with current knowledge of the political
crosscurrents in the South, the North, and the rest of the world. At the
very least, it points to reasons for doubting that there was a happy,
relatively costless solution to the moral dilemma posed by Stampp.

I have not, it should be emphasized, put forward the gloomiest view
of the alternative to the Civil War. The preceding sketch suggests an
indefinite but more or less peaceful continuation of slavery. It would not
be difficult to make a case for the proposition that peaceful secession
would merely have postponed the Civil War and that the delay would
have created circumstances far more favorable to a southern victory. In
that case aristocratic proslavery forces would have gained unchallenged
control of the richest and potentially the most powerful nation in the
world. Such an outcome not only would have greatly increased the
likelihood of rolling back the movement for working-class rights everywhere, but might have led to a loss of human lives far greater than the
toll of the Civil War.

As pacifists, Garrison and his followers had to confront the dilemma
posed by a violent confrontation with the Confederacy. They reluctantly
came to the conclusion that bloody as it might be, the Civil War was the
only realistic way of ridding the world of slavery. William E. Channing,
who had hoped against hope that slavery could be ended by moral
suasion alone, explained why the destruction of slavery was the moral
imperative of his age. "Slavery must fall," he said, "because it stands
in direct hostility to all the grand movements, principles, and reforms
of our age, because it stands in the way of an advancing world."[66]

What the Civil War achieved, then, was more than just inflated
wealth for northern capitalists and "half" freedom for blacks ("the
shoddy aristocracy of the North and the ragged children of the South").
It preserved and reinforced conditions favorable to a continued struggle
for the democratic rights of the lower classes, black and white alike, and
for the improvement of their economic condition, not only in America

but everywhere else in the world. The fall of slavery did not usher in the millennium, it produced no heaven on earth, but it vitalized all the grand movements, principles, and reforms of Channing's age and of our own.

ACKNOWLEDGMENTS

I have often been asked which of the ideas in *Time on the Cross* I was responsible for and which ideas were Engerman's. Between mid-1971 (when we began to write that manuscript) and July 1973 (when the last part was sent to the publisher) Engerman and I interacted so intensely and continually that it is impossible for me to distill our separate contributions. Since 1974 we have collaborated on scores of projects and papers dealing with the economics and demography of slavery, with slave culture, and with related topics whose findings are reflected in this book. Engerman also read the penultimate draft of the typescript and made numerous insightful suggestions.

Marilyn Coopersmith, the administrator for our slavery project from 1966 until the present, not only efficiently coordinated the many aspects of data collection and analysis, sometimes personally searching distant archives for useful data, but provided a drive and enthusiasm for the work that infected everybody associated with the project. Perhaps the best assessment of her contribution was the one made by Albert Fishlow in April 1973, when he and Robert Gallman spent a day providing me with their detailed criticisms of a draft of *Time on the Cross*. At the conclusion of our session, deeply appreciative of all that I had learned from their many points, I offered to supply them with copies of our computer tapes, adding that Engerman and I wanted to compete, not by hoarding the data, but by trying to be more thorough in the analysis of them. Fishlow cocked back his head for a moment and said: "Who are you trying to kid, Bob? You know that unless you also give us Marilyn Coopersmith it won't be a fair contest."

A few years ago Arcadius Kahan, my late colleague and close friend, told me that he considered it a privilege to teach students as bright as those we have at the University of Chicago. Under such circumstances teaching is a two-way process and it is far from clear that the students learn more from us than we do from them. Readers of *Evidence and Methods* or of the two volumes of *Technical Papers* can judge for themselves the quality of the contributions of those students who were collaborators on our project during the past two decades. As Engerman and

418

I have emphasized in the introduction to the companion volumes, they were often far ahead of us in recognizing major aspects of the operation of the slave system, in proposing novel approaches to the analysis of data, in discovering new data sets, and in offering probing criticisms.

It has been my good fortune to have had access not only to the pool of talented students at Chicago, but also to those at Rochester and Harvard. In addition to the current and former students whose works are represented in the companion volumes, I acknowledge my indebtedness to Andrea Atkin, Per Boje, Richard Clarke, Arlene Cliff, Fred Dong, Sheryl Dow, Michael Fishman, Thelma Foote, Caroline Ford, Grant Gardner, Eva Hale, Amos Hofman, Harry Holzer, Peter Ireland, John Komlos, Frank Lewis, Forest Nelson, Henry Otto, Hugh Rockoff, Joshua Rosett, Sushama Sabharwal, Kenneth L. Sokoloff, Lawrence Summers, Georgia C. Villaflor, Jenny Bourne Wahl, and James Walker.

Research during the last two-thirds of our project benefited from the vigorous debates touched off in 1974 by the publication of *Time on the Cross*. It was an exchange in which there were no losers. The detailed scrutiny of our preliminary findings pointed up numerous gaps that required additional data or different analytical approaches, and also broadened the range of issues that we investigated. Even after the debates of 1974–1976 died down we continued to benefit from the close reading given to both our published and unpublished papers by participants at numerous faculty colloquia, conferences, and seminars, and from written comments received from those who responded to working papers that were mailed to them.

Although it is not possible to acknowledge all the individuals from whom I learned during these debates, I incurred large debts to John W. Blassingame, Paul A. David, Lance E. Davis, Stephen J. DeCanio, Stefano Fenoaltea, Heywood Fleisig, Eric Foner, Elizabeth Fox-Genovese, John Hope Franklin, Eugene Genovese, the late Herbert Gutman, Thomas L. Haskall, Robert Higgs, Frank Knight, Winthrop D. Jordan, Christopher Lasch, Stanley Lebergott, Rah Lundstrom, Peter McClelland, Donald N. McCloskey, Duncan J. MacLeod, Sidney Mintz, William N. Parker, Roger Ransom, William K. Scarborough, Donald F. Schaefer, Harry Scheiber, Mark Schmitz, Kenneth M. Stampp, Richard Sutch, Peter Temin, Jan de Vries, Maris Vinovskis, Peter Wood, Harold Woodman, Gavin Wright, and Arthur Zilversmit.

A number of scholars provided me with detailed criticisms of the penultimate draft of *Without Consent or Contract* that improved both its content and style. Among these were Thomas A. Alexander, Allan G. Bogue, Jerome M. Clubb, John L. Comaroff, Seymour Drescher, Roderick Floud, Michael P. Fogel, J. David Greenstone, James Grossman, Richard Hellie, Michael F. Holt, Morton Keller, J. Morgan Kousser,

Allan Kulikoff, Arthur Mann, Douglass C. North, Herbert Shapiro, T. W. Schultz, and Thomas Weiss.

Others who commented on various drafts, pointed out errors, clarified conceptual issues, provided unpublished material, or suggested improvements in exposition include Ralph V. Anderson, Jeremy Atack, William O. Aydelotte, Bernard Bailyn, Fred Bateman, E. Van Den Boogaart, John Clive, Cheryll Ann Cody, Michael Craton, Joseph Cropsey, Phillip D. Curtin, David B. Davis, Carl Degler, Richard Dunn, David Eltis, G. R. Elton, Pieter Emmer, Richard Epstein, Elizabeth Field, the late Moses Finley, Enid Fogel, Charlotte Fogel, Ephim Fogel, Steven Fogel, James Foust, Norman Gash, David Geggus, Henry A. Gemery, Alan Green, Joan Hannon, John R. Hanson II, Barry W. Higman, Nathan I. Huggins, John James, David Katzman, Peter Laslett, Russell R. Menard, Sidney W. Mintz, Orlando Patterson, J. R. Pole, Clayne L. Pope, David Roediger, Armstead Robinson, Madelon Rosett, Roger Schofield, Robert W. Selenes, Richard H. Sewell, Richard B. Sheridan, Lee Soltow, George J. Stigler, J. M. Tanner, Howard Temperley, Mary Turner, Larry T. Wimmer, C. Vann Woodward, and E. A. Wrigley.

The editorial work on this volume has been particularly arduous, not only because of the diverse subject matter but because of complexities in connecting the material in this volume with the more technical material in the three companion volumes. The burden of this work was borne by Martha Hoffman, Anthony May, and Barbara Stufflebeem, whose dedication, persistence, and precision made it possible to meet difficult deadlines. The numerous drafts were quickly and efficiently typed by Kathleen Minchello McCauley, Katharine Mittelstadt, Carol Miterko, and Regina Strug.

Funding of the slavery project was made possible by grants from the National Science Foundation, the Ford Foundation, the Exxon Educational Foundation, the Walgreen Foundation, the University of Chicago, the University of Rochester, and Harvard University.

Our search for data was facilitated by officials at the U.S. National Archives, the Library of Congress, the Public Record Office (U.K.), the Library of the Genealogical Society of the Church of Latter-Day Saints, the Virginia Historical Society, the Virginia State Library, the North Carolina State Department of Archives and History, the Perkins Library of Duke University, the South Carolina Department of Archives and History, the Woodruff Library of Emory University, the Alabama Department of Archives and History, the Georgia Historical Society, the University of Alabama Library, the University of Texas Archives, the Southern Historical Collection at the University of North Carolina, the Georgia Department of Archives and History, the South Carolina Historical Society, the South Carolina Library of the University of South Carolina, the

Mississippi Department of Archives and History, the Department of Archives at Louisiana State University, the Widner, Littauer, Tozzer, Countway, and Lamont Libraries of Harvard University, the Regenstein and Crerar Libraries of the University of Chicago, and the Library of the University of Rochester.

I am grateful to the following publishers for their permission to quote text, to reproduce diagrams, and to republish parts of my earlier work or joint work with Stanley L. Engerman (numbers in parentheses refer to the pages in *Without Consent or Contract* on which the material appears): American Economics Association (79); Carnegie Institution of Washington (66, 305); *Journal of Social History* (157–168, 177–181); and W.W. Norton for material which originally appeared in *Time on the Cross* (17–21, 27–28, 30–34, 45, 72–73, 84–87, 94–97, 108–109, 155–156, 345–346, 352–353).

NOTES

ABBREVIATIONS AND CONVENTIONS FOLLOWED IN NOTES

In cross reference to companion volumes of *Without Consent or Contract,* titles are abbreviated to *EM* (*Evidence and Methods*) and *TP* (*Technical Papers*), and are immediately followed by the number of the *EM* entry or *TP* paper cited. Thus,

On the issue of slave occupations see *EM,* #7.

Or,

See Crawford, *TP,* #26, on ex-slave testimony.

Entry and paper numbers appear in the tables of contents to *EM* and *TP*. There are two volumes of *Technical Papers*. The volume titled *Markets and Production* contains papers #1–#16. The volume titled *Conditions of Slave Life and the Transition to Freedom* contains papers #17–#34.

Material reprinted or appearing for the first time in *EM* and *TP* is not listed in the references. Other reprinted sources are listed in notes by reprint date, but the original publication date will be found bracketed in the reference list entry. Sources for quotes in a paragraph will be found at the top of a note, except in rare cases where this would be misleading. Authors with identical last names are cited with initials if they have published in the same year.

FOREWORD: DISCOVERIES AND DILEMMAS

1. See *EM,* #1, on the struggle of American historians to break away from the long reach of the ideological issues produced by the Civil War and the political conflicts that preceded it.

2. Some aspects of the recent literature on slavery are discussed in Chapter 6 of this volume and in *EM,* #1, #14, #15, #16, #23, #32, #36, #70, #73, and #74.

3. Moral tension became acute during the antebellum era not because slavery failed as an economic system, but because it worked extremely well. If, in fact, slavery had not worked economically and if abolition would have increased the income and wealth not only of the slaves but of the slaveowners as well, the edge of the moral choice would have been dull. It was razor sharp precisely because the abolition of slavery involved great issues of equity, great changes in longstanding property rights in human capital, and a considerable threat to institutional arrangements based on private property, as well as to class relationships generally. Moral issues are discussed more fully in the Afterword to this volume and in *EM,* Part 10.

4. Cliometrics may be briefly defined as the application of the behavioral models and statistical methods of the social sciences to the study of history. For a more complete description see Fogel and Elton (1983) and Fogel (1982). The slavery research of cliometricians was originally focused on the United States and confined to a limited number of economic issues. Over the years the geographic scope of their

investigations has widened to include not only all of the New World but the entire Atlantic community. In recent years they have contributed to the analysis of such issues as the profitability, productivity, and economic viability of slavery in the British West Indies, Surinam, and Brazil; the economics of the Atlantic slave trade; and the internal and external factors influencing economic life in parts of West Africa. Cliometricians have also expanded the range of issues on which they are working. Indeed, the main thrust of cliometric research on slavery has shifted from purely economic issues to issues of demography and culture. Some of the most novel contributions of cliometricians in recent years have been on such topics as the influence of household structure on slave fertility rates; the effects of overwork and malnutrition on fetal, infant, and early childhood mortality rates; and the gap between the average age of slave women at menarche and at their first birth, which bears on the sexual mores of slaves.

CHAPTER 1. SLAVERY IN THE NEW WORLD

1. *Encyclopaedia Britannica* (1961), 20:776. For an alternative and lower estimate, see Hopkins (1978), 101. Estimates of the number of Romans that were slaves rest on shaky ground. But the point made by both Hopkins and Finley (1968b) that Roman Italy was one of the "five societies in which slaves played a considerable role in production" (Hopkins, 1978, 100) is well-founded. Compare Patterson (1982).

2. Curtin (1969) remains the foundation for current estimates of the Atlantic slave trade. New evidence uncovered since 1969 has led to the revision of various components of Curtin's estimates. Lovejoy's (1982) synthesis of Curtin and of the revisions raised Curtin's total for the number of black slaves imported into both the Old and the New World from 9,735,000 to 9,778,500. I have added 94,000 to Lovejoy's figure [based on *EM* #4 for the U.S. and Eltis (1987, 249) outside of the U.S. between 1811 and 1870], which brings the estimate of the total Atlantic slave trade to about 9,873,000. From this figure, 148,900 needs to be subtracted for imports into the Old World (Curtin, 1969, 116), which makes the figure for imports into the New World about 9,724,000.

    The slave import figures for the individual countries shown in Figure 1 were developed from the following sources. Sao Thomé: Curtin (1969), 116, 119. United States: *EM*, #4. Jamaica: 1660–1780, Galenson (1981), 218; 1781–1810, Eltis (1987), 247. Barbados: 1626–1650, Curtin (1969), 119; 1650–1780, Galenson (1981), 213; 1781–1810, Eltis (1987), 247. Haiti: 1651–1780, Curtin (1969), 119, 216; 1781–1800, Eltis (1987), 249. Brazil: 1551–1780, Curtin (1969), 116, 217, 235, 268; 1781–1860, Eltis (1987), 249. Cuba: before 1811, Curtin (1969), 40, 46; 1811–1870, Eltis (1987), 249. All figures for other countries are from Curtin (1969), 46, 268.

3. Estimates of the annual rate of increase in U.S. tobacco production during the eighteenth century, and the average production per hand, are based on the estimates of Jacob M. Price in a letter to RWF dated December 14, 1971; cf. *EM*, #8. See Gray (1958, 912, 1035) and U.S. Bureau of the Census (1960, 765–767). The assumption that the increase of slaves required for the increase in tobacco production could only be met out of imports biases the import requirement upward very considerably. As pointed out in Chapter 5 of this volume and in *EM*, #4, the estimated average annual rate of natural increase in the slave population in the United States between 1700 and 1800 was about 1.2 percent per annum, which is slighter greater than the average rate of increase in tobacco production during the same period. This suggests that even in the absence of increases in labor productivity and even if there had been no external slave trade, the share of U.S. slaves in tobacco production would have been lower in 1800 than it was in 1700.

4. Concerning the previous two paragraphs, see McCusker (1989); Drescher (1977), 48, 78.
5. Estimate from Sheridan (letters to RWF dated October 14, 1979, and September 5, 1988). Cf. Higman (1984), 67, 71, and Sheridan (1985), 8–9.
6. Boxer (1966), 113, 179, 220, 304; Klein (1986), esp. Ch. 6; Steckel (1971). See also *EM*, #9, #11.
7. Although there have been major advances in the quantification of economic and demographic aspects of slavery before 1800, the data for the seventeenth and eighteenth centuries are still sparse in comparison with those for the nineteenth century. The available data on the growth of the slave population throughout the New World from the earliest years are conveniently collated in Steckel (1971). See also McCusker (1989). For slavery in the Chesapeake during the seventeenth century, see Menard (1975a); for the eighteenth century see Kulikoff (1986). For South Carolina see Wood (1974). For Virginia see Rutman and Rutman (1984). For the West Indies in the late seventeenth and early eighteenth centuries, see Galenson (1986). For the shift from blacks to whites in immigration patterns between 1500 and 1900, see Galenson (1983); Eltis (1983).
8. In 1774 the value of total imports was £13,347,000, while the value of the imports of the five slave-produced commodities was £3,962,000. Mitchell and Deane (1962), 280, 286; Schumpeter (1960); Menard and McCusker (1985), Table 7.3.
9. Landes (1977), 13.
10. For the sugar plantation statistics, see Higman (1976), 13–14; on the exports of the thirteen colonies see U.S. Bureau of the Census (1960), 761.
11. The *median* plantation is defined as a plantation of such size that half of all the slaves in the region lived on plantations with fewer slaves than the median one, while the other half lived on plantations with more slaves than the median one. On the Chesapeake Bay plantations, see Kulikoff (1976), (1986).
12. Dunn (1972), Ch. 2, 3, esp. p. 96; Higman (1976), 275.
13. Knight (1970), 22, 60.
14. The value of the slaves on a Jamaican plantation of median size c.1770 was £7,641 (Sheridan, 1965, 301). Colquhoun (1815, 382) indicates that slaves represented 33.12 percent of all property in Jamaica. This figure implies that the capital value of the median sugar estate c.1770 was about £23,100 (7,641 ÷ 0.3312 ≈ 23,100). Fitting a log-normal curve to the distribution of inventories of personal property (Sheridan, 1965, Table 5) indicates that the average was approximately 14.5 percent greater than the median, so that the average value of a Jamaican sugar estate c.1770 was about £26,400 (23,071 × 1.1445 ≈ 26,400). The pound of c.1770 was converted into the pound of 1860 by splicing the Schumpeter-Gilboy index of consumer goods with the Rousseaux index, using the years 1816–1820 to make the splice (Mitchell and Deane, 1962, 468–469, 471–472). The resulting ratio of the 1860 pound to the 1770 pound was 1.2001 (1.8180 × 0.8185 × 0.8065 ≈ 1.2001), so that 26,400 in 1770 pounds was worth about 31,700 in 1860 pounds. Since the pound was worth $4.86 in 1860 (Friedman and Schwartz, 1963, 59), the value of a 1770 sugar estate in 1860 dollars was about $154,000 (31,700 × 4.86 ≈ 154,000). Since per capita income in 1860 was $128, a sugar estate was worth about 1,203 times per capita income. The last figure multiplied by 1986 per capita income in current dollars yields a figure of about $21 million (1,203 × 17,526 ≈ 21,000,000) (U.S. Bureau of the Census, 1987, 410).
15. The Boston Manufacturing Company was capitalized at $300,000 in 1813. Kirkland (1951), 300. Using Higman's (1976, 375) distribution of Jamaican slaveholdings and total capital investment per slave indicated in the previous note, there were about 34 Jamaican slaveholdings in 1832 worth more than $300,000. See U.S. Bureau of the Census (1862, 181) on the size of American cotton textile factories in 1860.

16. Craton (1974), 133. On pp. 132–139 Craton argues that the profits of sugar plantations have been underestimated, that profits were about 7.5 percent in 1790, 10 percent between 1750 and 1775, and as much as 20 percent before 1700; cf. *EM*, #17. The relative wealth of U.S. planters and northern merchants in 1860 is discussed on pp. 81–84 of the text. The relative wealth of West Indian planters and English noblemen is discussed in *EM*, #2.

17. Schmitz (1974), 24–31; Parry and Sherlock (1956), 145–147, 224.

18. Knight (1970), 32–33; see also 35, 37.

19. Schmitz (1974), 25–26; Fenichel (1967), 458. On the role of steam power see Knight (1970), 39. U.S. Bureau of the Census (1862), 180.

20. Various studies have focused new attention on the role of the factories as instruments for the transformation of the mode of labor, pointing out that the new labor discipline may have been a more crucial feature of the initial phases of the Industrial Revolution than changes in industrial hardware. See Thompson (1967); Landes (1969), (1986); Marglin (1976).

21. Ure (1835), 15–16.

22. Hammond and Hammond (1975), 16–17. Resistance was provoked partly by the extraordinary monotony of factory labor, for the efficiency of the system was related to the minute division of labor that required each worker to repeat over and over again the operation that he or she was instructed to perform. The incessant "joining of broken threads," said Friedrich Engels, or the "constant attention to the tireless machine is felt as the keenest torture by the operatives, and its action upon mind and body is in the long run stunting in the highest degree." Engels (1973), 213–214. Resistance was also provoked by the extraordinarily long hours of labor, 14 to 16 hours per day, and the intense rhythm of labor set by the machines.

23. A certain amount of force was also employed to compel the labor of factory operatives. The beating of children and adolescents, who constituted about a third of the hands, remained legal well into the nineteenth century and was used to discipline both operatives and apprentices. Factory owners called upon the courts for the imprisonment of hands who sought to quit (on the grounds of breach of contract), and the courts sanctioned the use of this instrument against older workers. Factory owners also instituted an elaborate system of fines covering the most minute infractions of labor discipline, with the heaviest penalties "reserved for absence (the cardinal sin, often worth several days' pay)." Landes (1969), 114. See Engels (1973), 180, on the employment and treatment of children; Deane and Cole (1969), Ch. 4, on the distribution of the labor force; Pollard (1965).

24. Large slave tobacco plantations had more of a division of labor than free farms, beginning in the 1750s or 1760s. Kulikoff (1986); Walsh (1977). The distinction between gang-system and other types of slavery is discussed in Patterson (1982), 455–456 n. 4. Finley (1968a) was one of the first scholars to draw a distinction between systems in which slavery was central to the economy and those in which slavery was marginal. Cf. Hopkins (1978), 100–101.

25. Metzer, *TP*, #10; Craton (1974), 123–125, 208–209; Kulikoff (1986), 396–408. See Ch. 2 of this volume for further discussion of the occupational distributions of slaves.

26. Bennet H. Barrow, as quoted by Metzer, *TP*, #10.

27. Russell (1857), 180.

28. Olmsted (1953), 452.

29. DeBow's *Review* VI, as quoted by Metzer, *TP*, #10.

30. Fogel and Engerman (1974), 1:204.

31. Metzer, *TP*, #10; Olson, *TP*, #8. Compare Phillips (1966), 370; Gray (1958), 547–550.

32. Metzer, *TP*, #10. Metzer's analysis of the cotton-picking rates of mothers in the

months immediately before and after childbirth is taken from the records of the
Leak plantation in North Carolina for the period 1841–1860.

33. Genovese (1974), 60–61; Bonner (1964), 201.

34. See Olson, *TP*, #11. In addition to those mentioned in the text, a further parallel
between the plantation and industrial systems of labor is drawn by Aufhauser
(1971, 37–38). Aufhauser compares comments made by Frederick Winslow Taylor
in his *Principles of Scientific Management* (New York, 1967) on the necessity of
careful instruction to replace a worker's own judgment to the attitude of slaveowners toward slaves. In both cases, workers were characterized as lazy and incapable
of initiative. For plantations using the gang system, calculation of the average slave
workweek includes some work done by slaves on their own time. For those using
the task system, our figure may overestimate total time worked. See pp. 192–194
on the task system.

35. On U.S. sugar production see Sitterson (1953) and Deerr (1949).

36. On the growth of the slave population in the West Indies see McCusker (1989),
548–767; Steckel (1971). The figures for the thirteen colonies are from the U.S.
Bureau of the Census (1960), 756.

37. See *EM*, #5, for the development of these estimates of the distribution of slaves
among crops. See also Fogel and Engerman, *TP*, #13.

38. Eltis (1987), 369 n.12; U.S. House of Representatives (1836), Table C; DeBow
(1854), Table 71 and p. 94; see also n.37 above, Ch. 2 below, and *EM*, #21.

39. The source for Figure 2 is Watkins (1895); compare Watkins (1969). Bales have
been converted to uniform weights of 400 pounds. The estimates of the white and
black population of the United States during the colonial era have been compiled
by Sutherland in U.S. Bureau of the Census (1960). The estimates for the Caribbean are those developed by McCusker (1989), 548–767.

40. On the Chesapeake, see Kulikoff (1986), 340, and the sources he cites 340 *n.* 50;
cf. Fogel and Engerman (1974), 1:21.

41. Menard (1975b), 51. Assuming the average size of a slave family in 1750 was 5
persons, there would be 4 families on a plantation of 20 slaves. The plantation
could instead consist of 3 complete families, 2 incomplete families, and a few
unrelated individuals.

42. The median in cotton was computed from the Parker Gallman sample. See Schmitz
(1974) on sugar and Swan (1972) on rice. Compare the discussion in the text on
pp. 185–188. It should be kept in mind that although sugar and rice plantations
were large there were relatively few of them in the U.S., so they accounted for only
a relatively small share of the slave population of the U.S.

43. See *EM*, #4, #6, for the estimates in this paragraph and the next three paragraphs,
as well as for Figures 3 and 4. See Kulikoff (1986, 71–74) for an alternative
procedure for estimating the proportion of slaves who were American born. This
procedure produces similar results.

44. See *EM*, #3, for a discussion of the importance of the smuggling of African slaves
into the U.S. before 1807, and its negligible dimensions thereafter except as a
political issue.

45. DeBow (1954), 63 and 82: See Ch. 5 below. Cf. *EM*, #4, #42.

46. The distribution of the slave and black populations in 1825 is based on an exhaus-
tive survey of population statistics carried out by Steckel (1971). Among Steckel's
principal sources were Curtin (1969), Deerr (1950), McCusker (1989), Rosenblat
(1954), and Zelinsky (1949).

47. There has been an impressive expansion of research into the factors influencing
the division of Atlantic migrants among slaves, indentured servants, and free labor.
Excellent summaries of this literature as well as insightful extensions of it include
Eltis (1983); Dunn (1984); Galenson (1984), (1986); McCusker and Menard (1985),
Ch. 5; Engerman (1986a, b).

48. Although the physical force permitted against indentured servants in America might not have been greater than that commonly used against workers in Europe, the legal constraints binding them to masters were probably stronger. The evidence on the latter issue is mixed. Standard sources on the treatment and legal status of indentured servants include, for England, Kussmaul (1981); Hartwell (1971); Pollard (1965); Lipson (1971). For the United States, primarily but not exclusively in the Chesapeake, see Farnam (1938); Smith (1971), Ch. 11 and 12; Morris (1965), 390–512; Semmes (1938), Ch. 5. More recent works which reflect conflicting opinion on the servant's lot are Morgan (1975), 123–130; Menard (1973), 48; Main (1982), 113–118.

    The legal position of indentured servants was not much different from that of freedmen under the apprenticeship system of gradual emancipation in the British West Indies. In both cases, masters might have responded to the limited time period of constrained service by forcing extreme amounts of work from their workers. They were within their legal limits to do so. On apprenticeship, see the sources cited below at p. 453 n.108, as well as those in Fogel and Engerman, *TP*, #29.

49. See Chapter 2, n. 2, below; *EM*, #9, #11.

50. The gang system was occasionally used in grain farming, but even on mixed grain/tobacco plantations, the gang system was uncommon. See Olmsted (1970). It is important to note that there were areas even in the U.S. South where the gang system was not used and slavery was marginal, primarily in areas of North Carolina and Tidewater Virginia. It is estimated that as many as 30 percent of American slaves in 1790 were in areas without a staple crop base. This percentage decreased later.

    Sarah Hughes (1978) found for Elizabeth City County, Virginia, that when the changeover from a tobacco monoculture to a variety of crops took place the ownership of slaves did not change significantly, although the distribution of them did. The units of farming became smaller, more akin to family farming, and having a few slaves was closer to having a few extra farmhands, resembling a system of hiring. Under these conditions, most natural increase of slaves would have been sold off. The explanation for why slavery did not die out entirely seems to lie in cultural expectations persisting despite economic disadvantages. I am indebted to Allan Kulikoff for bringing these issues to my attention.

51. Goldin (1976), 89–122. It is sometimes said that slaves were poorly represented in manufacturing, but that would not be correct if sugar mills, ginning mills, and artisan crafts are included in manufacturing. This complex issue is discussed more fully on pp. 103–104 of the text and in *EM*, #39.

52. Menard (1973b).

53. These characteristics limited the possibilities for the division of the production process into a series of routine operations. The problem is illustrated by the replanting procedure which took place about six weeks after the seeds were originally planted. The withdrawal of the plants from their beds could not be done gang style but required the judgment and skill of a highly trained hand. The replanting, however, was done by gangs; one gathered the plants into baskets and dropped them in the waiting hills; another closed the soil around the plants; a third was responsible for the setting operation. Topping (the removal of the upper part of the plant) is another operation that did not lend itself to the gang system, since not all the plants were topped in the same way. "Every tobacco plant must be treated differently in order to yield the maximum in quality" (Aufhauser, 1971, 113). While tobacco production thus involved some operations that could be performed on an assembly line basis, other operations remained on a handicraft basis. On the Chesapeake examples, see Kulikoff (1976), 7.14–7.15. On tobacco, see Schaefer (1978); Gray (1958), 775.

54. For this paragraph and the next one see Mintz (1969), 32; Dunn (1973); Sheridan (1974); E. Morgan (1975).

55. Deerr (1949); Palmer (1976); Bowser (1974); Parry (1979).
56. Klein (1966), 296, 297, 298, 306.
57. Mellafe (1975), 106.
58. Palmer (1976), 178. See also his Chapter 4 for the role of the Spanish Church in defending rights of slaves in Mexico. For a review of the debate over treatment of slaves in Protestant and Catholic countries, see Klein (1986). On the failure of the Catholic Church in Brazil to intervene on behalf of slave families, see Degler (1970). On the role of the Catholic Church in the U.S. see p. 397 in this volume and the sources cited there. See also p. 438, n. 31. The issue originated with Tannenbaum (1946). Compare North (1986); Parry (1979).
59. On the role of the British in this change, see Knight (1970), 6–24, esp. 7; Parry and Sherlock (1956), 222–230; Klein (1986), 86–88. The British promoted slavery when they occupied Cuba during the Seven Years' War.

CHAPTER 2. OCCUPATIONAL PATTERNS

1. For Jamaica, Surinam, and Trinidad, some of the comparisons are based on occupational censuses that covered the entire slave populations of the colonies. In Brazil the desired information is currently available only for a few large plantations specializing mainly in coffee and located mainly in the Campinas district (Slenes, 1975). In the United States, the information is most detailed in a sample of 60 intermediate and large plantations specializing in the production of either cotton, rice, sugar, or tobacco, which will be called the "Olson sample." Useful information is also contained in the larger sample of 570 slaveholdings drawn from the probate records of eight states, which will be called the "probate sample," as well as in the New Orleans slave invoices and in Union Army records. Since the information pools differ for the various economies, and because of the opportunities that exist for improving the data base, the discussion of occupational patterns presented in this chapter should be considered provisional. See *EM*, #7, for a discussion of the sources of data on slave occupations in the United States and the Caribbean.
2. Higman (1984, 93) estimated that c. 1830, some 9 percent of the slave population of the British West Indies lived in towns. Goldin (1976, 12) estimated that 4.0 percent of southern slaves lived in cities of 2,500 or more persons in 1850 and 3.6 percent did so in 1860. DeBow (1854, 94) put the town share at 12.5 percent, but his definition of towns apparently included nonagricultural communities ranging below 1,000 persons. In Cuba the urban share of slaves varied between 17.5 and 20.9 percent during 1855–1871 (Knight, 1970, 63). Higman's (1984) data for six British colonies with a combined population of 70,820 slaves indicates that 15.2 percent were domestics (computed from his Table 6.1). See also Bowser (1974), 100–101; Palmer (1976), 45–46; Klein (1967), 145; *EM*, #9. For another discussion and analysis of the probate records, see MacMillan (1988); cf. Olson, *TP*, #8.
3. See *EM*, #8.
4. Klein (1967), 144. See Goldin (1976), 30–31. See also *EM*, #9; for a discussion of slave-hiring practices, see *EM*, #8.
5. Higman (1976), 276–277; Fogel and Engerman (1974), 2:39–42; Craton (1978), 161. See *EM*, #9.
6. Mellafe (1975), 25–47; Bowser (1974), 5–10. During the Spanish conquest of South and Central America, the conquistadors often trusted their African slaves more than they did the native Americans. Black Cuban slaves took part in Cortés's conquest of Mexico in 1519 (Klein, 1967, 141), and Bowser reports that the Africans involved in the Spanish conquest of the Incas "identified with everything Spanish more rapidly than did the Indian—to the point, in fact, where many blacks, in imitation of their masters, terrorized native villages and even accumulated staffs

of cowed Indian servants. . . . Prized by the master for his fidelity, the black man rapidly came to occupy an intermediate position between Spaniard and Indian rather than the place beneath the Indian to which the law had consigned him" (Bowser, 1974, 7; see also Mellafe, 1975, 25–26). Slaves continued to serve the government and in the armed services in Peru and Cuba into the seventeenth century (Bowser, 1974, 105–107; Klein, 1967, 145–146). Between 1795 and 1815 the British organized 12 West India regiments composed of slaves, which in 1807 had an effective strength of just under 8,000 men. These regiments, over the objections of West India planters, formed a major part of the British Army in the West Indies during the Napoleanic Wars, and were acknowledged by the British high command as essential to the achievement of their objectives in the Caribbean (Buckley, 1979, esp. Ch. 5).

7. Dunn (1973), 242. The time frame of the shift to the dominance of slaves in crafts is drawn from evidence gathered by Galenson (1981), 128–134, 138–139, 177; Kulikoff (1976); Mullin (1972), 86–88, 94–98; Sheridan (1974); and other sources discussed in *EM*, Part 2.

8. Roughley (1823), 85. Menard (1975b, 51) points out that a tax list for Prince George's County, Maryland, in 1733 lists 37 of 79 quarters as having no taxable-age white population, suggesting a good proportion of black-filled supervisory positions. Cf. his comment on independent quarters (1975b, 36). See also Kulikoff (1986), 384–386; *EM*, #9.

9. It has been argued (Woodson, 1919b) that another factor that might have influenced the rise and fall in the proportion of overseers who were slaves is the rate of formation of new plantations. Newly settled plantations might have had to employ slaves as overseers out of necessity, for lack of available whites. If that were the case, however, there should have been a higher proportion of black overseers on the large plantations of the New South than on those of the Old South. But no such pattern has been detected. Moreover, in the West Indies the situation was exactly reversed. Originally, most of the higher ranking jobs were held by whites, then gradually transferred to blacks. In the West Indies there were very few whites at all on the plantations. See *EM*, #9, #10, #11, #12; Olson, *TP*, #8.

10. For data underlying this paragraph, see *EM*, #11, #12.

11. Higman (1976), 16. See also *EM*, #12, #27; Higman (1984).

12. Fogel and Engerman, *TP*, #13; Fogel and Engerman (1974), 2:37, 42. See also *EM*, #12, #27, #51. Allan Kulikoff has calculated occupational distributions for eighteenth-century tobacco plantations in the Chesapeake Bay region. For 1733, his estimate of the percentage of slaves engaged in field labor ranges from 74 to 90 percent. For the same region the estimates are 50 to 82 percent in the time period 1774–1791. See Kulikoff (1986).

13. See *EM*, #12, #27; Olson, *TP*, #8. For data underlying Figure 5, see *EM*, #12.

14. Olson, *TP*, #8; Metzer, *TP*, #10; Craton (1974), 208–209. See *EM*, #12.

15. "Elite occupations" not only involved release from gang labor, but were also considered by either the planters or the slaves, usually by both, to be preferable to gang labor. Such occupations carried a degree of status as well as material and other advantages not generally available to ordinary gang laborers. Van den Boogaart and Emmer (1977), 215; Carmichael (1834), 123.

16. Miller (1979), 42. Miller's studies on slave occupations are based on ex-slave narratives. Although the commentary quoted here refers to the South, it is equally applicable to the West Indies.

17. See *EM*, #12.

18. G. Friedman (1982), 488–493. It has been suggested that shorter males were chosen as domestics because owners preferred not to have large or imposing black men in the house.

19. *EM*, #12; cf. *EM*, #51; *TP*, #3, #8; Crawford (1980).

20. See *EM*, #12; Littlefield (1981), Ch. 2 and 4.
21. Olson, *TP*, #8; Kotlikoff, *TP*, #3; cf. *EM*, #12.
22. See *EM*, #7.
23. See *EM*, #9, #12; data for Figure 6 are in *EM*, #12.
24. Household servants were often children whose work would not be considered important in the field. In other cases, servants' work was also often physically taxing, and utilizing an adult worker in the house would be a necessity. Even given these factors, a domestic staff can still be seen as owner self-indulgence, since the labor does not produce income: It is a consumption good rather than a market good. In households with only one slave, according to the Parker-Gallman sample (of 5,200 farms in the cotton South in 1860), females were heavily overrepresented (see Foust, 1975, for a description of the Parker-Gallman sample). Some scholars have inferred it is because of this sexual imbalance that small slaveholdings had a disproportionate share of domestics. An alternative explanation is that the desire to have a domestic servant led these slave owners to purchase a female rather than a male slave.
25. For the data underlying the percentages in the preceding five paragraphs see *EM*, #12; Olson, *TP*, #8.
26. See *EM*, #12; *TP*, #8.
27. The lower ratio of field hands to drivers may reflect the desire and capacity of U.S. slaveowners to work their slaves far more intensely than was possible in the Caribbean. The stature and body mass of slaves in the United States permitted a level of work output far in excess of either Caribbean slaves or European workers. See *EM*, #47; Fogel (1987).
28. Olson, *TP*, #8; *EM*, #10, #12.
29. A cohort is a group of persons born during the same period and hence reaching a given age span at the same time. Cohorts are sometimes defined by their year of birth and sometimes by longer intervals. For example, slaves who were between ages 25 and 29 in 1839 belonged to the cohort born between 1810 and 1814.
30. Price-by-age profiles have been calculated for slaves listed with an age and price in probate samples following the procedure used by Fogel and Engerman in *Time on the Cross* (Fogel and Engerman, 1974, 1:21–26, 2:80–82). Age-earnings profiles can be calculated from the price-by-age profiles since the current price equals the present value of the future price plus current net earnings. In estimating labor force participation in the free economy, only production of goods for sale is considered. The labor of white farm women, since it was mostly non-field work and produced goods primarily for the family's consumption, is, therefore, seriously underestimated. Cf. *EM*, #12.
31. See pp. 27–28 of Chapter 1.
32. It is unlikely that children as young as that made significant contributions to output. Training, rather than current productivity, may have been the objective of such an early entry into jobs.
33. Roughley (1823), 103–109.
34. The early age of children beginning work is from Carmichael (1834). The data on the rate of entry into the labor force are from Crawford (1980); cf. Olson, *TP*, #8; *EM*, #12. Crawford's work is founded on the quantification of the information resulting from interviews of ex-slaves conducted by Fisk University and the Federal Writers Project of the WPA. Since patterns of answering questions might exist, information may be skewed along certain demographic lines. On the variables involved in the statistical evaluation of groups within the interviews, see *EM*, #51; Crawford (1980), 11–22. For discussion of other features of the samples and considerations in interpreting them, see Crawford (1980), 22–43; Escott (1979), 3–17. Johnson (1986) notes a similar pattern of entry into the work force in the mortality data from Mississippi, Georgia, and South Carolina. He finds that there was, statis-

tically, little sexual division of labor, although women dominated in the house staff and men in the skilled crafts.

35. See *EM*, #12, #13; *TP*, #8, #10. For the method of calculating the average net and gross "earnings" of children, see Fogel and Engerman (1974), 2:79–81.

36. Slenes (1975), 535; Kulikoff (1976), 7–31. See *EM*, #13, for a more detailed discussion of the life cycle in slave occupations.

37. The pattern of promotion of older slaves into elite positions reduces the "pay-back" period during which slaveowners can recoup their investment in training the slave to perform their craft. Promotion by seniority, however, may resemble the pattern of "job ladders" in twentieth-century American industry and corporate management. See Stone (1974); Doeringer and Piore (1971); Medoff and Abraham (1981). In many cases, sons appear to learn crafts from fathers. It is possible that later entry into crafts training reflects cases in which fathers were not artisans. In these cases, a young man might have been apprenticed to a craftsman who had no son of his own to train. See Johnson (1986), 343; Kulikoff (1986), Ch. 8 and 10.

38. Gutman (1975), 79–81.

39. Olson, *TP*, #8; Kotlikoff, *TP*, #3. See Ch. 3, *n*. 24, in this volume.

40. See Olson, *TP*, #8; Higman (1976); *EM*, #12, #13, which also deal with the issue of differential mortality rates.

41. See *EM*, #12.

42. Roughley (1823, 113–118) describes occupations thought fit for the aged.

43. Higman (1976, 144) estimated the number of whites per plantation by applying the 1844 Jamaican census regional distribution of the white population to the distribution of plantations in 1832. The distribution of whites across plantations in the United States South is based on the Parker-Gallman sample of plantations in the cotton states in 1859.

44. For examples of studies based on autobiographies and on ex-slave narratives see Blassingame (1977), (1975); Genovese (1974); Rawick (1972); Owens (1976). See Woodward (1974) for a review of Rawick's work. See *EM*, #51, Escott (1979), and Crawford (1980) for statistical analyses of the ex-slave narratives.

Chapter 3. Unraveling Some Economic Riddles

1. See Drescher (1977); Drescher (1986), 241–244, *n*.84, 328–330; cf. Sheridan (1981).

2. Garrison, as quoted by Thomas (1963), 326.

3. There were attempts to connect antislavery to economic issues before 1854, but these were desultory except in the South. See Chapter 10 in this volume for support for the assertion that the crucial switch took place between 1854 and 1856.

4. See *EM*, #14, #15. On the emergence of economic arguments as central aspects of northern antislavery politics, see pp. 344–348 of Chapter 10. Cf. *EM*, #16, #18.

5. Ward (1978); *EM*, #17, #18. On British restrictions see Eltis (1972), (1987).

6. For the econometric analysis underlying this paragraph, see *EM*, #19.

7. It might be argued that such constructs as real prices are the inventions of twentieth-century economists and have no applicability to the eighteenth or the early nineteenth century because planters, legislators, and others merely looked at money prices in making economic decisions. But workers who rioted in the nineteenth century because bread prices rose faster than their wages showed that they understood such concepts as real prices and real wages, and so did the government officials who pegged the amount of poor relief to the price of bread. See Rose (1961); Marshall (1968).

8. By 1812 these new lands accounted for a third of the sugar exports from Britain's Caribbean possessions; by 1833 the figure was up to 48 percent. To some extent the downward shift in the London price was due to the rise of sugar production

in Mauritius, Britain's slave colony in the Indian Ocean. For the sources supporting Figure 9 see *EM*, #19.

9. *Great Britain* (1837–1838, 369) contains prices of slaves in the British West Indies by island. These figures were assembled with a view toward estimating the compensation to slaveholders under a plan of emancipation. Eltis (1972); Ward (1978), 204, 207.

10. See *EM*, #20. U.S. rice production suffered from Oriental competition. Gray (1958), 610, 721–730, Ch. 26.

11. See *EM*, #21, #22; Berry (1943), 580–581; Gray (1958), 589, 605–606, Ch. 32; on 765 and 1038 Gray gives price trends over 1800–1861 for tobacco. Cf. Kotlikoff, *TP*, #3.

12. See *EM*, #22, for regional and southwide time series on the demand for slaves. See *TP*, #3, for an analysis of the course of slave prices in New Orleans.

13. Gray (1958), 610–611, 757.

14. Watkins (1908), 29–31. Excluding the French settlement around New Orleans, there was no count of whites or blacks in the Gulf states west of eastern Georgia in 1790. The estimated Indian population of all the Gulf states, including Florida, was about 114,000. *Encyclopaedia Britannica* (1961), V. 12, 203; U.S. Bureau of the Census (1960), 13; Rossiter (1909), 40, 69, 133.

15. The soils and climates of the various states were not equally advantageous to all southern crops. The Atlantic Coastal Plain just below the Mason-Dixon line and the Central Piedmont Plateau were favorable for raising tobacco and general farming, but could not support a cotton culture. Rice had its greatest advantage in the swamplands along the southeastern coastal flatwoods of Georgia and South Carolina and in the lower Gulf Coastal Plain. Sugar production was confined largely to a handful of parishes in the Mississippi Delta. On regional specialization, see *EM*, #21. Cf. Gray (1953), 684, 891, 652, 655.

16. Fogel and Engerman (1974), 1:46. This discussion of the interregional slave trade is based on the estimates of Claudia Goldin, which are presented in Fogel and Engerman (1974), 2:183–184.

17. Hunter (1949), Ch. 1 and 2; Haites, Mak, and Walton (1975), 60–69, 183–184.

18. Ratner, Soltow, and Sylla (1979), 118–119; Healy (1951), 127; U.S. Bureau of the Census (1862), 231. The mileage of track in Continental Europe is from Mulhall (1892), 495; in Britain, from Mitchell and Dean (1962), 225.

19. U.S. Bureau of the Census (1853), 106–118.

20. See, for example, Fogel and Engerman (1974), 2:53–54; Sutch (1975); Carstensen and Goodman (1977). For discussion of these estimates and the debate on these questions, see *EM*, #22, #23.

21. Davis (1975), 171; Miller (1977), 107. Cf. Richards (1979), 102–105.

22. Kotlikoff, *TP*, #3.

23. Figure 11 is taken from Fogel and Engerman (1974), 1:72. The curve was developed from data in probate records. For a discussion of Sutch's conjecture on the intercept of the price-by-age profile, see Fogel and Engerman, *TP*, #21, *n.* 9; *EM*, #23.

24. The premia and discounts shown in Figure 12 were estimated from data in the probate sample of slave prices by fitting sixth-order polynomials on age and using dummy variables for specific skills and defects. Separate regressions were run on each gender. That blacksmiths and carpenters brought such a large premium does not necessarily imply that more profit could be made by slaveowners if they sold such craftsmen than if they sold ordinary fieldhands, even leaving aside the incentive system described in Chapter 2. There was a cost to training craftsmen, which was the foregone product in other occupations during training. If markets were in equilibrium, then the profit rate on craftsmen would have been no greater than that on ordinary field hands.

25. Kotlikoff, *TP*, #3.
26. For an elaboration of this point, see Kotlikoff and Pinera, *TP*, #6.
27. The price planters received for tobacco depended on total output. Production of western tobacco lowered the price of tobacco on the world market. Slaves were valued by the output they could produce, but the increase in tobacco production, and decrease in price, could lower the price of slaves overall. If increases in quantity greatly reduced the price of tobacco, then the expansion of tobacco production into the West reduced the price of slaves. See Kotlikoff and Pinera, *TP*, #6. Cf. Passell and Wright (1972); Lee (1978); Schmitz and Schaefer (1981).
28. Phillips (1966), chart following 370. See *EM*, #22, #23, #35.
29. See *EM*, #21, #22, #35–#37.
30. Between 1840 and 1860 the productivity of agricultural labor increased nearly as rapidly in these states as in the Northeast, although productivity growth in both of the eastern regions lagged somewhat behind the pace of the North and the South Central states. Far from declining, the average value of farm lands in the three chief slave-exporting states (Virginia, North Carolina, and South Carolina) increased by 60 percent over the decade of the 1850s, nearly as much as the increase (79 percent) experienced by the three chief slave-importing states (Alabama, Mississippi, and Louisiana). See *EM*, #23, #40, #68; U.S. Bureau of the Census (1895), 84–100.
31. Fogel and Engerman, *TP*, #13; Anderson (1974), 53–70. Cf. *EM*, #23.
32. See Goldin, *TP*, #7, for a fuller discussion of the paradoxical effect of the combined rural and urban increases in the demand for slaves on the share of the slave labor force demanded by cotton planters. See also Fogel and Engerman, *TP*, #12.
33. Kotlikoff and Pinera, *TP*, #6. The main discussion of the critical political role of territorial issues is in Chapter 10, particularly pp. 325, 331, 335, 341–344, 349–354, 371–373, 378–383.
34. Smith (1937), 81. See Larabee and Bell (1961), 225–226; Davis (1966), 427, 431.
35. For further discussion, see Fogel and Engerman (1974), 2:126–130; *TP*, #12, #14, #15.
36. Olmsted (1953), 91.
37. On "hand" rating, see Ch. 1, pp. 27–28. On the procedure for computing Figure 13 from the Parker-Gallman sample see *EM*, #24. Cf. *EM*, #27.
38. For the procedures underlying this discussion see *EM*, #24–#31.
39. See *EM*, #24–#31.
40. It should be remembered that it was the greater intensity of slave labor per hour rather than longer hours that was the source of the greater productivity of the slaves.
41. Those who migrated to the West were also generally younger and a larger proportion of them were men. However, these demographic differences are controlled in the construction of the indexes and so do not affect the comparison.
42. Evans (1962), 197, 216. Since the hire rate reflects labor productivity, about two-thirds of total factor productivity was due to factors which made labor productivity higher in the New South than in the Old South.
43. For discussion of the elements contributing to the efficiency of slave farms, see Fogel and Engerman (1974), 1:191–209; *TP*, #12, #13. See also Fogel and Engerman (1974), 2:132–139.
44. For a discussion of the issues involved in the North-South comparison see David et al. (1976); David and Temin (1979); Wright (1979b); Schaefer and Schmitz (1979); Fogel and Engerman, *TP*, #12, #13; Yang, *TP*, #14.
45. For a discussion of some of these issues see *TP*, #12, #13.
46. Olson, *TP*, #11. It is important to note that these estimates of labor time refer mainly to the work of slaves on the master's account and probably exclude most

work on their own account, whether on or off the plantation. Cf. p. 28 and *n*. 34 of Chapter 1 above.

47. Olson, *TP*, #11.

48. U.S. Department of Agriculture (1912a), 35, 36, 43, 44. The relationships between the growing period, the growing season, and the period between seedtime and harvest are discussed on 14 of this source.

49. See Olson, *TP*, #11, for further discussion of the estimates of gross farm income originating in livestock and dairying in the North and the South.

50. Slaves' "pay" is the value of their maintenance plus some cash given to slaves as rewards. For the method of estimating the implicit income of slaves, see *EM*, #52; cf. Fogel and Engerman (1974), 2:116–117, 159–160. The term "equal-efficiency hour" refers to the adjustment for the higher intensity of labor by slaves than by free agricultural workers. See Olson, *TP*, #11, for a fuller treatment of this issue.

51. For a discussion of how caloric intake can be used to measure the intensity of labor, see Fogel (1987). The high body mass of slaves, which indicates that they consumed enough calories to sustain very intense labor, is discussed in *EM*, #47. Compare with Margo and Steckel (1982) and *TP*, #24.

Chapter 4. The Development of the Southern Economy

1. Beyond the purely economic motives for the commitment of masters to the slave system, there were political and cultural motivations. On the political motivations, see Chapters 9 and 10 of this volume and the sources cited there. On the cultural motivations, see Genovese (1965), (1971), (1974); Fox-Genovese and Genovese (1983); Roark (1977). For skeptical views of this cultural thesis, see Burton and McMath (1982); Thornton (1978); Hahn (1983).

2. Olmsted (1970), 16.

3. Wright (1978), 35. Wright based his statement on Soltow (1975, 65, 138–139), who reported that the average wealth of a northern adult male in 1860 was $2,040 and that the average value of a slave was $911. See *EM*, #32, #63, for the average wealth per household by various social groups cited in the text and graphed in Figure 15.

4. Cairnes (1969), 81.

5. It was the small-scale farmers of the South (both slaveowners and non-slaveowners), rather than the large-scale planters, who led the migration to the West. Foust (1975); Schaefer (1985).

6. Foust (1975), Ch. 7; Schaefer (1978); Soltow (1971a), 825. I have followed Soltow on the proportions of southern households that owned slaves in 1830 and 1860. Soltow's estimate for 1830 is based on a random sample of the 1830 census in 14 states and the District of Columbia. His figure for 1860 is from the distribution of slaveowning households in the eighth census, which covered 15 slave states and the District of Columbia. Olsen (1972), who limited himself to only the Confederate states, found that 31 percent of the households owned slaves (111). See also *EM*, #33.

7. Russell (1857), 284. Mere capitalization of the labor force did not add to the real wealth of the South, since the capitalized portion was merely a transfer of the property right from the slave to the master. Nevertheless, it was as much a part of the wealth of the masters as their securities, buildings, real estate, livestock, machinery, or other assets. Each master could have sold some or all of his slaves, converting that form of his wealth into another kind, and many did so. Cf. Wright (1986), Ch. 2; Ransom and Sutch (1983).

8. For discussion of the concept of yeoman in the antebellum context, see *EM*, #32, #33.

9. Wright (1978), 25.
10. See *EM*, #32, #33, #62.
11. See Soltow (1975, 99–101) and *EM*, #32, #33, #62, #63, for the sources of the calculations cited in the preceding three paragraphs. For example, in 1860 there "were 7,000 Americans (richest 0.1 percent of population) with wealth of $111,000 or more, 4,500 of whom lived in the South." Of the richest percentile in 1860, 59 percent were in the South; in 1870, 18 percent (Soltow, 1975, 101).
12. On this point, see Soltow (1975); *EM*, #33, #40; *TP*, #16, #31.
13. Economists generally prefer per capita income to total income in measuring the economic growth of nations, since per capita income is a better index of the ability of an economy to satisfy economic welfare. For example, the real national income of the United States rose during the Great Depression of the 1930s even though per capita income declined. This was because the population rose. Thus, it is possible for a nation's total income to increase even though each person in the nation is worse off economically. Per capita income is preferred also because it permits comparisons between the economic performance of large and small countries. The total income of India, for example, was 50 percent larger than that of Denmark in 1979. But economists obviously consider the economic performance of Denmark to be better than that of India, since Denmark produced $12,200 of income per capita while the per capita income of India was just $140. The discussion in the text, pp. 83–88, is an updated and revised version of Fogel and Engerman (1974), 1:247–257. For sources see Fogel and Engerman (1974), 2:162–167. GNP and per capita income of India and Denmark are from U.S. Central Intelligence Agency (1980), 48, 89.
14. Table 1 is from Fogel and Engerman (1971), Table 8, 335; cf. Table 4 of Fogel and Engerman (1974), 1:248, 2:162–164.
15. Cf. Fogel and Engerman (1971), 334 *n.* 35; Fogel and Engerman (1974), 2:117. See *n.* 50 of Chapter 3 on the estimation of slave income.
16. Genovese (1986).
17. Helper (1968), 25, 34. How to measure per capita income always involves inescapable ethical consideration. See Kuznets (1953); Studenski (1958).
18. For a discussion of the role of southern politicians in shaping the image of the poor South, see, among others, Wender (1930); Craven (1953), esp. 278. Both scholars note that control of the southern commercial conventions, originally lead by commercial circles who wanted to frame a political program to advance southern economic interests, gradually passed under the control of southern nationalists who maintained that only secession would free the South from the rule of northern politicians and permit the southern nation to realize its full economic potential. Cf. the discussion of southern economic grievances in Chapter 9, pp. 296–300.
19. Fogel and Engerman (1974), 1:251, 2:162–164; cf. Kuznets (1971), Table 1, 11–19.
20. And, it might be added, by most whites in the North as well.
21. For a further discussion of these issues, see Goldin (1976), Ch. 5; *TP*, #7. See also *EM*, #35, #66, #67.
22. Why the cause of the Confederacy enjoyed a strong support among non-slaveholding Southerners is still in dispute. Traditional interpretation of the loyalty of the southern "yeoman" to the regime stressed the commitment of the white South to racial supremacy (Eaton, 1967; Frederickson, 1971). Genovese (1975, 336) has argued that their loyalty stemmed from the desire to defend local rights against the pressures of centralization: "provincial rejection of an outside world which threatened to impinge on the culture as well as the material interests of the local community." More recent arguments stress that middle-class populism and Jacksonian democracy were the dominant political forces in most southern states and

the driving force toward southern nationalism. The attempt to restrict slavery was viewed by these classes as an effort to give the North a monopoly on new lands, thus striking at the rights of southern yeomen (Thornton, 1978; Cooper, 1978; Holt, 1978). Further studies of the regional differences in labor markets and voting behavior, with more precisely formulated hypotheses and quantitative tests, would be helpful in discriminating among these hypotheses.

23. Table 3 is compiled from Easterlin (1960, 1961, 1975); Engerman (1967). Cf. Fogel and Engerman (1974), 2:162–164; *EM*, #38.

24. Farm laborers' monthly wages (with board) increased by 43 percent, from $9.12 to $13.00, in the South between 1850 and 1860 and by 26 percent, from $10.85 to $13.66, in the nation as a whole. The wage data are from Lebergott (1964, 539). The national and southern averages were computed by weighting the figures for each state by its share of the agricultural labor force estimated by Easterlin (1975, 110). The southern income gap was obtained by taking the population-weighted average of the regional (South Atlantic, East South Central, West South Central) per capita income relative to the national per capita income. For 1960–1980, regional and national per capita income data are from U.S. Bureau of the Census (1981, 429); the regional population data are U.S. Bureau of the Census (1981, 9). For 1840–1940, population data are from U.S. Bureau of the Census (1975, 24–37, ser. A195). Income data for 1840–1860 are from Easterlin (1975, 528; 1960, 137), modified according to Fogel and Engerman (1974, 2:162–164) and Gallman (1966, Table A-1). Income relatives for 1880–1940 are from U.S. Bureau of the Census (1975, 242, ser. F292–294). See also *EM*, #38, #40. On the general tendency of per capita income to decline after emancipations, see Engerman (1982). For a discussion of the issue of labor withdrawal, see Moen, *TP*, #15.

25. For a further discussion of the issues in this paragraph and the next one, see *EM*, #38, #40.

26. See *EM*, #68, on northern growth in per capita income.

27. Cf. *EM*, #15, #35. For a modern version of the assertion that slavery retarded the growth of the southern free labor force, see Wright (1979a). He argued that in the North, breakthroughs in transportation and the opening of western lands to commercial agriculture undermined eastern farms, thereby creating a supply of "effectively cheap labor" for the factories. At the same time the South approached a "unified market in slave labor," making it difficult to find a local supply of cheap industrial labor (Wright, 1979a, 665). The long-run implication of this regional difference in the labor market for the timing of industrialization is discussed more fully in later sections of this chapter. More recently Wright has extended this point to argue that it was the effectiveness with which slaveowners responded to incentives to migrate to the West that was the barrier to southern industrialization. However, the findings of Foust (1975) and Schaefer (1985) indicate lower migration rates than those assumed by Wright, and that slaveowners were less likely to migrate than non-slaveowners (cf. *EM*, #35). For somewhat different interpretations of the relationship between labor supplies and industrialization see Goldin and Sokoloff (1982, 1984), who stress the difference in the ratio of the wages of women and children relative to those of men as the critical factor in industrialization. The role of the foreign born is discussed in Chapter 9, pp. 309–312.

28. For further discussion of these issues see *EM*, #23, #35, #36; *TP*, #6, #7.

29. As will be more fully discussed in Chapter 10, the glut of labor markets during 1851–1855 in the North Central states was a major factor in the rise of the Republican party. Native-born workers throughout the Midwest, who suffered unemployment and sharp declines in real wages as a consequence of the massive influx of Irish and German immigrants, bolted the two main parties (the Whigs and the Democrats) in droves as they sought a political solution to their economic

distress. For a further discussion of regional migration rates, see *EM*, #35, Table
35.1, which was computed from the data supplied by Lang (1971), Tables 3.7, 3.10,
3.11, 3.17, 3.18, C.8, C.9, D.1.

30. Evans (1961) estimated the costs of relocating slaves, which include brokerage fees,
maintenance, the cost of runaways, and the unproductive period during the trades.
Brokerage fees and costs of runaways, which do not exist in the case of free labor,
may have made the cost of migration greater for slaves than for free men. Cf. *EM*,
#35.

31. See Steckel (1983); Burnham (1955); Chapters 9 and 10 of this volume. Ironically,
the charge that immigrants went overwhelmingly to the North because they were
hostile to slavery was raised not by the antislavery leaders but by southern politicians who wanted to choke off continued immigration into the North (Bean, 1924,
325–329). Antislavery men in the North considered immigrants hostile to their
cause and one of the main props to the Democratic party. As one Republican leader
in Massachusetts put it in 1857, "the foreign vote at the present time constitutes
the cornerstone of American slavery, and could we knock that from under it, the
whole structure would come toppling to the ground" (Bean, 1924, 323–324). There
was "not in all America," said Theodore Parker, one of Garrison's supporters, "a
single Catholic newspaper hostile to slavery" (Bean, 1924, 322).

32. Cairnes (1969), 55. For a fuller discussion of Cairnes's view see *EM*, #15. Cf.
Fogel and Engerman (1974), 1:181–190. On Ramsdell and the "Phillips school,"
see Fogel and Engerman (1974), 2:185–186.

33. DeCanio (1974), 108. Traditional discussion of the crop mix or cotton "overproduction" of the postbellum South is summarized by DeCanio on pp. 99–118. Other
discussions of the issue include Wright (1978) and Ransom and Sutch (1975;
1977). Cf. Wright (1986).

34. See *EM*, #36.

35. See *EM*, #37.

36. The patterns of price and quantity movements that prevailed during the late 1850s
are typical of every boom expansion, regardless of crop, and by themselves offer
no basis for a prediction of a longrun tendency toward overproduction.

37. Figure 16 is reproduced from Figure 27 of Fogel and Engerman (1974), 1:91–92.

38. Figure 17 is reproduced from Figure 28 of Fogel and Engerman (1974), 1:92. For
discussion, see Fogel and Engerman (1974), 2:85–87.

39. Wright (1978), esp. 90–97.

40. Wright (1978), 96; Hanson (1979). See *EM*, #36, #37, on this paragraph and the
previous one.

41. See *EM*, #37. The data on cotton inventories in Britain are from Ellison (1968),
Appendix Tables 1 and 2. Cf. Hughes (1960), Ch. 4.

42. As to the role of the cotton boom in the increase in southern per capita income
between 1840 and 1860, the same approach that was used in Fogel and Engerman
(1971, 335n. 37) has been generalized and applied to decompose southern economic growth by sectors. The procedure indicates that less than one-fifth of the rise
in southern per capita income between 1840 and 1860 is attributable to the direct
effects of the cotton boom. However, this finding is provisional, pending improved
estimates of the aggregate variables on which it is based. For details of the computation and related discussion, see Fogel and Engerman, *EM*, #40. Cf. p. 101 in this
volume.

43. Much of the work has involved the screening of the data to eliminate incomplete
or erroneous information introduced either by the individuals who originally supplied the information or as a result of recording errors by the census takers or by
the cliometricians who have been processing the data. The samples drawn from the
1850 census are smaller than those for 1860, and little has as yet been done with
the 1870 census. A large sample has been drawn from the 1880 census but various

aspects of the sample design limit its applicability to the issues discussed here. Since both the 1850 and 1880 samples have deficiencies that impair their usefulness in productivity analysis, comparisons with the 1860 results are provisional and subject to change. Nevertheless, some findings have already emerged that seem likely to hold up since they are present in several different categories of data. See *EM*, #24–#31; Moen, *TP*, #15; Virts (1984).

44. See *EM*, #38, for a discussion of the computations. Cf. Moen, *TP*, #15.

45. See *EM*, #38; *TP*, #15. For further discussion of the squad system, see Shlomowitz, *TP*, #34; Holt (1982).

46. Had there been a withdrawal of one-third of the black labor force on top of the 25 percent decline in labor productivity, per capita income would have had to have been much lower than it actually was in 1880. A labor withdrawal of that magnitude is, however, consistent with the estimates of per capita income for 1870.

47. Cf. DeCanio (1974), 209–219; *EM*, #38; *TP*, #15.

48. Computed from *EM*, Table 38.3, using the weights from *EM*, Table 55.3.

49. According to the calculations of Moen, *TP*, #15, total factor productivity fell by 13 percent between 1860 and 1880 if measured by quantities, and by 35 percent if measured by the price dual. Cf. *EM*, #38; Jaynes (1986).

50. See Shlomowitz (1979); *TP*, #34.

51. For an explanation of the growth of southern per capita income between 1840 and 1860, and the allocation of that growth between various sectors of the economy, see Fogel and Engerman, *EM*, #40.

52. Ratner, Soltow, and Sylla (1979), 184.

53. The U.K.-U.S. urbanization comparison is from U.S. Bureau of the Census (1975), 8, 11–12. Cotton statistics are from Mulhall (1899), 156; Ellison (1968). Pig iron statistics are from Mulhall (1899), 332; Mitchell and Deane (1962), 131–132. See also Allen (1975). In addition, see sources cited in Fogel and Engerman (1974), 2:166–167. Lags in manufacturing are calculated on total production and consumption figures.

54. See Pitkin (1835, 492) for 1810 textile production, U.S. Bureau of the Census (1854, 180) for 1860 cotton mills in the Northeast, and U.S. Bureau of the Census (1854, 181) for the pig iron in Pennsylvania. See also Temin (1963).

55. See *EM*, #39, on Figure 18. Cf. Bateman and Weiss (1981).

56. For the purpose of this discussion, countries are defined by twentieth-century borders. For details of the estimating procedure, see Fogel and Engerman (1974), 2:166–167.

57. See *EM*, #39.

58. Fitzhugh (1857), 587.

59. See, for example, Lander (1969), esp. Ch. 4 and 5.

60. Whether the South bore a heavier burden than the North as a result of the iron and cotton tariffs depends not merely on its per capita consumption of the products but also on the degree to which it promoted import substitution. See pp. 297–298 of this volume and the sources cited there, which indicate that the burden of these tariffs fell largely on the slaveholders, and that wages and profits were raised in northern manufacturing.

61. Montgomery *Daily Confederation*, May 19, 1858, as quoted by Russel (1960).

62. Christy (1856), 164.

63. Hammond, as reprinted in McKitrick (1965), 121.

64. Cairnes (1969), 70; Starobin (1970); Dew (1974). See the discussion of Cairnes in *EM*, #15, which is adapted from Fogel and Engerman (1974), 1:97–102. See also Fogel and Engerman (1974), 1:234–238, 2:152–155.

65. As noted on p. 103 of this chapter, much of antebellum manufacturing was located in rural areas. Nevertheless, there has been a tendency to treat the industrialization and urbanization of the era as if each were a necessary condition, or at least a proxy,

for the other. See Russel (1938); Fischbaum and Rubin (1968); Genovese (1965), 24–25.

66. The discussion here and in the next four paragraphs is based on Goldin (1976), esp. Ch. 5, which is reprinted with revisions as #7 in *TP*. In the case of the top ten southern cities, demand for slaves declined in only four instances: in St. Louis during the decade of the 1830s, in New Orleans during the decade of the 1840s, and in Baltimore and Charleston during the 1850s. In all other decades these four cities experienced an increasing demand for slaves throughout the decades between 1820 and 1860.

67. It is often assumed that because slaves were withdrawn from the cities the nonagricultural sector was declining. Between 1840 and 1860, however, the nonagricultural sector of the South grew more than twice as rapidly as the agricultural sector and was the principal source of growth in per capita income. See pp. 101–102 of this chapter, and *EM*, #40.

68. It is sometimes assumed that because small plantations were less efficient than intermediate or large ones they should have disappeared. In fact, the share of slaves owned by small plantations and in cities was declining. Many factors, however, affected the rate of decline. For a further discussion of this issue, see Goldin, *TP*, #7; Fogel and Engerman (1974), 2:143–149, 167, and 1:255–257.

69. The gang system could only be made operational if planters were granted the power needed to compel labor. The authority to use force was granted, of course, but could be applied only to slaves. So force was not an incidental feature of slavery. Without force, the right to own slaves would have been worthless, at least insofar as it affected the plantation's capacity to produce. Since the right to use force did not significantly enhance the efficiency of urban firms or of farms too small to employ a gang system, such enterprises substituted free labor for slave labor whenever the prices of slaves rose more rapidly than the wages of free laborers. But variations in the ratio of slave prices to free wages had virtually no effect on the labor preferences of large plantations. Even when slave prices rose quite sharply relative to free wages, the labor force of the large plantations remained overwhelmingly slave, because free laborers would not work in gangs at any level of wages that plantations could afford to pay. See Fogel and Engerman (1974), 1:237, 255, 257.

   Recent cliometric research tried to explain the early start of industrialization in the Northeast and the lag in the South from many directions. Different scholars have emphasized different factors but they are by no means in conflict. For a brief survey of the hypotheses explaining the "backwardness" of southern manufacturing, see Bateman and Weiss (1981), Ch. 2.

70. Wright (1978), 114.

71. Ibid.

72. Fischbaum and Rubin (1968), esp. 124.

73. Cf. Parker (1970a); Wade (1964). Efforts to subject these and other theories about the lag in southern industrialization to rigorous quantitative tests are just getting under way. Large samples of manufacturing firms for both the North and the South have been drawn from the manufacturing censuses for the years 1820, 1832, 1840, 1850, and 1860 and are now on computer tapes. Bateman and Weiss (1981); Sokoloff (1982). Cf. *EM*, #68.

74. See *EM*, #40. Cf. *EM*, #36; *TP*, #16. Estimation of profit rates is a potentially effective but indirect way of testing the proposition that the ethos of planters prevented them from shifting their capital from agriculture to manufacturing. Some scholars consider a direct approach more promising. A procedure has been developed for estimating the degree of planter involvement in manufacturing that depends on searching for persons identified as heads of manufacturing firms in the manuscript schedules of the census of agriculture. The initial results of this work indicate that the share of manufacturing capital owned by planters ranged from 5

percent in Florida to 46 percent in South Carolina, and that planters were much more deeply involved in the manufacturing sector than were other types of farmers (Bateman, Foust, and Weiss, 1974). Although very useful, the census schedules are not the best source of information on the degree of interpretation of agricultural and manufacturing capital. These schedules do not identify all those who invested in manufacturing firms but only the heads of the firms. They do not reveal the full degree of investment in plantations from the commercial or manufacturing circles of southern states and miss nearly all such investments from the North. Nor do they reveal the extent to which planters invested in northern manufacturing and commercial enterprises. A more complete picture of the interpenetration of planter capital with commercial and manufacturing capital can be obtained from probate records, which give considerable detail on the composition of the assets of planters, including their investments in northern enterprises.

75. The fact that female wages were much lower relative to male wages in the North than in the South does not imply that female wages in factories were low relative to female wages in other northern occupations. Quite the contrary—the demand for women in the factories tended to raise women's wages elsewhere. In other words, women's wages in agriculture in the North were much lower before the factory created a new demand for the labor of women. See Goldin and Solokoff (1982).

76. This discussion of the role of women in the labor force has been cast purely in terms of the factors influencing the rise of manufacturing. There are also moral issues pertaining to the circumstances under which women, slave and free, were drawn into work in both the agricultural and the industrial sectors. Cf. Chapters 9 and 10 of this volume. See also *EM*, #73.

Regression analysis on the Parker-Gallman sample indicates that white women on the farms in the cotton belt had about one-half the labor participation rate of slave women. See Fogel and Engerman (1974) and *TP*, #12; Moen, *TP*, #15; *EM*, #24.

77. The literature on this and related issues is growing rapidly. Among others see Sabel and Zeitlin (1985); Greenberg (1982); Laurie and Schmitz (1981); A.J. Field (1985); Tolliday and Zeitlin (1986); Wiener (1981); Dellheim (1985); Sokoloff (1984), (1986); McPherson (1982), 20–21.

78. Barney, as quoted by Oakes (1984), 309.

79. Oakes (1984, 307) summarizes Thornton (1978). See further studies cited by Oakes, esp. Thornton (1978), Watson (1981), Hahn (1983), Schlotterbeck (1980), and Barney (1974).

80. Oakes (1984, 307, 310) summarizing Thornton (1978).

81. It may come as a surprise to some that wealthy slaveholders did not continually dominate the political process. However, the fact that they did not, and why they did not, is at the heart of the point that political historians have recently been making about the nature of southern populism. Office seekers who ignored the wishes of their electorate paid a heavy price.

Chapter 5. The Population Question

1. On the early history of population policies see Glass (1967), 86–95. Glass discusses various measures employed by the French government during the seventeenth century to encourage population growth. See also Hutchinson (1967), Ch. 2. On William Petty see Bonar (1966), 82–100. For Petty's influence on the American colonies during the seventeenth century see Cassedy (1969), 47–57. Petty called the statistical method that he suggested "political arithmetic," to underline the practical application of his calculations. Somewhat earlier than Petty was the work of John Graunt (1620–1674), considered by many to be the founder of demography. On John Graunt see Bonar (1966), 68–82, esp. 75–78.

2. On early American censuses see Cassedy (1969), Ch. 4. A detailed account is given in Wells (1975), esp. his general survey, 3–34. Most American colonies conducted 4 to 12 censuses between 1675 and 1775. In some cases only the total number of inhabitants in a given colony was reported. In other cases the population was broken down by age, gender, occupation, religion, servants, slaves, and convicts. Though first published in 1755, Franklin's essay was written in 1751 in response to the British Iron Act of 1750, which he saw as a deterrent to colonial growth. Larabee and Bell (1961), 225–226. For discussions of Franklin's statistics of population growth see Cassedy (1969), 158–172; Potter (1965), 633–663.

3. Cf. Potter (1965).

4. Cassedy (1969), 179, 181, 182. For a discussion of the economic costs and benefits to the American colonies of participation in the British imperial system see Hughes (1969); Reid (1970); McClelland (1969).

5. On the establishment of U.S. censuses, see Cassedy (1969), 213–216.

6. For Hume's analyses of demographic issues see his essay "Of the Populousness of Ancient Nations" (1764).

7. Smith (1937), 81.

8. Smith (1937), 364, 891–892. For a general survey of slavery and demographic theory see Higman, in Walvin (1982), Ch. 7. For a further discussion of Smith's views on slavery and the context in which they arose, see Drescher (1986), 133–134, 241 n. 84; Davis (1966), 422–438; Temperley (1977), (1980); Finley (1980).

9. Sheridan (1981), 265, 262–263.

10. The abolitionist pressure for the registration of slaves represents, in effect, a change of strategy on their part. Rather than emphasize the conditions of the African slave trade and the situation on slave ships, they turned their attention to the treatment of slaves after they reached the British colonies. See Walvin (1981), 67–71. Registration was a tactic invented by James Stephan as the opening wedge of a campaign for emancipation, although it was publicly advanced merely as a means of preventing smuggling. See pp. 218–220 of Chapter 7 of this volume and the sources in n. 46 there.

11. *Anti-Slavery Reporter*, as quoted by Mathieson (1967), 106.

12. Craton (1978), 97–99.

13. See pp. 324–329 of Chapter 10 of this volume. *American Slavery as It Is* operated in different ways among different antislavery audiences. It was a powerful weapon in encouraging potential allies within the northern evangelical churches toward a more militant position. See n. 133 of Chapter 8 below. At another level, Weld's population arguments provided an economic rationale for the alleged southern drive for territorial expansion. See the discussion on pp. 353–354 of Chapter 10 of this volume.

14. Quotes in the preceding three paragraphs are from Weld (1839), 39, 85, 182–183, 27, 40–44, 142, 183.

15. See DeBow (1966), 2:292–303.

16. On the treatment of slaves by slaveholders see Stampp (1956), 156–162, 228–231, 279–330; Fogel and Engerman (1974), 1:109–117, 239–242.

17. For a description of the debate over Malthusian theory among slaveholders see Spengler (1936), who quotes Tucker and DeBow. On the early opinions of Tucker and his supporters see Spengler (1936), 362–364. In 1847, DeBow's *Review*, a leading southern journal, published a prediction that by 1900 the U.S. population would reach 300 million, two-thirds of whom would live in cities.

18. Tucker, as quoted by Spengler (1936), 370.

19. DeBow (1966), 2:313.

20. The consequent advances in demographic knowledge rest partly on a more thorough analysis of the same published data in the registrations and censuses that

entered into the debates of the slave era. But many of the new findings are due to the availability of high-speed computers and modern statistical procedures which have made it possible to analyze large samples of data obtained from the original manuscript records of the enumerators. These samples (in one case the entire census has been put in machine-readable form) contain information on demographic behavior at the plantation level, including information on variations in the household structures of the slaves and in vital rates from plantation to plantation. Further information at the plantation and household level has been obtained from large samples of probate records and from the vital registers maintained by individual plantation owners, some of which make it possible to trace slave families over several generations. See *EM*, #42, and the sources cited there.

21. See Higman (1984), Ch. 4.
22. Figure 19 is based on data from the following sources. Jamaica: c.1700–c.1756 are from Crayton (1971), 24; c.1818 is from *EM*, Table 42.4. Bahamas: Higman (1984), 310. French West Indies: average for the period 1739–1788 was computed from data in Steckel (1971) and Curtin (1969), Table 65. Brazil: average for the period 1798–1825 was computed from data in Steckel (1971); Curtin (1969), Tables 62, 63, and 65; Eltis (1987), Tables I and V. Europe: Carr-Saunders (1964), 42; Glass and Grebenik (1965), 58; I have ignored emigration from Europe which averages less than 1 per 1,000 per annum during any of the 4 periods covered by this figure. U.S. whites: c.1685–c.1805 are computed from *EM*, Table 60.1; c.1825–c.1855 are from *EM*, Table 60.3; for c.1870–c.1900, the cbr's were computed from the equation in *EM*, #60, n. 4, using the child-woman ratios for white women in U.S. Bureau of the Census (1975), 54, while the cdr's were computed from the life tables in the unpublished appendix to Haines (1979), using the procedure outlined in *EM*, Table 4.1, with population shares taken from U.S. Bureau of the Census (1975), 16 U.S. blacks: c.1685–c.1855 are from *EM*, Table 4.1; c.1885–1895 are computed from Coale and Rives (1973), 21, on the assumption that the black population was virtually closed during this period. The 1860 census figure for blacks (U.S. Bureau of the Census, 1909, 80) was increased by a factor of 1.1003, which is the same factor as that obtained by Coale and Rives for the 1880 census. This revised figure for 1860 was then used in conjunction with the Coale and Rives figure for 1880 to compute the average rate of natural increase during those two decades.
23. See Menard (1975b); Kiple (1984), Ch. 7; Fogel and Engerman (1979); Sheridan (1985); John (1984); Higman (1984), Ch. 9.
24. For a discussion of the factors affecting the fertility of U.S. slaves see Steckel, *TP*, #17; Trussell and Steckel, *TP*, #20; Fogel and Engerman, *TP*, #21.
25. See Higman (1984), 26–34; John (1984). The comparisons in this section are limited mainly to the United States, Jamaica, and Trinidad, where the corrections of the records seem most reliable.
26. See the papers listed in *n*. 24 above for an explanation of the high birth rates of U.S. slaves. See *EM*, #42, for a discussion of the methods of correcting birth rates that did not include the births of children who subsequently died. Cf. Higman (1984); John (1984).
27. On the section just finished, "Population Trends," see Craton (1971, 11) for data on slave population and mortality in Jamaica before 1800; after 1800, see Higman (1976). Higman (1984, Ch. 4) provides revised estimates for Jamaica and other Caribbean islands, 1807–1834. Why the onset of positive natural increase came later for the slaves than it did for the whites in the South is still an unsolved problem. One possible factor is that slave imports into the South did not become substantial until several decades after the onset of substantial white immigration into the region. Such a lag in imports would have delayed the rise of a native-born

444   NOTES (pp. 127–132)

black population with lower death rates than Africans, but it would be premature to accept this as the main factor or even an important one. See *EM*, #4, #6, for estimates of the native share of the U.S. black population.

28. Percentages are from *EM*, #42. Cf. Higman (1976), 48, Table 5. See Higman (1984, 314–347) for a general survey of slave mortality in the Caribbean colonies.

29. On Jamaican mortality rates see Higman (1976), 121–124; the high mortality rate on sugar plantations can be obtained by comparing Higman's maps of natural increase (1976, 104, Figure 20) and of sugar and coffee production (1976, 19, 22, Figures 2, 3). On Trinidad, see Friedman (1980, 11–13) and John (1984). On the United States, see Steckel, *TP*, #18, #23; cf. *EM*, #4, #6, #41.

30. Higman (1976), 16–17, 123–124, 251–252. See also Craton (1978), 119–133. Caloric consumption above basal metabolism would be a better measure of the intensity of work than the value of output per worker, but such information is not available (cf. *EM*, #47). Variations in output per worker reflect not only variations in labor intensity but also factor proportions and the technological augmentation of other inputs.

31. Friedman (1980), 11 and Table 10; cf. John (1984) and *TP*, #19. On the use of fertilizers see Roughly (1823). On the relative importance of various diseases among adult slaves in the West Indies and the United States see Savitt (1978), 135–147; Tulloch (1838), (1841); Higman (1976), 109–115, and (1984), Table 9.8; Sheridan (1985); Kiple (1984), Ch. 8 and 9.

32. Klein (1978), 70–71, 90ff. The death rates of immigrants varied greatly over the months of the year and by the colony of destination. Below the Pennsylvania border, deaths were highest between the beginning of July and the end of September. Arrivals, therefore, tended to be concentrated in the fall and early winter. Annual death rates were correlated with latitude. The lowest migrant death rates were experienced in New England. The death rates in the Chesapeake region, just 300 miles to the south of Boston, were twice as high as in New England, and those in the West Indies were double those in the Chesapeake. The exceedingly high death rates in tropical climates, and during the hot months of temperate climates, appear to have been due in large measure to the prevalence of malaria, which not only was a direct cause of death but also weakened the ability of those who contracted it to resist other infectious diseases. See Fogel et al. (1978) and the sources cited there. On the trends in U.S. death rates over time, see Fogel (1986) and Pope (1986) for whites, and *TP*, #18, for slaves. Cf. Gemery (1980, 1984) and McCusker and Menard (1985), Ch. 10.

33. For reviews of the literature on slave mortality rates in the Atlantic trade see Eltis (1987), Ch. 8 and App. D. On the mortality rate of the crews of slave ships, see Steckel and Jensen (1986); Cohn (1984). Cf. Engerman and Klein, *TP*, #22.

34. See Davies (1975), esp. Table 3.

35. Kapp (1870). In this case it has been established that typhus epidemics that broke out on board the vessels were responsible for the deaths. Epidemics were probably caused by immigrants already infected with the deadly microorganisms, or infested with the lice that carry them, before they boarded. Cohn (1984); Galenson (1986a), 37–52, (1986b); Grubb (1987); Eltis (1987), Ch. 8.

36. See Eltis (1987), Ch. 8. Cf. Klein (1978); LeVeen (1971); Cohn and Jensen (1982); Engerman and Klein, *TP*, #22.

37. Tulloch (1838), (1841); Higman (1976), 113–115; Menard (1975a, b); Fogel and Engerman (1979); Higman (1984), 260–302, 314–347; Sheridan (1985), 9–41, 185–221; McCusker and Menard (1985), Ch. 10; Kulikoff (1985), 69, 168; Rutman and Rutman (1984), 2:37–60. Cf. Main (1982), 136–137.

38. Eltis (1972); Engerman (1976); Fogel et al. (1978); Fogel and Engerman (1979); G. Friedman (1980), (1982); Gemery (1980); Higman (1984), 43–45, 79–85; Sheridan (1985), 131–134, 187–188. The reduction in life expectancy caused by

moving from Jamaica to Trinidad is computed from life tables in *EM*, #42, and John (1984). It should be noted that life expectation of slaves in Jamaica at age 20 was about 7 years greater than at birth. Cf. Higman (1984), 32, 319.

39. Several different but generally complementary research strategies have been developed to investigate these nutritional issues. Some scholars have attempted to estimate the average quantities of the major foods actually consumed by one or another slave population and then have measured the nutritional content of these average or typical diets. Others have searched plantation records, medical reports, and death registers for information that would indicate the prevalence of diseases, such as scurvy, pellagra, and beriberi, which are now known to be caused by specific nutritional deficiencies. Still another task involves the use of data on the height and (when available) the weight of slaves at given ages as indexes of the average level of nutrition. Much information has also been derived from systematic studies of the narratives of ex-slaves about their conditions of life under slavery and from archaeological excavations of the grounds of former plantations. The narratives and the excavations have shed light on such matters as the range of foods consumed by slaves and the extent to which slaves were able, through their own efforts, to supplement the diets provided by masters. Although the several sources of information about diets vary in the quality and extent of the information they provide, and the findings based on alternative sources sometimes conflict, by and large the different studies have reinforced each other and collectively they provide a fairly detailed picture about the quantity and quality of slave diets, about their variations over time and place, and about the bearing of these diets on the mortality rates of slaves. See *EM*, Part 5; *TP*, Part 5.

40. The sources for Figure 21 are: U.S. slaves—Fogel and Engerman (1974), 2:97; Sutch (1976); Berlin, Antwerp, and Paris—Lis and Soly (1977), 466; U.S. Department of Agriculture (1907), Table 59 (the preparer of this USDA bulletin, George Holmes, believes that the figures are in pounds of dressed weight); Massachusetts workers—Mass. *Report of the Statistics of Labor* (1873), 118; Surinam slaves—Van den Boogaart and Emmer (1977), 212 (their figure for meat mandated by the 1851 law was divided by 1.28 to put it on a per capita basis); Cuba—Fraginals (1977), 200 (his figure was divided by 1.28 to shift it from a consuming unit to a per capita basis); see Fogel (1987) for a discussion of the 1.28 adjustment factor; all other data are from U.S. Department of Agriculture (1907), Table 59.

41. Richard B. Sheridan cites evidence suggesting that the average caloric intake of slaves in the Bahamas may have exceeded that of slaves in the sugar colonies by 75 percent. Sheridan (1985), 169–172. There is also evidence suggesting that during the decades of the rapid shift into sugar production, which extended from 1650 to 1750 depending on the colony, imports of meats, fish, and grains were insufficient to make up for the reduction of local food supplies. On the other hand, the food supplied to slaves in the Bahamas, which specialized in cotton and food crops rather than sugar, appears to have been relatively abundant. For reviews of these approaches see Kiple and King (1981); Reitz, Gibbs, and Rathbun (1985); *TP*, Part 5.

42. See Fogel and Engerman (1974), 1:109–117, 2:92–99; Sutch (1976), 261–268. Both studies followed the "disappearance procedure" developed by the U.S. Department of Agriculture that is currently used to estimate the U.S. national diet. The procedure employs various coefficients to transform data on heads of live cattle or swine into lean meat available for consumption. Similar coefficients are used to convert stocks of wheat or corn into flour and meal, taking account of the quantities of these grains used as animal feed and as seeds, as well as allowing for losses in milling and in inventory. Each study applied such coefficients to information on crop production and stocks of animals reported for large slave plantations and so produced estimates of the slave consumption of 11 principal foods enumerated in

the 1860 census, after making due allowance for the share of these foods consumed by the whites who lived on the test plantations. See Fogel and Engerman, *EM*, #43, for their response to Sutch's criticisms of their seed and feed allowance and their conversion ratios, as well as other issues.

43. Weld (1839), 28. For his general discussion of the "privations of slaves" with regard to food see Weld (1839), 27–35.

44. Sutch (1976), 234.

45. On niacin deficiency, see Sutch (1976), 270–274; on vitamin A deficiency, see 275–277; on thiamine deficiency, see 277–281. See *EM*, #43, for a response by Fogel and Engerman to issues raised by Sutch with respect to specific nutrients. Cf. Savitt (1978); Kiple and King (1981).

46. It might be argued that the narratives, by selecting slaves that had lived to an old age, also selected plantations that tended to have diets more varied than the average. Crawford (1980) and *EM*, #44, indicate a wide range of variation in the diets provided slaves by their masters. Although various characteristics of slave experience in the sample are correlated with their date of birth (and hence their age at the time of the interview), the quality of the diet provided by masters does not appear to have been one of them. Cf. *EM*, #51.

47. Crawford (1980), Ch. 4; *EM*, #43, #44, #51.

48. See Crawford (1980, Ch. 6) and *EM*, #51, for discussions of problems involved in interpreting the evidence in the ex-slave narratives. The 70 percent figure on other meats is obtained by dividing 59 by 84 (for pork). Regular consumption of milk was reported mainly by ex-slaves who were still children when slavery ended or by older slaves who reported their diet as children. This pattern is consistent with lactose intolerance among blacks and helps to explain the relatively low level of milk consumption reported by Fogel and Engerman (1974, 1:112). See Cardell and Hopkins, *EM*, #45.

49. Gibbs et al. (1980), 217; see also 205–217, esp. 212ff. See Reitz, Gibbs, and Rathbun (1985) for results from 20 plantations and 3 additional states. Results of this larger sample are similar to those from the four sites discussed in the 1980 paper.

50. On the nutritional value of slave diets, apart from the studies by Sutch and by Fogel and Engerman cited above, see Postell (1970), 85–86; Kiple and Kiple, (1977a, b), (1980); Gibbs et al. (1980); Savitt (1978), 86–98; Sheridan (1985), 200–219.

51. For an elaboration of the points made in this and the two previous paragraphs, see Tanner (1978), (1981); Fogel (1986); Floud, Wachter, and Gregory (1989). Cf. *EM*, #47.

52. On the Sierra Leone case, see Eltis (1982), 454. Eltis's data are from the records of 27,000 of the 57,000 freed blacks who were registered between 1819 and 1845.

53. The sources for Figure 24 are: France—LeRoy Ladurie (1979); U.S. northern whites—Gould (1869), Baxter (1875); U.S. slaves—Margo and Steckel (1982); Trinidad slaves—Friedman (1982); British town artisans—British Association for the Advancement of Science (1883), 3, 290; British non-sugar colonies—Higman (1984), 283; British Royal Marines—Fogel et al. (1978), 85, but cf. Floud, Wachter, and Gregory (1989); Cuba—Fraginals (1977), 198; Italy—SVIMEZ (1954), 49. The mean height of Africans was determined by weighting the mean height of given tribes as reported in Fogel et al. (1978, 86) by the distribution of U.S. imports by ethnicity given by Curtin (1969, 157). The heights of the Cubans may be too low. Africans destined for Cuba in the sample for Sierra Leone collected by Eltis (1972) had a mean height of 64.5 inches (letter from David Eltis to RWF dated August 23, 1983). On growth between age 20 and age at final height during the first half of the nineteenth century see Fogel (1987) and Floud, Wachter, and Gregory (1989). On the effect of early death on the distribution of final heights,

see G. Friedman (1982), 501–504; Robb, *EM*, #48. However, the 2.1-inch bias referred to by Friedman (p. 502) becomes negligible with life tables at Level West 7 or greater (Coale and Demeny, 1966). Similarly the effect on trends in final height over time also became negligible at such levels of life expectation. If slaves bound for the transatlantic trade were selected for height, as seems likely (Curtin, 1969, 156–158), the differential between the mean final heights of Africans and of U.S. slaves could have been greater than is indicated in Figure 24.

54. For a discussion of heights of slaves see G. Friedman (1982); Margo and Steckel (1982). A general review of the uses of data on height is Fogel, Engerman, and Trussell (1982). The present British standard of height is given in Tanner, White-house, and Takaishi (1966); for British heights by socioeconomic class, see Rona, Swan, and Altman (1978), 149.

55. The growth pattern reflects the interaction of genetic, environmental, and socioeco-nomic factors during the period of growth. According to Eveleth and Tanner (1976, 222):

> Such interaction may be complex. The genotypes which produce the same adult heights under optimal environmental circumstances may produce different heights under circumstances of privation. Thus, two children who would be the same height in a well-off community may not only be smaller under poor eco-nomic conditions, but one may be significantly smaller than the other. . . . If a particular environmental stimulus is lacking at a time when it is essential for the child (times known as "sensitive periods"), then the child's development may be shunted, as it were, from one line to another.

56. The map of centiles is from Tanner, Whitehouse, and Takaishi (1966). See G. Friedman (1982) for the Trinidad heights and Steckel, *TP*, #18, for the heights of U.S. slaves.

57. Crawford (1980), Ch. 2, on occupations. See also Steckel, *TP*, #23.

58. See Steckel (1986b); Steckel, *TP*, #23.

59. On intrauterine malnutrition see Tanner (1978), 210–211; Beal (1980), Ch. 3; Frisancho (1979), 184–186; Postell (1970), 122–124.

60. Blassingame (1977), 133; cf. Cody (1982), Ch. 4, on the "weaning crisis."

61. Kiple and King (1981), 112. See also Postell (1970), 123–124; Genovese (1974), 507–508; Kiple and King (1981), 111–113.

62. Crawford (1980), Ch. 4; *EM*, #43; Hilliard (1972), 55–62. See the discussion on body mass indexes in *EM*, #47.

63. Fogel and Engerman (1974), 2:101; Fogel and Engerman (1977), 286; Anderson (1974), 48ff.; Savitt (1978), 147. For data on mortality rates see *EM*, #41, and *TP*, #18.

64. See Metzer, *TP*, #10; Campbell (1984); Steckel (1986b); Postell (1970), 111.

65. See Naeye and Peters (1982), (1981). See also Beal (1980), 138; Hytten and Leitch (1971), 452–454. A study of peasants in Africa revealed that the weight gain of pregnant women during the heavy work of the rainy season was just half as much as the weight gain during the light work of the dry seasons. See Thomson et al. (1966). The African case suggests that the heavy work regime of pregnant slave women combined with insufficient dietary supplementation probably kept their weight gain during pregnancy extremely low, thus producing the tiny babies indica-ted by the anthropometric data. During the 1950s and 1960s U.S. obstetricians commonly set limits of 12 to 18 pounds on the weight gain of pregnant women (instead of current targets of 22 to 28 pounds) in the belief that a low weight gain would control certain ailments commonly associated with pregnancy. The practice was discontinued when research revealed that so low a weight gain compromised the viability of fetuses and infants. Beal (1980), 137–138.

66. Margo and Steckel (1982), Table 1; Steckel (1986), Table 2. See *EM*, #49, for a discussion of the overwork of pregnant slaves.

67. McKeown (1976), 121–123, 125–126, 138. On descriptions of childhood diseases, see Kiple (1984); Kiple and King (1981); Savitt (1978). Cody's work (1982) on the records of the Ball plantations in St. John's Berkeley Parish, South Carolina, suggests that children were breast-fed until 18 months, although partial weaning earlier is likely. It may be a mistake to assume that weaning meant a total removal of mother's milk. See Wray (1978).

68. On the Trinidad case, see G. Friedman (1982), 493–494, 506–508. On fetal alcohol syndrome see Tanner (1978), 47; Beal (1980), 147–148. It is doubtful that adult slaves in Trinidad could have worked harder than U.S. slaves; the nutrient value of their diet would not permit it. But in combination, the claims of work and disease left Trinidad slaves with a lower net nutrition than U.S. slaves to sustain an adolescent growth spurt. On rum consumption see McCusker (1989); Higman (1984), 205. Pieter Emmer suggests that females and children were more likely to receive molasses than rum (letter to RWF dated August 8, 1983). Cf. Fogel (1986), 480–484.

69. See n. 38 in this chapter.

70. See EM, #42, for a discussion of the procedures used to estimate the undercount of infant deaths in the slave populations. Cf. Wrigley and Schofield (1981), 97–100, and Fogel (1986), 518–519 n. 21.

71. The average age at which childbearing ended for U.S. slaves was 38. See Steckel, TP, #17. On Trinidad see Friedman (1980); John (1984), esp. Table A2.4.

72. Cf., for example, TP, #17, and Steckel (1985). Trussell and Steckel, TP, #20, discuss the age of slaves at their first births. On patterns of first birth and other determinants of fertility in non-industrial societies today and during the eighteenth and nineteenth centuries in Europe and America see Pebley, Casterline, and Trussell (1982); Talwar (1965); Levine (1978); Mokyr and Savin (1978); Mineau, Bean, and Skolnick (1979); Wrigley (1966); Wrigley and Schofield (1981).

73. Data for the computations underlying Table 4 are from Steckel (1985); TP, #17; EM, #41, #42; Friedman (1980); John (1984).

74. Craton (1979), esp. 28–29; Higman (1973), (1976), (1984); Crawford (1980).

75. Crawford (1980), 149–154, 164ff. Crawford grouped together two-parent, consolidated families and two-parent, divided families (i.e., when the father and mother did not live in the same plantations, but the father had visitation rights); see his pp. 150–154. For the Jamaican case see Higman (1973), esp. 535. Sheridan (1985, 134–141) points out that planters built houses or barracks for newly imported slaves, but creole slaves in the West Indies were generally expected to build their own houses, with some small help from their overseers or owners.

76. Computed by the procedures in United Nations (1983), Ch. 4, using the life tables in John (1984). Cf. Higman (1973), 535. See also Higman (1976), 156–173, esp. 168; Friedman (1980), Tables 9, 9b, 10.

77. Apart from the sources mentioned in the previous two notes, see Steckel (1985), esp. Ch. 5 and 6.

78. See TP, #21; EM, #50. See also the discussion on whether it was optimal to overwork pregnant slave women in EM, #49.

79. Steckel (1985), 203–206, 226–232. It should be remembered that a plantation with 100 slaves typically involved perhaps 15 families, some of which were related to each other. Since cousin marriages were generally excluded, confining the search for partners to persons living on the plantation severely limited choice.

80. Crawford (1980), 163–167. The last sentence implies that about 15 percent of slave marriages were destroyed by the slave trade.

81. Important progress has been made in tracing the fertility changes of U.S. slaves from the late seventeenth century on by making use of data in probate records and private plantation registers. See Kulikoff (1986); Cody (1982).

82. Steckel (1985), 185–196, 226–232.

CHAPTER 6. CHANGING INTERPRETATIONS OF SLAVE CULTURE

1. In this chapter I shift from presenting my own synthesis of recent scholarship to a review of the literature on slave culture. As I explained in the Foreword, differences of opinion among the experts on slave culture are still so wide that it would be premature to offer a synthesis. Readers should not infer that because I have proposed syntheses on the economic, demographic, and political aspects of slavery the disputes on these topics are minor. Quite the contrary, much of *EM* and *TP* is devoted to the analysis of debates in these fields, which are still vigorous.

2. The concentration camp metaphor was coined by Elkins (1968) and the resistance metaphor, inspired by events in Europe, was suggested by Herskovits (1958, 99–102). See also Bauer and Bauer (1942). These two new metaphors jointly replaced the previously reigning metaphor, found in Phillips (1966), which compared plantations to schools.

3. The juxtaposition of cliometrics and culture, which at first seemed odd to some scholars, is neither odd nor new. Franz Boas, the founder of cultural anthropology in the United States, made extensive use of statistical methods in his work. Culture does not exist in a vacuum; it is defined by the behavior, artifacts, institutions, and beliefs of a society. What frequently differentiates one culture from another is not so much the presence or absence of particular types of behavior, artifacts, or institutions but the frequency of their occurrence or their distribution over space and time. And much of what we know, or think we know, about the beliefs of a society is inferential, and turns on the study of the frequency of certain types of practices or artifacts. In applying quantitative methods to the study of slave culture, cliometricians were merely continuing an established and fruitful approach to cultural issues.

4. Rhodes (1928), 307, 309, 370.

5. DuBois (1918), 722.

6. Woodson (1919a), 102–103.

7. Woodson (1931), IV. See also Woodson (1919), (1921); Greene and Woodson (1930).

8. Woodson (1919b), 227–228.

9. Woodson (1919b), 85, 227–228.

10. Wesley (1927), 5–6.

11. Woodson (1927), 177.

12. Aptheker (1943), 50, 368.

13. Herskovits (1958), 99–102; Bauer and Bauer (1942), 388–419.

14. Herskovits (1958), 1–2, 99.

15. Stampp (1956), 108; see also his Ch. 2, esp. pp. 97–109, and his Ch. 3 and 9.

16. Stampp (1956), 334–336, 126–127; Stampp (1952), 618; Douglass (1969), 160; Frederickson and Lasch (1967), 315–329.

17. For a response to those who have questioned these findings see Fogel and Engerman, *TP*, #12, #13.

18. Genovese (1974), 65, 307–308; Crawford, *EM*, #51.

19. Crawford (1980), Ch. 3.

20. Genovese (1974), 286, 291, 315, 303, 292.

21. Genovese (1974), 292.

22. Genovese (1974), 311.

23. See, for example, Smith and Cole (1935); Berry (1943); American Iron and Steel Association (1856–1858), Tables A–K; Kuznets (1933), esp. 400, which shows that during the years 1925–1931 the monthly low in the production of passenger cars was 41 percent of the monthly high.

24. U.S. Department of Agriculture (1912), 14. I use the word *heavy* to mean that the

demand for labor was above average and found reflection in a hire price for labor that was above average. See Fogel and Engerman, *TP*, #12. Plantations satisfied peak labor demand primarily by more intense labor per hour rather than by more hours per day. See Olson, *TP*, #11.

25. Metzer, *TP*, #10; Olson, *TP*, #11.

26. Olmsted (1970), 452.

27. David and Temin (1975), 445–457; Genovese (1974), esp. 327–398; Crawford (1980); Olson, *TP*, #8. See *EM*, #43, for data on the effect of self-supplementation on the quality of the slave diet. Jonathan B. Pritchett, who has recently begun a new study of the New Orleans invoices, suggests in a letter to RWF of May 26, 1987, that there might have been undercounting of skilled occupations even in this source. This possibility cannot be ruled out, and Pritchett's study may shed new light on the issue. Undercounting of skills is a major problem in most bodies of records, although the undercount in the notarial records appears to be less than in other sources, because failure to insist on a guarantee of a skill would undermine the legal claim of a purchaser in the event of a suit. On undercounting of skills and on approaches to the estimation of the extent of undercounting see Olson, *TP*, #8; McMillan, (1988). Cf. Kotlikoff, *TP*, #3; Margo, *TP*, #9.

28. The discussion in this section focuses on a limited set of issues that have been at the center of the controversy about the effect of slavery on the integrity of slave families. These issues have been so all-consuming that they have impeded the development of a more complete view of the life and mentalité of slave women and their specific contributions to the development of an independent slave culture. For two studies that have begun to fill the void, see Jones (1985) and White (1985).

29. Rhodes (1928), 318, 332, 335; see Phillips (1918), 342–343 and Ch. 22.

30. DuBois (1970a), 47, 49.

31. DuBois (1970a), 152.

32. Frazier (1939), 483.

33. Frazier (1939), 23–25, 29, 30; see also Frazier (1930), 198–259. With the possible exception of Carter Woodson, Frazier was the first scholar to examine systematically and employ the printed autobiographies of ex-slaves as a source of information on the slave family. Frazier reported the results of his examination in a long article published in 1930, generally accepting the autobiographies as authentic reflections of slave family life, although he recognized that at least some had been influenced by the antislavery critics who edited them.

34. Stampp (1956), 340, 343–348.

35. Gutman's extensive remarks in a symposium held in November 1971 and one of his papers from this period have appeared in print; Engerman et al. (1972), 22–41; Gutman (1972), 1197–1218. This paper was republished in English, with the addition of an introductory footnote; see Gutman (1976b).

36. Blassingame (1972), 79.

37. Genovese (1974), 450, 451–452.

38. Engerman et al. (1972), 25, 26.

39. Elkins (1975), 47; Gutman (1976), esp. Ch. 2.

40. Blassingame (1972), 87. In the 1979 edition of his book Blassingame reconsidered the dual-model approach, pointing out that much of what had been described as the loose morality of the quarters reflected not a destabilization of the slave family, but the increasing effort by white churches to exercise moral influence in slave quarters. This perceived "increase" in moral laxity reflected an increase in awareness of the conflict between family patterns in the slave quarters and Christian precepts, due to increased involvement of the white church. Blassingame (1979), 170.

41. Genovese (1974), 459, 465–466.

42. Genovese (1974), 415, 452, 483, 489.

43. Genovese (1974), 457.
44. Blassingame (1972), 91. If the destruction of marriages was as extensive as Blassingame indicated, surely Stampp's case for the widespread demoralization of family life would gain credence, while the credence of Gutman's and Genovese's contention that the black family emerged from slavery with a "remarkably stable base" would be diminished (Genovese, 1974, 452). Nor does it seem plausible that with such extensive destruction of marriages marital fidelity could have been so strong or adultery so rare as Genovese suggested. Certainly the extent to which slave fathers were able to affect the fortunes of their families would have been far less than Genovese suggested.
45. My point here is not necessarily that all these issues can, in fact, be resolved by quantification, but that knowledge of distributions of slave responses (or of some of their parameters) has been implicitly assumed by disputants, even on issues as difficult to quantify as the expectations and fears of slaves about the threat of family dissolution.
46. Stampp (1956), 54, 81, 327, 329.
47. Stampp (1956), 78, 81.
48. Stampp (1956), 331.
49. Stampp (1956), 332, 335, 374, 378; see also Frazier (1940).
50. Stampp (1956), 367–369.
51. Stampp (1956), 361.
52. Stampp (1956), 362, 364.
53. Elkins (1968), 86.
54. Fredrickson and Lasch (1967), 325–328.
55. Webber (1978), xii–xiii.
56. Webber (1978), 26.
57. Webber (1978), 71.
58. Stampp (1956), 146.
59. Webber (1978), 91, 133.
60. Webber (1978), xii.
61. Webber (1978), 191–192, 205–206.
62. Webber (1978), 215, 222, 223.
63. Genovese (1974), 675.
64. Blassingame (1979), 367.
65. Genovese (1974), 675.
66. Blassingame (1977), li. See *EM*, #51, and Escott (1979, 3–14) for a brief description of the various collections of ex-slave narratives, a comparison of the locations of interviewees during slavery and during interviews, and tables of information given in relation to the race of the interviewers.
67. Blassingame (1977), xliii–lvii. It has been argued that since most of the interviewees were children when slavery ended, they were less likely to emphasize work and more likely to suggest a paternalistic relationship between masters and slaves. Crawford reports on his investigation of this issue in *EM*, #51, and *TP*, #26. See also Crawford (1980), 34.
68. Stuckey (1973), 134.
69. Levine (1977), xi–xii.
70. Levine (1977), xiii.
71. Genovese (1974), 676.
72. Webber (1978), 267.
73. Genovese (1974), 675–676.
74. I have relied primarily on Crawford's work on the quantification of the ex-slave narratives because he addresses the points at issue here more directly than Escott (1979). Where they overlap, however, Crawford's findings are quite similar to Escott's. See Crawford (1980), 244. Rawick (1972, V. 1) was skeptical of the

suitability of the narratives for quantification, but that judgment was made before either the Escott or the Crawford studies were completed.

75. In quantification, an attribute is any characteristic of a slave that can be identified, such as the age at which he or she left the parental household. The distributions give, for example, the percentage who left the household at each specific age.

76. Crawford, *EM*, #51 Although cotton producers began to feel the impact of competition from rayon in the 1920s, black workers were far better off during this decade than during the depression decade, since farm income from cotton and tobacco remained relatively high during most of the 1920s. U.S. Bureau of the Census (1975), 485. Cf. Soule (1947), Ch. 11; Mitchell (1947), Ch. 6.

77. Crawford (1980), 38.

78. Crawford (1980), 32.

79. The statements in this and the next paragraph are based on distributions computed from the data set underlying Crawford (1980).

80. Gutman (1976), xxii.

81. Plantation growth rates were computed from data in the Steckel (1985, Table 2) collection of large plantations with demographic data; Gutman (1975), 147; Gutman and Sutch (1976), 145–146; Trussell and Steckel, *TP*, #20.

82. Gutman (1975), 147, (1976) 58–61ff; cf. Gutman and Sutch (1976), 145–146.

83. The discussion in this and the next three paragraphs is based on Steckel (1985); Steckel, *TP*, #17.

84. Tanner (1981), 167; see also Trussell and Steckel, *TP*, #20. From these studies, the age of menarche appears to have been 1.5 to 2.5 years below the range conjectured by Gutman (see sources in n.82 of this chapter).

85. In a letter to RWF of February 5, 1987, J. Morgan Kousser points out that South Carolina allowed interracial marriages in the antebellum period.

86. Crawford (1980); Steckel (1980).

87. For a discussion of methodology, including the singulate mean, see Trussell and Steckel, *TP*, #20; cf. Fogel (1982), 90–94.

88. Stampp (1956), 333.

89. Webber (1978), 3.

90. Webber (1978), xii. On p. x, Webber defines the slave quarter community as:
    those slaves throughout the South who related to a slave quarter as the center of their social activities and relationships, who shared a common set of values and attitudes, were organized in a familiar social structure, and displayed an awareness of their uniqueness and separate identity as a group. In general, the forming of a quarter community necessitated a plantation population of between fifteen and twenty slaves.

91. The proportion of adult slaves was somewhat lower on small plantations than on large ones, because fertility rates were lower, and infant death rates probably higher, on the larger plantations than on the smaller ones. For a fuller discussion of this question, see *TP*, #17, #18, #23, #24; cf. Margo and Steckel (1982).

92. Owens (1976), 137.

93. Rawick (1972), 19:170, as quoted by Owens (1976), 136.

94. For the United States, see *EM*, #55. The Jamaican data are from Higman (1976), 274–275.

95. I do not mean to suggest that important elements of a black culture could not have arisen in a world of small plantations, especially when slaves had opportunities to move freely about the countryside after work and on weekends. In such circumstances, however, slaves also had much more contact with whites than was typical on large plantations and were less likely to develop cultures with a high degree of autonomy. Although the separation of blacks from whites on large plantations allowed a more autonomous slave culture, it would be wrong to assume that slaves in other circumstances did not have a role in shaping their culture. The interaction

of master and servant was affected by action and response on both sides. For a discussion of this issue, especially as it affects the possibilities of resistance and is affected by the American character, see Kolchin (1978), 470–479. Cf. Kulikoff (1986) and Kolchin (1987).

96. Gray (1958), 538–539. See Phillips (1966), 230–231, and Olson, *TP*, #8. Cf. *EM*, #12.

97. One can only conjecture as to why abolitionist editors and the later interviewers found the big plantations so compelling. However, it was the wealthy planters, not the petty slaveowners, that were the prime targets of the abolitionists. It was easier to rouse the support of petty northern farmers and artisans by promoting their populism than by seeking to arouse them against southern yeomen farmers with whom they could more easily identify. As a result, large plantations became the quintessence of slavery, even in the United States where they contained only a relatively small percentage of the slaves. That tradition carries down to this day and may be sturdy enough to withstand many critiques to the contrary. For a discussion of the procedures used to estimate the distribution of slaves, see *EM*, #55. The data on the ex-slaves are from Crawford (1980).

98. See the reviews by Elkins (1975); Davis (1977); Engerman (1978).

99. Patterson (1982), 11; Genovese (1971), 89–90. For a critique of Elkin's thesis of slave personality, see Genovese (1971), Ch. 4. See also Engerman et al. (1972), 39–41, esp. Genovese's comments on 41. For this paragraph and the next one, see *TP*, #4.

100. For a brief history of concentration camps see *Encyclopaedia Britannica* (1961), 6: 191–192.

101. Engerman et al. (1972), 41.

102. Mintz (1979), 222–223.

103. Mintz and Hall (1960), 11.

104. Mintz (1978), 93, 94–96.

105. Mintz (1974), 200–201, 205–207.

106. The rebellion of 1831 was also called the "Baptist War" because of the involvement of preachers, especially its leader, Sam Sharpe, an urban slave and mission-based Native Baptist preacher. ["Native Baptist" is a "generic term for a proliferation of sects in which the slaves developed religious forms . . . that reflected their needs more closely than the orthodox churches" (Turner, 1982, 58; see also 94).] The organization and freedom of activity that the churches allowed slaves made them part of the proto-peasant experience that contributed to the atmosphere of revolt. The role of the rebellion in encouraging British emancipation is discussed in Chapter 7 of this volume, pp. 228–230. See also Drescher (1986, 110) and, for a more detailed discussion, especially of the role of missionaries, Turner (1982).

107. Genovese (1979), 102.

108. Apprenticeship was a system of gradual emancipation instituted in the British West Indies. The system freed slaves on August 1, 1834, but required the freedmen to work for their former masters, a period of six years for agricultural workers and of four years for craftsmen and domestics. There were many abuses of the system, such as masters reclassifying slaves as field workers in order to command their labor longer, and much outcry against it, with the result that total abolition was decreed in 1838. See Green (1976), 156ff.; Craton (1978), 275. For a brief description of the apprenticeship system, see Mintz (1974), 206–207. Cf. Fogel and Engerman, *TP*, #29; *EM*, #18.

Serfdom in Russia could be interpreted as a prolonged instance of apprenticeship, given the endurance of major elements of the system long after the formal emancipation of the serfs. Cf. Gerschenkron (1968), Ch. 7. For a comparison of the defenses of slavery in the southern United States and of serfdom in Russia, see Kolchin (1980), (1987).

109. Davis (1943), 52, 139, 412, 414. See Gutman (1975, 17–28, 30–35, 39–42, 44–46) for criticism of this use of Barrow's records. See *EM*, #52, for evidence indicating that in c.1860 the "extra" income of most slave households exceeded $20 per year. For a discussion of the underlying moral issues in this debate, see *EM*, #72.

110. For an explanation of the computation of the "basic income," and the comparison of top income to basic income for slaves, see *EM*, #52.

111. See *n.* 109 and *n.* 110 above; Devereux (1839–1864).

112. Crawford (1980), 104–105. The limitations put on proto-peasant activities by masters are a further example of the extent of the drive to dehumanize slaves in the American system. For examples of the rights allowed to slaves in other systems, see Hellie (1982), 1–26 and Part 1; Hellie (1989).

113. Morgan (1982), 588; cf. *EM*, #52.

114. Gray (1958), 556.

115. Morgan (1982), 578. See also Morgan (1983), concerning property usage and ownership by slaves and recently freed slaves.

116. Phillips (1966), 248. Phillips cites Olmsted (1968), 436.

117. I have put the word "concessions" in quotation marks to emphasize that what southern slaveholders viewed as concessions were common in other slave systems. Under gang-system slavery, the dehumanization of slaves was pushed so far that granting rights normally exercised by slaves in other systems was considered, and sometimes became, a threat to stability. See Hellie (1982), (1989); Patterson (1982); Finley (1968a), (1980).

118. There were, however, fairly high instances of manumission in Virginia between 1780 and 1805, as well as in Maryland and in New Orleans during the antebellum era. Some of these occurred through religion convictions, primarily of Quakers and Methodists. Whatever the source, it seems likely that manumission occurred for ideological reasons since it cannot have been economically sound, unless free blacks were strongly represented among buyers. See Albert (1976); Kotlikoff and Rupert, *TP*, #30; Patterson (1982), 296.

119. See *EM*, #54.

120. *Plantation and Farm Instruction, Regulation, Record, Inventory, and Account Book* (1852), 4–5.

121. Kahn, *TP*, #25. Linear programming is the mathematical procedure used to find the least expensive diet that will satisfy nutritional standards or any other set of constraints.

122. From the writings of Solon Robinson, a northern agriculturist, in Kellar (1936), 149.

123. Savitt (1978), 95, 93.

124. Elkins (1975), 54, 53, 41. That U.S. slaves faced more uncertainty than other laborers is open to question, and was in fact questioned by Greeley, Engels, Marx, and other critics of the operation of wage labor markets at the time.

125. Degler (1978), 279–280.

126. In all forms of slave systems, it is overwhelmingly the case that elite slaves led any rebellions that occurred. See Hellie (1982), (1987); Patterson (1982); Finley (1980); Genovese (1979).

127. Genovese (1979), 28.

128. Patterson (1982), 97. Although resistance to degradation would seem to be universally the case, the urge for freedom definitely would have been diminished in slave societies, such as Russia, where it was common for people to sell themselves into slavery in times of difficulty. It was also true, however, that in Russia flight from slavery was more common and more easily undertaken than in other slave cultures. See Hellie (1982).

129. For a brief account of the 1831 slave revolt in Jamaica, see Reckord (1968), 117–119; for a fuller account, see Turner (1982).

130. In some cases, slave resistance encouraged external intervention.

CHAPTER 7. THE BRITISH CAMPAIGN

1. Aristotle, Politics I, 1254b. For discussions of the nature of slavery in ancient Greece and Rome, see Davis (1966); Finley (1968), (1980); Hopkins (1978); Patterson (1982).
2. Davis (1966), 86, 165; slavery in Christian doctrine is discussed on 84ff.
3. Davis (1966), 100–101.
4. Thomas More's *Utopia*, as quoted by Davis (1966), 107.
5. Davis (1966), 106.
6. Davis (1966), 119, also 118–121. For a somewhat different interpretation of Locke's attitude toward slavery, see Drescher (1986), 23–24, 184 n. 69.
7. Davis (1984), 135–136. See also Hellie (1989).
8. Davis (1984), 26–27. Cf. Drescher (1986), 12–24; Gay (1977), 2:407–423.
9. Davis (1984), 54, 59.
10. Davis (1984), 76. On the proportion of households owning slaves in northern colonies, and on the proportion of slaves in their population and labor forces, see 75.
11. Davis (1966), 291. Gay (1977), 2:406–422.
12. On Sewall see Davis (1966), 342–348; on the Quakers, see his Ch. 10. See also Drake (1965), esp. Ch. 1 and 4; Zilversmit (1967), 58–60. Cf. Soderlund (1985).
13. For sources for Table 6 see Davis (1975), 23–36; Drescher (1977), 189–192; Drescher (1986), xiii–xv; Lovejoy (1983), 283–287. For general descriptions of the course of emancipation see Davis (1975), Ch. 1; Fogel and Engerman (1974), 1:29–37; Austen (1981); Franklin (1967).
14. For a discussion of the economics of gradual emancipation see *TP*, #29. On Haiti see James (1963); Genovese (1979); Geggus (1982). On Cuba, see Knight (1970); Scott (1985). On other regions of Latin America, see Klein (1986).
15. Fogel and Engerman, *TP*, #29.
16. Steckel (1971).
17. I use the term "civility" to describe not merely those who officially had the right to shape the political process but also those who, although officially denied that right, sought to have it and de facto wielded great influence on the process. During the first three or four decades of the reign of George III, various groups in the middle class and in the labor aristocracy began to emerge as major blocs in the struggle for power even though they were excluded from the electorate. These groups were not merely manipulated by members of the establishment who were in the opposition, but they gradually acquired an independent political consciousness and influence. The civility of the time thus included not just the electors but those members of the middle class and labor aristocracy who counted politically, who were on the threshold but not yet within the political nation.
18. For a brief survey of the history of Britain in the eighteenth century see Plumb (1974); on the rise of party politics see Brewer (1976), Ch. 1; cf. Christie (1982).
19. Plumb (1974), Part 2, Ch. 6; Brewer (1976), Ch. 8–12, esp. Ch. 9.
20. Plumb (1974), 155–162; Christie (1982), Ch. 12, esp. 295–305; cf. Hobsbawm (1976); Anstey (1980), (1981); Drescher (1986), Ch. 3–6.
21. Davis (1966), 300.
22. Davis (1966), 303; see also his 299–306 for a discussion of the Quaker dilemmas about slavery and their views of authority.
23. Davis (1966), 330–332; see also Anstey (1975), Ch. 9, esp. 209. Cf. Soderlund

(1985), who emphasizes the complexities of the antislavery movement among American Quakers.

24. Anstey (1975), 222–263; on the 1783 Committee see 229; on the members of the 1787 Committee see 249, n. 37; on the Committee's membership in 1791 see 261–262. Cf. Drescher (1986, Ch. 6), who emphasizes the difference between the strong antislavery stance of the Methodists in Britain and their accommodationist position in the West Indies and the South. He suggests that Methodist clergy in Britain did not lead the abolitionist movement but responded to the antislavery militancy of their working-class parishioners.

25. John Wesley, as quoted by Green (1964), 156. See also Plumb (1974), 94–95.

26. Walvin (1981), 64–67; see also Anstey (1975), 255ff., esp. 262–267, 272–278; Wrigley and Schofield (1981), 529; Drescher (1986), 67–88; Christie (1982), 135–138, 210.

27. Walvin (1981), 65. Anstey (1975, 180, 276–278) and Walvin (1981, 65–67) discuss the influence of the French Revolution on the abolitionists. Christie (1982, Ch. 9) discusses the general issue of British politics and the French Revolution.

28. Anstey (1975), 273, 280, 282–285, 321. Anstey notes that in 1802 the bill was introduced too late in the session for effective action to be taken on it.

29. Anstey (1975), 344–346; Davis (1975), 443; Howse (1952), 58–60.

30. Howse (1952), 60–61. See Anstey (1975). For the economic factors influencing these decisions see Drescher (1977), 76–83, 170–174, 193–204; Davis (1975), 437–443.

31. See Christie (1982, 271–280), which describes the changes in British politics after Pitt's death. For a somewhat different view, see Drescher (1986). See also Anstey (1975), 357–413; EM, #58.

32. The Duke of Norfolk, as quoted by Davis (1975), 449.

33. W. E. H. Leckey, as quoted by Anstey (1968), 307.

34. Lord Dartmouth, president of the Board of Trade, as quoted by Mathieson (1967), 15.

35. For the problem of sugar production in the West Indies and the slave trade see Davis (1975), 441; Drescher (1977), 139, 170–174; DuBois (1969), Ch. 5, esp. 41–42; Mathieson (1967), 28; Anstey (1975), 340–341, 394–395. See the estimates of the elasticity of demand for West Indian sugar and its implications for profits, EM, #19; cf. EM, #17, #18.

36. The ban on the inter-island slave trade and other injunctions did, however, significantly impair the operation of West Indian plantations. See Eltis (1972), (1987); EM, #17–#19; TP, #29.

37. Williams (1966), 210–211; Drescher (1977), 4–6. See also Anstey (1968), 307, and EM, #58.

38. Davis (1984), 174–175.

39. Temperley (1972), 7–9; Eltis (1987), 249.

40. Walvin (1981), 67–68. The number of names contained in the petitions is from Drescher (1986), 82.

41. Bethell (1970), 12.

42. Bethell (1970), 16–19; Eltis (1987), Ch. 6 and 7; LeVeen (1971), Table II.

43. Eltis (1987), Table 4, p. 99, states that from 1811 to 1867, 1,588 ships were detained by the British Navy; 152,600 slaves were liberated from 576 of these ships, while the remaining 1,012 ships were detained without slave cargo on board. Not having slaves on board did not exempt a ship from prosecution, however, as the possession of slave trading implements was sufficient to subject a ship to confiscation.

   While the British were the most active force in the suppression movement, they were not entirely alone. The United States, France, Portugal, Spain, and Brazil each participated in relatively small ways, as a group bearing about 10 percent of the total direct cost of the suppression effort. "Between 1808 and 1870 . . . the international effort against slave trade resulted in 1,635 ships being condemned . . . or [lost by their owners]." This count omits several ships which were detained, but for which no records of court decisions survive (Eltis, 1987, 97; see also 96).

44. Although the slave trade was abolished in Cuba in 1862, smuggling continued until 1867. Scott (1985), 10, 38, 93; Eltis (1987), 14, 218–221.

45. For data in this paragraph see Eltis (1987), 92, 96; LeVeen (1971), 61–73 and Tables 1, 7, 11, 12; Lloyd (1949), App. A and B; Mitchell and Deane (1962), 410 (table reporting relief for the poor in England). For a discussion of the estimates of Eltis and LeVeen, see *EM*, #57.

46. Davis (1984), 176, 99ff.; Coupland (1933), 115ff.; Mathieson (1967), 26–29.

47. Anstey (1981), 43; Mathieson (1967), 111–114.

48. Anstey (1981, 44) quotes instructions attributed to Watson, found in *The Works of the Reverend Richard Watson* (1834–1837), 1:280.

49. On the composition of the London Antislavery Committee of 1823 see Mathieson (1967), 115–119, esp. 118–119.

50. Mathieson (1967), 127.

51. Gash (1979), 118, esp. 63–64, 135–137; Gash is referring to influence, not to enrollment. For estimates of Methodist enrollment in 1832 as well as their share in the electorate see Anstey (1981), 51–53. The Methodists alone had close to a million adherents and a strong central administration that made them both a formidable religious force and "the most powerful vehicle for protest, petition, and publicity in British society" (Gash, 1979, 65).

52. Gash (1979), 140, 142. The Catholic Emancipation Act was pushed through Parliament by a coalition of Whig and Tory leaders who recognized the popular hostility to the measure but who believed that the alternative was even more threatening to the established order.

53. On the development of trade unions see Cole and Postgate (1976), Ch. 20, esp. 232–240.

54. Cole and Postgate (1976), 240, see 239–241. See also Ward (1972), 122–124; Gayer, Rostow, and Schwartz (1975), 535; Floud and Wachter (1982), 435, Figure 2. For a more general description of class riots and revolts see Hobsbawm and Rudé (1975), esp. 112–113, 119–120, 153–154, 158–159, 262 for examples of specific revolts and data about those tried and punished. See Newman (1975) on the connection between evangelicalism, anti-Gallic propaganda in Britain, and the rise of organized working-class protest. See Gash (1956) on the relative importance of Catholic emancipation, and the French Revolution of July 1830, in the movement for parliamentary reform during the election of 1830. In discussing Borougham's campaign for Parliament from Yorkshire, Gash (1956, 284) notes that merchants and manufacturers were mainly concerned with parliamentary and economic reform, despite the concern of dissenters and Quakers with the slavery question. However, abolition of slavery was included in the reform package and these reforms were supported by many electors and candidates "irrespective of party" (Gash, 1956, 287).

55. Cole and Postgate (1975), 250. See 241ff., esp. 249–250. See also Thompson (1975), 890–899; Gash (1979), 150–152.

56. On the Reform Act (1832) see Gash (1971), Ch. 1; Cole and Postgate (1976), 250–251, 255. The proportion of contested elections rose from just over a quarter in 1830 to 71 percent in 1832, but fell off to 49 percent in 1841. See Gash (1956), 261; Gash (1971), 239; Aydelotte (1971), 102, which contains a table of contested constituencies between 1832 and 1864. When the new House met in 1833, its composition was much like the old one. A third of the seats were held by baronets or sons of peers, just about the same proportion as in the old House. Indeed, it has been pointed out that down into the 1840s, the House of Commons was

"overwhelmingly aristocratic in composition." When a count was made not only of the titled members and the children of peers but also of the direct descendants of the other families listed in Burke's *Landed Gentry*, it turned out that at least 80 percent of MPs belonged to the "aristocratic or landed class" (Aydelotte, 1954, 255, 254).

57. Gash (1971), 10; see pp. 88–89. The middle class was "offered full partnership" (Cole and Postgate, 1976, 251), not in governing society, which remained in the hands of the gentry, but in deciding which members of the gentry should represent them. Urban and rural laborers as well as the small farmers were still left voteless, but this was precisely what Thomas Babington Macaulay, newly elected to Parliament, had in mind when he said that the Reform Act had done "all that was necessary for the removing of a great practical evil, and no more than was necessary" (Gash, 1971, 12).

58. For an interpretation of the events leading up to the Emancipation Act of 1833 that is somewhat different from that put forward in the next 10 paragraphs, see Drescher (1986), esp. Ch. 5–7.

59. On the composition of West Indian planters and merchants committed to gradual amelioration in the condition of slaves see Ragatz (1928), 411.

60. Ragatz (1928), 134–136.

61. Mathieson (1967), 195; Coupland (1933), 131; Anstey (1981), 45.

62. Anstey (1981), 46.

63. Watson, as quoted by Anstey (1981), 46, 57 *n*. 26.

64. Anstey (1981), 46.

65. Mathieson (1967), 199, 203–204, see 195–207.

66. On the uprising in Jamaica see Turner (1982); Mathieson (1967), 208–220; Ragatz (1928), 443–444; Wright (1973), 109.

67. Letter from Zachary Macaulay to Brougham as quoted by Anstey (1980), 28.

68. For these figures see Anstey (1981), 48, 50; Temperley (1972), 192 *n*. 44.

69. Davis (1984), 200.

70. Green (1976, 114–115 *n*. 149) quotes Viscount Howick's words at a private meeting, December 1832 (from Colonial Office papers).

71. Anstey (1980), 29.

72. Craton (1974), 278; Temperley (1972), 17–18.

73. Temperley (1972), 17–18; Green (1976), 120.

74. Williams (1966), 136, 139. The sugar prices were computed from Sheridan (1976), Table 3. On the conditions in the West Indian sugar plantations after emancipation see also Engerman (1982), esp. 196–199; Engerman (1984).

75. See *n*. 56 above.

76. The discussion in this paragraph and the next one is based on Webb, *TP*, #28. Webb's stress is on his finding that capitalists and religious dissenters were more likely to vote for emancipation than others. I agree with that point but focus on another of his findings: that members of these groups represented a small part of the total vote in favor of emancipation, so small that the bill would have passed overwhelmingly without their vote.

77. Grey, as quoted by Gash (1979), 147. See also Anstey (1981, 53–54) on the percentage of dissenters in the English electorate. On related issues in these and the following paragraphs see Hobsbawm (1976), Ch. 3, esp. 27–29; Gilbert (1976), Ch. 6, esp. 126–129; Ward (1972), 127–128. See also *EM*, #58.

78. Watson, as quoted by Ward (1972), 128.

79. See Armstrong (1973), 196–197; Cowherd (1956), 59–60; Drescher (1982), 30–35; Wright (1973), 123–125; Drescher (1986), esp. Ch. 6.

80. Anstey (1980), 29.

81. Hollis (1980), 302.

82. Drescher (1982), 42–45. For the estimate of the share of British wealth represented by slaves and the contrasting U.S. case, see *EM*, #56; cf. *TP*, #29.

83. Howse (1952), 126, 129. On the question of the altruism and philanthropy of the "saints" see his 124–137. On Macaulay's financial difficulties see Clive (1973), 60, 100, 247. Eltis (1987, 110–111, 333 *n.* 12, 335 *n.* 40) suggests that Zachary Macaulay made as much from his abolitionist activities as he expended on them.

84. Clive (1975), 43.

85. Temperley (1972), 23, cf. xii.

86. Temperley (1972), 185–190; see also Drescher (1982), 42–45, and (1986), 53–57. On Guizot and the events described here see also *Encyclopaedia Britannica* (1962), 9:626, 11:1–2.

87. Temperley (1972), 27, esp. xiii–xiv, 20–29, 191–220.

88. *Encyclopaedia Britannica* (1962), 12:167, see also 12:165–169.

89. Temperley (1972), 95, see also 93–110.

90. Austen (1979); the summary estimates of the trans-Saharan slave trade between 1650 and 1900 are in Table 2.8, 66; Table 2.9, 68, gives the estimates of the East African trade.

91. Coupland (1933), 210, 211; on David Livingstone see 206ff. See also *Encyclopaedia Britannica* (1962), 14:239–240.

92. Miers (1975), 25.

93. On the Berlin Conference and after see Miers (1975), Ch. 4 and 5.

CHAPTER 8. THE AMERICAN CAMPAIGN: FROM THE REVOLUTION
TO THE ABOLITIONIST CRUSADE

1. Martineau (1839), 3–4. The whole of Martineau's comparison is:
   Before we fix our attention on the history of the [American abolitionists], it may be remarked that it is a totally different thing to be an abolitionist on a soil actually trodden by slaves, and in a far-off country, where opinion is already on the side of emancipation, or ready to be converted; where only a fraction of society, instead of the whole, has to be convicted of guilt; and where no interests are put in jeopardy but pecuniary ones, and those limited and remote. Great honor is due to the first movers in the anti-slavery cause in every land: but those of European countries may take rank with the philanthropists of America who may espouse the cause of the aborigines: while the primary abolitionists of the United States have encountered, with steady purpose, such opposition as might here await assailants of the whole set of aristocratic institutions at once, from the throne to pauper apprenticeship. Slavery is as thoroughly interwoven with American institutions—ramifies as extensively through American society, as the aristocratic spirit pervades Great Britain.

2. See Robinson (1979), Ch. 6 and 7; Wiecek (1977) for discussions of the relationship between federal powers in the American Constitution and the institution of slavery.

3. I was tempted to expand the "three overlapping fields" to four by adding "social history," but decided instead to emphasize how the sociological approach has infiltrated the other three fields.

4. Perry Miller, as quoted by Essig (1982), xii.

5. Robinson (1979), 79.

6. For an overview of the views and actions of the Virginia legislature affecting the prohibition of the slave trade see MacLeod (1974), 31–32, 38–39, 192 *n.* 52; Robinson (1979), 78–79.

7. See Bailyn (1967, 232–238, 241, 246), who identifies attacks on slavery in this period with the logic of Revolutionary ideology.

8. On Freemasonry among the signers of the Declaration, see Albanese (1981), 290; Ahlstrom (1975), 1:444, 446 *n.* 4. American deism and its main proponents are discussed by Nye (1960), 209–211.

9. MacLeod (1974), 16, see 15–17; Jordan (1969), 350–352; Bailyn (1967), 232–234, 238, 246. Nevertheless, the Declaration of Independence and the preamble to the Constitution had a potential for reinvigorating the spiritual content of the antislavery struggle. As became apparent during the debates over the admission of Missouri, the new nationist ideology of American freedom provided an important stimulus for a more radical attack on the slave issue. See pp. 294–296 of this volume.

10. MacLeod (1974), 46–47, 78–81, 167–169; Fogel and Engerman, *TP*, #29; Locke (1901), 74–75, 184. For John Locke's views on slavery and the social compact see Davis (1966), 119; for a somewhat different interpretation, see Drescher (1986), 23, 184 *n.* 69.

11. Jordan (1969), 351.

12. MacLeod (1974), 20, see also 99; Jordan (1969), 343.

13. Robinson (1979), 170–175.

14. Wiecek (1977), 62, 64, see Ch. 3, esp. 62–64.

15. It should be remembered that although the Northwest Ordinance prohibited the importation of slaves into the region, whether from abroad or from other states in the Confederation, it was not a sweeping antislavery document. The Ordinance did not affect slaves already living in the Northwest. Moreover the Ordinance introduced the concept of a "fugitive slave" into American law, giving national sanction to property in slaves. When the fugitive slave provision was subsequently incorporated into the Constitution, it became unlawful for a state to free a slave owned by a master residing in a state where slavery was recognized. Davis (1975), 129; Robinson (1979), 228–229.

16. Robinson (1979), 240–241, see Ch. 6 and 7, esp. 228; Davis (1975), 127.

17. Robinson (1979), 228.

18. Zilversmit (1967), 125, see 109–117, 124–137; Wiecek (1977), 48, 89–90; Fogel and Engerman, *TP*, #29.

19. Ahlstrom (1975), 1:442, see 442–459; Zilversmit (1967), 127. Ahlstrom, in particular, emphasizes the "religious depression" of the Revolutionary period. The decline in influence was only transitory, however, since the Revolutionary jeremiads of the northern clergy later influenced the antislavery, feminist, and other liberation movements. I am indebted to J. David Greenstone for calling this point to my attention.

20. Locke (1901), 97–101. See *EM*, #4.

21. Locke (1901), 100, see also 99–101; Dumond (1966), 46–48.

22. Locke (1901), 115.

23. Dumond (1966), 53.

24. Robinson (1979), 304–305.

25. Locke (1901), 99–102, 106, 114–115, 139–140; Robinson (1979), 303–312; Dumond (1966), 53–57.

26. Dumond (1961), 58, see 48; Locke (1901), 101, 141–142.

27. Robinson (1979), 318–319; Locke (1901), 158–159. See *EM*, #3, #4.

28. Robinson (1979), 337, see 324–341 and 334 for a discussion of the "critical vote"; Dumond (1966), 81, 84–86.

29. Robinson (1979), 292, see 286–292; Dumond (1966), 58–64, 72–75; Wiecek (1977), 90–105.

30. MacLeod (1974), 123, 124, see 78–79, 120–121, 123–124, 128, 147.

31. Locke (1901), 110, see 109–111; MacLeod (1974), 124.

32. Smith (1972), 44–45, see 42–44.

33. MacLeod (1974), 35.

34. Essig (1982), 91.
35. For a discussion of Hopkins (1721–1803), see Ahlstrom (1975), 1: 494–496, and for leaders of the Second Great Awakening, 509–512. See also McLoughlin (1978), 69–70, 78–79, 118–119; Essig (1982), 88–94; Jordan (1969), 298–299.
36. Essig (1982), 92, 93, 162, see 134–139; Ahlstrom (1975), 1:512–520.
37. Essig (1982), 145, see 143–146.
38. Drake (1965), 118, 119, see 115–119.
39. Drake (1965), 121, see 119–132; Jordan (1969), 550; Meltzer and Holland (1982), 42–45.
40. Essig (1982), 135.
41. Howse (1952), 47, 46.
42. Essig (1982), 136, see 135–139; Temperley (1972), 7–8; Howse (1952), 45–47.
43. Adams (1908), 199–202; Dumond (1966), 129; Drake (1965), 124–127, 129–130; Davis (1975), 334–335; Fox (1919), 90–91; Frederickson (1971), 6–8. "The colonization movement drew not only on the evangelical antislavery strain . . . but also on a merger of Christian missionary zeal with American nationalist evangelicalism: the Word to be spread was to be an *American* Christian Word. Both the new abolitionism and the popular reaction against it were nourished by the spread of a popular American nationalism during the early 19th century." I am indebted to Morton Keller for calling this point to my attention (letter of June 4, 1987).
44. Frederickson (1971), 9–10. See also Adams (1908), 202–204; Fox (1919), 79; Sydnor (1966), 96–97. *New American Cyclopaedia* (1866), 5:488.
45. Drake (1965), 126; Smith (1972), 70.
46. Different forces conflicted to shape the direction of the American Colonization Society. In the context of the increasingly militant proslavery South, it was militant, it was a potential threat, and it did encourage abolitionist forces. See MacLeod (1981) on the need for a reassessment.
47. Freehling (1966), 122, see 122–125; Fox (1919), 77–78; Staudenraus (1961), 171–178.
48. Freehling (1966), 122, see 122–125.
49. Sydnor (1966), 185, 186. Staudenraus (1961), 171–178.
50. Frederickson (1971), 27, see 27–28; Thomas (1963), 78, 121; Kraditor (1970), 4; Fox (1919), 88–89.
51. See McKivigan (1984, 203–220) for religious affiliations of the officers of the four national abolition societies, 1833–1864.
52. See Walzer (1965) on the role of Calvinist elitism in promoting the radical reforms of the sixteenth and seventeenth centuries. Cf. Gay (1977), V. 2. For brief descriptions of the Puritan Awakening of 1610–1640 and the First Great Awakening of 1730–1760 see McLoughlin (1978), Ch. 1–3.
53. Marty (1970).
54. Gaustad (1962), 76, see 75–78.
55. Gaustad (1962), 78. These figures include both the northern and southern wings of the Methodist and Baptist churches, which split in the 1840s. See pp. 275–277 of this chapter.
56. Ahlstrom (1975), 1:399.
57. Cross and Livingstone (1983), 1063, see 223–224, 1064; Smith (1957), 114–118.
58. Gaustad (1962), 4, 10–13, 15; Ahlstrom (1975), 1:390–392, 455–456; McLoughlin (1978), 89–94.
59. Mathews (1977), 24; Gaustad (1962), 13, 57.
60. Ahlstrom (1975), 495, 472, 512, see 525–528, 531, 536, 538.
61. Cross (1982), 18–19.
62. Liberalization of the conditions of sale by the federal government of small parcels of public lands also spurred the movement of New Englanders to the frontier. Gates (1968), 131–137.

63. Ahlstrom (1975), 1:551–552, see 492–512; Mathews (1977), xi; Fogel et al. (1983), 445–481; Easterlin (1976a), 45–75; Easterlin (1976b), 600–614; see also Villaflor and Sokoloff (1982), 539–570. See *EM*, #59, for the method of estimating New England's contribution to the growth of population in the eight states designated as the New England diaspora.

64. Ryan (1981), 75.

65. Cross (1982), 22–23, see 19–23.

66. Miller (1965), 9.

67. Cross (1982), 152, see 151–157.

68. McLoughlin (1978), 123, see 122–125.

69. Cross (1982), 174–184.

70. McLoughlin (1978), 128, 129, see 128–130.

71. Cross (1982), 198, see 198–199, 268.

72. Nye (1960), 212–213; Miller (1965), 4; Hofstadter (1965), 10–13.

73. Hofstadter (1965), 13.

74. Miller (1960), 231.

75. Miller (1960), 229–232; Kerber (1970), 173–184; Fischer (1965), 287; Griffin (1960), 5–18; Cole (1954), 132–134.

76. Ahlstrom (1975), 1:478. See also Marty (1970), 67–71.

77. Marty (1970), 67.

78. Ahlstrom (1975), 1:515, see 515–516. See also Foster (1960), 106–107; Banner (1977), 303–305; Cole (1954), 109; Howse (1952), 95–99.

79. Foster (1960), 134, 135, see also 130–135.

80. Foster (1960), 130–132; *Dictionary of American Biography* (1933) 10:11–12, (1935) 17:270–271, (1936) 18:298–301, 303–304; *New American Cyclopaedia* (1871), 8:504–505; Banner (1977), 304–306; Freehling (1966), 180–182.

81. Cole (1954), 9; Foster (1960), 224–227, 171–178; Griffin (1960), 118–142. Single-issue organizations established in the United States in the years 1810–1828 included the American Board of Commissioners for Foreign Missions, 1810; the American Educational Society, 1815; the American Bible Association, 1816; the American Colonization Society, 1817; the American Tract Society, 1824; the American Sunday School Union, 1824; the American Temperence Union, 1826; the Sabbath Union, 1828; and the American Home Missionary Society, 1828. See Bodo (1980), 18–20.

82. Tocqueville (1969), 1:293, 295, 291, see 291–296.

83. Tocqueville also exaggerated the "voluntary" component in the political restraint of the clergy and he overlooked the influence in politics of the devout laity. His failure to recognize the enmity between Protestant denominations as well as the fierce rivalries between factions within denominations reflected the extent to which these tensions were suppressed during the era of "the Evangelical United Front," but they broke into the open shortly after Tocqueville returned to his native France. Tocqueville might have been less sanguine about the prospects for religious harmony if he had read the "Associates Creed" of the Andover Seminary. Consisting of 36 points of detailed doctrine, this Creed required faculty members to pledge resolute "opposition, not only to Atheists and Infidels, but to Jews, Papists, Mahometans, Arians, Pelagians, Antinomians, Arminians, Socinians, Sabellians, Unitarians, and Universalists, and to all heresies and errors, ancient or modern" (Bodo, 1980, 4).

84. Bodo (1980), 69.

85. Ahlstrom (1975), 1:672.

86. Billington, (1964), 108.

87. Bodo (1980), 69; Billington (1964), 53–58, 67–76, 91–100, 122–127; Ahlstrom (1975), 1:670–676; Holt (1978), 158–169.

88. The religious affiliations of the officers of the four national abolition societies in the

years 1833–1864 are given by McKivigan (1984), 203–220. Of the 406 officers for whom religious affiliations are known, approximately 49 percent were of the Congregational-Presbyterian-Unitarian rubric, 20 percent Quaker, 12 percent Baptist, 6 percent Methodist, 5 percent Comeouters, 2 percent Episcopalian, and those remaining of such churches and denominations as Universalist, Union Church, Spiritualist, and Free Thinker. There were no Catholics or Lutherans in the number.

89. See Barnes (1964, 38–58) for a discussion of the new abolitionist movement in 1833. See also Dumond (1966), 172, 177–180; Dillon (1974), 39, 49; L. Friedman (1982), 68–70, 46–47.

90. L. Friedman (1982), 115–116, see 96–99, 102–116; Cross (1982); Harlow (1939), 46–60, 67–79, 115–124, 138–148.

91. Walters (1976), xi. Despite their slogan of "immediate emancipation," the abolitionists were not out to bankrupt the slaveowners. The full slogan was "immediate emancipation gradually obtained," by which they meant an immediate agreement to eventual emancipation. They wanted the masters to recognize their sin and immediately begin on a program of repentance, but such a program need not require masters to sacrifice all their worldly wealth to atone for their sin.

92. Davis (1984), 188, see 186–189. See Smith (1972, 65) for the influence of Bourne on Garrison. See also Thomas (1963), 97–105.

93. Cross (1982), 238.

94. Mathews (1977), 62. For two insightful but different views of the interrelationship of slavery and the distinctive development of evangelical Protestantism in the South, see Oakes (1982), Ch. 4; Genovese and Fox-Genovese (1986).

95. Wish (1950), 247–251, 407–414.

96. Cross (1982), 275.

97. Foster (1960), 171.

98. Cross (1982), 130, 211.

99. Foster (1960), 175. Arthur Tappan, whose involvement in the temperance movement preceded his leadership of the abolitionist crusade, offered a special donation to any church "under A.H.M.S. supervision" if they made abstinence a condition of "the admission of persons to the communion." Some ultraists, striving to follow the principle of total abstinence to its logical conclusion, called for an immediate end to the use of wine in the Eucharist. Although many supporters of the temperance movement were shocked by a demand that was a direct violation of scripture, Gerrit Smith was not. Since temperance crusaders "knew more about the evils of alcohol than did Jesus," he argued, "they would sin in following His practice." Cross (1982), 213, 216.

100. Walters (1976), 38.

101. Wiecek (1977), 150.

102. Davis (1975), 200, 332. See Davis (1975, 200–201) and Dumond (1966, 93) on Bourne, and Thomas (1963, 97–105) for Garrison's view of immediate emancipation.

103. McKivigan (1984), 20. It has been suggested that Garrison thought that slavery was against natural law. That is correct only in the theological sense of the term, as "God's law," not in its secular sense. Compare with the discussion on pp. 330–332 of this volume.

104. Cross and Livingston (1983), 1278.

105. Thomas (1963), 213.

106. Kraditor (1970), 91, see 90–91.

107. McKivigan (1984), 22, 21.

108. McKivigan (1984), 26, see 25–27, 203–220; Davis (1984), 143.

109. Donald (1978), 17. Statistics of abolitionist societies are from Temperly (1972), 192, and Drescher (1982), 24; see also Bemis (1956), 336; Van Deusen (1959),

108, 133–134. I have followed Drescher's figures on the number of locals, which are much higher than Temperley's. The British may have had more signatures on their petitions than the AASS. The AASS, however, treated various local collections of signatures as separate petitions, a device that served to clog the congressional machinery.

110. Thomas (1963), 203–204, see also 200–207; Temperley (1972), 192; Barnes (1964), 48, 59, 81, 162; Dillon (1974), 93–95.

111. Dillon (1974), 98, see 93; Ratner (1968), 80–81; Thomas (1963), 207.

112. Thomas (1963), 100. See Dillon (1974), 89–91; Wyatt-Brown (1969), 152–156; Temperley (1972), 196–197.

113. Wyatt-Brown (1969), 149, see 143–163, 145 for the number of pamphlets. See also Temperley (1972), 196–197; Dillon (1974), 89–91.

114. Wyatt-Brown (1969), 152, 153, see 152–156.

115. Smith (1972), 115.

116. McKivigan (1984), 45.

117. Smith (1972), 77, see 77–78, 114–117.

118. McKivigan (1984), 46, 48, see 43–46, 91–92.

119. Smith (1972), 84, 88, see 77–94; Ahlstrom (1975), 2:105–106; McKivigan (1984), 82–84, 92. With almost solid southern support the General Assembly expelled "the synods of Western Reserve, Utica, Geneva, and Genesee, thereby separating from the denomination more than five hundred ministers and nearly sixty thousand communicants," which was about a fifth of the Presbyterian membership. Shortly thereafter the remainder of the New Schoolmen joined the expelled synods and formed "an independent General Assembly" which, like the Old School Assembly, retained the "original denominational name" (Smith 1972, 87, 89).

120. Smith (1972), 43, 45, 101, 102.

121. Smith (1972), 111, see 43, 45, 89, 94–114; Ahlstrom (1975), 1:106–109.

122. McKivigan (1984), 88.

123. Ahlstrom (1975), 2:110, see 109–111.

124. McKivigan (1984), 88, see 87–90, 92. See also Smith (1972), 112–127.

125. Cole (1954), 212, see 212–217.

126. Smith (1972), 127, 128.

127. Cole (1954), 211, 213.

128. Kraditor (1970), 92, see 41–55.

129. Griffin (1960), 154. See Thomas (1963), 318–323; McKivigan (1984), 64–73.

130. McKivigan (1984), 65.

131. Thomas (1963), 330, 326, see 330–371.

132. Abzug (1980), 129, 134, see 126–135.

133. Abzug (1980), 211–212, see 210–218. One indication of the far-reaching impact of Weld's book is found in the contrast between its argument and that of *Remarks on the Slavery Question* by William E. Channing. Channing's pamphlet includes long passages on the immorality of property rights in man and on the psychic damage the unequal power relationships wrought on a slave even "though little of what is called cruelty enters into his lot" (Channing, 1841, 39). Channing conceded that with respect to physical and material conditions, "slavery wore a milder aspect" in the South "than in other countries" and that the "condition of the slave continues to improve" (33), although he attributed much of the "kindness" practiced by masters to the attention drawn to the evil system by the abolitionists (34). As his pamphlet was going to press, Channing learned of *American Slavery as It Is* and added the following note (1841, 5:106):

> I have allowed on this page, that slavery wears a milder aspect at the South than in other countries. I ought to inform my readers, that this is denied by some who have inquired into the matter. A pamphlet or larger volume is announced at New York, in which the subject of the *treatment* of slaves is to be particularly consid-

ered. The work is said to be the result of patient inquiries, and full proofs of its statements are promised. Those at the North, who believe in the mildness of Southern Slavery, will do well to examine the publication.

If Channing's view of slavery reflected the older abolitionist argument, the impact of Weld's book helped form the new. While Channing strongly stressed the immorality inherent in the personal relations required by the structure of slavery and discounted cruelty as a central factor, the next thrust of the antislavery argument emphasized the physical hardships endured by slaves, in the manner formulated by Weld. Cf. *EM*, #71.

134. Dumond (1966), 249.
135. Weld (1839), 8–9, 115.
136. Abzug (1980), 135, see 210–218, ix, x; Wyatt-Brown (1969), 193–195, 198–199.
137. Dumond (1966), 297, see 290–297.
138. Sewell (1976), 79.
139. Thomas (1963), 326.
140. Wyatt-Brown (1969), 269.

Chapter 9. The American Campaign: Breaching the Barriers to Antislavery Politics

1. Petersen (1963), 24–27; see the *Tribune Almanac* for the years 1841 and 1845. Cf. Kraut (1979) for insights into the sources of Liberty party support.
2. Wiecek (1977), 169.
3. Wiecek (1977), 169, 239, see 228–248.
4. Cross (1982), 225.
5. Barnes (1964), 162.
6. See Silbey (1967, 20–21) for percentages of presidential votes by region from 1836 to 1852.
7. The characterizations of the Whig and Democratic parties that follow represent my attempt to synthesize the recent literature on the second American party system. However, I do not mean to suggest a general consensus on all the points discussed in the balance of this section. Where experts are in disagreement, I threaded the eye of the needle as best I could. The notes indicate how I combined disparate views. For further discussion of the second party system, see pp. 301–322 of this volume.
8. Cited by Baker (1983), 143, 144, 146, see 143–148 for a discussion of the prewar political ideology of Democrats. See also Holt (1973b) and *Encyclopaedia Britannica* (1961), 12:1851–1853.
9. Van Deusen (1963), 97. Cf. Van Deusen (1973).
10. Howe (1979), 17. See Bensen (1969, 10–14) for a discussion of Democratic populism and egalitarianism, and Smith (1965, 239–242, 333) for a description of a gradual broadening of the franchise at the state level. See Van Deusen (1963, 97) for a discussion of Whiggery in the Jacksonian era; for differences between Whig and Democrat ideology and constituencies, see Howe (1979, 17–18); for Whig and Democrat voting on "pro-Negro" issues, see Ershkwitz and Shade (1971, 611–612) and Richards (1979).
11. I am indebted to J. David Greenstone for calling this point to my attention.
12. Howe (1979), 210, 217, 190, 191, 107–108, 21.
13. Benson (1969), 225.
14. Baker (1983), 319.
15. Howe (1979), 8, 21.
16. Formisano (1983), 276, see 275–276.
17. Van Deusen (1963), 66.

18. Howe (1979), 30; on the influence of moral philosophy, and particularly "faculty psychology" on Whig political values, see 28–31.

19. Benson (1969), 250, see 225–226 on the Democratic party's self-portrait in 1844.

20. Howe (1979), 18, see also 164. McCarthy (1903), 369–374, 386, 396; Griffin (1960), 116ff.; Van Deusen (1963), 55–57.

21. The quote is from Howe (1979), 35. See Howe (1979), 18, 35, for the religious affiliation of Whigs nation-wide and 20 for Whig attitudes toward the state. On the evangelical support of Whiggery in Michigan, see Formisano (1971), 160–164; for Whig religious affiliation in Massachusetts, see Formisano (1983), 291–292. In Hunterdon County, New Jersey, however, Democrats had no predominant religious affiliation, though nationwide Catholics, Episcopalians, and German Lutherans tended to be Democrats; see Baker (1983), 47–48. See Benson (1969), 166–207, for an analysis of voting patterns by ethnic groups and religious affiliations in the 1844 election in New York, and esp. 185 for a breakdown of estimated party percentages by ethnic groups in that election. For a critique of Benson's estimates, see Kousser (1986). For a more optimistic review of the literature on the political tendencies of various denominations, see Swierenga (1988). On Pittsburgh, see Holt (1969). For the mid-1850s, see Gienapp (1987), 507–508. For further discussion of religious and ethnic voting patterns, see *EM*, #69.

22. For an overview of economic development in the United States see Fite and Reese (1959), 118–119, 123–126; for a discussion of the crisis of 1819, 1837, 1839, and 1857 see Taylor (1958), 334–346. On the Jacksonian boom and bust, see Temin (1969) and Rockoff (1971). See also Chapter 3 of this volume. See Chapter 10 of this volume for a discussion of the crisis of 1853–1855.

23. The quote is from Silbey (1967), 54; for his analysis of party votes on the issues in Congress, see 51–55.

24. Silbey (1967), 59, 142, see 53–54.

25. The quotes are from Howe (1979), 63; see 62–68 for Howe's assessment of Adams's views on the antislavery issue. See also Adams (1877), IV 530–531, VII 229–230, IX 23, 289, XI 79–80, 284, 377–378, XII 57, 171–172; Bemis (1956). See also pp. 335–346 of this volume.

26. Hofstadter (1973), 108.

27. Banner (1970); Robinson (1979); Meyers (1960); Howe (1979); Wiecek (1977).

28. See *n.* 14 to Chapter 8 of this volume for a fuller discussion of the slavery provisions of the Northwest Ordinance.

29. Robinson (1979), 379–391; the quote is from 391. Cf. Fehrenbacher (1978), 84–89.

30. Robinson (1979), 392, 394, 393, see 392–396; Fehrenbacher (1978), 97ff.

31. Robinson (1979), 379, 395, 396. See Fehrenbacher (1978), 89–97.

32. Fehrenbacher (1978), 96, 94, 96.

33. Fehrenbacher (1978), 100–101; see Wiecek (1977), 107–110; Berwanger (1971), 7–14.

34. Wiecek (1977), 122, see 110–123; Fehrenbacher (1978), 100–110; Robinson (1979), 402–421.

35. Moore (1953), 171–174; see 170–186 for the extent of public indifference to the Missouri controversy, esp. 173. The resentment expressed in Congress over southern domination during the Missouri crisis was not translated into votes during the elections of 1820. Monroe was swept back into office, winning all but one electoral vote. There was little change in the House, although Federalists lost two seats to the Jeffersonian party. Petersen (1963), 16; *Encyclopaedia Britannica* (1962), 23:-845.

36. Hofstadter (1973), 89.

37. Freehling (1966), 109, 121, see 89–126.

38. The southern willingness to compromise can be seen by the southern vote on the

proviso by Senator Jesse Thomas (IL) to prohibit slavery north of 36°30′. The vote
of the southern members of the Senate was 14 for and 8 against the compromise. In
the House the margin of passing was smaller, 39 for and 37 against, with Virginia
strongly affecting that margin by voting 18 to 4 against. Moore (1953), 109, 111.
See also Fehrenbacher (1978); Robinson (1979); Wiecek (1977).

39. Jefferson, as quoted by Fehrenbacher (1978), 111. For a discussion of new party
formations in New York see McCormick (1966), 111–123; for Jefferson's response
to the Missouri controversy see Miller (1977), 221ff.

40. Jefferson, as quoted by Fehrenbacher (1978), 111. For congressional debates and
action on the Missouri Compromise see Wiecek (1977), 112–122.

41. Wiecek (1977), 112.

42. Quotes are from Wiecek (1977), 120–121; see his 119–120 for a summary of
arguments on the illegitimacy of slavery based on the Constitution.

43. Davis (1975), 332. On King's speeches and Vesey see Robinson (1979), 415–416;
Freehling (1966), 54; Craven (1953), 123.

44. For southern "Old Republicans" one lesson of the Missouri crisis was that a party
based firmly on the states' rights principles of the Virginia and Kentucky resolutions of 1798 was essential to the defense of slavery from outside interference.
Together with Martin Van Buren and others of like mind, southern Old Republicans like Thomas Ritchie set out to form an alliance between "the planters of the
South and the plain Republicans of the North," an alliance largely responsible for
Andrew Jackson's victory in 1828. See Brown (1966), 55–72; the quote is on 69,
from a letter of Van Buren to Ritchie in January of 1827. I am indebted to Richard
Sewell for calling this point to my attention.

45. The development of sectional supremacy was not, of course, Jefferson's principal
motive for founding a university. See Malone (1981), esp. 233–282, 365–380, on
his dedication to education.

46. Sydnor (1966), 137, see 135. For the impact of the Missouri issue on the views
of southern leaders, see Moore (1953), 251–256, and on Jefferson, 253–256. For
Pinckney's atitude toward the Missouri Compromise see Freehling (1966), 109.

47. Sydnor (1966), 138, 139; on the general survey bill see 138–141.

48. Freehling (1966), 93. See Wiltse (1944), V. I. For a classic characterization of
Calhoun's fundamental political philosophy, see Current (1943).

49. Current (1963), 13. For the rejection of nationalist dogma by South Carolina
planters and by Calhoun, in particular, see Freehling (1966), 116–133.

50. Taussig (1964), 18, 86; U.S. Bureau of the Census (1975), 888.

51. See James (1981, 732, Figure 3) for consumer real income indexes as a function
of the tariff rate. For the nature of the 1824 congressional tariff debate, see
Edwards (1970), 804–821, 830–838. See McCardell (1979, 15) on Jefferson's
attitude toward the tariff, and Pope (1975, 4–9, 12–16) for an appraisal of Calhoun's analysis of the adverse effects of the tariff. See also Bils (1984).

52. Freehling (1966), 294, see also his discussion of the nullification crisis on 260–263
and 292–297; Current (1963), 13–19; Bemis (1956), 267–269.

53. Freehling (1966), 257, see 254–257. South Carolina's position as the leading
cotton-producing state from 1800 to 1820 made its leaders especially determined
opponents of the tariff. See Watkins (1969), 71, 75, 77; James (1978), 231–256,
esp. 249; James (1981), 726–734.

54. Robinson (1979), 242.

55. Wiecek (1977), 72.

56. Robinson (1979), 210, see 210–211, 242–243; Dodd (1911), 139; Watkins (1969),
71.

57. Dodd (1911), 139. Such positive defenses of slavery did not become systematic
until after the nullification crisis, which coincided with the imminent victory of
British abolitionism. See Freehling (1966, 79–82) on the struggle in southern

ideology that preceded the general acceptance of the positive good theory. Compare with McCardell (1979), 44–71.

58. Robert J. Turnbull, as quoted by Freehling (1966), 123. Sydnor (1949); Freehling (1966); McCardell (1979), Ch. 1.

59. Freehling (1966), 307, 308.

60. Freehling (1966), 110–111. The quoted arguments are paraphrases or direct quotes of arguments put forward by Robert Hayne, Whitemarsh Seabrook, Robert Turnbull, and Arthur Hayne in Congress, in published essays, and in private correspondence.

61. On the ups and downs of economic arguments about slavery within the South, see pp. 61–64, 68–71, and 105–107 of this volume. See also *EM*, #15. On the Virginia debate over the merits of the gradual abolition of slavery during 1831–1832, see Robert (1941); Bruce (1982), Ch. 6; Freehling (1982).

62. See *TP*, #29, and *EM*, #18, on the British West Indies. See DeMello, *TP*, #5, #32, on the impact of an antislavery ideology on the decline of slave prices in Brazil. Cf. Reis (1977); Schwartz (1985), 439–467; Correa do Lago (1978). On the attitudes of Jamaican planters see Green (1976).

63. See Silbey (1967, 60–62) for an analysis of party and sectional divisions in votes on the expansion issue. Also see Bemis (1956), 364–370. For the debate and vote on Texas see Bemis (1956), 462–473; Wiltse (1949), 291, 386–388. Eaton (1966), 324–325. On the economic concerns, see Dorfman (1966), 2:941.

64. Fehrenbacher (1978), 127.

65. Bemis (1956), 416, 478, see also his discussion on 487; see Eaton (1966), 324–331.

66. Current (1963), 28.

67. See Chapter 10 of this volume for a fuller discussion of the effects of the Mexican War, the Compromise of 1850, and the Kansas-Nebraska Act on the destabilization of the second party system.

68. Silbey (1967), Ch. 5 and 6; Van Deusen (1963); Temin (1969), 172–177; Rockoff (1972); Rockoff (1971), 448–458; Nevins (1950), 1:176–197.

69. See U.S. Bureau of the Census (1975), 88, for the value of merchandise imports and duties for these years, and 1104. On the iron industry, see Fogel (1964), 151–166; Fogel and Engerman (1969).

70. Goodrich (1960), Ch. 5; Meyer (1948), 523–528; Fogel (1960), 25–39.

71. Hunter (1949); U.S. Bureau of the Census (1975), 22–37; Steckel (1983); Chudacoff (1975), 56. See also *EM*, #35, #59.

72. See Bidwell and Falconer (1941), 306. On migration patterns, see *EM*, #35, #59, #60, and Steckel (1983); cf. Burnham (1955), Foner (1970), 107–108, and McPherson (1982), 20–21. On the development of the canal system in the Midwest see Cranmer (1960); Ransom (1963). See also Taylor (1951), 52, 56–67, 79, 156–164, 169–172; Hunter (1949); Fogel (1964).

73. Nevins (1947), 2:207–214. See Fishlow (1965b, 196) for comparisons by region of international merchandise trade flow from 1839 to 1860. See also Bidwell and Falconer (1941), 310–311. Before 1825 both the Midwest and the Northeast conducted more of their interregional business with the South than with each other. By the eve of the Civil War the magnitude of trade between the Midwest and the South had fallen to barely a fifth of the trade between the Midwest and the Northeast. Most of the shift from a North-South axis in trade to an East-West axis had already occurred by 1849. Although the South was no longer a major trading partner of the West after the 1830s, it remained an important market for northeastern commodities down to the eve of the Civil War, which might explain the deep concern expressed by many northeastern merchants over the increasing political tensions between the North and the South during the 1850s. See Foner (1968).

74. Meyers (1960), 239–240, see 61–64, 239–241; Pessen (1978), 23–25.

75. The quoted phrases are Benjamin Franklin's, as cited by Field (1978), 146. The term "redundant" was used by Alexander Hamilton, cited by Goldin and Sokoloff (1984), 461.
76. G. Taylor (1958), 6–9; Handlin (1979).
77. Goldin (1976), 13, see 11–16, 52–53. On the urban wealth distribution, see *EM*, #62.
78. See Howe (1979, 116–117) for a discussion of Whig distrust of the moral and political effects of large cities. See also G. Taylor (1958), 6–9, 388–392; Nye (1960), 126–128; Rothman (1971), 57–59; Chudacoff (1975), 36–45; Pessen (1978), 54–59; Nye (1974), 126–129, 146–147. This antipathy to big-city life reflected social and moral problems of unprecedented scope and severity. In New York City crime rates during the 1820s and 1830s rose more than four times as rapidly as the population, overwhelming the capacity of the semiprofessional police force to cope with the phenomenon. By the early 1840s, newspapers and governmental investigating committees were decrying the uncontrolled and unpunished spate of murders and riots, the commercialized vice, and the incessant robberies of both dwellings and businesses. Official estimates put the number of prostitutes in New York at 10,000 in 1844, some of them "not even into the teens." Drunkenness was widespread with one saloon "for every fifty persons in the city over the age of fifteen." And there was a mounting problem of "vagrant and criminal children" (estimated by police at over 3,000), some organized into rings of thieves by professional criminals, others individually engaged in acts "which for vileness and deep depravity, would absolutely stagger belief." Richardson (1970), 25–28, 52–53; the quotes are from 27 and 52.
79. Parrington (1930), 347; for quite similar views expressed by Franklin see 173. For statistics on urban and rural mortality rates during the antebellum era, see Jaffe and Lourie (1942), 352–371; Vinovskis (1972), 184–213; Fogel (1986), 465; Fogel et al. (1978), 78; Fogel and Engerman (1974), 1:125; Ware (1924), 14. Life expectation at birth for U.S. slaves c.1830 was about 30 years. See *EM*, #41, for the method of estimating slave life expectancy.
80. Ernst (1949), 48. New York's cellar population tripled in less than a decade, reaching about 29,000 persons at the mid-century—a number large enough to make New York's underground population by itself one of the nation's 20 largest cities. Indeed, the number of people who lived in the cellars of New York at the end of the 1840s probably exceeded the entire urban population of that city on the eve of the Constitutional Convention. Warner (1968), 52–53; Glaab (1963), 116; Chudacoff (1975), 56; U.S. Bureau of the Census (1909), 15; Ernst (1949), 29.
81. Tocqueville (1969), 278. See Glaab (1963, 52–54) for the views of Thomas Jefferson and Benjamin Rush on cities. On the creation of armed, uniformed police, see Monkkonen (1981).
82. Monkkonen (1981), esp. Ch. 1 and the sources cited there; Pessen (1977), (1978). For a discussion of the European sources of America's labor thinkers see Dorfman (1966), 2:637–695; Warner (1968), 91–98.
83. Warner (1968), 152.
84. Benson (1969), 121; see 114–122 for a discussion of the American Republican party. See Warner (1968, 143–144, 152–157) for the case of Philadelphia.
85. Potter (1965), 645; see Fogel et al. (1978), 100; Gemery (1984); U.S. Bureau of the Census (1975), 106; U.S. Bureau of the Census (1854), 61, 114, 116–118; Galenson (1981), 216–217.
86. See Handlin (1979, 54–55) for the case of Boston. The foreign-born proportion in the rural areas was computed from the Bateman-Foust sample. The percentage of foreign-born workers in New York is computed from Ernst (1949), 193, 214–217. For different definitions of urban, the Moen sample of urban households yields the following figures for 1860:

Urban Definition	% of Population Foreign Born	Labor Force Participation Rate	
		Foreign Born	Native Born
≥ 3,000 inhabitants	25.0	0.540	0.277
≥ 10,000 "	36.8	0.521	0.245
≥ 25,000 "	40.5	0.518	0.235
≥ 100,000 "	42.5	0.517	0.224
New York City	47.5	0.522	0.214

Using published census figures for New York City, which show the percentage of foreign born as 47.63, does not change the figure for the fraction of the work force that was foreign born indicated in the text.

I am indebted to Nathaniel Wilcox for supplying me with these figures.

For further analysis of the urban occupational and wealth distribution by ethnicity in 1860, see *EM*, #62, #63. See *EM* #60 on the sources, and #69 on the political consequences, of population growth in the North.

87. For occupational structure in Philadelphia see Nash (1979), 387–391; Warner (1968), 13, 15, 18. The New York figures were computed from Ernst (1949), 214–217.

88. The process of displacing native workers is illustrated by the experience in the textile mills of Lowell, Massachusetts, which prior to 1840 employed very few Irish women, relying instead on the daughters of New England farmers. As late as 1845 less than 10 percent of the female operatives were Irish, but by the end of the heavy immigration of 1846–1854, "half the Lowell operatives were of that nationality." New England girls left the mills both because they refused to work for wages as low as those accepted by Irish girls and because of Yankee prejudices against close association with Catholic immigrants. The development of improved looms which could be operated by less skilled hands also served to undermine the wages and working conditions of native operators, as less skilled Irish girls were substituted for more skilled Yankees. On the Lowell mills see Dublin (1979), 160–164; Lazonick and Brush (1985). For the defensive creation of trade organizations see Ware (1924), 229–235.

89. Dublin (1979), 142–143; Field (1978), esp. 160ff. For the development of the factory system see G. Taylor (1958), Ch. 10 and 11. For the role of women and children in the industrial process see Goldin and Sokoloff (1982), 741–774, and (1984), 461–487. For the conditions and wages of laborers in the 1840s and 1850s see Ware (1924), 67–70; Margo and Villaflor (1987); Lazonick and Brush (1985).

90. Figure 27 is computed from data in Ernst (1949), 214–217. The direct competition of the foreign born for craft jobs substantially lowered the earnings of native-born craftsmen. In 1846 native-born cabinetmakers in New York City complained that the competition from immigrants had lowered their wages by a third to a half during the preceding decade. The willingness of immigrants to accept such low wages from "any one who offers them immediate and permanent employment," they charged, had "ruined the Cabinet-Making business." Native-born artisans also complained that these aliens "broke down the apprenticeship system in the skilled trades," broke craft monopolies, undermined their social status, and destroyed the "mechanic's reputation." Still another grievance was the willingness of immigrants, particularly "newly arrived 'Dutchmen,' " a derogatory term for Germans, "to act as strikebreakers," although many German immigrants were in the forefront of the unionization movement. Ernst (1949), 103, 107, see 102–107. Cf. Ware (1924), 38–67. See *EM*, #63, for a discussion of the ethnic distribution of occupations in cities in 1860.

91. Taft (1964), 8, 20–34. Cf. Wilentz (1984); Montgomery (1968).

92. Feldberg (1975), 47, see 47–48. See also Lebergott (1971), 78–79, 82–83.

93. Feldberg (1975), 55–56, 51, see 49–58. For other cities, see Holt (1973c), 309–331; Pessen (1978), 279–283; Ernst (1949), 135–136, 271 *n.* 2; for the case of Boston see Handlin (1979), 180–206, 349 *n.* 11.
94. Quotations are from Pessen (1978), 270, 273, 272, 274, 279; see 272 and 275 for election returns. Taft (1964), 17–18.
95. Seward's proposal did not breach established standards regarding the separation of church and state, since public funds were already being expended to support the distribution of the Protestant version of the Bible. However, Seward's gesture could not offset Tammany Hall's smoothly working political organization for converting "aliens into naturalized citizens and naturalized citizens into steadfast Democrats" (Benson 1969, 118). Tammany cemented its hold over the foreign-born vote by liberally granting them market licenses and petty offices, which nativists condemned as payments for votes and as the most conspicuous signs of the general corruption of both parties in the running of city and state governments. The program of the American Republican party in the New York elections of 1844, therefore, combined the condemnation of toadying to foreigners with a call for the general reform of city government. It also called for a change in the naturalization laws so that the right to vote would be withheld from immigrants for 21 years, a step intended to debase the coin with which immigrants purchased licenses and offices. Other demands included the restriction of local offices to natives and the continuation of the King James version of the Bible as a schoolbook. See Benson (1969), 118–122; Billington (1964), 199–205; Griffin (1960), 141–142; Pessen (1978), 279–283.
96. Benson (1969), 121, see 121–122. For more on the growth of nativism, see Chapter 10 of this volume. Cf. Pessen (1978), 280–282; Billington (1964), 199–205; *EM,* #69.
97. Claiming 110,000 votes in the polling places of 14 states, the nativists held a national convention which met in Philadelphia in July of 1845, proclaimed a new national party, and sought to implement their program in Washington. In the Senate, which was controlled by the Whigs, the judiciary committee responded to a resolution calling on it to extend the period of naturalization, to eliminate the fraud in both the naturalization process and in elections, "and to prohibit the introduction of foreign convicts into the United States," although its sympathetic report produced no legislation. In the House, which was controlled by the Democrats, the judiciary committee produced a report that categorically stated that "no alteration of the naturalization laws is necessary for the preservation of the rights, interests and morals of the people, or from the guarding of the ballot-box against every improper influence." Although nativists condemned the House report as a "servile, truckling, pope's-toe-kissing resolution," efforts to stir popular support for their program came to naught. The American Republican party was turned out of power in the New York City elections of 1845, and the national movement expired during the next three years. Billington (1964), 206, 209, see also 205–211; Pessen (1978), 283.
98. See Fogel (1964, 159–166) for a discussion of the boom in the pig iron industry; Smith (1851) on the manufacture of iron in Pennsylvania; Davis and Stettler (1966, 221) for textile output by region, 1826–1860; Fishlow (1965a, 397–399) for railroad construction. For investment in construction in Ohio see Gottlieb (1966), 250. For the distribution of gross investment see Fishlow (1965a), 397–398; Wicker (1960), 516; Cranmer (1960), 556. See U.S. Bureau of the Census (1975, 164, 201) for daily wage rates on the Erie Canal and wholesale price indexes for this period. For a fuller review of these wage trends, see Margo and Villaflor (1987).
99. Pessen (1978), 282. For an example on one senator's land speculation, see Current (1955), 92–93, on Daniel Webster. Information regarding rents can be found in Ernst (1949), 49–50. Daily wage is taken at $0.58 to $1.25 and weekly rental of

a room was in the same range; see Margo and Villaflor (1987). For New York, see Ernst (1949), 70–71, 21, 22, 24, 13; Ware (1924), 14–17, 26–37, 50, 67–70, esp. 68–69, which points out that New York laborers worked about 200 days per year, often for as little as $0.65 per day. Hence,

$$\frac{\$0.65 \times 200}{365} = \$0.356 \text{ and } \frac{\$1.25}{7 \times \$0.356} = 0.50.$$

For a further discussion of this issue see *EM*, #61.

100. Howe (1979), 162, 165, see 162–165. Approaches that were acceptable to the upper-class Protestant crusaders included the formation of organizations such as the American Protestant Association which was dedicated to "alerting the public to the evil teachings of popery through lecture, publication, Sunday schools, revivals, and the reinstitution of the Sabbath as a day of piety." Feldberg (1975), 87. They also favored programs developed by the Home Missionary Society and the American Tract Society that aimed to convert Catholic immigrants by disseminating tracts in their native languages "designed to show by Biblical quotations that everything about the Roman religion was wrong." Griffin (1960), 211.

101. Griffin (1960), 213.

102. Howe (1979), 202.

103. Bodo (1980), 78, 83.

104. One of the most ominous features of the nativist movement was its radical overtone. On economic issues, "the American party adopted antimonopoly, antielitist, anti-Bank, pro-hard money positions" (Feldberg, 1975, 71) that strongly resembled the Locofoco wing of the Democratic party. Like the Locofocos, the nativists began to articulate the idea that the conflict between the wage laborer and his employer was deeper and more bitter than any other conflict in American society. For a discussion of the Locofocos see Dorfman (1966), 652ff.

105. Van Deusen (1964), 97–105, 110–114, quotations from 97–98, 98–99, 104. On Greeley's support of land reform, see Robbins (1933). The tariff remained a big issue in the iron regions, especially in Pennsylvania. See Holt (1969), 275–280. For a discussion of the severe effect of the Walker tariff of 1846 on the iron industry see Fogel (1964), 151–166; Fogel and Engerman (1971), 148–162.

106. Howe (1979), 138. Van Deusen (1963), 41–42, 129–130. For the congressional vote on the land issue see Silbey (1967), 87, 252 *n.* 20; Bemis (1956), 440–444; Robbins (1962), 37–50.

107. Van Deusen (1964), 101, 102, 117, see 101–118.

108. Dorfman (1966), 684–685, 686. See also Robbins (1942), 103.

109. Van Deusen (1964), 112.

110. Robbins (1962), 102, 101, 107, see 101–109.

111. Van Deusen (1964), 118.

112. Robbins (1962), 37, see 37–50. Silbey (1967), 107–136, 189–212.

113. Robbins (1962), 176. See pp. 349–351 of Chapter 10 of this volume.

114. See *EM*, #69, for the estimates of the number of native bolters and foreign additions to Democratic support. The complexity of the position of southern Democrats on immigration is discussed further in Chapter 10 of this volume. Because the Whigs in the South Central states entered en masse into the Know-Nothing party, they had to develop an argument that opposed nativism while at the same time explaining their switch on land policy. Compare with Thornton (1978, 352–360), who describes how the bulk of the Whigs in Alabama sought to capture nativists deflecting from the Democrats by entering the Know-Nothings while the Democrats sought to capture the conservative Whigs who refused to do so. See also Robbins (1962), 111–116, 176–179.

115. See *EM*, #60, #69.

CHAPTER 10. THE AMERICAN CAMPAIGN: FORGING A VICTORIOUS ANTISLAVERY COALITION

1. Silbey (1967), 91. On the Wilmot Proviso, see Foner (1969); Morrison (1967).
2. The respite was brief. The territorial issue soon erupted with more explosive force than ever before because of the way it was transformed by the economic and social issues that wracked the North. Much of this chapter deals with this transformation in the territorial issue. See especially pp. 326–327, 331–332, 335–337, 342–344, 347–354, 371–373, 378–383.
3. Silbey (1967), 134, 135.
4. Thomas (1963), 326–327.
5. For an insightful discussion of the divisions among the abolitionists on principles and tactics in the political arena, see Kraditor (1973).
6. Wyatt-Brown (1969), 289–292. Kraditor (1970), 255–260. For a recent discussion of the similarities and differences in northern and southern culture, see Pessen (1980).
7. Garrison, as cited by Davis (1984), 143–144; Current (1963), 22–24; Freehling (1966), 348–356; Wiltse (1949), 2:275–286; Cooper (1978), 88–93; Dillon (1974), 91–98, 101–107.
8. Kraditor (1970), 198. See also Dillon (1974), 153.
9. Kraditor (1970), 205, see 204–205. Lipset and Raab (1978), 44–47, 62–63, 84–121; Banner (1970), 147–167, 302–350; Bodo (1980), 221; Cole (1954), 216–217.
10. Wyatt-Brown (1969), 290, 291.
11. Kraditor (1970), 258, 259.
12. Hammond (1972), 82–83; Kraditor (1970), 259. See Cross (1982, 173–184) on religious revivalism.
13. Weld (1839), 117, 114.
14. The arguments of Bourne, Henry C. Wright, and Thomas W. Higginson are cited by Walters (1976), 77, 80, 81–82, 74; Wyatt-Brown (1982a), 278–281.
15. Olmsted (1970), 104; Cairnes (1969), 44; Bertelson (1967), 179–183; Clay (1969), 204.
16. From a speech given by James Henry Hammond to Congress on March 4, 1858, as reprinted in McKitrick (1965), 121.
17. Dumond (1966), 264–267; Nye (1963), 117–122.
18. Nye (1963), 121.
19. From a speech given by John C. Calhoun to the Senate on February 6, 1837, as reprinted in McKitrick (1965), 12.
20. Lowell (1858), 249.
21. Wiecek (1977), 16.
22. Wiecek (1977), 239, 245.
23. Wiecek (1977), 232, 239, 240, 241, 244–246. In this and the preceding paragraph, quotes are of Garrison, Phillips, Adams, and an AASS tract of 1845, as cited by Wiecek, or are Wiecek's presentation of their arguments.
24. Banner (1970), 84–85.
25. Banner (1970), 112–117; McCormick (1982), 106.
26. Channing, as quoted by Donald (1960), 133. See Wiecek (1977, 237) on Wendell Phillips's anti-Constitution rhetoric.
27. Wiecek (1977), 272, see also 259–261, 266–274.
28. Wiecek (1977), 251–258.
29. Wiecek (1977), 259, 260. See Cross and Livingstone (1983, 956) for a brief discussion of the concept of natural law.
30. Perry (1973), 195.
31. Spooner (1860), 5–8.

474 NOTES (pp. 333-338)

32. Spooner (1860), 17–18, 117, 58, 59.
33. From Madison's letter to Robert Walsh, dated November 27, 1819, reproduced in Meyers (1981), 321.
34. Spooner (1860), 59.
35. Phillips (1969), 45–46.
36. Phillips (1969), 65–67.
37. Wiecek (1977), 251; Burnham (1955), 893–953; Petersen (1963), 29, 31, 34, 37.
38. Wiecek (1977), 202–209.
39. I have designated Adams, Giddings, and Chase as the principal figures in the development of the moderate antislavery theory of the Constitution not because they were the original formulators of the theory but because they elevated it to the center of politics. Elements of the theory had been in the air for decades. As I noted in Chapter 9, many of the elements were set out in the congressional debates over Missouri. Betty Fladeland (1955, 148–149, 152) believes that James G. Birney outlined the theory most fully in 1836. According to Barnes (1964, 137–138), Weld's pamphlet *The Power of Congress over the District of Columbia* (1838) was the first full articulation of the theory. Foner (1970, 74–84) names Weld, Stanton, Goodell, Birney, and Thomas Morris as early formulators of the theory, but credits Chase for its elaboration, for some of the most compelling phrasing of the theory, and for developing it in a way that maximized its political potential.
40. Bemis (1956), 368, see 334–347, 361–370; Filler (1960), 106–107.
41. Filler (1960), 99–102.
42. The full composition of the antislavery bloc in the House during the 27th Congress is somewhat unclear. Barnes (1964) names Andrews and N.B. Borden (MA), Gates, Giddings, and F. James (PA), and J. Mattocks and Slade (VT) on 181–82; on 193 he adds D. D. Barnard and S.N. Clarke (NY), W. B. Calhoun (MA), and Robert C. Winthrop (MA). Bemis (1956, 424) states that Adams was a member of the "Select Committee on Slavery" or the "Insurgency" as members of the bloc referred to it. However, Stewart (1970, 70) states that although Adams worked with members of the Insurgency he "never joined their group."
43. Barnes (1964), 182, see 178–182; Bemis (1956), 420–425; Friedman (1982), 69–73. Barnes calls Giddings one of Weld's converts, but Stewart (1970, 29–31) disagrees with this "tradition." He cites, in particular, Giddings's membership in the Colonization Society, to which most strong abolitionists of the time were opposed. He also points out the lapse of time between the meeting of the two men and Giddings's first extensive statement of abolitionist views, the lack of significant antislavery sentiment in his personal correspondence before 1837, and personal traits that would have eventually led him to an antislavery position of his own understanding, with or without Weld's influence.
44. Julian (1892), 134, see 111–135; Barnes (1964), 182–84, 187–88, 286–287 *n.* 33.
45. Julian (1892), 119.
46. Sydnor (1966), 237, 246–248; Barnes (1964), 187–189; Nye (1963), 51–53. Technically, the gag rule forbade only antislavery petitions, but it was used to halt antislavery speeches as well.
47. Foner (1970), 77; Julian (1892), 134–135.
48. Ludlum (1936), esp. 51–52.
49. Wiecek (1977) on 217 quotes from the "Address" of the Portland Anti-Slavery Society reprinted in the *Liberator* of October 3, 1835; see also 213–216.
50. Nye (1963), 282–283.
51. The resentment expressed over southern domination in Congress during the Missouri crisis was not translated into votes during the elections of 1820. Monroe was swept back into office, winning all but one electoral vote. There was little change in the House, although Federalists lost two seats to the Jeffersonian party (Petersen, 1963, 16; *Encyclopaedia Britannica*, 1962, 23:845).

52. Leavitt (1965), 71; Jay (1853), 218–220. The incorrect figure of 45 electoral votes in Leavitt is apparently a printer's error.
53. Phillips (1969), esp. 38–49.
54. Leavitt (1965), 71, 73; Jay (1853), 227–229.
55. Jay (1853), 220.
56. From a letter of Albert G. Riddle to Joshua Giddings, quoted by Gara (1969), 18.
57. Leavitt, cited by Foner (1970), 93.
58. Bemis (1956), 337–340. On Adams see pp. 334–335 of this chapter and the sources cited in *n.* 25 to Chapter 9.
59. Holt (1978), 82, see 67–99; Potter (1976), 97–120; Fehrenbacher (1978), 142–145, 155–177.
60. Potter (1976), 130, 131, see 130–134. Sewell (1976), 236–251; Petersen (1963), 29, 31 (tables).
61. Potter (1976), 131, 132, 140. See Dillon (1974), 175–176. There were approximately 2.5 million families in the Northeast and North Central states in 1850 (DeBow, 1854, 99–100), thus the figure for copies of *Uncle Tom's Cabin* per household.
62. Nevins (1947), 2:112, see 111–112.
63. The events that led to the expansion of the antislavery coalition and the formation of the Republican party in 1856 are discussed on pp. 371–380 of this chapter.
64. Lincoln, in Angle (1958), 7, see 6–7; Fehrenbacher (1962), 78–82.
65. The quotation is from southern arguments cited by Wilson in the *Congressional Globe*, March 20, 1858, 170.
66. The Richmond *Enquirer* and the New Orleans *Delta,* cited by Nye (1963), 304.
67. Also cited by Wilson, see *n.* 65 above.
68. The Richmond *Enquirer* and J.H. Hammond, cited by Nye (1963), 305, see 301–315. See also Gara (1969), 14–16.
69. Although cliometricians have made a considerable contribution to the analysis and testing of the various elements in the economic indictment of slavery, they did so by tearing the issues from the political context in which they arose. While such an approach may have assisted in the evaluation of the factual basis of the economic indictment, it also contributed to a misunderstanding of the way in which the economic issues arose, tending to reinforce the view that economic issues were intrinsic to the struggle over slavery, even though their technical findings indicated that slavery was economically vigorous. The cliometric approach tended to obscure the asymmetry between the central role of economic issues in the antislavery movement after 1854 and their relative unimportance before then, giving economic issues a more fundamental role and a greater degree of continuity than they actually had.
70. Bretz (1929), 252; Temin (1969), 15–27; Pessen (1978), 197–232; Rockoff (1971), 449–450; McFaul (1972); Fogel and Engerman (1974), 1:92. The Specie Circular was an order requiring payment in gold or silver for the purchase of federal land.
71. Bretz (1929), 254. A sample of probate records drawn from the collection at the state archives of North Carolina in Raleigh indicated that northern railroad securities held by decedents substantially exceeded the debts to Northerners. However, the information needed to compute the balance was not retained.
72. Bretz (1929), 256. See Sewell (1976, 103–106) for a cogent description of the attempts of abolitionists before 1844 to pin the blame for economic hard times on the "Slave Power." He characterizes the Liberty party's arguments during this period as

> often naive, simplistic, or downright faulty. They grossly exaggerated the extent and the impact of Southern indebtedness and belittled the importance of free white labor. . . . They seriously distorted the tariff history of the early republic, for example blaming proslavery interests for the Tariff of 1816 although in fact

476 NOTES (pp. 345–351)

Southern Congressmen had voted heavily against that measure. And they wholly ignored the repressive influence of the North on economic development in the South. Yet for all that—perhaps in part because of it—such arguments possessed a substantial appeal, especially at a time of economic hardship.

73. The idealization of the cities was primarily a feature of the late nineteenth and early twentieth centuries. During the antebellum era cities were viewed far more critically, and large cities were held responsible for the physical, mental, and moral deterioration of society. See Weber (1967), Ch. 7; Schlesinger (1933), Ch. 3; Rosenberg (1971); Higgs (1979); Meckel (1985); White and White (1961), 148–154; Smillie (1955), Ch. 15–28.

Although some eastern urban workers (especially Irish and German immigrants lured to work on the railroads) moved west, the number drained off was too few to solve the social, economic, and demographic crises in eastern cities. However, migration intensified the crises in Cincinnati, Chicago, St. Louis, and other midwestern cities. See pp. 356–371 of this chapter and the sources cited there.

74. Stewart (1970), 85, see 85–86. Bretz (1929), 258; Fogel and Engerman (1974), 1:92.

75. Clay (1969), 204, 205, 224.

76. Porter and Johnson (1966), 13; Silbey (1967), Ch. 4–6.

77. Robbins (1962), 106, see 82–109. Commons et al. (1918), 1:522–535, 562–563; Dorfman (1966), 684–686; Cole (1984), 408–419; Stephenson (1917), 136–138; Thornton (1978), 365.

78. In emphasizing the central role of economic issues in the antislavery appeal after 1854, I do not mean to slight the importance of anti-southern appeals or the alarms over the political conspiracy of the slave power and of the papal conspiracy. All of these arguments were important in luring the Know-Nothings, the radical Whigs, and the radical land reform Democrats to the Republican fold. Quantification of the relative importance of these arguments in the unification of the antislavery coalition, while feasible in principle, is beyond practical implementation, unless some new body of data is developed. See pp. 367–379 of this chapter for a discussion of the role of the Know-Nothing movement and of the radical land reformers in the emergence of the Republican party.

79. Van Deusen (1964), 12, 13, 14, see Ch. 1 and 2.

80. Van Deusen (1964), 51, see 21. *Encyclopaedia Britannica* (1961), 10:850–851; Howe (1979), 184–197.

81. Van Deusen (1964), 31–32.

82. Van Deusen (1964), 90, see 64, 95; Commons et al. (1918), 1:498–506.

83. Commons et al. (1910), 7:213; see his 188, 203, 205, 213, and 217 for examples of the arguments that form the context of Greeley's ambivalence to the antislavery movement.

84. Stephenson (1917), 173–174; Robbins (1962), 110–116, 174–177; Hibbard (1939), 371.

85. Stephenson (1917), 172.

86. Rayback (1943), 156, see 153–156.

87. Kriege, as quoted by DuBois (1970b), 23, see 22–25.

88. Commons et al. (1918), 1:522–535; Commons (1910), 7:36–37; Robbins (1962), 110–111.

89. Stephenson (1917), 146–147. See Mandel (1955), 120–122. The extent of the defection of native urban workers from the Democratic party in the presidential elections of 1856 and 1860 has been underestimated because of an underestimation of the increased voter participation of immigrants who voted overwhelmingly for the Democrats in New York and other major northern cities. This issue is addressed in *EM*, #69.

90. Rayback (1943), 161; Isely (1947), 84–85, 132–137; Commons (1918), 1:537,

547. On Bovay's connection with the land reform movement and his role in the formation of the Republican party, see Ware (1924), 184; Commons et al. (1918), 1:532, 547, 549; Crandall (1930), 20–21; Commons (1909), 484; Isley (1947), 84.

91. Silbey (1985), 141; Stephenson (1917), 174; Robbins (1962), 176–177, 179–180.

92. Isely (1947), 206–210; Commons (1910), 7:33–40; Van Deusen (1964), 213.

93. Helper (1968), 35, 111, 116.

94. Despite their questionable economic validity, Helper's arguments were influential not only during antebellum times but also in much of the scholarship on the South during the twentieth century. See Woodman (1963); Frederickson's introduction to Helper (1968). For a recent critique of Helper's arguments, see Fogel and Engerman (1974), 1:161–169.

95. Isely (1947), 263, see 258–264. Van Deusen (1964), 213–232.

96. The melding of the economic (or class) and ethnocultural approaches developed in the balance of this chapter reflects both an old and a new approach in historical research. This melding is found in such classics as Commons et al. (1918) and Perlman (1923), and in such more recent works as Dorfman (1966); Holt (1969), (1973a,c), (1978); Foner (1970); Montgomery (1972); Pessen (1978), (1980); Laurie (1974); Feldberg (1975); Wilentz (1984); Bridges (1987); Ashworth (1987). Cf. Dublin (1985); Watson (1985); Wilentz (1986). The list could be extended many-fold.

   Frankly, I find in the works of what are supposed to be conflicting schools much more of a melding than the authors acknowledge in their programmatic declarations. In reading the work of Benson, Silbey, and Formisano, I find considerable recognition of the role of class; and in reading the work of Kousser and Foner, I find considerable recognition of ethnocultural factors. Although the implicit weights assigned to economic and ethnocultural factors vary, the evidence currently in hand is not of a nature that produces confidence limits so tight that one set of weights necessarily rules out the validity of the other.

97. Warren and Pearson (1933), 92; Rockoff (1972); G.R. Taylor (1958), 346.

98. G.R. Taylor (1958), 346–347. U.S. Bureau of the Census (1975), 731, 754; Gallman (1960), 61, Table A-8; Mitchell (1975), 581–582; Gottlieb (1964), 61–81.

99. Bidwell and Falconer (1941), 497–504; Gray (1958), 1039. The New Orleans prices cited by Gray were governed by Cincinnati prices since Cincinnati remained the main source of wheat and flour received in New Orleans. Gates (1968), 180–218, 276–284; U.S. Bureau of the Census (1975), 201, 209, 523–524; Ernst (1949). On the rural land speculators, petty and great, see Carstensen (1963, esp. 205–432) and Swierenga (1968).

100. See *EM*, #65–#68; Goldin (1976), 29–33, 42–50, 106–108; Pessen (1977). Cf. *EM*, #60.

101. For an analysis of the ethnic composition of the labor force in northern cities in 1860, see Wilcox's discussion in *EM*, #63. Information on the ethnic composition of the northern cities is found in U.S. Bureau of the Census (1854), 116–118. The speed with which the influx of immigrants transformed the cities is well described for Milwaukee in Conzen (1976) and in Ross (1985) for Cincinnati. On the growth of relief in New York, see Hannon (1984), (1985).

102. U.S. Bureau of the Census (1975), 106; Thorp (1926), 123–124; Fogel (1964), 117–121, 127–129, 151–166; Hannon (1985); Lazonick and Brush (1985); Williamson (1976), 333; Margo and Villaflor (1987). For a discussion of the problems involved in measuring trends in the real wage 1840–1860 by region, see *EM*, #61, #67.

103. Hoagland (1913), 297–299; Thorp (1926), 124; Smith (1951), 574–581; Fogel (1964), 152–166; Holt (1969), 89.

104. See Smith (1963, esp. 304, 310) for the movement of real wages in New York. Margo and Villaflor (1987) find quite similar patterns in the movement of real

wages between 1840 and 1856 in both the cities and the rural areas of the Midwest and Northeast. Compare with Ross (1985), Ch. 6 and 7, and *EM*, #67.

105. Lazonick and Brush (1985); Hoagland (1913); Ernst (1949); Ross (1985).

106. Fishlow (1965a), 118–120, 172; Thorp (1926), 125–126. For discussion of the cycles in midwestern railroad construction and aspects of the market for railroad labor see Paxson (1914); Fogel (1960), (1964), esp. Ch. 5; Licht (1983); Fishlow (1965a), esp. Ch. 4, and the sources cited there. For the method of estimating the labor requirements of the railroads and the number laid off as the building boom subsided, see *EM*, #66. Although some of the discharged immigrants moved westward to work on other railroads, after 1854 mileage added in the Midwest declined sharply, falling to hardly 40 percent of the peak by 1857 (Fishlow, 1965a, 172). Consequently, the majority of the railroad workers laid off were forced to find employment elsewhere. Even at the peak of the boom, however, turnover in the railroad gangs was high since, for many of the immigrants, work on the railroad was merely a ticket to the Midwest. Moreover, since railroad work was seasonal, midwestern labor markets were under especially heavy pressure during the off season. Cf. Wilentz (1984), Ch. 10; Commons et al. (1918), V. 1, Pt. 4, Ch. 7; Ross (1985), Ch. 6 and 7.

107. Between 1820 and 1860, immigration increased the average annual rate of growth of the northern labor force by 65 percent (*EM*, Table 60.9). It might be argued that in the long run supply creates its own demand, so that the large influx of immigrants could have been absorbed into the economy. In the long run, they were. Nevertheless, in the short and medium run the economy could not smoothly absorb additions to the labor force as rapidly as they were increasing, and distress was widespread in the North in the 1840s and 1850s. Hannon (1985), Ch. 1, 62, 82; Boyer (1978), 68–80; Schneider (1938), 254–281.

108. Hoagland (1913), 302–303.

109. U.S. Bureau of the Census (1864), xxxiv, cxl–cxli; Gates (1960), 166–167; Thorp (1926), 124–126; Commons et al. (1918), 1:607 *n.*83; Bidwell and Falconer (1941), 312, 315; Berry (1943), 564; Warren and Pearson (1933), 25–26.

110. See *EM*, #67, for a discussion of the evidence bearing on the magnitude of the decline in the real wages of native-born craftsmen. The high levels of economic inequality in northern cities are analyzed in *EM*, #62.

111. See Smillie (1955), esp. Ch. 9 and 10.

112. Fogel (1986), 465; Pope (1986).

113. Rosenberg (1971), 137; U.S. Surgeon General (1875), 608–621.

114. Smillie (1955), 120–140; U.S. Surgeon General (1875), 608–621.

115. Holt (1969), 89; see Ware (1924), 235.

116. Commons et al. (1918), 1:576–607; Wilentz (1984), Ch. 10; Ross (1985), Ch. 6 and 7.

117. Commons et al. (1918), 1:576–607, esp. 576, 587, 590, 593; Thorp (1926), 125–126.

118. Commons et al. (1918), 1:536–546; Ware (1924), 154–162.

119. Commons et al. (1918), 1:531, see 531–535, 558–563. DuBois (1970b), 22–24; Robbins (1962); Stephenson (1917); Mandel (1955). On the early history of the land reform movement and the basis for the popularity of agrarianism among urban artisans, see Ashworth (1987).

120. Hennesey (1981), 108, see 108–109. Commons et al. (1918), 1:181–184, 321–325, 469–471; Billington (1964), 142–158.

121. Commons et al. (1918), 1:85, see 84–87, 552–554. In New York in 1850, the cordwainers, painters, bricklayers and plasterers, sashmakers and blindmakers, carpenters, plumbers, jewelers, printers, cabinetmakers, boilermakers, and tailors each had their independent benevolent organization. Cf. Wilentz (1984, 344, 364–372), who, perhaps more than any other scholar in recent years, has recog-

nized the significance of the benevolent organizations in the antebellum labor movement. On their critical role in the early British labor movement, see Cole and Postgate (1976).

122. Billington (1964), 336, see 336–337. About early German fraternal organizations, see Schuelter (1913), 70–78. Ware (1924), 233.

123. Commons et al. (1918), 1:578, see 578–579.

124. Commons et al. (1918), 1:559, see 552–559.

125. Pessen (1977), 244, 246, 251, 254; quotations are from 251 and 254.

126. Scisco (1901), 64–67.

127. For examples of propaganda and counterpropaganda see Abbott (1926, 292–337) and Berger (1946).

128. Laurie and Schmitz (1981), 54–55; see Ernst (1949), 213–217, 223; Handlin (1979), 253; Whitney (1856), 261, 272–273. See *EM*, #65, for estimates of the distribution of craftsmen between the urban and rural areas of the North. For an estimate of the proportion of northern voters who were native born, see *EM*, #69; cf. *EM*, #60, #65.

129. Scisco (1901), 72–73, 77–83; Whitney (1856), 277–279.

130. Formisano (1983), 330–334.

131. Scisco (1901), 88, 90, see 81–83.

132. Formisano (1971), 224, 225, see 222–229.

133. Holt (1969), 111, see 110–116. Holt (1973c), 313; Maizlish (1983), 191–192; Billington (1964), 300–314, about anti-Catholic violence; Johnson (1972), 147–150. Cf. Senning (1914) and Schafer (1924).

134. Whitney (1856).

135. Whitney (1856), 280–282.

136. Billington (1964), 389, see 388–389. Gienapp (1985), 530–531; Holt (1973a), 594, 601–603, 606–607, 612–613; *Congressional Globe* (1856), 352.

137. Sewell (1976), 249–253.

138. Isely (1947), 39–42; Van Deusen (1964), 168–172; Stephenson (1917), 144–148; Robbins (1962), 110–111; Porter and Johnson (1966), 18–20.

139. Fehrenbacher (1978), 181–187; Mandel (1955), 120–122.

140. In emphasizing the role of manual workers and petty proprietors in the anti-Nebraska movement I do not mean to slight the role of farmers, especially those of Yankee stock, in this movement, which I alluded to in Chapter 8, pp. 257–258, and Chapter 9, pp. 304–307 and n. 78, but to call attention to an underestimation of the role played by artisans in both the cities and the rural areas. In the pages that follow and in *EM*, #69, evidence which indicates that nativist urban workers represented the swing vote that gave the Republicans their margin of victory in 1860 is set forth. The statistical basis for previous underestimates of the size of the nativist defection in the cities is also discussed.

141. Mandel (1955), 120–121.

142. Ibid. For the views of labor leaders regarding the antislavery movement in the 1840s and early 1850s, see Foner (1980b). For the views of abolitionists regarding the condition and prospects of free labor in the North see Glickstein (1979).

143. Schuelter (1913), 76.

144. Mandel (1955), 120–121; Gienapp (1987), 240–248, 540–547. See *EM*, #69.

145. Dannenbaum (1978).

146. Handlin (1979), 201–202; Formisano (1983), 332–333; Haynes (1897), (1898); cf. Sweeney (1976); Baum (1978).

147. Holt (1973a), 604.

148. Gienapp (1985), 535, see 532–535. For Douglas's view of the fusion tickets, see *Congressional Globe* (1855), 216.

149. In focusing on the Free Soilers I do not mean to slight the role of such antislavery Whigs as Greeley, Thaddeus Stevens (PA), and Schuyler Colfax (IN), and

such Democrats as Lyman Trumball (IL), Preston King (NY), and Francis P. Blair (MO). However, it was the Free Soilers who had the clearest vision of the antislavery coalition that eventually emerged and who led the drive to bring it into existence.

150. Foner (1970), 233.
151. Scisco (1901), 153–168; Foner (1970), 226–241; Gienapp (1985), 536–537.
152. Holt (1969), 171, see 161–162, 171–174. Gienapp (1985), 539.
153. Crandall (1930), 269, 270; Foner (1970), 202, 237–248.
154. Crandall (1930), 25, 34; Gienapp (1985), 540–547; Brand (1922), 304.
155. Harrington (1948), 22–24.
156. Bean (1924), 329, see 328–331. Cooper (1978), 363–369.
157. Holt (1973a), 609.
158. Holt (1973a), 607, see 607–612. Wilson (1874), 2:431–434; Scisco (1901), 133–147; Gienapp (1987), 261–263.
159. Wilson (1874), 2:433, see 419–434. Holt (1973a), 607.
160. Gienapp (1985), 538. See also Gienapp (1984), 7–28; Foner (1970), 244–245.
161. Even in Ohio, Chase's margin of victory was considerably below that of Republicans who were also Know-Nothings. Gienapp (1987), 200–202.
162. The *Tribune Almanac* (1855, 5) lists nine anti-Nebraska Democrats at the end of 1855. They are Fuller (ME); Wheeler, Spinner, Oliver, and Williams (NY); Hickman and Barclay (PA); Trumball (IL); and Wells (WI).
163. Gienapp (1987), 240–248; Nevins (1947), 1:170; Isley (1947), 142–147.
164. Gienapp (1987), 240–248. Banks also played a critical role in delivering the Know-Nothings to the Republican party in June 1856. See Harrington (1939). On Know-Nothing strength in the 34th Congress, see *Congressional Globe* (1856), 352.
165. Crandall (1930), 49–61; Scisco (1901), 172–173; Holt (1973a), 613–615.
166. U.S. Bureau of the Census (1975), 106, 201; Fogel (1964), 166; Berry (1943), 564, 572–573.
167. Nevins (1947), 2:474, see 472–475. Gienapp (1987), 296–299; Craven (1953), 209–226. The phrase "sack of Lawrence" is used by Gienapp (1987) on 298 and elsewhere.
168. Nevins (1947), 2:437–446; Gienapp (1987), 299–303, the quote is from 300; Donald (1960), 288–311; Craven (1953), 223–228.
169. Craven (1953), 217, 231, see 217–218, 228–236. Thornton (1978), 350–352; Nevins (1947), 2:431; Gienapp (1987), 300–303.
170. Gienapp (1987), 303, see 300–303.
171. Isley (1947), 188, see 175–189.
172. *Tribune Almanac* (1861), 34, 64; Petersen (1963), 35–38; Fite (1911), 233.
173. The northern Democratic vote in 1852 (including California in the North) was approximately 1,196,000. The 210,000 Democratic bolters include new voters (mainly native children of native parents) who in 1852 would have been expected to vote largely as their parents had. Work on the estimation and identification of bolters is still in progress. The number of Democratic bolters may have been somewhat larger than indicated in Table 7, but offset by foreign-born Whigs and their children who switched to the Democrats because of Republican concessions to the nativists. The interim figure, 210,000, is best interpreted as the net Democratic defection to the Republicans. The results presented in Table 7 are provisional and subject to changes which are not expected to affect significantly the interpretation of the table presented in the text. For the latest results and for a more detailed analysis, see *EM*, #69. There have been extensive debates as to the value of using regression analysis and other quantitative methods to interpret popular and legislative voting patterns as well as of the problems and advantages of alternative statistical procedures. See Foner (1974); Kousser (1976); Shade (1981); Kousser and

Lichtman (1983); Bogue (1983); Winkle (1983); Fehrenbacher (1985); Benson (1984); Kousser (1986).

174. Cooper (1978), 339–344, 355–362.

175. See *EM*, #69. Cf. *Tribune Almanac* (1855), 40–41.

176. Schuelter (1913), 77, see 77–79. Dawley (1982), 99–104; Huston (1982), 200–202.

177. Gienapp (1985); Foner (1970), 245.

178. Isely (1947), 249, 250, see 248–252. Silbey (1985), 141–147.

179. Isely (1947), 292, see 290–292, 218–222. Formisano (1983), 331–339.

180. U.S. Bureau of the Census (1975), 106. *EM*, #65. Lebergott (1971), 79.

181. Boatner (1973), 17–21. The Republican party, which controlled the executive and Congress, did not immediately move to abolish slavery after the war broke out and might not have done so if the North had not been forced to use emancipation as a means of raising troops. On the struggles over emancipation in the 37th and 38th Congresses, see Bogue (1982), (1989); Silbey (1977); McPherson (1982), Ch. 16–20.

182. Lipset and Raab (1978), 73.

183. Litwack (1961), 277, see 268–279; McPherson (1982), 276–278.

AFTERWORD: THE MORAL PROBLEM OF SLAVERY

1. Pope, *Essay on Criticism*, Pt. II, 1:215. T.H. Huxley's variant is also to the point: "If a little knowledge is dangerous, where is the man who has so much as to be out of danger?" Huxley (1894), 300.

2. Benedict and Weltfish (1943); Myrdal (1944).

3. Conrad and Meyer (1958). Cf. Engerman (1967).

4. See *EM*, #70.

5. The conclusion that slavery was profitable was not novel. It was precisely the point Stampp had made in 1956 when he rejected the numerous "myths" about the negative economic consequences of slavery (cf. Gray, 1958) and reasserted the moral foundation for the condemnation of slavery. The fact is that down to 1968 few historians dealing with the ideological and political aspects of slavery viewed the work of the cliometricians as particularly relevant to their concerns. Stampp welcomed the evidence they uncovered, for it supported his interpretation of the nature of southern slavery. Genovese (1965; and in Engerman et al., 1972) was critical of their findings, but thought they were irrelevant to the interpretation of the sectional conflict that precipitated the Civil War. The "general crisis" that confronted American slaveowners, said Genovese, was not primarily economic, but political and ideological. Elkins (1968), like Genovese, argued that the southern commitment to slavery transcended purely economic considerations and was uncertain as to what implications cliometric research had for the broader issue.

6. Fogel (1966), 647.

7. Conrad and Meyer (1958), 99.

8. The entire quote is: "Power tends to corrupt; absolute power corrupts absolutely" (Lord Acton, in a letter to Bishop Mandell Creighton, 1887).

9. For an elaboration of this point see Chapter 5 of this volume; *EM*, Part 5; *TP*, Parts 4 and 5.

10. See Crawford, *TP*, #26; Kahn, *TP*, #27.

11. Weld (1839), 15, 110, 167, 175. Less than 1 percent of the profits of slaveholders is attributable to the interstate slave trade. See *TP*, #6, #21; *EM*, #23, #49, #50.

12. William E. Channing made precisely this point in the late 1830s. See *EM*, #71.

13. See Fogel and Engerman (1974), 1:29–35, 105–109, 144–147, 153–159, 177–181, 215–219, 223–232, 236–240, 244–246, 258–264; 2:3–6, 16–19, 87–90,

119–125, 155–161, 171–177, 185–187, 220–225, 245–246. For examples of
other discussions between the late 1950s and the mid-1970s of moral and ideological issues in the historiography of slavery see Fogel and Engerman (1974), 2:App.
C; Davis (1974); Fogel (1975); Elkins (1959), Ch. 1; Degler (1976).

14. See *EM*, #74.

15. Davis (1984), 114; Davis (1966), 306.

16. Elkins (1975), 54; see also Stampp (1956), 327. For additional comments on
Elkins's argument, see Degler (1976); Lane (1971). Others, often following Jefferson, place emphasis on the "pathological" effects of slavery on the masters. However, both characterizations seem overdrawn to me. Whatever the limitations, I see
little warrant in medical or social evidence to suggest that the ruling elites and the
lower classes of the past were somehow more deficient personalities than those of
our day. Certainly there was no shortage of revolutionary spirit among the Haitian
slaves, oppressed peasants of France, or the workers of Germany during the late
eighteenth and the nineteenth centuries. Nor is there evidence of especially sick
intellects and personalities among such slaveholders and defenders of slavery as
Aristotle, Plato, Washington, Jefferson, Madison, and Jackson. The prominent role
of slaveholders in American politics during the first five decades of nationhood, and
their popularity with voters, even in the North, suggests that they were considered
among the most admirable of personalities.

17. Davis (1975), 561.

18. This point was made by Channing (1848, 6:387–390), who not only rejected
material treatment as an adequate basis for either a moral defense or a moral
indictment of slavery, but condemned such arguments as moral "insults." For his
full statement on this question see *EM*, #71.

19. Floud and Wachter (1982); see also Cunliffe (1979), 19–25; Hollis (1980), 296;
Fogel et al. (1983); Fogel (1987); Floud, Wachter, and Gregory (1989); Chapter
5 of this volume; *EM*, Part #5. It might be argued that comparing the malnutrition
of peasants or free urban workers with that of slaves is compounding one evil with
another. The point at issue, however, is whether, with respect to the consumption of
food, etc., lower classes under slavery suffered more than other lower classes of the
age, not whether some theoretical system might have provided better conditions for
all lower classes than actually prevailed. In utopias conditions are invariably better,
and measurement is unnecessary.

20. Had there been economic decline, competition would have led to the immiseration
of the laboring classes and slavery would have been more appealing to the starving
multitudes, as it was in India. See *n.* 22 below.

21. On the subject of the progress of the laboring classes see Thernstrom (1973), esp.
Ch. 9; Kearl, Pope, and Wimmer (1980); Kearl and Pope (1981a, b), (1983a, b);
and the sources cited in these works.

22. Margo and Steckel (1982). The argument for the second count presupposes the
technological changes and rapid economic growth actually experienced in Western
Europe and America during the nineteenth and twentieth centuries. See *EM*, #52,
#72, for a discussion of the income distribution of U.S. slaves c.1860 and its moral
implications.

23. On the question of slavery and citizenship and the legal status of slaves in general
see Genovese (1971), Ch. 7; Klein (1967), esp. Parts 2 and 3; Klein (1986); Davis
(1966), 54–58; Farnam (1938), Ch. 14 and 15; Morgan (1975); Dunn (1973);
Tushnet (1981). On the role of the Catholic Church in the United States see
Hennesey (1981), Ch. 12; cf. *n.* 31 in Ch. 4, above.

24. On the Protestant churches and the rights of slaves see Blassingame (1979),
269–271; Drake (1965), esp. Ch. 7 and 8; Woodson (1919), esp. Ch. 2 and 8.

25. On popular agitation by Europe's lower classes see pp. 208–213 and 222–223 of
Chapter 7 of this volume and the relevant notes. See also Bohstedt (1983), esp. Ch.

NOTES (pp. 400–402)   483

1 and 9; Gash (1979). On the legal proscription of the rights of free blacks in the North and South see Farnam (1938), 204–224.

26. Franklin (1967), 217–241, 249–260. Cf. the descriptions of working-class culture in Thompson (1975), *passim.*

27. For discussions of slave religion as an expression of cultural autonomy see Genovese (1974), 161–284; Blassingame (1979), 130–137. Higman (1975), who describes slave families of the British West Indies, indicates that their structure was more stable and organized than suggested by previous research.

28. My intent in this paragraph and in the remainder of this section is not to belittle the foes of slavery or to engage in self-flattery but to emphasize why the indictment developed to meet the exigencies of the antislavery struggle does not adequately serve the moral needs of our own age. While it is easy to criticize the actual indictment, I am hard put to suggest one that would have worked better in building a winning antislavery coalition. On that criterion, the purchase of consistency at the expense of the support needed to defeat the proslavery forces would have been a disaster. See the discussion of the moral problem of the Civil War on pp. 409–416 below. However, too much of what was expedient in the 1850s continues to contaminate current interpretations of the moral legacy of the antislavery struggle. My points are directed not at the moralists of the past but at our own deficiencies.

29. The evangelicals were not against economic opportunity per se, which they believed was an individual matter and which could be obtained by individuals who diligently sought it. What they opposed were economic doctrines that proposed to elevate the poor en masse to a higher social condition. Such change they believed could be accomplished only by force and by appropriation from others. I am indebted to Norman Gash for calling this distinction to my attention.

30. Foner (1970), 16.

31. James Birney, as quoted by Walters (1976), 117.

32. William Garrison, as quoted by Walters (1976), 116.

33. Quoted by L. Friedman (1982, 240), who discusses the racial views of Preston King, William Seward, Owen Lovejoy, and others.

34. I am treading on unsettled terrain here—on points that specialists on the antislavery movement and antebellum politics generally still do not fully agree on. For evidence on the strength of racism within the Republican party see Mandel (1955); McPherson (1964); Zilversmit (1967); Berwanger (1971); Voegeli (1967); Woodward (1971); L. Friedman (1982). Other specialists have argued that this emphasis has been overdone. See Fehrenbacher (1962, esp. 156–157); Foner (1970); Sewell (1976); Maizlish (1986). This point was made forcefully to me by J. Morgan Kousser. In a letter to RWF of February 5, 1987, he argued that if Republicans such as Sumner, Wilson, and Chase were added to my list of Republicans who supported full equal rights for blacks and closet egalitarians (such as Indiana war governor Oliver P. Morton), who were "always ready to endorse as much equality for blacks as they could get while still retaining office," then my "minority" of Republican leaders might become a "majority."

It would, however, be misleading to treat even such defenders of black equality as Garrison as though they embraced the anti-racist views found in the late twentieth century. See Litwack (1961, Ch. 7) for a cogent and balanced assessment of the sometimes uneasy relationship between black and white abolitionists. Moreover, as Richard H. Sewell recently pointed out to me, in a letter of March 18, 1987, even such staunch defenders of equal rights as Garrison sometimes equivocated, as in 1864 when he "publicly expressed doubts about the instant enfranchisement of freedmen." See Woodward (1968, 89–91), who discusses Garrison's equivocation and similar equivocations by Sumner and Greeley.

35. Lincoln and Douglass are quoted by Handlin and Handlin (1980), 156–157. On the March 1862 vote see Bogue (1982), 156.

36. David Davis's letter to Lincoln, August 3, 1858, quoted by Foner (1970), 265.
37. Birney, as quoted by Sewell (1976), 98–99. Sewell quotes a pamphlet published by Birney in 1850 entitled "Examination of the Decision of the Supreme Court . . . in the Case of Strader, Gorman (and others) . . . Concluding with an Address to the Free Colored People, Advising Them to Remove to Liberia."
38. Gerrit Smith, as quoted by Litwack (1961), 215.
39. Macaulay's letter to Henry S. Rendall, May 23, 1857, is quoted by Huston (1983), 38.
40. Walters (1976), 55–56, see also 12–13. Walters discusses the arguments of Theodore Dwight Weld, James Birney, Wendell Phillips, and other abolitionists.
41. Lewis Tappan, as quoted by Walters (1976), 56.
42. Walters (1976), 12, 30, 32. Walters quotes resolutions made by the Massachusetts Anti-Slavery Society in 1857.
43. Harriet Beecher Stowe's letter to Garrison is cited by Litwack (1961), 243.
44. Temperley (1980), 346–347.
45. L. Friedman (1982), 193–194. Of course abolitionists were not unique in their desire to bring their civilization to other cultures. That desire has been prominent among elitists in numerous countries throughout the ages.
46. See EM, #71–#74, for further discussion of these issues.
47. At some point exaggeration of the brutality and material deprivations of slavery becomes transformed from an antislavery weapon to apologetics for the injustices against the underprivileged in free society. Whether or not these exaggerations were warranted during the antebellum era in order to promote the antislavery coalition, honoring them as fact long after the destruction of slavery and its ruling class serves only to make all that came afterward appear as an improvement. However, in those post-emancipation societies so far studied, the actual situation was far more complex. Although freedom provided the basis for the ultimate improvement of the living conditions of slaves and their descendants, the immediate consequence was often deeper impoverishment, new social and political restrictions, and a reduced life expectation. Some of the questions are discussed in Moohr (1972); Adamson (1972); Engerman (1982), (1984), (1986a); Craton (1978); Green (1976).
48. Cf. Bok (1978).
49. On this type of deception in the case of Wilberforce, see Mathieson (1967), 20; Coupland (1933), 112.
50. Temperley (1972), 119–120.
51. Sewell (1976), 92; L. Friedman (1982), 238.
52. Foner (1970), 100. On migration patterns, see EM, #35, and the sources cited there.
53. Gerrit Smith, as quoted by Foner (1970), 302; see also L. Friedman (1982), 239.
54. Lydia Maria Child's letter to Smith, January 7, 1862, is cited by L. Friedman (1982), 260.
55. In arguing that only a "negrophobic" strategy could have produced a Republican victory, I do not mean to suggest that the Republican party had a hidden agenda or that a Republican victory made emancipation a foregone conclusion. In the end, emancipation was a product of the exigencies of the war. For a discussion of the complexities of the emancipation issue in the 37th and 38th Congresses see Bogue (1982), (1989); cf. McPherson (1982), 275–279, 293–298.
56. For a discussion of the connections between free labor and economic changes (in relation to the abolitionist claims) in this and the following paragraphs see Green (1976); Ch. 7; Temperley (1972), Ch. 6, esp. 115–122.
57. Potter (1976), 583.
58. Potter (1962), xxi.
59. Wender (1930); Stampp (1970), 136; Eaton (1954), Ch. 1–3; McCardell (1979);

Alexander and Beringer (1972), esp. Ch. 12. I do not mean to imply that the views summarized in this paragraph were universal in the South, even among planters, but only that they were the politically reigning views.

60. Stampp (1970), xvii.

61. Stampp (1970), 136. Although the majority for secession was overwhelming in some states, in others the majority was small. See Eaton (1954); Alexander and Beringer (1972). On southern attitudes before the 1860 election and during the secession crisis see Degler (1982), who describes various forms of opposition to slavery by a minority of dissenters within the South between 1830 and the Civil War. Franklin (1976) describes the defense of slavery by prominent Southerners who traveled to the North and then returned home to rally southern opinion behind militant proslavery policies.

62. Bowden, Karpovich, and Usher (1969), 259–279, 474–493; Porter (1918); Baum (1978), 974; Eaton (1954), 53–54.

63. On Greeley's attitude toward strikes see Ware (1924), 230–231; Commons et al. (1918), 1:576–577.

64. For discussions of the strong expansionist movements in the South between 1846 and 1861, especially during the last half of the 1850s, see Wender (1930), 207–236; Nevins (1947), 2:368–374, 405–408; Fornell (1956); Fuller (1934); Takaki (1971); May (1973); McCardell (1979), 263–267, 273–276. There was nearly 2 to 1 support in the Senate in 1859 for the annexation of Cuba (May, 1973, 182–183).

65. The strength of the northern peace movement during the Civil War suggests the pressures that would have arisen for a modus vivendi. Cf. Silby (1977); McPherson (1982); Bogue (1989).

66. Channing (1848), 81.

REFERENCES

Abbot, Edith, ed. 1926. *Historical aspects of the immigration problem: Selected documents.* Chicago: University of Chicago Press.

Abzug, Robert H. 1980. *Passionate liberator: Theodore Dwight Weld and the dilemma of reform.* New York and Oxford: Oxford University Press.

Adams, Alice Dana. 1908. *The neglected period of anti-slavery in America, 1808–1831.* Boston: Ginn.

Adams, Charles Francis, ed. 1877. *Memoirs of John Quincy Adams, comprising portions of his diary from 1795 to 1848,* 12 vols. Philadelphia: J.B. Lippincott and Co.

Adamson, Alan H. 1972. *Sugar without slaves: The political economy of British Guiana, 1838–1904.* New Haven: Yale University Press.

Ahlstrom, Sydney E. 1975. *A religious history of the American people,* 2 vols. Garden City, NJ: Image Books.

Albanese, Catherine L. 1981. *America: Religions and religion.* Belmont, CA: Wadsworth.

Albert, Peter Joseph. 1976. The protean institution: The geography, economy, and ideology of slavery in post-Revolutionary Virginia. Ph.D. dissertation, University of Maryland.

Alexander, Thomas B. 1967. *Sectional stress and party strength: A study of roll-call voting patterns in the United States House of Representatives, 1836–1860.* Nashville: Vanderbilt University Press.

Alexander, Thomas B., and Richard E. Beringer. 1972. *The anatomy of the Confederate congress: A study of the influences of member characteristics on legislative voting behavior, 1861–1865.* Nashville: Vanderbilt University Press.

Allen, Robert C. 1975. International competition and the growth of the British iron and steel industry: 1830–1913. Ph.D. dissertation, Harvard University.

American Iron and Steel Association. 1856–1858. Bulletin of the American Iron Association. Philadelphia.

Anderson, Ralph V. 1974. Labor utilization and productivity, diversification and self-sufficiency, southern plantations, 1800–1840. Ph.D. dissertation, University of North Carolina, Chapel Hill.

Angle, Paul M., ed. 1958. *Created equal?: The complete Lincoln-Douglas debates of 1858.* Chicago: The University of Chicago Press.

Anstey, Roger T. 1968. Capitalism and slavery: A critique. *Economic History Review* 21:307–320.

———. 1972. A reinterpretation of the abolition of the British slave trade, 1806–1807. *English Historical Review* 87 (April):304–332.

———. 1975. *The Atlantic slave trade and British abolition 1760–1810.* Atlantic Highlands, NJ: Humanities Press.

———. 1980. The pattern of British abolitionism in the eighteenth and nineteenth centuries. In Christine Bolt and Seymour Drescher, eds., *Anti-slavery, religion and reform.* Folkestone, UK: W. Dawson.

————. 1981. Religion and British slave emancipation. In David Eltis and James Walvin eds., *The abolition of the Atlantic slave trade*. Madison: University of Wisconsin Press.

Aptheker, Herbert. 1943. *American Negro slave revolts*. New York: Columbia University Press.

Armstrong, Anthony. 1973. *The Church of England, the Methodists and society, 1700–1850*. Totowa, NJ: Rowman and Littlefield.

Ashworth, John. [1983] 1987. *'Agrarians' and 'Aristocrats': Party political ideology in the United States, 1837–1846*. Cambridge: Cambridge University Press.

Atack, Jeremy, and Fred Bateman. 1981a. The "Egalitarian Ideal" and the distribution of wealth in the northern agricultural community: A backward look. *Review of Economics and Statistics* 63:124–129.

————. 1981b. Egalitarianism, inequality, and age: The rural North in 1860. *Journal of Economic History* 41:85–93.

Aufhauser, Robert K. 1971. Work and slavery: Profitability, discipline, and technology on Caribbean plantations. Ph.D. dissertation, Harvard University.

————. 1974. The distribution of income and leisure after emancipation in Louisiana and the Caribbean. Typescript.

Austen, Ralph A. 1979. The trans-Saharan slave trade: A tentative census. In Henry Gemery and Jan Hogendorn, eds., *The uncommon market: Essays in the economic history of the Atlantic slave trade*. New York: Academic Press.

————. 1981. From the Atlantic to the Indian Ocean: European abolition, the African slave trade, and Asian economic structures. In David Eltis and James Walvin, eds., *The abolition of the Atlantic slave trade*. Madison: University of Wisconsin Press.

Aydelotte, William O. 1954. The House of Commons in the 1840's. *History* 39:249–262.

————. 1971. *Quantification in history*. Reading, MA: Addison-Wesley Publishing Company.

Bailey, David T. 1980. A divided prism: Two sources of black testimony on slavery. *Journal of Southern History* 46:381–404.

Bailyn, Bernard. 1967. *The ideological origins of the American revolution*. Cambridge: The Belknap Press of Harvard University Press.

Baker, Jean H. 1983. *Affairs of party: The political culture of northern Democrats in the mid-nineteenth century*. Ithaca: Cornell University Press.

Banner, James M., Jr. 1970. *To the Hartford Convention: The Federalists and the origins of party politics in Massachusetts, 1789–1815*. New York: Alfred A. Knopf.

Banner, Lois W. 1977. Religious benevolence as social control: A critique of an interpretation. In Edward Pessen, ed., *The many-faceted Jacksonian era: New interpretations*. Westport, CT: Greenwood Press.

Barnes, Gilbert Hobbs. [1933] 1964. *The anti-slavery impulse, 1830–1844*. New York: Harcourt, Brace, & World.

Barney, William L. 1974. *The secessionist impulse: Alabama and Mississippi in 1860*. Princeton: Princeton University Press.

Bateman, Fred, and Jeremy Atack. 1979. The profitability of northern agriculture in 1860. *Research in Economic History* 4:87–125.

Bateman, Fred, and James D. Foust. 1974. A sample of rural households selected from the 1860 manuscript censuses. *Agricultural History* 48:75–93.

Bateman, Fred, James D. Foust, and Thomas Weiss. 1971. Large scale manufacturing in the South and West, 1850–1860. *Business History Review* 45:1–17.

————. 1974. The participation of planters in manufacturing in the antebellum South. *Agricultural History* 48:277–297.

————. 1975. Profitability in southern manufacturing: Estimates for 1860. *Explorations in Economic History* 12:211–231.

Bateman, Fred, and Thomas Weiss. 1975. Comparative regional development in antebellum manufacturing. *Journal of Economic History* 35:182–208.

————. 1976. Manufacturing in the antebellum South. *Research in Economic History* 1:1–44.

————. 1981. *A deplorable scarcity: The failure of industrialization in the slave economy.* Chapel Hill: University of North Carolina Press.

Bauer, Raymond A., and Alice H. Bauer. 1942. Day to day resistance to slavery. *Journal of Negro History* 2:388–419.

Baum, Dale. 1978. Know-Nothingism and the Republican majority in Massachusetts: The political realignment of the 1850s. *Journal of American History* 64:959–986.

Baxter, Jedediah H. 1875. *Statistics, medical and anthropological, of the Provost-Marshal-General's bureau, derived from records of the examination for military service in the armies of the United States during the late war of the rebellion of over a million recruits, drafted men, substitutes, and enrolled men.* Washington, D.C.

Beal, Virginia A. 1980. *Nutrition in the life span.* New York: John Wiley and Sons.

Bean, William G. 1924. An aspect of Know Nothingism: The immigrant and slavery. *The South Atlantic Quarterly* 23:319–334.

Bemis, Samuel Flagg. 1956. *John Quincy Adams and the union.* New York: Alfred A. Knopf.

Benedict, Ruth, and Gene Weltfish. 1943. *The races of mankind.* New York: Public Affairs Committee (Pamphlet No. 85).

Bennett, J. Harry. 1958. *Bondsmen and bishops: Slavery and apprenticeship on the Codrington plantations of Barbados, 1710–1838.* Berkeley: University of California Press.

Benson, Lee. 1969. *The concept of Jacksonian democracy: New York as a test case.* New York: Atheneum.

————. 1984. The mistransference fallacy in explanations of human behavior. *Historical Methods* 17:118–131.

Berger, Max. 1946. The Irish emigrant and American nativism as seen by British visitors, 1836–1860. *The Pennsylvania Magazine of History and Biography* 70:146–160.

Berlin, Ira. 1974. *Slaves without masters.* New York: Pantheon.

Berry, Thomas Senior. 1943. *Western prices before 1861: A study of the Cincinnati market.* Cambridge: Harvard University Press.

Bertelson, David. 1967. *The lazy South.* New York: Oxford University Press.

Berthoff, R.T. 1951. Southern attitudes toward immigration, 1865–1914. *Journal of Southern History* 17:330–360.

Berwanger, Eugene H. 1971. *The frontier against slavery: Western anti-Negro prejudice and the slavery extension controversy.* Urbana: University of Illinois Press.

Bethell, Leslie, 1970. *The abolition of the Brazilian slave trade.* Cambridge: Cambridge University Press.

Beveridge, Charles E., and Charles Copen McLaughlin, eds. 1981. *The papers of Frederick Law Olmsted:* Vol. 2, *Slavery and the South, 1852–1857.* Baltimore: Johns Hopkins University Press.

Bidwell, Percy Wells, and John I. Falconer. 1941. *History of agriculture in the northern United States, 1620–1860.* New York: Peter Smith.

Billington, Ray Allen. 1964. *The Protestant crusade, 1800–1860: A study of the origins of American nativism.* Chicago: Quadrangle.

Bils, Mark. 1984. Tariff protection and production in the early U.S. cotton textile industry. *Journal of Economic History* 44:1033–1045.

Blackett, R.J.M. 1983. *Building an antislavery wall: Black Americans in the Atlantic abolitionist movement, 1830–1860.* Baton Rouge: Louisiana State University Press.

Blassingame, John W. 1972. *The slave community: Plantation life in the antebellum South.* New York: Oxford University Press.

————. 1975. Using the testimony of ex-slaves. *Journal of Southern History* 41:473–492.

————, ed. 1977. *Slave testimony: Two centuries of letters, speeches, interviews, and autobiographies.* Baton Rouge: Louisiana State University Press.

————. 1979. *The slave community: Plantation life in the antebellum South.* Revised and enlarged edition. New York: Oxford University Press.

Boatner, Mark Mayo. 1973. *Cassell's biographical dictionary of the American Civil War 1861–1865.* London: Cassell.

Bode, Frederick A., and Donald E. Ginter. 1984. A critique of landholding variables in the 1860 census and the Parker-Gallman sample. *Journal of Interdisciplinary History* 15:277–295.

Bodo, John R. 1980. *The Protestant clergy and public issues, 1812–1848.* Philadelphia: Porcupine.

Bogue, Allan G. 1982. *The earnest men: Republicans of the Civil War Senate.* Ithaca: Cornell University Press.

————. 1983. *Clio and the bitch goddess: Quantification in American political history.* Beverly Hills: SAGE Publications.

————. 1989. *The congressman's Civil War.* Cambridge: Cambridge University Press.

Bohstedt, John. 1983. *Riots and community politics in England and Wales, 1790–1810.* Cambridge: Harvard University Press.

Bok, Sissela. 1978. *Lying: Moral choice in public and private life.* New York: Pantheon.

Bolt, Christine, and Seymour Drescher, eds. 1980. *Anti-slavery, religion, and reform.* Folkestone, UK: W. Dawson.

Bonar, James. [1931] 1966. *Theories of population from Raleigh to Arthur Young.* London: Frank Cass and Co.

Bonner, James C. 1964. *A history of Georgia agriculture, 1732–1860.* Athens: University of Georgia Press.

Bowden, Witt, Michael Karpovich, and Abbott Payson Usher [1937] 1969. *An economic history of Europe since 1750.* New York: Howard Fertig.

Bowser, Frederick P. 1974. *The African slave in colonial Peru, 1524–1650.* Stanford, CA: Stanford University Press.

Boxer, C.R. 1966. *The Spanish seaborne empire: The history of human society.* New York: Alfred A. Knopf.

Boyer, Paul. 1978. *Urban masses and moral order in America, 1820–1920.* Cambridge, MA: Harvard University Press.

Brand, Carl Fremont. 1922. The history of the Know Nothing Party in Indiana. *Indiana Magazine of History* 18:47–81, 177–206, 266–306.

Bretz, Julian P. 1929. The economic background of the Liberty Party. *American Historical Review* 36:250–264.

Brewer, John. 1976. *Party ideology and popular politics at the accession of George III.* Cambridge: Cambridge University Press.

Bridges, Amy. 1987. *A city in the republic: Antebellum New York and the origins of machine politics.* Ithaca: Cornell University Press.

British Association for the Advancement of Science. 1883. *Report of the 53rd meeting.* London: John Murray, Albemarle St.

Brown, Richard H. 1966. The Missouri crisis, slavery, and the politics of Jacksonianism. *South Atlantic Quarterly* 65:55–72.

Bruce, Dickson D., Jr. 1982. *The rhetoric of conservatism: The Virginia Convention of 1829–30 and the conservative tradition in the South.* San Marino, CA: The Huntington Library.

Buckley, Roger Norman. 1969. *Slaves in red coats: The British West India regiments, 1795–1815.* New Haven and London: Yale University Press.

Burnham, W. Dean. 1955. *Presidential ballots, 1836–1892.* Baltimore: Johns Hopkins University Press.

Burton, Orville Vernon, and Robert C. McMath, Jr., eds. 1982. *Class, conflict, and consensus: Antebellum southern community studies.* Westport, CT, and London: Greenwood Press.

Cairnes, J.E. [1862] 1969. *The slave power: Its character, career, and probable designs: Being an attempt to explain the real issues involved in the American contest.* Introduction by Harold D. Woodman. New York: Harper & Row.

Campbell, John. 1984. Work, pregnancy, and infant mortality among Southern slaves. *Journal of Interdisciplinary History* 14:793–812.

Campbell, R.B., and R.G. Lowe. 1977. *Wealth and power in antebellum Texas.* College Station: Texas A & M University Press.

Cardell, Nicholas Scott, and Mark Myron Hopkins. 1978. The effect of milk intolerance on the consumption of milk by slaves in 1860. *Journal of Interdisciplinary History* 8:507–513.

Carmichael, Anne. 1834. *Five years in Trinidad and St. Vincent.* London: Whittaker.

Carr-Saunders, A.M. 1964. *World population: Past growth and present trends.* London: Frank Cass.

Carstensen, Vernon, ed. 1963. *The public lands: Studies in the history of the public domain.* Madison: University of Madison Press.

Carstensen, Vernon, and S.E. Goodman. 1977. Trouble on the auction block: Interregional slave sales and the reliability of a linear equation. *Journal of Interdisciplinary History* 8:315–318.

Cassedy, James H. 1969. *Demography in early America: Beginnings of the statistical mind 1600–1800.* Cambridge: Harvard University Press.

Chandler, Alfred. 1977. *The visible hand.* Cambridge: Harvard University Press.

Channing, William E. 1841. *The works of William E. Channing, D.D.*, Vol. 5. Boston: James Munroe and Company.

———. 1848. *The works of William E. Channing, D.D.*, Vol. 6. Boston: James Munroe and Company.

Child, Lydia Maria. 1982. *Lydia Maria Child: Selected letters, 1817–1880.* Milton Meltzer and Patricia Holland, eds. Amherst: University of Massachusetts Press.

Christie, Ian. 1982. *Wars and revolutions: Britain 1760–1815.* Cambridge: Harvard University Press.

Christy, David. 1856. *Cotton is king: Or the culture of cotton, and its relation to agriculture, manufactures and commerce.* New York: Derby and Jackson.

Chudacoff, Howard P. 1975. *The evolution of American urban society.* Englewood Cliffs, NJ: Prentice-Hall.

Clark, Blanche Henry. 1942. *The Tennessee yeoman, 1840–1860.* Nashville: Vanderbilt University Press.

Clay, Cassius Marcellus. [1848] 1969. *The writings of Cassius Marcellus Clay.* New York: Negro Universities Press.

Clive, John. 1973. *Macaulay: The shaping of the historian.* New York: Vintage Books.

Coale, A.J., and P. Demeny. 1966. *Regional model life tables and stable populations.* Princeton: Princeton University Press.

Coale, Ansley J., and Norfleet W. Rives, Jr. 1973. A statistical reconstruction of the black population of the United States 1880–1970: Estimates of the true numbers by age and sex, birth rates, and total fertility. *Population Index* 39:3–36.

Cody, Cheryll Ann. 1982. Slave demography and family formation: A community study of the Ball family plantations, 1720–1896. Ph.D. dissertation, University of Minnesota.

Cogswell, Seddie, Jr. 1975. *Tenure, nativity and age as factors in Iowa agriculture: 1850–1880.* Ames: Iowa State University Press.

Cohn, Raymond L. 1984. Mortality on immigrant voyages to New York, 1836–1853. *Journal of Economic History* 44:289–300.

———. 1985. Deaths of slaves in the middle passage. *Journal of Economic History* 45:685–692.

Cohn, Raymond L., and Richard A. Jensen. 1982. The determinants of slave mortality rates on the middle passage. *Explorations in Economic History* 19:269–282.

Cole, Arthur Charles. 1934. *The irrepressible conflict, 1850–1865.* New York: Macmillan.

Cole, Charles C., Jr. 1954. *The social ideas of the northern evangelists, 1826–1860.* New York: Columbia University Press.

Cole, Donald B. 1984. *Martin Van Buren and the American political system.* Princeton: Princeton University Press.

Cole, G.D.H., and Raymond Postgate. [1938] 1976. *The common people, 1746–1946.* London: Methuen.

Coles, Harry L., Jr. 1943. Some notes on slaveownership and landownership in Louisiana, 1850–1860. *Journal of Southern History* 9:381–394.

Collins, Dr. 1811. *Practical rules for the management and medical treatment of Negro slaves in the sugar colonies.* London: J. Barfield.

Colquhoun, P. 1814. *Treatise on the wealth, power, and resources of the British Empire.* London: Joseph Mawmay.

Commons, John R. 1909. Horace Greeley and the working class origins of the Republican Party. *Political Science Quarterly* 24:468–488.

Commons, John R., Ulrich B. Phillips, Eugene A. Gilmore, Helen L. Sumner, and John B. Andrews, eds. 1910. *A documentary history of American industrial society,* 10 vols. Cleveland: The Arthur H. Clark Company.

Commons, John R., David J. Saposs, Helen J. Sumner, E.B. Mittelman, H.E. Hoagland, John B. Andrews, and Selig Perlman. 1918. *History of labour in the United States,* 2 vols. New York: Macmillan.

Congressional Globe. 1855. Appendix. Washington, D.C.: John C. Rives.

Congressional Globe. 1856. Appendix. Washington, D.C.: John C. Rives.

Conrad, Alfred H., and John R. Meyer. 1958. The economics of slavery in the antebellum South. *Journal of Political Economy* 66:95–130.

———. [1958] 1964. *The economics of slavery and other studies in econometric history.* Chicago: Aldine.

Conzen, Kathleen Neils. 1976. *Immigrant Milwaukee, 1836–1860: Accommodation and community in a frontier city.* Cambridge: Harvard University Press.

Cooper, William J., Jr. 1978. *The South and the politics of slavery, 1828–1856.* Baton Rouge: Louisiana State University Press.

Correa do Lago, Luiz Aranha. 1978. The transition from slave to free labor in agriculture in the southern and coffee regions of Brazil: A global and theoretical approach and regional case studies. Ph.D. dissertation, Harvard University.

Coupland, R. 1933. *The British anti-slavery movement.* London: Thornton, Butterworth, Ltd.

Cowherd, Raymond G. 1956. *The politics of English dissent.* New York: New York University Press.

Cramner, H. Jerome. 1960. Canal investment, 1815–1860. In *Trends in the American economy in the nineteenth century.* Conference on Research in Income and Wealth, Vol. 24. Princeton: Princeton University Press (for NBER).

Crandall, Andrew Wallace. 1930. *The early history of the Republican Party, 1854–1856.* Boston: The Gorham Press.

Craton, Michael. 1971. Jamaican slave mortality: Fresh light from Worthy Park, Longville, and the Tharp estates. *Journal of Caribbean History* 3:1–27.

———. 1974. *Sinews of empire: A short history of British slavery.* Garden City, NY: Anchor Press.

———. 1978. *Searching for the invisible man: Slaves and plantation life in Jamaica.* Cambridge: Harvard University Press.

———. 1979. Changing patterns of slave families in the British West Indies. *Journal of Interdisciplinary History* 10:1–35.

Craton, Michael, and James Walvin. 1970. *A Jamaican plantation: The history of Worthy Park, 1670–1970.* London: W.H. Allen.

Craven, Avery. 1953. *The growth of southern nationalism, 1848–1861,* Vol. VI of *A History of the South.* Edited by Wendell Holmes Stephenson and E. Merton Coulter. Baton Rouge: Louisiana State University Press.

Crawford, Stephen C. 1974. Toward a quantitative analysis of the data contained in the W.P.A. and Fish University narratives of ex-slaves: Some preliminary findings. Photocopy, University of Chicago.

————. 1980. Quantified memory: A study of the WPA and Fisk University slave narrative collections. Ph.D. dissertation, University of Chicago.

Cross, F.L., and E.P. Livingstone, eds. 1983. *The Oxford dictionary of the Christian church,* 2nd ed. Oxford: Oxford University Press.

Cross, Whitney R. [1950] 1982. *The burned-over district: The social and intellectual history of enthusiastic religion in western New York, 1800–1850.* Ithaca: Cornell Paperbacks.

Cunliffe, Marcus. 1979. *Chattel slavery and wage slavery: The Anglo-American context, 1830–1860.* Athens: The University of Georgia Press.

Current, Richard N. 1943. John C. Calhoun, philosopher of reaction. *Antioch Review* 3:223–234.

————. 1955. *Daniel Webster and the rise of national conservatism.* Boston: Little, Brown.

————. 1963. *John C. Calhoun.* New York: Washington Square Press.

Curtin, Phillip D. 1968. Epidemiology and the slave trade. *Political Science Quarterly* 83:190–216.

————. 1969. *The Atlantic slave trade: A census.* Madison: University of Wisconsin Press.

————. 1975. Measuring the Atlantic slave trade. In Stanley Engleman and Eugene Genovese, eds., *Race and slavery in the Western hemisphere: Quantitative studies.* Princeton: Princeton University Press.

Dannenbaum, Jed. 1978. Immigrants and temperance: Ethnocultural conflict in Cincinnati, 1845–1860. *Ohio History* 87:125–139.

David, Paul A., Herbert G. Gutman, Richard Sutch, Peter Temin, and Gavin Wright. 1976. *Reckoning with slavery: A critical study in the quantitative history of American Negro slavery.* New York: Oxford University Press.

David, Paul A., and Peter Temin. 1975. Capitalist masters, bourgeois slaves. *Journal of Interdisciplinary History* 5 (Winter):445–457.

————. 1979. Explaining the relative efficiency of slave agriculture in the antebellum South: Comment. *American Economic Review* 69:213–218.

Davies, K.G. 1975. The living and the dead: White mortality in West Africa, 1684–1732. In Stanley Engleman and Eugene Genovese, eds., *Race and slavery in the Western hemisphere: Quantitative studies.* Princeton: Princeton University Press.

Davis, David Brion. 1966. *The problem of slavery in Western culture.* Ithaca: Cornell University Press.

————. 1974. Slavery and the post–World War II historians. *Daedalus* (Spring):1–16.

————. 1975. *The problem of slavery in the age of revolution, 1770–1823.* Ithaca: Cornell University Press.

————. 1977. Review of *The black family in slavery and freedom, 1750–1925,* by Herbert G. Gutman. *American Historical Review* 82:744–745.

————. 1984. *Slavery and human progress.* New York: Oxford University Press.

Davis, E.A. 1943. *Plantation life in the Florida parishes of Louisiana 1836–1844 as reflected in the diary of Bennet H. Barrow.* New York: Columbia University Press.

Davis, Lance E., Richard A. Easterlin, William N. Parker, Dorothy S. Brady, Albert Fishlow, Robert E. Gallman, Stanley Lebergott, Robert E. Lipsey, Douglass C. North, Nathan Rosenberg, Eugene Smolensky, and Peter Temin. 1972. *American economic growth: An economist's history of the United States.* New York: Harper and Row.

Davis, Lance E., and H. Louis Stettler III. 1966. The New England textile industry, 1825–1860: Trends and fluctuations. In *Output, Employment, and Productivity in the United States after 1800.* Conference on Research in Income and Wealth, Vol. 30. New York: Columbia University Press (for NBER).

Dawley, Alan. 1982. *Class and community: The Industrial Revolution in Lynn.* Cambridge: Harvard University Press.

Deane, Phyllis, and W.A. Cole. 1969. *British economic growth, 1688–1959,* 2nd ed. Cambridge: Cambridge University Press.

Debien, Gabriel. 1974. *Les esclaves aux Antilles françaises XVIIe–XVIIIe siècles.* Basse-Terre: Societé d'histoire de la Guadeloupe.

DeBow, James D.B. 1854. *Statistical view of the United States: Compendium of the Seventh Census.* Washington: Beverley Tucker.

———, ed. 1857. *DeBow's review: Agricultural, commercial, industrial progress and resources.* 23, 3rd ser.:3–6. New Orleans: The Office of DeBow's Review.

———. [1854] 1966. *The industrial resources, statistics, etc. of the United States, and more particularly of the southern and western states,* 3rd ed., 3 vols. New York: Augustus M. Kelley, Publishers.

DeCanio, Stephen J. 1974. *Agriculture in the postbellum South: The economics of production and supply.* Cambridge: MIT Press.

Deerr, Noel. 1949. *History of sugar.* London: Chapman and Hall.

Degler, Carl N. 1970. Slavery in Brazil and the United States: An essay in comparative history. *American Historical Review* 75:1004–1028.

———. 1971. *Neither black nor white: Slavery and race relations in Brazil and the United States.* New York: Macmillan.

———. 1976. Why historians change their minds. *Pacific Historical Review* 45:167–184.

———. 1978. Experiencing slavery. *Reviews in American History* 6:277–282.

———. [1974] 1982. *The other South: Southern dissenters in the nineteenth century.* Boston: Northeastern University Press.

Dellheim, Charles. 1985. Notes on industrialism and culture in nineteenth-century Britain. *Notebooks in Cultural Analysis* 2:227–247.

De Mello, Pedro Carvalho. 1977. The economics of labor in Brazilian coffee plantations, 1850–1888. Ph.D. dissertation, University of Chicago.

Devereux, Julian S. 1839–1864. *Record Book.* Box B6/40. Barker-Texas Historical Collection.

Dew, Charles B. 1974. Disciplining slave ironworkers in the antebellum South: Coercion, conciliation, and accommodation. *American Historical Review* 79:393–418.

Dictionary of American Biography. 1928–1937. 20 vols. Dumas Malone and Allen Johnson, eds. New York: Charles Scribner's Sons.

Dillon, Merton L. 1974. *The abolitionists: The growth of a dissenting minority.* New York: W. W. Norton.

Ditchfield, G.M. 1980. Repeal, abolition, and reform: A study in the interaction of reforming movements in the Parliament of 1790–1796. In Christine Bolt and Seymour Drescher, eds., *Anti-slavery, religion, and reform.* Folkestone, UK: W. Dawson.

Dodd, William E. 1911. *Statesmen of the South or from radicalism to conservative revolt.* New York: Macmillan.

Doeringer, Peter, and Michael J. Piore. 1971. *Internal labor markets and manpower analysis.* Lexington, MA: D.C. Heath and Co.

Donald, David Herbert. 1960. *Charles Sumner and the coming of the Civil War.* Chicago: University of Chicago Press.

————. 1978. *Liberty and union: The crisis of popular government, 1830–1890.* Boston: Little, Brown.

Dorfman, Joseph. 1966. *The economic mind in American civilization, 1606–1865,* Vol. II. New York: Augustus M. Kelley.

Douglass, Frederick [1855] 1969. *My bondage and freedom.* New York: Dover Publications.

Drake, Thomas E. [1950] 1965. *Quakers and slavery in America.* Gloucester, MA: Peter Smith.

Drescher, Seymour. 1977. *Econocide: British slavery in the era of abolition.* Pittsburgh: University of Pittsburgh Press.

————. 1982. Public opinion and the destruction of British colonial slavery. In James Walvin, ed., *Slavery and British society, 1776–1846.* London: Macmillan.

————. 1986. *Capitalism and antislavery.* London: Macmillan Press.

Dublin, Thomas. 1979. *Women at work: The transformation of work and community in Lowell, Massachusetts, 1826–1860.* New York: Columbia University Press.

————. 1985. Republicanism and the making of the American working class. *Reviews in American History* (March):43–47.

DuBois, W.E.B. 1910. Reconstruction and its benefits. *American Historical Review* 4:781–799.

————. 1918. Review of *American Negro slavery. American Political Science Review* 12 (November):722–726.

————. [1896] 1969. *The suppression of the African slave trade to the United States of America, 1638–1870.* Baton Rouge: Louisiana State University Press.

————, ed. [1909] 1970a. *The Negro American family.* Cambridge: MIT Press.

————. [1935] 1970b. *Black reconstruction in America.* New York: Atheneum.

Dumond, Dwight Lowell. [1961] 1966. *Antislavery: The crusade for freedom in America.* New York: W. W. Norton.

Dunlevy, James A. 1983. Regional preferences and migrant settlement: On the avoidance of the South by nineteenth-century immigrants. *Research in Economic History* 8:217–251.

Dunlevy, James A., and Henry A. Gemery. 1978. Economic opportunity and the responses of "old" and "new" migrants to the United States. *Journal of Economic History* 38:901–917.

Dunn, Richard S. 1973. *Sugar and slaves: The rise of the planter class in the British West Indies, 1624–1713.* New York: W.W. Norton.

————. 1984. Servants and slaves: The recruitment and employment of labor. In Jack P. Greene and J.R. Pole, eds., *Colonial British America: Essays in the new history of the early modern era.* Baltimore: Johns Hopkins University Press.

Easterlin, Richard A. 1960. Interregional differences in per capita income, population, and total income, 1840–1950. In *Trends in the American economy in the nineteenth century.* Conference on Research in Income and Wealth, Vol. 24. Princeton: Princeton University Press (for NBER).

————. 1961. Regional income trends, 1840–1950. In Seymour Harris, ed., *American Economic History.* New York: McGraw-Hill.

————. 1975. Farm production and income in old and new areas at mid-century. In David Klingaman and Richard Vedder, eds., *Essays in nineteenth century economic history: The old Northwest.* Athens: Ohio University Press.

————. 1976a. Factors in the decline of farm family fertility in the United States: Some preliminary research results. *Journal of American History* 53:600–614.

————. 1976b. Population change and farm settlement in the northern United States. *Journal of Economic History* 36:45–75.

Eaton, Clement. 1954. *A history of the Southern Confederacy.* New York: Macmillan.

————. 1966. *A history of the old South.* New York: Macmillan.

———. 1967. *The mind of the old South,* rev. ed. Baton Rouge: Louisiana State University Press.

Edwards, Richard C. 1970. Economic sophistication in nineteenth century Congressional tariff debates. *Journal of Economic History* 30:802–838.

Elkins, Stanley M. 1959. *Slavery: A problem in American institutional and intellectual life.* Chicago: University of Chicago Press.

———. 1968. *Slavery: A problem in American institutional and intellectual life,* 2nd ed. Chicago: University of Chicago Press.

———. 1975. The slavery debate. *Commentary* 60 (No. 6; December):40–54.

Ellison, Thomas. [1886] 1968. *The cotton trade of Great Britain.* New York: Augustus M. Kelley.

Eltis, David. 1972. The traffic in slaves between the British West Indian colonies, 1807–1833. *Economic History Review* 25:55–64.

———. 1982. Nutritional trends in Africa and the Americas: Heights of Africans, 1819–1839. *Journal of Interdisciplinary History* 12:453–475.

———. 1983. Free and coerced transatlantic migrations: Some comparisons. *American Historical Review* 88:251–280.

———. 1987. *Economic growth and the ending of the transatlantic slave trade.* New York: Oxford University Press.

Eltis, David, and James Walvin, eds. 1981. *The abolition of the Atlantic slave trade.* Madison: University of Wisconsin Press.

Encyclopaedia Britannica. 1961. Chicago: William Benton.

Engels, Friêdrich. [1892] 1973. *The condition of the working-class in England.* Moscow: Progress Publishers.

Engerman, Stanley L. 1967. The effects of slavery upon the southern economy. *Explorations in Entrepreneurial History* 4:71–97.

———. 1975. A reconsideration of southern economic growth, 1770–1860. *Agricultural History* 49:343–1361.

———. 1976. Some economic and demographic comparisons of slavery in the United States and the British West Indies. *Economic History Review* 29:258–1275.

———. 1977. Black fertility and family structure in the U.S., 1880–1940. *Journal of Family History* 2:117–138.

———. 1978. Studying the black family. *Journal of Family History* 3 (Spring):78–101.

———. 1982. Economic adjustments to emancipation in the United States and British West Indies. *Journal of Interdisciplinary History* 12:191–220.

———. 1983. Contract labor, sugar, and technology in the nineteenth century. *Journal of Economic History* 43:635–660.

———. 1984. Economic change and contract labor in the British Caribbean: The end of slavery and the adjustment to emancipation. *Explorations in Economic History* 21:133–150.

———. 1986a. Slavery and emancipation in comparative perspective: A look at some recent debates. *Journal of Economic History* 46:317–339.

———. 1986b. Servants to slaves to servants: Contract labour and European expansion. In P.C. Emmer, ed., *Colonialism and migration: Indentured labor before and after slavery.* Dordrecht, the Netherlands: Martinus Nijhoff Publishers.

Engerman, Stanley L., and David Eltis. 1980. Economic aspects of the abolition debate. In Christine Bolt and Seymour Drescher, eds., *Anti-slavery, religion, and reform.* Folkestone, UK: W. Dawson.

Engerman, Stanley L., Robert Fogel, Eugene Genovese, and Herbert Gutman. 1972. New directions in black history. *Forum: A Journal of Social Commentary and the Arts* 1:22–41.

Engerman, Stanley L., and Robert E. Gallman. 1983. U.S. economic growth, 1783–1860. *Research in Economic History* 8:1–46.

———, eds. 1986. *Long-term factors in American economic growth.* Conference on Research in Income and Wealth, Vol. 51. Chicago: University of Chicago Press (for NBER).

Engerman, Stanley L., and Eugene D. Genovese, eds. 1975. *Race and slavery in the Western hemisphere: Quantitative studies.* Princeton: Princeton University Press.

Ernst, Robert. 1949. *Immigrant life in New York City, 1825–1863.* New York: King's Crown Press, Columbia University.

Ershkowitz, Herbert, and William G. Shade. 1971. Consensus or conflict? Political behavior in the state legislatures during the Jacksonian era. *Journal of American History* 58:591–621.

Escott, Paul D. 1979. *Slavery remembered: A record of twentieth century slave narratives.* Chapel Hill: The University of North Carolina Press.

Essig, James D. 1982. *The bonds of wickedness: American evangelicals against slavery, 1770–1808.* Philadelphia: Temple University Press.

Evans, Robert, Jr. 1961. Some economic aspects of the domestic slave trade. *Southern Economic Journal* 27:329–337.

———. 1962. The economics of American Negro slavery. In *Aspects of Labor Economics.* Universities-National Bureau Committee for Economic Research. Princeton: Princeton University Press.

Eveleth, Phyllis B., and J.M. Tanner. 1976. *Worldwide variations in human growth.* Cambridge: Cambridge University Press.

Farnam, Henry W. 1938. *Chapters in the history of social legislation in the United States to 1860.* Washington, D.C.: Carnegie Institution of Washington.

Fehrenbacher, Don E. 1962. *Prelude to greatness: Lincoln in the 1850's.* Stanford: Stanford University Press.

———. 1978. *The Dred Scott case: Its significance in American law and politics.* New York: Oxford University Press.

———. 1985. The new political history and the coming of the Civil War. *Pacific Historical Review* 54:117–142.

Feldberg, Michael. 1975. *The Philadelphia riots of 1844: A study of ethnic conflict.* Contributions to American History, No. 43. Westport, CT: Greenwood Press.

Fenichel, Allen H. 1967. Growth and diffusion of power in manufacturing, 1838–1919. In *Output, employment, and productivity in the United States after 1800.* Conference on Research in Income and Wealth, Vol. 30. New York: Columbia University Press (for NBER).

Field, Alexander James. 1978. Sectoral shift in antebellum Massachusetts: A reconsideration. *Explorations in Economic History* 15:146–171.

———. 1985. On the unimportance of machinery. *Explorations in Economic History* 22:378–401.

Field, Elizabeth B. 1985. Elasticities of complementarity and returns to scale in antebellum cotton agriculture. Ph.D. dissertation, Duke University.

Fields, Barbara Jeanne. 1985. *Slavery and freedom on the middle ground: Maryland during the nineteenth century.* New Haven: Yale University Press.

Filler, Louis. 1960. *The crusade against slavery.* New York: Harper & Row.

Finley, M.I. 1968a. Slavery. In *International encyclopedia of the social sciences*, Vol. 14. New York: Macmillan.

———. 1968b. *Slavery in classical antiquity.* Cambridge: Cambridge University Press.

———. 1980. *Ancient slavery and modern ideology.* New York: Viking Press.

Fischbaum, Marvin, and Julius Rubin. 1968. Slavery and the economic development of the American South. *Explorations in Economic History* 6:116–127.

Fischer, David Hackett. 1965. *The revolution of American conservatism: The Federalist party in the era of Jeffersonian democracy.* New York: Harper & Row.

Fisher, Franklin M., and Peter Temin. 1970. Regional specialization and the supply of wheat in the United States, 1867–1914. *Review of Economics and Statistics* 52:134–149.

Fishlow, Albert. 1965a. *American railroads and the transformation of the antebellum economy.* Cambridge: Harvard University Press.

———. 1965b. Antebellum interregional trade reconsidered. In Ralph Andreano, ed., *New views on American economic development.* Cambridge, MA: Schenkman.

Fite, Emerson David. 1911. *The presidential campaign of 1860.* New York: Macmillan.

Fite, Gilbert C., and Jim E. Reese. 1959. *An economic history of the United States.* Boston: Houghton Mifflin.

Fitzhugh, George. 1857. Wealth of the South and the North. *DeBow's Review* 23:587–596.

Fladeland, Betty. 1955. *James Gillespie Birney: Slaveholder to abolitionist.* Ithaca: Cornell University Press.

Fleisig, Heywood. 1976. Slavery, the supply of agricultural labor, and the industrialization of the South. *Journal of Economic History* 36:572–597.

Floud, Roderick, and Kenneth W. Wachter. 1982. Poverty and physical stature: Evidence on the standard of living of London boys 1770–1870. *Social Science History* 6:422–452.

Floud, Roderick, Kenneth W. Wachter, and Annabel Gregory. 1989. *Height, health and history: Nutritional status in Britain, 1750–1980.* Forthcoming, Cambridge University Press.

Fogel, Robert William. 1960. *The Union Pacific railroad: A case in premature enterprise.* Baltimore: Johns Hopkins University Press.

———. 1964. *Railroads and American economic growth: Essays in econometric history.* Baltimore: Johns Hopkins University Press.

———. 1966. The new economic history. *Economic History Review* 19:642–656.

———. 1975. From the Marxists to the Mormons. *Times Literary Supplement,* June 13.

———. 1982. Circumstantial evidence in "scientific" and traditional history. In David Carr, William Dray, and Theodore Geraets, eds., *Philosophy of history and contemporary historiography.* Ottawa: University of Ottawa Press.

———. 1986. Nutrition and the decline in mortality since 1700: Some additional findings. In Stanley Engerman and Robert Gallman, eds., *Long term factors in American economic growth.* Conference on Research in Income and Wealth, Vol. 51. Chicago: University of Chicago Press (for NBER).

———. 1987. Biomedical approaches to the estimation and interpretation of secular trends in equity, morbidity, mortality, and labor productivity in Europe, 1750–1980. Typescript.

Fogel, Robert W., and G.R. Elton. 1983. *Which road to the past?: Two views of history.* New Haven and London: Yale University Press.

Fogel, Robert W., and Stanley L. Engerman. 1969. A model for the explanation of industrial expansion during the nineteenth century: With an application to the American iron industry. *Journal of Political Economy* 77:306–328.

———, eds. 1971. *The reinterpretation of American economic history.* New York: Harper & Row.

———. 1974. *Time on the cross: The economics of American Negro slavery,* 2 vols. Boston: Little, Brown.

———, eds. 1979. Recent findings in the study of slave demography and family structure. *Sociology and Social Research* 63:569–74.

Fogel, Robert W., Stanley L. Engerman, and James Trussell. 1982. Exploring the uses of data on height: The analysis of long-term trends in nutrition, labor welfare, and labor productivity. *Social Science History* 6:401–421.

Fogel, Robert W., Stanley L. Engerman, James Trussell, Roderick Floud, Clayne L. Pope, and Larry T. Wimmer. 1978. The economics of mortality in North America, 1650–1910: A description of a research project. *Historical Methods* 11:75–109.

Fogel, Robert W., Stanley L. Engerman, Roderick Floud, Gerald Friedman, Robert A. Margo, Kenneth Sokoloff, Richard H. Steckel, James Trussell, Georgia Villeflor, and

Kenneth W. Wachter. 1983. Secular changes in American and British stature and nutrition. *Journal of Interdisciplinary History* 14:445–481.

Foner, Eric. 1969. The Wilmot Proviso revisited. *Journal of American History* 56:262–279.

———. 1970. *Free soil, free labor, free men: The ideology of the Republican party before the Civil War.* New York: Oxford University Press.

———. 1974. The causes of the American Civil War: Recent interpretations and new directions. *Civil War History* 20:197–214.

———. 1980a. *Politics and ideology in the age of the Civil War.* New York: Oxford University Press.

———. 1980b. Abolitionism and the labor movement in antebellum America. In Christine Bolt and Seymour Drescher, eds., *Anti-slavery, religion, and reform.* Folkestone, UK: W. Dawson.

Foner, Philip S. 1968. *Business and slavery: The New York merchants and the irrepressible conflict.* New York: Russell & Russel.

Formisano, Ronald P. 1971. *The birth of mass political parties: Michigan, 1827–1861.* Princeton: Princeton University Press.

———. 1983. *Transformation of political culture: Massachusetts parties, 1790s–1840s.* New York: Oxford University Press.

Fornell, Earl W. 1956. Agitation in Texas for reopening the slave trade. *Southwestern Historical Review* 60:245–259.

Foster, Charles I. 1960. *An errand of mercy: The Evangelical United Front, 1790–1837.* Chapel Hill: University of North Carolina Press.

Foust, James D. 1975. *The yeoman farmer and westward expansion of U.S. cotton production.* New York: Arno Press.

Fox, Early Lee. 1919. *The American Colonization Society, 1817–1840.* Baltimore: Johns Hopkins University Press.

Fox-Genovese, Elizabeth, and Eugene D. Genovese. 1983. *Fruits of merchant capital.* Oxford: Oxford University Press.

Fraginals, Manuel M. 1977. Africa in Cuba: A quantitative analysis of the African population in the island of Cuba. *Annals of the New York Academy of Science* 292:187–201.

Franklin, Benjamin. In Leonard Larabee and Whitfield Bell, eds., *The papers of Benjamin Franklin.* New Haven: Yale University Press.

Franklin, John Hope. 1943. *The free Negro in North Carolina, 1790–1860.* Chapel Hill: University of North Carolina Press.

———. 1967. *From slavery to freedom: A history of Negro Americans,* 3rd ed. New York: Alfred A. Knopf.

———. 1976. *A southern odyssey: Travellers in the antebellum North.* Baton Rouge: Louisiana State University Press.

Frazier, E. Franklin. 1930. The Negro slave family. *Journal of Negro History* 15:198–259.

———. 1939. *The Negro family in the United States.* Chicago: University of Chicago Press.

———. 1940. *Negro youth at the crossways.* Washington, D.C.: American Council on Education.

Frederickson, George M. 1971. *The black image in the white mind: The debate on Afro-American character and destiny, 1817–1914.* New York: Harper & Row.

Frederickson, George M., and Christopher Lasch. 1967. Resistance to slavery. *Civil War History* 13:315–329.

Freehling, Alison Goodyear. 1982. *Drift toward dissolution: The Virginia slavery debate of 1831–1832.* Baton Rouge: Louisiana State University Press.

Freehling, William W. 1966. *Prelude to civil war: The nullification controversy in South Carolina, 1816–1836.* New York: Harper.

Freyre, Gilberto. 1964. *The masters and the slaves.* New York: Alfred A. Knopf.

Friedman, Gerald C. 1980. The demography of Trinidad slavery. Photocopy, Workshop in Economic History, Harvard University.

————. 1982. The heights of slaves in Trinidad. *Social Science History* 6:482–515.

Friedman, Lawrence J. 1982. *Gregarious saints: Self and community in American abolitionism, 1830–1870.* Cambridge: Cambridge University Press.

Friedman, Milton, and Anna Jacobson Schwartz. 1963. *A monetary history of the United States 1867–1960.* Princeton: Princeton University Press.

Frisancho, Roberto A. 1979. *Human adaptation: A functional interpretation.* St. Louis: C.V. Mosby Co.

Fuller, John D.P. 1934. The slavery question and the movement to acquire Mexico, 1846–1848. *Mississippi Valley Historical Review* 21:31–48.

Galenson, David W. 1981. *White servitude in colonial America: An economic analysis.* Cambridge: Cambridge University Press.

————. 1983. On the age at leaving home in the early 19th century: Evidence from the lives of New England manufacturers. Workshop in Economic History Paper No. 8384–01. University of Chicago Department of Economics.

————. 1984. The rise and fall of indentured servitude in the Americas: An economic analysis. *Journal of Economic History* 44:13–24.

————. 1986a. *Traders, planters and slaves: Market behavior in early English America.* New York: Cambridge University Press.

————. 1986b. Labor market behavior in Colonial America. Workshop in Economic History Paper No. 8687-02. University of Chicago Department of Economics.

Galenson, David, and Russell Menard. 1977. Economics and early American history. *The Newberry Papers in Family and Community History,* Paper 77-4E.

Gallman, Robert E. 1960. Commodity output 1839–1899. In *Trends in the American economy in the nineteenth century.* Conference on Research in Income and Wealth. Princeton: Princeton University Press.

————. 1966. Gross national product in the United States. In *Output, employment and productivity in the United States after 1800.* Conference on Research in Income and Wealth, Vol. 30. New York: Columbia University Press.

————. 1969. Trends in the size distribution of wealth in the nineteenth century: Some speculations. In *Six Papers on the Size Distribution of Wealth and Income.* Conference on Research in Income and Wealth, Vol. 33. New York: Columbia University Press (for NBER).

————. 1978. Professor Pessen on the "egalitarian myth." *Social Science History* 2:194–207.

————. 1981. The "egalitarian myth," once again. *Social Science History* 5:223–234.

————. 1982. Professor Blumin on age and inequality: Antebellum America. *Social Science History* 6:381–384.

Gallman, Robert E., and Ralph V. Anderson. 1977. Slavery as fixed capital: Slave labor and southern economic development. *Journal of American History* 64:24–46.

Gara, Larry. 1969. Slavery and the slave power: A crucial distinction. *Civil War History* 15:5–18.

Gash, Norman. 1956. English reform and French revolution in the general election of 1830. In Richard Pares and A.J.P. Taylor, eds., *Essays presented to Sir Lewis Namier.* London: St. Martin's Press.

————. [1953] 1971. *Politics in the age of Peel.* New York: W.W. Norton.

————. 1979. *Aristocracy and the people: Britain, 1815–1865.* Cambridge: Harvard University Press.

Gates, Paul W. 1960. *The farmer's age: Agriculture, 1815–1860,* Vol. III in *The economic history of the United States.* New York: Holt, Reinhart, & Winston.

————. 1968. *History of public land law development.* Washington, D.C.: U.S. Government Printing Office.

Gaustad, Edwin Scott. 1962. *Historical atlas of religion in America.* New York: Harper & Row.

Gay, Peter. 1977. *The Enlightenment: An interpretation,* 2 vols. New York: W. W. Norton.

Gayer, Arthur D., W.W. Rostow, and Anna Jacobson Schwartz. 1975. *The growth and fluctuation of the British economy, 1790–1850.* New York: Harper & Row.

Geggus, David Patrick. 1982. *Slavery, war, and revolution.* Oxford: Clarendon Press.

Gemery, Henry A. 1980. Emigration from the British Isles to the new world, 1630–1700: Inferences from colonial populations. *Research in Economic History* 5:179–231.

————. 1984. European emigration to North America, 1700–1820: Numbers and quasi-numbers. *Perspectives in American History,* New Series, Vol. I.

Gemery, Henry A., and Jan S. Hogendorn, eds. 1979. *The uncommon market: Essays in the economic history of the Atlantic slave trade.* New York: Academic Press.

Genovese, Eugene D. 1965. *The political economy of slavery: Studies in the economy and society of the slave South.* New York: Pantheon.

————. 1969. *The world the slaveholders made.* New York: Vintage Books.

————. 1971. *In red and black: Marxian explorations in southern and Afro-American history.* New York: Vintage Books.

————. 1974. *Roll, Jordan, roll: The world the slaves made.* New York: Pantheon Books.

————. 1975. Yeoman farmers in a slaveholders' democracy. *Agricultural History* 49:-331–342.

————. 1979. *From rebellion to revolution: Afro-American slave revolts in the making of the modern world.* Baton Rouge: Louisiana State University Press.

————. 1986. Western civilization through slaveholder eyes: The social and historical thought of Thomas Roderick Dew. Andrew W. Mellon Lecture, Tulane University.

Genovese, Eugene D., and Elizabeth Fox-Genovese. 1986. The religious ideals of Southern slave society. *The Georgia Historical Quarterly* 70, 1:1–16.

Gershenkron, Alexander. 1968. *Continuity in history and other essays.* Cambridge, MA: Belknap Press.

Gibbs, Tyson, Kathleen Cargill, Leslie Sue Lieberman, and Elizabeth Reitz. 1980. Nutrition in a slave population: An anthropological examination. *Medical Anthropology* (Spring):175–262.

Gienapp, William E. 1984. Salmon P. Chase, nativism, and the formation of the Republican Party in Ohio. *Ohio History* 93:5–39.

————. 1985. Nativism and the creation of a Republican majority in the North before the Civil War. *Journal of American History* 72:529–559.

————. 1987. *The origins of the Republican party, 1852–1856.* New York: Oxford University Press.

Gilbert, Alan D. 1976. *Religion and society in industrial England: Church, chapel, and social change, 1740–1914.* London: Longman.

Ginter, Donald E. 1980. A critique of landholding variables in the 1860 census and the Parker-Gallman sample. Paper presented at the 95th Annual Meeting of the American Historical Association, Washington, D.C.

Glaab, Charles N. 1963. *The American city: A documentary history.* Homewood, IL: Dorsey.

Glass, D. V. 1967. *Population policies and movements in Europe.* London: Frank Cass and Co.

————. 1973. *Numbering the people: The eighteenth-century population controversy and the development of census and vital statistics in Britain.* Farnborough: D.C. Heath.

Glass, D.V., and D.E.C. Eversley, eds. 1965. *Population in history: Essays in historical demography.* Chicago: Aldine Publishing Co.

Glass, D.V., and E. Grebenik. 1965. World population, 1800–1950. In H.J. Habakkuk and M. Postan, eds., *The Cambridge economic history of Europe,* Vol. 6: *The industrial revolution and after.* Cambridge: Cambridge University Press.

Glickstein, Jonathan A. 1979. "Poverty is not slavery": American abolitionists and the competitive labor market. In Lewis Perry and Michael Fellman, eds., *Antislavery reconsidered: New perspectives on the abolitionists.* Baton Rouge: Louisiana State University Press.

Goldin, Claudia Dale. 1976. *Urban slavery in the American South, 1820–1860: A quantitative history.* Chicago: University of Chicago Press.

Goldin, Claudia, and Kenneth Sokoloff. 1982. Women, children, and industrialization in the early republic: Evidence from the manufacturing censuses. *Journal of Economic History* 42:741–774.

———. 1984. The relative productivity hypothesis of industrialization: The American case, 1820 to 1850. *Quarterly Journal of Economics* 49:461–487.

Goodman, Paul. 1980. White over white: Planters, yeomen, and the coming of the Civil War: A review essay. *Agricultural History* 54:446–452.

Goodrich, Carter. 1960. *Government promotion of American canals and railroads, 1800–1890.* New York: Columbia University Press.

Gottlieb, Manuel. 1964. *Estimates of residential building, United States, 1840–1939.* Technical paper 17, National Bureau of Economic Research. New York: Columbia University Press.

———. 1966. Building in Ohio between 1857 and 1914. In *Output, employment, and productivity in the United States after 1800.* Conference on Research in Income and Wealth, Vol. 30. New York: District of Columbia University Press (for NBER).

Gould, B.A. 1869. *Investigations in the military and anthropological statistics of American soldiers.* Cambridge, MA: Riverside Press.

Goveia, Elsa. 1969. *Slave society in the British Leeward Islands at the end of the eighteenth century.* New Haven: Yale University Press.

Gray, Lewis Cecil. [1933] 1958. *History of agriculture in the southern United States to 1860,* 2 vols. Gloucester, MA: Peter Smith.

Great Britain. 1837–1838. *Parliamentary papers,* Vol. 48. London.

Green, Vivian Hubert Howard. 1964. *John Wesley.* London: Nelson.

Green, William A. 1976. *British slave emancipation: The sugar colonies and the great experiment, 1830–1865.* Oxford: Clarendon Press.

Greenberg, Dolores. 1982. Reassessing the power patterns of the industrial revolution: An Anglo-American comparison. *American Historical Review* 87:1237–1261.

Greene, Lorenzo J., and Carter G. Woodson. 1930. *The Negro wage earner.* Washington, D.C.: The Association for the Study of Negro Life and History.

Griffin, Clifford S. 1960. *Their brothers' keepers: Moral stewardship in the United States, 1800–1865.* New Brunswick, NJ: Rutgers University Press.

Griscom, John H. [1845] 1970. *The sanitary condition of the laboring class of New York, with suggestions for its improvement.* New York: Arno.

Grubb, Farley. 1987. Morbidity and mortality on the North-Atlantic passage: Eighteenth century German immigration. *Journal of Interdisciplinary History* 17:565–586.

Gutman, Herbert G. 1972. Le phenomène invisible: La composition de la famille et du foyer noirs après la guerre de secession. *Annales E.S.C.* 26:1197–1218.

———. 1975. *Slavery and the numbers game: A critique of Time on the Cross.* Urbana: University of Illinois Press.

———. 1976a. *The black family in slavery and freedom, 1750–1925.* New York: Pantheon.

———. 1976b. Persistent myths about the Afro-American family. *Journal of Interdisciplinary History* 6:181–210.

Gutman, Herbert, and Richard Sutch. 1976. Sambo makes good, or were slaves imbued with the Protestant work ethic. In Paul David et al., eds., *Reckoning with slavery: A critical study in the quantitative history of American Negro slavery.* New York: Oxford University Press.

Hahn, Steven H. 1979. The roots of southern populism: Yeoman farmers and the transformation of Georgia's upper Piedmont, 1850–1890. Ph.D. dissertation, Yale University.

———. 1983. Capitalists all! *Reviews in American History* 11:219–225.

Hahn, Steven. 1983. *The roots of southern populism: Yeoman farmers and the transformation of the Georgia Upcountry, 1850–1890.* New York: Oxford University Press.

Haines, Michael. 1979. The use of model life tables to estimate mortality for the United States in the late nineteenth century. *Demography* 16:289–312.

Haites, Erik F., James Mak, and Gary M. Walton. 1975. *Western river transportation: The era of early internal development, 1810–1860.* Baltimore: Johns Hopkins University Press.

Hall, Gwendolyn. 1971. *Social control in slave plantation societies.* Baltimore: Johns Hopkins University Press.

Hammond, James Henry. 1858. In *Congressional Globe*, 35th Congress, 1st Session, 961–962.

Hammond, John Lockwood, Jr. 1972. The Revivalist political ethos. Ph.D. dissertation, University of Chicago.

———. 1974. Revival religion and antislavery politics. *American Sociological Review* 39:175–186.

Hammond, John Lawrence, and Barbara Hammond. 1975. *The town labourer: The new civilization 1760–1832.* Gloucester, MA: Peter Smith.

Handler, Jerome S., and Frederick W. Lange. 1978. *Plantation slavery in Barbados: An archaeological and historical investigation.* Cambridge: Harvard University Press.

Handlin, Oscar. 1979. *Boston's immigrants, 1790–1880: A study in acculturation.* Cambridge: Belknap Press of Harvard University Press.

Handlin, Oscar, and Lillian Handlin. 1980. *Abraham Lincoln and the union.* Boston: Little, Brown.

Hannon, Joan Underhill. 1984. Poverty in the antebellum Northeast: The view from New York State's poor relief rolls. *Journal of Economic History* 44:1007–1032.

———. 1985. Relief or social control?: A political economy of public poor relief policy in nineteenth-century New York state. Photocopy, University of California, Berkeley.

Hanson, John R., II. 1979. World demand for cotton during the nineteenth century: Wright's estimates reexamined. *Journal of Economic History* 39:1015–1021.

Harlow, Ralph Volney. 1939. *Gerrit Smith: Philanthropist and reformer.* New York: Henry Holt.

Harrington, Fred Harvey. 1939. Frémont and the North Americans. *American Historical Review* 44:842–848.

———. 1948. *Fighting politician: Major General N.P. Banks.* Philadelphia: University of Pennsylvania Press.

Hartwell, R.M. 1971. *The Industrial Revolution and economic growth.* London: Methuen.

Haynes, George H. 1897. A Know-Nothing legislature. In *Annual report of the American Historical Association for the year 1896.* Washington, D.C.

———. 1898. The causes of Know-Nothing success in Massachusetts. *American Historical Review* 3:67–82.

Healy, Kent T. 1951. American transportation before the Civil War. In Harold F. Williamson, ed., *The growth of the American economy.* Englewood Cliffs, NJ: Prentice-Hall, Inc.

Hellie, Richard. 1982. *Slavery in Russia: 1450–1725.* Chicago: University of Chicago Press.

———. 1989, forthcoming. *Encyclopaedia Britannica*, 15th ed., s. v. Slavery.

Helper, Hinton Rowan. [1857] 1968. *The impending crisis of the South: How to meet it.* Edited by George M. Frederickson. Cambridge: Belknap Press.

Hennesey, James S.J. 1981. *American Catholics: A history of the Roman Catholic community in the United States.* Oxford: Oxford University Press.

Hershberg, Theodore, ed. 1981. *Philadelphia: Work, space, family, and group experience in the nineteenth century.* Oxford: Oxford University Press.

Herskovits, Melville J. [1941] 1958. *The myth of the Negro past.* Boston: Beacon Press.

Hibbard, Benjamin Horace. 1939. *A history of the public land policies.* New York: Peter Smith.

Higgs, Robert. 1979. Cycles and trends of mortality in eighteen large American cities, 1871–1900. *Explorations in Economic History* 16:381–408.

Higman, Barry W. 1973. Household structure and fertility on Jamaican slave plantations: A nineteenth century example. *Population Studies* 27:527–550.

――――. 1975. The slave family and household in the British West Indies, 1800–1834. *Journal of Interdisciplinary History* 6:261–287.

――――. 1976. *Slave population and economy in Jamaica, 1807–1834.* Cambridge: Cambridge University Press.

――――. 1982. Slavery and the development of demographic theory in the age of the Industrial Revolution. In James Walvin, ed., *Slavery and British society, 1776–1846.* London: Macmillan.

――――. 1984. *Slave populations of the British Caribbean, 1807–1834.* Baltimore: Johns Hopkins University Press.

――――. 1986. Population and labour in the British Caribbean in the early nineteenth century. In Stanley Engerman and Robert Gallman, eds., *Long-term factors in American economic growth.* Conference on Research in Income and Wealth, Vol. 51. Chicago: University of Chicago Press (for NBER).

Hilliard, Sam Bowers. 1972. *Hog meat and hoecake: Food supply in the old South, 1840–1860.* Carbondale: Southern Illinois University Press.

Hoagland, H.E. 1913. The rise of the Iron Molders' International Union. *American Economic Review* 3:296–313.

Hobsbawm, E.J. [1964] 1976. *Labouring men: Studies in the history of labour.* London: Weidenfeld and Nicolson.

Hobsbawm, E.J., and George Rudé. 1975. *Captain Swing.* New York: W.W. Norton.

Hofstadter, Richard. 1944. U.B. Phillips and the plantation legend. *Journal of Negro History* 29:109–124.

――――. 1965. *The paranoid style in American politics.* New York: Alfred A. Knopf.

――――. 1973. *The American political tradition and the men who made it.* New York: Vintage Books.

Holbrook, S.H. 1950. *The Yankee exodus: An account of migration from New England.* New York: Macmillan.

Hollis, Patricia. 1980. Anti-slavery and British working-class radicalism in the years of reform. In Christine Bolt and Seymour Drescher, eds., *Anti-slavery, religion and reform.* Folkestone, UK: W. Dawson.

Holmes, George K. 1907. Meat supply and surplus. U.S. Department of Agriculture, Bureau of Statistics, *Bulletin,* No. 55. Washington, D.C.: Government Printing Office.

――――. 1912. *Wages of farm labor.* U.S. Department of Agriculture, *Bulletin,* No. 99. Washington, D.C.: Government Printing Office.

Holt, Michael F. 1969. *Forging a majority: The formation of the Republican Party in Pittsburgh, 1848–1860.* New Haven: Yale University Press.

――――. 1973a. The Antimasonic and Know Nothing parties. In Arthur Schlesinger, ed., *History of U.S. political parties,* Vol. I. New York: Chelsea House Publishing.

――――. 1973b. The Democratic party, 1828–1860. In Arthur Schlesinger, ed., *History of U.S. political parties,* Vol. I. New York: Chelsea House Publishing.

――――. 1973c. The politics of impatience: The origins of know nothingism. *Journal of American History* 60:309–331.

――――. 1978. *The political crisis of the 1850s.* New York: John Wiley & Sons.

Holt, Thomas C. 1982. "An empire over the mind": Emancipation, race, and ideology in the British West Indies and the American South. In J. Morgan Kousser and James

McPherson, eds., *Religion, race, and reconstruction.* New York: Oxford University Press.

Hopkins, Keith. 1978. *Conquerors and slaves.* Cambridge: Cambridge University Press.

Howe, Daniel Walker. 1979. *The political culture of the American whigs.* Chicago: University of Chicago Press.

Howse, Ernest Marshall. 1952. *Saints in politics: The "Clapham Sect" and the growth of freedom.* Toronto: University of Toronto Press.

Huffman, F.J., Jr. 1974. Old South, new South: Continuity and change in a Georgia county, 1850–1880. Ph.D. dissertation, Yale University.

Huggins, Nathan I. 1979. *Black odyssey: The Afro-American ordeal in slavery.* New York: Vintage Books.

Hughes, J.R.T. 1960. Fluctuations in trade, industry and finance: A study of British economic development, 1850–1860. Oxford: Clarendon Press.

―――. 1969. Discussion of McClelland's paper. *American Economic Review Proceedings* 59:382–385.

Hughes, Sarah S. 1978. Slaves for hire: The allocation of black labor in Elizabeth City County, Virginia, 1782–1810. *William and Mary Quarterly* 35:260–286.

Hume, David. 1764. On the populousness of ancient nations. In *Essays, Moral, Political and Literary.* London.

Hunter, Louis C. 1949. *Steamboats on the western rivers.* Cambridge: Harvard University Press.

Huston, James L. 1982. Facing an angry labor: The American public interprets the shoemakers' strike of 1860. *Civil War History,* 28:197–212.

―――. 1983. A political response to industrialism: The Republican embrace of protectionist labor doctrines. *Journal of American History* 70:35–57.

Hutchinson, E.P. 1967. *The population debate: The development of conflicting theories up to 1900.* Boston: Houghton Mifflin.

Huxley, Thomas Henry. [1877] 1894. On elemental instruction in physiology. In *Science and education: Essays.* New York: D. Appleton & Co.

Hyde, John, and James L. Watkins, preparers. 1899. U.S. Department of Agriculture: *The Cost of cotton production.* Misc. Senes Bulletin No. 16. Washington, D.C.

Hytten, Frank E., and Isabella Leitch. 1971. *The physiology of human pregnancy.* Oxford: Blackwell.

Isley, Jeter Allen. 1947. *Horace Greeley and the Republican Party, 1853–1861.* Princeton: Princeton University Press.

Jaffe, A.J., and W.I. Lourie, Jr. 1942. An abridged life table for the white population of the United States in 1830. *Human Biology* 14:352–371.

James, C.L.R. 1963. *The black Jacobins.* New York: Vintage Books.

James, John A. 1978. The welfare effects of the antebellum tariff: A general equilibrium analysis. *Explorations in Economic History* 15:231–256.

―――. 1981. The optimal tariff in the antebellum United States. *American Economic Review* 71:726–734.

Jay, William. 1853. *Miscellaneous writings on slavery.* Boston: John J. Jewett & Company.

Jaynes, Gerald David. 1986. *Branches without roots: Genesis of the black working class in the American South, 1862–1882.* Oxford and New York: Oxford University Press.

John, Ann Meredith. 1984. The demography of slavery in nineteenth century Trinidad. Ph.D. dissertation, Princeton University.

―――. *The plantation slave population of Trinidad, 1783–1816.* Forthcoming.

Johnson, David R. 1972. The search for an urban discipline: Police reform as a response to crime in American cities, 1800–1875. Ph.D. dissertation, University of Chicago.

Johnson, Michael P. 1986. Work, culture, and the slave community: Slave occupations in the cotton belt in 1860. *Labor History* 27:325–355.

Jones, Jacqueline. 1985. *Labor of love, labor of sorrow: Black women, work, and the family from slavery to the present.* New York: Basic Books.

Jordan, Winthrop D. 1962. American chiaroscuro: The status and definition of mulattos in the British colonies. *William and Mary Quarterly* 19:183–200.

———. 1968. *White over black: American attitudes toward the Negro, 1550–1812.* Chapel Hill: University of North Carolina Press.

Julian, George W. 1892. *The life of Joshua R. Giddings.* Chicago: A.C. McClurg.

Kapp, Friedrick. 1870. *Immigration and the commissioners of emigration of the state of New York.* New York: n.p.

Karasch, Mary C. 1987. *Slave life in Rio de Janeiro, 1808–1850.* Princeton: Princeton University Press.

Kearl, J.R., and Clayne L. Pope. 1981a. Individual choices and aggregate distributions. Typescript.

———. 1981b. Intergenerational effects on the distribution of income and wealth: The Utah experience 1850–1900. National Bureau of Economic Research, Working Paper No. 754.

———. 1983a. The life cycle in economic history. *Journal of Economic History* 43:149–158.

———. 1983b. Wealth mobility: The missing element. *Journal of Interdisciplinary History* 13:461–488.

Kearl, J.R., Clayne L. Pope, and Larry T. Wimmer. 1980. Household wealth in a settlement economy: Utah, 1850–1870. *Journal of Economic History* 40:477–496.

Kellar, Herbert Anthony, ed. 1936. *Solon Robinson, pioneer and agriculturist: Selected writings*, Vol. II. Indianapolis: Indiana Historical Bureau.

Kerber, Linda K. 1970. *Federalists in dissent: Imagery and ideology in Jeffersonian America.* Ithaca: Cornell University Press.

Kiple, Kenneth F. 1976. *Blacks in colonial Cuba, 1774–1899.* Gainsville: University Presses of Florida.

———. 1984. *The Caribbean slave: A biological history.* Cambridge: Cambridge University Press.

Kiple, Kenneth F., and Virginia H. King. 1981. *Another dimension to the black diaspora: Diet, disease, and racism.* Cambridge: Cambridge University Press.

Kiple, Kenneth F., and Virginia H. Kiple. 1977a. Slave child mortality: Some nutritional answers to a perennial puzzle. *Journal of Social History* 10:284–309.

———. 1977b. Black yellow fever immunities, innate and acquired, as revealed in the American South. *Social Science History* 1:419–436.

———. 1980. Deficiency diseases in the Caribbean. *Journal of Interdisciplinary History* 11:197–215.

Kirkland, Edward C. 1951. *A history of American life*, 3rd ed. New York: Appleton-Century-Crofts.

Klein, Herbert S. 1966. Anglicanism, Catholicism, and the Negro slave. *Comparative Studies in Society and History* 8:295–327.

———. 1967. *Slavery in the Americas: A comparative study of Virginia and Cuba.* Chicago: University of Chicago Press.

———. 1978. *The middle passage: Comparative studies in the Atlantic slave trade.* Princeton: Princeton University Press.

———. 1986. *African slavery in Latin America and the Caribbean.* New York: Oxford University Press.

Kleppner, Paul. 1979. *The third electoral system, 1853–1892: Parties, voters, and political cultures.* Chapel Hill: University of North Carolina Press.

Klingaman, David C. 1975. Individual wealth in Ohio in 1860. In David C. Klingaman and Richard K. Vedder, eds., *Essays in nineteenth century economic history: The old Northwest.* Athens: Ohio University Press.

Knight, Franklin W. 1970. *Slave society in Cuba during the nineteenth century.* Madison: University of Wisconsin Press.

Knowles, George, ed. 1965. *Crisis of the union.* Baton Rouge: Louisiana State University Press.

Kolchin, Peter. 1978. The process of confrontation: Patterns of resistance to bondage in nineteenth-century Russia and the United States. *Journal of Social History* 11:-457–490.

———. 1980. In defense of servitude: American proslavery and Russian proserfdom arguments, 1760–1860. *American Historical Review* 85:809–827.

———. 1987. *Unfree labor: American slavery and Russian serfdom.* Cambridge and London: Harvard University Press.

Kousser, J. Morgan. 1976. The "new political history": A methodological critique. *Reviews in American History* 4:1–14.

———. 1986. Must historians regress? An answer to Lee Benson. *Historical Methods* 19:62–81.

———. 1987. The supremacy of equal rights. California Institute of Technology: Social Science Working Paper 620.

Kousser, J. Morgan, and Allan J. Lichtman. 1983. "New political history": Some statistical questions answered. *Social Science History* 7:321–344.

Kousser, J. Morgan, and James M. McPherson, eds. 1982. *Region, race, and reconstruction.* New York: Oxford University Press.

Kraditor, Aileen S. 1970. *Means and ends in American abolitionism: Garrison and his critics on strategy and tactics, 1834–1850.* New York: Vintage Books/Random House.

———. 1973. The Liberty and Free Soil parties. In Arthur Schlesinger, ed., *History of U.S. political parties,* Vol. I. New York: Chelsea House Publishing.

Kraut, Alan M. 1979. The forgotten reformers: A profile of third party abolitionists in antebellum New York. In Lewis Perry and Michael Fellman, eds., *Antislavery reconsidered: New perspectives on the abolitionists.* Baton Rouge: Louisiana State University Press.

Kulikoff, Alan. 1976. Tobacco and slaves: Population, economy and society in eighteenth-century Prince George's County, Maryland. Ph.D. dissertation, Brandeis University.

———. 1986. *Tobacco and slaves: The development of southern cultures in the Chesapeake, 1680–1800.* Chapel Hill: University of North Carolina Press.

Kussmaul, Ann. 1981. *Servants in husbandry in early modern England.* Interdisciplinary Perspectives on Modern History. Cambridge: Cambridge University Press.

Kuznets, Simon. 1933. *Seasonal variations in industry and trade.* New York: NBER.

———. 1953. National income and economic welfare. In his *Economic change: Selected essays in business cycles, national income, and economic growth.* New York: W.W. Norton.

———. 1971. *The economic growth of nations: Total output and production structure.* Cambridge, MA: Belknap Press.

Lander, Ernest McPherson, Jr. 1969. *The textile industry in antebellum South Carolina.* Baton Rouge: Louisiana State University Press.

Landes, David S. 1969. *The unbound Prometheus: Technological change and industrial development in Western Europe from 1750 to the present.* Cambridge: Cambridge University Press.

———. 1980. The "great drain" and industrialisation: Commodity flows from periphery to centre in historical perspective. In R.C.O. Mathews, eds., *Economic growth and resources.* New York: St. Martin's Press.

———. 1986. What do bosses really do? *Journal of Economic History* 46:585–623.

Lane, Ann J., ed. 1971. *The debate over slavery: Stanley Elkins and his critics.* Urbana: University of Illinois Press.

Lang, Edith Mae. 1971. The effects of net interregional migration on agricultural income growth: The United States, 1850–1860. Ph.D. dissertation, University of Rochester.

Larabee, Leonard W., and Whitfield J. Bell, eds. 1961. *The papers of Benjamin Franklin.* New Haven: Yale University Press.

Laurie, Bruce. 1974. "Nothing on compulsion": Lifestyles of Philadelphia artisans, 1820–1850. *Labor History* 15:337–366.

Laurie, Bruce, and Mark Schmitz. 1981. Manufacture and productivity: The making of an industrial base, Philadelphia, 1850–1880. In Theodore Hershberg, ed., *Philadelphia: Work, space, family, and group experience in the 19th century.* Oxford: Oxford University Press.

Lazonick, William, and Thomas Brush. 1985. The "Horndal Effect" in early U.S. manufacturing. *Explorations in Economic History* 22:53–96.

Leavitt, Joshua. [1840] 1965. Joshua Leavitt warns of a slave-power conspiracy. In John L. Thomas, ed., *Slavery attacked: The abolitionist crusade.* Englewood Cliffs, NJ: Prentice-Hall.

Lebergott, Stanley. 1964. *Manpower in economic growth: The American record since 1800.* New York: McGraw-Hill.

———. 1971. Changes in unemployment, 1800–1960. In Robert Fogel and Stanley Engerman, eds., *The reinterpretation of American economic history.* New York: Harper & Row.

Lee, Susan Previant. 1978. Antebellum land expansion: Another view. *Agricultural History* 52:488–502.

Le Roy Ladurie, Emmannuel. 1979. The conscripts of 1868: A study of the correlation between geographical mobility, delinquency and physical stature, and other aspects of the situation of the young Frenchmen called to do military service in that year. In E. Le Roy Ladurie, Ben Reynolds, and Siam Reynolds, trans., *The territory of the historian.* Sussex: Harvester Press, Ltd.

LeVeen, Phillip E. 1971. British slave trade suppression policies, 1821–1865: Impact and implications. Ph.D. dissertation, University of Chicago.

Levine, David. 1978. Some competing models of population growth during the first industrial revolution. *Journal of European Economic History* 7:499–516.

Levine, Lawrence W. 1977. *Black culture and black consciousness: Afro-American folk thought from slavery to freedom.* New York: Oxford University Press.

Licht, Walter. 1983. *Working for the railroad: The organization of work in the nineteenth century.* Princeton: Princeton University Press.

Lipset, Seymour Martin, and Earl Raab. 1978. *The politics of unreason: Right wing extremism in America, 1790–1977.* 2nd ed. Chicago: University of Chicago Press.

Lipson, E. 1971. *The economic history of England:* Vols. 2 and 3, *The age of mercantilism.* London: Adam and Charles Black.

Lis, C., and H. Soly. 1977. Food consumption in Antwerp between 1807 and 1859: A contribution to the standard of living debate. *Economic History Review* 30:460–486.

Littlefield, Daniel C. 1981. *Rice and slaves: Ethnicity and the slave trade in colonial South Carolina.* Baton Rouge: Louisiana State University Press.

Litwack, Leon F. 1961. *North of slavery: The Negro in the free states, 1790–1860.* Chicago: University of Chicago Press.

Lloyd, Christopher. 1949. *The Navy and the slave trade: The suppression of the African slave trade in the nineteenth century.* London: Longman, Green and Co.

Locke, Mary Stoughton. 1901. *Slavery in America from the introduction of African slaves to the prohibition of the slave trade (1619–1808).* Boston: Ginn.

Long, Edward. 1774. *A history of Jamaica.* London. (n.p.).

Lovejoy, Paul E. 1982. The volume of the Atlantic slave trade: A synthesis. *Journal of African History* 23:473–501.

———. 1983. *Transformations in slavery: A history of slavery in Africa.* Cambridge: Cambridge University Press.

Lowell, James Russell. 1858. The American tract society. *Atlantic Monthly* 2:246–251.

Ludlum, Robert P. 1936. Joshua R. Giddings, radical. *Mississippi Valley Historical Review* 23:49–60.

McCardell, John. 1979. *The idea of a southern nation: Southern nationalists and southern nationalism, 1830–1860.* New York: W.W. Norton.

McCarthy, Charles. 1903. The Antimasonic Party. In *Annual report of the American Historical Association for the year 1902,* Vol. 1. Washington, D.C.: Government Printing Office.

McClelland, P.D. 1969. The cost to America of British imperial policy. *American Economic Review Proceedings* 59:370–381.

McCormick, Richard P. 1966. *The second American party system: Party formation in the Jacksonian era.* Chapel Hill: University of North Carolina Press.

———. 1969. New perspectives on Jacksonian politics. In Don Karl Rowney and James Q. Graham, Jr., eds., *Quantitative history: Selected readings in the quantitative analysis of historical data.* Homewood, IL: Dorsey Press.

———. 1982. *The presidential game: The origins of American presidential politics.* New York: Oxford University Press.

McCusker, John James. 1989. *Rum and the American Revolution: The rum trade and the balance of payments of the thirteen continental colonies, 1660–1775.* New York: Garland.

McCusker, John James, and Russell R. Menard. 1985. *The economy of British America, 1607–1789.* Chapel Hill: University of North Carolina Press.

McFaul, John M. 1972. *The politics of Jacksonian finance.* Ithaca: Cornell University press.

McKeown, Thomas. 1976. *The modern rise of population.* New York and San Francisco: Academic Press.

McKitrick, Eric L., ed. 1965. *Slavery defended: The views of the old South.* Englewood Cliffs, NJ: Prentice-Hall.

McKivigan, John K. 1984. *The war against proslavery religion: Abolitionism and the northern churches, 1830–1865.* Ithaca: Cornell University Press.

MacLeod, Duncan J. 1974. *Slavery, race and the American Revolution.* London: Cambridge University Press.

———. 1981. From gradualism to immediatism: Another look. *Abolition and Slavery* 2:140–152.

———. 1983. The triple crisis. In R. Jeffreys-Jones and Bruce Collins, eds., *The growth of federal power in American history.* Edinburgh: Scottish Academic Press.

McLoughlin, William G. 1978. *Revivals, awakenings, and reform: An essay on religion and social change in America, 1607–1977.* Chicago: University of Chicago Press.

McMillan, John. 1988. Slave skills on southern plantations: Inference from incomplete records. Typescript.

McPherson, James M. 1964. *The struggle for equality: Abolitionists and the Negro in the Civil War and Reconstruction.* Princeton: Princeton University Press.

———. 1982. *Ordeal by fire: The Civil War and Reconstruction.* New York: Alfred A. Knopf.

Main, Gloria L. 1982. *Tobacco colony: Life in early Maryland, 1650–1720.* Princeton: Princeton University Press.

Maizlish, Stephen E. 1983. *The triumph of sectionalism: The transformation of Ohio politics 1844–1856.* Kent, OH: Kent State University Press.

———. 1986. Race and politics in the northern democracy: 1854–1860. In Robert H. Abzug and Stephen E. Maizlish, eds., *New perspectives on race and slavery in America.* Lexington: University Press of Kentucky.

Malone, Dumas, ed. 1936. *Dictionary of American biography,* Vol. 18. New York: Charles Scribner and Sons.

————. 1981. *The sage of Monticello,* Vol. 6 in *Jefferson and his time.* Boston: Little, Brown.

Mandel, Bernard. 1955. *Labor: Free and slave.* New York: Associated Authors.

Mann, James A. 1860. *The cotton trade of Great Britain: Its rise, progress and present extent.* London: Snupkin, Marshall & Co.

Marglin, Stephen. 1976. What do bosses do? In Andre Gorz, ed., *The division of labour: The labour process and class struggle in modern capitalism.* London: Harvester.

Margo, Robert A., and Richard H. Steckel. 1982. The heights of American slaves: New evidence on slave nutrition and health. *Social Science History* 6:516–538.

Margo, Robert A., and Georgia C. Villaflor. 1987. The growth of wages in antebellum America: New evidence. *Journal of Economic History* 47:873–895.

Martin, R. Montgomery. 1835. *The British Colonial Library: History of the West Indies,* Vol. 6. London: Whittaker and Co.

Martineau, Harriet. 1839. *The martyr age of the United States.* New York: J.S. Taylor.

Martis, Kenneth C. 1982. *The historical atlas of United States congressional districts, 1789–1983.* New York: Free Press.

Marty, Martin E. 1970. *Righteous empire: The Protestant experience in America.* New York: Dial Press.

Mathews, Donald G. 1977. *Religion in the old South.* Chicago: University of Chicago Press.

Mathieson, William Law. [1926] 1967. *British slavery and its abolition 1823–1838.* New York: Octagon Books.

Matthaei, Julie. 1982. *An economic history of women in America.* New York: Schocken Books.

Matthews, K.K. 1909. *The expansion of New England.* Boston: Houghton Mifflin.

May, Robert E. 1973. *The southern dream of a Caribbean empire, 1854–1861.* Baton Rouge: Louisiana State University Press.

Meckel, R.A. 1985. Immigration, mortality, and population growth in Boston, 1840–1880. *Journal of Interdisciplinary History* 15:393–417.

Medoff, James, and Katheryn Abraham. 1981. Are those paid more really more productive? *Journal of Human Resources* 16:186–216.

Meeker, Edward. 1976. Mortality trend of southern blacks. *Explorations in Economic History* 13:13–42.

Mellafe, Rolando. 1975. *Negro slavery in Latin America.* Trans. by J.W.S. Judge. Berkeley: University of California Press.

Meltzer, Milton, and Patricia G. Holland, eds. 1982. *Lydia Maria Child: Selected letters, 1817–1880.* Amherst: University of Massachusetts Press.

Menard, Russell Robert. 1973a. From servant to freeholder: Status mobility and property accumulation in seventeenth century Maryland. *William and Mary Quarterly* 30:37–64.

————. 1973b. From servants to slaves: The transformation of the Chespeake labor system. *Southern Studies* 16:355–390.

————. 1975a. Economy and society in early colonial Maryland. Ph.D. dissertation, University of Iowa.

————. 1975b. The Maryland slave population, 1658 to 1730: A demographic profile of blacks in four counties. *William and Mary Quarterly,* 3rd series, 32, 1:29–54.

Meyer, Balthasar Henry, ed., with Caroline E. McGill and Staff. 1948. *History of transportation in the United States before 1860.* Washington, D.C.: Peter Smith.

Meyers, Marvin. 1960. *The Jacksonian persuasion: Politics and belief.* Stanford, CA: Stanford University Press.

————. 1981. *The mind of the founder: Sources of the political thought of James Madison.* Hanover: University Press of New England.

Miers, Suzanne. 1975. *Britain and the ending of the slave trade.* New York: Africana Publishing Co.

Miller, John Chester. 1960. *The Federalist era, 1789–1801.* New York: Harper.

———. 1977. *The wolf by the ears: Thomas Jefferson and slavery.* New York: Meridian.

Miller, Perry. 1965. *The life of the mind in America from the Revolution to the Civil War.* San Diego: Harvest.

Miller, Randall M. 1979. The man in the middle: The black slave driver. *American Heritage* 30:40–49.

Mineau, G.P., L.L. Bean, and M. Skolnick. 1979. Mormon demographic history: II, The family life cycle and natural fertility. *Population Studies* 33:429–446.

Mintz, Sidney W. 1969. Slavery and emergent capitalism. In Laura Foner and Eugene D. Genovese, eds., *Slavery in the new world.* Englewood Cliffs, NJ: Prentice-Hall.

———. 1974. *Caribbean transformations.* Chicago: Aldine Publishing Co.

———. 1978. Was the plantation slave a proletarian? *Review* 2:81–98.

———. 1979. Slavery and the rise of peasantries. *Historical Reflections* 6.

———. 1985. *Sweetness and power.* New York: Viking Penguin Inc.

Mintz, Sidney, and Douglas Hall. 1960. *The origins of the Jamaican internal marketing system.* New Haven: Yale University Press.

Mitchell, B.R. 1975. *European historical statistics, 1750–1970.* London: Macmillan.

Mitchell, B.R., and Phyllis Deane. 1962. *Abstract of British historical statistics.* Cambridge: Cambridge University Press.

Mitchell, Broadus. 1947. *Depression decade: From New Era through New Deal, 1929–1941,* Vol. 9 in *The Economic History of the United States.* New York and Toronto: Rinehart.

Miyao, Takahiro. 1976. A further look at antebellum cotton supply. Working paper in economics #59. University of California at Santa Barbara. Typescript.

Mokyr, Joel, and Eugene N. Savin. 1978. Some econometric problems in the standard of living controversy. *Journal of European Economic History* 7:517–525.

Monkkonen, Eric H. 1981. *Police in urban America, 1860–1920.* Cambridge: Cambridge University Press.

Montgomery, David. 1968. The working classes of the pre-industrial American city, 1780–1830. *Labor History* 9:3–22.

———. 1972. The shuttle and the cross. *Journal of Social History* 5:411–446.

Moohr, Michael. 1972. The economic impact of slave emancipation in British Guiana, 1832–1852. *Economic History Review* 25:588–607.

Moore, Glover. 1953. *The Missouri controversy, 1819–1821.* Lexington: University of Kentucky Press.

Morgan, Edmund S. 1975. *American slavery, American freedom: The ordeal of colonial Virginia.* New York: W. W. Norton.

———. 1985. Our town. *New York Review of Books,* January 17, 44–45.

Morgan, Philip D. 1982. Work and culture: The task system and the world of low country blacks, 1700 to 1880. *William and Mary Quarterly* 39:563–599.

———. 1983. The ownership of property by slaves in the mid-nineteenth-century low country. *Journal of Southern History,* 49 (August):399–420

Morris, Richard Brandon. 1965. *Government and labor in early America.* New York: Octagon Books.

Morrison, Chaplain W. 1967. *Democratic politics and sectionalism: The Wilmot Proviso controversy.* Chapel Hill: University of North Carolina Press.

Mulhall, Michael G. 1892. 1899. *The dictionary of statistics.* London: George Routledge and Sons.

Mullin, Gerald W. 1972. *Flight and rebellion: Slave resistance in eighteenth-century Virginia.* New York: Oxford University Press.

Murray, D.J. 1965. *The West Indies and the development of colonial government, 1801–34.* Oxford: Clarendon Press.

Myrdal, Gunnar. 1944. *An American dilemma: The Negro problem and modern democracy.* New York: Harper & Row.

Naeye, Richard L., and Ellen C. Peters. 1981. Maternal nutritional status and fetal outcome. *American Journal of Clinical Nutrition* 34:708–721.

———. 1982. Working during pregnancy: Effects on the fetus. *Pediatrics* 69:724–727.

Namier, Lewis, and John Brooke. 1964. *The House of Commons, 1754–1790.* London: Her Majesty's Stationery Office.

Nash, Gary B. 1979. *The urban crucible: Social change, political consciousness, and the origins of the American Revolution.* Cambridge: Harvard University Press.

Nevins, Allan. 1947. *Ordeal of the union,* 2 vols. New York: Charles Scribner and Sons.

———. 1950. *The emergence of Lincoln,* 2 vols. New York: Charles Scribner and Sons.

New American Cyclopaedia: A popular dictionary of general knowledge. 1866. Vol. V. George Ripley and Charles A. Dana, eds. New York: D. Appleton and Company.

———. 1871. Vol. VIII. George Ripley and Charles A. Dana, eds. New York: D. Appleton and Company.

Newman, Gerald. 1975. Anti-French propaganda and British Liberal Nationalism in the early nineteenth century: Suggestions toward a general interpretation. *Victorian Studies* 18:385–418.

Niemi, Albert. 1977. Inequality in the distribution of slave wealth: The cotton South and other southern agricultural regions. *Journal of Economic History* 37:747–754.

North, Douglass C. 1986. Institutions, economic growth, and freedom: An historical introduction. Workshop in Economic History Paper No. 8687–04. University of Chicago Department of Economics.

Nye, Russell Blaine. 1960. *The cultural life of the new nation, 1776–1830.* New York: Harper & Row.

———. 1963. *Fettered freedom: Civil liberties and the slavery controversy 1830–1860.* East Lansing: Michigan State University Press.

———. 1974. *Society and culture in America, 1830–1860.* New York: Harper & Row.

Oakes, James. 1982. *The ruling race: A history of American slaveholders.* New York: Alfred A. Knopf.

———. 1983. The muted fireball of old Virginia. *Reviews in American History* 11:381–385.

———. 1984. The politics of economic development in the antebellum South. *Journal of Interdisciplinary History* 15:305–316.

Olmsted, Frederick Law. [1856] 1968. *A journey in the seaboard slave states.* New York: Negro Universities Press.

———. [1861] 1970. *The cotton kingdom.* Edited, with an introduction, by Arthur M. Schlesinger. New York: Alfred A. Knopf, Borzoi Books.

Olsen, Otto H. 1972. Historians and the extent of slave ownership in the southern United States. *Civil War History* 18:101–116.

Olson, John F. 1983. The occupational structure of plantation slave labor in the late antebellum era. Ph.D. dissertation, University of Rochester.

Owens, Leslie H. 1976. *This species of property: Slave life and culture in the old South.* New York: Oxford University Press.

Owsley, Frank Lawrence. 1949. *Plain folks of the old South.* Baton Rouge: Louisiana State University Press.

Palmer, Colin A. 1976. *Slaves of the white god: Blacks in Mexico, 1570–1650.* Cambridge: Harvard University Press.

Pares, Richard. 1950. *A West Indian fortune.* London: Longman's Green.

Parker, William N. 1970a. Slavery and southern economic development: An hypothesis and some evidence. *Agricultural History* 44:115–125.

———, ed. 1970b. *The structure of the cotton economy of the antebellum South.* Washington, D.C.: Agricultural History Society.

Parrington, Vernon Louis. 1930. *Main currents in American thought: An interpretation of American literature from the beginnings to 1920:* Vol. I, *1620–1800: The colonial mind.* New York: Harcourt, Brace, and Company.

Parry, J.H. 1979. *The Spanish seaborne empire.* New York: Alfred A. Knopf.

Parry, J.H., and P.M. Sherlock. 1956. *A short history of the West Indies.* London: Macmillan.

Passel, Peter, and Gavin Wright. 1972. The effects of pre–Civil War territorial expansion on the price of slaves. *Journal of Political Economy* 80:1188–1202.

Patterson, Orlando. 1972. *The sociology of slavery.* New York: Academic Press.

———. 1982. *Slavery and social death: A comparative study.* Cambridge: Harvard University Press.

Paxson, Frederick L. 1914. The railroads of the "Old Northwest" before the Civil War. *Transactions, Wisconsin Academy of Sciences, Arts, and Letters* 17:243–274.

Pebley, Anne R., John B. Casterline, and James Trussell. 1982. Age at first birth in 19 countries. *International Family Planning Perspectives* 8:2–7.

Perlman, Selig. 1923. *A history of trade unionism in the United States.* New York: Macmillan.

Perry, Lewis. 1973. *Radical abolitionism: Anarchy and the government of God in antislavery thought.* Ithaca: Cornell University Press.

Perry, Lewis, and Michael Fellman, eds. 1979. *Antislavery reconsidered: New perspectives on the abolitionists.* Baton Rouge: Louisiana State University Press.

Pessen, Edward. 1973. *Riches, class, and power before the Civil War.* Lexington: D.C. Heath & Co.

———. 1977. Who governed the nation's cities in the "Era of the Common Man"? In Edward Pessen, ed., *The many faceted Jacksonian era: New interpretations.* Westport, CT: Greenwood Press.

———. 1978. *Jacksonian America: Society, personality, and politics.* Homewood, IL: Dorsey.

———. 1979. On a recent cliometric attempt to resurrect the myth of antebellum egalitarianism. *Social Science History* 3:208–227.

———. 1980. How different from each other were the antebellum North and South? *American Historical Review* 85:1119–1149.

Petersen, Svend. 1963. *A statistical history of the American presidential elections.* New York: Frederick Ungar Publishing Co.

Phillips, Ulrich Bonnell. 1906. The origin and growth of the southern black belts. *American Historical Review* 11:798–816.

———. 1907. Slave labor in the Charleston district. *Political Science Quarterly* 22:416–439.

———. [1918] 1966. *American Negro slavery: A survey of the supply, employment and control of Negro labor as determined by the plantation regime.* Baton Rouge: Louisiana State University Press.

Phillips, Wendel. 1969. *Review of Lysander Spooner's essay on the unconstitutionality of slavery.* New York: Arno Press.

Pitkin, Timothy. 1835. *A statistical view of the commerce of the United States of America.* New Haven: Durrie and Peck.

Plantation and farm instruction, regulation, record, inventory and account book. 1852. Richmond: J.W. Randolph.

Plumb, J.H. [1950] 1974. *England in the eighteenth century.* Harmondsworth: Penguin Books.

Pollard, Sidney. 1965. *The genesis of modern management: A study of the Industrial Revolution in Great Britain.* London: Edward Arnold.

Pope, Clayne L. 1975. *The impact of the ante-bellum tariff on income distribution.* New York: Arno Press.

Porter, Kirk H. 1918. *A history of suffrage in the United States.* Chicago: University of Chicago Press.

Porter, Kirk H., and Donald Bruce Johnson. 1966. *National party platforms, 1840–1964.* Urbana: University of Illinois Press.

Postell, William D. [1951] 1970. *The health of slaves on southern plantations*. Gloucester, MA: Peter Smith.

Potter, David M. 1962. *Lincoln and his party in the secession crisis*. New Haven: Yale University Press.

———. 1976. *The impending crisis: 1848–1861*. New York: Harper.

Potter, J. 1965. The growth of population in America, 1700–1860. In D.V. Eversley and D.E.C. Eversley, eds., *Population in history: Essays in historical demography*. Chicago: Aldine.

Quarles, Benjamin. 1969. *Black abolitionists*. New York: Oxford University Press.

Ragatz, Lowell J. 1928a. *The fall of the planter class in the British Caribbean, 1763–1833: A study in social and economic history*. New York: Century Company.

———. 1928b. *Statistics for the study of British Caribbean economic history, 1763–1833*. London: Bryan Edwards Press.

Ransom, Roger L. 1963. Government investment in canals: A study of the Ohio canal. Ph.D. dissertation, University of Washington.

Ransom, Roger L., and Richard Sutch. 1975. The "lock-in" mechanism and overproduction of cotton in the postbellum South. *Agricultural History* 49:405–425.

———. 1977. *One kind of freedom: The economic consequence of emancipation*. Cambridge: Cambridge University Press.

———. 1983. The long-run implications of capital absorption in slave labor. Presented to the annual meeting of the Cliometric Society, May 1983. Photocopy.

Ratner, Lorman. 1968. *Powder keg: Northern opposition to the antislavery movement, 1831–1840*. New York: Basic Books.

Ratner, Sidney, James H. Soltow, and Richard Sylla. 1979. *The evolution of the American economy: Growth, welfare, and decision making*. New York: Basic Books.

Rawick, George P., ed. 1972. *The American slave: A composite autobiography:* Vol. 1, *From sundown to sunup: The making of the black community;* Vol. 19, *God struck me dead.* Contributions in Afro-American and African studies, No. 11. Westport, CT: Greenwood Press.

Rayback, Joseph G. 1943. The American workingman and the antislavery crusade. *Journal of Economic History* 3:152–163.

Reckord, Mary. 1968. The Jamaica slave rebellion of 1831. *Past and Present* 40:108–125.

Reid, Joseph D. 1970. On navigating the navigation acts with Peter D. McClelland: Comment. *American Economic Review* 60:949–955.

Reis, Jaime. 1977. The impact of abolitionism in northeast Brazil: A quantitative approach. *Annals of the New York Academy of Science* 292:107–122.

Reitz, Elizabeth J., Tyson Gibbs, and Ted A. Rathbun. 1985. Archeological evidence for subsistence on coastal plantations. In Theresa A. Singleton, ed., *The archaeology of slavery and plantation life*. Studies in Historical Archaeology. London: Academic Press.

Rhodes, James Ford. [1893] 1928. *History of the United States from the Compromise of 1850:* Vol. 1, *1850–1854*. New York: Macmillan.

Richards, Leonard L. 1979. The Jacksonians and slavery. In Lewis Perry and Michael Fellman, eds., *Antislavery reconsidered: New perspectives on the abolitionists*. Baton Rouge: Louisiana State University Press.

Richardson, James F. 1970. *The New York police: Colonial times to 1901*. New York: Oxford University Press.

Ripley, C. Peter, Jeffery S. Rossbach, Roy E. Finkenbine, and Fiona E. Spiers, eds., with Debra Susie. *The black abolitionist papers:* Vol. I, *The British Isles, 1830–1865*. Chapel Hill: University of North Carolina Press.

Roark, James L. 1977. *Masters without slaves: Southern planters in the Civil War and Reconstruction*. New York: W. W. Norton.

Robbins, Roy M. 1933. Horace Greeley: Land reform and unemployment, 1837–1862. *Agricultural History* 7:18–41.

————. 1962. *Our landed heritage: The public domain, 1776–1936.* Lincoln: University of Nebraska Press.

Robert, Joseph Clarke. 1941. *The road from Monticello: A study of the Virginia slavery debate of 1832.* Durham: Duke University Press.

Robinson, Donald. 1979. *Slavery in the structure of American politics, 1765–1820.* New York: W. W. Norton.

Rockoff, Hugh. 1971. Money, prices, and banks in the Jacksonian era. In Robert Fogel and Stanley Engerman, eds., *The reinterpretation of American economic history.* New York: Harper & Row.

————. 1972. The free banking era: A reexamination. Ph.D. dissertation, University of Chicago.

Rona, R.J., A.V. Swan, and D.G. Altman. 1978. Social factors and height of primary school children in England and Scotland. *Journal of Epidemiology and Community Health* 32:147–154.

Rose, R.B. 1961. Eighteenth century price riots and public policy in England. *International Review of Social History* 6:277–292.

Rosenberg, Charles E. 1971. *The cholera years: The United States in 1832, 1849, and 1866.* Chicago: University of Chicago Press.

Rosenblat, Angel. 1954. *La Pablación Indigena y El Mestizaje en America,* 2 vols. Buenos Aires: Editorial Nova.

Ross, Steven J. 1985. *Workers on the edge: Work, leisure, and politics in industrializing Cincinnati, 1788–1840.* New York: Columbia University Press.

Rossiter, W.S., preparer. 1909. U.S. Bureau of the Census: *A century of population growth.* Washington, D.C.: Government Printing Office.

Rothman, David J. 1971. *The discovery of the asylum: Social order and disorder in the new republic.* Boston: Little, Brown.

Roughley, T. 1823. *The Jamaica planter's guide.* London: Longman, Hurst, Rees, Orme, and Brown.

Russel, Robert Royal. 1938. The general effects of slavery upon southern economic progress. *Journal of Southern History* 4:34–54.

————. [1922] 1960. *Economic aspects of Southern sectionalism 1840–1861.* New York: Russell and Russell.

Russell, Robert. 1857. *North America: Its agriculture and climate.* Edinburgh: Adam and Charles Black.

Rutman, Darnett B., and Anita H. Rutman. 1984. *A place in time: Middlesex County, Virginia, 1650–1750,* 2 vols. New York and London: W. W. Norton.

Ryan, Mary P. 1981. *Cradle of the middle class: The family in Oneida County, New York, 1790–1865.* Cambridge: Cambridge University Press.

Sabel, Charles, and Jonathan Zeitlin. 1985. Historical alternatives to mass production: Politics, markets and technology in nineteenth-century industrialization. *Past and Present* 108:133–176.

Savitt, Todd L. 1978. *Medicine and slavery: The diseases and health care of blacks in antebellum Virginia.* Urbana: University of Illinois Press.

Scarano, Francisco A. 1984. *Sugar and slavery in Puerto Rico, the plantation economy of Ponce, 1800–1850.* Madison: University of Wisconsin Press.

Scarborough, William K. 1966. *The overseer: Plantation management in the old South.* Baton Rouge: Louisiana State University Press.

Schaefer, Donald F. 1978. Yeoman farmers and economic democracy: A study of wealth and economic mobility in the western tobacco region, 1850 to 1860. *Explorations in Economic History* 15:421–437.

————. 1985. A statistical profile of frontier and New South migration: 1850–1860. *Agricultural History* 59:563–578.

Schaefer, Donald F., and Mark D. Schmitz. 1979. The relative efficiency of slave agriculture: A comment. *American Economic Review* 69:208–212.

Schafer, Joseph. 1924. Know-Nothingism in Wisconsin. *Wisconsin Magazine of History* 8:3–21.

Schlesinger, Arthur Meier. 1933. *The rise of the city, 1878–1898.* New York: Macmillan.

Schlesinger, Arthur M., Jr., ed. 1973. *History of U.S. political parties,* Vol. I. New York: Chelsea House Publishing.

Schlomowitz, Ralph. 1979. The transition from slave to freedom: Labor arrangements in southern agriculture, 1865–1870. Ph.D. dissertation, University of Chicago.

Schlotterbeck, John T. 1980. Plantation and farm: Social and economic change in Orange and Green Counties, Virginia, 1716–1860. Ph.D. dissertation, Johns Hopkins University.

Schlueter, Herman. 1913. *Lincoln, labor and slavery.* New York: Socialist Literature Co.

Schmitz, Mark. 1974. Economic analysis of antebellum sugar plantations in Louisiana. Ph.D. dissertation, University of North Carolina at Chapel Hill.

Schmitz, Mark, and Donald Schaefer. 1981. Paradox lost: Westward expansion and slave prices before the Civil War: Discussion. *Journal of Economic History* 41:402–407.

Schneider, David M. 1938. *The history of public welfare in New York State, 1609–1866.* Chicago: University of Chicago Press.

Schumpeter, Elizabeth B. 1960. *English overseas trade statistics 1697–1808.* Oxford: Clarendon.

Schwartz, Stuart B. 1985. *Sugar plantations in the formation of Brazilian society: Bahia, 1550–1835.* Cambridge: Cambridge University Press.

Scisco, Louis Dow. 1901. *Political nativism in New York State.* New York: Columbia University Press.

Scott, Rebecca J. 1985. *Slave emancipation in Cuba: The transition to free labor, 1860–1899.* Princeton: Princeton University Press.

Semmes, Raphael. 1938. *Crime and punishment in early Maryland.* Baltimore: Johns Hopkins University Press.

Senning, John. 1914. The Know-Nothing movement in Illinois. *Illinois State Historical Society Journal* 7:9–33.

Sewell, Richard H. 1965. *John P. Hale and the politics of abolition.* Cambridge: Harvard University Press.

––––––. 1976. *Ballots for freedom: Antislavery politics in the United States, 1837–1860.* New York: Oxford University Press.

Shade, W.A. 1981. "New political history": Some statistical questions raised. *Social Science History* 5:171–196.

Sheridan, Richard B. 1974. *Sugar and slavery: An economic history of the British West Indies 1623–1775.* Aylesbury, UK: Ginn and Company.

––––––. 1976. "Sweet malefactor": The social costs of slavery and sugar in Jamaica and Cuba, 1807–54. *Economic History Review* 29:236–257.

––––––. 1981. Slave demography in the British West Indies and the abolition of the slave trade. In David Eltis and James Walvin, eds., *The abolition of the Atlantic slave trade.* Madison: University of Wisconsin Press.

––––––. 1985. *Doctors and slaves: A medical and demographic history of slavery in the British West Indies 1680–1834.* Cambridge: Cambridge University Press.

Silbey, Joel H. 1967. *The shrine of party: Congressional voting behavior, 1841–1852.* Pittsburgh: University of Pittsburgh Press.

––––––. 1977. *A respectable minority: The Democratic Party in the Civil War era, 1860–1868.* New York: W. W. Norton.

––––––. 1985. *The partisan imperative: The dynamics of American politics before the Civil War.* New York: Oxford University Press.

Sitterson, J. Carlyle. 1953. *Sugar country: The cane sugar industry in the South, 1753–1950.* Lexington: University of Kentucky Press.

Slenes, Robert Wayne. 1975. The demography and economics of Brazilian slavery: 1850–1888. Ph.D. dissertation, Stanford University.

Smillie, Wilson G. 1955. *Public health: Its promise for the future.* New York: Macmillan.

Smith, Abbot Emerson. 1971. *Colonists in bondage: White servitude and convict labor in America, 1607–1776.* New York: W. W. Norton.

Smith, Adam. [1776] 1937. *The wealth of nations.* New York: Modern Library.

Smith, Charles E. 1851. The manufacture of iron in Pennsylvania. *Hunt's Merchants' Magazine* 25:574–581.

Smith, H. Shelton. 1972. *In his image, but . . .: Racism in southern religion, 1780–1910.* Durham, NC: Duke University Press.

Smith, J. Allen. 1965. *The spirit of American government.* Cambridge, MA: Belknap Press.

Smith, Timothy L. 1957. *Revivalism and social reform in mid-nineteenth century America.* New York: Abingdon.

Smith, Walter B. 1963. Wage rates on the Erie Canal, 1828–1881. *Journal of Economic History* 23:298–311.

Smith, Walter Buckingham, and Arthur Harrison Cole. 1935. *Fluctuations in American business, 1790–1860.* Cambridge: Harvard University Press.

Soderlund, Jean R. 1985. *Quakers & slavery: A divided spirit.* Princeton: Princeton University Press.

Sokoloff, Kenneth L. 1982. Industrialization and the growth of the manufacturing sector in the Northeast, 1820–1850. Ph. D. dissertation, Harvard University.

———. 1984. Was the transition from artisanal shop to the non-mechanized factory associated with gains in efficiency? Evidence from the U.S. manufacturing censuses of 1820 and 1850. *Explorations in Economic History* 21:351–382.

———. 1986. Productivity growth in manufacturing during early industrialization: Evidence from the American Northeast, 1820–1860. In Stanley Engerman and Robert Gallman, eds., *Long-term factors in American economic growth.* Conference on Research in Income and Wealth, Vol. 51. Chicago: University of Chicago Press (for NBER).

Soltow, Lee. 1971a. Economic inequality in the United States in the period from 1790 to 1860. *Journal of Economic History* 31:822–839.

———. 1971b. *Patterns of wealthholding in Wisconsin since 1850.* Madison: University of Wisconsin Press.

———. 1975. *Men and wealth in the United States, 1850–1870.* New Haven: Yale University Press.

Soule, George. 1947. *Prosperity decade: From war to depression, 1917–1929,* Vol. 8 in *The Economic History of the United States.* New York and London: Harper.

Spengler, Joseph J. 1936. Population theory in the ante-bellum South. *Journal of Southern History* 2:360–389.

Spooner, Lysander. 1860. *The unconstitutionality of slavery.* New York: Burt Franklin.

Stampp, Kenneth M. 1952. The historian and southern Negro slavery. *American Historical Review* 57:618–624.

———. 1956. *The peculiar institution: Slavery in the antebellum South.* New York: Alfred A. Knopf.

———. 1970. *And the war came.* Baton Rouge: Louisiana State University Press.

———. 1976. Introduction. In Paul David et al., *Reckoning with slavery: A critical study in the quantitative history of American Negro slavery.* New York: Oxford University Press.

Starobin, Robert S. 1970. *Industrial slavery in the old South.* New York: Oxford University Press.

Staudenraus, P.J. 1961. *The African colonization movement, 1816–1865.* New York: Columbia University Press.

Steckel, Richard H. 1971. Negro slavery in the Western Hemisphere. Typescript.

———. 1979. Slave height profiles from coastwise manifests. *Explorations in Economic History* 16:363–380.

————. 1980. Miscegenation and the American slave schedules. *Journal of Interdisciplinary History* 11:251–263.

————. 1983. The economic foundations of East-West migration during the 19th century. *Explorations in Economic History* 20:14–36.

————. 1985. *The economics of U.S. slave and southern white fertility.* New York: Garland Publishing, Inc.

————. 1986a. A peculiar population. *Journal of Economic History* 46:721–741.

————. 1986b. Birth weights and infant mortality among American slaves. *Explorations in Economic History* 23:173–198.

Steckel, Richard, and Richard Jensen. 1986. New evidence on the causes of slave and crew mortality in the Atlantic slave trade. *Journal of Economic History* 46:57–77.

Stephen, James. 1814. Reasons for establishing a registry of slaves in the British colonies. *Pamphleteer* 7:13.

Stephenson, George M. 1917. *The political history of the Public Lands from 1840 to 1862.* Boston: Richard G. Badger.

————. 1926. *A history of American immigration, 1820–1924.* Boston: Ginn & Co.

Stewart, James Brewer. 1970. *Joshua R. Giddings and the tactics of radical politics.* Cleveland: Case Western Reserve University Press.

Stone, Katherine. 1974. Origins of job structures in the steel industry. *Review of Radical Political Economy* 6:113–174.

Stuckey, Sterling. [1968] 1973. Through the prism of folklore: The black ethos in slavery. In A. Weinstein and F.O. Gatell, eds., *American Negro Slavery.* New York: Oxford University Press.

————. 1987. *Slave culture: Nationalist theory and the foundations of black America.* New York: Oxford University Press.

Studenski, Paul. 1958. *The income of nations:* Part I, *History.* New York: New York University Press.

Sutch, Richard. 1974. The treatment received by American slaves: A critical review of the Fogel-Engerman thesis. Manuscript presented at the Rochester Conference.

————. 1975. The treatment received by American slaves: A critical review of the evidence presented in *Time on the cross. Explorations in Economic History* 12:335–438.

————. 1976. The care and feeding of slaves. In Paul David et al., eds., *Reckoning with slavery: A critical study in the quantitative history of American Negro slavery.* New York: Oxford University Press.

SVIMEZ (Associazione per lo Sviluppo Dell'Industria nel Mezzogiorno). 1954. *Statistiche sul mezzogiorno d'Italia, 1861–1953.* Rome: SVIMEZ.

Swan, Dale E. 1972. The structure and profitability of the antebellum rice industry: 1859. Ph.D. dissertation, University of North Carolina.

Sweeney, Kevin. 1976. Rum, Romanism, representation, and reform: Coalition politics in Massachusetts, 1847–1853. *Civil War History* 22:116–137.

Swierenga, Robert P. 1968. *Pioneers and profits: Land speculation on the Iowa frontier.* Ames: Iowa State University Press.

————. 1988. Religion and political behavior in the nineteenth century: Voting, values, cultures. Presented at the Conference on Religion and American Politics, Institute for the Study of American Evangelicals, Wheaton, IL, March 18.

Sydnor, Charles S. [1933] 1965. *Slavery in Mississippi.* New York: D. Appleton Co.

————. [1948] 1966. *A history of the South:* Vol. 5, *The development of southern sectionalism, 1819–1848.* Baton Rouge: Louisiana State University Press.

Taft, Philip. 1964. *Organized labor in American history.* New York: Harper & Row.

Takaki, Ronald T. 1971. *A pro-slavery crusade: The agitation to reopen the African slave trade.* New York: Free Press.

Talwar, P.P. 1965. Adolescent sterility in an Indian population. *Human Biology* 37:256–261.

Tannenbaum, Frank. 1946. *Slave and citizen.* New York: Vintage Books.

Tanner, J.M. 1978. *Fetus into man: Physical growth from conception to maturity.* Cambridge: Harvard University Press.

———. 1981. *A history of the study of human growth.* Cambridge: Cambridge University Press.

Tanner, J.M., R.H. Whitehouse, and M. Takaishi. 1966. Standards from birth to maturity for height, weight, height velocity, weight velocity: British children, 1965. *Archives of Diseases of Childhood* 41:454–471, 613–635.

Tappan, Lewis. 1870. *The life of Arthur Tappan.* New York: Hurd and Houghton.

Taussig, F.W. [1892] 1964. *The tariff history of the United States.* New York: Capricorn.

Taylor, George Rogers. [1951] 1958. *The transportation revolution, 1815–1860:* Vol. IV, *The economic history of the United States.* New York: Rinehart & Co.

Taylor, Orville W. 1958. *Negro slavery in Arkansas.* Durham: Duke University Press.

Temin, Peter. 1963. *Iron and steel in nineteenth century America: An economic inquiry.* Cambridge: MIT Press.

———. 1969. *The Jacksonian economy.* New York: W. W. Norton.

———. 1979. Freedom and coercion: Notes on the analysis of debt peonage in *One kind of freedom. Explorations in Economic History* 16:56–63.

Temperley, Howard. 1972. *British antislavery: 1833–1870.* Columbia, SC: University of South Carolina Press.

———. 1977. Capitalism, slavery, and ideology. *Past and Present* 75:94–118.

———. 1980. Anti-slavery as a form of cultural imperialism. In Christine Bolt and Seymour Drescher, eds., *Anti-slavery, religion and reform.* Folkestone, UK: W. Dawson.

Thernstrom, Stephan. 1973. *The other Bostonians: Poverty and progress in the American metropolis, 1880–1970.* Cambridge: Harvard University Press.

Thomas, John L. 1963. *The liberator: William Lloyd Garrison, a biography.* Boston: Little, Brown.

———. 1965. *Slavery attacked: The abolitionist crusade.* Englewood Cliffs, NJ: Prentice-Hall.

Thompson, Edward P. 1967. Time, work discipline and industrial capitalism. *Past and Present* 38:56–97.

———. 1975. *The making of the English working class.* Middlesex, UK: Penguin Books.

Thomson, A.M., W.Z. Billewicz, B. Thompson, and I.A. McGregor. 1966. Body weight changes during pregnancy and lactation in rural African (Gambian) women. *Journal of Obstetrics and Gynecology of the British Commonwealth* 73:724–733.

Thornton, J. Mills, III. 1978. *Politics and power in a slave society: Alabama, 1800–1860.* Baton Rouge: Louisiana State University Press.

Thorp, William Long. 1926. *Business annals.* New York: National Bureau of Economic Research, Inc.

Tocqueville, Alexis de. [1835] 1969. *Democracy in America.* Translated by George Lawrence and J.P. Mayer, eds. Garden City, NY: Doubleday.

Tolliday, Steven, and Jonathan Zeitlin. 1986. *The automobile industry and its workers: Between Fordism and flexibility.* Cambridge, UK: Polity Press.

Towne, Marvin W., and Wayne D. Rasmussen. 1960. Farm product and gross investment in the nineteenth century. In *Trends in the American Economy in the Nineteenth Century.* Conference on Research in Income and Wealth, Vol. 24. Princeton: Princeton University Press (for NBER).

Tribune almanac, for the years 1838 to 1868, inclusive. 1868. New York: New York Tribune.

Tucker, George. 1843. *Progress of the United States in population and wealth in 50 years, as exhibited by the decennial census.* New York: Press of Hunt's Merchants' Magazine.

Tulloch, A.M. 1838. On the sickness and mortality among the troops in the West Indies, Pt. 1–3. *Journal of the Statistical Society of London* 1:129–142, 216–230, 428–443.

———. 1841. Comparison of the sickness, mortality, and prevailing diseases among seamen and soldiers, as shewn by the naval and military statistical reports. *Journal of the Statistical Society of London* 4:1–16.

Turner, Mary. 1982. *Slaves and missions: The disintegration of the Jamaican slave society, 1787–1834.* Urbana: University of Illinois Press.

Tushnet, Mark. 1981. *The American law of slavery, 1810–1860: Considerations of humanity and interest.* Princeton: Princeton University Press.

United Nations. 1983. *Manual X: Indirect techniques for demographic estimation.* New York: United Nations Publications.

United States Bureau of the Census. 1853. *Abstract of the seventh census.* Washington, D.C.: Robert Armstrong.

———. 1854. *Compendium of the seventh census, 1850.* Washington, D.C.: Government Printing Office.

———. 1862. *Preliminary report of the eighth census, 1860.* Washington, D.C.: Government Printing Office.

———. 1864. *Census of agriculture in 1860.* Washington, D.C.: Government Printing Office.

———. 1895. *Report on the statistics of agriculture in the United States.* Washington, D.C.: Government Printing Office.

———. 1909. *A century of population growth.* Prepared by W.S. Rossiter. Washington, D.C.: Government Printing Office.

———. 1960. *Historical statistics of the United States, colonial times to 1957.* Washington, D.C.: Government Printing Office.

———. 1975. *Historical statistics of the United States, colonial times to 1970.* Bicentennial Edition, Pt. I and II. Washington, D.C.: Government Printing Office.

———. 1981. *Statistical abstract of the United States, 1981*, 102d ed. Washington, D.C.: Government Printing Office.

———. 1987. *Statistical abstract of the United States: 1988*, 108th ed. Washington, D.C.: Government Printing Office.

United States Central Intelligence Agency. 1980. *National intelligence fact book.* Washington, D.C.: Government Printing Office.

United States Department of Agriculture. 1895. *Production and prices of cotton for one hundred years.* Prepared by James L. Watkins. Misc. Series Bulletin No. 9. Washington, D.C.

———. 1899. *The cost of cotton production.* Prepared by John Hyde and James L. Watkins. Misc. Series Bulletin No. 16. Washington, D.C.

———. 1907. *Meat supply and surplus.* Prepared by George K. Holmes. Bureau of Statistics Bulletin No. 55. Washington, D.C.: Government Printing Office.

———. 1912a. *Seedtime and harvest.* Prepared by James R. Covert. Bulletin 85. Washington, D.C.: Bureau of Statistics.

———. 1912b. *Wages of farm labor.* Prepared by George K. Holmes. Bulletin No. 99. Washington, D.C.: Government Printing Office.

United States House of Representatives. 1836. *Letter from the Secretary of the Treasury transmitting tables and notes on the cultivation, manufacture, and foreign trade of cotton.* Document No. 146, 24th Congress, 1st Session.

United States Surgeon General's Office. 1875. *The cholera epidemic of 1873 in the United States.* Washington, D.C.: Government Printing Office.

Ure, Andrew. 1835. *The philosophy of manufacturers.* London: Charles Knight.

Van DeBurg, William L. 1979. *The slave drivers: Black agricultural labor supervisors in the ante bellum South.* Westport, CT: Greenwood Press.

Van den Boogaart, E., and P.C. Emmer. 1977. Plantation slavery in Surinam in the last

decade before emancipation: The case of Catherine Sophie. In Vera Rubin and
    Arthur Tuden, eds., *Comparative perspectives on slavery in new world plantation socie-
    ties.* New York: New York Academy of Sciences.
Van Deusen, Glyndon G. 1947. *Thurlow Weed: Wizard of the lobby.* Boston: Little,
    Brown.
————. 1963. *The Jacksonian era, 1828–1848.* New York: Harper.
————. 1964. *Horace Greeley: Nineteenth-century crusader.* New York: Hill and Wang.
————. 1967. *William Henry Seward.* New York: Oxford University Press.
————. 1973. The Whig party. In Arthur Schlesinger, Jr., ed., *History of U.S. political
    parties,* Vol. I. New York: Chelsea House Publishing.
Vedder, Richard K., and L.E. Gallaway. 1972. The geographical distribution of British
    and Irish emigrants to the United States after 1800. *Scottish Journal of Political
    Economy* 19:19–35.
————. 1980. The profitability of antebellum manufacturing: Some new estimates.
    Business History Review 54:92–103.
Villaflor, Georgia C. 1985. Changing patterns of migration in nineteenth-century Amer-
    ica. Typescript. Harvard University.
Villaflor, Georgia C., and Kenneth L. Sokoloff. 1982. Migration in colonial America:
    Evidence from the militia muster rolls. *Social Science History* 6:539–570.
Vinovskis, Maris A. 1972. Mortality rates and trends in Massachusetts before 1860.
    Journal of Economic History 32 (March):184–213.
Voegli, V. Jacque. 1967. *Free but not equal: The Midwest and the Negro during the Civil
    War.* Chicago: University of Chicago Press.
Wade, Richard C. 1964. *Slavery in the cities: The South 1820–1860.* New York: Oxford
    University Press.
Walsh, Lorena Seebach. 1977. Charles County, Maryland, 1658–1705: A study of
    Chesapeake social and political structure. Ph.D. dissertation, Michigan State Univer-
    sity.
Walters, Ronald G. 1976. *The antislavery appeal: American abolitionism after 1830.*
    Baltimore: Johns Hopkins University Press.
Walvin, James. 1981. The public campaign in England against slavery, 1787–1834. In
    David Eltis and James Walvin, eds., *The abolition of the Atlantic slave trade.* Madi-
    son: University of Wisconsin Press.
————, ed. 1982. *Slavery and British society, 1776–1846.* London: Macmillan.
Walzer, Michael. 1965. *The revolution of the saints: A study in the origin of radical politics.*
    Cambridge: Harvard University Press.
Ward, J.R. 1978. The profitability of sugar planting in the British West Indies, 1650–
    1834. *Economic History Review* 31:197–213.
Ward, W.R. 1972. *Religion and society in England, 1790–1850.* London: B.T. Batsford
    Ltd.
Warden, Robert B. 1874. *An account of the private life and public services of Salmon
    Portland Chase.* Cincinnati: Wilstach, Baldwin & Co.
Ware, Norman. 1924. *The industrial worker, 1840–1860: The reaction of American indus-
    trial society to the advance of the Industrial Revolution.* Boston: Houghton Mifflin.
Warner, Sam Bass, Jr. 1968. *The private city: Philadelphia in three periods of its growth.*
    Philadelphia: University of Pennsylvania Press.
Warren, George F., and Frank A. Pearson. 1933. *Prices.* New York: John Wiley & Sons.
Watkins, James L., preparer. 1895. U.S. Department of Agriculture: *Production and
    prices of cotton for one hundred years.* Misc. Series Bulletin No. 9. Washington, D.C.
————. [1908] 1969. *King cotton: A historical and statistical review, 1790 to 1908.* New
    York: Negro Universities Press.
Watson, Harry L. 1981. *Jacksonian politics and community conflict: The emergence of the
    second American party system in Cumberland County, North Carolina.* Baton Rouge:
    Louisiana State University Press.

————. 1985. Parties count. *Reviews in American History* 13:538–544.

Weaver, Herbert. [1945] 1968. *Mississippi farmers, 1850–1860.* Nashville: Vanderbilt University Press.

Webber, Thomas L. 1978. *Deep like the rivers.* New York: W. W. Norton.

Weber, Adna Ferrin. [1899] 1967. *The growth of cities in the nineteenth century, a study in statistics.* Ithaca: Cornell Paperbacks.

Weiman, David F. 1983. Petty commodity production in the cotton South: Upcountry farmers in the Georgia economy, 1840 to 1880. Ph.D. dissertation, Stanford University.

Weld, Theodore Dwight. 1839. *American slavery as it is: Testimony of a thousand witnesses.* New York: American Anti-Slavery Society.

Wells, Robert V. 1975. *The population of the British colonies in America before 1776.* Princeton: Princeton University Press.

Wender, Herbert. 1930. *Southern commercial conventions 1837–1859.* Baltimore: Johns Hopkins University Press.

Wesley, Charles H. 1927. *Negro labor in the United States, 1850–1925: A study in American economic history.* New York: Vanguard Press.

White, Deborah Gray. 1985. *Ar'n't I a woman? Female slaves in the plantation South.* New York: W. W. Norton.

White, Morton, and Lucia White. 1961. The American intellectual versus the American city. *Daedalus* 90:166–179.

Whitney, Thomas R. 1856. *A defense of the American policy.* New York: De Witt & Davenport.

Wicker, E.R. 1960. Railroad investment before the Civil War. In *Trends in the American Economy in the Nineteenth Century.* Conference on Research in Income and Wealth, Vol. 24. Princeton, NJ: Princeton University Press (for NBER).

Wiecek, William M. 1977. *The sources of antislavery constitutionalism in America, 1760–1848.* Ithaca: Cornell University Press.

Wiener, Martin J. 1981. *English culture and the decline of the industrial spirit, 1850–1980.* Cambridge: Cambridge University Press.

Wilentz, Sean. 1984. *Chants democratic: New York City and the rise of the American working class, 1788–1850.* New York: Oxford University Press.

————. 1986. Land, labor, and politics in the age of Jackson. *Reviews in American History* (June):200–209.

Williams, Eric. [1944] 1966. *Capitalism and slavery.* New York: Capricorn Books.

Williamson, Jeffrey G. 1976. American prices and urban inequality since 1820. *Journal of Economic History* 36:303–333.

Wilson, Henry. 1872–1877. *Rise and fall of the slave power in America,* 3 vols. Boston: Houghton Mifflin.

Wiltse, Charles M. 1944–1951. *John C. Calhoun,* 3 vols. Indianapolis: Bobbs-Merrill.

Winkle, Kenneth J. 1983. A social analysis of voter turnout in Ohio, 1850–1860. *Journal of Interdisciplinary History* 13:411–435.

Winters, Donald L. 1978. *Farmers without farms: Agricultural tenancy in nineteenth century Iowa.* Westport, CT: Greenwood Press.

Wish, Harvey. 1950. *Society and thought in early America: A social and intellectual history of the American people through 1865.* New York: Longman Green and co.

Wood, Peter. 1974. *Black majority: Negroes in colonial South Carolina from 1670 through the Stone rebellion.* New York: W. W. Norton.

Woodman, Harold D. 1963. The profitability of slavery: A historical perennial. *Journal of Southern History* 29:303–325.

————. 1968. *King cotton and his retainers.* Lexington: University of Kentucky Press.

Woodson, Carter G. 1919a. Review of *American Negro slavery. Journal of Negro History* 4:102–103.

————. 1919b. *The education of the Negro prior to 1861: A history of the educations of the colored people of the United States from the beginning of slavery to the Civil War,* 2nd ed. Washington, D.C.: Associated Publishers.

———. 1921. *The history of the Negro church.* Washington, D.C.: Associated Publishers.

———. [1922] 1927 1931. *The Negro in our history,* 3rd and 4th editions. Washington, D.C.: Associated Publishers.

Woodward, C. Vann. [1960] 1968. *The burden of southern history.* Baton Rouge: Louisiana State University Press.

———. 1971. *American counterpoint: Slavery and racism in the North-South dialogue.* Boston: Little, Brown.

———. 1974. History from slave sources. *American Historical Review* 79:470–481.

Wray, Joe D. 1978. Maternal nutrition, breast-feeding, and infant survival. In W. Henry Mosely, ed., *Nutrition and human reproduction.* New York: Plenum Press.

Wright, Carrol D. 1900. *History and growth of the United States census.* Washington, D.C.: Government Printing Office.

Wright, Gavin. 1970. "Economic democracy" and the concentration of agricultural wealth in the cotton South, 1850–1860. *Agricultural History* 44:63–94.

———. 1971. An econometric study of cotton production and trade, 1830–1860. *Review of Economics and Statistics* 53:111–120.

———. 1974. Cotton competition and the postbellum recovery of the American South. *Journal of Economic History* 34:610–635.

———. 1978. *Political economy of the cotton South: Households, markets, and wealth in the nineteenth century.* New York: W. W. Norton.

———. 1979a. Cheap labor and southern textiles before 1880. *Journal of Economic History* 39:655–680.

———. 1979b. The efficiency of slavery: Another interpretation. *American Economic Review* 69:219–226.

———. 1986. *Old South, new South: Revolutions in the southern economy since the Civil War.* New York: Basic Books.

———. 1987. Capitalism and slavery on the islands: A lesson from the mainland. *Journal of Interdisciplinary History* 17:851–870.

Wright, Philip. 1973. *Knibb "the notorious": Slaves' missionary 1803–1845.* London: Sidgwick and Jackson.

Wrigley, E.A. 1966. Family limitation in pre-industrial England. *Economic History Review* 19:82–109.

Wrigley, E.A., and R.S. Schofield. 1981. *The population history of England, 1541–1871: A reconstruction.* Cambridge: Harvard University Press.

Wyatt-Brown, Bertram. 1969. *Lewis Tappan and the evangelical war against slavery.* Cleveland: Case Western Reserve University Press.

———. 1982a. *Southern honor: Ethics and behavior in the Old South.* New York: Oxford University Press.

———. 1982b. Modernizing southern slavery: The proslavery argument reinterpreted. In J. Morgan Kousser and James McPherson, eds., *Race, region, and reconstruction.* New York: Oxford University Press.

Yang, Donghyu. 1984. Aspects of United States agriculture circa 1860. Ph.D. dissertation, Harvard University.

———. 1985. The Parker-Gallman sample and wealth distributions for the antebellum South: A reply. *Explorations in Economic History* 22:227–231.

Zelinsky, Wilbur. 1949. The historical geography of the Negro population of Latin America. *Journal of Negro History* 34:153–221.

Zilversmit, Arthur. 1967. *The first emancipation: The abolition of slavery in the North.* Chicago: University of Chicago Press.

INDEX

italicized page numbers refer to tables and figures

Lowell, James Russell, 329
Lownes, William, 295–96
Lundy, Benjamin, 251, 253
Luther, Martin, 202

Macaulay, Thomas Babington, 231, 232, 403, 414
Macaulay, Zachary, 227, 232, 233, 236, 251
McConnell, Felix G., 347
McNeimar, Richard, 268
Madeiras Islands, 17, 20
Madison, James, 245, 252, 282, 295, 333
Maine, 291
malnutrition, see under diets of slaves
Malthus, Thomas, 120
manumission, 35, 38, 194
Marshall, John, 294
Martineau, Harriet, 238
Marx, Karl, 317
Maryland, 55, 64, 65, 252
Massachusetts, 102, 246, 310, 330–31, 363, 364, 369, 372, 373, 384
material improvements identified with slavery, 203–4
Methodist Episcopal Church, South, 275
Methodists:
  in British antislavery movement, 210, 212, 219, 225–26, 227, 230–31
  schisms due to abolitionism, 274–75
  in U.S. antislavery movement, 250, 270, 274
  U.S. membership, growth of, 255–56
Mexican War, 301, 320, 331, 340
Mexico, 20, 35
  free blacks, 34–35
  occupations of slaves, 41, 42
  slave codes, 37, 38–39
Meyer, John R., 390, 391
mining, 21, 37
Mintz, Sidney, 189, 190, 197
missionaries, 219, 227, 397
Mississippi, 65
Missouri Compromise, 290–92, 293, 338
moderate constitutional antislavery, 334–38
modern view of slavery, see new indictment of slavery
Monk, Maria, 264
Monroe, James, 249
moral problem of slavery, 9–10
  Civil War, moral problem of, 411–17
  cliometric findings and, 390–93
  deception and compromise, abolitionists' use of, 406–9

efficiency of slave labor as amoral issue, 409–11
  see also new indictment of slavery
More, Thomas, 201
Morgan, Philip D., 193
Morse, Jedidiah, 261
mortality rates on Atlantic crossings, 129–31
mortality rates of slaves:
  crop type, relation to, 127–28
  disease-specific causes of death, 128
  fertility rates, relation to, 147–48, 151
  infants and children, 128, 142–48
  malnutrition and, 142–47
  mortality over time, 128
  natural decrease of slave population, 116–19, 123, 124
  slave trade and, 118, 129–32
Myrdal, Gunnar, 389

National Era (antislavery newspaper), 342
National Political Union, 227
National Reform Association, 363
nativist movement:
  anti-Catholicism, 263–64, 315–16, 364, 368
  economic conditions giving rise to, 355–62
  education issues, 364, 366–68
  emergence of, 313–16, 347
  labor actions, 362–65
  political activities, 308–9, 363–64, 365–69
  see also Know-Nothing (American) party
natural increase, see demography of slavery
natural law, 332
natural rights doctrine, 10, 242, 243, 244
The Negro American Family (DuBois), 163–64
The Negro Family in the United States (Frazier), 164
The Negro in Our History (Woodson), 156, 157
Netherlands, 22, 217
  colonies of, 20, 21
New England Anti-Slavery Society, 265
New England Tract Society, 262
New Hampshire, 246, 363, 369
new indictment of slavery:
  abolitionist indictment, comparison with, 400–406
  citizenship denied to slaves (3rd count), 396–98, 402–3
  cultural self-identification denied to slaves (4th count), 398–400, 403–5
  economic opportunity denied to slaves (2nd count), 395–96, 401–2
  need for, 389–92

natural increase experienced by slaves,
32–34
occupations of slaves, 42, 44–45, 46–47,
46, 49–52, 54, 55
ratios of blacks to total population, 30
Utopia (More), 201

Van Buren, Martin, 324, 339, 347
Venetian slavery, 203
Venezuela, 205
Vermont, 246, 373
Vesey, Denmark, 294
violence against abolitionists, 271–72,
378–80
Virginia, 29, 64, 65, 69–70, 112, 242, 249,
252, 292
virtue rewarded and evil punished, theology
of, 410–11

Walker, Isaac A., 351
Walker, Robert J., 347
Washington, Bushrod, 252
Washington, George, 68, 256
Watson, Richard, 231
Wayland, Francis, 275, 276, 282, 325
Webber, Thomas L., 172–75, 177, 184
Webster, Daniel, 285, 286, 315, 341
Weed, Thurlow, 285, 314, 316, 317, 349,
385
weeding gangs, 54
Weitling, Wilhelm, 350
Weld, Theodore, 119–21, 265, 268, 269,
271, 273, 277–79, 323, 335, 392
Wellington, Duke of, 216, 228
Weltfish, Gene, 389
Wesley, John, 212
Wesleyan Methodist Connection of America,
274–75
Wesleyans, 256
West Indies, see British colonies
westward movement of slavery:
cotton industry, 65, 66, 70–72
mortality rates, 131
southern economic growth, impact on,
90–92
tobacco industry, 69–70
see also territorial issue

Whig party:
destruction as national party, 383–84
economic policies, 285–86, 302, 344,
345–46
ethnic issues, approach to, 308–9
"exclusiveness," religious tradition of,
330
franchise policy, 283–84
immigrant support, 314
internal improvements policy, 303
Kansas-Nebraska Act, position on, 370
land policy, 316–19
nativist parties, relations with, 314,
315–16
party cohesion, disappearance of, 320–21,
367–68, 370, 371, 375
realignment within, 316–18
religious/ethnic support, 284–85
slavery, position on, 282–83, 286–87
social philosophy, 284
territorial expansion policy, 300–301
Wilberforce, William, 211, 213, 214, 217,
219, 220, 225, 236, 251, 298, 405,
407
Wilkes, John, 209
William III, king of England, 209
William Frederick, Prince, Duke of
Gloucester, 220
Williams, Eric, 215, 228
Wilmot Proviso, 320, 341
Wilson, Henry, 376
women's rights, 276–77
Woodson, Carter, 44, 155–57
work ethic of slaves:
education and vocational skills, acquisition
of, 156–57
incompetence of blacks, myth of, 155
regularity system, avoidance of, 161–62
resistance work ethic, 157–61, 162
seasonal work rhythm of slaves, 161–62
Working Men's parties, 313
workweek of slaves, average, 28–29,
77–79

Yankee exodus from New England,
257–58
yeomen, relative prosperity of, 82–83